AND GOD CREATED
LENIN

AND GOD CREATED
LENIN

Marxism vs. Religion
in
Russia, 1917–1929

PAUL GABEL

Prometheus Books

59 John Glenn Drive
Amherst, New York 14228-2197

Published 2005 by Prometheus Books

Inquiries should be addressed to
Prometheus Books
59 John Glenn Drive
Amherst, New York 14228–2197
VOICE: 716–691–0133, ext. 207
FAX: 716–564–2711
WWW.PROMETHEUSBOOKS.COM

09 08 07 06 05   5 4 3 2 1

Library of Congress Cataloging-in-Publication Data

Gabel, Paul.
And God created Lenin : Marxism vs. religion in Russia, 1917–1929 / Paul Gabel.
   p. cm.
Includes bibliographical references and index.
ISBN 1–59102–306–8 (hardcover : alk. paper)
   1. Communism and Christianity—Soviet Union—History. 2. Church and state—Soviet Union—History. 3. Persecution—Soviet Union—History. 4. Soviet Union—Church history. 5. Soviet Union—Politics and government—1917–1936. I. Title.
BR936.G27 2005
322'.1'094709042—dc22

2005012215

Printed in the United States of America on acid-free paper

To Song, for her love of knowledge

CONTENTS

ACKNOWLEDGMENTS

First and foremost, I would like to thank Sharlynn Mar of San Jose, California, for her thorough and excellent proofreading of the manuscript. Mary Gabel of Kensington, California, also contributed to this effort. Will Reaves of Campbell, California, deserves a mention for his macrocritique of the ideas included. David King of London was generous both with his time and with the graphics from his outstanding collection of Russian photographs and posters. Everybody at Prometheus Books has been considerate and helpful all along the way, and I am grateful.

I maintain that nothing [worldly] need be destroyed, that we only need to destroy the ideal of God in man, that's how we have to set to work. It's that we must begin with. Oh, blind race of men who have no understanding! As soon as men have all of them denied God—and I believe that period, analogous with geological periods, will come to pass—the old conception of the universe will fall of itself . . . and what's more the old morality, and everything will begin anew. Men will unite to take from life all it can give, but only for joy and happiness in the present world. Man will be lifted up with a spirit of the divine. Titanic pride and the man-god will appear. From hour to hour extending his conquest of nature infinitely by his will and his science, man will feel such lofty joy from hour to hour in doing it that it will make up for all his old dreams of the joys of heaven. Everyone will know that he is mortal and will accept death proudly and serenely like a god. His pride will teach him that it's useless for him to repine at life's being a moment, and he will love his brother without need of reward. Love will be sufficient only for a moment of life, but the very consciousness of its momentariness will intensify its fire, which now is dissipated in dreams of eternal love beyond the grave.

—Ivan's devilish ghost in Dostoevsky's
The Brothers Karamazov, 1880

The nation will not stand infinitely such atheistic scoffing at its beliefs. It will rise like the biblical pillar of fire and with its big broad hand it will deal such a blow in the face of the red monkey-buffoon that the whole world will tremble.

—A. Valentinov, *The Assault of Heaven*, 1923

THE STRENGTH OF MEN'S CONVICTIONS IS NOT IN PROPORTION TO THE COHERENCE AND VALIDITY OF THE BELIEFS THEY HOLD

—J. C. Rees

INTRODUCTION

THE QUESTION

We have finished with the earthly tsars; now we shall deal with the heavenly tsars.

—*Bezbozhnik (The Godless), January 1923*

On virtually the same day, Vladimir Ilyich Ulyanov, better known as Lenin, and Vasily Vasilyevich Belavin, better known as Tikhon, assumed power.* The former replaced almost a thousand years of tsardom with a socialist government, while the latter restored the Russian Orthodox Patriarchate, which had been vacant for over two hundred years. Lenin reached the pinnacle of success through conspiracy and violence, while Tikhon rose, as he believed, by the hand of God. As one might imagine, their courses would be diametrically opposed.

World-embracing ideologies are powerful things, and ideologues who promulgate them, when challenged, say that capitulation is unthinkable. Yet the conflict between the atheistic Bolsheviks and the Russian Orthodox Church is metaphorically reminiscent of the ancient Chinese wisdom of the I-Ching: the yang and the yin. The yang is the male, whose principles include the sun, illumination, aggression, control, hardness, and rationalism. The yin is the female, whose principles include the moon, darkness, passivity, submission, softness, and feeling. The beleaguered dots convey the idea that each force contains the seed of the other and that each in a sense becomes the other. Neither side is pure, neither continually dominates, and the two forces constantly ebb and flow. As

---

*That is, on November 18 (new calendar) the Bolsheviks consolidated their power in Moscow, and Tikhon's name was chosen by lot to become patriarch.

15

will become apparent in our story, the Communists, despite their rigid ideology, could not completely separate themselves from religion in their practical affairs, and the church contained within itself many atheistic attributes. The yang and the yin, always in a state of flux, were especially so during the 1920s.

At the time, of course, neither Communists nor Christians would have accepted the yang-yin metaphor. The Communists viscerally felt the power of history on their side and were confident of ultimate victory. But the church was also confident—not so much of victory but of its ability to endure. The patriarch often repeated Christ's message, "I shall establish my church, and the gates of hell shall not prevail against it" (Matthew 16:18).

I am inviting you to join in an investigation of these questions:

Using either immoral or moral means, did the Bolsheviks have a realistic chance of creating an institutionally and psychologically secular society? If they had played their unique hand of history differently, could atheism have succeeded? And, ultimately, is such a society even possible?

Neither before the 1920s nor since has any national leadership felt the need to eliminate religion—*all* religion—from a land.* With several decades of preparation, a well-thought-out ideology, highly motivated followers, a ruthless mentality, and vulnerable opponents, Lenin and his successors should have been able to pull it off. The fiercely determined Bolsheviks faced a corrupted church; they seemingly had the power to crush its institutions easily and penetrate deep into the souls of Russia's 180 million people. After all, we were already in an age when totalitarianism was technically feasible.

Straightaway, Lenin put his program into motion. The day after the successful storming of the Winter Palace in Petrograd on November 7, 1917, the new government proclaimed its official policy: conversion of the masses from a backwards, heaven-based superstition to a progressive, Earth-based, materialist understanding of life. At issue was whether religion answered to a basic human need and was thus universal, or was merely a product of economic conditions at a certain stage of history and hence could be dispensed with when that stage had receded into the past. The eager Bolsheviks were sure it was the latter. Religion was not only inconsistent with the socialistic goals of the new society; it was doomed. A new society would be built on the ashes of the old. Humanity was not dependent upon God; man was self-sufficient. All remnants of the corrupt tsarist order and the backwardness of the East—of which religion was an integral part—would be not only neutralized but eliminated beyond all hope of revival. Rationalism and materialism would prevail; theory demanded it.

---

*A possible exception might be during the French Revolution when its leaders assaulted the Catholic Church, but this attack was more anticlerical in nature, and its incoherence and brevity made it not a true test.

Although Lenin was fired up, religion was here first and had gotten a head start, extending uninterrupted at least from the days of the Cro-Magnon and the Lascaux cave paintings. Religion's history, its pervasiveness, and the lack of new societies to experiment on meant that the only way to answer the above questions would be to remove faiths from *existing* societies. When I began writing this book I was convinced that it must be *possible* for a civilized people to live without religion. The first dozen years of the Communist Revolution were the opportunity not just of a lifetime but of all recorded history, and there might never be another. Of course religious societies would always exist, but it seemed there must be one place and time in the history of man where someone would show that secularism could prevail. Then it would at least be an option.*

I am not equating my interest in the feasibility of a purely secular society with the motives of the Bolsheviks—Marxist theory, anticlericalism, a longing for material progress, and an urge to power drove them onward. I am driven by a curiosity that makes me wonder *why* they failed and whether failure was caused by the Bolsheviks shooting themselves in the foot or by inevitable causes over which they had no control. At first I found excuses for the Bolsheviks—inadequate theory, wartime devastation, an unfortunate penchant for violence, a perversely stubborn religious opposition, or Lenin's premature death in January 1924. If only he had lived to see seventy-five, I thought, the implementation of his atheistic agenda might have succeeded.

However, the more I read and the more I wrote, the more convinced I became that this best-of-all-possible opportunities had merely a modest chance of success, if any. While it is true that Marxist-atheist theory contained major flaws, that Lenin had to contend with man-made and natural disasters, and that he made many tactical mistakes, what if the Bolsheviks had acted more wisely? But even if Lenin's health had been strong and all these natural and man-made impediments had magically disappeared, I had to face the reality that no more than a dent—maybe a significant dent—could have been hammered into the Russian religious mind.

Lenin's problem was essentially one of the limits of idealism. Consider this story about St. Augustine. In 391 CE, he returned to North Africa from a five-year sojourn in Rome full of "philosophical reflection and divine wisdom." Before, he had been confident that the social order on Earth could mirror the cosmic order in the heavens. If church and state were "organized according to the rationality of God's creation, human society could be in harmony with the order of the universe." But he had matured while abroad; once back in Alexandria his eyes opened, and he saw that the church was not "a pure vessel for the saved." Instead, it was "a microcosm of the world, incorporating the mixed and messy state of the human condition." Realizing that the church was imperfect, but that its sacraments were a prerequisite for salvation, he began to justify coercion. Sin-

---

*Throughout this book I use the term "secularism" to mean not just the separation of church and state but the absence of religious institutions and thought.

ners and heretics, he argued, must be forced into joining—or rejoining—the church for their own good: "Compel them to come in."[1] Fifteen hundred years later, Lenin would follow a parallel path—ideology clashing with the messiness of the human condition. Only his message was: "Compel them to come out."*

I am not writing to support any suppressed church, though I do feel sympathy for those who were persecuted. And I am not writing to support the Bolsheviks, though I do find *some* of their goals laudable. It is my intent that light be shed on both sides of the story, for, if truth be told, both antagonists were guilty of sins and were seekers of justice. What I am really searching for is an understanding of why the Bolsheviks could not win this war, why they failed in their obsession to wipe clean the religious mind of Russia. And was their failure a failure of tactics, a failure of will, or a stupid banging of their heads against the stone wall of human nature?

FOCUS AND SCOPE

A system of universal propaganda, brought to perfection, built on state-organized false-hood, deception, temptations, and terror, together with the diabolically cruel, perfected system of torture and torments, being systematically and by principle used by the Soviet state for the glory of atheism, is a phenomenon which is absolutely new and by nature profoundly different from all known aspects of cruelty and force in world history.[2]

—Ivan Andreyev

During the 1920s, especially in England and America, there was considerable interest in the Soviet antireligious experiment. This interest could be attributed to either the possibility that the Bolshevik government might not survive the civil war raging against it—the hoped-for outcome—or that the Bolshevik government might succeed in its antireligious (and anticapitalist) crusade. Interest in the religious issue waned, however, as the 1930s brought the reign of Joseph Stalin, the show trials, and the Nazi threat. Books have been written on the career of Lenin, the interventions in the Russian Civil War, and the foreign policy of the Soviet Union, but modern historians have paid only modest attention to the conflict between church and state during the years 1917 to 1929, and what has been written is often inaccessible to the general reader. My aim is to fill this gap.

The focus is on these dozen or so years, though ample background and updates will be presented. There are two discernible periods within this range: November 1917 to January 1924 (while Lenin lived) and the post-Lenin years up

---

*St. Augustine may have justified compulsion from his reading of Luke 19:27, where Jesus is presumed to have said: "But those mine enemies which would not that I should reign over them, bring hither and slay them before me."

to 1929 when there was much confusion of leadership. Another way to divide this period is between War Communism from 1918 through 1921, when Lenin felt compelled to use ruthless methods for his party's survival, and the New Economic Policy (NEP) from 1922 through 1928, when some laxity and experimentation were needed for the nation's survival.

The year 1929 is a convenient outer limit to this study. In this year Stalin consolidated his rule and imposed the first Five-Year Plan and collectivization of agriculture. But, of course, the sweep of Russian history is extensive and twelve years cannot be understood in isolation. The first four chapters can be considered prologue, dealing with religion and atheism in tsarist Russia and analyzing the Marxist-Leninist contribution to the latter. The last three chapters will discuss the meaning of it all—developments in the continuing struggle in the Soviet Union until its collapse as well as some personal reflections on the strengths of human nature and the weaknesses of social engineering.

These twelve years were when the major elements of the antireligious struggle were created and applied. During the Stalinist period and beyond there would be few departures from the original form, only shifts in enforcement for domestic or foreign policy reasons and, oddly, occasional retrogression to tactics that had already proven worthless. The collectivization of agriculture became a vehicle for religious oppression, but World War II necessitated an almost tsarist appeal to the people for the defense of "Holy Mother Russia." In the postwar period antireligious zeal turned to lethargy, and gradually accommodations with organized religion were worked out. Clearly, in the end, Lenin's initial dream of religious obliteration fell short.

Irregular waves of religious persecution did roll through Russia under Communist control, but I would like to emphasize that the Bolsheviks did not introduce this practice. It had been going on since at least 988 CE—and probably long before—when Vladimir I (allegedly) drove Kievan pagans into the Dnieper River at sword point to be baptized as Christians. The Bolshevik innovation was *indiscriminate* persecution; Marx was talking about every single religion when he described them all as "the opium of the people," so there was no issue of conversion to a "true" faith. Yet much was perceived as persecution that actually may not have been, and often the Bolsheviks did discriminate between religions for *tactical* reasons.

For a thousand years, the Russian Orthodox Church had been the national church of the land—the established church—and it therefore bore the brunt of Communist attack; therefore this book shall concentrate on it as well. When I use the term "the church," it means the Russian Orthodox Church in chapters 1 through 19. In chapters 20 and 21 this term refers to the Catholic Church. When I discuss the (mostly Protestant) sectarians in chapter 22, I will not use the term at all, as the sects were diverse.

Originally I wrote chapters on Russian Jews, Muslims, and Buddhists but have decided to omit them for several reasons. The major problem with covering these religions within this book's context (and length) is that their tenets were (and still are) so tightly tied to ethnicity and nationality that it becomes virtually impossible to disentangle them. For example, when the Bolsheviks closed down a synagogue, did the urge come from hatred of the Jewish "nation" or from loathing of particular aspects of their religious ritual (or from the fact that they *had* a ritual)? Was Bolshevik pressure on Muslims to strengthen women's rights an attempt to integrate Muslim women into the greater Russian community or a blatant violation of Koranic teaching? For Muslims, especially, there was no historical distinction between church and state, and the mullahs held both religious and secular power. Attempts to suppress this power might be interpreted by the Russian government as being political, while Muslims always interpreted it as antireligious. The Bolsheviks, too, sidestepped the issue of non-Christian minorities, at least until the late 1920s when they felt strong enough to confront it.

Another reason for dealing only with Russia's Christians is that once the Bolshevik-Christian dynamic is understood, there is little that is really new. To the extent that Bolshevik policies were truly antireligious and not antinationality, they tried the same tricks that they had perfected earlier in the decade. If we concentrate on attempts to suppress Christianity, we can deal with a *pure case*. If it were not for their Christian faith, the Bolsheviks would have had nothing against either the Christian clergy or the laity. (The only exceptions were the issue of bourgeois social class among a very few of the clergy and the issue of the Polish nationality of much of Russia's Catholic population.)

This, then, is not a book about all Marxist theory, about the entire Bolshevik program, or about the full scope of Russian history during the period under study. It is a book about the clash between the Bolshevik Party and the Christian denominations in Russia between 1917 and 1929. That was bloody enough.

THE MEANING OF RELIGION

[Religion is] belief in a nonexistent, supernatural world, supposedly inhabited by gods, spirits, angels, saints, the souls of the dead, or other supernatural beings.[3]

—a Soviet handbook

Even though this book deals specifically with Christianity, it is also a book about religion in general. So far I have mentioned "religion" as if it were a catchall term, simple to comprehend. This is not the case, and what is meant by the term may well determine the extent to which we finally judge any Communist success or failure. Consider these two hypothetical examples. After a certain number of years of Communist rule, every church was closed, causing church attendance to plummet to zero. Would that indicate success in the antireligious crusade? Conversely, if every Orthodox Church member kept an ikon of the Virgin Mary in his home, celebrated every saint day, and observed all required fasts, would that indicate a healthy and vigorous religious sentiment? A moment's reflection should lead to negative answers to both questions.

Even though the term "religion" appears throughout this book, we should consider what it might really mean within its various contexts. Perhaps simply a deistic sense that there is a great power out there who created the universe but cares little about its daily workings and cares even less about the mundane activities of man. "Religious" could describe perfunctory but dutiful believers, who go through the motions and respond positively when asked about their faith but who rarely think about God and seldom pray. There are institutional believers, who are primarily concerned with the survival of the church, and there are those who use religion to further their careers or their political agendas; we will meet all these types. Religion also encompasses deep thinkers and those who seek profound spiritual experiences, a connection with Universal Truth and the Eternal, or perhaps have concluded that there would be nothing for man but futility and existentialist despair without reliance upon God—what the German philosopher Oswald Spengler called "the loneliness of the ego in the cosmos."[4] Believers might include fanatics, even those who believe because of mental instabilities. Then there are the missionaries. The Bolsheviks, of course, did not much concern themselves with these distinctions. Lenin voiced his universal repulsion, "Every religious idea, every idea of God, even flirting with the idea of God, is unutterable vileness, vileness of the most dangerous kind, contagion of the most abominable kind."[5]

The anthropologist Robin Horton, writing in the 1960s, offered a definition of religion that has some application to our study: "[Religion is] the extension of the field of people's social relationships beyond the confines of purely human society." People turn to these "outside" relationships when human relationships fail to meet their needs. People who live in small and simple societies, such as Russian villages, are good at creating intimacies and friendships but poor at meeting their technological needs, so for them religion serves the purpose of improving technological control of the world around them. God takes care of the weather, controls agricultural pests, and prevents or cures illnesses.[6]*

Some scholars charge the Bolsheviks with establishing a substitute religion in a feeble attempt to answer a universal need in man for faith in something larger than himself—Marx's "power of history," for example, or the worship of Lenin. This is sometimes referred to as a "civil religion" or a "secular religion." But history is not a supernatural being and Lenin was no deity; only a very loose definition of religion would support such speculation. Some philosophers argue

---

*Conversely, people in technologically advanced societies, alone and alienated, use religion to build personal relationships with God.

that any conflict between Good and Evil is religious, one even arguing that since "communism offers a goal for life," it is religious.[7] Paradoxically, *religious* writers are more inclined to view Bolshevism as a religion, perhaps because this line of thinking leads to acceptance of a universality of religion or because there is some pride in being mimicked. Nicolas Berdyaev, at various times of his life either a Marxist or a religious thinker, offered a good example of this approach:

> One can comprehend the passionate tone of antireligious propaganda and per-secution in Soviet Russia [only] if one sees communism as a religion that is striving to take the place of Christianity. Only a religion is characterized by the claim to possess absolute truth; no political or economic movement can claim that. Only a religion can be exclusive. Only a religion has a catechism that is obligatory for everyone. Only a religion can claim to possess the very depths of the human soul. . . . Communism persecutes all religions because it is itself a religion. Recognizing itself as the one true religion, it cannot suffer other false religions alongside of it.[8]

As we shall see, "Leninism" developed many of the external trappings of religion—rites, ceremonies, and even worship of the fallen leader. Some Communists even twisted atheist materialism to fill the void left by the loss of religion—creating a Communist cult. But I am going to take Marx and Lenin at their word. I want to see if their theories could have been effective; perversions of their theories will be considered weaknesses of implementation. Clearly, if the Bolsheviks simply replaced an awe of Divine Providence with an awe of Soviet Power, there is no victory that they could legitimately claim. But atheism does not require an act of faith; it is the negation of faith.

Another point: All that we will be able to investigate in this book is the outward manifestation of an inward spirit (or lack of it). We should try to look deep into the actions of Russia's people, into their motives, whether they are believers or not, but ultimately we can only judge them by what they do, what actions they take. All ideas left unexpressed will remain a mystery to us.

PRACTICAL MATTERS

A little refresher on nomenclature should be helpful. The term "Bolshevik," meaning majority, refers to Lenin's faction of the prerevolutionary Russian Social Democratic Labor Party. The term was used extensively in 1917 and the years immediately following. Although in the spring of 1918 the official name was changed to the Communist Party, only gradually did popular usage make the switch. The term "Soviets," meaning representative councils of workers (prole-tarians) or peasants, existed as early as the unsuccessful 1905 Revolution and was revived in 1917. When capitalized, Soviet refers to the national level of government; a lowercase soviet is a local government organization that sends delegates to the national level. The term "Soviet Union," or Union of Soviet Socialist Republics (USSR), became official in December 1922. "Sovnarkom" is an abbreviation for the government's Council of People's Commissars, or council of ministers.

The Politburo (Political Bureau) headed the Communist Party and held absolute power. In 1919 it was composed of Lenin, Trotsky, Lev Kamenev, Stalin, and Nikolai Krestinsky, with Grigory Zinoviev, Nikolai Bukharin, and Mikhail Kalinin as alternates. The Cheka was Lenin's secret police organization—the "sword and shield" of the Communist Party. From 1918 until February 1922 (the Civil War years) it administered the Red Terror. The people called its agents the "peaked-heads" for their easily recognizable high-peaked caps, but its full name was the All-Russian Extraordinary Commission for Fighting Counter-revolution, Sabotage, Speculation, and Misconduct in Office. It was superseded by the GPU, a Russian abbreviation for the State Political Administration, which handled government security until 1934, when it was replaced by Stalin's NKVD. (Technically, it was the GPU from February 1922 until November 1923 and then the OGPU until 1934.) These secret police forces operated against the church, as well as against "socially alien" elements, kulaks ("rich" peasants), party deviants, and common criminals. They could convict and sentence without public trial.

It can be confusing when switching back and forth between references to the party and the state. In theory, they were parallel organizations that fulfilled the dialectical process (see chapter 3). The government legislated what it thought was good for the people, while the party—the "vanguard of the proletariat"—pushed for as much of its theoretical program as could realistically be implemented. The party, with 800,000 full members in 1927, was the "leading nucleus" in government and as such pushed for the elimination of religion, while the government was supposed to regard religion as a private matter. In practice, there was a significant overlap—an interlocking directorate—and no *meaningful* distinction at all, as theorists took positions of administrative power and the party line was always followed by the government. A 1945 government document regulating church-state relations put it succinctly:

> The efficient and well-coordinated work of the Soviet state organs would be impossible without a single guiding and organizing force. The guiding force is the Communist Party.[9]

The party itself did not allow for freedom of conscience. Its purpose was to realize the one and only scientifically correct world outlook—Marxism/Leninism.

As for terms involving a lack of religious sentiment, "anticlericalism" is used to denote opposition to the practices of the clergy, as opposed to a denial of the existence of God. From the Soviet perspective anticlericalism and atheism resulted in similar policies, but from the peasantry's point of view anticlericalism did not imply a lack of religious belief; many devout peasants were anticlerical, depending largely on the character of their priest. "Materialism" means any theory that considers the facts of the universe to be sufficiently explained by the existence of nature and matter. For the materialist, the human mind is considered a product of the development of matter and its movement, with no reference to soul or spirit. For economic materialists the substructure of material relationships determines the superstructure of societal values (including religious "superstitions"). Marxists often referred to themselves as materialists rather than atheists because the former seemed more positive and revealed more about man's destiny. I will define atheism very simply as an individual's affirmation that he does not believe in the existence of any god or supernatural force. This definition rejects the assertion made by some Christians that nobody can *really* be an atheist. Some certainly can—the issue here is whether a whole society can. Bolsheviks who attacked both religious belief and practice were true atheists.

Even more practical matters have to do with city names, currency exchange rates, and the calendar. The city built out of Baltic swamps by Peter the Great (with slave labor) was called St. Petersburg until 1914, when World War I required rejection of the Germanic form. It was then Russianized to Petrograd. With the death of Lenin in 1924 the city was named Leningrad in his honor. (And with the end of Commumist power it has reverted to the name that Peter gave it in the early eighteenth century.) During the 1920s, the Communists honored other leaders and celebrities; for example, they changed Nizhny-Novgorod to Gorky and Tver to Kalinin. And they moved the capital from Petrograd to Moscow in March 1918.

It is difficult to pinpoint the exact exchange rate between Russian rubles and any other currency either before the Revolution or during the 1920s. This is made doubly difficult because some sources do not distinguish between gold and paper rubles—it was paper rubles that horribly inflated during the early 1920s. Nikolai Bukharin described the paper ruble as one hundred times more valuable in tsarist times than it was during the 1920s, and this was certainly an understatement.[10] At the end of November 1922 the State Bank introduced a new denomination of notes equal to the gold content of the prewar ten-ruble gold coin, but by the end of the year there were five different currencies being used in trade, varying according to how close or distant one was from the capital. So, admittedly, when I refer to rubles it will be difficult to determine their buying power compared with modern currencies.

The Bolsheviks changed the Russian calendar almost immediately after their coup. The Julian calendar had been established during the rule of Julius Caesar in 46 BCE and had been adopted by the Council of Nicaea in 325 CE. By the sixteenth century, however, it had fallen behind the true date (determined by the Earth's revolution around the sun) by eleven days. The discrepancy was removed when Pope Gregory XIII introduced a new calendar, but by the twentieth century neither the tsarist government nor the Russian Orthodox Church had accepted this reform, and by this time the gap had crept up to thirteen days. "For the purpose of being in harmony with all the civilized countries of the world," Lenin declared that the day after February 1, 1918 (old calendar), would be February 14 (new calendar).[11] The difficulty for today's researcher is that primary (and sometimes secondary) sources often fail to mention which calendar they are using during the transitional period. To compound the problem, when the Russian Orthodox Church split into two factions in 1922, one retained the Julian calendar (and still does today), and the other switched to the Gregorian. I will use the Gregorian calendar for all dates—even before the Bolshevik synchronization with the West—thus referring to the 1917 seizure of power in Petrograd as occurring on November 7 rather than October 25. An interesting side note is that Christmas in Communist Russia (to the extent that it was tolerated at all) was officially on December 25, the same as the rest of the world, but the Orthodox Church celebrated it on January 7 (Gregorian calendar), the day that it would have been on according to the Julian calendar if thirteen days had not been lost.

For the convenience of the Western reader, I will usually use the "s" form for Russian plurals instead of the "i" form, which I assume is unfamiliar—thus "Bolsheviks" not "Bolsheviki."

Short passages of historical fiction—realistic stories within the context of the narrative—are included at various places in the book. These are based on actual events and are meant to be illustrative of them. Think of them as textual paintings—actual scenes portrayed with a little license. To further distinguish them from the main narrative, they will be set off in this letter style. At the end of the book you will find some useful resources, including two glossaries and a time line.

And a final caveat: these were difficult and messy times, and *objective* information is hard to come by. Almost everyone who wrote in this period or of this period had an ax to grind. Many sources are in irreconcilable conflict. World War I, the 1917 Revolution, the Red Terror, the Civil War, famine, along with social and economic experimentation, rendered record keeping a low priority. As the historian Joseph McCabe put it, "The period in question is still as obscure as some parts of ancient history, for the confusion was such that few authentic records were kept while the intense passion on both sides gave rise to vast quantities of reckless rumors."[12] I hope that I have not perpetuated any of these.

PART I
PRELUDE

1

A FOURTH THERE WILL NEVER BE

A Brief History of Russian Orthodoxy

W hen Lenin's Bolshevik faction of the Russian Social Democratic Labor Party seized power in Petrograd in November 1917, its first priority was to stay in power. Beyond that imperative, however, lay, like an itch that could never be adequately scratched, the ongoing irritation of modern-day religion—specifically, the Russian Orthodox Church, which made up at least 70 percent of the population. What was the nature of this church that it should arouse such atheistic passion in the minds of the nation's new rulers?

EAST AND WEST I

To approach that question we must first journey back to the early Christian councils held in the vicinity of Constantinople. The first of these councils gathered at Nicaea in 325 CE and was most famous for its declaration of the triune nature of the Godhead. By the time the fourth council met at nearby Chalcedon in 451, the essential dogma of the Christian Church was firmly established in the middle ground between competing heresies.[1] While earlier councils had formalized the system of church hierarchy, regulated the conduct of the clergy, and ruled on the treatment of heretics, the Chalcedon Council instituted the office of the patriarchate. The seventh Ecumenical Council (and the last to be recognized by the whole of the Eastern, or Greek, Orthodox Church) met once again at Nicaea in 787, sanctioning the veneration of sacred pictures, or ikons. During the subsequent twelve centuries the Orthodox branch of Christianity fervently preserved what it had established; dynamism was replaced with stasis—the truth was now known.

Christian influence penetrated Russia over a thousand years ago, in the very period when Russian national identity was being forged. It accompanied Byzan-

29

tine traders in their commercial travels up the Dnieper River into Kievan Rus. But the Christianity that developed in the East diverged over the centuries from the Christianity developing in the West. This early branching will help to explain a thousand years later the inability of Western, rationalist Communists and Eastern, spiritualist Orthodox to understand each other.

By the ninth century, the long-simmering dispute between the papacy in Rome and the emperor in Constantinople could no longer be hidden under the rug. Cultural divergence, political rivalries, and quarrels over papal claims of universal jurisdiction were making unity difficult enough, but theological trinitarian disputes hardened these differences. As early as the sixth century, Catholics in Spain had added three words to the fourth-century Nicene Creed, stating in its new form that the Holy Spirit emanates from both the Father *and the Son* (Latin: *filioque*)—not just the Father. Although the Spanish made this change to thwart the Arian heresy, the iconoclastic Charlemagne adopted it in the late eighth century as part of his bid for independence from Rome. With characteristic boldness, the king of the Franks accused the Greek Church of heresy for not accepting the *revised* Nicene Creed. Although the pope did not insist on inclusion of the *filioque* until the early eleventh century, by 850 the Orthodox Church considered the gauntlet to have been thrown down.[2]

When the Eastern Church finally focused on this issue, the *filioque* developed into a major theological *and practical* division between East and West. Among Catholics the Holy Spirit was subordinated, as it could emanate from Jesus, but for the Orthodox the Spirit could be called upon by Jesus but emanated only from the Father; therefore it played a more exalted role in their daily lives. The *filioque* also implied a forced unity of the three persons of the Godhead, whereas the Orthodox stressed more distinctiveness of personality. The Catholic view, the Orthodox believed, led to the Western church's rigid institutionalization, excessive centralization, and acceptance of papal supremacy. All Eastern Churches repudiated these innovations as well as their practical consequences.[3]

The Byzantine Orthodox Church continued to win converts among the Slavs. By the late tenth century Vladimir, Grand Prince of Kiev, decided to abandon outdated paganism and convert to one of the major religions pressing upon him from every side. Reportedly, he sent emissaries to the world's religious centers, asking for reports on their churches. They were unimpressed with Catholics, Jews, and Muslims, but when they entered the Cathedral of St. Sophia in Constantinople they were awestruck, reporting to Vladimir that they had not known whether they were "in Heaven or on Earth." Vladimir may have been influenced by this news, but he was certainly more strongly influenced by his realization that Russia's commercial interests lay to the south and east, with the Byzantine Empire, not to the west or in the Arab world. He chose for his people Constantinople's Eastern Orthodox Church.

In 988 Vladimir ordered the statue of the pagan god Perun dragged by horses from its perch and plunged into the cold waters of the Dnieper. The citizens of Kievan Russia were "encouraged"—in part by mass baptisms—to abandon the old faith and accept the new. Tsar Ivan IV, in the early sixteenth century, circulated an alternate version of Russia's conversion to Christianity. This story—with a transparent purpose—told of the journey up the Dnieper by St. Andrew, the brother of the Apostle Peter, immediately after the Crucifixion, thus eliminating any connection to the Catholic West. In either case, any remaining bridge between the Eastern and Western churches had been burned when in 1054 the pope in Rome and the patriarch in Constantinople anathematized each other, or separated the other from his church.[4] The situation certainly did not improve when in 1204 European Crusaders, who were supposed to be liberating the Holy Land from the Muslims, attacked Constantinople instead.*

Opposition to Christianity in Russia was stiff, and an admixture of pagan and Christian beliefs lingered for centuries—indeed, a millennium—referred to as the "double faith."[5] Over the years the number of Christian believers in Russia steadily grew, attracted by the beauty and emotional appeal of the church service, not by any theological considerations.

The prestige of Kiev also grew among Christian nations. Soon the city had its own cathedrals and its own saints, emerging strong enough to enter into that dispute, which over its long history would prove the nemesis of the entire Christian faith: the yearning for national autonomy. Russia's concerns were not doctrinal but geopolitical. The Eastern Orthodox Church had four ancient religious centers: Constantinople, Antioch, Alexandria, and Jerusalem. Russia hoped that there might soon be a fifth, Kiev, and that the Russian Church soon might boast of its own patriarch and of autonomy within the Orthodox world. Already the city was the "soul of Russian Orthodoxy."

This autocephalous dream was to be put on hold for a few centuries, however, when endless armies of Mongols came streaming out of Central Asia. Between the thirteenth and the fifteenth centuries, descendants of Genghis Khan ruled Russia's southlands, holding them in subjugation from their military capital at Sarai on the lower Volga. Because Mongol khans were more interested in commercial tribute than interference with Russian culture, they did not attempt to destroy the Russian Orthodox Church or proselytize among its members. The period of the Mongol Yoke allowed for a deepening and maturing of Russian faith, as people turned to the church for solace and relief from their sufferings. A new spirituality settled over the land. St. Sergius established a monastery north of Moscow and inspired thousands with his humility and piety. During the fourteenth century, religious strength gradually melded into military strength as cracks were revealed in the armor of the Mongol Empire. Sergius blessed Moscow's troops as Prince Dmitry Donskoy departed for the Battle of Kulikovo

---

*Though Eastern and Western union has still not been achieved, in a rare act of ecumenism the anathemas were mutually lifted in 1965.

Pole in 1380. Victory there and in subsequent battles prepared the way for the demise of Mongol power in Russia in the fifteenth century.[6]

Waning Mongol hegemony in Russia left a power vacuum that would be filled by the city of Moscow's expanding strength. Muscovite ascendancy coincided with not only Mongol but also Byzantine decline. At the Council of Florence in 1439 the Byzantine patriarch consented to reconciliation between the Eastern and Western churches. This was part political consideration and part military expediency, as Muslim Turks now threatened both the Eastern and Western churches. Russians, however, regarded reconciliation as nothing less than capitulation—even treason. When Turks overran Constantinople in 1453, Russians viewed it as divine retribution for the city's betrayal, and the authority of the Eastern patriarchate further diminished in their eyes.

The Greek patriarch continued nominal rule from the fallen city, but the Russian Church was becoming increasingly self-sufficient. Rome, Russians believed, had fallen into heresy, and the "second Rome" had fallen to the infidels. The monk Philotheus of Pskov wrote to Tsar Vasily III in 1510:

> I wish to add a few words on the present Orthodox Empire of our ruler: He is on Earth the sole Emperor of the Christians, the leader of the Apostolic Church which stands no longer in Rome or in Constantinople, but in the blessed city of Moscow. She alone shines in the whole world brighter than the sun. . . . All Christian empires are fallen [including Alexandria, Antioch, and Jerusalem] and in their stead stands alone the empire of our ruler in accordance with the prophetic books. Two Romes have fallen, but a third stands and a fourth there will never be.[7]

As a part of this developing religious patriotism, the Russian Church became aware that the saints it venerated were all of Greek origin. Where were Russia's "holy witnesses" to the truth of God's love? A search began for local holy men who had perhaps been overlooked, and in 1547 a council of bishops in Moscow revealed twenty-two new and purely Russian saints, further boosting the case for autocephaly. Finally, in 1589, Boris Godunov, pretender to the Russian throne, obtained approval from Constantinople for a separate Russian patriarchate. Enthronement of the Patriarch Job settled the matter for the time being.[8]

TSAR AND CHURCH

The Emperor of all the Russias is an autocratic and absolute monarch. His supreme power must be obeyed not only out of fear but with heart and soul, for this is the command of God himself.[9]

—The Fundamental Law of the Russian Empire

The Russian Church achieved its ecclesiastical independence by becoming a National Church, and this meant that its destiny was directly tied to the destiny of the Russian nation and the Russian government. Between 988, when a secular prince chose the Christian faith, and 1917, when the Russian monarchy fell to armed revolution, church and state were welded as one. As the state grew stronger, the church grew stronger with it. Autocracy was justified as being the model of heaven, where one God ruled with one law. On Earth as well there should be one ruler, the head of both the state and the church, governing with one law.[10]

The Orthodox hierarchy relied upon the state in its disputes with Constantinople and was indebted to it for its aid in rooting out heretics. The church, in turn, upheld the majesty and legitimacy of the tsars. This synergistic relationship, however, had its downside. With the autocratic support of the tsarist state, the church never had to compete in the marketplace of ideas; its enemies were simply persecuted by the government; in the long run this weakened Russian Orthodoxy and failed to prepare it for the trials ahead.

In the seventeenth century this mutually reinforcing relationship protected the church when a schism developed between the doctrinally conservative Old Believers and the reformist New Believers (more on this in chapter 22). Irreparable damage might have been inflicted had the strong arm of the state not protected the "new believing" reformers. This century also saw the height of feudalism, and under tsarist patronage the Orthodox Church with all its monasteries owned close to one million serfs—about 8 percent of the entire population.[11]

In spite of having already canonized 230 saints, by the early eighteenth century the power and influence of the Orthodox Church reached its nadir. Tsar Peter I (the Great) disdained the church's backwardness and showed off his low opinion in drunken debauches where men of the court dressed as monks and the loosest available women as nuns.[12] The Orthodox patriarchate had been formalized for only 120 years, but after Patriarch Adrian died in 1700 Peter declined to appoint a successor. He hoped to Westernize, secularize, and "enlighten" Russia and rejected the idea of competing with a "Russian Pope" for power in the process. The matter remained in limbo until 1721, when Peter felt strong enough to issue the *Ecclesiastical Regulation*, formally abolishing the patriarchate and decapitating the Russian Church. (The patriarchy would not reappear, ironically, until the first year of Communist rule.)

It was not Peter's intent to weaken the bonds between church and state but to tighten them, or rather to place the church under the control of the state. It was his purpose, moreover, to drive a wedge between the church and the people. While he declared the vernacular dialect the official language of the civil government and literature, he commanded the church to continue its use of ancient Church Slavonic in the liturgy—making services unintelligible to the common people—and ordered courses in seminaries to be taught in Latin. As the vernacular evolved and church languages did not, the clergy became increasingly inward looking and isolated.[13]

Peter created in the patriarch's place a governing commission—the Holy Synod—modeled after the Lutheran Church's organization in Prussia and Sweden, countries he had visited as a youth. He appointed and dismissed its twelve members (bishops, heads of monasteries, married clergy) at will, rather than allow church control. The Synod had all the powers of the former patriarchs but without having this power concentrated in a rival personality. It was responsible for maintaining the True Faith and conducting trials involving cases of witchcraft, heresy, or blasphemy. It selected bishops, administered the church, operated parochial schools and seminaries, regulated marriages, and published devotional books—censoring those it found offensive. The *Ecclesiastical Regulation* was a controlling document, clearly regarding with suspicion the church as an institution, as well as its individual members. The Synod took little interest in altering doctrine or changing liturgy. Peter and his successors had no interest in directly meddling in church policy; they simply wanted the church to contribute to an orderly and obedient society.[14]

At the head of the Synod was the chief procurator—the "eye of the tsar"—responsible to the emperor alone. Frequently military men were given this post so that the clergy might feel the impact of martial discipline.[15] The chief procurator was, in effect, a minister of religion, ensuring that all church affairs were conducted in conformity with imperial decrees. Not only the church hierarchy, but also village priests were treated as an arm of the state. The tsar expected them to post governmental decrees and proclamations in church buildings; the bureaucracy expected them to provide statistical data on the condition of their parishes; and the police expected them to inform on persons who, in the privacy of the confessional, revealed thoughts of "evil intent toward the regime" and did not repent them.

In 1906 ultraconservatives formed the Union of the Russian People, called the "Black Hundred Party" by their adversaries. It set up fascistic organizations supporting autocracy, anti-Semitism, and nationalism. Some portions of the church willingly supported this group, with many clergy even participating in government-sanctioned pogroms.[16]

Nicholas II, the last of the Romanov Dynasty (reigned 1894–1917), further bound the church to the state when he approved state payments of clerical salaries. The announced purpose of this move was to improve the economic security of the priesthood, but its no-doubt intended effect was to force the clergy into even greater dependence on state "generosity," turning it even more into a pliable arm of autocracy. Priests were transformed into "state officials of the twentieth category" and became indistinguishable from any other department in the state bureaucracy. So tight was the connection that one archbishop declared "a priest dared not preach against drunkenness, since that might be harmful to the state vodka monopoly."[17]

In February 1912 Nicholas issued Decree #1198, giving the Minister of the Interior "the right to be kept fully and everywhere informed about every manifestation of the religious life of heterodox religions."[18]

The philosopher John Dewey noted:

Nowhere in the modern world, not even in Old Mexico at its height, was the union of institutional religion and the established political and economic regime as close as in Russia.[19]

EAST AND WEST II

The Eastern Orthodox Church (Russian, Greek, Serbian, etc.) considered itself the One True Church. The Catholic Church to the west was a heresy, and Protestants were a heresy of a heresy. The Orthodox believed that differences between East and West reduced to three levels: ritual, dogma, and spirituality—in ascending order of importance. Although various ecumenical councils had tried and failed to resolve issues of ritual, in the grand scheme of things this was of little consequence. Issues of dogma were more serious.

In 1854 Pope Pius IX declared that Mary was immaculately conceived—that is, not only did she commit no actual sin, but she did not inherit original sin. The new Catholic view was not a doctrine of the Orthodox Church, nor did the Orthodox have a doctrine against it, but most members of the Eastern Church did not accept this notion because it too strongly separated Mary from Adam.[20] The *filioque* and new doctrines of Mary were suspect innovations. But these paled compared with the 1870 doctrine of papal infallibility; it is on the edge of impossibility that the Orthodox Church will ever accept it.

Overall, the Orthodox perceived themselves as less dependent on and less reverential toward dogma than Catholics—and as having less of it. Orthodoxy considered only the Nicene Creed ("I believe in . . . one Holy, Catholic [universal], and Apostolic Church. . . .") and the definitions agreed upon at the first seven ecumenical councils as absolutely necessary dogma; all else was theological teaching that left room for minor variations. The Orthodox theologian Sergius Bulgakov wrote that his church "is a stranger to the legalistic spirit, even in the matter of doctrine."[21]* These concerns, of course, mainly affected the hierarchy of the church. If we think of the *people* as the church, they prayed to God that it would rain when their crops needed water; issues of dogma were far from their minds.

From the Orthodox perspective, spirituality was the *essential* difference between themselves and Catholics. They believed that the East retained a deepness of connection to God that was lost in the West. This spiritual connection was

---

*Bulgakov had been secretary to Leo Tolstoy until the latter's death.

lost even in the Russian theological seminaries, which were so influenced by Western ways of learning and Western knowledge. Only the Russian peasants really understood and lived this pure spiritual relationship with God. "Degenerate" Catholic teachings and corrupt leadership all occurred *after* its historical separation from Orthodoxy.

Western Christianity was, according to the Orthodox, more concerned with happiness here on Earth, extracting those aspects of Christian teachings that would lead to and support a pleasant earthly experience. Orthodoxy, on the other hand, was ascetic in the sense that the aim of Christianity was the moral perfection of the individual. Asceticism—or "spiritual heroism," as Metropolitan Anthony of Kiev called it—was aimed at suppressing and destroying the passions of fornication, pride, spite, envy, gluttony, and laziness. Thus asceticism meant constant warfare with one's thoughts and a vision fixed on life after death. In many ways the Orthodox were (and still are) "renunciationists," seeing the present life as a "vanishing vapor" (James 4:14).

The Orthodox view on love and compassion was that they should be applied not just to those who suffered external misfortune but to those who cried over their own sins—that is, to people who were already practicing the ideal of asceticism. Orthodoxy held that Westerners were too individualistic; too much emphasis was put on "the feeling of personal worth" and the achievement of saving one's own soul. Orthodox asceticism aimed at individual perfection, but that perfection was a state of humility and spiritual union with God—and a mystical unity with all the other saved souls of the universe. The Holy Spirit would descend upon them. This may be why in Orthodoxy there is no doctrine of purgatory between Earth and heaven.[22]

The Russian Church also placed a heavy emphasis on repentance and forgiveness. It saw Catholic communion as tending toward the mechanical and perfunctory, whereas communion within Orthodoxy was taken only after great soul searching, often requiring months of preparation, as the sacrament should not be taken until all who have sinned against you have been forgiven. Forgiveness was a powerful virtue. The story goes that in 1943 emaciated German POWs were being marched across Red Square in Moscow, when Russian Orthodox women rushed out to hand them bread in spite of the family losses they had suffered during the war.[23]

Both Catholicism and Protestantism were simply mistaken about the method of achieving salvation. Church historian Edward Roslof described the Orthodox view:

> The Orthodox Eucharist is a series of manifestations of divine immanence through the performance of ritualistic acts. Salvation in this tradition comes not from grace dispensed by the true church, as in Catholicism, or from belief evoked by preaching the Word of God, as in Protestantism. Rather, Orthodox believers are saved by the proper and corporate completion of liturgical acts in which God himself is present.[24]

As for Protestantism specifically, it was disdained for two interconnected reasons. The first was at the root of the problem: *sola scriptura* (scripture alone). Protestants contended that the scriptures were open to new interpretations and that certain passages of scripture could be emphasized at the expense of others, outside of the body of tradition. This, the Orthodox maintained, led to the sins of arrogance and modernity—arrogance in believing that your denomination or sect had discovered something that for centuries others had missed and modernity in the sense of believing that anything in the Bible could be understood separated from the wisdom of the church fathers.

The second reason for disdain was the divisions and multiplicity that *sola scriptura* caused. There were hundreds of disparate groups within the general category of Protestantism. The Orthodox believed that since they could not all be right, none were right. Each disagreed with the others as to what the Bible said and what it meant, but they all agreed on one thing—the Bible was to be interpreted "on your own," apart from church tradition. Orthodoxy, on the other hand, pointed to St. Ignatius of Antioch (presumably a disciple of the Apostle John), who warned, "Make no mistake brethren, no one who follows another into a schism will inherit the Kingdom of God." (Of course, the Orthodox Church would suffer through its own schisms in the seventeenth and twentieth centuries.)

Orthodox theologians were not as harsh as one might suspect with Martin Luther, the founder of the Protestant Reformation. Considering the state of the church in Rome at the time, it was thought reasonable that he sought reform. He was not directly accused of *sola scriptura*, and he never tried to eliminate tradition altogether; he merely hoped to rid Roman tradition of corruptions. Others, however, took the idea of *sola scriptura* to its logical conclusion.

The longer the river of history flowed, the more errors had a chance to enter the stream. Orthodoxy desired to remain at the headwaters and saw Protestantism struggling downstream into the widely dispersed waters of the delta. The fathers of Orthodoxy had proclaimed the tenets of their faith as inviolable, thus no deviation could be tolerated. It was not the job of the individual to strive for originality but to convey to the next generation what was already understood. The Orthodox Church alone preserved the divine doctrines just as they were committed to her and would preserve them without an iota of change to the end of the ages. Bulgakov explained:

> Retaining these forms [of the ancient ecumenical councils] is not an archaism,
> for their supreme verity still imposes itself upon the religious and philosophical
> conscience of our time.[25]

Orthodoxy was also highly critical of modern Protestantism's attitude toward science. Attempts by archaeologists to unearth artifacts from biblical times to put biblical events within a solid historical context might be interesting but were certainly not necessary. The Orthodox approach to scripture was not based on scientific research, but rather, as its theologians said, upon the church's "unique relationship with the Author of the Scriptures." They proclaimed the Orthodox Church to be the body of Christ and the pillar of Truth. It was the inheritor of a single living tradition beginning with Adam and stretching through all time. It could not be proven in the lab but must be mystically experienced through the descent of the Holy Spirit into the soul.

These theologians subscribed to St. Augustine's teaching that more important than intellectual knowledge was the kinds of persons who received the knowledge. They should love God with their whole heart, be empty of pride, keep a pure mind dead to worldly temptations, neither fear men nor seek to please them, thirst for righteousness, and show mercy and love through their works. And they should be "doers of the Word and not hearers only" (James 1:22).[26] As for the divisive issue of faith, works, and merit, Orthodoxy found itself on middle ground between Catholics and Calvinists. Good works would not get you into heaven, nor had your salvation been predetermined. Bulgakov again: "Faith . . . is an enduring state which is constantly reaffirmed; and to be affirmed, faith should be active; it must include good works."[27]*

The Orthodox Church was not enthralled with the concept of ecumenism, calling it a false unity. Christ came to Earth to build his church, not to establish various schools of thought that compromised with each other for the sake of an artificial peace. Orthodoxy said it provided an organic unity, not a mechanical unification of internally divided persons. Unity was sought in the Eucharist as it was celebrated in a local church; the Apostles, the Church Fathers, and the saints in heaven were considered to be there with worshipers as much as, or even more than, those physically present.

SIZE AND ORGANIZATION

In 1917 there were around 48,000 functioning Russian Orthodox churches (perhaps 54,000 if we include monastery churches and various chapels). As for the church hierarchy, at the bottom was the parish laity, comprising perhaps 117 million persons. The next step up was the church deacons, who, combined with the priesthood, may have numbered around 50,000. The country was partitioned into sixty-seven dioceses, each containing around twenty parishes. Each diocese sup-

---

*Actually, Section 2016 of the Catechism of the Catholic Church reads: "The children of our holy mother the Church rightly hope for the grace of final perseverance and the recompense of God their Father for the good works accomplished *with his grace in communion with Jesus* [emphasis added]." So Orthodoxy is closer to the Catholic view than to the Protestant view.

ported a bishop, but there were also many auxiliary bishops—the total coming to 130.[28] The title of archbishop was personal and referred to no local jurisdiction. Bishops and archbishops served under one of the three metropolitans, each the head of one of the three greater monasteries in Russia: the Pechersky (Cave) Monastery at Kiev, founded in 1051 CE; the St. Sergius-Trinity Monastery just north of Moscow, and the St. Alexander Nevsky Monastery in St. Petersburg/Petrograd. Around 20,000 monks and 60,000 nuns served in 550 monasteries and 475 convents. All—laity, clergy, and hierarchs alike—were subject to the overarching Holy Synod and its chief procurator.[29]

The major organizational split within the framework of the Orthodox Church was between the white clergy (priests) and the black clergy (monks). The white clergy were parish priests who were required to marry before ordination (and allowed to marry but once). If a priest's wife died, canon law theoretically allowed him to take monastic vows, but this seldom occurred in practice.[30] Before reforms in the 1860s, priests were legally rooted to their occupations, as were serfs, unable to move or advance in any way. Even in later years the white clergy found their road to ecclesiastical advancement effectively blocked, as, its members being married, they could not receive the monastic tonsure and thus could not become bishops.

Priests' sons became priests, were conscripted into the army, or, after the end of serfdom in 1861, just wandered away into towns. Many, though having no calling for the church, were pressured into seminaries anyway. Seminaries provided them a free education, but as secular higher education became increasingly available many a priest's son was lured away to a secular career. This trend left behind the least competent sons to follow in the footsteps of their fathers. Often bishops would automatically appoint a son upon his father's death, even if he showed no evidence of learning or pastoral skills. In many parishes, priestly dynasties flowed through the generations in this way.[31]

Until 1917 white clergy felt they had no say in the operation of the church. They certainly felt no respect from petty church officials whose sole responsibility was to the chief procurator or to the police. Their social class was essentially that of the peasantry they served, and the respect they received within this social class was often not great. The only saving grace was that congregations usually forgave their priests their sins and drew a distinction between the priest and the religion he represented.[32]

The Russian priesthood has been described as "ignorant, envious, and powerless," which explains why some of its members gravitated toward movements promising sweeping social change. Among these was the priest Georgy Gapon, leader of the protest march on January 22, 1905—"Bloody Sunday"—that inaugurated the abortive 1905 Revolution. Another, though only a seminarian, was Joseph Vissarionovich Djugashvili—Stalin.

The black clergy—monks who had taken vows of celibacy—was itself divided. Traditional monasticism expected humility, poverty, piety, and a life of quiet contemplation, but in the seventeenth century academic monasticism, borrowed from Roman Catholics, entered Russia by way of the Kiev Theological Academy. The emphasis here was on learning and advancement. The tonsure was taken specifically to ensure promotion through the episcopal ranks. Piety became suspect when power and ambition were the chief motivators.[33]

From the black clergy came the church's bishops, who often enjoyed the promotion but found themselves in an uncomfortable position. They tended to come from the clerical class, either as unmarried or (rarely) widowed priests. Though often men of intelligence, learning, and devotion to the church, they endured lonely lives, never meeting in larger convocations and seldom familiar with the people of their own diocese. This was church historian Nicolas Zernov's description:

> [The bishops] were seen only as enigmatic figures, dressed in their gorgeous robes, when they celebrated the divine offices. The external pomp that surrounded them emphasized their helplessness and isolation.[34]

Ambitious bishops sometimes attained high church office but then were frequently accused of possessing or developing unchristian political instincts. Some did develop an arrogant attitude toward the lowly priesthood.

The Synod was reasonably effective as a church administrator, yet it managed this only by maintaining a colossal bureaucracy. Most of these church officials were laymen, with a smattering of senior priests. No action could be taken involving the affairs of the church without the consent of the chief procurator; he could veto any synodal decision he believed failed to conform to the laws of the state.

Although the Synod shaped nineteenth-century Russian attitudes, it was the patriarchate, reestablished in November 1917, that the Bolsheviks would have to battle. Clearly, the more malleable Synod would have presented an easier target for Soviet manipulation, lacking the moral authority and potential for martyrdom that a patriarch would possess. As will be discussed in chapter 5, however, the patriarchate was not re-created for the purpose of combating Bolshevik power. This change of church leadership emerged from long-standing grievances that were being worked out concurrently with the assault on the Winter Palace in Petrograd.

By the early twentieth century, the church epitomized all that liberals, progressives, and radicals abhorred within the imperial system. As the intelligentsia's rebellion against state repression escalated, the "unholy alliance" between church and state confirmed their alienation from both. They saw tsarist Russia and her national church as the bulwark of the most backward social system since the Turkish Empire.

2

THEY RESIGN THEIR LIVES TO PROVIDENCE

Weaknesses in Church and Culture

The Russian Church was a part of Russian society and both, relative to the West, were something of a cultural backwater. The waves of rationalism that swept over Western Europe in the seventeenth and eighteenth centuries barely dampened the Russian landscape. But even nonrationalists found much to criticize in the condition of Orthodoxy. When the church excommunicated Leo Tolstoy in 1901, he answered back:

> I am convinced that the teaching of the church is theoretically a crafty and injurious falsehood, and practically a conglomeration of gross superstitions and sorceries beneath which true Christianity has utterly disappeared. . . . If one ventures to remind men that all these prayers, masses, candles, and images have no connection with the teachings of Christ, that he simply commanded men to love one another, not to return evil for evil, and not to kill their fellows, then immediately all those who profit by the lie burst into indignation and protest with incredible boldness saying that Christ taught none of these things. . . . If Christ should return today and see what is done in his name in the churches, he would not fail to fling [all this paraphernalia] away from him.[1]

But Orthodoxy in Russian is *pravoslavie*, which means the "the correct way to exalt God," and no matter what its weaknesses the Russian Orthodox Church had a monopoly on it.

The Forbidding (1912)

On the great plain northeast of Moscow the wheat billowed in the wind as far as the eye could see in any direction. On this sweltering August day, many in the village languished in the heat, but most were bustling with activity. Today, Father Michael had said, is the day to prevent from happening what had happened last year and two years prior to that.

41

Giggling children emerged from the church as the priest berated them to be careful. Four chubby hands were firmly latched onto the four corners of each of the ikons of the nation's saints and local holy men of past ages. Settling down somewhat, considering the seriousness of their work this day, they joined the gathering procession as it moved gently, kicking up dust, toward the dividing line between the village and its fields. The vivid colors of the women's dresses contrasted nicely with the uniformity of the grain.

For nine months these peasants had labored—clearing, sowing, cultivating, and watching as their sustenance for the coming winter grew lush upon its stems. Last year at this time—actually eleven and a half months ago—just as the heads were maturing to brown, locusts appeared, millions (it seemed), and devoured their crops in two days. Of course, the procession had entered the fields last year, too, but this time, with God's good grace (and perhaps less sinning in the village), it might be different. Father Michael, carrying the most valuable ikon of St. Sergius himself, led the marchers a little way around one edge of the first field then gathered all about him for a preliminary prayer:

> Today we invoke the name of Holy Triphon and ask him to pray for us. Let the Earth bring forth its fruits at the proper time. Have mercy upon us and deliver us from those enemies that would deny these good people what they have toiled so hard to obtain. Holy Triphon, pray for us.

Then he explained what they already knew, that by using holy water, crosses, candles, and prayer they would erect a magical barrier around their crops that no insect, worm, mouse, ant, or caterpillar—not even a dry, burning wind—could cross.

Triphon was a third-century Christian martyr in Asia Minor who had saved his own crops with appeals to the Lord against marauding insects before he gave up his own life to the Romans. That this technique would still work seventeen centuries later was not doubted by any in the procession. The priest led them farther around the fields, even as the midday sun beat down and made their loads heavier. Wasn't the efficacy of this effort at least partly determined by the suffering that went along with it? The other part, of course, depended on following established procedure to the letter. No short cuts. No rest stops. No jollity—except for the children who were difficult to control.

After walking for hours and many miles, they were allowed to stop at a brook, drink of it, and prepare for the main prayer—the one that would erect the impenetrable barrier. Father Michael called out in a loud voice (glancing in a small book to get the names right):

Worms and grasshoppers!
Mice and rats!
Ants, moles, and reptiles!
Flies and horseflies and hornets!
And all the flying things that wreak destruction ...

I forbid you in the name of the Savior come on Earth to suffer for men. I forbid you in the name of the all-seeing cherubim and seraphim, who fly around the heavenly throne. I forbid you in the name of the angels and the millions of heavenly spirits standing in the glory of God. I forbid you to touch any tree, fruitful or unfruitful, or leaf or plant or flower. I forbid you to bring any woe upon the fields of these people.

He dipped his long-handled brush into the holy water and flung the spray far to the north, south, east, and west. Then he said another prayer, more threatening this time. If all these pests did not obey him and flee to the barren wastelands where no crop can grow, then the God of Abraham, Isaac, and Jacob would bring terrible birds to gobble them up. "Like wax before fire, melt and disappear! Away from these fields! Away and perish!"

Father Michael inwardly hoped that his invocations would work this time, lest it be the faith of the people that perished.[2]

SUPERSTITION AND FATALISM

The peasant with his childlike soul will believe in miracles. The poor, robbed by the nobility, cheated by the officials, deceived by the emancipation act, exhausted from endless labor, from inescapable poverty, the peasant will believe. He is too crushed, too unhappy not to be superstitious. Not knowing where to lay his head at heavy moments when human needs ask for rest and for hope; surrounded by a pack of ferocious enemies, he will come to drop a hot tear to the dumb sarcophagus, to the dumb body of the saint; and by this relic, by this sarcophagus, he will be deceived, he will be comforted so as not to fall into other comforts.[3]

—Alexander Herzen

There is some dispute over the depth of religious feeling among Russia's peasantry. Vissarion Belinsky, Chekhov, and Lenin emphasized rural superstition, with the implication that once it was exposed their faith would falter. Fyodor Dostoevsky, however, was certain that the *true* Christian Church in Russia dwelt among the peasants.[4]

The Beauty of Myth

There was a strong tendency during the late nineteenth and early twentieth centuries to idealize and romanticize the peasant and his presumed deep spirituality. Listen to the words of the British traveler and journalist Stephen Graham gushing in 1914 about peasant women:

> During all their life they never forget God, they never sully themselves, they are never tempted by evil. Simply and tranquilly they live, their eyes full of light because their hearts are pure. Because of them the woodsman is strong and happy. Because of them Russia is strong. Because of them the sun shines freshly and the birds sing.[5]

And a certain bishop wrote:

> [Peasants] study in prayer with humility and diligence and are enlightened by the Holy Spirit and are wiser than the philosophers of this age; they are devout and holy and beloved of God; although these do not know the alphabet, they well comprehend everything; they speak simply, crudely, but they live beautifully and auspiciously. These, O Christian, emulate.[6]

The peasantry, though generally good natured and hospitable, was also mythologized as peaceful—even to the extent of being the hope of the world. But reality was contrary to romance. Just as Japanese men in China and Southeast Asia during World War II, released from geographical and social constraints, showed a brutal savagery that few—including these men themselves—knew was latent within them, the same was true of Russian peasants during the few periods of their history when suppression was lifted long enough for them to act. As we shall see, the horrors of the Civil War offered vivid testimony to this fact. Maurice Hindus, a traveler in Russia during the 1920s, called foreign-born sentiments "mawkish myth."[7] Most peasants lived a life of parochial drudgery punctuated by an abundance of holy days where drinking, gossip, and quarreling occupied more of their time than worship inside the church. Their life was full of Christian nostrums, prescribed fasting, and church attendance—religious form without spiritual substance.

Rebaptizing the Pagan Spirits

Church historian George Fedotov wrote of Russia's agricultural society, "In Mother Earth, who remains the core of Russian religion, converge the most secret and deep religious feelings of the folk."[8] Most peasants would ask the Earth for forgiveness *before* submitting to the Christian confession.[9] Russian conversion to Christianity in the tenth century entailed few modifications of this mindset. The new teachings blended nicely with pagan beliefs. Russians simplified and nationalized Byzantine Christianity and mingled it with what they knew. Former gods were now termed "God with many angels," and they were still revered. Evil spirits, now called demons, were still feared. Belief in the efficacy of all these supernatural beings never faltered. An example of this syncretization is the worship of the fertility god Kupalo in pre-Christian Ukraine. Christian bishops, disgusted with libertine fertility festivals honoring this god, suppressed them by merging Kupalo Day with the feast of the Nativity of John the Baptist, calling it Ivana Kupala and toning down its pagan voluptuous nature.[10]*

Christian saints often emerged from rebaptized pagan gods. Perun, the ancient god of thunder and lightning, now became Elijah roaring in the heavens. Earlier fetish worship continued with new symbols: the cross, ikons, relics of saints, holy water, communion wafers, incense, and the Bible. To the majority of the masses these objects were magic. According to Hindus, the clergy did little to disabuse the peasantry of the powers of "witches, sorcerers [and] magicians, . . . charmers that infested the villages and preyed on the *muzhik* [peasant]."[11] It was in the interests of Russian Christianity, as it had been for all Christianity since Constantine, to incorporate what was unavoidable into the new faith.

Two British travelers in prerevolutionary Russia described the peasant way of thinking. Donald Mackenzie Wallace wrote in 1877:

> The Russian Church has always paid inordinate attention to ceremonial observances and somewhat neglected the doctrinal and moral elements of the faith which it professes. This peculiarity greatly facilitated the spread of its influence among the people accustomed to pagan rites and magical incantations, but it had the pernicious effect of confirming in the new converts their superstitious belief in the virtue of mere ceremonies.
>
> Thus the Russians became zealous Christians in all manners of external observance, without knowing much about the spiritual meaning of the rites which they practiced. They looked upon the rites and sacraments as mysterious charms which preserved them from evil influences, . . . and they believed that these charms would inevitably lose their efficacy if modified in the slightest degree.[12]

And Bernard Pares observed in 1905:

> The peasant is even more ignorant [than the lower monks]. His mind is often full of a whole host of non-Christian superstitions, of native poetic traditions, glen and wood and water fairies, and curious prejudices as to "luck." Luck is more often than not "bad luck."[13]

Surviving from some ancient time was the belief that crops should be sown on Mondays or Thursdays and that a bright moon on Christmas Eve was a sign

---

*A subdued version of this festival is still practiced in Russia.

of good harvests the following year.[14] Like many traditions, the origins were lost in time. The modern writer Moshe Lewin put it this way:

> The church adapted herself and adopted popular customs in order to rule and maintain its monopoly over the supernatural and the sacred as defined in its own terms. In turn, the rural world did its part from the other end. They accepted, selectively, the official new creed, but chewed up and transformed many of its elements. The peasants also preserved many components from their own old religion and carried them down through the centuries into our own time.[15]

The best occasion to observe the full extent of surviving pagan beliefs was ironically the "Christian" festivals held in villages throughout the year on saint days. Although Orthodox dogma held that the departed were still members of the Christian community, the village's pagan-based ancestor cult far exceeded anything the church could officially tolerate. Peasants left food out for departed relatives, chatted with them at their tables, and sent them kisses at their graves.[16] Few decisions were made without consultation with those who had lived before.

To the Western mind, the Russian peasantry was riddled with superstition, but the bias of the Western perspective must be recognized. As is commonly said, "One man's religion is another man's superstition"—and vice versa. From the atheist's point of view, the whole body of organized (and unorganized) religion, even faith-based spirituality, was superstition. The term has a pejorative sense. For our purposes this definition should suffice: "Superstition is an irrational but usually deep-seated belief in the magical effects of a particular action or ritual, especially in the likelihood that good or bad luck will result from performing it." (Of course, prayer would come awfully close to qualifying under this definition.) The priest himself was seen as something of a magician. Utilizing ikons, crosses, holy water, and certain magical signs, he could bring God's grace from Heaven to Earth. The priest's actual holiness mattered little. A fee was paid, the magic was performed, and the peasant was protected and satisfied. It was not just the blessing of cows and crops; all the Christian sacraments were magical as well. The peasant participating in these rituals was not thinking of how they fit into God's heavenly plan. He was expecting practical results and even material gain.[17]

Due to the generally low level of cultural development in rural Russia and the prevalence of poverty and illiteracy, superstitions remained at the root of the peasants' faith. The Soviet sociological study *The Village of Viriatino* (1958) told of the Christmas mass when everyone would go to the river for a ritual called the "Blessing of the Water." They would collect this holy water, bring it home, wash themselves in it, and sprinkle it on their livestock. They stored the sacred water for a year, and if anyone should fall ill during this time he or she would be washed again with it. On Christmas morning the head of the household sprinkled some of the holy water on unthreshed grain and breadcrumbs and fed it to his animals.[18]

Albert Rhys Williams, a Congregational minister from Boston with extensive experience in Russia, told this story of a conversation in the village of Salvation on the Vladimir plains in the mid-1920s. He and a Communist guide were discussing the Doctrine of Holy Water with the village priest:

> "Take two bottles," [the priest] explained to me, as an outsider. "Fill one with just ordinary water. Fill the other with water that has been blessed in the proper way. Let them stand a few months—the ordinary water may be spoiled, but the consecrated water will be just as fresh as new."

"Did you ever do that experiment?" asked the Communist. Father Popov was dumbfounded. For to him, as to tens of millions of members of the Orthodox Church, this was a plain matter of fact. This was the way water acted. Heat water and it boils, freeze water and it solidifies into ice, and consecrate water and it stays unspoiled. What was there to experiment about?[19]

"The priest goes his way, the Devil his own" was a common folk saying. The peasant's hut was infiltrated and surrounded by demons, few of which were benign: There was the house spirit; the bathhouse spirit; the grain dryer spirit; and the spirits of woods, fields, and even women working in the fields (a particularly dangerous one). Illnesses—especially mental illnesses—were all attributable to angry demons, just as they were in first-century Galilee. Many could transform themselves into any object or person, useful for explaining unexpected pregnancies. Demons, the "evil eye," and unfriendly spirits could, of course, be placated, bribed, scared off, or outsmarted, and the peasants put much effort into this. Often this was accomplished with Christian symbols. Similar to Western custom, peasants crossed their mouths after a yawn to protect against demonic entry,[20] but contrary to the West these rituals were performed assiduously and seriously well into the nineteenth century and in some areas right on through the 1917 Revolution.

Many peasant superstitions had a material tinge to them, as if there were something corporeal about a spiritual experience. In rural areas around Samara, even into the Communist period, a peasant family would invite the village priest to bless their house, filling it with God's grace. Then, as soon as he left, they would plug up the chimney and any cracks in the walls to prevent any "grace" from escaping.[21]

Fortune-telling and divining were widespread among the rural population, especially among the women. In Viriatino, a girl used a chicken to foretell the quality of her husband-to-be. She would spread grain on the floor along with a randomly placed looking glass, a piece of charcoal, and a small dish of water; then the chicken would be allowed in. If it first approached the looking glass, the husband would be a handsome and elegant man; if it moved toward the charcoal, he would be a coal miner; and if toward the water, a drunkard. Then she would toss a boot in front of the gate—the toe magically pointing in the direction of the girl's future home.[22]

Fatalism suffused the peasantry's attitude toward nature and the elements. In the Kirsanovsk District of Tambov Province, to estimate the yield of future harvests the oldest family member would leave a few grains of rye overnight in the snow. If there was a slight covering of ice on the grains in the morning, he assumed that there would be plenty of grain for bread the following year. If not, once the prediction was made he was unlikely to consider that more vigorous work in the fields could significantly alter the result.[23]

Instead of encouraging innovative agricultural techniques, village priests urged reliance upon faith and the priests' own talents in interceding with God. Often, this dependence could work to the peasants' detriment and the priests' profit. In the early 1920s there were reports in the Tver newspapers that a few priests had secretly purchased barometers. When the mercury fell they agreed to pray for rain, otherwise they found an excuse. Their "miraculous" skills in bringing sorely needed precipitation earned them extra donations of food.[24] Soviet agricultural agents attempted to convince farmers that they could defeat drought if only they would plow deeper. The typical reply:

> Rain is God's gift; it is impious to try to circumvent his will. If he sends rain the crops will grow; if not, it is a sign that we must suffer for our sins. There is, in emergencies, only one hopeful course—the bishop must pray for rain.[25]

Bernard Pares did unearth a few priests whose work he respected. Some would read aloud to the whole village from manuals on modern crop-planting techniques, and others devoted great effort to eliminate the scourge of drunkenness— the greatest destroyer of productivity.[26]

In rural villages the Russian priesthood revealed few signs of a profoundly spiritual life. For the most part they reflected and perpetuated the abject fatalism and naivete of the peasants. Through the priesthood, the church taught that progress and success could *not* be achieved by man's efforts. Rewards in this life came from participating in fasts prescribed on the church calendar and from praying in front of paintings of saints.

Ikons

Veneration of ikons lay at the heart of the peasant's faith. They transmitted grace from God, through the pictured saint, to the worshiper. Officially sanctioned at the seventh Ecumenical Council in 787, ikons were paintings of Christ, the Apostles, or saints meant to be venerated, not worshiped. Believers brought the Vladimir ikon—a portrait of the Virgin Mary, thought to have been painted by St. Luke and presented to the Mother of God in person—from Constantinople to Russia during the twelfth century. It reputedly saved Moscow, and Russian Christianity itself, from the Mongol Tamerlane's onslaught in 1395 when it was moved from the city of Vladimir to Moscow just in time to cause Tamerlane to suffer a nightmarish vision of impending defeat and to vacate the battlefield the next morning. It was hidden again in Vladimir during the Napoleonic invasion and, when returned to Moscow, became the holiest object in Russia. In Russian iconography Mary was a "super-saint."[27]

The power of an originally painted ikon was, with the proper blessing, transferable to copies made for the home.[28] Stephen Graham wrote in 1914:

> The ikons in the churches, cathedrals, monasteries, and shrines are the symbols of the saints and of God. The ikons in the homes are the symbols of the ikons in the churches . . . as all crosses may be understood as [symbols] of the original Cross on Calvary.
>
> Every Russian home has ikons. . . . The ikon claims the home and the man for God; it indicates God's ownership. . . . In every Russian room there is an ikon. . . . It occupies what is known as the front corner of every room; that is the corner towards the rising sun. . . . If you sleep in a Russian home, the ikon with its little lamp before it looks down upon you all night and guards you from evil. It teaches little children not to be afraid of the dark.[29]

The home ikon was imbued with the power to see and hear the grievances and the prayers of family members. It was living. (Even into the 1950s, older peasant women kept ikons in the home. They no longer prayed before them and, to visitors, espoused the goals of communism, but, as one woman said, "An empty corner without ikons doesn't look right.") Ikons were even placed in the barn with the hope of driving away mice.[30]

In the West, ikons, in addition to their beauty, were thought to have a pedagogical function—like stained-glass windows, they instructed the illiterate. In the East priests hung them on the iconostasis (separating the congregation from the sanctuary), and they were thought of as "windows to God," or sometimes as doors to the heavenly kingdom through which one became aware of the presence of God.[31] They were not the deity itself, though this theological distinction may have been lost on the average worker or peasant. Among thousands of ikons, the church held that 241 were painted by God himself—often portraying the Virgin Mary—and possessed miracle-working powers. The people placed implicit faith in them, and they played an important part in everyday life. Some monasteries even sold, for a *kopeck* (penny), small ikons of these saints painted on white wood that could be carried in one's pocket.[32]

One observer witnessed a group of peasants trying to halt the progress of a fire by placing the ikon of a saint between a burning house and the next building. But the notion of the power of God working through a saint and his venerated image transcended social class. Prince N. Zhevakhov, associate procurator of the Holy Synod during World War I, believed, and persuaded Tsarina Alexandra to believe, that the war had not been concluded successfully because an ikon of St.

Joseph had not been paraded along the army front as ordered by this saint in one of Zhevakhov's dreams.

Similar trust was placed in the power of the cross, and most Orthodox faithful wore their baptismal crosses around their necks day and night from infancy. Few would have taken the chance of diving into a lake or river for a swim without one.

Belief in the power of prayer for the dearly departed was also widespread. Much of the church's wealth grew from this practice, as worshipers were expected to bring gifts when church prayers were offered. The clergy frequently took advantage of its "powers" by convincing parishioners that more prayers, and hence more gifts, would enhance the chances that their departed relatives would be relieved of punishment for their mortal sins. The saying in the country-side was, "For the priest, the unenlightened people is a source of income."[33]

Russian peasants would have been condemned as heretics if they had lived in the Catholic West. The Orthodox Church, by intention and of necessity, toler-ated wildly divergent practices as long as one called himself a member of the National Church. When the Englishman Edward Daniel Clarke traveled across the Russian continent in the nineteenth century, he commented:

> The wild, untutored savage of South America, who prostrates himself before the sun and pays his adoration to that which he believes to be the source of life and light, exercises more rational devotion than the Russian, who is all day crossing himself . . . and sticking farthing candles before a picture of St. Alexander Nevsky.[34]

HUMILITY AND SUFFERING

For unto you it is given on behalf of Christ, not only to believe in him, but also to suffer for his sake.

—Philippians 1:29

The church taught that the body is opposed to the "spiritual man" and must be sacrificed to save the soul. Piety in Russia meant the cross, sorrow, mortification of the flesh, and death. Where was the joy of living? The church hierarch Anthony Khrapovitsky answered during the 1905 uprisings that "we were sent to Earth by God not for happiness."[35] And an Orthodox cleric wrote in 1913:

> Asceticism is the foundation of historical Christianity. It is its principal peculi-arity; it is its pillar of truth, and in Russia it has received a particular emphasis. . . . In asceticism, in the merging of the body into the mystery of Christ, in this beautiful sorrow lies the true life of a Christian; besides such mode of life he

does not want any other, for his kingdom is not of this world. Death and the Russian soul are inseparable.[36]

From a theological perspective, of course, remaining humble and enduring suffering were not thought of as weaknesses but as strengths. But from a historical point of view these "virtues" put the church in an awkward position, both in relation to its secular enemies and its religious rivals.

The peasant remained humble because he knew that he was filled with sin. Church attendance provided relief from past sin and a fortress against future sin. For a while he might ignore the church, or even ridicule it, but when the inevitable sin returned he would be back in church where he knew that he could be cleansed. The priest was indulgent of this human cycle, this indulgence being part of the power that the church had over the peasantry.[37]

Asceticism did not mean that one had to live in caves and practice flagellation, but it was necessary to "bear the cross of suffering"—to practice self-reproach, self-abasement, self-resistance, and self-constraint. Metropolitan Benjamin (who will play an important role in chapters 11 and 12) reflected upon his youthful reading of the lives of the saints:

> With all my heart I sorrowed over the fact that times had changed and one no longer had to suffer what they suffered. Times have changed again [after the Bolshevik Revolution], and the opportunity has been opened to suffer for Christ [once more].[38]

And in one of his letters while awaiting execution by the Soviet government:

> It is difficult, hard to suffer, but according to the measure of my sufferings, consolation abounds from God. . . . [When one gives oneself over wholly to the will of God] man abounds in consolation and does not even feel the greatest sufferings; filled as he is in the midst of sufferings by an inner peace, he draws others to sufferings so that they should imitate that condition in which the happy sufferer finds himself.[39]

CHRISTIAN ILLITERACY AND THE PRESERVATION OF TRUTH

Heavily endowed by the state, the Russian Church did as the state bade it, endorsed every action of the government, and threw all the weight of its influence against progressive and liberating movements.[40]

—William Henry Chamberlin, 1926

Perhaps 85 percent of the rural population was illiterate in the mid-nineteenth century and 70 percent of the whole population—especially the elderly—in 1917.[41] During the previous half century, locally run *zemstvo* schools and church parish schools had made great progress, but ironically the educational attainment of parish priests declined markedly during the last twenty-five years of tsarist rule. Ignorance of the written language, however, was only one of the problems. Visitors to Russia in the seventeenth century were appalled that only one person in ten knew the "Our Father," the Ten Commandments, or the Creed.[42] One would have been hard pressed to discover a single peasant who had even heard of the Sermon on the Mount. A Dane visiting Russia in the eighteenth century concluded, "Our thirteen-year-olds with any education at all know more about the subject [of the Bible] than most Russian adults."[43]

Another reason for Christian illiteracy was that the entire Bible was not translated into modern Russian from the unintelligible Old Church Slavonic until the mid-nineteenth century and was thus unavailable even to the literate.[44] The overarching reason, though, was the complete absence of sermons in church services. When the seventeenth-century visitors asked why sermonizing was ignored, they were told that religion was too high a science for ordinary peasants and that it was reserved for the tsar, the nobility, and the clergy itself. Visitors who tried to engage Russian priests in discussions of God and morality found the conversation diverted to issues of fasting and eliciting the intervention of saints.[45]

In the first years of the twentieth century Constantine Pobedonostsev, chief procurator of the Orthodox Church, described with a clear conscience what he considered the religious mentality of the peasantry:

> Our clergy teaches little and seldom. The Bible does not exist for the illiterate people. . . . In far off parts of the country the people understand absolutely nothing as to the meaning of the words of the service, not even the Lord's Prayer, which is often repeated with alterations which altogether destroy its meaning. And yet, in all those primitive minds there is erected, as in ancient Athens, an altar to the unknown God, and they resign their lives to Providence.[46]

Bible reading in the common language was not considered necessary for the church service, and anyway it was suspect as a Protestant innovation.[47] Consequently, the teachings of Jesus had little effect on the moral code of the people or their social behavior, concepts of right and wrong instead being shaped by time-honored customs and by ancient proverbs and folk sayings. These maxims, handed down over generations, offered prescriptions and proscriptions for almost every aspect of daily living. To the extent that villagers were aware of Christian concepts and biblical teachings at all, they simply synchronized them with what they already knew.[48]

Theological questions did not concern the common people—only the ritual of daily living. Their faith was essentially functional and utilitarian. Ikon and relic "worship," feast days, and sacerdotal functions served to keep the evil spirits away and to prevent disease and famine. The peasants' interests were of such a practical nature—mainly the protection and fertility of their crops—that under some definitions they would not be considered religious at all. Maurice Hindus reported many cases of peasants "invoking the aid of God for success in robbery, arson, and murder."[49]

Critics of the Orthodox Church in the early twentieth century described an institution in a rather low moral state. Francis McCullagh, a British correspondent traveling through Russia in the early 1920s, observed, "The average [priest] had as little spirituality as the average shoemaker."[50] The church took the peasants' money to build magnificent churches and left them to dwell in miserable straw-thatched huts. It mesmerized them with mystic rites, church bells, and incense, while over three-quarters of them were unable to read and write. It offered them ikons to help ward off disease and left them to the ravages of plague and disaster. It held imposing ceremonies on feast days and left peasants wallowing in drunkenness. It encouraged passivity and resignation to fate at a time when the peasantry needed to be shaken out of its stupor if it was to survive.

On the other hand, it was the people's church. By 1917 out of 145 million citizens of the Russian Empire there were 100 million members of the Orthodox Church. They understood its imperfections as well as the imperfections of the priests for whom they prayed. The British writer Maurice Baring observed the Russian people on the eve of revolution and said, "Their Church smells of the poor,"[51] but it was the devotion of these poor that constituted the soul of the church.

There is a Western geographical bias inherent in this allegation of backwardness and reaction. In medieval Russia there was no St. Thomas Aquinas, no *Divine Comedy*, and there were no Gothic cathedrals. As briefly mentioned at the beginning of this chapter, the Renaissance, the Reformation, the Enlightenment, the French Revolution, and the Industrial Revolution shaped the Western European mind, making virtues of logic, rationalism, and the scientific method, exalting the concepts of progress and reform, but the Russian mind was barely touched by these forces and remained Byzantine in outlook. It made virtues out of the very qualities that Westerners so systematically attacked, characterizing them positively as stability and security and viewing progress with repugnance. This deeply felt need for continuity and tradition, which others called inertia and obscurantism, grew out of reverence for the pronouncements of the ancient Christian Ecumenical Councils. The fathers of the church had entrusted the clergy with the truth, and they struggled to maintain it in an unadulterated state; there were no new truths to discover. Instead there was simple Christian humility, contemplation, and the calling of the Holy Spirit. The Russian peasant was essentially a denizen of the Middle Ages well into the nineteenth century.

Because the Orthodox hierarchy perceived its mission as preserving the truth instead of searching for it, theologians adopted an apologetic function, attempting to guard against innovation. Thus the church had little need of a seminarian-trained, learned clergy. Church leaders expected scholarship to perpetuate traditional theology and to guard against heresy. In Russian monasteries excessive "book cunning" was looked upon with suspicion. A monk who did educate himself could be accused of spiritual pride, and, having been tempted by the Devil, liable to be dragged to perdition. The Russian historian Paul Miliukov made the point that this aversion to learning not only prevented Russian Orthodox theology from developing beyond the Council of Nicaea, it precluded efforts to preserve in pure form what it already had. He also argued that this ignorance led to the gradual "materializing" of Russian Orthodoxy— for example, its tendency to venerate relics and ikons while losing the spiritual meaning associated with them. Even the soul was seen with a pagan lack of sophistication; somehow it had more substance and location within the body than in the Catholic or Protestant West.[52]

The following example will illustrate the vulnerability of the Orthodox Church as it entered the twentieth century. The antidemocratic monk Konstantin Leontev (1831–1891) championed the Byzantine thinking that permeated the church at all levels. He taught that man was inwardly corrupt and hence could not be expected to easily believe in God. He must force himself into this belief, and he must force others to follow after him. For Leontev, God could not be known through reason, but only through mystical intuition. Neither philosophy nor science could lead to true knowledge of God, thus they were both antagonistic to religion. His conclusion was that Russia's overwhelming illiteracy was in reality Russia's good fortune, for it preserved its people from sin (at least the sin that seemed to bother him most—the sin of intellectual pride).

WEALTH AND POVERTY

The priests and monks lived on the fat of the land, with a superfluity of the goods of this world; abbots of monasteries and bishops especially wallowed in luxury. The eloquent preacher Gideon Krinovsky, archimandrite of the monastery of St. Sergius and later bishop of Pskov, wore diamond buckles in his shoes![53]

—anonymous, written shortly after the death of Peter the Great in 1725

Rubles

It is difficult to deal with the Orthodox Church's material assets as it was paradoxically floating in luxury and sinking in poverty. Like the Catholic Church in the West (but not Catholics in Russia), the Orthodox Church as an institution had become bloated with wealth. During the seventeenth century, as the tsars and the nobility steadily forced the peasantry into subjugation, serfdom was reaching its peak. The Orthodox Church exploited this economic system by skimming off its share of the spoils. Using biblical justifications, the patriarchate, the bishops, and the monasteries owned one-third of the Russian land. A small portion of this wealth was lost in the eighteenth century to the confiscations of Catherine II and her successor, who turned some church-owned land and 50,000 serfs over to their favorites among the nobility. In the nineteenth century, monasteries alone still owned millions of acres.[54] In addition to income from the land came payments from the faithful for candles, communion loaves, ikons, and pilgrimages to sacred places and relics.

In 1892 the Holy Synod, stung by criticism of venality, issued this description of the problem:

> Information has repeatedly come to the knowledge of the Holy Synod from our bishops that fathers and mothers-superior, to whom the custody of monasteries has been entrusted, keep monastery funds in their cells intermingled with their personal monies and expend these trust funds on the purchase of articles, the enjoyment of which is entirely out of keeping with clerical simplicity—such as adornment of the cells of the superiors with expensive furniture, carpets, and paintings, sometimes in gaudy hues, keeping expensive horses and carriages, and arranging luxurious dinners at which rare foreign wines are served. There have even been cases of ikons and crucifixes being sold by fathers and mothers-superior for their personal gain.[55]

Although the hierarchs acknowledged the abuses of avarice and gluttony, they moved sporadically and halfheartedly to correct them.

Church income was derived from endowments, income from landed estates, voluntary offerings, the profits from candle and ikon manufacturing, and government subsidies. According to its own report, the church hauled in 500 million rubles in 1914, around 60 million rubles of this sum having been contributed by the government. (Half of the government's subsidy went to church schools.) When Orthodox Church bank funds were nationalized by the Bolsheviks in 1918, they amounted to over eight billion rubles.[56]

Yet despite accumulated wealth, most individual priests came from the lower ranks of society, lived penurious lives, and were little respected. Lack of respect was demonstrated in these two Russian proverbs: "To be a priest one needs a big beard, a big voice, and a big stomach" and "For the priest the unenlightened people is a source of income."[57] This lack of respect came from the local clergy's common drunkenness, perceived greed—though not wealth— and generally low level of education. Usually he was the son of the village priest before him. Priests were married with large families, and in poorer regions they suffered from lower incomes. I. Belliustin, a rural priest during the mid-nineteenth century, kept notes intended for the eyes of the tsar:

The priest administers a short prayer service and thrusts out his hand for a reward; he accompanies a deceased person to his eternal resting place, and again he holds out his hand; a wedding ceremony has to be performed, and he even bargains over his fee; and on holidays he goes about the parish with the sole purpose of collecting money. . . .

Is he not simply a hireling? And how must the parishioners look upon him? Walk across Russia from end to end and listen to how they revile the clergy because of these accursed emoluments. After all this, what benefit is to be gained from the priest's service? What moral influence can he exert on the parishioners when they understand perfectly the primary goal of all his actions?[58]

In the village of Viriatino in Tambov province, the priest took a cart with him as he made the rounds of each peasant's home to bless it. Villagers were expected to pile the cart high with food, and the priest kept careful watch over who contributed and who did not. If food was not forthcoming, a young man or woman might find that the marriage sacrament was withheld until the deficit was made up.[59] Although the peasants grumbled and cursed at these perpetual extortions, in the end they realized that his services were indispensable.

The greatest source of income for both the white and black clergy was in collecting fees for saying prayers for the dead. At least once a year families paid the priest to pray for their departed, and the wealthy sometimes endowed whole monasteries on the condition that resident monks offer daily prayers for ancestors. One's salvation might well depend on the number of prayers said over a lifetime, as well as the number said for the departed.[60]

To supplement their incomes, most village priests farmed—or bought vodka with which to pay villagers to farm—a small plot of land attached to the church. From this they obtained produce for their families and perhaps a bit left over for sale. But Belliustin saw this, too, as a degradation of the priesthood. How could a clergyman be a man of God when he was covered with the filth of his fields or encouraged village drunkenness? How could he exercise pastoral care when that meant time (and energy) away from cultivating the crops needed to feed his family? After a few years of this life, he would assimilate the coarseness of the peasantry whom he was meant to uplift.[61]

Belliustin's solution for the priests' predicament was the payment of a salary by the church or the state. Especially for the rural clergy, this income would gain them the dignity needed for respect. But for a thousand years the *church* rarely offered a salary, and it was 1893, the last year of Tsar Alexander III's rule, before the *state* offered a stipend. In 1903 the government officially fixed an amount of 300 rubles for a priest, though in wealthier regions this may have reached 700 rubles (in the latter case putting the priest's salary well above that of the average peasant farmer or factory worker). At the top of the hierarchy and the high end of the salary scale the metropolitan of Kiev received 4,000 rubles, with another 50,000 rubles in income from the Pechersky Monastery.[62]

A salary enabled the priest to chastise the villagers for their sins without endangering his source of income, but there was a downside as well. Prince Eugene Trubetzkoy summed up the dilemma in 1919:

> To whatever degree a priest retains a lively sense of his sacred character, his subservience to the secular power becomes psychologically impossible. Moreover, the transformation of the priest into an employee of the state is always accompanied by the loss of his influence over the masses.[63]

Of course, salaries paid by the Moscow Patriarchate could have avoided the latter problem, but they were not forthcoming. With the Bolshevik coup in 1917 they *could* not be forthcoming, for, as we have already seen, the church was stripped of its financial resources.

The Case of St. John of Kronstadt

John of Kronstadt (named after an island near St. Petersburg) became a religious hero to the Russian people. According to his modern-day followers, John was born in the village of Soura in North Russia in 1829 and, as he grew up, was loved by both rich and poor, by noblemen and beggars. After entering the priesthood, thousands flocked to the cathedral in Archangelsk when he celebrated the Divine Liturgy. During the last years of his life he constantly predicted the approach of terrible events in Russia. At his death in December 1908, over 60,000 people attended his funeral. His hagiographers marveled at his character:

> He was a righteous man. His whole life he tried to keep God's commandments and to do everything as God had commanded. . . . He fervently raised up prayers to God, assiduously kept the church regulations, was truly an image and example for all sacred ministers. . . . He was the incarnation of mercy, took pity on everyone, helped everyone. He sought out the needy. . . . He was also a stern denouncer of human sins, like unto the Prophet Elias and John the Baptist, not fearing to speak the truth openly to someone's face. Kind to the repentant, no matter how great their sins were, he could not bear obstinacy in sin.[64]

John said, "The Holy men of God would not betray the Faith by even so much as a word."

Yet in 1934 the Bolshevik antireligious leader Emelyan Yaroslavsky told a different story. After John's death there ensued a quarrel over his estate, and the matter went to court. An inventory of his belongings revealed (among other items) 260 bottles of very expensive wine, 150 new shirts of the finest material, and a well-stocked haberdashery. His comb was set in gold and studded with large jewels. The 1908 court record revealed a home not only in disarray but full of garbage and filth. Hats, boots, linen, jam, tea, gem-encrusted crosses, dried mushrooms, eiderdown-lined silk trousers, dried sturgeon bones, and the remains of recent meals were all "piled up indiscriminately." Bank notes totaling 13,162 rubles were found in a drawer under some old letters.

Apparently large sums of money had been donated to his secretaries as well as various courtesans and prostitutes. One secretary built a 900,000-ruble home in Kronstadt, and all had additional country homes. The prostitutes allegedly participated in parties thrown on the premises. Yaroslavsky rubbed it in:

> So the ribald tales of the midnight orgies celebrated in the luxurious apartments of this prototype of Christian saintliness, all the gossip about loose women and the wine parties given there, were not just idle talk, but a true contemporary evaluation of the supposedly sacrosanct lives of all these "saints" and "princes" of the church.[65]

ORTHODOX ANTI-SEMITISM

Although the Orthodox Church as an institution never officially supported anti-Semitic pogroms, neither did it chastise renegade priests who indulged in them or propose toleration to the tsarist government that did, at times, officially support these atrocities. The church hierarchy allowed its priests to blame Jews for the execution of Christ, and it was around Easter that the worst of the pogroms occurred.[66]

Philip Bernstein wrote for *Harpers Magazine* in 1930:

> The church was criminally responsible for most of the outrages perpetrated on the Jews, because it taught the Russian masses to hate this people who were responsible, it believed, for the death of Jesus. . . . Many of the pogroms were actually instigated by the priests, and frequently the pogromists would fall upon a Jewish community with the priests at their head and with the name of their Savior on their lips.[67]

POBEDONOSTSEV

The late Constantine Pobedonostsev transformed Orthodoxy under the Romanovs into a handful of dry bones.[68]

—correspondent for the London *Morning Post*, early 1920

The height of church reaction emerged during the administration of Chief Procurator of the Holy Synod Constantine Pobedonostsev, who ran the government's religious bureaucracy from 1880 until 1905. A great scholar, but at the same time a confessed pessimist and a devoted advocate of the state-run church, he enjoyed the complete confidence of Nicholas II and the imperial family, therefore managing to carry out his repressive policies unhindered. To prevent rival power centers from developing, he transferred bishops from see to see, ignoring the requirements of canon law, and saw to it that no bishop traveled outside of his diocese without the chief procurator's explicit approval. He persecuted Jews and sectarians and convinced himself that Truth could be apprehended only through the mediation of the Orthodox Church.[69]

Bernard Pares was harsh in his criticism of the chief procurator and the effects of his policies, charging that he had "raised [his post] to the first importance by his sinister policy of using the authority of the church as an instrument of governmental repression." He quoted from Pobedonostsev's own book, *Reflections of a Russian Statesman*:

> Among the falsest of political principles is the principle of the sovereignty of the people. . . . Thence proceeds the theory of parliamentarism, which up to the present day has deluded much of the so-called Intelligence [intelligentsia] and unhappily infatuated certain foolish Russians.[70]

Pares believed that true religion was needed in Russia but detested Pobedonostsev for seeing "a chance of putting religion into conflict with modern ideals, using it as a political asset and supporting his conception of it with the full force of the police."[71] Again from the chief procurator's book:

> How many men, how many institutions, have been perverted in the course of a false development! For these rooted principles in our religious institutions are, of all things, the most precious. May God prevent them from ever being destroyed by the untimely reformation of our church.[72]

Pobedonostsev, a layman, even had a hand in the selection of saints, persuading the Holy Synod to canonize a peasant named Seraphim, who, though a good man, was ignorant and superstitious. Yet Seraphim was Pobedonostsev's role model for society. He talked the tsar into going out to the countryside to pray at Seraphim's tomb. When in the next year an heir to the throne was born, the Moscow *Gazette* ascribed this blessing to the new saint.[73]

REFORM AND RETRACTION

I write not so much with sadness as with the indignation of a person whose holy of holies, whose soul, was mocked. We have to say that the Orthodox Faith had become a weapon in agile and shameless hands for the oppression of younger brethren. We merited the lack of confidence and even anger with which we were met.

—Father G. Kazansky, writing in the Orthodox Church press, February 17, 1918

From 1904 into 1906 pent-up frustrations over failures in the Russo-Japanese War and the far-too-slow emergence of social justice led to rioting in the streets and mutiny in the navy. After the tsar's troops fired on peaceful demonstrators in January 1905, the situation worsened. Finally in April, Nicholas issued a statement granting religious freedom to all citizens, including the right to change communions, proselytize among the Orthodox, and deliver uncensored sermons—now that sermons were becoming more fashionable. A flood of religious publications appeared that promoted every variety of opinion but especially exulted in freedom. In his October Manifesto, Nicholas allowed a freely elected Duma (Parliament) and a Constituent Assembly to decide the future course of the nation, and, as a part of these general reforms, Pobedonostsev was forced into retirement.[74]

Although these religious reforms had mixed implications for Orthodoxy, thirty-two progressive St. Petersburg priests signed a letter in the *Church Messenger.*

> The forthcoming liberation of the religious conscience from external restraints . . . is welcomed with great joy by all true members of the Orthodox Church. . . . The Church is at last acquitted of the heavy charge of violating and suppressing religious freedom. This was formerly done in her name, . . . but it was done against her will and against her spirit.[75]

During this (brief) liberalization period, progressive church officials gained control of Orthodox seminaries and academies, but reform was like trying to pry open the jaws of a clam. In 1907 the retired (and dying) Pobedonostsev denounced the spirit of change:

> Inertia sustains humanity in the crises of its history, and so indispensable has it become that without it all measured progress would be impossible. . . . It is absolutely essential to the prosperity of society.[76]

In 1908 the Synod appointed a committee of conservatives to recommend a sweeping rollback of all theological training school reforms. In 1910, when these recommendations were ready for implementation, the Third Duma saw them as too severe, but when V. Sabler took office as the new chief procurator he appraised these illiberal regulations as not nearly severe enough. He saw to it that they were superseded by "Changes in the Constitution of Theological Academies," which placed all such schools directly in the hands of their monastic superiors. As a result, liberal professors were dismissed and new rules were imposed to drive out all remnants of progressive thought. Now professors could belong to no political parties unless they were previously given a stamp of approval by ecclesiastical authorities. As for the main body of the Orthodox Church, the power to censor *all* religious publications in the empire was conferred upon it, and once again it was officially permitted to proselytize among other Christian churches while reciprocity was forbidden.[77]

*   *   *

By the reign of Alexander I (1801–1825), Russia's upper classes were already alienated from the spirituality of the Orthodox Church, though they kept up with their duties on various solemn occasions. But a greater tragedy for the church was the alienation of the intellectuals—not necessarily the same people—from the church. The shepherds of the church had not attempted to win into their fold these young, educated, yet restless souls who sought spirituality. Socially, the church drove the intelligentsia from its midst by its failure to participate on an institutional level with the reform movements of the day. The intelligentsia would have preferred to see Christ's Kingdom established here on Earth, but the church looked upon this world as hopelessly lost. The Christian's duty was to deny this world, save one's soul, and prepare for the heavenly experience. Now, in the years between 1905 and 1917, the church once again was repressing free thought, free discussion, and questioning minds.

RASPUTIN

Lord, preserve me from all earthly ties, and no evil spirits shall harm me. There are evil spirits in earthly ties, and such ties are indeed the vanities of the world.[78]

—Rasputin, 1915

During the final years of Nicholas's rule, scandal rocked the capital. Eventually its effects would work their way across the nation and seriously undermine the dignity of both tsar and church. This was the notorious Rasputin Affair. Grigory Rasputin was a mystic Siberian lay elder (not a monk, as is often supposed). His morals were reminiscent of the Khlysty sect, which held it was necessary to sin so that one could be forgiven for sins—the more sins, the more forgiveness. He managed to ingratiate himself into the court of Tsar Nicholas II and Tsarina Alexandra by playing upon her superstitious nature, credulity, and desire to provide a (surviving) male heir to the throne. After four daughters, the Tsarevich Alexis was born, but doctors soon discovered that he was stricken with hemophilia, a genetic disease carried though the male line that prevented blood clotting after internal or external injury. Rasputin convinced the tsarina that he, and he alone, could stop the bleeding and save the boy's life. He gained her confidence on not only medical questions but also state affairs.

Though licentious, dirty, and ignorant, Rasputin possessed a charismatic, compelling, and hypnotizing personality, and he soon became a power in the court. Referring to him as "our friend," the strong-willed tsarina pressured her more compliant husband to follow Rasputin's wishes concerning key political appointments. Few favors were refused. To gain office one had to seek out Rasputin and ply him with flattery and entreaties, for this was the path to power. In 1911 Rasputin was able to gain the appointment of V. Sabler (mentioned above) as chief procurator, and in 1915 he was able just as easily and arbitrarily to have him removed from office. A. Samarin took his place but foolishly defied Rasputin and soon went the way of his predecessor. Two more chief procurators met a similar fate. Rasputin's appointees were frequently men of dubious worth. Vladimir Sukhomlinov, his choice for minister of war, was disastrously incompetent and criminally negligent in the matter of caring for army equipment, but it did not seem to matter; at the height of Rasputin's power even the prime minister was putty in his hands.

Rasputin's career affected the reputation of the church, as he was considered a representative of the black clergy. His immoral ways and insinuating ambition appalled those who expected decency from an Orthodox "monk." The church was also weakened by its obvious inability, despite its closeness to the state, to impede his corrupting influence and ruinous policies. When he was finally stopped in 1916, it was not by church authorities but by patriotic assassins at the house of Prince Felix Yusopov, the husband of the tsar's niece. After Rasputin was gone, the church seemed apathetic in response to the damage he had done. It was as if the church was waiting patiently for a preordained revolution.

In the second half of the nineteenth century, the thoughts of the intelligentsia (and many of the workers) were turning to that revolution. A handful of influential thinkers—non-Marxist and Marxist—described how rejection of religion would fan the flames of drastic change.

3

REFLECTIONS IN THE MINDS OF MEN

An Introduction to Marxists on Religion

Into the tumult that was Russia during the 1890s crept the Western European ideas of Karl Marx and Friedrich Engels. While Marx's political and economic concepts were new to Russia, the atheist core of Marxism was not. However, Russia's peasant atheism was more superstitious and Russia's exiles were more sentimental than the rationalist atheism that Marxism would bring— or, more accurately, impose.

PRE-MARXIST ATHEIST THINKERS

Absolute atheism is the sole inheritance that has been preserved intact by the new generation, and I need scarcely point out how much advantage the modern revolutionary movement has derived from it.[1]

—Stepniak

Four Russians

Nineteenth-century, pre-Marxist Russian atheism was of two types: The first was traditional and anticlerical, while the second was philosophical. Peasant atheism, the first type, was seldom articulated, except in the privacy of the home when the village priest came to collect his fees. Even the most uneducated peasant was aware of the abuses and the unchristian conduct of many of the representatives of the official church. Perhaps anticlericalism would not have become so pervasive had Peter I kept his hands off the patriarchate. His substitution of the Holy Synod in 1721 gave the church no choice but to become the pillar of the state and become identified with the evils of the state in the people's minds. This was the religion described in the previous chapter, a practice of tradition, superstition, and ritual, with little or no personal relationship with God. Prayers had largely been supplanted by invocations and the duty of church attendance. Leon Trotsky characterized these ancient attitudes as pseudobelief, but, as we shall see later, they could not be so easily dismissed.

Among the intelligentsia, anticlericalism shared a place with philosophical atheism, much of it based on readings of French and German materialists. Vissarion Belinsky, Alexander Herzen, Michael Bakunin, and Nikolai Chernyshevsky incorporated atheism into their dreams of revolution. Paradoxically, though their views were deeply Russian, they would have little direct influence on the masses of the Russian people. Their audience was those fellow countrymen who were eager for change.

Vissarion Belinsky's short life ended in 1848—the year of the failed socialist uprising in Western Europe—due to a losing battle with tuberculosis. Like most of the exiled revolutionaries, he had moved in fits and starts from belief to nonbelief. Also like the others, he was propelled by the existence of suffering. While the Orthodox Church nurtured the sense of suffering, Belinsky was appalled by it. How could God choose favorites, enriching some while allowing thousands to perish in famine, illness, and war? Clearly God was man's attempt to bolster a miserable state of affairs by attaching a divine quality to it.

Belinsky's atheism, true to the Russian tradition, was also strongly anticlerical, as revealed in this 1847 letter to the Russian writer Nicolai Gogol:

> Do you really mean to say that you do not know that our clergy is held in universal contempt by Russian society and the Russian people? Of whom do the Russian people relate obscene stories? Of the priest, the priest's wife, the priest's daughter, and the priest's farm hand. Does not the priest in Russia represent for all Russians the embodiment of gluttony, avarice, servility, and shamelessness? According to you, the Russian people are the most religious in the world. That is a lie! The basis of religion is pietism, reverence, fear of God. The Russian man utters the name of the Lord while scratching himself somewhere. He says of the ikon, "If it isn't good for praying, it's good for covering the pots." Take a close look at the Russian people and you will see that, by nature, they are profoundly atheistic people. Among them there is still much superstition, but not a trace of real religiousness.[2]

The most influential Russian revolutionary during the 1840s and 1850s was Alexander Herzen (1812–1870). He lived freely and in internal exile until 1847, when he left for the centers of radical thinking in Western Europe, never to return. His first anticlerical experience was at age fourteen when he watched the Orthodox Church offering a *Te Deum* as the tsarist government hanged five leaders of the 1825 Decembrist Revolt. It pained him to watch the church prostitute itself in the service of the state. He later wrote: "The Metropolitan Philaret thanked God for the murders. . . . On that very day I vowed vengeance and pledged myself to fight against this throne and this altar."[3] Later, he wondered what could be meant by Christ's injunction to "lose your life in order that it might be saved,"[4] and he rejected the sop to the poor that their rewards would come in the next world. The historian E. Lampert said of Herzen:

> He was . . . quite unacquainted with atheism as a spectacular event in his life—it was in a sense inborn in him, instinctive, precisely because he was too incredulous, too distrustful, too questioning, too aware to be satisfied with master keys or, to use his own expression, "the wholesale solution of things."[5]

Michael Bakunin (1814–1876) was an anarchistic socialist who lived a life of constant rebellion against authority. He participated in the revolutions of 1848 and the Polish uprising of 1863, and at one time or another was jailed by Russia, Prussia, and Austria. He learned from the French anarchist Pierre Proudhon to become not merely an atheist but an antitheist, believing God to be a personification of evil. He wrote in *God or Labor: The Two Camps*:

> We pride ourselves on being Atheists. Atheism is Truth—or rather the basis of all Truths. We do not stoop to consider practical consequences. We want Truth above everything. Truth for all![6]

In 1866 Bakunin published *A Revolutionary Catechism*, declaring reason and human conscience to be the sole criteria of truth. He insisted on the "annihilation and dissolution" of the state, which was the twin partner of the church and as such "the permanent source of pauperism, deception, and enslavement of the peoples."[7] Religious influences had destroyed man's ability to reason—the chief instrument of human freedom—and "by filling man's mind with divine absurdities, [they had] reduced the people to imbecility, which is the foundation of slavery." As long as people were sunk in religious superstition, he argued, they would be pliable instruments in the hands of all despotic powers leagued against the emancipation of humanity. Once any god became established on his throne, he became the "curse of mankind."[8]

Bakunin's rejection of God was psychologically profound, all-encompassing, and complete, and he held onto these views tenaciously. It cannot be argued that there was some form of *pure* Christianity somewhere that Bakunin had missed, for it was the very essence of religious belief in any form that he militantly opposed.

Nihilism was a philosophical movement that struggled to emancipate intelligence from every form of dependence. It was the negation in the name of individual liberty of all obligations imposed on the individual by society, religion, and family life. It fought both political and moral despotism. The nihilists were not so much opposed to Christianity in particular, or even religion in particular, as they were to *principles*. They believed in scientifically tested *facts* only. They rejected all the foggy notions of the 1840s and 1850s, and Christianity, like the others, was a superstitious, idealist principle to be consigned to the garbage heap of history. They took atheism to a new extreme, yet were less penetrating and analytical than the three revolutionaries considered so far. The nihilists of the 1860s took religion to be pure anthropomorphism—man's creation of God in his own image.[9]

Nikolai Chernyshevsky (1828–1889) was the most prominent and influential of the nihilists and had more effect on the late-nineteenth-century Russian intelligentsia than did either Belinsky or Herzen. He also probed more deeply into the nature of religious belief. Born the son of an Orthodox priest, and perhaps attributable to his upbringing, he maintained an ascetic mental outlook throughout life. His friends and acquaintances saw him as honest, pure, and self-sacrificing. Although he would not have appreciated the remark, when police officers took him into Siberian exile, they said, "Our orders were to bring a criminal and we are bringing a saint."[10]

Chernyshevsky's natural skepticism developed into a deepening materialistic atheism. In 1860 he wrote that science "can provide us with information only about external material nature and about man as an earthly and material being"—he assumed that was all one needed to know. In that same year he attacked, as had Herzen, the dualism of body and spirit. He described in *The Anthropological Principle of Philosophy* how physiology and medicine had revealed that the human organism was "an extremely complex chemical combination that goes through an extremely complex chemical process that we call life." Twenty-four years later he was still arguing that "mountains and lakes, grass and flowers, animals and humans, were all simply diverse combinations of matter." There were no spiritual forces in nature.[11] In his "Essay on the Gogol Period of Russian Literature," he wrote, "Man by himself is very feeble; he obtains all his strength only from his knowledge of real life."[12] All this, and the way that Chernyshevsky lived his life, made a strong impression on the young Vladimir Ilyich Ulyanov—Lenin.

One German

Ludwig Feuerbach (1804–1872) grew up about forty miles northeast of Munich in Landshut, Bavaria. Studying theology and philosophy at Heidelberg and Berlin, he gradually developed a humanistic and anthropological explanation for the origins of religion, which he explained in his most famous work *The Essence of Christianity* (1841). Although Marx approved of Feuerbach's explanation of how man had created the imaginary world of God, he felt that Feuerbach had not gone far enough in explaining how contradictions in the real (earthly) world had led to this fancy. In other words, Feuerbach had exposed man's mistake, but where was the *revolution* going to come from? Marx was more interested in the societal origins of religion than the individual ones. Friedrich Engels accused

Feuerbach of "combating religion not in order to destroy it but in order to renovate it," as Feuerbach claimed that a thorough subjective understanding of it
would render it easier to appreciate.

Feuerbach moved to Nuremberg in 1860 and remained there until his death
twelve years later.

*   *   *

Revolution can occur within a *Christian* context, but it was not likely to have
achieved much success in nineteenth- and early-twentieth-century Russia within
such a context. A church-led revolution can occur when there is a deep split
within the established church or when a large segment of the lower class is outside the body of the church, but these conditions did not exist then in Russia. The
Orthodox Church had too strong a hold on the minds of the peasantry. The revolutionary agent would have to be an atheistic, educated class (the intelligentsia)
that could reject the submissiveness required by the church and by the state that
it supported.

This intelligentsia was not bothered by the conflict between scientific
knowledge and religious faith to the extent western Europeans—especially Germans—were. Bakunin was the only Russian atheist to have dealt extensively
with this subject, and, like Lenin, he learned this dichotomy in the West.
Nihilists idealized science in their writings, but the science versus faith conflict
was not foremost in their minds. For Russian intellectuals, atheism's roots were
in the conflict between Christianity and *social truth*—the conviction that Christianity supported social *un*truth. Their atheism mostly dealt with the existence
of misery and suffering; for them, God did not exist because it was impossible
to conceive of a God who would tolerate so much evil in a world that he had
created. As we shall see, one of the reasons that Marxist atheism had a hard time
thriving on Russian soil was that it was based on the science-faith dichotomy
and not on the misery-faith dichotomy.

The Russian scholar Nicolas Berdyaev wrote on this subject:

> The Marxian type of atheism is not moved at all by pity; on the contrary, it is
> pitiless. In order to procure power and riches for the social collectivity, it pro-
> claims ruthless cruelty towards men. There is no humanitarian element left in it.
> . . . [Marx] is not so much moved by pity for the suffering, humiliated prole-
> tariat, longing to alleviate its sufferings and liberate it from humiliation, as by
> the idea of the coming might and power of the proletariat. . . . The intellectual
> elements prevailed over the sentimental.[13]

Nineteenth-century atheism was a prerequisite for the success of the revolutionary movement in Russia. It enabled progressive and radical thinkers to cut
emotional ties to the autocratic regime. It enabled them to believe that they, as

men, with no omniscient and omnipotent God watching from above, could alter their own social and political environment. Atheism gave men the confidence to seek rational change.

Imagine nineteenth-century Russian atheism as a pair of shears, severing the chains that had bound men's minds to the old order. Beyond the cutting there was no inherent direction in it—Russia might well have traveled a different course. Had Marxist theory not entered the country during the 1880s and 1890s, the people might well have disposed of the tsar's power through a more humanitarian and less strident revolution. Had Herzen's and Bakunin's teachings on religious belief been given time and a more secular educational system—and not been overshadowed by Marxism—the people might have been provided with a deeper understanding of the connection between despotism and the established church.

Atheism itself did not predestine Russia to a future of despotic rule. Pre-Marxist atheists were leading Russia toward a revolution favoring compassion and social justice—they believed in freedom within socialism. The new Marxist atheism would contain no element of pity; it was instead chiefly concerned with strength—the power of organized society. For Marxists and Leninists, God was to be destroyed so that society could become mentally and physically healthy and so human life could be organized and rationalized and moved forward. Russia's humanitarian atheistic tradition, in the sense of caring for the lives of individual people, had ended. Marxist atheism, which we shall investigate next, was a negation of the traditional *humanist* atheism and the substitution of another more *scientific* type.

MARXIST ATHEIST THINKERS

Within the philosophical system of Marx and Lenin, and at the heart of their psychology, hatred of God is their principal driving force, more fundamental than all their political and economic pretensions. Militant atheism is not merely incidental or marginal to Communist policy. It is not a side effect, but the central pivot.

—Alexander Solzhenitsyn

Marx believed that he had discovered—not created—a system explaining all history, all economy, and all society and that socialist victory was inevitable. This sense of certainty, but little else, he had in common with Christianity. While Feuerbach had tended toward abstraction in his writings, Marx and his apostles analyzed the condition of real men in real societies. Lenin took on the most concrete of all challenges—actually attaining power in a specific place and time—then, once in power, striving to prove that his predecessors, on the religious issue and all others, were correct.

Karl Marx

Karl Marx (1818–1883) was born and raised in the west Prussian city of Trier. His parents were Jewish, both his father and mother having been born into families of rabbis, but one year before Karl's birth his father had converted to the Lutheran faith for career reasons. Karl was baptized at the age of six, but his parents—though well educated in Enlightenment literature—never provided him with either a Jewish or a Christian education. In his youth he never had anything close to a personal religious experience, therefore in adulthood he never had to convert to atheism.[14] Europe's prevailing anti-Semitism never seriously affected him. Studying Marx's Jewish background would not take one very far in understanding what motivated him.

At seventeen Marx wrote *The Union of Believers with Christ* as a school assignment. Strangely, he spoke of the warmth of the bond felt among all Christians that resulted from Christ's sacrifice on the cross.

> [This bond could bring] comfort in sorrow, calm trust, and a heart susceptible to human love, . . . everything noble and great, not for the sake of ambition and glory, but only for the sake of Christ.[15]

This sounds like a young man still in the thralls of religious idealism, but some historians—most likely trying to preserve the great man's purity—have called it Marx's first parody of Christianity. Others have noted that the essay, taken as a whole, reveals a young man who is dealing with religion as an abstraction or at best a method of self-improvement.[16]

Marx studied briefly at the University of Bonn, but his father ordered him home due to his excessive drinking, rowdiness, and debt. At the University of Berlin he developed into a serious intellectual, trained in the law and philosophy, but he became increasingly subversive as he took up dialectics and materialism (see below). He soon rejected any and all deities.[17] Included in his doctoral dissertation, written at the University of Jena in 1841, was the statement (borrowed from Aeschylus): "In one word—I hate all the gods."[18] The gist of his paper was a debunking of known "proofs" of the existence of God. But as he matured, he did not repeat such emotional outbursts, and his attitude toward religion became almost benign—in the sense that atheism was so obvious that it hardly needed further elucidation.

Marx developed a fascination with "laws of history" that those who had come before him had failed to discover. Francis Randall wrote:

> He came to believe that all the various sciences and philosophies were part of one overarching system, which, when completed, would give a true and total picture of the universe and man. . . . He came to believe that nature and man

evolve according to certain inexorable scientific laws whose working-out can be embodied but not opposed by even the greatest men.[19]

In his late twenties he renounced his citizenship in the reactionary Prussian state. His editing of radical newspapers then led to expulsion from Germany. He fled first to Paris and then to Brussels, where he and Friedrich Engels wrote *The Communist Manifesto* with its "specter of communism" haunting Europe and its overwhelmingly false assertion that nationalism was dead and the rise of internationalism imminent. Its publication in 1848 led to his deportation from Belgium and the moving of his family to England, where he spent the next thirty-four years reading, writing, and communicating with the socialist savants of Europe. He studied economics and published the first of three volumes of *Capital* in 1867. Suffering from ill health during the last decade of his life, he passed away in London in 1883. Years later Bakunin, who had known Marx in Paris, wrote, "[Marx] called me a sentimental idealist and was right; I called him a sinister, disloyal, and vain man and was equally right."[20] Marx, like Bakunin, was a difficult man to live with or love.

Friedrich Engels

Marx's collaborator in Belgium and in England was Friedrich Engels (1820–1895), an expert on the religious issue. He was born to a tyrannical Calvinist father in Barmen, Prussia, and was intently religious in his youth. At age nineteen he described himself as praying "every day, indeed, almost all day."[21] For Engels, as for Feuerbach, adult atheism meant overcoming the legacy of childhood.

Barmen was a developing industrial region in the Ruhr Valley, and his father owned cotton mills there as well as in Manchester, England. During a sojourn at the University of Berlin, Engels, like Marx, adopted radical views, causing his father to ship him off to England to learn a practical trade in his mills. As he absorbed the textile business, he also picked up a working knowledge of the grim lives led by workers on the factory floor, deepening his distrust of the capitalist system. Further alienating him from Victorian society was social disapproval of his long-term unmarried relationship with Mary Burns, an Irish girl whom he met in the mills.

Engels worked so intimately with Marx that it is difficult to disentangle their thinking and writing, though Engels himself gave Marx the greater share of credit. He once said: "Karl Marx is a genius. He stands higher, sees farther and takes a wider and quicker view than all the rest of us put together."[22] After 1842 Engels remained mostly in England, where in 1870 the two collaborators founded the First International to spread their theories. After Marx's death, Engels spent his waning years editing his colleague's writings.

George Plekhanov

George Plekhanov (1856–1918) was an early importer of Marxist ideology to Russia. Educated in St. Petersburg, he dropped out of the university to work with the People's Will Party (populists), which struggled for the emancipation of the peasantry through rural education and agitation. By reading the works of Marx and Engels he deduced that socialist revolution could not be achieved through the peasantry, as the People's Will had hoped, but only through the organization and long-term support of the proletariat.

Pursued by the *Okhrana* (the tsarist secret police), Plekhanov fled from Russia to Switzerland in 1880, not returning until the March Revolution in 1917. While in exile he translated Marx's *Communist Manifesto* into Russian and, in 1883, helped form the first Russian Marxist organization—the Emancipation of Labor. This group gave rise, in 1898, to the formation of the Russian Social Democratic Labor Party. When, at its second Party Congress in London in 1903, the party split, Plekhanov sided against Lenin's Bolshevik faction. In 1904 he lectured on socialism and religion at a socialist conference in Zurich and afterwards published *On the So-Called Religious Quests in Russia*. This work was in the vein of Feuerbach, but updated and advanced.[23] Plekhanov believed that morality came prior to religion and thus could not be dependent on it. Churches later enforced morality but were unnecessary for its sustenance. He viewed religion as a matter of ignorance, failing to focus on the class struggle as its cause, as did other Marxists. The "cure" for religion was enlightenment—in this sense he was closer to the eighteenth-century French Encyclopedists than he was to Marx.

In prerevolutionary days, Lenin frequently quarreled with Plekhanov, but the former was greatly influenced by the latter and strove to master his skills of agitation and party building. Ultimately, though, it was Lenin, the man of action, who brought Western Marxist ideas to Slavic Russia.

Vladimir Lenin

Vladimir Ilyich Ulyanov (1870–1924) was born to an Orthodox father and a Lutheran mother in Simbirsk, on the Volga River south of Kazan. He later claimed that he broke with religion at the tender age of sixteen, before his acceptance of Marxism; if so, he still received high grades in his high school religious studies. He took the revolutionary name Lenin after the government hanged his older brother in May 1887 for involvement in a crude and hopeless plot to assassinate Tsar Alexander III. Studying at Kazan and St. Petersburg universities, he graduated with a degree in law, but he spent the last three years of the nineteenth century in Siberian exile for participation in underground revolutionary activities. In a town on the banks of the Yenisey River he married his companion Nadezhda Krupskaya in an Orthodox Church ceremony in 1898.[24]

At the 1903 Russian Social Democratic Labor Party Congress, held in London and Brussels, Lenin forced a split into the Menshevik and Bolshevik factions. The Bolsheviks argued that they could carry out a Marxist, socialist revolution with what the Mensheviks thought to be an insufficiently developed proletariat. The Menshevik view was consistent with the letter of Marxist theory, but the Bolshevik view was consistent with its spirit. Marx himself had never visited Russia and would most likely have condemned a revolution at this stage as woefully premature. However, the impatient Lenin—the ageing crusader—pushed forward; revolution could not wait.

While languishing in exile in Geneva, he read in a newspaper that Nicholas II had been overthrown by angry crowds in the streets of Petrograd. Although hard at war with Russia, the Germans—aware of his antiwar views and hoping his "defeatism" would destabilize their enemy—agreed in April 1917 to spirit Lenin and his entourage in a "sealed train" (to prevent him from ideologically infecting Germans) across their country to the Russian capital. Under the slogan "All Power to the Soviets," his Bolshevik Party managed to overthrow Kerensky's Provisional Government in November, and Lenin took power. Victorious in the subsequent four-year Civil War, he and his power were secure.

His health, however, was fragile. After his death in January 1924, Joseph Stalin gradually accumulated power. He ordered Lenin's body embalmed and it—or something resembling it—still lies in a mausoleum in Red Square in Moscow. In his honor Petrograd was renamed Leningrad.

Although Lenin never met Marx, Marxism provided the theoretical premise for all of Lenin's activities, both before and after his Bolshevik Party took power. Marx and Lenin saw eye-to-eye on the religious question. Lenin added nothing theoretical to Marx's explanation of religion because he concurred with the Master, and he wrote next to nothing on the history of religion because he saw it as being derived from a misery that the building of socialism would soon alleviate. But there was a shift in emphasis in Lenin's approach. Marx was primarily a theorist and only secondarily concerned with the practical difficulties of implementation. He was even less willing to spell out in detail what a postrevolutionary society would look like; essentially, one could not tell until one got there. He did not expect to see the fruition of his theories in his lifetime. Lenin, on the other hand, was secondarily a theorist—or, to put it differently, relied mainly on Marx's theories—and was primarily concerned with the practicality of overthrowing a specific government. Except on issues of timing and tactics, Lenin's essential views on religion underwent no change upon taking power.

DOCTRINE

Marxism-Leninism has no beauty, nor has it any mystical value. It is only extremely useful. [25]

—Mao Zedong

The whole of Marxist theory is, of course, far beyond the scope of this book and irrelevant besides. The following six topics, however, are crucial to an understanding of what Lenin was trying to accomplish in Russia on the antireligious front. The first three have to do with history—its basis and the causes of its change over time. The following three have to do with the condition of man—how he related to himself and his fellow man.

Materialism: Two Meanings

Marx did not reject religion out of a simple anticlericalism. It would never have occurred to him to argue that God existed but could not be held responsible for the mistakes of his representatives on Earth. He never asked himself whether he was objecting to a perverted manifestation of religion. His rejection of religion was entirely unrelated to the historical practices of priests and monks; rather it was of a fundamental philosophical nature. Although he attacked the entire structure of society, of which religion was only a part, his atheism was essential (his other theories could not have stood without it), radical (the probability of the existence of God was zero), and integral (man's life held no room for religion in any form).[26]

"Marxism is materialism," Lenin wrote in 1909.[27] To acknowledge reality was to acknowledge materialism. Man's task was to understand the physical and chemical forces that provided for his existence and then to use them through the socialist application of technology. Lenin was a thoroughgoing materialist in the sense that *all* was natural and nothing that could be called supernatural existed outside of imagination. No proof was offered of this; it was simply a metaphysical assertion that nature explained all and the supernatural explained nothing. For Marx and Lenin materialism was an objective truth—a cold, hard fact.*

In *Three Sources and Three Essential Elements of Marxism* (1913), Lenin defended the concept:

> Materialism turned out to be the only consistent philosophy true to all the teachings of natural science, inimical to superstition, magic, etc. The enemies of [socialist] democracy endeavored therefore by every means to disprove,

---

*At times, though, Marx felt the muse of poetry. Coming right before his famous line about religion as the opium of the people, he wrote, "Religion is the sigh of the harassed creature, the heart of a heartless world, as it is the spirit of soulless stagnation."

undercut, and slander materialism, and defended various forms of philosophical idealism, which always amounted in the end to be a defense or support of religion.[28]

It was after Lenin took power that the Bolsheviks used the term "materialism" in a second, nonphilosophical sense. The peasants were not going to be won over with abstract argument, so they were persuaded to adopt materialism in the Western sense of acquisitiveness of *things*. Communism brought radios, sewing machines, and tractors. Acceptance of science rather than faith would lead to the possession of laborsaving devices that, once owned, would be difficult to give up.[29] With this definition, every peasant could quickly become a "materialist."

Dialectics: Beyond Formal Logic

Dialectics is a system of logical thought originating with the ancient Greeks but formalized by Hegel in nineteenth-century Prussia. It postulates a method of historical development where we can call any given economic, social, or political structure, or any idea, a "thesis." Since a thesis is riddled with internal contradictions and history is dynamic, it will in time engender an antithesis or counterthesis that will develop its own internal contradictions. Although the antithesis is thought to negate the original thesis, it does not completely cancel it out. Both the original thesis and the antithesis contain some truth and some falsehood. A third thesis will develop—the synthesis—that will incorporate the truth from both earlier theses, leaving falsehoods in the dustbin of history. This synthesis now becomes a new thesis and the process continues. All Marxists are convinced that this process accounts for the progress of history.

Marx took dialectics to be the iron law of history he had long sought and used it to shed light on the class struggle. Internal contradictions within the thesis of feudalism (perhaps an arbitrary starting point) engendered the antithesis of capitalism; both were riddled with the internal contradictions of the class struggle between oppressors and oppressed. But the Great Revolution, contrary to earlier cycles, would bring to birth a contradictionless synthesis of socialism where there would be no class struggle. The bourgeoisie would be eliminated and the world would be peopled with harmonious workers only. With internal contradiction ended, the dialectical process would stop and history would be fulfilled. Government and religion had existed only to aid the ruling class in its oppression of the ruled class, so in the synthesis of socialism/communism (in the truly Marxist sense) both would disappear. Personal freedom would be a meaningless concept (nothing to compare it to), and all citizens would automatically take actions to benefit the world society. Everyone would live happily.

For many Marxists, dialectics was simply a useful tool, an aid to thinking about progress in history, but for Lenin it was dogma. Every social development that he encountered, including religious faith in Russia, was stuffed into its confines.

Determinism: Driver of History

Economic determinism is the belief that economic relationships within a society (one of the theses) are foundations that determine the entire superstructure of that society. The superstructure can consist of anything from the judicial system to marriage customs, but it definitely includes religion. Marx believed religion to be "an invalid form of consciousness"[30] based on the internally contradicted foundations of presocialist societies. Since religion was a reflection of the internal contradiction of class struggle, there could be no dialectical process within religion (though some Marxists have tried to create one). Religion changed only with changing economic foundations. Thus the rise of nations led to national gods and the rise of the Roman Empire led to the international faith of Christianity. Communism, since it was classless and without internal contradictions, could not generate a superstructure that included religion.

Religion did not just spring fully formed into the mind of man. It was the result of a particular historical process and arose at a particular point in human history. Religion was not in and of itself evil—it was the result of evil systems that had to be dialectically and historically worked through. Two postrevolutionary examples illustrate this point:

- "Religion is by no means the result of exceptional ignorance and darkness, just as it is not a question of simple logic, the result of false thinking. It has its roots in the social life, in the conditions of existence; it grows upon the soil of definite social relations and is determined by the class position in society of the one or the other group."[31]—Communist Party Conference on Antireligious Propaganda, Article IX, April 1926
- "To the query, 'Does modern civilization need religion?' the Communist answer is 'yes,' so far as decaying capitalist civilization is concerned. There, under pressure of crisis, in an atmosphere of uncertainty and fear, religion serves as an escape mechanism for the classes which history has already condemned."[32]—Julius Hecker, 1933

Religious belief, along with all the ideas contained in the superstructures of earlier societies, had its limited and temporary usefulness; it was good in the sense that it was necessary. Feuerbach observed—and Marxists agreed—that in his "childlike condition of humanity" religion is a necessary step in man's historical journey toward self-awareness. In a certain sense, Marx also saw religion as true. Although it was objectively false, even laughable, it was true for people living in a precommunistic world because it was historically necessary and because it was a perfect reflection of a world that was primitive, conflicted, and terribly wrong. It was true in the same sense that when man acts like a brute, the statement "there is little difference between man and animal" is true—the man has made it true. Only a social revolution could make religion *genuinely* false. The delusions of a delirious person are true at the time, but after the cure (revolution) it would be hard for him to imagine what he had previously "seen."[33]

Alienation: The Splitting of the Self

Marx and Engels theorized that religion was born from feelings of helplessness and frustration experienced by primitive peoples when they encountered forces of nature beyond their control. To combat these, man conjured his own external forces, his gods, to defend and comfort him. Early religion was therefore emotional in nature. Engels wrote in 1853:

> At present, every religion is nothing other than the reflection in the minds of men of those external forces that dominate them in their daily life, a reflection in which earthly forces take on the form of unearthly.[34]

Engels described man as gaining self-knowledge through contact and encounters with others; ultimately he was a social, communal being. Yet, before he could achieve self-knowledge he became alienated from his fellow man in a profound way. He was isolated, vulnerable, and limited in the face of nature, running up against the finiteness of his existence; he was still full of passion and short on the ability to reason.

During this growing process, humans expressed their unmet needs, their limitations, and their emptiness through imagination. They created an object of imagination that fulfilled their inward sense of deficiency. This overcame the sense of finiteness and became limitless; it was a projected concept of God (or gods), expressing infinity and perfection. Seeming real and objective, it was in truth but "the dream of the human mind."[35] One might believe that such dreams were harmless, but religion was an interruption of growth. Even worse, as he made God larger man allowed himself to shrink in stature; humility, sacrifice, poverty, and longing for a different world became virtues. To be *fully* human required rejection of the story of Creation—the belief that God created the world out of nothing and that God did all the work, not man. God's efforts denigrated human importance and human power. Man had forgone the possibility of his own perfection by creating a perfect God and sublimating his own miserable condition.[36]

We might expect man to have made advances through the dialectical process. He should have evolved through and beyond the unreflective, sentient level of self-knowledge, the emotionality of religion. Theologians—especially medieval scholastics—however, stifled this process by rationalizing what had been mere feelings, thus turning emotions into "logical truths." Theology prevented the awareness of self. This made progress difficult and stunted man's growth; the development of self-confidence was postponed.

On the other hand, although it was an irrational expression of the imagination, Feuerbach held that dreaming of God was positive in the sense of pointing to the essence of humanity. As man matured through history and developed his religious understanding, he actually learned more about himself: "Every advance in religion is therefore a deeper self-knowledge." The highest and fullest advancement, however, would be when man, achieving reason, comprehended that the qualities being projected onto God were in fact *inherent in himself.* He wrote, "In the personality of God man consecrates the supernaturalness, immortality, independence, unlimitedness of his own personality."[37]

It was his inability to know his true self that led him to project his ideal qualities onto a fictitious supreme "Other." Feuerbach held that religion was neither myth nor literature; it was anthropology. The characteristics of God were exactly the characteristics of man, which was only natural since man anthropomorphically invented God and projected his attributes onto him. Religion was an externalization of the self, and this self-alienation had become rigidly fixed in the dogma of the church. In one of many examples, Feuerbach offered Western religion's repression of man's natural sexuality. This was certainly a major theme in the early Christian church and still exists today:

> The monks made a vow of chastity to God; they mortified the sexual passions in themselves, but therefore they had in heaven the Virgin Mary, the image of a woman—an image of love. . . . The more the sexual tendencies are renounced, the more sensual is the God to whom they are sacrificed.[38]

To Feuerbach, Marx, and Engels, religion was the very essence of alienation.

After the dialectically determined final revolution, man would attain full comprehension. The epiphany would occur when he looked "for a superman in the fantastic reality of heaven" and found nothing there but the reflection of himself. He would not be satisfied with the reflection and would seek his *true reality.*[39] Eventually reason would reveal that man had created God in his own image and that transcendent, superior beings were all illusion. By creating God, man had wounded and corrupted himself, but man could also find the cure: self-sufficiency of production and autonomy from God. Then he would reach his true potential. The compensatory God—making up for man's perceived shortcomings—would no longer be relevant. Man would have achieved dignity.

But the forces evoking fear could come from society as well as nature. Marx expanded Feuerbach's concept of alienation by considering its roots in political, economic, and social injustice. As we shall see next, the elimination of alienation and illusion required the destruction of the economic and social foundation upon which the corrupt superstructure of religion had been built.

Man was alienated from his fellow man because of the divisive, competitive, and profit-minded nature of capitalism: the economic forces of uncaring capitalists and absentee landlords. Man was alienated from his work because, from the perspective of his workplace, the forces driving capitalism were opaque. Despite the publication of Adam Smith's *The Wealth of Nations* (1776), the market system remained a mystery. Who could understand why prices rose or fell, why surpluses or shortages occurred, or why unemployment vacillated? Waldemar Gurian wrote in 1933:

> [For Marx], religion corresponds to a social order in which things, commodities, still rule man, who is therefore confronted at every turn in his social life with the unexpected and the enigmatic. It serves as the opium which renders those enigmas and shocks endurable by pointing to another world and explaining them as effects of divine Providence, or as God's punishment for sin.[40]

Economic worries led baffled workers to seek supernatural explanations—solace in God—or, even better, divine intervention.

Class: The Explanation of Everything

The cleavages and contradictions within capitalist society were the result of oppression by the bourgeoisie of the proletariat. The bourgeoisie had evangelized workers to secure them in their place (just as American slave owners had evangelized slaves so they would seek consolation in heaven and not on Earth). Marx wrote, "The mortgage the peasant has on heavenly goods gives guaranty to the mortgage the bourgeoisie has on the peasant's earthly goods."[41] And Emelyan Yaroslavsky, the head of the Bolshevik League of the Godless, added:

> [The church taught that] Christ came to Earth not in order to abolish slavery, but in order to make the bad slave a good slave. . . . Ought the slave to strive for freedom? The priest taught him that the slave, the serf, ought to remain such for all time. "Let every man abide in the same calling wherein he was called. Art thou called being a servant? Care not for it" (I Corinthians 7:20).[42]*

In his earliest writings Lenin had acknowledged a "democratic revolutionary spirit" among Christians into the third century and later contended, "Christianity

---

*This Bible citation is unfair, however, as three verses later Paul explained that servants should "care not for it" because all, rich and poor alike, *are servants of the Lord.* Thus in the eyes of the Lord there were no class divisions—just what the Communists were seeking.

had lost value on the day when Constantine promised it revenue and a place at court."[43] When a Roman emperor first accepted the faith it had become a tool of the ruling class. One of the ways that the rulers used the faith was to suppress the worst profligacy and debauchery of their class, thus hiding their true vileness. The elimination of religion would remove the wool from the eyes of the oppressed and expose the rulers to the wrath they deserved.

From the Bolsheviks' class-struggle perspective, the tsar and the landed aristocracy of Russia had purposefully stifled any sign of cultural development among the masses. The rulers' major weapons were illiteracy, exhaustion, and religion—each reinforcing the others. Lenin offered this simple proof of religion's role: "Whoever consoles a slave instead of raising him up to an uprising against slavery, helps the slaveholder."[44] In May 1909 he authored an article in the periodical *Proletariat* titled "The Attitude of the Workers' Party to Religion," which was a critique of a speech made in the Russian Duma by the Social Democrat, Surkov. Here Lenin laid out his views on the religious question and attempted to haul Social Democrats back to the pure and strict Marxism from which they had wandered. He cautioned against befuddlement:

> The deepest root of religion is the socially downtrodden condition of the working masses and their apparently complete helplessness in the face of the blind forces of capitalism, which every day and every hour inflicts upon ordinary working people the most horrible suffering and the most savage torment, a thousand times more severe than those inflicted by extraordinary events, such as wars [and] earthquakes.[45]

He went on to explain the origin of religion, not in terms of primitive ignorance, but as a social phenomenon:

> Fear made the gods. Fear of the blind force of capital—blind because it cannot be foreseen by the masses of the people—a force which at every step in the life of the proletarian and small proprietor threatens to inflict, and does inflict, sudden, unexpected, accidental ruin, destruction, pauperism, prostitution, death from starvation. Such is the root of modern religion.[46]

Lenin distinguished between the Western—especially the German—Social Democratic policies and those that were applicable in Russia. In the West the bourgeoisie had undertaken the attack upon religion by separating church from state and declaring religious belief a private matter of the conscience. (Lenin, too, had espoused this view, but only tactically, whereas European Social Democrats were sincere.) The European position, Lenin continued, led to aberrations of anarchist, militant atheism (counterproductive) and bourgeois anticlericalism (useless); neither would advance the cause of socialism. Since in Russia the petty bourgeoisie and the populists had done little to thwart religious prejudice, the task fell to the revolutionary party of the proletarians—the Bolsheviks. They would lead the Russian struggle against medievalism and obscurantism, and would protect the people from any attempt to revive the old state religion or to renovate it.

Reformation of religion was to be avoided. Lenin worried that in Russia an introduction of bourgeois anticlericalism would lead to curbing the excesses and corruption of the church and would therefore work toward its *improvement*. An improved church would blur class divisions and set back the class struggle. Better that the church remain active in politics; that way its self-serving policies would be apparent to all. He preferred that the church use crude, antiquated, and played-out methods of "stupefying the people," rather than more subtle, clever, and advanced methods. He especially feared a "religion of love" led by morally upright priests, calling such a faith "loathsome." To compromise religion, the party should even tolerate "a priest who violates young girls" because that priest can be exposed and thus weaken religion. A well-educated, charming, and popular priest was the one to fear.[47] Lenin's worry was that the "foolish religion" of his times—what he sometimes referred to as "medieval mildew"—might be "superseded by a new and more subtle one which the proletariat could not so easily reject."[48] The more refined and cultivated the religion, the more difficult it would be to expose the reactionary motives lurking behind it. He wrote to his somewhat heretical friend Maxim Gorky in November 1913:

> [Liberal theology is] the most dangerous vulgarity, the foulest infection, because every religious idea, any idea of any god, any flirtation with the idea of a god is an unspeakable vulgarity willingly tolerated and often enthusiastically accepted by the democratic bourgeoisie. A million sins, bestialities, rapes, and infections of a physical kind are more easily seen through by the crowd, and are therefore less dangerous, than the refined spiritualized idea of God decked out in the most gorgeous costume.[49]

The class struggle required the presentation of black-and-white options to the masses—with the church painted black.

Under capitalism, besieged as it was by fear and anxiety, religion was a necessary "escape mechanism." Under oppressive conditions, Marx wrote, religion served real needs and it would continue to do so until "the practical relations of everyday life offer to man none but perfectly intelligible and reasonable relations with regard to his fellow men and to nature."[50] Although religion was required in class-conflicted societies, at the same time it must not become so well entrenched that it refuses to go when its time is up. After all, Lenin wrote:

> [The idea of God is made up of] filth, prejudices, sanctification of ignorance, and stupor on the one hand and of serfdom and monarchy on the other.[51]

He also referred to all devils and gods as "spiritual necrophilia."[52]

The concept of class led to one final objection to religion, but this was a practical point that trumped the theoretical. Class implied division, but religion often brought with it a sense of unity between classes and even a sense of national unity. To achieve and maintain power, the Bolsheviks (at least until World War II) depended upon turning one class against another and *avoiding* unity. It could be explained theoretically that oppressed workers and peasants would soon understand how the bourgeoisie had used religion to exploit them, but pragmatically the party had to ensure that no unifying, nationwide institution remained to rival its power. Eugene Trubetzkoy told the following story in 1919:

> One day a commissariat in Moscow nationalized the auditorium of the Church of St. Barbe, where religious addresses were being given to the people. The Orthodox workingmen who had founded the auditorium demanded the restitution of their property, insisting that they had a right to it as members of the proletariat. They were met with a formal refusal, the motives of which are interesting. "This auditorium," they were told, "had become a place for peaceful meetings and for friendly intercourse between the bourgeoisie and the proletariat; from the revolutionary point of view, nothing could be more inadmissible."[53]

Morality: No Absolute Ethics

Feuerbach wrote, "The belief that God is the necessary condition of virtue is the belief in the nothingness of virtue itself."[54] Man had transported his natural virtues above the clouds and onto God and debased and diminished himself to the extent that his virtue could come *only* from God's threats of punishment or promises of glory. Without self-respect, man's innate virtue could not be expressed.

Theology not only prevented self-awareness, it discouraged moral behavior because the source of good behavior was seen as external, artificial, and alien. The beatitudes spoken by Jesus in the Sermon on the Mount did not speak of virtue for its own sake but of promises of spiritual gain such as "Blessed are the pure in heart, for they shall see God," and "Blessed are they who are persecuted for righteousness's sake, for theirs is the kingdom of heaven" (Matthew 5:8, 10). Professor of philosophy Richard Lichtman summarized Marx's views on morality:

> The wellspring of Marxian morality is its contention that man's dignity and fulfillment are possible only under conditions which he rationally and freely imposes upon himself, for his own end and under canons which are intrinsic to his nature.[55]

True morality and true love, then, could only exist among unalienated, self-conscious men living within communal and atheist societies.

For Lenin the only morality was class morality, meaning what served the interests of the proletariat was moral. There were no absolute ethical standards. He wrote:

> Morality is that which serves to destroy the old exploiting society. . . . We deny all morality that is drawn from some conception beyond men, beyond class. We say that it is a deception, . . . a fraud and a stultification of the minds of the workers and peasants in the interests of the landowners and capitalists.[56]

What of Marxism's direct relationship with Christianity? Were Marx and Lenin—perhaps inadvertently—proposing a substitute for religion? And when should the triumph of atheism be expected?

4

THE FOG OF RELIGION

Marxists on Christianity, and Theories of Revolutionary Timing

A DEBATE

Both Christianity and workers' socialism preach forthcoming salvation from bondage and misery; Christianity places this in a life beyond, after death, in heaven; socialism places it in this world, in a transformation of society. . . . [Early Christian writings] could just as well have been written by one of the prophetically minded enthusiasts of the [Communist] International.[1]

—Engels, *On the History of Early Christianity*

The subject of the following short debate may at first seem odd, but there is a point to it that relates to the credentials of Marx and Lenin as antireligious proselytizers. The point will also make some topics later in this book more clear.

Resolved: Jesus and Marx Were Both
Religious Missionaries with Similar Messages

PRO: Good evening, ladies and gentlemen. My first contention is that Karl Marx owes a debt to Jesus Christ that neither he nor his followers have been willing to acknowledge. Marx was raised in a household at first Jewish and later Lutheran, so he was well steeped in the Judeo-Christian ethic that he later so rebelliously rejected. Whether consciously or subconsciously, he knew of Jesus as a revolutionary concerned with the plight of the poor and downtrodden—in other words, preproletarians. The community Jesus formed was communistic in the sense of sharing worldly possessions. My second contention is that Marx himself had a religious character. Marx was messianic—a modern-day Messiah. Just as the Gospels portray the Apostles as never fully understanding their Master, Marx knew that the workingmen of Europe were not wading through Das Kapital. They, too, could accept him only through faith.

Both Jesus and Marx promised an imminent, apocalyptic event that would lead to a Golden Age (paradise/communism), where man would live on Earth for a millennium (or, in Marx's case, forever) in peace and harmony. Both foresaw a great moral transformation in man, and both believed he was perfectible.

CON: Good evening. My purpose is to show you enough of my opponent's errors in knowledge and reasoning that you will reject the resolution as farfetched and ridiculous. First of all, Jesus counseled his followers to accept their stations in life and to render unto Caesar what was his due—hardly a revolutionary proposal. Jesus's postcrucifixion followers in Jerusalem had no interest in overthrowing anything, as they expected the Second Coming any day. Second, Marx was about as thoroughly unreligious as one can get. His approach to understanding was historical and scientific, with faith playing no role whatsoever. He distinguished his socialism from that of others as being scientific, not emotional or utopian. For example, through the use of historical dialectics he demonstrated how the forces needed to free workers (and slaves) were nowhere near sufficiently developed 1,900 years ago, and he thus explained Jesus's failure. Marx owes Jesus nothing, nor was he a missionary for any faith.

PRO: Sorry; Marx may have been a philosophical visionary—a prophet—but he was no scientist. He couldn't have been a scientist because he didn't adjust his conclusions as facts and events unfolded. Instead he claimed personal knowledge of The Truth and ignored facts that failed to fit into his picture of the world. Scientists are impartial, but Marx pushed for the most biased of propaganda and claimed that it was historically justified. No matter that he rejected God's existence; his character and motives were religious.

CON: It violates all common sense to say that a man who invoked no supernatural forces and relied totally upon logic and history was religious. My opponent's difficulty is mixing passion with religion. It should be obvious that religious people can be dispassionate, and passionate people, like Michael Bakunin, can be forceful atheists.

No matter what we read as the deep psychological origins of Marx's and Lenin's thoughts on religion, it is what they avowed that mattered for history.

CHRISTIANITY IN PARTICULAR

Do you offer your right cheek when you are struck upon the left, or do you not institute proceedings for assault? Yet the Gospels forbid that.[2]

—Karl Marx*

---

*The historian Edward Hulmes observed that Marx "repudiated biblical teaching by means of quotation out of context, carefully selected allusions, a tendentious use of theological interpretation and outright parody."

At times Marx stated that religious faith was so absurd that it needed no refutation. He tended to downplay its importance and granted it little respect. He never saw religion as an independent entity—something of substance to be assaulted. It was merely the "spiritual aroma" of a wretched and soon-to-be-replaced society, and there was no reason to spend much intellectual effort denouncing it. This attitude reflected not just Marx's mastery of dialectics but also his dearth of religious experience and knowledge. Engels, who between the partners was considered the religion expert, called faith "a necessary but transitory stage of civilization."[3]

As has been mentioned, Engels made a distinction between early Christianity (the first three hundred years) and Christianity after it became the state religion under Constantine in the early fourth century. He drew parallels between the suffering of early Christians and those of the modern working class. Christianity was the religion of the oppressed: slaves, ex-slaves, the poor, and victims of Roman expansion. He wrote, "Both Christianity and the workers' socialism preach forthcoming salvation from bondage and misery."[4] But early Christians did not choose to revolt against social oppression; instead they turned to heaven and belief in escape by bodily resurrection after death.

Engels also wrote of Christian eschatology—the passionate trust of the disciples that Jesus's Second Coming was just around the corner and that all to whom God had shown grace would soon be living in the Heavenly Kingdom. He described Paul as the "thirteenth apostle," spreading the word that the dead would soon be raised, the living transformed, and the children of God seated beside him (Mark 9:1, Mark 13:30, and Matthew 10:23). Engels found no sense in Paul of social transformation in the here and now and no concern for the long-term moral improvement of man in his present world; all was preparation for the End Times.[5] How could it be otherwise if Jesus had said: "He that findeth his life shall lose it, and he that loseth his life for my sake shall find it" (Matthew 10:39) and "What shall it profit a man if he shall gain the whole world and lose his own soul?" (Mark 8:36).

Engels pointed to the obvious: The End Times never came, and man was stuck on Earth with a religion not created for these conditions. Christians lived another two millennia with a religion awkwardly and hypocritically trying to fit itself into the worldly kingdom, without the tools of social change. Marx claimed that Christian morality was based on preparation for the Kingdom of God and not on building better societies on Earth. Why else, for example, would Jesus preach to abandon one's mother and father—patently immoral in the earthly sense—and follow him (Matthew 10:37–38)?

Marx and Engels contended that it was this absence of a *social plan* that led to Christianity's perverse adaptability and corruption. The historian Richard Lichtman wrote:

It was precisely the social vacuousness of the original teachings of Christianity that so simplified the process of adapting them to any conceivable status quo. In other words, it was because the religious motive of total transcendence was so radical in Christianity that it lent itself so readily to the politically conservative function of accepting or sanctioning any existing social order.[6]

For example, Marx held that Christianity clung to any social system that would preserve its prerogatives:

The social principles of Christianity justified the slavery of Antiquity, glorified the serfdom of the Middle Ages, and equally know, when necessary, how to defend the oppression of the proletariat, although they make a pitiful face over it. . . . The social principles of Christianity declare all vile acts of the oppressors against the oppressed to be either the just punishment of original sin or trials that the Lord in his infinite wisdom imposes on those redeemed.[7]

Christianity, Marxists contended, was hypocritical for forgetting its roots in slavery, martyrdom, and oppression. No sooner than it had gained the protection of the state under Constantine than it began its own persecution of heretics and infidels. By the early Middle Ages the Catholic Church, and a little later the Orthodox Church, had become staunch supporters of feudalism and, remarkably, owners of serfs. Marx and Engels pointed out that Christianity should be thought of as "the religious counterpart to [feudalism], with a corresponding feudal hierarchy."[8] Too much attention was being paid to Paul's admonition, "Render therefore to all their dues—tribute to whom tribute is due; custom to whom custom; fear to whom fear; honor to whom honor" (Romans 13:1–7). What had happened to the Christian sense of injustice?

Christian teaching on original sin encouraged believers to meekly accept the wretchedness of their surroundings as fit punishment. Christian teaching on humility, meekness, obedience, and acceptance of suffering kept workers from protesting against these conditions. As for the bourgeoisie, church attendance assuaged their guilt. Lenin put it this way:

Those who toil and live in want all their lives are taught by religion to be submissive and patient while here on Earth and take comfort in the hope of being rewarded in heaven. But those who live by the labor of others are taught by religion to practice charity while on Earth, thus offering them a very cheap way of justifying their entire existence as exploiters and selling them, at a moderate price, tickets to heavenly bliss.[9]

Marx *condemned* Christians for their charity—it would not have been necessary had the church fought to achieve social justice so that man could earn his way in this world. The point was not to provide alms for the poor but to eliminate those economic and social conditions that bred the need for alms.[10]

In spite of almsgiving, Marx considered greed a major motivator for the church as an institution. In *Capital*, he wrote, "The English Established Church will more readily pardon an attack on thirty-eight of its thirty-nine articles than one thirty-ninth of its income." And he accused the Church of England of hypocritically sanctifying the Sabbath while its leading members in Parliament voted to allow work on that day to increase their capital.[11] Sarcastically, he wrote:

> The "holy ones" . . . show their Christianity by the humility with which they bear the overwork, the privations and the hunger of others.[12]

According to the Marxist analysis, greed traveled right along with the Christian—especially Protestant—emphasis on private property. An overweening concern for the salvation of one's own soul reinforced the psychology of personal possessions. In this sense Christianity worked against the dreamed-of communality of the future.

Engels tackled the issue of equality, arguing that the only equality Christians acknowledged was that of all being equally guilty of original sin. He ascribed the presumed social equality, sharing, and communality of the earliest Christian communities to their having been ostracized from both Jewish and Roman society. As soon as they began distinguishing between priests and laity, inequality made its appearance.[13] Equality among believers was possible only through the Christian teaching that all were equal before God, or, to put it negatively, all were equally distant from God's perfection and equally needy of God's redemption. But even if men *were* equal in that sense, it did not imply an equal receipt of God's grace. Predestination, championed by the early church and some modern Protestant denominations (such as Calvinists), removed the whole discussion of equality from the table. Some were saved and some were not, and it was beyond the ability of man to fathom the criteria applied. In any case, there was no attempt within the historical church to fundamentally alter society so that men could approach equality in a material—or even in a legal—sense.

Marx was provoked to anger by the mere thought of that greatest of inequalities, the Inquisition—that epitome of institutionalized arrogance. The church had "developed" to such a point that it thought it could force people into "correct belief" through threat of fire and thereby save those who believed they were just fine the way they were. For Marx and Marxists, all theology was as dangerous and obsolete as the Inquisition. The modern world had passed by theology's most highly developed form, Christianity, and this church had become a relic, as irrelevant for man as tales of God's incarnation, the trinity, and the existence of angels; he referred to it as "a snakeskin to be shed by history."[14] By the nineteenth century, all religion was anachronism, Marx contended, and the only reason it had lasted so long was the continued existence of the class struggle.

As might be expected, Marx also rejected deism, that "rational religion" emerging from the Enlightenment and the French Revolution, which was predicted to supplant Christianity. Although deism deified reason, it did nothing to change society or remove the workers' burden of oppression. It proclaimed man's liberty but did nothing about it.[15]

ACTION AND TIMING

Economic slavery is the true source of the religious humbugging of man. . . . The proletariat of today takes the side of socialism, which enlists science in the battle against the fog of religion and frees the workers from their belief in life after death by welding them together to fight in the present for a better life on Earth.

—Lenin, *Socialism and Religion*, 1905

Marx did not predict the demise of Christianity (and all other religions) just because he wished people to hold the "correct view." Lenin did not reject individual atheism—where a man sat in his armchair feeling smug about his intellectual achievement—just because he thought it bourgeois. The point of philosophy was to apply it to society not to understand society but to *change it*. Therefore materialism must contribute to building the future socialist society. God was not in control of the forces of nature, man was. As long as man regarded his stay here on Earth as only a necessary prelude to eternal life in heaven, where would he find the motivation to improve his lot on this planet? Religion hampered his talents and obstructed his freedom; it condemned him to accept what he was, blocking his impulse to construct something new. The "opium" that affected not only the oppressed but also the oppressor could be shaken off only through vigorous action.

Already in 1853 Engels anticipated that the task of taking power would someday become immediate; the point would eventually be to "achieve subordination of society to social forces."

> And when this action takes place, when society, taking in hand the whole range of the means of production and using them systematically, liberating thereby itself and all its members from slavery . . . only then will the last external force vanish, which up to that time expressed itself in religion, and with it will vanish the religious image itself.[16]

Thinking in the present but looking to the future, Marx saw no place for religion in the modern scientific and industrial world. Having explained how religion occurred in history, he saw the culminating phase of social progress as making better use of the material contributions of capitalism and making no use at all of the religion capitalism had succored—dialectics in action. After Marx's death in 1883, it would be up to Lenin to nudge along the inexorable flow of history.

But what was the relationship between religion and the revolution? Which came first? Was eliminating religion a prerequisite to revolution? Or must the revolution be accomplished before creating the historical conditions to eliminate religion? The answer depended upon circumstances and who was telling the story and when.

Revolution First

In his early writings (1840s) Marx worried that religion would negate the self-realization and self-determination that man needed to overthrow the state, therefore atheism must come first, but in his mature writings (1860s) he concluded that revolution would create the conditions for the death of faith. He stressed a sequence of events whereby revolution would eliminate the social and economic roots upon which religion was built and thrived; when these roots were cut religion would wither away and die—the resulting transformation of society would make religion superfluous. The Old Bolshevik* Nikolai Bukharin put it succinctly:

> The transition from the society that makes an end of capitalism to the society that is completely free from all traces of class division and class struggle will bring about the natural death of all religion and all superstition.[17]

Theoretically, the demise of religion need not involve antireligious education, as education was just another part of the superstructure that was soon to change. In any case, there should certainly be no need of persecution. Those who truly understood the causes of religion could afford to wait.

The genesis of this approach must have come at least in part from the experiences of the French Revolution. Although remote from us now, when Marx matured during the mid-1800s the lessons of France were vividly in mind. Terror against the Catholic Church had failed to destroy it, instead driving belief into the privacy of the home, and rash attacks against religion had been one of the causes of the revolution's eventual collapse.[18] Thus Marx explicitly opposed professional atheists or "religious atheists"—those who attacked God with religious fervor. Besides, too vigorous an assault would be taking religion too seriously. Of course, it was easier for Marx to be patient, since he had no immediate prospects of overthrowing a European government. But as we shall see in later chapters, Marxist Bolsheviks, once in power, found it difficult to adhere to the master's sentiments.

Lenin lived in two successive worlds: first, as an exile in Europe (like Marx) theorizing and plotting and wondering whether he would live long enough to see the downfall of autocracy in Russia; and second, as the leader of a successful revolution facing immediate problems where on-the-spot decisions had to be made.

---

*A term used for those who were with Lenin in internal or external exile, contrasted with those who joined the party after the Revolution.

If the Orthodox Church were not crushed, or at least rendered impotent, it might rally the people to undo his great accomplishment. Ever the model of theoretical rigidity but tactical flexibility, he acted contingent on the circumstances.

In the prerevolutionary period, when party unity was the major concern, Lenin paradoxically both upgraded and downgraded the religious question. He made the struggle against religion and the church *more* significant within the revolutionary movement than had Marx, who had concentrated his intellectual efforts on the "mundane origin of the religious illusion" and on establishing the class context of religious belief. But Lenin also thought of religion as *less* important, as seen in this 1909 polemic:

> The combating of religion cannot be confined to abstract ideological preaching.
> . . . It must be linked up with the concrete practice of the class movement, which
> aims at eliminating the social roots of religion. . . . It means that Social Democ-
> racy's atheist propaganda must be *subordinated* to its basic task—the develop-
> ment of the class struggle of the exploited masses against the exploiters.[19]

Lenin also argued that atheism should not be required for party membership, though his two reasons for this apparent toleration had little to do with religion as such. First, he did not want to divide the revolutionary workers' movement along believer/unbeliever lines, and second, he did want to divide the Bolsheviks from Bakunin's anarchists, who were more stringent on the issue of membership. He not only professed a willingness to allow believing workers into the Russian Social Democratic Labor Party but urged that they be *recruited*. No offense should be given to their religious beliefs, he wrote, but they should be educated "in the spirit of our program."* In prerevolutionary days, Lenin was even willing to admit *priests* into the party, as long as they abstained from spreading religious views through his organization.[20]

Still years from power, Lenin concentrated on practical ways of combating religious belief through the development of class-consciousness and "patiently preaching proletarian solidarity and the scientific world outlook."[21] He persuaded his followers that knowing how to combat religion meant explaining to the masses the source of faith *in a materialist way*. He harked back to Engels and his attacks on "left revolutionaries," warning against "dilettantes and ignoramuses" in the present who loudly proclaimed atheism and declared all-out war on religion:

> "Down with religion and long live atheism; the dissemination of atheist views
> is our chief task!" The Marxist says that this is not true, that it is a superficial

---

*This was perhaps a precursor to Stalin's reply when he met with a group of visiting American workers in 1928. Asked if church members could join the Communist Party, he replied that of course they could, as long as they swore to support the party program. He failed to add that the party program explicitly endorsed atheism and condemned religion.

view, the view of narrow bourgeois uplifters. It does not explain the roots of religion profoundly enough; it explains them not in a materialist but in an idealist way.[22]

Lenin's apparent prerevolutionary moderation was not softness on religion, nor was it based on fear of scaring off converts to the party; it was not even a political tactic. Dialectical materialism required the primacy of the class struggle, and it required that he subordinate idealism and theory to practicality and flexibility. He offered this hypothetical example:

> The proletariat in a particular region and in a particular industry is divided, let us assume, into an advanced section of fairly class-conscious Social Democrats, who are of course atheists, and rather backward workers who are still connected with the countryside and with the peasantry, and who believe in God, go to church, or are even under the direct influence of the local priest, who, let us suppose, is organizing a Christian labor union. Let us assume furthermore that the economic struggle in this locality has resulted in a strike.
>
> It is the duty of a Marxist to place the success of the strike movement above everything else, vigorously to counteract the division of the workers in this struggle into atheists and Christians. . . .
>
> Atheist propaganda in such circumstances may be both unnecessary and harmful . . . out of consideration for the real progress of the class struggle, which in the conditions of modern capitalist society will convert Christian workers to Social Democracy and atheism a hundred times better than bald atheist propaganda. To preach atheism at such a moment and in such circumstances would only be playing into the hands of the priest and the priests, who desire nothing better than that the division of the workers according to their participation in the strike movement should be replaced by their division according to their belief in God.[23]

Lenin reminded his followers of Bismarck's mistake in 1870 when he attacked the Catholic Party in Germany, resulting in a resurgence of clericalism.[24] Overzealous stupidity would "be the best way to revive interest in religion and to prevent it from really dying out." But far more importantly, it was a denial of fundamental Marxist tenets. "Only the class struggle of the working masses could, by comprehensively drawing the widest strata of the proletariat into conscious and revolutionary social *practice*, really free the oppressed masses from the yoke of religion." In other words, the answer was that revolution, of dialectical necessity, must precede atheism. The gamble of antireligious war should be avoided. The prerevolutionary Lenin clinched his point:

> Why do we not declare in our program that we are atheists? . . . Unity in the revolutionary struggle of the oppressed class for the creation of a paradise on Earth is more important to us than unity of opinion among the proletarians about a paradise in heaven.[25]

Atheism First

But a contradictory thread runs through the thinking of Marx's disciples—that workers have to be free from the entangling web of religion *before* they can become effective fighters in the revolutionary cause. How could nonmaterialists even carry out such an uprising? And, after political power had been achieved, should they merely sit on their hands waiting for faith to disappear through historical processes?

Before 1917 there were no successful socialist revolutions in Europe, and Marxists sought explanations for the failure of their teacher's predictions to materialize. The settled-upon rationalization was that, since modern Christianity was inherently antirevolutionary, it had developed into a powerful roadblock to the path that history must eventually take. In other words, it had become a more obstinate enemy than Marx had anticipated. At the very least, after the seizure of power revolutionaries would have to be free of religion to carry on the crusade for "socialist construction," which would—on the basis of new economic foundations—*eventually* be free of religion.

Although Lenin was theoretically patient on the religious issue (as we saw above), he was also temperamentally impatient. After taking power, he realized that religion was a little more tenacious than theory had predicted and the withering away of faith through the restructuring of economic relationships would need a significant shove. As the historian David Powell put it:

> If man cannot alter the laws of nature or social development, he can act as an agent of the historical process and thus bring about the results that the laws of history themselves require.[26]

As it turned out, the Communist leadership would still need antireligious propaganda into the 1920s and beyond. A rationalization could be found in Marx's unelaborated concept of the Dictatorship of the Proletariat, when, after the fall of oppressive governments, some time (duration unmentioned) would be required in the victorious socialist society to clean up the vestiges of capitalism's malignant superstructure. The 1919 Program and Rules of the Communist Party was a testament to the continuing, indeed perpetual, process of the "shove":

> The Communist Party of the Soviet Union is guided by the conviction that only conscious and deliberate planning of all the social and economic activities of the masses will cause religious prejudices to die out.[27]

Even after their national success, Bolshevik leaders resented religion because it sapped the fighting spirit of the world's oppressed classes. Thus, in April 1923, the author of the article "Who Wants the Fable of the Resurrection of Christ, and What For?" in the periodical *Bezbozhnik* (*The Godless*) still felt compelled to write:

> The bosses of all countries whose chief concern is to enslave the laboring masses always looked upon religion as a ring in the bull's nose. The idea of the sufferings of God, the Savior of all the laboring and needy, is more destructive of the spirit of activity than all the physical whippings. . . . For that reason the employers of all countries, the bloodsuckers who feed on the sweat of the oppressed laboring classes, were always convinced Christians and spent large amounts of money on the propaganda of the religion of Christ among the workers, thus undermining their will to struggle.[28]

(Marx, who wrote *The Communist Manifesto* at the height of the abolitionist movement in the United States, applied this same logic to the American racial class system.)

THE NATURE OF BOLSHEVISM

Nothing in thought or aspiration seemed to Lenin more incomprehensible than tolerance. For him it was indistinguishable from lack of principle. It was the beginning of contemptible surrender.[29]

—Valeriu Marcu, *Lenin 1870–1924* (1928)

Approaching the end of Part I (Prelude), we should look at some characteristics that are not just Marxist but particular to the political party that appointed itself to put Marxism and Marxist atheism into power. What was peculiarly "Bolshevik" about the Bolsheviks?

Cultural Isolation

They thought of themselves as an elite and as a vanguard. The perceived necessity of avoiding a mass membership party is one reason that Lenin broke up the Russian Social Democrats into Mensheviks and Bolsheviks in 1903. He was convinced that an effective revolutionary party would have to consist of *only* those who were totally dedicated to the cause. To include all Marxists would blunt the party's fighting edge. To permit a membership of sympathizers and passively interested reformers would reduce the party to merely the expression of majority opinion. The party and the revolutionary movement it led would become inert. Only a dedicated and fully focused leadership could master Marxist theory and, through its esoteric knowledge, discover the inner dynamics of any historical situation. Once having chosen the correct course of action, this vanguard would manipulate the masses accordingly. The party leadership should draw strength from the masses and keep in constant contact with them, but the masses should never be consulted on the making of any specific decision. They could later be induced to accept and approve it. In *Mastering Bolshevism* (1937), Stalin boasted:

> [Bolsheviks] are strong in that they maintained their contact with their mother, the masses which gave them birth, fed them, and brought them up. As long as they maintain the link with their mother, the people, they will have every chance of remaining invincible. This is the key to the invincibility of the Bolshevik leadership.[30]

The truth, however, was that the Old Bolsheviks—Lenin, Stalin, Grigory Zinoviev, Lev Kamenev, the urbane and cultivated Anatoly Lunacharsky, and others—were far removed from the social lives of the people they ruled. In fact, the early leadership rapidly became estranged even from the lower ranks of its own party, and the lower ranks became estranged from the Russian masses. By 1921, the beginning of the New Economic Policy,* true working-class support for the Bolsheviks had all but disappeared. The historian Roger Pethybridge wrote of the Bolsheviks' limited experience in Russia:

> Repression, imprisonment, and exile had induced them to formulate abstract, preconceived ideas about the nature of Russian society, since it could not be studied at close hand [or] at the grass roots level for much of the time. During the periods when they managed to be politically active in Russia, they were forced to adopt secretive underground methods, which they found hard or impossible to discard once they achieved power in 1917.[31]

This cultural isolation meant that Lenin and the top Bolsheviks had no first-hand experience with the religious mentality of the people and, even worse, no convenient way of obtaining it. What scanty evidence they did absorb became virtually useless as it refracted through their ideological prism, and it provided no guidelines as to which antireligious approach would be most effective. Faced with a recalcitrant society, the Old Bolsheviks resorted to trial and error for short-term solutions, and, when these failed—as they usually did—they often resorted to dreaming, as in prerevolutionary times, of how they would shape the future society where problems seemed, with distance, less intractable.[32]

On the other hand, Stalin's 1937 disingenuous statement was correct in a Leninist sense because contact with the masses was permissible; it was taking advice or direction from them that was not. The party leadership did not represent the people in the Western democratic sense. Instead, it acted "in their interests."

---

*The attempt during the mid-1920s to restore economic prosperity by temporarily allowing limited capitalism.

In *The Foundations of Leninism* (1939), Stalin wrote that the party could not be a real party if it "limits itself to registering what the masses of the working class think or experience, if it drags along at the tail of the spontaneous movement."[33]

Regardless of theory, imposing Marxist principles—or what passed for Marxist principles—on the people was not going to happen anywhere near as expediently as had the November 1917 government takeover in Petrograd.

Obsolete Stereotypes

Bolsheviks acknowledged the stereotypical Russian national character as portrayed in Ivan Goncharov's novel *Oblamov* (1859). In the story, Oblamov spent his days lying on the couch in his dressing gown and slippers, orating about ambitious plans and complex projects. One plan followed another in rapid succession, each holding the promise of great activity and impending, earthshaking events. But he seldom *raised* himself from the couch. What was the point in doing so? Any effort would be fruitless in the face of inexorable fate. No one could really change the world; better to let it go its way. Although action was perceived as part of Russian character, it was action undirected and soon dissipated. Oblamov would throw himself up from his couch in a frenzy of activity, without plan or forethought. Then he would give up before accomplishing anything.

Bolsheviks pledged to create a new type of Russian. They struggled against "Oblamovism" within themselves and within others. Ideal Bolsheviks were the antithesis of Oblamov. They forced themselves into a mold that they termed "German character"—cultivating traits of careful planning and attention to the successful completion of a set goal. They would not allow themselves to be diverted by moods of pessimism or despair; they trained themselves to work methodically to the end.

Another theme running through much of nineteenth-century Russian literature was the lack of distinction between motivation and action. A good motivation implied a good action ("He meant well"), and a bad motivation implied a bad action. All intentions inevitably led to consistent actions. Influenced by European (especially German) rationalism, Bolsheviks rejected this ethic. They argued that one must distinguish between motivation and action and, in practice, elevate the distinction to a real separation. They considered subjective intention to be morally irrelevant and focused exclusively on action. Any action that furthered Bolshevik ends was morally acceptable, regardless of why the action was first contemplated.

Stereotypically, Russians reacted to the individual failures and social blunders of others with a tempering penchant for forgiveness. Man was by nature sinful, but when he repented his sins his fellow man would take great joy in forgiving him. But Bolsheviks had no stomach for forgiveness, especially when confronted with collective wallowing in guilt. Expecting results, they were intolerant of failure, or even of error. Forgiveness might be used as a political expedient but never celebrated as a moral virtue.

Typical Russians were usually thought of as experiencing great and recurring emotional crises when attempting to find their place and role in society. Bolsheviks tried to steer away from these traumas of self-doubt. After all, they based their party and its principles on Marx and Engel's "scientific socialism," which should eschew doubt. In the prerevolutionary and immediate postrevolutionary periods, party leaders expected members to indulge in constant self-appraisal, but only to ensure that they were taking the historically correct route. It was not long, however, before the doctrine of "party conscience" appeared—subsequently, the tenets of the party were to be taken as empirical fact. The bases for all actions were no longer to be questioned or evaluated by individuals. The party member should be concerned only that he was effective.

*   *   *

Tactics were central to Lenin's approach to the religious question. Since the founding of the Bolshevik movement, Lenin had called for "the propagation of atheism" in party propaganda. But atheism was not an ideology in itself; rather it was a part of the larger Marxist system. This meant that the pure philosophy never changed, but day-to-day tactics did. No matter what abrupt changes occurred on the antireligious front, Lenin always saw consistency.

Even within the same year he made tactical adjustments. In April 1909 he lashed out against an alleged revival of "militant clericalism" in the Third Duma. Later in that same year he softened his tone, not wanting Bolsheviks to sound like the despised anarchists, who were even more radical on the religious question. Disciplining himself to stay within the more moderate boundaries of previous socialist statements, he now contended that antireligious propaganda must not be overemphasized; the proletariat would be educated in atheism primarily by "its own struggle against the dark forces of capitalism." This tactical concession did nothing, however, to alter Lenin's deeply held conviction that the working class could not develop socialist consciousness through its own efforts, nor could it spontaneously emancipate itself from religious illusion. The party must impregnate the masses with a scientific, atheist worldview by the process of class warfare led by a revolutionary vanguard.[34]

We are now prepared to jump into the narrative—the actual clash between the Bolsheviks and the Orthodox Church. The story naturally begins with the overthrow of the tsar, Nicholas II.

PART II
CONFLICT

5

WE HAVE A TSAR NO MORE

The Importance of the First Church Sobor

T he narrative of our story begins with the two revolutions of 1917—the overthrow of the monarchy in March and the overthrow of the democratic Provisional Government in November—and the meeting of the Russian Orthodox Church's All-Russian Church Council (sobor) in the midst of the second revolution. It did not take long for the Bolsheviks and the church to clash.

THE PROVISIONAL GOVERNMENT AND THE CHURCH

I came not to send peace, but a sword.

—Jesus according to Matthew 10:34, quoted by an Orthodox priest in his message to Russian troops while trying to persuade them to keep fighting against the Germans after the March 1917 Revolution

If you want to fight, take the rifle and go into the trenches, for we are going home.

—Russian soldier at the front to a priest who was trying to convince him of his duty, summer 1917

On March 15, 1917, Nicholas II abdicated in favor of his brother Michael, who immediately abdicated as well. Mob rule on the streets of Petrograd had won a sudden victory. The monarchy was over. Nicolas Zernov described its passing, "It fell as an old tree falls, rotted at the heart by weather and time."[1] Prince Vladimir Lvov, the new procurator of the Holy Synod, informed the nation that the will of God had been accomplished and ordered all prayers for the tsar replaced with blessings for the "true believing Provisional Government."[2]

Oddly, the Orthodox hierarchy, which had been so intimately wedded to the tsarist state, at first made little commotion or protest over its potential loss of position and attempted no restoration of the monarchy. The fall of the tsar, the "anointed of God," merited not even a comment from the Holy Synod. For the moment it seemed as if church leaders were either numb or indifferent. Perhaps the form of government was of no consequence as long as the church's interests and privileges continued uninterrupted.[3] Or perhaps the Provisional Government's struggle to stay in the world war initially misled the hierarchs into thinking that church reform was not on the new government's agenda.

It was not until April 28 that Lvov, backed by soldiers, announced to the Holy Synod that he was canceling all future sessions and involuntarily retiring all but two of its current members. Of these two, Lvov's sparing of Metropolitan Sergei (Stragorodsky) of Vladimir was the most significant for the Orthodox Church's future. Placed in charge of the reconstituted Holy Synod, Sergei made a formal request for a sobor and accepted the principle of election of bishops, which, as this reform spread throughout the country, diminished the power of the episcopate and increased the power of the newly enfranchised parish councils.[4]

In June the Provisional Government abolished the Holy Synod, replacing it with a Ministry of Religion whose job description was to look out for the interests of *all* Russian religions and show no favoritism toward Orthodoxy. (Though Sergei was temporarily deposed, we will hear much more from him later.) Orthodox hierarchs deeply resented this policy and refused to relinquish their privileged position among the faiths. They also expressed their unwillingness to be denied the financial support they were used to. In addition, the government ruled on the "Law of God"—the Orthodox catechism taught by priests in the schools—making it optional, not required.[5] The catechism, the church knew, was vital to bringing up the next generation within its theological framework. (Within a few months the Bolsheviks would completely remove this catechism from the schools.)

In mid-June, an All-Russian Congress of clergy and laity met in Moscow for ten days to discuss plans for the upcoming church sobor. Many within the clergy hoped the much-anticipated sobor would restore the patriarchate, abolished by Peter the Great. But, with Archbishop Sergei at its head, this group issued a report on July 26 that called such a restoration "anti-Christian"—meaning anti-democratic, as the early church was considered to have been perfectly democratic. For two decades a debate had churned its way through Russia's intelligentsia concerning the correct balance between the power of the individual and *sobornost*—collectiveness and conciliarity. Those who favored *sobornost* were fearful of granting too much power to a patriarch lest he begin to resemble a Catholic pope, a personage who Orthodox clergy felt had usurped God's position as the emissary of grace. Those who favored restoration of the patriarchate cited canon law, church dogma, and church history (with arguments too numerous to go into here) and were heavily represented by the lay peasantry. As a second revolution approached, the issue would be decided less by theology and more by practical concerns. There would be a need for a strong leader, but there also had to be compromise. Perhaps a patriarch could serve as a symbol of the wholeness of the church without violating the *sobornost* imperative.[6]

The above-mentioned conference report then took on the Provisional Government in a contest over who was going to control the daily lives of the people. It demanded that the Orthodox Church have legal precedence over all other religions in Russia and that it retain autonomy in internal affairs. The state must continue to recognize church regulations on marriage and divorce and honor church registration of these events, maintain compulsory Orthodox religious instruction in all religious and secular schools, and allow no interruption in existing levels of church subsidies.[7] Still, the Pre-Sobor Conference leaned more toward church reform than would the upcoming sobor.

On July 30 the Duma shocked the established church by granting full religious liberty—abolishing all civil limitations based on religious belief. Not only was the right to pass from one religious communion to another proclaimed but in addition the right to hold no religious belief at all. Up to this point, the right to atheism had never been legally recognized. The Duma still compelled citizens to resort to the church, however, for marriages and divorces. Out of fear of losing influence to secular forces, the church labeled this legislation a gross injustice. The new laws went into effect, however, over its protests. Perhaps church bitterness was somewhat assuaged when Alexander Kerensky took over the Provisional Government in July and signed a check for 1 million rubles to cover the expenses of the first All-Russian Sobor since 1667.[8]

By summer the church finally awakened from its slumber and realized the danger posed by the Provisional Government. The conflict began over control of the educational system. There were thirty-seven thousand church-run, but state-supported, schools in Russia, about one-third of all schools. On August 3 the government required that schools supported by public funds be put under the control of the Ministry of Education and that all parochial school buildings and equipment be turned over to the state. Churches of all faiths lost control of the education of their young, but the Orthodox Church, having the most to lose, protested the loudest. At this point many in the church spoke out in favor of getting rid of the democratically elected soviets of people's deputies and finding a strong military leader to rule.[9]

THE FIRST CHURCH SOBOR

We have a tsar no more; no father whom we may love. It is impossible to love a synod, and therefore we, the peasants, want a patriarch.[10]

—a peasant speaking at the sobor

Organization

The sobor convened on the second floor of the Uspensky Cathedral within Moscow's Kremlin walls on August 28, 1917. The cathedral—officially the Cathedral of the Falling Asleep (Dormition) of the Mother of God—had been built in 1326 during the period of the Mongol Yoke. Having missed two and a half centuries, the sobor had much work to do—work that could take up to a year to accomplish and would have to be conducted in the much larger Cathedral of Christ the Savior, just southwest of the Kremlin.

Delegates were democratically elected and were representative of the church as a whole—each of the 66 dioceses, for example, sent its bishop, 2 priests, and 3 laymen. The 564 delegates included 80 bishops; altogether there were 250 clerical delegates and 314 lay delegates. Observers of socialist persuasion emphasized the capitalist and bourgeois nature of the delegation, listing 11 princes and counts, 10 generals and other army officers, 132 former tsarist civil officials, 22 big landowners, 17 manufacturers and bankers, and 69 bourgeois intellectuals. This breakdown, though, amounts to less than half of the delegates and could even include some overlap.[11]

By an overwhelming vote the sobor elected Tikhon, the new metropolitan of Moscow, to preside. Delegates among the upper hierarchy were dominated by the more conservative elements of the Orthodox Church, led by Metropolitan Anthony (Khrapovitsky) of Kharkov. They were by now fully alarmed and ready to do political battle. Eugene Trubetzkoy and Father Sergius Bulgakov led a centrist party, though on major issues it differed little from the conservatives. Working-class and academic delegates tended "irresistibly to the left." There was also a radical party, led by Boris Titlinov, with a negligible following.[12]

Conservative hierarchs wanted church independence from state power, but they did not intend to grant democratic control of the church to the lower clergy. They pushed for the restoration of a strong patriarchate with weak advisory councils. Theological professors urged a more democratic and representative (conciliar) synod at the head of the church. The overarching mood seemed to be repentance for the sins of the Russian people (the alleged cause of revolution and chaos) and joy at the opportunity to rebuild the church through the actions of the sobor. For conservatives, however, rejuvenating the church did not mean progress; it meant a deepening of devotion in the traditional manner. Nothing too forward-looking was likely to pass, as all resolutions ultimately had to be approved by the Council of Bishops, who held veto power.[13]

Thomas Whittemore, reporting for *National Geographic*, attended many of the sessions. Predisposed toward a good impression, he described the scene:

> Although there are perhaps no conspicuously outstanding and dominant figures in the assembly, it reaches as a whole the highest level of the Russian mind. . . . It is an all-Russian assembly. There are many strong personalities and many men marked by singularly beautiful and consecrated devotion to their task. . . . I heard no uncommonly stirring speechmakers, but a good deal of clear, cogent statement. It is because there is nothing noisy or spectacular about the [sobor] that it evokes profound respect as the sanest and most democratic, as well as the most spiritual, body of men now assembled in Russia.[14]

Electing a Patriarch and Other Duties

As mentioned, there was a strong impetus toward electing a patriarch, that office having been empty—actually nonexistent—since Patriarch Adrian died in 1700. Since the Provisional Government had been steadily encroaching on church prerogatives, and nobody knew what the Bolsheviks were up to, delegates increasingly redefined *sobornost* to include a patriarch. Mitrofan, bishop of Astrakhan, told the sobor:

> We need a patriarch as a spiritual leader and counselor, who would lift the hearts of the Russian people, would summon them to a better life and to great deeds, and would himself lead the way.[15]

The majority of delegates were determined to bring forth a steadfast and energetic leader who would assert the church position. He was to transcend mere administrative function and become a savior to his people. To do this he would have to set the church against the ever-more-aggressive Provisional Government. Yet a minority persistently urged a conciliar form of church government—councils without a head—that would be more consistent both with early Christianity and democratic trends in the twentieth century.[16] They also felt it highly unlikely that a strong savior could be found.

Then, on November 7, news reached the delegates in Moscow of the Bolshevik seizure of power in Petrograd. There was once again, and even more oddly, initial silence—though each delegate's mind was no doubt filled with anxiety for the future. At first, Bolsheviks in Moscow made no move against the sobor. Although worried, delegates tried to ignore the shouting of revolutionary slogans by exhilarated and angry throngs of workers. They hoped that this was merely a minor coup that would not survive in Petrograd's tumultuous atmosphere. At first the sobor made pronouncements with utter disregard for the new government, addressing itself instead to a more conservative government that assuredly would follow. But by November 12 the delegates felt a sudden sense of urgency and hastily voted to reinstate the patriarchate. Most bishops and (nonacademic) lay delegates voted for it, while the white clergy was divided and most academics voted against it.[17]

The new patriarch would be considered a "first among equals" within the episcopacy and thus hold less power than his seventeenth-century predecessors. He would be charged with caring for the general welfare of the church but would also be the chairman of both the Holy Synod (responsible for missionary work, church appointments, and educational policy) and the Higher Church Administration (responsible for temporal issues such as finance, administration, and ecclesiastical justice). Although he would have veto power over advisory council's decisions, at the same time he would be expected to cooperate with these two bodies, which would have to sanction any proposals made by him. Once his policies were in effect, only the next regularly convened sobor would be authorized to overturn them.[18] The patriarch would represent the church in its dealings with the state and would communicate with other autocephalic Orthodox churches (for example, in Greece and Bulgaria). He would fill episcopal vacancies and settle disputes among bishops. Symbolically, however, the patriarchate would transcend these administrative functions.

After preliminary balloting, the sobor reduced the nominees to three: Metropolitan Tikhon of Moscow, Archbishop Arseny of Novgorod, and Archbishop Anthony of Kharkov—the last nominated with the largest vote. The names of the nominees were written on strips of paper and placed inside an urn, which was then left all night in front of the Vladimir Ikon of the Virgin Mary in the Cathedral of Christ the Savior. On November 18, as the guns of revolution blazed in Moscow's streets, the saintly monk Aleksy thrust his hand into the urn. The "Hand of God"—or chance—guided the monk toward the name of Tikhon, age fifty-two, who among the three nominees had received the least number of votes.[19] Upon hearing the news, he responded with the ancient formula:

> Since the Sacred Council judged me, although unworthy, to be in this ministry,
> I thank, accept, and say nothing to the contrary."[20]

Although election of a patriarch was seen as a portent of church revival, Bishop Evlogy later reported that there was a portent of disaster as well. As the hierarchs filed out of the church, a fanatical woman with long, flowing hair rushed forward and shouted, "Not long, not long will you celebrate! Soon your bishop will be murdered."[21]

Three days later, as the fighting died down and the Bolshevik Red Guards consolidated control of Moscow, emissaries from the sobor sought and received permission from the city's Military Revolutionary Committee to consider the

Kremlin and its churches neutral ground for the installation ceremony. It was held on December 4 inside the Uspensky Cathedral, whose dome was freshly pierced by a Bolshevik shell. Tikhon sat on the patriarchal throne, preserved from the days of Peter the Great, where he accepted the pastoral staff and donned the ancient, patriarchal white mantle and blue velvet cowl.[22] Until his death in the mid-1920s, he would be the only person in Russia given power by freely elected representatives of the people. On this day Red Guards posted at the gate smoked and joked, but on December 9, as the church's new leader conducted a huge procession around the Kremlin and sprinkled holy water on its walls, he approached more friendly and respectful soldiers. They pulled off their caps and rushed toward him, stretching out their hands for a blessing (which they received).[23] He prayed for strength in the task ahead.

Tikhon's acceptance speech to the sobor is one of the few surviving records of his personal words, for he wrote little and usually spoke extemporaneously. He again likened his difficulties to those of Moses, quoting from the Old Testament's Book of Numbers:

> "And Moses said unto the Lord, wherefore hast thou afflicted thy servant? And wherefore have I not found favor in thy sight, that thou layest the burden of all these people upon me? . . . I am not able to bear all these people alone, because it is too heavy for me." From now on I am entrusted with the care for all the Russian [Orthodox] churches, and what awaits me is the gradual dying for them all my days.[24]

He consoled himself with the thought that he had not sought the election—that it was God's will. God would make his burden lighter.

The sobor then held a public funeral for the military cadets who had perished defending the ancient fortress, and afterward, at the request of relatives, another public funeral for the Bolsheviks who had perished trying to kill the cadets.[25] The Revolution was very young.

Moving against bureaucratic centralization, the sobor then restored much of the independence of local parishes that Peter the Great and a long string of chief procurators had usurped, and it mandated that every Orthodox parish in Russia organize a membership list. Formerly any citizen could attend any church service—though, of course, in villages there *was* only one church—but now each citizen in town and country would have to register with a *specific* church and thereby assume an obligation to support that church. This was obviously going to be necessary with the withdrawal of state subsidies. (Later, after the Bolsheviks closed down many churches, crowded Easter services often admitted only those who were registered with the open church.)[26]

The sobor delved into the progressive issue of sermon reform on December 14. As was mentioned earlier, preaching had become virtually a lost art in tsarist times, mostly due to what authorities feared might be said. Now the sobor encouraged everyone from bishops to laymen to preach the word of God at every liturgical service—not just on Sundays and feast days—and to speak in the local dialect (though in many areas this was already being done) and emphasize communication and comprehension.[27]

On December 15 the sobor once again took up the issue of Orthodox ascendancy, resolving:

> The Russian Orthodox Church should have a privileged position in the Russian State as compared to other churches and yet be free and independent of the state.[28]

Its position was that "in its teachings of faith and morals, divine service, internal church discipline and its connection with other autocephalic churches [the Orthodox Church] is independent of civil authority and . . . has the right of self-determination and self-direction."[29]

In two dozen more paragraphs it detailed further demands that the delegates naively thought the Bolsheviks would consider. Among them were the "rights" to:

- receive state subsidies, while avoiding taxation on all but income property
- obtain clerical exemption from military service (required by the eighty-third canon of the Holy Apostles)
- have all church decrees, so long as they did not violate otherwise legitimate state laws, be binding and enforceable by the state, while having the power of prior approval of all state legislation affecting the church
- continue operation of religious schools on an equal basis with secular schools and have all religious holidays remain state holidays
- require the head of the Russian state and the ministers of education and religion to be members of the Orthodox Church.[30]

Simply put, the Orthodox Church was asserting its prerogative to be "the sole ordering principle in society."[31] In light of later developments, it is hard to grasp how sobor delegates could have supported such an unlikely resolution, but it must be understood how wobbly the Bolshevik regime was only a month into power.

The Rise of Vasily Belavin

Tikhon was born Vasily Belavin and began life's long journey in 1865 in the town of Toropets, Pskov District, about two hundred miles (as the crow flies) south of St. Petersburg. His father had been a local priest, and the boy—with few options—decided to follow in this profession. His hagiographers describe his deeply religious nature at an early age, his simplicity of taste, his readiness to laugh, and his willingness to help slower students—traits that endeared him to his fellow students then and the clergy later. He entered the Pskov Theological Seminary in 1878 and was soon dubbed "the bishop." After graduating in 1884, he was accepted at the age of nineteen to the St. Petersburg Theological Academy, where he was good-naturedly promoted to "patriarch," not so much as a prophecy but as a kindly tribute to his leadership and bearing. He earned his Master of Dogmatic and Moral Theology degree in 1888 and headed back to Pskov to teach. Three years later he took his monastic vows and was ordained, taking the name Tikhon ("peaceful") in honor of the eighteenth-century Saint Tikhon of Zadonsk.[32]

Tikhon then took the job of inspector (and later rector) of the Kholm Seminary, near the Austrian border, where he was known, again, as a "good, jolly, kindly person."[33] He moved up the church hierarchy quickly, becoming—one year younger than was canonically allowed—first bishop of the Polish, but Russian-controlled, city of Lublin in 1897. Later he headed the Russian Church on the North American continent. In 1905 he returned to Russia to be elevated to the office of archbishop at the age of forty; then he resumed his duties abroad. After nine years in America, during which he lived briefly in San Francisco and New York City, he acknowledged that his experiences and world outlook had been considerably broadened. Returning to Russia for good in January 1907, Tikhon administered the eparchy of Yaroslavl for six years and then was transferred to Vilna in Russian-controlled Lithuania. There he gained extensive experience with Roman Catholics and Eastern Rite Catholics,* as well as with the Orthodox Russians who were in bitter conflict with the city's Polish population. He was expected to show great formality and the dignity befitting his office, but this was difficult for a man whose natural character was unpretentious and humble. Soon his warmhearted and affable ways, along with his habit of walking the streets dressed in plain monk's frock and cap, won over even those of non-Orthodox faiths.[34]

Just as he felt he was making real progress in the conflicted city, war broke out in Europe. Caught in the crossfire, Tikhon was forced to retreat to Moscow. During the fighting, however, he visited the front to bless the troops and aid refugees and was awarded a military medal for distinguished conduct. After the first of the 1917 revolutions, when the Provisional Government replaced key Rasputin appointees, Tikhon was selected as head of all Russian eparchies and given a seat on the Holy Synod. In March 1917, as mentioned earlier, he was elected metropolitan of Moscow. This was the position he held—strategically placed for his role in history—when the church sobor convened in August 1917.[35] He was to be, as we all are, a man of the time and place in which he lived, but his times would undergo dramatic change.

---

*Those who followed the Orthodox liturgy and rites but acknowledged the primacy of the Roman pope.

When Aleksy drew Tikhon's name from the urn, most delegates felt that the wrong choice had been made, yet they were reluctant to gainsay God's decision. Tikhon was the least popular among the three final candidates. Why had they not chosen a tough fighter like Anthony? As mentioned, Tikhon was known to have a kindly, none-too-aggressive character, and he might be easily swayed by those around him. For balance, the delegates appointed strong men to the two newly created advisory councils.[36]

Among those who knew him, each saw Tikhon in a different light, though some of his qualities were universally recognized. Metropolitan Anastasy (Gribanovsky) told of a tall, blond man with a broad Slavic nose in the center of a kindly face. His hair was slightly curled, and his beard was shorter than usual for an Orthodox hierarch.[37] His most striking feature was his deep-set blue eyes. Donald Lowrie, who interviewed the patriarch twice—in 1918 and in 1920—wrote in admiration:

> [He is] an erect, well-built man in a black robe with grey hair and beard, which at first glance make him appear older than his 56 years. [He has] a firm handclasp and kindly eyes with a decided trace of humor and ever a hint of fire in the back of them; those are your first impressions; that and his beaming smile. . . . [He appeared] calm, unhurried, and fearless.[38]

Lowrie saw Tikhon as accessible to the people and devoted to justice. He could not think of a better man to lead the church through challenging times. Tikhon told Lowrie in November 1920, "They think 'Oh, he's an old chap; he'll die soon . . . we won't bother him.'" The patriarch gesticulated, "Wait and see, I'll show them, yet."[39]

In her biography of Tikhon, Jane Swan stressed his sense of duty and his humility:

> One of the most striking peculiarities of his character was an absolute necessity for the patriarch constantly to be conducting liturgies, a duty which so many bishops have little time for. From the time he became a monk, Tikhon went out of his way to take part in services either in his own church or as a visiting priest to another church.
>
> When he became Metropolitan of Moscow, people were at first confused by the appearance of such a high dignitary constantly officiating in one church or another, seldom missing a day. He would not recognize bodily discomfort as an impediment to his priestly serving, and his intense spiritual development was easily felt by the people, all the more since he dispensed with the usual formal manner and ceremony normally associated with high church dignitaries. His habit of traveling almost unattended, quietly bowing and blessing all who approached, was not only unique but, in the revolutionary times, precisely what was needed to disprove the Bolshevik picture of the fat, selfish monk concerned only with his own importance and the church possessions for his use.[40]

The journalist Francis McCullagh also interviewed Tikhon in 1920 and described him with a slightly critical eye:

> He is a tall man of about sixty, with shrewd gray eyes and a florid, healthy face—the face of a peasant. In the conversation, he struck me as simple in the ways of the world, but fearless and sincere. . . . Patriarch Tikhon is a pious, unsophisticated monk . . . with more than a touch of Russian fatalism and apathy. . . . [He] is a holy man, but not a great man. He cannot do the great thing in a great way. He is apathetic. He lacks initiative and personal magnetism.[41]

While acknowledging that part of the problem was the weakness of the patriarch's church, McCullagh added the rather harsh observation, "Tikhon's death [martyrdom] would have given life to the church; his life may mean the church's death."[42]

Those who were close to him saw a man neither vain nor ambitious. "For the love of God," he is once supposed to have said, "don't make an idol of me." Yet the question remained: Could a man of indisputable honesty, humility, and goodness lead the church out of danger? Trubetzkoy, a Tikhon supporter, was initially dubious:

> Even his most ardent admirers could not help asking if this gentle soul could be the hero we expected, if he indeed possessed the qualities needed to steer the ship of the church through the hurricane.[43]

Trubetzkoy saw other qualities in Tikhon, however, which boded well for the future. He was a man of courage and self-abnegation. He thought of his office as the cross that he was doomed to bear, but he would carry it as would a pastor caring for his spiritual children. Personal considerations were set aside as he sacrificed for church and Mother Russia—identical in his mind. Trubetzkoy added to his analysis:

> [Tikhon's] serenity is undisturbed in the most dangerous situations. Never have I met a man with such a power of calming those about him. Standing in his presence, one has the feeling of certainty that the fatherland will be saved.[44]

Tikhon's easygoing ways caused his opponents to underestimate him. His weakness was his strength. Although he disliked reading long and tedious reports (often signing them with a cursory glance) and frequently wavered (seeking advice and following the majority), he had a streak of stubbornness that he occasionally displayed.[45] His humility was not timidity. Besides, if he had been completely unbending the Bolsheviks might have broken him—as in the proverb of the oak and the willow. In the end he was able to oppose the new government more effectively than anyone would have supposed on the day he assumed office. The historian Matthew Spinka, a close observer of Tikhon, wrote:

Had Anthony Khrapovitsky been elected patriarch, and had he actually persisted in his monarchical and anti-Soviet policy come what may, such a course would have been suicidal for the church.[46]

Venturing into Politics

The Bolsheviks and the church were natural enemies, and any policy of accommodation would be awhile coming. The Bolshevik Vladimir Bonch-Bruevich wrote in his memoirs how within days of the coup in Petrograd the priests were preaching vitriolic sermons against them:

Everywhere in Petrograd and even in the most remote back streets printed proclamations appeared in which Soviet power was cursed and which called for bringing down God's anger on the heads of "atheists and terrorists."[47]

These placards, instructing the people not to obey the new government, were posted by *babushkas* in headscarves. When Bonch-Bruevich's agents arrested these women, they were terrified, but when the agents offered them tea at the police station they confessed all and implicated the capital's top clergy.[48]

During the final days of November 1917, just after Tikhon's coronation, the sobor addressed a letter to the faithful condemning the Bolshevik seizure of power. It referred to the revolutionaries as "descended from the Antichrist and possessed by atheism":

No earthly kingdom founded on ungodliness can ever survive; it will perish from internal strife and party dissension. Thus, because of its frenzy of atheism, the state of Russia will fall.[49]

In a speech on Russia's New Year's Day, Tikhon issued his own tirade against the godless Bolsheviks:

Have we heard from the lips of our rulers the holy name of the Lord in our numerous councils, parliaments, and committees? No, they rely solely on their own strength. . . . We have forgotten God! We have been hunting a new happiness, running after deceptive shadows, have got drunk on the wine of freedom. . . . We warn most decisively that there will be no success until we remember God.[50]

For the first few months after Tikhon's election, the sobor's leadership threw caution to the wind. V. Vostokov called for the return of a wise Orthodox Russian tsar. A. Vasiliev referred to the Bolsheviks as the second stage in a national tragedy. The Provisional Government, the first stage, had begun "this terrible work of pillage and blasphemy." Archpriest I. Tsvetkov proposed referring openly to the Bolsheviks as "Satan."[51]

On February 1, 1918,* Tikhon fired off a pastoral letter—to be read in every church—anathematizing the entire Bolshevik Party, though he did not mention the party by name.

> By the authority invested in me by God, we forbid you [the Bolsheviks] to approach the Mysteries of Christ [the liturgy and sacraments]; we declare you anathema, if you still bear the name of Christians, even if merely on account of your baptism you still belong to the Orthodox Church.[52]

Two days later Metropolitan Benjamin read this letter to the crowds—reportedly numbering several hundred thousand—in Red Square. Reacting first to the loss of respect for law and then to the rampant brutality of the new regime, he declared: "It is a hard time the Holy Church of Christ is now going through. The Commandments of Christ to love one's neighbor are forgotten and trampled underfoot." He described the sacrileges of the Red Guards, the rejection of the "blessed mysteries" of baptism and marriage, and the conversion of seminaries into "schools of atheism or into nurseries of immorality." But in the end Orthodoxy would triumph. To some he was reminiscent of the prophet Elijah calling down the fire of heaven against the pagan god Baal, but he certainly was less effective.[53]

The following day Tikhon, rising to a new level of defiance, delivered a sermon:

> All into the churches! All to prayer meetings! By religious procession, petitions, declarations, protests, resolutions, messages to the authorities—by decisive force, by all that is permitted by Christian conscience, we can and are obliged to fight for faith and church, for the trampled treasures of our soul. . . . Let them cross our dead bodies. Let them shoot us, shoot innocent children and women. Let us go with crosses, ikons, unarmed, with prayers and hymns—let Cain and Judas kill us! The time has come to go to martyrdom and suffering![54]

The sobor, back in session on February 2 (after the Christmas recess), enthusiastically supported the anathema. Priest Tsvetkov announced that this first "collision with the servants of Satan will serve as the beginning of saving the nation and the church from the enemy."[55] Many prayed for the return of a tsar. Full of vainglorious indignation, the sobor's official resolution read in part:

---

*Remember the thirteen-day calendar discrepancy. The anathema was read on January 19, 1918, on the old Julian calendar, which the Russians had been using. This would make it February 1 on the new Gregorian calendar that most of the world was using. The Bolsheviks updated their calendar on February 1 (old calendar), skipping thirteen days, so that the next day was February 14 (new calendar). Thus, technically, there were no dates between February 1 and February 14. Nonetheless, I will use these dates when adding thirteen days to a late-January old calendar date. This should be understood when I use any date between February 2 and February 13, 1918.

> The Holy Sobor of the Russian Orthodox Church lovingly welcomes the procla-
> mation of the holy Patriarch Tikhon, punishing the malicious evildoers and con-
> victing the enemies of the Church of Christ. From the elevation of the patriar-
> chal throne a word of warning has thundered and the spiritual sword is raised
> against those who are constantly scoffing at the sanctities of the national faith
> and conscience.[56]

The resolution (accurately) concluded, "Even the Tatars had more respect for our
holy creed than our present law-givers."[57]

Dedicated Bolsheviks hardly felt imperiled; it could even be said that "the
threat of divine punishment only excited their antireligious fervor."[58] Nonetheless, though phrased in religious terms, the anathema should be considered a
political act—Tikhon was rendering the masses less amenable to Bolshevik influence. When he proclaimed in the anathema, "Cast out the wicked from among
you" (I Corinthians 5:13), he was in effect saying that the government had no
moral authority and that citizens owed absolutely no obedience to the Soviet
state.[59] Yet the anathema was in no way ideological. None of the patriarch's statements, even in those impassioned times, ever directly attacked, or even criticized, socialism or the tenets of Marxist theory, except as they immediately
affected the survival of the Orthodox Church. Nonetheless, such damning letters,
speeches, and other condemnations of the party in power were bound to bring
repercussions.

Concern for the patriarch's safety increased. On February 7, 1918, the sobor
asked Tikhon to make a secret list of three men who might succeed him as locum
tenens,* one after the other, in case he died, was incapacitated, or was imprisoned before a new sobor could be called. The envelope containing this list was
to be opened only upon Tikhon's death, when the next chosen would be informed
of his destiny. In chapter 16 we will see the names on the list—or perhaps a new
list—and how this procedure played out. (Such a list was technically uncanonical, as no bishop could appoint another as his successor, but these were extraordinary times and canons were to be applied "for the good of the church." It could
be considered "uncanonical" to strictly and literally apply the canons in a way
that would lead to the destruction of the church.)[60]

On March 18, 1918, Tikhon again crossed the line between religion and politics by denouncing the Brest-Litovsk Treaty, which relinquished over 300,000
square miles of Russian land and 56 million inhabitants in exchange for peace
with Germany (and, not incidentally, saved the Bolsheviks' skin). He called it a
"shameful peace" and rhetorically wondered, "They say peace, peace, but there
is no peace" (Jeremiah 6:14).[61] From Tikhon's perspective, the treaty cut away
and abandoned much of his church, but from the government's point of view

---

*After the death of a patriarch, this is the guardian of the church or temporary patri-
arch, presiding only until the next sobor can elect a replacement.

these statements could be justifiably construed as meddling in politics and going beyond the competency of the church. Later this "meddling" would come back to haunt Tikhon.

Three months after taking power, the government had separated church and state (the topic of chapter 7). A month and a half later, on March 28, seven churchmen (four from the sobor) consulted on the subject with three commissars inside the Kremlin. The commissars were warm and comradely, expressing the hope that the separation decree might actually clear up differences between the church and the government. The government was still trying not to frighten the church. Both sides aired their grievances, the clergy stressing the closing of diocesan courts that handled marriage and divorce, and the commissars emphasizing the reactionary preaching of a particular priest. But in the end the commissars likened their efforts to those of Christ—"a fellow socialist"—and one of the church negotiators concluded that the government's "attitude toward the church and its interests is benevolent."[62]

Although the government forbade the traditional Good Friday ride on an ass from St. Basil's Cathedral into the Kremlin, it did permit Tikhon to celebrate an Easter 1918 mass. The war-damaged Uspensky Cathedral overflowed with worshipers responding to his intonation of "Christ is risen." In May he journeyed to Petrograd. After entering the city, he stood in his open carriage the entire way to the St. Alexander Nevsky Monastery, blessing the crowds that knelt and waved along his route.[63]

In spite of his popularity, there were renewed efforts within the church to protect him. During the summer the Moscow Council of United Parishes was formed, providing Tikhon with a permanent, around-the-clock, unarmed bodyguard of twenty-four men split into two shifts. It arranged for the ringing of alarm bells when he moved from place to place so that friendly crowds could gather around to protect him. Even that was not always successful. A year later, in June 1919, as Tikhon walked down the steps of the Cathedral of Christ the Savior, a crazed woman (though not a Bolshevik) jumped into his carriage and thrust a knife into him. She pierced more clothing than flesh, and Tikhon received only a slight wound.[64]

Tikhon ventured into the political realm yet again when he dispensed communion wafers to Nicholas II and his family imprisoned in Ekaterinburg. Then in July, in Moscow's Kazan Cathedral, he openly denounced their murder by labeling the shooting a heinous crime, and he warned, "Whoever does not condemn it will be guilty of his blood." He challenged the government, "They may accuse me of counterrevolution, they may shoot me, but no threat shall hinder me from speaking the naked truth." Later he celebrated a requiem mass for the deceased royal family and referred to the killings as "regicide."[65]

Rumors of the patriarch's imminent arrest now spread through Moscow— the new capital.[66] Some members of the Synod woke him in the night, begging him to flee, but Tikhon said that he would rather sleep and replied: "The flight of the patriarch would play into the hands of the enemies of the church. Let them do with me what they want."[67]

Tikhon addressed "all the faithful children of the Russian Orthodox Church" on August 8, bewailing the spiritual state of the people:

> Sin has fanned everywhere the flame of the passions, enmity, and wrath; brother has risen up against brother; the prisons are filled with captives; the Earth is soaked in innocent blood, shed by a brother's hand; it is defiled by violence, pillaging, fornication, and every uncleanness.

He grieved over the people's turning away from God to grasp for material things. Christ had resisted temptation while in the wilderness, and the people should resist the temptation to build a paradise on Earth. "Sin," he concluded, "heavy and unrepented of, had summoned Satan from the abyss, and he is now bellowing his slander against the Lord."[68]

The sobor closed in September 1918, suffering from diminishing delegate attendance and an empty cash box. The Kerensky contribution had been exhausted, and church bank accounts had been nationalized.[69] The delegates gave up their initial optimism about the Bolsheviks' quick demise and felt forebodings of defeat.

GETTING THE REVOLUTION UNDER CONTROL

A year shall come, our blackest year of all, in which the Crown of Russia's Tsars shall fall,
The mob shall change its old confiding mood, and death and blood shall be our daily food
. . . Red flames shall grow upon our streams that hour, and then shall stand revealed the
Man of Power.

—Mikhail Lermontov, 1831

Lenin could never have thought of the antireligious struggle as anything but a single aspect, albeit an important aspect, of the larger struggle. Before 1917 the overall focus had to be on gaining power and after 1917 on consolidating power. Once the coup was complete and the euphoria faded, hard realities faced the Bolshevik elite. This is what the historian Roger Pethybridge meant when he said:

> In their time the early Bolsheviks possessed a single theory, which, for all its brilliance, contained the inevitable crudities of pioneer theories, and it fitted Russian social conditions like a saddle on a cow's back. With limited practical experience and an ill-adapted theory that had already suffered at the hands of vulgarizers and revisionists, the Bolsheviks introduced radical changes whose consequences were of necessity very hard to calculate.[70]

Events moved faster than politicians could manage. Early acts against religion were not official acts at all, but instead were defilements of churches and clerics by overzealous revolutionaries, not necessarily even party affiliated. In many cases the defilers were simply hooligans. Liberated from the social bonds that had restrained them and certainly not motivated by any understanding of Marxist antireligious theory, long-suppressed youth, workers, and soldiers all too often went wild. At times their antireligious activities were innocuous, being little more than pranks. In one church they substituted a statue of Judas Iscariot for that of Christ. But mostly they were more serious.

As mentioned above, fighting in the streets raged all around and within the Kremlin as the November 1917 patriarchal election was taking place. The seventy-acre triangular fortress was defended by a small number of military officers and cadets, but rather than take this center of resistance by a direct assault Bolshevik forces chose to shell the defenders into submission. This could be considered a cautious military strategy, but Thomas Whittemore, as he toured the sites of destruction, was outraged at the wanton destruction of the many churches and cathedrals within the walls:

> A sacrilegious attack upon [the Kremlin] could be made only by madmen or by men to whom nothing is holy and who are incapable of understanding . . . the significance and importance of this monument of Russian history. It cannot be considered a sufficient reason that the artillery fire directed against the Kremlin had for its object to crush the handful of officers and cadets who were within.[71]

A shell pierced one of the domes of the Uspensky Cathedral, dropping rubble into the interior. The Chudov Monastery, the Church of the Annunciation, the Church of the Archangel, the Church of the Twelve Apostles, the Church of St. Nicholas, and many others were severely damaged. Giving added weight to the charge of *purposeful* destruction was the nature and extent of the vandalism and looting that occurred once Red troops were inside. Soldiers covered church walls with graffiti, defecated behind the iconostases, smashed glass cases to steal their contents, and gouged gems out of religious ornaments and ikons.[72]

The Commissariat of Justice, seeing no benefit to the Revolution in outrages against the citizenry, rebuked young marauders in the pages of *Revolution and the Church*:

> They took away from churches the vestments, episcopal mantles, and altar cloths, sewed them up into revolutionary flags, and, as if to intentionally outrage the feelings of believers, hung them out in squares in the busiest streets of the city and village settlements. . . . In one city draperies from the biers of relics . . . were hung up to decorate the walls of the local Office of Public Education.[73]

Outrages proliferated across the country. The following are three testimonials collected by the anti-Bolshevik White Army at the height of the Civil War (1918–1921) and later published as *Protocols of the Special Commission of Investigation of the Outrages Committed by the Bolsheviks in the South of Russia.* (Many elements in the White Armies were fighting to restore the tsar, so the potential for exaggeration in these accounts has to be kept in mind.)

- From the Don River region near Kharkov: "Sailor Dybenko, his comrades and paramours entered the church with their hats on, smoked there, using bad language and blasphemies against the Virgin Mary; they upset the altar, stole some of the sacred objects, and pierced through with a knife the image of the Savior. After their departure some excrements were found in the vestry."
- From the Uspensky Convent in Sviatogorsk: "Five monks' corpses were found near the ikon which stood in a pool of blood. . . . The monks had been made to smoke, to dance, even to drink the ink. . . . One of the Communists put on a robe and a miter, climbed to the altar, and began to peruse the Gospels, while the others, also clad in robes, imitated the service, accompanying it with indecent songs."
- From Mikulinskaya in the Don region: "In the local church a wedding of a priest and a mare was arranged by the Bolsheviks. A cross was held to the lips of the horse, which was brought into the church, so that the animal should be able to kiss it. The orchestra played in the meantime. After the ceremony, the 'newly married priest' was led off to be shot."[74]

Clearly murder cannot be considered a prank. Metropolitan Vladimir of Kiev was assassinated, Bishop Andronik of Perm was horribly tortured and killed, and Bishop Ephraim of Irkutsk, Bishop Hermogen of Saratov, and Archbishop Vasily of Chernigov were executed for their "counterrevolutionary activities."[75] There were incidents of eyes being gouged out and tongues being cut off before priests were paraded through the streets, then shot. During 1918 and 1919 the Bolsheviks executed at least twenty-eight bishops and thousands of clergy and laity for what the condemned felt were purely religious activities. Between February and May 1918 there existed a Don Soviet Republic within which fifteen priests were killed as a result of lawlessness. In December 1918, Bishop John of Penza urged renewed missionary work in the provinces because "godlessness is growing among the youth, not by the day but by the hour; hooliganism is expanding, moral law . . . has lost any meaning [and] true patriotism is languishing."[76]

The government endeavored to put these incidents in the best possible light, especially when they might reach foreign ears. But party leaders had to deal with the larger theoretical question as to whether hooliganism and murder were appropriate forms for an antireligious offensive. It seemed dubious that this behavior would achieve long-term practical results. From the strictly Marxist perspective, they had clearly put the wrong foot forward. Persecution of believers, Engels had argued, would only lead to a martyr's complex among believers and prolong religion's reign.

Lenin addressed the first All-Russian Congress of Working Women in November 1918:

> We must be extremely careful in fighting religious prejudices; some people cause a lot of harm in this struggle by offending religious feelings. We must use propaganda and education. By lending too sharp an edge to the struggle we may only arouse popular resentment; such methods of struggle tend to perpetuate the division of the people along religious lines, whereas our strength lies in unity. The deepest source of religious prejudice is poverty and ignorance; and that is the evil we have to combat.[77]

On another occasion he remarked, "A noisy declaration of war on religion is the best way to enliven interest in it." He pushed for subtler tactics, but he was not always successful.

As mentioned earlier, Lenin may have also downplayed antireligious zealotry as a way to refute rival anarchistic theories. Marx and Bakunin had engaged in a long-running philosophical dispute, with Marxist-Leninists disdainful of anarchist idealism when compared with the practicality of professional revolutionaries. Lenin wrote disdainfully, "Anarchy, by proclaiming a life and death struggle against God would help fundamentally the [Orthodox clergy] and the bourgeoisie."[78] He considered anarchists to be incomplete materialists and abstract utopians who mistakenly believed that concepts were independently operating entities rather than the result of economic conditions. A "pure materialist," he commented, would not make such an error.[79]

In addition to taming zealots, Lenin emphasized the need for flexibility in dealing with "religious prejudices." This approach seemed consistent with Marxist "economic determinism," whereby the economic structure in a region determined its people's particular culture, customs, and attitudes. Where economic conditions differed, so, too, would the nature and intensity of religious belief. Proceeding with this logic, techniques used to combat religion and the intensity of that combat must vary from place to place. In other words, he was looking at the uneven growth of socialism in Russia, so he felt he needed to apply antireligious methods in uneven ways. Through newspapers, pamphlets, and party meetings, antireligious propagandists were advised to stamp out hooliganism and to use instead variable and creative methods. An approach effective with a peasant or workman might not be effective with a student or a Red Guard; what worked with the old might not work with the young.[80]

The party theorist Nikolai Bukharin, while indoctrinating Bolshevik recruits, asked them to distinguish between the struggle with the church and the struggle with the deeply ingrained religious feelings of the masses. The former he defined as "a special organization existing for religious propaganda," which must be dealt with sternly.[81] The latter could be treated with understanding. At times party workers were encouraged to support the lower "democratic" parish clergy and concentrate their attacks on church hierarchs. Although the policy was to go slowly with the education of the masses, acceleration of propaganda was required within the party membership. Yet even here there was a certain leeway. The Party Central Committee decided in August 1921 that, while educated party members could not be believers, uneducated and believing new members could be temporarily tolerated:

> Religious believers may in individual cases, as an exception, be admitted into the party if by their revolutionary struggle or work for the Revolution and its defense in its most dangerous moments they have proven their devotion to communism.[82]

And, of course, if they would subject themselves to "re-education."

Flexibility, however, did not mean vacillation of intent or "Oblamovism." Early on, when there was a division among the Bolshevik leadership as to whether they should treat religion as moribund and outmoded (just sitting back and watching it die a natural death) or pursue it aggressively with propaganda and legislation, the latter view won a decisive and permanent victory.

*   *   *

During the bloody Civil War period, Lenin and his comrades had more immediate life-and-death concerns than religion. Fighting raged to the north, south, east, and west. After initial decrees on the religious question, Lenin delegated implementation to his lieutenants: Nikolai Bukharin, Evgeny Preobrazhensky, Peter Krasikov, Emelyan Yaroslavsky, Vladimir Bonch-Bruevich, Ivan Skvortsov-Stepanov, and Anatoly Lunacharsky. Lenin put Trotsky in charge of antireligious propaganda from 1921 to 1922, until the formation in October 1922 of the Party Central Committee's "Commission on Antireligious Propaganda" under Yaroslavsky.

How did the Civil War affect the Russian Church, and what was the church's role in that war? One of the conflict's consequences was the emigration of many clergy members, whose later attempts to influence Russian politics would stir up more trouble for the Bolsheviks *and for the patriarch.*

6

SHEDDING TEARS OF MY SUFFERING SOUL

The Civil War, Émigré, and Ukrainian Churches

A brutal civil war raged along the borders of the centralized Bolshevik state from 1918 through 1921, and much of the conflict was fought on the southern Ukrainian front. Although the church suffered mightily during the Civil War, it also gained a new respect and authority among rural populations. Just as Lenin had feared, wartime chaos created martyrs. Anticlericalism in the villages, which had been on the rise during the nineteenth century, now receded as local clergy stood up to the Bolsheviks and suffered for it.

THE CHURCH IN THE CIVIL WAR

[The church has appealed to] Kerensky, Kornilov, Skoropadsky, the Constituent Assembly, the Czechoslovaks, the Germans, the French, the English, Zulus and Hottentots, Kolchak and Denikin.[1]

—*Revolution and the Church*
(published by the Comissariat of Justice), 1919

The Civil War

Marx had taught class warfare and had specifically rejected warfare among nations. But for the workers and peasants of Russia—turned into soldiers during World War I—this was not a theoretical issue. They were poorly trained, poorly equipped, and poorly led and subscribed to the adage: "A rich man's war but a poor man's fight." They "voted with their feet" and retreated all along Russia's Western Front, often killing their officers in the process. After the November coup, Lenin was desperate to get out of the war and salvage his fragile revolution. To extricate himself, he signed the Treaty of Brest-Litovsk in February

1918, trading a huge swath of Russian territory to the Germans in exchange for peace. (Temporarily as it turned out, for in the Treaty of Versailles the Germans had to give it all back, and more.) To many the Brest-Litovsk Treaty was cynical opportunism and a violation of the territory of sacred Mother Russia, but to the Bolsheviks and many of the antitsarist troops who supported them it was the only way to survive.

The White Armies grew from officer corps opposition to Bolshevism but soon included supporters of a hodgepodge of causes: monarchists (those who were bent on restoring Nicholas II to the throne or, after he and his family were murdered in July 1918, some other Romanov), supporters of Western-style democracy (those in Kerensky's Provisional Government who hoped to call a national Constituent Assembly), former landowners who simply wanted their already-nationalized land back, and nationalists on Russia's periphery who saw an opportunity to achieve independence from Moscow. Some were military men who were in it for the glory and because fighting was what they knew how to do, but most were conscripted peasants who would rather be home with their families and farms. Besides the Whites, there were also bands of Blacks—anarchists roaming the countryside of the Ukraine and southern Russia—and independent peasant armies who resisted all sides to protect their villages and keep their harvests from being requisitioned. Villages were reduced to starvation as they were taken by the Reds and punished for aiding the Whites, then taken by the Whites and punished for aiding the Reds. Hundreds of peasant revolts occurred during 1919 and 1920, but their lack of coordination doomed them to frustration and failure. The historian Lynne Viola wrote, "Three of the four horsemen of the apocalypse—war, famine, and disease—stalked the Russian land in an all too literal orgy of death and destruction." Nine million died of their wounds, of starvation, or in epidemics.[2]*

There were three major fronts. Admiral Kolchak led the White Army in the East, along the Trans-Siberian Railroad; General Denikin, and later General Wrangel, led the Whites coming from the south, and General Yudenich attacked from the northwest. Americans, British, French, and Japanese contributed large amounts of munitions and small numbers of troops to the White cause, first, to keep Russia in the war and their Eastern Front active and, second, to topple Bolshevism. Geography, however, worked against anti-Bolshevik forces. Communications among the separated White Armies across the vast Russian landscape were nearly impossible. Coordination was so lacking that the three fronts were in effect three separate wars. At the same time, the Red Army held the interior ground with a vastly superior population and more food and industrial resources. The Red Army outnumbered the *combined* White Armies ten to one.

---

*Usually the Four Horsemen are interpreted as Conquest, War, Famine, and Death (Revelation 6).

In the end, White Army leaders failed to generate sufficient popular support, partly due to their refusal to accept minority-nationality independence. The slogan "Russia, one and indivisible" alienated the Cossacks, for example. And aristocratic White leaders refused to accept land reform, thus disaffecting the peasantry, who then gravitated toward the socialist Red Army as the lesser of two evils.[3]

The Church's Dilemma

It is not hard to imagine that pronouncements and decrees emanating from Moscow on religious issues (and everything else) were unevenly enforced. During this period, called War Communism, the Bolsheviks ignored separation of church and state requirements when it suited their military purposes. Popular support was crucial to victory, and victory was an absolute precondition for long-range implementation of the separation decrees.[4]

In 1918 the survival of Bolshevism was still an open question, and its leaders were on a hair trigger. They issued hasty decrees that seem, in retrospect, to have been overreactions. Article 237 of the Penal Code, for example, forbade religious processions that might impede the movement of citizens; impeders were subject to six months' hard labor. In August it was forbidden to ring church bells outside of service hours lest "the sounding of the tocsin" lead to insurrection against the young regime. But the government, preoccupied with fending off opposition armies in every direction, put more emphasis on announcing the Bolshevik position than it did on implementation and enforcement. It almost appeared as if Tikhon's anathema had been forgiven. The main problem for the church, as mentioned in the previous chapter, came from rank-and-file Bolsheviks and Red Guards who, newly caught up in the ideology of working-class liberation, far exceeded the letter of the law.

Considering the state of war, there were times when the church, too, seemed a little touchy. To support the war effort the government imposed compulsory labor equally upon all "capable members of the community for the sake of the socialistic society." Many clergymen took exception to this practice, arguing that being denied exemptions amounted to persecution. The Commissariat of Justice rejoined that the rules concerning exemption from military duty had no special clause concerning ministers of worship. If compulsory labor conflicted with the hours of religious service, the clergy should rearrange their ecclesiastical duties so as to have time free for public works.

In the heat of combat, both Reds and Whites perpetrated countless atrocities. Local Orthodox priests suffered more at the hands of Red Army commanders, and Ukrainian Jews suffered more at the hands of White Army commanders. The intense hatred felt for the church by some Red commanders led them to view a priest as counterrevolutionary by the mere fact of his existence. Denikin published statistics from his own commission showing that 28 bishops and 1,215 priests had been shot during 1918 and 1919,[5] but it is not clear whether he was including the entire country, whether he was including all faiths, and whether he was relying on verifiable data.

Denikin himself was anti-Semitic. Although he once spoke out—purely for foreign consumption—against the rampant Ukrainian pogroms, he was known to tolerate these atrocities, partly because of his lack of personal concern but also partly because of his lack of any other method of paying his troops other than allowing them to loot Jewish communities. Perhaps for this reason, and certainly for the reason stated below, in late 1918 Tikhon specifically refused to send requested blessings to General Denikin. Prince Gregory Trubetzkoy* related the story:

> I requested the permission of His Holiness to give in his name a blessing personally to one of the outstanding leaders of the White Movement, under conditions of maintaining absolute secrecy. However, the patriarch did not find even this possible, so strongly did he hold himself aloof from any sort of politics.[6]

Metropolitan Benjamin of Petrograd even promised that if the government left the sacred relics of St. Alexander Nevsky unharmed and unprofaned he would suspend any cleric who aided the White Army.

As Red Army violence against church and clergy escalated, however, Tikhon felt compelled in October 1918 to ask the government for mercy. By September 1919 he appealed to church members to avoid any activity that might provoke the suspicion of Soviet authorities, and he instructed his followers to fulfill all civil obligations as long as they were not contrary to the practices of their faith. If local priests went over to the Whites, the patriarch claimed that the Orthodox Church as an institution could not be held responsible. If *Te Deums* were performed in areas under White control, then they were at the behest of the local people or mandated by the general in charge. The church hierarchy, he claimed, never instigated them.[8]

Tikhon never outwardly stepped over the line to support the White cause, but his inward prayers we can easily imagine. Although he could not possibly be informed of every incident across the country, his statement of clerical noninstigation was certainly not true. Here are some examples:

- The Bishop of Ufa made xenophobic and anti-Bolshevik speeches and rallied the people to the White cause in 1918.
- The Archbishop of Ekaterinburg (in the Ural Mountains) organized protest demonstrations when he learned of the Romanov family execution in July 1918, and he held a victory celebration when Admiral Kolchak took the city in February 1919.[9]

---

*Brother of Eugene Trubetzkoy, already mentioned.

- Sixty churchmen organized a conference in Stavropol (in the northern Caucasus) on June 3, 1919, and listened to Denikin speak on the church's and the White Army's common need to eradicate Bolshevism.[10]
- In both the Siberian and the Ukrainian campaigns, "Jesus Christ Regiments," organized by Orthodox hierarchs on the scene, aided White Armies. And the patriarch's anathema of the Bolsheviks was used as propaganda to boost the morale of soldiers under Denikin and Kolchak.[11]
- Metropolitan Anthony of Kharkov delivered lectures in Rostov claiming that Christ was a counterrevolutionary and told the Kuban Cossacks: "Our common calamity will not last forever. The Russian people will throw off the hated yoke of the godless and again will take up their blessed labors and will defend their freedom."[12]
- When the White Army established a commission to investigate Bolshevik terror in the countryside, many Orthodox priests participated. Their presence made the commission's findings more credible.[13]
- In December 1918 the priest Georgy Shavelsky joined the propaganda agency of the White government in the South.[14]
- The Red Army claimed (though evidence is lacking) that many bishops and priests spied for White Army generals.[15]

Pleas for Intervention

Other Orthodox clergy sent appeals to the Americans and the British to step up intervention on the Whites' behalf. Metropolitan Platon of Odessa appealed from Denikin's camp:

> Here I am kneeling down before you and shedding tears of my suffering soul. I implore you, help the tormented Russian people. There is still a power in Russia which can defeat the Bolsheviks. . . . Consider this army as yours, give it your support, give it everything it needs.[16]

In mid-February 1919 Archbishop Sylvester, president of the Higher Church Administration, wrote from Omsk to Pope Benedict XV concerning the grievous oppression of the Orthodox Church. His emphasis was on Bolshevik cruelty:

> The churches of the Kremlin in Moscow and of the towns of Yaroslavl and Simferopol were ransacked, many temples sacrilegiously stained [with blood], and historical sacristies as well as the libraries of the patriarchs in Moscow and Petrograd looted. The Metropolitan Vladimir of Kiev, nearly twenty bishops, and hundreds of priests were assassinated. Before the executions, the Bolsheviks bind the legs and arms of their victims; some are buried alive. . . . In areas where Bolshevik Authorities rule, the Christian Church is persecuted with more ferocity than in the first three centuries of the Christian era.[17]

In March Cardinal Gasparri sent a telegram from the Vatican to Lenin imploring him to "issue strict orders that ministers of all religions be respected." George Chicherin, Commissar of Foreign Affairs, replied in April that unfortunately the cardinal had been misled. Religion in Russia was being treated as a purely private matter:

> Thus, it is absolutely erroneous to talk about the persecution of clergymen. . . . I can guarantee you that no clergyman of this [Orthodox] religion has suffered because of his religious convictions.[18]

But naturally, Chicherin continued, those clergymen who had participated in "conspiracies against the state" would have to be treated in the same manner as anyone else. With the separation of church and state, no special privileges could be granted to the clergy.[19] Unwritten in Chicherin's letter was the stark fact that the party was pledged to atheism, and the party was the constant guide and monitor of the state. Any propagation of religious beliefs could very easily be construed as a conspiracy in itself. A priest, once accused, would have a difficult if not impossible time clearing himself of the "counterrevolutionary" charge.

A church group within territory controlled by Kolchak in the East appealed to the Anglican Church, reciting numerous stories of the Red Army's pillage of churches, persecution of believers, and even "the nationalization of women."* Orthodox clergy in the far northern city of Archangel made a similar appeal in September 1919:

> In this solemn hour the Archangel Christians ask the Christians in England to ask their government to leave the British troops in northern Russia until after the storm has passed and the position of the Russian people has become clear.[20]

The Archbishop of Canterbury promised to do all he could to influence the British government.[21]†

In April 1920 a parish conference in Chita (about 300 miles east of Lake Baikal in Siberia) was so desperate for protection that it supported Japanese occupation of Russian coastal cities and ports:

---

*The latter was a common atrocity story; this practice was actually contemplated by some Bolsheviks but never implemented.

†There was much hypocrisy on the part of Western critics of Bolshevik rule. Chicherin inquired in his letter to the pope whether the Holy Father had protested when Kolchak, Denikin, and the Ukrainian leader Simon Petliura committed atrocities against the Russian people during the Civil War. And Emelyan Yaroslavsky, in his book *Religion in the USSR*, offered the example of a bill introduced in January 1929 in the British parliament to end all punishments for heretics and blasphemers of the Church of England. Since the bill was soundly defeated, how could the British be worldwide champions of freedom of religion?

The priests of the Orthodox Church and its faithful sons welcome the Japanese
policy, which is designed to defend the property, life, and faith of the fathers of
the Russian people from persecution and oppression.[22]

Abroad, anti-Bolshevik propagandists exaggerated atrocity stories, though
some such events were no doubt occurring. The Northcliffe Press in London carried lurid accounts of thousands of priests having their eyes gouged out and their
ears and noses sliced off, then being buried alive. The *Hibbert Journal* in late
1919 described priests having their tongues cut out for speaking in defense of
their church or being bayoneted for locking their church doors against
"marauders bent on pillaging."[23]

When White Armies, émigré clergy, and believers inside Russia appealed to
Western powers, it was not just violent persecution that was the basis of their
plea. They also appealed to the deeply ingrained European prejudice that civilization was *not possible* without religion of some sort. Religion, true or not, was
the basis of morality and order in society. The English and the Americans were
sure that Russia was being dragged from the civilized world.

Regardless of their motives, however, all appeals for foreign protection
merely supported the Bolshevik contention that they were not persecuting religious believers but were prosecuting counterrevolutionaries. And there was
plenty of evidence that the Red Army was suppressing not just religious freedom
but out-and-out monarchism. Although Tikhon forthrightly opposed the monarchist cause, church excesses were beyond central control. Thus Father Vostokov
formed the Brotherhood of the Living Cross, whose aims were to restore the
Romanov Dynasty and combat "Jewish Freemasonry." After Baron Wrangel took
over in the Crimea in March 1920, Vostokov suggested that an army of unarmed
clergy march against the Reds, who, he was certain, would thrust their bayonets
into the ground and prostrate themselves before Orthodox ikons. Wrangel,
though monarchist and deeply religious, restrained Vostokov and opted to fight.[24]

The peasantry, however, was not nearly as devoted as Father Vostokov. After
the Civil War ended Maurice Hindus asked groups of villagers why there were
no Bibles to be found. The reply in several villages was that they had been
smoked; the Good Book's thin pages made up for the shortage of cigarette paper
during the years of deprivation.[25]

The Monk Nikolsky

The government was constantly distracted by problems with the church that were
tangential to their Civil War effort. One occurred far north of Moscow during the
summer of 1919. It concerned a monk named Nikolsky who was rather well educated but, before the world war, had been expelled from his monastery for
preaching heresy. He vehemently opposed the atheistic Bolsheviks and proposed

his own form of social organization: The civil authorities of this world, he said, have proven themselves unfit to rule and should be replaced by religious chiefs. He manufactured rosaries with five beads and taught his followers to chant "Tsars, Dumas, Soviets, Self, God," representing the movement from autocracy through democracy to eventual theocracy. The government decided to seize him and circulated leaflets describing him as a spy in the pay of the British and Americans (who had bases along the nearby White Sea). All attempts to capture the religious "bandit" failed. When the fall rainy season rendered the roads impassable, thus holding the Red Guards at bay, Nikolsky and his followers established their authority over a thousand-square-mile territory on the North Dvina River (between Moscow and Archangel). They levied taxes, developed cooperative societies, and so thoroughly controlled the food supply that members of local soviets had to flee or face starvation. Nikolsky eventually met his end when a false devotee turned him in. He was shot, allegedly during an escape attempt, in January 1920.[26]

THE ÉMIGRÉ CHURCH

To all Christians of the Western world: realize the common danger; join us in a united struggle against the common enemy.[27]

—Orthodox bishops behind White Army lines

The Civil War raged on, but by late 1920 all anti-Bolshevik forces were in retreat. Many of the Orthodox clergy who fled in their wake settled in Constantinople; others fled to Western or Eastern Europe. These émigrés became a source of constant irritation for both the Bolsheviks *and the Orthodox Church.*

From Southern Church Council to Karlovtzy Sobor

There were two significant schisms within the Russian Orthodox Church during the 1920s. The first, dealt with here, involved émigré clergy who fled to the newly created Yugoslavia. This was the "rightist schism." The second, the "leftist schism," will be discussed in chapters 13 through 16. Our interest in both of these divisions within the church concerns how the Bolsheviks manipulated schismatic activities for antireligious purposes.

While the Reds held the core of Russia, and the Whites under Denikin held the South, Patriarch Tikhon and his administration were cut off from the church in the lower Volga region. Southern bishops felt justified in organizing a temporary synod under the presidency of Metropolitan Platon until the Whites could reunite the church. For this purpose they organized the Southern Church Council, headed by Anthony Khrapovitsky, which in May 1919 held its first session in Novocherkassk and created the first of several temporary Higher Church Administrations.[28] The bishops thought of themselves as forming a de facto church government while the patriarch was temporarily held captive by revolutionary forces. They were initially optimistic, as Denikin was approaching Moscow from the south and Kolchak was advancing from the east. The Council sent a message to White Army generals fighting a little farther north along the Don River:

> May your labors in defense of the outraged Orthodox faith and church, and for the sake of the revival of great, indivisible Russia, be blessed by God.[29]

But the longer the war lasted, the gloomier the White's chances appeared. General Wrangel let himself get pinned down in the Crimea and was on the verge of collapse. Tikhon foresaw abandonment of the southern front as leading to his own arrest and complete loss of contact with his bishops.[30] As a preemptive move, he issued *Ukaz* #362 on November 20, 1920:

> In the event that a diocese . . . finds itself completely out of contact with the [Moscow] Higher Church Administration, or if the Higher Church Administration itself, headed by his Holiness the Patriarch, for any reason whatsoever ceases its activity, the diocesan bishop shall immediately enter into relations with the bishops of neighboring dioceses for the purposes of organizing a higher ecclesiastical authority. [If this proves impossible, each diocesan bishop should] take upon himself all the fullness of authority.[31]

The Southern Church Council reasonably concluded that Tikhon's ruling applied to their situation. Southern White Armies were soon routed, forcing the bishops who supported them to face the dilemma of where to go. In 1921 some deserted their flocks and fled to Constantinople, where the ecumenical patriarch authorized a Temporary Higher Russian Church Administration Abroad. This became one of the nuclei of the rightist émigré schism. Others headed west by sea to Yugoslavia. Accepting the hospitality of the Serbian patriarch, they settled in an old monastery at Sremski-Karlovtzy, a few miles north of Belgrade, and claimed that they had brought the Constantinople-based organization with them in their baggage.[32] This church leadership became known as the Karlovtzy Synod; ironically, it would play an important role in Tikhon's undoing.

Ignoring their debt to Constantinople and citing Tikhon's *ukaz*, they asserted their power to act in the name of the Russian Church on matters outside of the country. Critics, however, claimed that there was no canonical authority to assume jurisdiction in a *foreign land* without the group being explicitly authorized to do so by its superior (Tikhon). In addition, the émigrés, in violation of canon law, had abandoned their dioceses (others, after all, had remained behind to face their fate at the hands of the Bolsheviks).[33]* While in the eyes of many

---

*The canons require that a bishop "be married to his diocese." He cannot voluntarily move and take his authority with him.

hierarchs and clergy there was a stain of illegitimacy on the Karlovtzy Synod, those who had fled their homeland became fiery and tendentious.

In December 1921, after the Civil War had ground to a halt, the émigré bishops convened an uncanonical Karlovtzy Sobor under the leadership of Metropolitan Anthony. Its illegitimacy under church canons was due to Anthony's abandonment of his diocese and his technical subordination to the Serbian patriarch, where he was in no position to be calling church councils.[34]

Anthony came from the Novgorod region, born to educated and deeply religious parents. He took his tonsure in 1885 and then served the church in both Volhynia and Kharkov. According to his admirers, he preached Christian love, kindness, and humility, while giving money to poor priests, poor students, and destitute widows. During the early 1890s he labored to refute the anti-Orthodox views of Leo Tolstoy and his followers (though he was an enthusiast of the more Orthodox Fyodor Dostoevsky). Rising to become a bishop at age thirty-four and an archbishop fifteen years later, at one time or another he was on the faculty of all four of Russia's theological academies. Some in the clergy had hoped that Anthony would be the reformer the church had longed for, but he turned into an unrepentant monarchist and disparager of the liberal and progressive movement. He believed that the pending 1917–1918 sobor should be a "council of bishops" and resisted the move toward more lay power in the church. Although he vigorously protested being tarred with the brush of anti-Semitism, he had been a prominent member of the Black Hundreds. The radical priest Grigory Petrov wrote in 1911 that Anthony had sunk to being "a defender of courts-martial and executions, a hater of foreigners and the non-Orthodox, and a collaborator of Pobedonostsev."[35]

In 1917 Anthony was a monastic delegate to the First Church Sobor and had pushed hard for restoration of the patriarchate. As mentioned earlier, when votes were taken for the three patriarchal candidates, Anthony received the highest number (a majority), losing to Tikhon in the end only because the choice was made by lot. It is difficult to believe that he had no inner hope of filling the position himself. Perhaps out of both respect and consolation, in the final days of the sobor he was appointed metropolitan of Kiev and Galicia.

Upon returning to the Ukraine, Anthony and Archbishop Evlogy were captured by Simon Petliura's Ukrainian nationalist army, shipped off to Lvov, and, when the Poles took that city, imprisoned in Krakow. They were released in the spring of 1919 and returned to the Ukraine just in time to be forced by the onslaught of the Red Army to flee to Yugoslavia.[36]

Returning to the story of the 1921 Karlovtzy Sobor, approximately one hundred persons attended, eighty-five of them voting delegates. Among these were Metropolitan Evlogy, nine archbishops, one archimandrite, eighteen bishops, and many other high-placed ecclesiastical leaders. Among the lay delegates, Count Volzhin, former chief procurator of the Holy Synod, was the most prominent.

Among the laity were some who had not even been practicing Orthodox Christians before 1917 but had subsequently joined the church when it was the only fragment of the Old World left to them. Many—clergy and nonclergy—had been members of the notorious Black Hundred Party, and thirty were active monarchists, fresh from a meeting in Bavaria, where they had set up the Higher Monarchist Council. Anthony sponsored the monarchists' membership in the sobor and guaranteed their voting rights.[37]

A twist to the sobor's delegate list was the rumor that Bolshevik agents had infiltrated its ranks. The purpose of these agents provocateurs, so the story went, was to inspire chauvinistic attitudes and provoke counterrevolutionary statements by the sobor. These could then be used to incriminate clergy in Russia who might have been in communication with the sobor. Given their powerful pro-tsarist propensities, though, it seems unlikely that these delegates would have needed much encouragement. Here is a sample sobor resolution to illustrate the point:

> Let our increasing prayer be that the Lord shall show us the way to save and build up our native country; that He shall give protection to Faith and Church and our entire country, and that He shall enlighten the heart of the Nation; that He shall return to the Throne of All-Russia His anointed, strong in the love of the people, the lawful Orthodox Tsar of the House of Romanov [that is, a relative or heir of the executed family].[38]

As we will see in later chapters, this resolution would cause major problems for Orthodox hierarchs remaining in Russia because Anthony insisted that all declarations and resolutions include the phrase "By the blessings of the patriarch" (who was not even there). Before the sobor ended on December 15, 1921, Anthony was named vice-regent of the All-Russian Patriarch—of course, without Tikhon's knowledge or approval.[39] Tikhon's opposition to Anthony's assumption of the office of president of the Russian Orthodox Church Outside of Russia—and the "Vice-Regency," once the word got out—was not due to any personal rivalry but to Anthony's hard line against the Bolshevik regime. Such an attitude could topple Tikhon from the tight wire he was walking between the Bolsheviks and conservative church hierarchs.

Karlovtzy versus the Bolsheviks

From April 10 to May 11, 1922, a postwar economic conference was held in Genoa, Italy. The United States did not attend, but Britain, France, and Germany did. Lenin eagerly accepted the invitation extended to the Russians, anxious to establish normal relations with the bourgeois powers—at least until he could overthrow them. Although during the year or so after their seizure of power the Bolsheviks ignored accusations of maltreatment of the church, by 1919–1920 the government was thinking about the advantages of international acceptance, diplomatic recognition, and commercial treaties. In the opening days of the conference Chicherin, the head of Russia's delegation, was sensitive about persecution charges reaching the ears of outsiders and insisted that complete religious freedom existed in Russia. At this point émigré clerics dispatched a letter to the conference pointing to Denikin's (unverified) figure of 28 bishops and 1,215 priests executed by the Bolsheviks.[40]

Metropolitan Anthony then issued a proclamation to the delegates cautioning them not to grant Communist Russia diplomatic recognition. He warned that doing so would stimulate socialist uprisings in other European lands and suggested preemptive armed intervention against the outlaw regime:

> Peoples of Europe and of the world, have pity upon this nation and equip its sons with arms; then they together with their dear comrades, officers, generals, and soldiers will be ready to spring up and march into Russia to rescue it from its enslavement by the robbers![41]

He begged nations attending the conference to help drive Bolshevism—"this cult of killing, looting, and blasphemy"—out of the country.[42]

Anthony further expressed the wish that the "terrible havoc wrought by the famine, cold, and epidemic at present devastating Russia" should topple the Communists from power (more on the famine in chapter 11). Although Lenin was certainly not above using natural calamities to further his political interests, he reacted violently to this suggestion from the Karlovtzy Synod. The Bolsheviks pointed to this statement as proof that the church was interested only in exploiting the tragedy for its own political gain. When the government began confiscating church valuables, ostensibly for famine relief, Anthony suggested that the money gained from the sale of these valuables be used instead to finance the struggle against Soviet power. He claimed that the most serious disease in Russia was not the famine; it was communism. Blame for the famine in the first place, Anthony continued, should be placed at the feet of "the perverted, bloody regime of the butchers of Russia." But Anthony and the Karlovtzy Synod were far removed from the *anti*-interventionist reality of current European politics.

Were there connections between the Orthodox clergy in Karlovtzy and Patriarch Tikhon in Moscow—connections that the Bolsheviks could exploit? Communications were weak and compliance with the wishes of the patriarch was negligible, but there were rumors that Bishop Venyamin, living in Constantinople, was a liaison between Karlovtzy and Tikhon. However, Venyamin opposed the connection between Karlovtzy and the supporters of a Romanov restoration.

Having been recently placed under house arrest—and thus under great pressure—Tikhon tried to deal with the issue. On May 5, 1922, he repudiated the major resolutions emanating from Karlovtzy, claiming émigrés had no right to speak on behalf of the Russian Orthodox Church. At the same time he issued one of several decrees dissolving the Karlovtzy Synod (insofar as this was within his power) and turned over all church operations in Western Europe to Metropolitan Evlogy, headquartered in Paris. Tikhon felt that he had adequately cut himself off from the unduly politicized émigrés in Yugoslavia.[43] But Anthony was not about to go quietly into obscurity. In November 1922 the Karlovtzy Synod issued this interpretation:

> In future cases those orders from His Holiness [the patriarch] relating to the Orthodox Church Abroad which would be insulting to her honor and bearing clear features of direct pressure upon the Holy Patriarch's conscience on the part of Christ's foes, should be ignored as originating not from the patriarch's will but from a completely different [Bolshevik] will. At the same time full respect and devotion should be rendered to the person of the innocently suffering Holy Patriarch.[44]

The continuing stream of radically conservative pronouncements radiating from Anthony's organization convinced the Soviets—or so they said—that they were faced with a church conspiracy. In his book *On The Church Front* (1923), Commissar of Justice Peter Krasikov directly accused Tikhon of collusion with the émigré group. When the patriarch protested his innocence, Krasikov challenged him to either acknowledge his communications with Karlovtzy or excommunicate all its members. Tikhon protested that he could not accomplish the latter as they were living beyond his jurisdiction, but Krasikov was not satisfied with this canonically correct answer. Tikhon was in disagreement not so much with the inner convictions and sympathies of the Karlovtzy clergy as he was with their penchant for bold pronouncements calling for a Romanov return.[45] His position became even more precarious when the government mounted a massive propaganda campaign portraying him as an unrepentant monarchist linked with émigré monarchists. Tikhon's followers were worried that he might suffer the same fate as the tsar.

In spite of Anthony's protestations, after Tikhon's censure of the Karlovtzy Synod in May 1922, it began a long downhill slide. Except for a few parishes deep in the Balkans and a few scattered elsewhere, Anthony's synod really had no power base. The émigré center of gravity had been shifting westward to Berlin and Paris, where only a few felt that Anthony spoke for them. Émigrés in Paris joined the Orthodox Theological Institute of St. Sergius or the Religious Philosophical Academy (after the latter moved from Berlin in 1924). Metropolitan Platon was sent to the United States as head of the Russian Orthodox Church of North America. Both Evlogy in France and Platon in America broke with Anthony in the summer of 1926.[46] Ultimately, the existence of the Karlovtzy Sobor was more of a win for Soviet antireligious propaganda than a furtherance of the church's agenda.

Tumult and confusion rolled not only through the émigré communities to the west of Russia but through the region they had abandoned as well: the Ukraine.

TROUBLE IN THE UKRAINE

The principality of Kiev had been the headquarters of Russian Orthodoxy from Vladimir's conversion in 988 CE until the rise of Muscovy in the thirteenth century. Its distinct language and culture allowed it to retain a large measure of independence for centuries afterward. Kiev began and remained the "soul of the faith."

With the overthrow of the tsar, a non-Bolshevik Orthodox priest became the Provisional Government's Ukrainian Commissar for Ecclesiastical Affairs. He spent his days and nights driving around Kiev in frantic searches for counterrevolutionary or pogromist materials hidden in the city's churches. This commissar, and the Executive Committee of Clergy and Laymen that he headed, stood in direct opposition to Metropolitan Vladimir, a member of the Holy Synod in Moscow. Returning to Kiev after attending the First Church Sobor, Vladimir was disgusted with the liberalism and separatism of the Executive Committee, calling it "an illegitimate institution which is trying gradually to expand its power and to usurp prerogatives which do not belong to it."

In August 1917 a Ukrainian Orthodox (Regional) Sobor met in Kiev, apparently dominated by those same forces that Vladimir loathed. He sent this sobor a pastoral letter expressing puzzlement that so many believed in their *personal* interpretations of God's One True Faith and befuddlement that the unity of the Russian Orthodox Church could so easily be tossed aside in the name of Ukrainian autocephaly. Then he journeyed back to Moscow's sobor and later led the enthronement rites of Patriarch Tikhon. The regional sobor in Kiev never completed its work, having been disrupted by the political tumult surrounding it.[47]

After the Provisional Government fell in November, both the Ukrainian government and the Ukrainian Church seized the opportunity to declare independence from Moscow.* Church separation, however, engendered great controversy. Many feared that autocephaly might lead to joining with the Eastern Rite Catholics and submission to the pope. At the end of the month Metropolitan Vladimir again returned to Kiev, wishing to guide the tumultuous situation as best he could.

In 1920 a newly formed (and Bolshevik-infiltrated) organization called the Union of Orthodox Parish Councils tried to remove Vladimir as metropolitan.

---

*Ukrainians declared national independence on January 22, 1918, which lasted officially until the formation of the USSR in December 1922.

When its efforts failed, the Union offered—for an exorbitant amount of church treasure—to make him patriarch of a separated Ukrainian Orthodox Church. When he refused to cooperate, they tried to eject him from Kiev. Reportedly, Vladimir approached a member of the ejection delegation, pointed his finger at the man's chest, and said, "Do you know that the first revolutionary was the devil, and you are making a revolution in the Church of Christ?" He refused to leave the city, saying, as was expected among church hierarchs, that he would suffer to the very end and willingly give his life for Christ. Then he wept bitterly for the loss of church unity.[48]

Vladimir resided at the Pechersky (Caves) Monastery in Kiev, which by late January 1918 was being shelled in the first of the Civil War battles to reach the city. During the first week of February, Bolshevik armies broke into the monastery and wreaked an awful destruction on everything in sight. They looted treasures, executed monks, and performed outrageous acts of sacrilege. On February 6, six men in military uniforms came for the metropolitan. There are several differing versions of ensuing events. According to one witness, the Bolsheviks tortured Vladimir in his room (probably to force him to reveal the location of hidden wealth) and then escorted him to a monastery wall and shot him multiple times. Another witness, a clergyman who later claimed he had seen this as a child, described angry soldiers encircling Vladimir in the courtyard and shouting questions at the old man. Each time he answered unsatisfactorily they stabbed him with a bayonet, until he died. Three days later, the Moscow sobor dedicated its session to his memory.[49]

A Ukrainian Autocephalous Orthodox Church, separate from and independent of the Moscow patriarchate, was finally organized by the Ukrainian nationalist government on January 1, 1919, during the height of the Civil War. Metropolitan Vasily (Lipkovsky) organized its first sobor in Kiev in October 1921. Born of nationalism, the new church required priests to pledge their love for "independent Mother Ukraine" and labeled any opposition to the use of the Ukrainian language in the churches "an offense against the Holy Spirit."[50] Since no Russian Orthodox bishops would join this separatist church, it had to create its hierarchy—uncanonically—without the laying on of hands. At its height in the early 1920s, it had 2,500 priests and over 2,000 parishes.[51]

When the Soviets regained control of the Ukraine in late 1921, it might have seemed that they would mercilessly crush a separatist Orthodox Church, but that was not the case. The government "supported" any Orthodox organization that would drive a wedge into Orthodox solidarity.[52] This wedge was doubly effective because not only would Tikhon not recognize Ukrainian autocephaly, but his conservatism would not allow him to accept the Ukrainian Autocephalous Orthodox Church's ideologically progressive and liturgically radical views. Liberal-minded Ukrainian Church leaders naively sought ideological reconciliation with communism and believed that Ukrainian culture might be allowed to thrive within the Soviet system. After the formation of the USSR, the Ukrainian Church offered to support the government of the Ukrainian Soviet Socialist Republic, which "gives the population the possibility of organizing its ecclesiastical and religious life according to its wishes." It trusted that any religious persecution in the Ukraine would be directed at Tikhonites in their midst. In 1924 the Ukrainian Church admitted that in tsarist times the Russian Orthodox Church had oppressed the working class and national minorities.[53]

Paradoxically, Bishop Theophilus (Buldovsky) tried to unify Orthodoxy by creating another Ukrainian autocephalous church, this time one that the Moscow patriarchate recognized. Father Vasily (Zelentsov), a popular pro-Tikhon priest in the Ukraine, tried to mend Orthodox schisms, but the Bolsheviks arrested and tried him in 1922 on political charges; in all cases the Soviets preferred church schism to church unity. At the end of Vasily's trial, and under duress, he declared his loyalty to the Soviet state but slipped in a final comment:

> It would be shamefully sinful for me, as a warrior of Christ, bearing this cross on my breast, to defend myself personally at a time when our enemies have taken up arms and declared war against Christ himself.[54]

Vasily survived the trial and in 1925 was elevated to the episcopacy, where he continued to struggle against what he termed the "satanic, bloodsucking, fiendish" power of Bolshevism until he was martyred in Moscow in 1930.[55]

Moving through the 1920s, the Bolsheviks at first welcomed the Ukrainian Church schism, then moved to toleration, and finally rose to condemnation. As Stalin amassed power he slowly turned his eye southward, infiltrating some churches and inching toward the massive church closings and clerical arrests of the first Five-Year Plan. Metropolitan Lipkovsky was forced out in October 1928 and replaced with a more pro-Soviet church leader.

In early 1929 Stalin wielded the tax weapon, assessing all the region's churches 5,000 to 40,000 rubles—far in excess of what congregations could raise. Later in the year he began a purge of Ukrainian nationalists, and the church was caught up in an alleged anti-Soviet conspiracy. In January 1930 the Ukrainian Autocephalous Orthodox Church met in an "extraordinary sobor" and decided to dissolve itself in an attempt to preempt arrests of its members.[56] Soviet authorities forced the dissolved church to merge with the national Russian Orthodox Church. By 1932 there was not a surviving Autocephalous Orthodox priest or bishop in the Ukraine—unless he had dug very far underground.[57]

A forceful weapon that the Soviet government used against all Russian churches was one that, in milder form, was perfectly acceptable in the West, but this democratic reform was perverted in Soviet hands.

7

A STONE
INSTEAD OF BREAD
Separation of Church and State

When the Bolsheviks took power in November 1917, they had few immediately available weapons with which to attack the influence of the Orthodox Church. But among their untried arsenal was one weapon that had a certain beauty to it—the separation of church and state. Its attractiveness was its apparent rationality and, even more, its acceptance in the West; it logically flowed from the teachings of Thomas Jefferson and the lessons of the French Revolution. Indeed, Peter Krasikov let slip that the Soviets intended to model their separation decree on the American system.[1] Yet in the hands of the Bolsheviks, separation of church and state was intended not so much as a protection for the state but as a weapon used by the state; it was the first official arrow shot in what would become a full-quivered assault on the existence of the church as an institution and the presence of religious faith in the minds of the citizenry.

PROBLEMS OF CHURCH AND STATE

Only the complete fulfillment of these [separation] demands can put an end to the shameful and accursed past when the church lived in feudal dependence on the state, and Russian citizens lived in feudal dependence on the established church. . . . Complete separation of church and state is what the socialist proletariat demands of the modern state and the modern church.

—Lenin, *Socialism and Religion*, 1905

As others had before and after him, Marx saw a historically inevitable and universal—but nonetheless insidious—connection between the state and organized religion. Although his experience was mainly of the established Lutheran Church in northern Germany, he defined *all* churches as groups of people united by particular sources of income at the cost of the faithful. The church assisted the state, capitalists, and landlords in the oppression of workers and peasants.

Marx's Interpretation

According to the founder of modern communist theory, feudal power—kings, princes, and landowners—exterminated the lower clergy and placed the church under its iron rule. Then this power began to share the fruits of victory with bishops, archbishops, and other *ecclesiastical* princes, the latter becoming servants of the state not only by submitting to its whim and fancy in secular matters but also by allowing the state to interfere in religious and ecclesiastical affairs. At least on the surface, a mutual admiration society formed between secular and religious aristocracy.

Marx knew that within the capitalist system's liberal democracies the bourgeoisie often pushed for separation of church and state. But its motives, though historically determined, were not pure. The urban middle class merely coveted the vast wealth that the church had accumulated under feudalism; wealth derived directly from the state and indirectly from land the state had given to the church. Marx contested not just the connection between church and state; he saw the church and the faith it engendered as *tools* used by the state (especially in Germany) to protect its privileged position and keep proletarians and peasants in their place.

For Marx mere separation of church and state was totally insufficient, as this arrangement would allow the basic error of religion to be perpetuated. With communism's fruition, "religion as a private affair" and "freedom of religion" would be antithetical to *real* freedom.

Lenin's Interpretation

Both Marx in considering Western churches and Lenin in considering Russian churches realized that the welding of church and state provided not only theoretical difficulties but also practical ones. On tactical grounds, both revolutionaries knew that Western and Eastern churches were committed to the status quo. Lenin knew that the Russian Orthodox hierarchy had received huge subsidies from the tsarist government, that the church's landholdings were protected by law, that bishops were named only with the tsar's consent, and that priests were required to report the political activities of parish members to tsarist authorities. The church thus favored stagnation and was unlikely to develop sympathy for revolution.

In December 1905—twelve years away from power—Lenin wrote the essay "Socialism and Religion," published in *New Life* (*Novaya Zhizn*). It contained a general statement of his views on the religious question for members of the

Russian Social Democratic Labor Party. Interestingly, and cleverly, he put forth a belief in religious tolerance—not of religion itself, but in the sense of treating all faiths equally—and challenged those clergy in Russia who were anticipating freedom from autocratic and bureaucratic control to "put their money where their mouths were." They should openly agitate for—indeed demand—the complete separation of church and state; that is, the disestablishment of the Orthodox Church. Lenin instructed party workers to say to the clergy:

> If you are sincere, you must stand for a complete separation of the church from the state, for a separation of the school from the church, and insist that religion be regarded *entirely and unconditionally* as a private matter. If you do not accept these consistent demands of liberty, it means you are still a slave to inquisitorial traditions. It means that you are still hankering after government posts and the revenues attached to them, it means that you do not believe in the spiritual force of your weapon and that you still wish to take bribes from the government. If this is so, the class-conscious Russian workers will declare ruthless war on you.[2]

But Lenin made this distinction: Religion was a private matter for the *state* but not for the *party*. While he wrote that state discrimination against any religion was "wholly intolerable" and insisted that the bare mention in any government document of the religion or denomination to which a citizen belonged should "unquestioningly be eliminated," he added this caveat:

> Our party is a league of conscious, leading fighters for the liberation of the working class. Such a league cannot and must not be indifferent to lack of consciousness, ignorance, or obscurantism in the shape of religious beliefs.[3]

The party *should* keep records of citizen's religious affiliation for use at a later date.

The Church's Changing Viewpoint

In earlier centuries the church had no quarrel with the unity of church and state. The Russian Church was derived from the Greek Church, which was encompassed within the Byzantine theocracy. In Byzantium, however, the church was in the dominant position—the ruler held his power through the grace of the church. But this arrangement became twisted around in Russia, as church leaders gradually found themselves subservient to the whims of tsars. This reversal of power became institutionalized when Peter issued the Ecclesiastical Regulation in 1721, abandoning the patriarchate and forcing the church to become an arm of government policy. The church was now separated from the state only in the sense that Peter had ended the period of church-state co-rule and set in motion two hundred years of church *dependence* on the state.

A separation proposal was presented to Nicholas II, the last tsar, who apparently gave it serious consideration. The proposal died, however, when Rasputin turned against it. During the Provisional Government period, the First Church Sobor also listed separation on its agenda—at least in the sense that the election of a patriarch would give the church a more independent position relative to the new democratic state. The Provisional Government itself favored a gradual separation from the church, but it failed to provide the driving force necessary for implementation. It passed the issue off to the abortive Constituent Assembly.

With the successful Bolshevik takeover, church leaders began to waver, then completely changed their position. They had envisaged a separated church, with a patriarch at its head, as a stronger church. Now they were faced with a *complete* separation of church and state—a total cutting loose from state support. The Bolshevik plan was that the church, "if it continued to exist at all, would exist as a loose, anonymous community of believers and not as an institution or organization."[4] Religious groups would become "absolutely free associations of like-minded citizens," and all Russians would be free to become atheists.

SEPARATION OF CHURCH AND STATE: A BLIZZARD OF DECREES

The separation of the church from the state, which we have established once and for all, by no means signifies that the state is indifferent to what is happening in the church.[5]

—Leon Trotsky in a letter to Lenin, May 14, 1922

What was meant by separation of church and state under Bolshevik rule was the termination of even dependence. The church was to be set adrift. This was explained in a later issue of *Izvestia*:

> The existence in this country of a "church hierarchy" as such is impossible. The [government] allows the existence of separate religious communities, not joined together by any administrative authority and freely electing their clergy, who most certainly must not be confirmed by Episcopal Councils.[6]

The concept was immediately apparent, the laws soon followed, but implementation would be awhile in coming.

On the day after taking power Lenin nationalized all land, which included church and monastery land that alone was worth perhaps $4 billion.[7] The "Decree on Land Nationalization" read in part:

> The monastic and church lands, with all their livestock, implements, farm buildings, and everything pertaining thereto, shall be placed under the control of the

village land committees and the district Soviets of Peasants' Deputies, pending the meeting of the Constituent Assembly.[8]

One factory worker commented on a Soviet questionnaire, "Not God gave the peasants the land of the lords, but the godless Bolsheviks."[9]

Then, a week after taking power, Lenin issued the "Declaration of the Rights of the People of Russia." Among other provisions, it took aim at the church by denying it, as had the Provisional Government, the privileged status it had held under the tsars. All religions (or "cults," as they were called) would stand—or fall—as equals.[10] The government then began issuing a series of specifically *anti*-religious decrees.

On December 24 Lenin ordered religious schools, including Orthodox seminaries, turned over to the Commissariat of Education. On December 29 he ordered divorce laws liberalized and secularized and births out of wedlock legitimized.[11] On December 31 he required the civil registration of birth, marriage, and death and soon thereafter mandated that hundreds of years of past church records be turned over to the state (more on this in chapter 10).

Religious feelings were now running high and were bold in their challenge to fledgling Soviet authority. Nonetheless, the government proceeded on January 26, 1918, with its first physical attempt to take over church property. Alexandra Kollontai, Commissar of Welfare, dispatched a squad of Kronstadt sailors to the St. Alexander Nevsky Monastery in Petrograd. The medieval hero Prince Alexander Nevsky was buried there, and it had become a symbol of the old order that the Bolsheviks were in a hurry to replace; Kollontai intended to convert the building into a rest home for war invalids.

When the sailors demanded the monastery's cash and other assets—another motive—the head of the monastery refused, as he had been instructed by a vote of his monastic community. The sailors left, but six days later Bolshevik Red Guards arrived at the monastery's door and were greeted by the pealing of church bells—a traditional cry for help. Thousands of nearby residents—and even some soldiers—formed an angry crowd to resist the Red Guards, resulting in one of the defending clerics, Dean Skipetrov, being shot and killed. Yet again the monastery was left untouched. Two more days passed, then another crowd of believers, organized by Metropolitan Benjamin, gathered in the monastery square for a peaceful demonstration, vowing that they would walk directly into rifle fire if necessary. Vladimir Bonch-Bruevich, fearing a repeat of Bloody Sunday thirteen years before, restrained the military and told the believers that he was not an enemy of religion.[12] Government sources released a sanitized version of this incident to the Associated Press claiming that ringing the church bells constituted forcible resistance and the incitement of violence. It declared that the monks attacked the Red Guards, and they fired in self-defense.

A week later similar mass protests against Bolshevik church policy took place in Moscow. There was also a major disturbance in the Petrozavodsk region of Olonets Province, where the Union for the Defense of the Alexander Svirsky Monastery aroused thousands in defiance of the law. After the Red Army was called to subdue the mob, five of the ringleaders were arrested and executed.[13]

The party sensed the threat and quickly decided to present a more organized and coherent program. The next decree, on February 2, terminated financial support for the clergy and denied state funds for the upkeep of church buildings.[14] Lenin's staff then drafted an early version of a comprehensive decree modeled after those issued by the Paris Commune in 1871. Originally called "On Freedom of Conscience, Church and Religious Organizations," it was printed in *Izvestia*, but Lenin was not satisfied. Accusing his staff of missing the point, and perhaps of omitting a little revolutionary zeal, he started over, this time putting some teeth into it. It emerged on February 5—four days after Tikhon's anathema of the Bolsheviks—as "Separating the Church from the State and the School from the Church" (henceforth referred to here as the "separation decree"). This decree contained not a word about persecution of any faith; on its face it was nonreligious rather than antireligious, but its purpose was the secularization of Russian society.

Not through yet, on February 10 the government nationalized the bank accounts of all "religious associations" and in March rescinded all credit. Also in March, Commissar of War Trotsky dismissed all chaplains serving with troops (unless military units wanted to pay for their upkeep themselves) and confiscated all church property associated with the military.[15] (Later, in May 1923, the government closed all chapels connected to hospitals. No places of worship were to be attached to any state institution.)

After the separation decree, church leaders, now fully aware of their predicament, turned defensive. Metropolitan Benjamin publicly predicted that if the decree led to the confiscation of church valuables, the faithful would not stand for it. He issued a warning that the people's excitement might "develop into an elemental movement and bring on an uprising with serious consequences." No power on Earth would be able to impede it, once begun. Tikhon issued instructions for all parishes to organize local defense committees of at least twelve members to protect churches from marauding government agents. The church need not have been so *immediately* worried, however, as the government at this point had nowhere near the capacity to enforce the separation decree, especially in rural areas. It would not be until 1919–1920 that the Cheka—the secret police—could finally take up the slack.[16]

Nonetheless, the separation decree was law, entrusted for implementation to Krasikov in the Commissariat of Justice. On April 26, 1918, he created a special commission to apply the separation decree in individual cases, and in his capacity as editor of the commissariat's journal *Revolution and the Church* (1919 to 1924) he produced a steady flow of articles providing details and specifics for carrying out the program.[17]

And what exactly was the program?

- Article 3 of the separation decree read: "Every citizen may profess any religion or none at all. Any legal disabilities connected with the profession of any religion or none are abolished."[18] Henceforth, state records would make no mention of a citizen's religious affiliation.
- Article 5 included this rather vague guarantee: "The free observance of religious customs is guaranteed in so far as the same do not disturb the public order and are not accompanied by attempts upon the rights of the citizens of the Soviet Republic."[19] A quick look at this article might lead one to believe that Lenin was simply following through with his prerevolutionary statements about the "privacy" of religious belief—privacy from the government, that is, not from the party. But this article caused trouble for the church later due to its ambiguity of interpretation and potential for abuse.
- Religious vows were declared invalid—for example, in court—and religious ceremonies could not accompany any governmental events. On April 12, 1918, all religious plaques, insignias, crosses, and ikons were ordered removed from public buildings (including schools and hospitals).[20]
- Religious objections to performing state-required duties—for example, military service—were restricted. (Orthodox believers could not get draft exemptions or conscientious objector status, as the church had historically raised no objections to fighting in "imperialist wars.")
- It was illegal to incite the people against the government by ringing church bells.
- As mentioned, births, marriages, and deaths had to be recorded at civil registration bureaus. Divorces were removed from the old ecclesiastical courts and placed in the new people's courts where uniform laws could be administered.
- All state subsidies for religious groups were cut off.
- Compulsory collection of money for national religious purposes was forbidden. Purely voluntary local collections, for firewood, church furnishing, and so on, were permissible.
- All property held by religious associations, including church buildings and the objects inside churches, was declared to be part of the "national wealth."
- While it was legal for a citizen to proclaim religious communion, churches on both the national and local levels lost their status as legal entities ("juridical persons").[21] The Commissariat of Justice put it plainly: "All mandates, certificates, etc., issued by religious corporations have no legal force in Soviet institutions. They may deal only with religious affairs."

Eventually the RSFSR (Russian Soviet Federated Socialist Republic) Criminal Code would provide penalties for violations. The assumption by the church of "a public legal character" or "the rights of juridical persons"—which could be interpreted as any *church*, as opposed to *individual*, action—could result in forced labor in the gulag for up to six months and the confiscation of church property involved in the crime. Who would do the labor and how church *property* could be involved in "the crime" remained unclear.

On July 10, 1918, the essence of the separation decree was incorporated into Article 13 of the new constitution of the RSFSR,[22] or, simply, the overwhelmingly Russian part of what would in a few years officially become the Soviet Union. Moderates on the constitutional committee insisted on including that old phrase "religion is a private affair of the citizens"—harking back to Lenin's prerevolutionary slogan, but their leader was now in power and he declared this wording unacceptable. So the final version simply stated:

> In order to ensure genuine freedom of conscience for the working people, the church is separated from the state and the school from the church, and freedom of religious and antireligious propaganda is recognized for all citizens.[23]

Although this might seem fair enough on its face, the right to religious propaganda was given to a church whose strength was daily being sapped, while the right to antireligious propaganda was granted to a state with the Bolshevik Party and Red Army propping it up. The "rights" granted to the church would be insufficient to defend it from the separation decree's detrimental enforcement. Virtually all future assaults on religion in Russia would use the decree as their justification. Ironically, armed with this decree and the Constitution's statement on freedom of religious propaganda, the government could somewhat successfully defend itself against foreign charges of religious persecution. Ultimately, though, "freedom of religious propaganda" was insincere. Krasikov wrote in *Revolution and the Church* in early 1919 that it was a temporary concession to "the age-long religious prejudices still so strong in the Russian village."[24]

On August 24, 1918, the Commissariat of Justice published in *Izvestia* an "Ordinance" (officially called "On the Procedure for the Implementation of the Decree on the Separation of Church from State and School from Church") that clarified and elaborated the new laws. It was more a response to church obstructionism and stalling tactics than it was a blueprint for the future, and it reiterated that *every* religious organization, denomination, or sect—no matter what it called itself—was covered under the new law. The Ordinance tightened up rules forbidding religious education of the young (discussed in the next chapter) and imposed heavier burdens on parish laity. It required the removal of all church monuments or tablets that commemorated the glories of the tsarist regime, as they were considered "insulting to the revolutionary sensibilities of the working masses." Violation of these provisions would void the church's lease and the building would be closed.[25]

The final decree in the "separation series" was issued on December 7, a year after the campaign began. It nationalized all burial grounds, including church-yards, and set up civil procedures for burial.

Despite slow implementation, the party made its long-term commitment clear at its Eighth Congress in 1919:

> As far as religion is concerned, the Russian Communist Party will not be satisfied by the decreed separation of church and state. . . . The party aims at the complete destruction of links between the exploiting classes and [the workers and peasants].[26]

Finally, in the fall of 1922, the party set up an enforcement agency—aptly named the Commission to Establish Separation of Church and State. It held its first meeting in October and quickly emerged as the most powerful force on the antireligious effort, issuing proposals, recommendations, and suggestions to state agencies. It answered only to the party's Agitation and Propaganda (Agitprop) Department, which itself answered to the Politburo. Emelyan Yaroslavsky chaired the Commission, which included Yevgeny Tuchkov, Peter Krasikov, T. Samsonov, and Peter Smidovich. Soon its name was shortened to the Antireligious Commission, and under this name it continued its work until 1929 when it was disbanded.[27]

CLOSING MONASTERIES AND CHURCHES

The separation of church and state was so construed by the state that the churches themselves and everything that hung in them, was installed in them, and painted in them belonged to the state, and the only church remaining was that church which, in accordance with the Scriptures, lay within the heart.[25]

—Alexander Solzhenitsyn

Motives

One could argue that the separation decree was not antireligious at all. Perhaps the new laws were designed to protect both the church and the state. Could it be that the Bolsheviks were just taking back the ill-gotten gains of the corrupt feudal period? Maybe they were simply more effective at carrying out the program laid down by the Provisional Government but never implemented. Kerensky had wished to secularize the state, and he had attempted to deprive the Orthodox Church of its unfair advantages and privileges. And, on paper at least, Bolshevik restrictions operated both ways. After all, Article 125 of the RSFSR Criminal Code stated:

> Hindering the performance of religious rites, as far as they do not disturb the public peace and are not accompanied by infractions of the rights of citizens, is punishable by forced labor up to six months.[29]

Or one could argue that the separation decree was not antireligious because, consistent with Marxist theory, the government was simply attempting to remove *all* private and corporate control of productive property. The church just happened to be the largest corporate owner of productive property in the tsarist system.

However, the confiscation of monasteries, churches, their treasures, and their land was not simply an inadvertent aspect of a general process. Marxists were convinced that religion—especially Christianity—was a pillar upholding capitalism, and weakening this pillar would hasten the collapse of capitalist remnants in Soviet Russia. This process would also set an example for workers in foreign countries, speeding the spread of worldwide revolution.

In *ABC of Communism* (1919), Bukharin affected concern for Catholics, Jews, and Muslims, whom the tsarist government had taxed and had thus indirectly forced to support the established Orthodox Church: "This money was used by the Orthodox clergy to demonstrate that all other faiths were false."[30] Yet a basic sense of fairness and concern over the misspending of money could hardly have been the government's major concern. There were also pecuniary motives behind monastery and church closures. The government converted many religious buildings to schools, shops, asylums, and museums, so perhaps some degree of sincerity can be attributed to its leaders; that is, they were primarily interested in the alternative value of these properties. Clerical and monastic buildings provided secular meeting places for Komsomol (Communist Youth Organization) and workers. And every church converted into a grain storage warehouse was a warehouse that the government, on a national or local level, did not have to spend scarce resources building.

In any case, party leaders would have closed churches even if it there were no alternative uses. The party suffered no compunctions; closings of buildings and confiscations of land were administrative measures in its antireligious struggle.

Monasteries

In 1920 the Commissariat of Justice issued this statement:

[We call for] painless but full liquidation of the monasteries, as chief centers of the influence of the churchmen, as nurseries of parasitism, as powerful screws in the exploiting machine of the old ruling classes.[31]

But this was a subsequent justification; monasteries and convents were being closed within weeks of the Bolshevik assumption of power, and they were closed even before the churches. The fired-up Bolsheviks no doubt saw monasteries as the starkest symbols of nonproductive labor and religious mysticism, or—at least as important—they knew most were found in out-of-the-way places where public clamor could be avoided. The Bolshevik revolutionary slogan "Land, Bread, and Peace" implied that there would be land redistribution to the peasants, and the land had to come from somewhere.

In the summer of 1918 the government emptied many monasteries of monks and nuns and filled them with prisoners of the Cheka-driven Red Terror. With their high walls and solid construction, monasteries were easily converted to concentration camps. In September, *Krasnaya Gazeta* (*Red Gazette*) described the first of these detention areas: an empty nunnery near Nizhny-Novgorod planned for an initial population of 5,000 prisoners. A convent in Ryazan was used in the same manner. The Boris and Gleb Monastery in Torzhok became a transit camp to more distant camps, and the Valdai Monastery was put to use as a facility for juvenile offenders. In 1921, when more and remoter camps were needed for the burgeoning prison population, one of many Northern Special Purpose Camps was built in and around the monastery on the Solovetsky Islands in the White Sea, a few dozen miles from the mainland and frozen in for half the year.[32] This became a favorite long-term holding facility for recalcitrant clergy. Besides being designated as incarceration sites, the August 1918 Ordinance stipulated that all confiscated monastic property be turned over to local soviets for whatever "socially useful" purposes their members agreed upon.

Monasteries could not invoke the law guaranteeing freedom of worship; that was allowed only for parish churches. Of course, monasteries also had attached churches, but a 1921 law provided that these, too, be closed, except where closure would be a hardship on local peasants. Even then, they had to be walled off from the monastery, have a separate entrance, and ring no bells.[33]

Two years into the Revolution:

- over 2.3 million acres of monastery and convent land had been handed over to the state in the name of Russia's peasantry. (Eventually all 10.8 million acres the monasteries had owned would be lost to them.)
- out of 1,025 monasteries existing before World War I, 673 had been dissolved.
- the state had stripped from the monasteries 1,112 leased houses, 708 hotels, 602 cattle sheds, 435 dairy farms, 311 beehives, 277 hospitals and asylums, and 84 factories.[34]

By 1923 there was very little left. Most monastic property either had been appropriated by peasants at the time of the Revolution or had been confiscated by the state during the following four years. Any land left to the monks was too remote to be of any use to the government. Although the land was gone, most of the buildings remained with somewhat altered functions. An Orthodox writer sent this report out of the country in early 1926:

> Not all monasteries are closed. Here and there they still exist under the name of "laboring communities." Even in the capitals they are still to be found. Of course the number of ikons has been very much reduced. Sometimes the monasteries have been transformed into colonies where aged cripples or invalids are allowed to pass the remainder of their lives in the guise of custodians and keepers of the sacred objects and relics that have been declared to be objects of art and worthy of being kept in museums.[35]

Thirty-four more monasteries were closed in 1927 and 48 in 1928.[36] In April 1928, *Komsomolskaya Pravda* boasted:

> The monasteries are no more centers of propaganda preaching; they have been transformed into museums, established to preach against God. Many excursions come to visit them.[37]

In May the same newspaper added that the soviet in Kazan had decided to confiscate all the monasteries in the city and the surrounding districts so they could be transformed into homes for workmen, who were in great need of suitable quarters. The thirteenth-century Danilov Monastery, a mile south of the Moscow Kremlin, was closed in stages between 1929 and 1932. Its fate: a prison for juvenile delinquents.[38]

Throngs of monks poured into the countryside, wandering from village to village seeking something useful (and remunerative) to do. A 1926 newspaper wrote, "The black clergy were scattered over the face of the Russian land like cockroaches swept out from under the stove by the hand of a tidy housewife." Some entered the workforce (or were drafted into labor battalions), some became wandering mystics, and some, as mentioned in the quotation above, organized "monasteries" disguised as economic collectives or labor communes on the Soviet model (these, too, were eventually closed). Some monks cut their hair and became true farmers, and some nuns married.[39]

The Committees of Twenty

After, in the name of "the people," the government confiscated every church building in Russia, it leased most of them back to their congregations free of charge; back, that is, to parish communities represented by an elected Committee of Twenty. These twenty parishioners had to bind themselves by contract with the local soviet to be responsible for the material condition of the building and all that took place within it. The government demanded complete information on the individual members of the Committee of Twenty, especially emphasizing their—and their parents'—class and social status and their prerevolutionary property ownership. Lease contracts forbade meetings, speeches, sermons, books, or pamphlets hostile to the government and required that state ownership be acknowledged. Clearly, the government did not freely lease the land beneath the churches, rather it was rented at moderate to high rates (in effect, a tax). In urban areas church buildings were locally taxed (outside of the lease). The government required churches to carry fire insurance, and in December 1923 it ordered insurance companies to pay benefits to the state when a church burned to the ground even though the parishioners had paid the premiums. It was, after all, government property that had been lost.[40]

In most areas the Twenty supported the priest and never stopped believing that the church building, the land it sat on, holy ikons, robes, and instruments of worship belonged to those who prayed there.[41] Some Twenties, however, were either sympathetic to the Bolsheviks—possibly because they were infiltrated by them—or were directly under the thumb of the local soviets. But no matter what the Twenty's attitude, the local soviet was authorized to make sure that the government's interests were protected. The priest had no power to prevent closure and was not represented in the soviet. In practice, a zealous soviet could close a church on its own if it felt doing so reflected "the wishes of the workers," and in many instances soviets were more draconian than the central government intended and had to be restrained.[42] But it was not always mean-spirited soviets that instigated church closures; in many areas, due to antireligious propaganda or even in its absence, attendance was too low to justify the expense of keeping a church open. Buildings were just left to rot.

Commissar of Education Lunacharsky distributed a circular in December 1921 titled "On the Use of Buildings Formerly Religious." Churches were converted to grain storage warehouses, textile mills, electric power plants, stables, clubhouses, libraries, children's homes, mental health asylums, health clinics, and restaurants. For those left open, when the Twenty signed its contract it consented to alternative uses of the building on days other than Sunday. During the other six days of the week it could be used for political meetings, lectures, concerts, plays, dances, and cinema. Many congregations refused to avail themselves of their churches after they had been so "desecrated," whereupon the government would say that they had been voluntarily closed. Decrees further clarifying church use were issued on April 27 and June 19, 1923.[43]

Church property not directly connected to worship, such as church-owned hotels, hospitals, and candle factories, was confiscated without lease-back rights. Candle factories had been a major source of church income, but the government took over and operated these facilities, along with incense and olive oil production, and then sold the manufactured items back to the churches at higher prices. Church cemeteries were also confiscated and then rented back to the highest bidder.[44]

Later the government had to deal with special situations. If there were fewer than twenty lay representatives to take responsibility for the church, this smaller group could form its own congregation and meet in private homes, but the church building was subject to closure. If there were more than twenty lay members but there was no church building, they were also permitted to worship in private homes, but either way home worship required a report to local authorities as to the time and place of each meeting. There were many instances where the Twenty simply could not keep up with the financial burden of maintenance, so it had no choice but to hand the church back to the government.[45]

The system of Twenties was progressive in one sense—it was a democratic reform providing laity with a stronger voice in church affairs. Since they, and not the priest alone, were responsible to the government, they deserved some decision-making power. In some regions they usurped the bishop's authority to call and dismiss priests, who could retain their posts only if they earned the moral and religious respect of their parishioners. Even regarding ritualistic practices, the voices of laity often dominated. Of course, on the clerical level this was not seen as progressive at all.

On the other hand, since the government no longer officially dealt with the church hierarchy, but only with Twenty as the legal trustee of individual churches, the Orthodox Church was vulnerable to fragmentation while the government remained intact. Indeed, this was the plan. Looking at it this way, the Bolshevik separation decree and its implementation made the Orthodox Church *more* dependent on the state than it had been under the tsars. In prerevolutionary times, the church was dependent on the state for financial subsidies, but after the Revolution the church—broken up into isolated pockets of parish self-rule— became dependent upon the state for its very legal existence and the use of church buildings. One could even argue that this contrived dependence was a violation of the separation decree itself, though there was no legal way to make the case.

By 1929 the law required that if one of the Twenty were arrested, defected from the parish, or died, the contract be invalidated; the entire bureaucratically rigorous and costly registration/contract process had to begin anew, including long questionnaires on the history of the parish and information on every member in it. Also, since the Twenty itself was not a legal entity (even though the government negotiated with it), each individual within it could be held liable for damage to the church or its contents—all government property.[46]

Churches and Bells

In 1914 there were almost 91,000 Orthodox churches and chapels in the entire expanse of Russia.[47] What kind of a dent in this number could Bolshevik administrative closings make? Although confiscation of church buildings and property occurred throughout the period under consideration and beyond, the half-dozen years following the end of the Civil War were the most "productive." Now the government could focus on the issue with less distraction.

The government seldom shut down churches by relying on brute force alone; usually it used one devious method or another to show the people that it stayed within the law ("Communist legality"). According to the separation decree, church closings were to be voted on by the affected communities, but there were many ways around this legal requirement. The most common method was to hold the vote at a time or place least likely to have believers present—at the workers' club or the factory (where believing workers, fearful of losing their jobs or promotions, would often abstain) or even at antireligious lectures. Another problem for the Orthodox faithful was that native and Protestant sectarians, perhaps still bitter over their treatment under the tsars, would sometimes vote with atheists to shut down their rival's churches (and sometimes vice versa).[48] In some localities the formality of a vote was simply dispensed with.

One rationale for closure was the condemnation of old and dilapidated church buildings to ensure public safety. In the past, subsidies from the tsarist state had paid for repairs, but these funds were no longer available. Many buildings had been constructed centuries ago, were made of wood in an extremely cold climate, and were true candidates for demolition, but soviets sometimes certified these buildings as dangerous long before this was technically true. Fifty of Moscow's churches, including the Chapel of Alexander II, were condemned by this method and leveled in December 1922.

In 1923 a new threat to church buildings emerged. The Supreme Soviet passed a law requiring fifty members of every congregation to fill out and sign a detailed questionnaire, which included queries into each member's past and present political beliefs. Parishioners, frightened by this intrusion even if their lives had been blameless, were nonetheless under great pressure to comply. Soviet authorities announced that if all the questionnaires were not completed by August, the church would be closed.[49] Perhaps government sociologists had valid reasons for gathering this data, but it fit in very neatly with the harassment of the antireligious campaign.

The press was anxious to report on church closures, as these five samples from various 1923 newspapers show:

1) Today the military cathedral was solemnly handed over to Komsomol. In the presence of a huge mass of workers, Red Army soldiers, Commu-

nists, and others, the president of the town council, Comrade Pievsov, handed over to the representatives of Komsomol the keys of the cathedral. The "Internationale" resounded from the belfries, performed by the wind orchestra. Red flags were hoisted. In the evening, the former military cathedral—from now on the Komsomol Club—lit up brightly with electricity. Over a sea of lights presided the red Communist Star.

2) The population in one of the villages in Ossetia has expelled the priest. The church property has been divided between the poorest [in the] population.

3) By order of the Moscow Soviet the Pymen Church has been closed. The Moscow soviet has issued an order for the closing of the Church of St. Alexander of Neva in village Vsesviatskoye [near Moscow] that is to be handed over to the "isolator" factory to be turned into a workers' club.

4) The Home Commissariat of the Crimea has declared the Cathedral of St. Alexander of Neva [in Simferopol] to be henceforth the Central State Museum for objects of religious worship. It is not to be used for religious services.

5) A great meeting was held at Petropavlovsk by the railway men of that station, at which almost all of them were present, over six hundred men. At that meeting was discussed the question of the church at Petropavlovsk. The workmen saw no use in keeping a church that was not visited by anybody except a few old women. When the question was put up at the meeting, only fifteen out of six hundred voted against closing the church. . . . The next question was what to do with the church. There were several proposals. The majority was for changing it into a club of the Communist Youth. The church with its golden cupola stands on a hill and overlooks the whole settlement. The golden cross on the cupola was hateful to the Communists and it was decided to remove it. Shortly afterwards, by means of a rope, a couple of men reached the cupola and removed the cross and hoisted the red flag instead. Only a few toothless women were crying. . . . The old folks standing outside were expecting God's punishment but nothing came.[50]

In May 1923 the government attempted to slow down the pace of church closures or at least to keep them legal.

[The Party Central Committee ordered the GPU] to investigate all cases of closure of churches. Should these have taken place with abuse of the Soviet legislation on the cults, the guilty ones ought to be made responsible for their acts.[51]

In June this message was dispatched to all party branches, but as it was never made public it would have been difficult for any church organization to take advantage of its protection.

What Happened to 1,003 Closed Orthodox Churches in 29 Provinces in 1925?

Source: "Statistical Review," July–September 1925, published by the Commissariat of Domestic Affairs

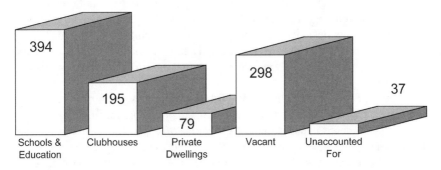

Schools & Education	Clubhouses	Private Dwellings	Vacant	Unaccounted For
394	195	79	298	37

In 1925 the government surveyed 29 out of 87 provinces as to the number of religious buildings seized to date. Closures in just those areas amounted to 1,003 Orthodox churches and 27 Old Believers' churches.

During 1927 only seventeen Orthodox churches were shut down, showing that the rate of closures had stalled.[52] One Western observer noted that of Moscow's 460 churches, most were still opened for services in that year, however many of the more beautiful churches, or those with great historical value, had been turned into state-operated museums depicting church exploitation of the people under tsarist rule. In Moscow the Uspensky Cathedral and the Arkhangelsky Cathedral inside the Kremlin as well as the Cathedral of Basil the Blessed on Red Square achieved this distinction.

The pace of closures picked up again in 1928, as authorities seized 359 Orthodox churches. *Komsomolskaya Pravda* reported in June that the city of Murmansk was left without a single church. When some "middle-class shopkeepers" announced their desire to build a new one, the city's soviet passed a sharply worded resolution preventing any such construction.[53]

The most disastrous year from the perspective of those trying to save their religious structures was 1929. With Stalin firmly in power and the collectivization of agriculture under way, there was a renewed effort to stamp out the alleged evils of faith. Church property suffered proportionately. As of 1928 over 2,000 Orthodox churches had been closed, but during 1929 alone 1,119 churches (of all Christian faiths) were shut down or converted to secular uses. The authorities closed seventy-three churches in Moscow alone during this year. Two of these closures involved traffic congestion:

- The Chapel of the Iberian Virgin had stood guard at the entrance of Red Square since 1669. Ivan the Terrible had prayed there after murdering his son, and Alexander I had prayed there as Napoleon's troops neared the capital. Soviet authorities now saw it as a public nuisance, calling it "the haunt of unclean beggars." In its position between two arched gateways, it also obstructed traffic, so one morning in July 1929 demolition began.

• Another church had been built by Alexander I to celebrate a military victory, but its designers purposely projected the edifice into the road so all who passed by would have to stop and admire its handsome green roof and gold onion domes. It, too, was demolished during the summer of 1929.[54]

Official Soviet figures list 3,350 Orthodox churches taken over during the first twelve years of the Revolution, while others put the figure slightly higher. In 1931 Stalin ordered even Moscow's Cathedral of Christ the Savior blown up. The planned replacement—a Palace of the Soviets mounted by a towering statue of Lenin three times higher than the Statue of Liberty—was never built. Later an outdoor swimming pool was constructed on the site.[55]*

Although one might easily consider Stalin himself to be the great abuser of "church property," he seemed to find this fault in others. In January 1930 he fumed that "great confusion" was pervasive in the atheist movement and that "extraordinarily stupid acts are sometimes committed which play into the hands of our enemies."[56] He insisted that church closings be consistent with the law. In March the Party Central Committee instructed local party organizations:

> Positively put an end to the practice of closing churches forcibly, fictitiously disguising it as the public and voluntary wish of the population. [You must] permit the closing of churches only when this is the genuine desire of an overwhelming majority of the peasants. . . . [We will] bring to the strictest accountability those guilty of mocking the religious feelings of peasant men and women.[57]

The Sixteenth Party Congress, also in March, supported this enjoinder and added that closings must follow approval by the regional, not just the local, soviet.[58]

Although the number of closures may seem quite substantial, it does not appear as sizeable when compared with the multitude of churches in all Russia. In tsarist times Moscow alone had been known, with some exaggeration, as "the city of forty times forty churches." Although the government listed 3,350 Orthodox churches shut down across the land, it also listed 35,000 remaining open. Of the 54,174 existing Orthodox churches at the start of World War I, only 6 to 8 percent had been lost, and, since the highest closure rates were in cities, rates in the countryside must have been much less. Thus Soviet accomplishments were hardly dramatic. The British journalist Henry Noel Brailsford observed in 1929, "Churches are as numerous in a Russian city, even in a big village, as

---

*The Cathedral of Christ the Savior was completely and faithfully rebuilt in 1995.

saloons are in England."[59]* Closures did not make church attendance impossible, just inconvenient.

Besides the buildings, there was the issue of revenue. Separation of the church from the state resulted in a tremendous loss of church income. As we saw earlier, by the end of the nineteenth century the Romanov Dynasty had been subsidizing the Orthodox Church (including paying the salaries of priests and supporting church schools) in amounts as high as 60 million rubles a year.[60] When the Bolsheviks cut off those subsidies, and other income was reduced, cathedrals that had cost fortunes to build could not be maintained. St. Basil's in Red Square had to suspend services, and the government, as noted, eventually converted it to a museum. When a lack of funds forced the closure of local churches, clergymen who depended on them for their incomes sank into destitution; their robes grew shabby and their faces became haggard and malnourished. Classified as nonworkers, they were often ineligible for ration cards during the post–Civil War famine.

What about building new churches? During the mid-1920s tens of thousands of peasants poured out of the countryside into the cities and industrial centers, and they brought their faiths with them. So in spite of old churches having been closed, these migrants collected money to erect new ones, often right next to the factories they worked in. Peasant pressure must have been great, because in 1928 the government stated that new houses of worship could be erected "without any hindrance"[61] and that when older church buildings were closed congregations could take all ikons, robes, and banners to their new churches. But a more accurate appraisal of government intentions can be gleaned from reading an article in *Bezbozhnik* published a week before this law took effect. If government policy was to close the churches, the author asked, why were new churches going to be permitted, and who was going to construct them? The author provided the answer to the second question: the abominable priests, merchants, and kulaks (wealthy peasants). He cited this example:

> In the village of Sheldan of Penza Province [southeast of Moscow], the kulaks have unlawfully fixed a certain sum to be given for the repairs of the church. When the poorest peasants proposed to help in building a steam mill and an electrical station instead of repairing the church, the kulaks did not allow them to speak.

The article ended by lambasting "counterrevolutionary church builders" and con-

---

*When counting, we must also consider the reliability of information. Some of the available data comes from Soviet sources, some from the Moscow Patriarchate, and some from overseas anti-Soviet publications. These sources, each for its own reason, exaggerated governmental success. In addition, some sources are unclear as to whether they are referring to the closure of only Orthodox churches, those of all Christian denominations, or those of all faiths. In any case, the vast preponderance of churches was Orthodox.

cluded that the *working class* did not need church buildings. Only "exploiters" were interested in taking the new law at face value!

The spate of church building was indeed brief. Believers in Odessa raised 100,000 rubles for a new church, and buildings were erected in Vyatka, Novgorod, and around Moscow. In Vladimir Province seven new churches were erected in 1928.[62] But RSFSR legislation passed in April 1929 put a quick end to the trend, requiring that for any new church construction an unspecified sum of money had to be deposited in the state treasury to "guarantee completion." By manipulating the sum, the government could effectively deny permission.

A final irony: There were many instances where soviet guards were called in to resist the depredations *of church members*, that is, protecting abandoned church buildings from the ravages of peasant looting. If lack of attendance had emptied a church, nearby villages would often strip it of valuable building materials—tin, iron, glass, lumber—and furniture. A soldier with a rifle posted outside was the only way to halt the destructive process.[63] In such cases, of course, the soviets were not guardians of the faith but rather protectors of an alternative use of the buildings.

*　　*　　*

Along with the closure and conversion of churches came the removal of their bells (usually atop a freestanding bell tower), but sometimes it was just the bells that were sought, and the church was left untouched. The purpose was not straightforwardly antireligious; Soviet industry was not yet producing at prewar levels, and there was a crying need for nonferrous metals to refuel it. Church bells happened to be made out of copper and bronze, and there were lots of them. Yaroslavsky estimated that if all the church bells in Russia were melted down they would provide over 300,000 tons of metals for the industry-starved nation. The slogan was: "Put bells in the smelters and put tractors in the fields." Although this plan was only partially implemented, many a bell ended up in the body of a tractor, an airplane, or a gun. When criticized, the government justified itself by pointing to the same practice during the French Revolution.[64]

For villagers there was quite an emotional attachment to the clarions that had called them to service for generations. Although the government was sensitive to the potential for disturbances and made all arrangements in secret, there was violence. During the winter of 1928–1929, *Komsomolskaya Pravda* reported an incident in a village in the Yegoryevsky district (near Moscow) in which the soviet decided to turn a church into a school. The church bell was lowered to the ground, but when a cart was brought to take it away the population became very distressed. Someone rang the village alarm bell, and peasants from miles around converged on the site. The newspaper described the scene:

They ran breathless for two or three miles, some were on horseback—two men riding one horse—disheveled women rushed along the village street weeping and wailing. One peasant threw himself on the bell and put his arms round it shouting, "Good Christians, Christ has suffered for faith and I too will die here."

The men who came to get the bell were beaten, and for two weeks the authorities could do nothing to quell the riotous situation. The peasants said they would hold onto the bell until spring when there would be war; then the godless government would fall. As always, the defenders of the bell were eventually overcome; in this case some of those arrested and tried received three to eight years' imprisonment, but one priest and one peasant were condemned to death and shot.[65]

RESISTANCE TO THE SEPARATION DECREE

Now then to you, who use power for persecuting your neighbors and for wiping out the innocent, we extend a word of admonition: celebrate the anniversary of your taking power by releasing the imprisoned, by ceasing bloodshed, violence, havoc, and restriction of the faith. . . . Otherwise all righteous blood shed by you will cry out against you [Luke 11:51], and with the sword will perish you who have taken up the sword [Matthew 25:52].

—Tikhon's November 8, 1918, letter to the Council of People's Commissars
(Sovnarkom)

Neither clergy nor laity accepted the takeover of church property without defiance and resistance. The sobor, while still in session, issued a vehement denunciation of the separation decree, and on February 7, 1918, Eugene Trubetzkoy read a list of grievances to the assembled delegates, characterizing the decree as hiding in a cloak of liberty and conscience while, in fact, attempting to murder the church:

> [The decree is] an act of open persecution of the Orthodox Church. . . . Those
> in power are threatening the very essence of the church and have issued the
> decree in pursuance of this satanic design.[66]

The sobor issued instructions on how to deal with government attacks, admonishing the priesthood "not to surrender anything whatsoever voluntarily to the plunderers of the church but to guard it according to the example of our pious ancestors." If forcible demand was made of any part of ecclesiastical or monastic property, the priest or monk was to refuse, "turning on the violators with appropriate words of exhortation," and parishioners were to sound the alarm by ringing church bells and sending out runners for assistance. Vessels and other objects necessary for the church service "should be protected by all possible means against desecration and destruction." Any attempt to remove a priest in a church or a teacher in a religious school should immediately be reported to higher church authorities. Tikhon also called for parish defense committees to protect church property and belongings (but to refer to these groups, for security reasons, as charitable and educational organizations).[67]

In spite of these brave exhortations, the hierarchy had a tough time persuading the clergy to adopt an uncompromising stand. Many village priests found it convenient to cooperate with the authorities, and certainly less dangerous. As a result, in April 1918 the sobor adopted disciplinary measures. Bishops, clerics, monks, and laity who resisted the authority of the church in this matter were required to appear before ecclesiastical courts. If found guilty they were forbidden to officiate; if they refused to repent they were defrocked. The sobor's disciplinary resolution threatened any community that had participated in violence and looting against their church with the closure of that church and the withdrawal of its clergy until all had repented and returned the stolen property.

Tikhon warned the laity that cooperating with the separation decree's implementation would be grounds for the heaviest penalties, including excommunication. To walk the fine line between the church's demand for resistance and the government's demand for compliance, opposition had to be expressed more subtly. Priests without a church or a parish became wanderers (as with the monks mentioned above). They would hide their cassocks in their bundles and dress as itinerant laborers, living off the donations of the faithful. They held services and conducted baptisms and weddings in believers' homes. In extreme cases, a wandering priest would have a wedding ring sent to him for a blessing and then send it back where a priestless ceremony would take place, or he would bless some Earth from a grave before sending it back for a funeral.[68]

Resistance often involved nonparticipation, as when Tikhon ordered believers not to be involved in government May Day celebrations in 1918, when the socialist holiday happened to fall on Wednesday of Holy Week. Sometimes resistance became obstructionist in nature, as when priests issued their own versions of the separation decree, sowing confusion among the population. They also wrangled with government agents over the details and dreamed up endless delaying tactics.[69]

Just as a criminal sentenced to hard time might use the prison's law library to file an endless stream of appeals, literate believers used the government's own proclamations, decrees, and laws (the letter of the law) to reverse their intent (the spirit of the law). As mentioned above, the government was concerned about adhering to "revolutionary legality" and thus found it difficult to ignore correctly filed petitions to the state's Central Executive Committee asking for a reversal of its own policies—the reopening of closed churches. When petitions and appeals were directed to head-of-state Mikhail Kalinin, who was known during the 1920s as having somewhat of a "soft heart" in this area, they were often successful.

Once this was understood, parishes sometimes abused Kalinin's weakness, bypassing intermediate levels of authority and going straight to the top. And sometimes they filled their petitions with exaggerations and obfuscations of the truth.[70]

But nonparticipation and obstruction were not sufficient, and violence ensued. In Voronezh a government agent was sent to a local monastery where an angry crowd promptly killed him. The Bolsheviks fired on religious processions in Orel and Kharkov. There were eleven deaths in Tula.[71] Nuns at the Krestod-vizhensk Monastery blocked the path of an approaching commissar and rang the alarm bells. Believers rushed to the rescue, and in the resulting confrontation a citizen was killed by gunfire and a Red Guard wounded. The sobor resolved on May 3, 1918, that priests in every parish should say special prayers for the "persecuted faithful and the martyrs" and hold a special mass every year on February 7 in memory of those who had died defending their faith.

On November 8, during celebrations of the first anniversary of the Petrograd uprising, Tikhon wrote a letter to the Council of People's Commissars (partially quoted in the epigraph above):

> The attacks on freedom in matters of faith are particularly painful and cruel. Not a day passes but the most monstrous calumnies against the church of God; angry blasphemy and sacrilege appear in your press. You mock the servants of the church. You force bishops to dig trenches and set priests to perform the meanest tasks. You have laid your hands upon the inheritance of the church, gathered together by generations of the faithful. . . .
>
> You have closed a whole series of monasteries and chapels without any pretext or reason. You have forbidden access to the Moscow Kremlin—that sacred patrimony of all the faithful. You are destroying the traditional framework of the ecclesiastical community—the parish. You are closing down brotherhoods and other charitable and educational institutions maintained by the church. . . .
>
> The blood of our brothers shed in rivers at your order cries to heaven and compels us to speak the bitter words of truth. You have given the people a stone instead of bread, a serpent instead of a fish. You have exchanged Christian love for hatred; in the place of peace you have kindled the flames of class enmity.[72]*

Since the government forbade church ownership of printing presses, hand-typed copies of the letter were distributed to bishops.[73]

As a direct result of his tirade, Tikhon was placed under house arrest in a Moscow facility owned by the St. Sergius-Trinity Monastery. Three Red Army soldiers guarded him day and night, and parishioner-bodyguards also watched over him. Since he had been deprived of his ration card, they made sure that he was brought food. (The authorities would release him the following spring in time for Easter.)[74]

---

*Another part of this letter forms this section's epigraph.

By now Tikhon was seeing the wisdom of modifying his rhetoric; struggle seemed less likely to result in success. He began urging his clergy to offer no provocation to government authorities, reminding them of the New Testament passage: "Submit yourselves to every ordinance of man" (I Peter 2:13). When Francis McCullagh interviewed Tikhon in April 1920, the patriarch commented:

> The state has separated itself from the church, and I think it has acted wisely; but it should therefore refrain from continually meddling, as it does, in ecclesiastical affairs.[75]

This meddling was based upon Lenin's analysis: "We have separated the church from the state, but we have not yet separated the people from religion."[76]

Church adjustments to Soviet reality would become a little easier over time, as more of those hierarchs who were unable to reconcile their religion with the Soviet system ended up either in prison, in exile, or dead. But die-hard Tikhonites held on to the antagonistic words of their leader's first year in office and ignored his later moderation. They were certain that the Bolsheviks would "break their necks on the church."[77]

Separation of church and state also meant separation of the school from the church. This would prove to be the more difficult of the two tasks.

8

HOW, THEN, ABOUT ELIJAH?

Religion and the Schools

The Bolshevik leadership was certainly aware that no religion could long survive without the capability of teaching its faith to its young. This was because conversion was rare, and church membership had to come from within the religious community. If only the mass and an occasional prayer remained, many would grow up outside of church influence. To ensure that this would happen, the government separated not only the church from the state but also the school from the church. As in any country, however, education was an entrenched system; getting rid of religion within the school system would be a slow process. Actually, the process had begun before the Bolshevik seizure of power, as on July 3, 1917, the Provisional Government had expropriated the entire Orthodox parish school system (which provided half of the elementary school education in Russia). When, in October, sobor delegates met with Alexander Kerensky over the issue, he was rude, informing them that this was the price of the church's freedom.[1] But before the sobor's objections could gather a head of steam, the church had to face a new enemy.

Although this chapter is not about the widespread problem of illiteracy, a brief mention should be made of the Bolsheviks' sincere desire to raise the cultural level of the Russian people, and the first step was learning to read. Aside from remaining in power, their primary goal was modernization. That, in turn, was impossible without first creating a literate society; their goal of spreading atheism throughout the school system was secondary. Literacy was pushed so hard that during the second year of the 1922–1923 famine, food in many districts was provided only for those men and women who showed up at school.[2]

IN PRAISE OF INERTIA

Thanks to the union of school and church, our young people were from their earliest years thralls to religious superstition, thus making it practically impossible to convey to their

159

minds any integral outlook upon the universe. To one and the same question (for instance concerning the origin of the world) religion and science give conflicting answers, so that the impressionable mind of the pupil becomes a battleground between exact knowledge and the gross errors of obscurantists.[3]

—Bukharin in *The ABC of Communism*, 1922

Secular education in the Western sense ran contrary to the entire spirit of Orthodoxy—it interfered with piety. Even within the realm of religious subjects, the church had never been a teaching institution. Through the mid-nineteenth century, the state, too, had resisted educational progress. Recall Chief Procurator Pobedonostsev—a holdover from the earlier approach—championing inertia and fulminating against rationalism. In his writings he pronounced "the spread of public education positively harmful."

But it was already too late for such a view. During the latter half of the nineteenth century it had become increasingly clear how far Russia lagged behind the West in every secular subject. Thus the tsarist government had begun constructing a broad, secular public education system through local self-government agencies known as *zemstva*. The new schools had a decidedly anticlerical bent, but religion was still a required part of the curriculum. To counter this trend, or at least compete with it, the Orthodox Church developed its own nationwide system of religious schools, applying for and (paradoxically) receiving large grants from the state. Pobedonostsev then betrayed his own government's efforts by suppressing public schools and backing parochial school development under the control of parish priests. By 1917 the church had created 59 seminaries (for 20,000 students), 200 ecclesiastical schools, and over 40,000 primary education parochial schools open to the common people, with several million students in attendance.[4]

Parochial schools not only propagated governmental decrees but also taught that the tsar was God's representative on Earth. They validated the Fundamental Laws (as revised in 1906), declaring that the tsar was to be obeyed out of duty recommended by God himself, and through the tsar God carried out his will for Russia. Paragraph 64 of these laws defined the tsar as the supreme protector and guardian of the dogmas of the Greek-Russian faith. Religious education had turned into a spiritual police force.

TEACHERS: NO TURNING ON A DIME

Religion is a brutalization of the people. Education must be so directed as to efface from the people's minds this humiliation and this idiocy.[5]

—from a December 26, 1922, Soviet decree

When the Bolsheviks took over the educational system at the end of 1917, they faced the challenge of undoing the work that the church, Pobedonostsev, and the Fundamental Laws had begun. On December 24 Lenin ordered the new Commissar of Education,* Anatoly Lunacharsky, to convert the 40,000 church schools into public schools and make certain that none of the 5 million students in *all* types of schools received any religious instruction.[6] The first task would be to teach the teachers, many of whom continued on with religious instruction no matter what the government ordered. The only way to ensure purely secular instruction was to hire purely secular instructors who would inculcate "a moral aversion to religion." Yet the requisite number of qualified atheistic instructors was never available during the 1920s.

Lenin's wife, Nadezhda Krupskaya, working in the Commissariat of Education, made a six-week school tour in the summer of 1919, and she was irritated to find ikons hanging in many schools.[7] And Bukharin, in his *ABC of Communism*, expressed exasperation that the religious outlook of the parents at home would immediately undermine the scientific outlook taught at school. He labeled the liberation of children from the influence of their reactionary parents as one of the highest priorities of the Soviet state and argued, "From the very onset the children's minds shall be rendered immune to all those religious fairy tales, which many grownups continue to regard as truth."[8]

The All-Russian Teachers' Union strongly opposed the abandonment of state-run religious education, to the point of calling strikes in four cities in early 1918. The government answered by forming a rival teachers' union—the All-Russian Union of Teachers-Internationalists—that was willing to cooperate. This tactic must have been ineffective, however, as when Soviet schoolteachers held their first congress in 1925 they still refused to endorse the separation decree and insisted that religion continue to be taught in the public schools. Lenin, Krupskaya, and Lunacharsky delivered antireligious lectures at teacher conferences in many cities trying to quell the disturbances.[9]

The problem was that almost all teachers subscribed to "rightist" views. Many were reluctantly willing to teach their subjects in a nonreligious manner, but most were loath to teach *anti*-religion, as was increasingly expected of them. Their reluctance was a matter of principle; there was a sincere belief that teaching so negatively was bad for the children. If religion was supposed to become less important in their pupils' minds, then it should be accomplished by instruction in the natural sciences.[10]

But there was also a matter of practicality. Many teachers feared their students' parents, both for the sake of the school and for themselves. As some irritably replied to Krupskaya, the ikons had to remain hanging to avoid parental rebellion.

---

*The Commissariat of Education was often referred to as the Commissariat of Enlightenment.

In many areas the community refused to support a school "where there was no law of God." They allowed the school building to deteriorate, refused to provide firewood for heating in the wintertime, or simply withdrew their children and sent them to the priest for a proper moral—though less academic—education.[11] And teachers had to live in the communities where they taught. Yaroslavsky described cases where the local soviet sent teachers packing when they were discovered to be antireligious propagandists.[12] Teachers also complained that their curriculum was already full, leaving no room for new subjects. In any case, pushing for *anti*-religion in the classroom ran counter to the party's recommendation for a "gentler approach," which will be discussed when we look at atheistic propaganda techniques in chapter 18. It was not so much that teachers were *counter*-revolutionary as it was that they were *un*-revolutionary (and often unpaid).

Although clergy of any denomination or rank were excluded from teaching, if an applicant renounced his ordination and left his former position he could teach, provided he received Commissariat of Education clearance. The Thirteenth Party Congress in 1924 estimated that at least 50 percent of Russia's public school teachers were the children of priests, and Lunacharsky conservatively estimated in 1929 that 30 to 40 percent of teachers were still believers.[13] He complained:

> The believing teacher in the Soviet school is an awkward contradiction, and departments of popular education are bound to use every opportunity to replace such teachers with new ones, of antireligious sentiments.[14]

Across the country there was no end to reports of teachers escorting their students to church during school hours and continuing the practice of classroom singing of religious hymns. Theoretically, if they could not bring themselves to teach as ordered they were either restricted in the subjects they could teach or were weeded out altogether. The Criminal Code formalized the punishment for teaching religion to children of tender age in public or private schools—"forced labor for a period not exceeding one year"—but the law was unenforceable. Full implementation would have decimated the teacher corps.[15]

To stimulate the educational bureaucracy, in March 1923 *Pravda* announced a contest to determine the best teacher in each area of the country, with one (of several) criterion of judging being "whether the teacher is endeavoring to eradicate the religious prejudices with which the surrounding milieu infects the children." The winner in Minsk province was V. Minkevich, whose merits included his success at teaching children not to cross themselves before meals and not to remove their hats before ikons.[16] *Pravda* described the province of Stavropol's winner—V. Malinotchka:

> [He was praised because] he systematically studies with other teachers the doctrine of historical materialism, gradually disposing . . . of idealistic notions.

Before Easter he gave a series of lectures . . . on antireligious subjects, and thus in an easy and interesting way exposed the cunning devices of the priests.[17]

Yaroslavsky told a story illustrating how frustrating nonreligious teaching could be. A second-grade teacher was explaining to the class the scientific origin of rain and thunder. She taught it practically and theoretically and was sure all the children understood, but before she could move on to the next subject a little boy suddenly asked, "How, then, about Elijah the Prophet?" Taken aback, she asked why he spoke about such fairy tales. The boy replied, "Oh, you must not say this; these are not fairy tales." It turned out that all the children had been taught at home or in church that thunder was caused when Judas, with fetters on his feet, ran away from hell with the Prophet Elijah shouting and chasing after him. He never caught up with Judas, and they continually ran around the world in this way spreading the sound of thunder.[18] In another instance, a militantly antireligious teacher put great effort into her final weekly lesson—an attack on priests. When she was finished and the school day ended, the students shouted in unison: "Tomorrow we go to church! Tomorrow we go to church!"[19]

Not only did the government have the problem of eliminating religious teachers, but also it had to get rid of the religious textbooks that the teachers used. It was a simple step to remove Bibles and religious works from school libraries so that children would not be subject to their "pernicious influence," but removal of textbooks was more problematic. Every book's lessons were riddled with religious imagery and examples. Warehousing or destroying these texts was unthinkable as there was nothing to replace them, nor would there be for quite a while.

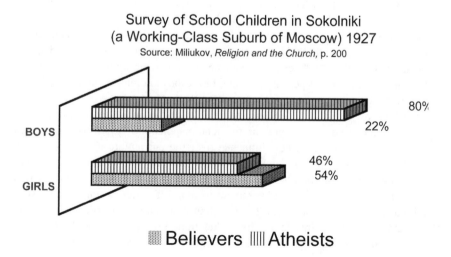

**Survey of School Children in Sokolniki
(a Working-Class Suburb of Moscow) 1927**
Source: Miliukov, *Religion and the Church*, p. 200

BOYS — 80% / 22%

GIRLS — 46% / 54%

▓ Believers ⦀ Atheists

POLICY AND METHODS

In [the Bolshevik] method of attack they proceed on the theory that religion is not the result of an inborn force or impulse, but of training, of something that is superimposed from without. If children, they declare, are reared without religious guidance, they will grow up to be nonreligious, and then religion will dry up at the source and will die of its own accord.

—Maurice Hindus, *Humanity Uprooted*, 1929

Public schools had to change if atheistic goals were to be reached. The separation decree barred the teaching of any religious dogma or religious prejudice in any state school or in any private school where general subjects were taught. Although this sounded clear enough, there was continued confusion as to exactly what was intended, and many controversies erupted over implementation. In March 1919 the Commissariat of Education issued a clarification (or reiteration): "The state is neutral in matters of religion . . . and hence it follows that the government cannot take upon itself the religious education of children."[20] Bukharin argued that if religious instruction in state-run schools were tolerated, the state would be offering "a ready-made audience of children" and free facilities to the teachers of "religious poison."[21] Later in the year the party program called for a completely proletarian and nonreligious education, but efforts in this area were perfunctory. While the Civil War was still being fought, Soviet newspapers reassured the peasantry that it would take a generation of rational education before religion in the schools could be eliminated.

As the war ended the task was begun in earnest. In 1921, following the Western penchant for "progressive education," the government introduced into the schools the Complex Method. The idea was to move beyond rote memorization and advance toward critical thinking. Students would learn through direct involvement in constructive projects and would have to figure things out for themselves. Lunacharsky argued that this, of necessity, removed religion from the curriculum, as the church already "knew" all those answers, leaving nothing to investigate. Religious instruction, if permitted, would block the children's natural curiosity.[22]

But there was also a step backward in 1921. Broke at the end of the Civil War, Moscow decided to decentralize funding of the public school system. An unintended consequence of passing financial responsibility to local communities was that it also passed a new influence over the curriculum to the religiously minded parents of the students (as we saw above). Monks and priests were increasingly brought into the schools to teach religious lessons.[23] And there was constant backsliding for the government to fend off. After having initially submitted to Moscow's mandates, the Karelian Autonomous Territory (bordering Finland) applied to reinstate religious education in its secular schools. The government, not willing to give anything back, sent this no-nonsense reply:

The idea that man can fulfill his high destiny only on the basis of the Gospel is erroneous. It is obvious that religious education results in stupidity. As the Soviet government is responsible for the children of the country, it must prevent the minds of these children from being darkened by religious superstition.[24]

At the Twelfth Party Congress in 1923 members were reminded that "all our antireligious agitation and propaganda will fail to affect the masses until the program of urban and rural education . . . moves off dead center"[25] and that religious prejudices could not be eradicated until illiteracy had been eradicated.

As mentioned above, there had been a push through the mid-1920s to switch from simply eliminating the religious message in the schools to an active assault on religious thinking among students. By 1927–1928 this was slowly being implemented. Instead of insisting that all instruction be merely "nonreligious," Lunacharsky sent out directives that all primary and secondary schools develop a 100 percent antireligious program, whether or not they had the teachers to teach it, but this did not stop Yaroslavsky from complaining at a December 1928 Party Central Committee meeting about Lunacharsky's tolerance of lingering "neutrality" in the schools.[26] Partly due to policy confusion and personal rivalries, by 1929 this program, as well as the teaching of evolution, was just getting under way. But at least by 1929 religious holidays (temporarily) could no longer be school holidays, and all public schools were free of overt (if not covert) religious instruction.

RELIGIOUS INSTRUCTION OUTSIDE OF PUBLIC SCHOOLS

The teaching of religious doctrine to persons under age in public and private schools is to be punished by hard labor for a maximum term of one year.[27]

—Article 121 of the 1922 Criminal Code

Another educational issue the Soviets had to deal with was the constitutionally protected right of religious propaganda *outside* of the public schools. What could this propaganda entail and to whom could it be directed? The 1918 separation decree allowed religious instruction to those under eighteen in private homes, but a Commissariat of Education decree in March 1919 contradicted this provision by stating, "Teaching religious doctrine to persons younger than eighteen years is not permitted." Confusion reigned for two years, as some interpreted the law to mean no *organized* religious education in private homes was permissible, while others thought that none at all was allowed. Finally, on April 23, 1921, a clarification was issued, stating that homes should not become "regularly functioning educational institutions managed by the clergy."[28]

Trying to get it right, the government issued a follow-up decree in January 1922 forbidding the teaching of religion to children before or during school age when assembled in churches and other ecclesiastical buildings. It further stated that all churches, prayer houses, chapels, temples, and synagogues were confined to "confessional associations." These buildings could be used *only* for religious services and ceremonies, not to educate the young. To do otherwise, the decree explained, would allow education previously banned in church schools to simply continue inside the churches.

In September 1923 the Commissariat of Justice promulgated a new law, going even further: Children under eighteen legally belonged to no religion whatsoever, the protestations of their parents notwithstanding. The penal code mandated forced labor for up to a year for any parent making such an assertion, the same penalty mandated for teaching religious doctrine to persons under age in public and in private schools. In July 1924 another decree forbade teaching religion inside church buildings, and in September yet another decree limited the number of children who could be given private religious lessons in a home to the children who lived in that home plus three neighbors.[29]

When challenged on the contradiction between the constitutional guarantees of religious propaganda and the obstacles placed in the way of teaching religion to minors (when its effectiveness was greatest), a spokesman for the Commissariat of Justice pointed out with some justification that the ingrained conservatism of the church prevented it from taking advantage of opportunities that still existed. Why, he asked, had the church not adapted to conditions by offering religious instruction within the church service? He knew, of course, that sermons were only recently being experimented with as a part of the Orthodox liturgy. One opportunity that the church did take advantage of was simply disobeying the law by taking church schools underground. It was impossible for Soviet authorities to ferret out even a minority of these secret academies.

UNIVERSITIES AND SEMINARIES

By the late 1920s deeply religious parents were not only having difficulty with public primary and secondary schools but also were finding it increasingly difficult to get their children into universities. When the doors of higher education were closed to them they faced a cruel dilemma: whether to deny their faith or deny their children a future.

Within the universities themselves, there were two developments: the renewed teaching of religion (for atheistic purposes) in regular universities and the creation of special antireligious universities. Higher education no longer abandoned instruction on religion but created chairs for the History of Religion—essentially, chairs of Atheism. They taught courses in primitive religion, ancient Eastern religions, the religions of Greece and Rome, old Israelite religion, and the origin and development of Christianity. Yaroslavsky created an antireligious seminar within the Sverdlov Communist University in 1921. Moscow's Antireligious Seminary opened its doors in November 1922, with courses taught by such luminaries as Ivan Skvortsov-Stepanov, Peter Krasikov, and A. V. Galkin.[30] Armed with an impressive antireligious library, the seminary's purpose was to train propagandists and agitators to take the atheist case into the field.

In 1924 the government founded the Society of Militant Materialists (not to be confused with the League of Militant Atheists) to spread materialism among university professors, scholars, and scientists. The group was associated with the periodical *Under the Banner of Marxism*.[31] Atheism was especially stressed, of course, at the Institute of Red Professors (1921–1938), which supplied the political and economic elite for the new Soviet empire. By the end of 1926 there were sixty-eight antireligious seminaries in Russia. The trade unions even operated Evening Universities of Atheism for workers not on the academic track.[32]

By 1929 there were arrests in the universities of believing professors. The Russian Academy of Sciences was purged, with many scholars shipped off to Siberian camps.[33]

*   *   *

When a student reached eighteen, he could attend special theological courses preparing him for the priesthood, providing that the curriculum hewed closely to theological subjects and did not cut too wide a path encompassing politics or full scholastic instruction. No adult religious instruction was permitted outside of the seminaries.[34]

In early May 1923 the Commissariat of Justice narrowed the opportunities open to aspiring priests, requiring that theological courses be organized only in large cities (presumably so they could be watched more closely) by small groups of private citizens (not the church hierarchy). They had to list the details of the curriculum, the conditions under which the courses were to be presented, and the instructors' names. With this information in hand, applicants still required consent from the provincial Executive Committee and the Commissariats of Education and Justice.

By 1927 there was no theological training facility run by the traditional Orthodox Church.

Whether in Great Russia, White Russia, or the Ukraine, the suppression of Orthodox clergy could not be accomplished unless their status in communities was lowered and respect for them diminished. What techniques could the Bolsheviks use to degrade the hierarchs and the priests in the people's eyes?

9

PARADES MOVING ALONG EMPTY STREETS

Bolshevik Attempts to Socially Undermine the Clergy

Mikhail Bukharin noted in 1919 that the separation of church and state had been relatively easy so far—almost an "effortless task for the proletarian power." But he knew that it would be incomparably more difficult to fight against the intractable religious prejudices whose roots had burrowed deeply within the mass consciousness. He urged patience and firmness, but he realized that little could be accomplished until the entire church hierarchy was demystified and discredited. This chapter probes the methods the party and the government used to undermine the clergy—sapping, in the military sense, until all above ground collapsed. Their techniques ranged from exposing fraud within the monasteries to creating substitutes for Christian holidays.

RESIDENCE, CITIZENSHIP, WORK, AND TAXES

All persons engaged in nonproductive labor and not living on labor wages, . . . are not entitled to enjoy full civil rights on equal terms with the working population of the Republic.

—the Commissariat of Justice, April 1920

A significant step in removing clergy from the social life of the nation was denying them the normal rights of citizenship. The government declared archbishops, bishops, priests, deacons, monks, and ministers to be "servitors of the cult," among those without rights. The restrictions placed upon them involved residence, citizenship, work, and taxes. The party even exhorted its members not to marry their children.

Consistent with the Soviet claim that there was no such thing as a national church organization—only local parishes—the government prevented bishops from living in their dioceses. Especially from the mid-1920s on, Russian bishops were confined to Moscow, and Ukrainian bishops were held in Kharkov. By the end of the decade over sixty diocesan bishops were stuck in Moscow.[1]

According to Article 65 of the 1918 Constitution, along with imbeciles, criminals, capitalists, and former members of the tsar's secret police, "monks and spiritual servitors of churches and religious cults have no vote and no right to be elected to the soviets."[2] Losing the vote within a Communist system may not seem like a great loss, but symbolically it was a demotion to the lowest ranks of society. Whereas in bourgeois countries the franchise was determined by gender, educational background, property ownership, income, or age, in socialist Russia it was based upon the nature of one's work. Only those engaged in "productive labor" were entitled to the full rights of citizenship; from the Bolshevik perspective "servitors of the cult" were clearly nonproductive. According to a Commissariat of Justice decree in July 1920, if a cleric refused to accept compensation for religious duties and found a constructive job his right to vote would be restored.[3] (In the Stalin Constitution of 1936, with Europe in turmoil and national unity paramount, the right of priests to vote was restored. It removed the category of "those deprived of rights.")

During the hungry times of the 1920s, priests were permitted only the smallest food rations and were frequently refused ration cards altogether. Even with ration cards, priests could not always count on government stores selling to them. A 1928 law required priests purchasing food in cooperative stores to pay a special deposit in advance or be denied the privilege of shopping there. Although occasionally they were allowed to work for the government, they were banned from the Commissariats of Education, Justice, and Agriculture. Priests were not permitted anywhere near the state educational system, and even ex-priests could teach only with special dispensation. Their children were often denied access to schools above elementary grades. The tremendous pressures on priests forced many family quarrels. Children often begged their fathers to defrock themselves, or, short of that, asked that they be adopted by nonclerical aunts and uncles to hide their family origins and improve their job prospects.[4]

In February 1921 Sovnarkom forbade priests from working in any capacity whatsoever on a collective agricultural unit (this law had little practical effect, however, until the actual collectivization of agriculture in 1929). Since they could not join trade unions,* many churchmen had to resort to manual labor to stay alive. Any such civilian work would be at the provincial level where priests were required to wear civilian clothes. In April 1923, for example, *Izvestia* reported the case of an unemployed priest who applied for work as an ordinary laborer in the Zadonsky Mines; the workers' committee consented to give him the job, but only on the condition that he first doff his cassock. Occasionally longhaired men in robes were seen selling newspapers on the streets.[5]

---

*These were not unions in the capitalist sense. Obviously workers could not be allowed to go on strike against management when management was the state. They were more like factory clubs and were conduits for indoctrination.

In 1922 the government ordered that no one under eighteen was to be employed on church premises. Priests were barred from joining local cultural or enlightenment groups. Too much damage might be done by allowing close contact with workers or peasants who were still unsophisticated and politically naive. Thus priests became pariahs in their own communities.

All through the 1920s higher tax rates for priests (as well as other "class enemies") persisted. In 1928 the government passed an additional law requiring that priests pay taxes on all sources of income, and the information upon which these taxes were based could come from any "information available to the fiscal authorities," thus opening the law to arbitrary interpretation and abuse. A Sovnarkom decree in May 1929 classified even poor priests as kulaks and raised their taxes even higher. For many in the clergy these taxes rose to prohibitive levels, and, since tax increases were concurrent with rent increases, many were forced out of their homes.[6]

All these discriminatory practices were perfectly consistent with the RSFSR Constitution. Article 23 read:

> Where the interests of the working class as a whole are threatened, the RSFSR has the right to deprive particular individuals or particular groups of individuals of the rights which they abuse to the detriment of the Revolution and of the Soviet Republic.

The quasi-governmental League of Militant Atheists, at its Second Congress in 1929, even resolved that the clergy should be completely ostracized, suggesting, for example, that workers and peasants never invite a priest into their homes.[7]

The laws seem, however, to have gone too far too soon, and the resultant backlash forced reconsideration. *Izvestia* on March 23, 1930, published the government's retraction. The Presidium of the Central Executive Committee of Soviets announced "the unconditional elimination of additional restrictions" on priests and their families.[8]

MOCKERY

The population, and not only the faithful, looked upon this hideous carnival with dumb horror. There were no protests from the silent streets—the years of terror had done their work—but nearly everyone tried to turn off the road when they met this shocking procession. I, personally, as a witness of the Moscow carnival, may certify that there was not a drop of popular pleasure in it. The parade moved along empty streets, and its attempts at creating laughter or provocation were met with dull silence on the part of the occasional witness.[9]

—George Fedotov

In Petrograd during 1919 and 1920, Lunacharsky staged impressive festivals—street theater—emphasizing the party's purity and its heroic martyrs. Lenin, however, squelched these non-Marxist, nonmaterialist, and utterly idealistic efforts, at least while he was still healthy enough to care. When he fell ill in late 1921 these spectacles returned with a vengeance, most noticeably the Komsomol Christmas that ran from December 25, 1922, through January 7, 1923.[10] Dreamed up by Ivan Skvortsov-Stepanov several years earlier, the spectacle was now hurriedly organized by Komsomol, whose branches received instructions to "put on mass carnivals portraying the ancient pagan gods as prototypes of Christ"[11] and to satirize them. Presumably ridiculing all the "dead" gods and parodying the clergy would make a strong antireligious point with the masses. But these demonstrations were badly conceived and poorly prepared. They quickly got out of control.

Wild pageants erupted in the largest cities, mocking and ridiculing the Christian celebration of Jesus's birth. Young, working-class atheists paraded through the streets carrying effigies of God, Jesus, the Virgin Mary, and religious leaders of every other faith they could think of. They dressed up as priests, monks, rabbis, mullahs, and shamans, while others taunted and mocked them. An article in *Izvestia* described some of the characters: a yellow-robed Buddha, a Marduk of Babylon, the Mother of God, the pope in a fancy motor car blessing the people, the monk riding on a coffin full of holy relics, a priest offering to marry anyone for a price, a Protestant pastor, a Jewish rabbi, and a group of devils with long tails and horns bringing up the rear. Many revelers paraded up and down the streets carrying red Christmas trees. Open trucks rolled by with clowns mocking God. One showed God embracing a naked woman; others carried "priests" shouting parodies of church liturgy. Caught up in their own gaiety, they turned town dwellers' pigs loose in the streets and ripped crosses off churches. Some Komsomol youth stood outside churches during services, singing loudly, "Down with the priests, down with the monks. We will climb to heaven and chase away the gods."[12] After dark in Moscow the revelers threw cardboard effigies of the gods into a bonfire, and *Pravda* reported, "They burned as though they were alive; they shriveled, their heads drooped, and their hands shook." Then the hell-raisers danced around the fire singing atheist parodies of Christmas carols. The original goal was to demonstrate that all religions had a common origin and that all clergy exhibited common behavior, but it turned into an officially sanctioned drunken street party.[13]

There seemed no end to the fun for mockers and despoilers, but would pranks, burlesques, and insults to the vast majority of viewers contribute to atheistic conversions? Initially the Soviet press reported that Komsomol Christmases had been staged all over Russia—a frequently quoted number was 417 cities—but within a few weeks there were admissions that the figure was much smaller and that in Moscow itself attendance had been disappointing. The blunt approach was clearly a disaster. Besides Lenin's theoretical and practical objections, there was the superficial nature of these events. Urban parades and hoopla were inadequate to compete with centuries-old traditions in the villages tied to the Orthodox Church calendar. As we have seen, peasant life was connected to an unvarying cycle of backbreaking work punctuated by feasts held on saints' days or other religious holidays. Feasts were intimately social and often morally permissive, featuring drinking, brawling, and a little illicit sex. The next day they would all be forgiven. A Bolshevik street spectacle was nonparticipatory; observers simply watched others perform. There was nothing endearing or enduring to it.

The Party Commission on the Separation of Church and State denounced the Komsomol Christmas in February 1923, before the Komsomol Easter even got started. It portrayed this winter "carnival" as frivolous, urged the production of more substantial propaganda, and asked whether insulting the population was the correct method of winning it over to materialist thinking. (No such events were held from 1924 through 1927, but they resumed in 1928 under different circumstances, to be discussed later.)[14]

THE USES OF PAPIER-MÂCHÉ

Whosoever uses fraudulent devices to excite the superstitious spirit of the masses or to obtain profit for himself is liable to imprisonment or hard labor for a maximum term of one year.

—Article 120 of the 1922 Criminal Code

Raising the Dead (1919)

A banging on the door jarred Father Theodosius awake. This was a monastery of little importance, on the gentle slopes of the Ural Mountains near Ekaterinburg, so who could be calling so rudely and so early? Donning his black robe and brushing down his matted hair with his hands, he pulled hard to open the wooden door and found himself facing an official delegation.

There stood Vasily Alexandrovich Kuskov—whom the monk vaguely remembered as chairman of the local soviet—backed up by a Bolshevik official from the regional soviet, a crowd of around ten unknown persons, and a film crew. Theodosius knew that at this hour he should have been at prayer—perhaps this was God's long-awaited punishment. Kuskov demanded access to the reliquary, where the "incorruptible" body of St. Philip of Moscow had been shown to the faithful—and had healed the faithful—for over a hundred years.

Not sure of what response to make, and with the other monks praying out of earshot on the far side of the monastery, Theodosius reluctantly accepted his punishment and turned the key to the door of the stone-block building. The cinematographer set up his tripod with a clear view of all that would transpire and turned on his battery-operated lights to overcome the darkness inside. A sarcophagus, apparently constructed of papier-mâché, sat in the center of the room. On its top was a hole about two inches square through which peasants from many generations and miles around had peered, straining in the candlelight to glimpse the holy relic. On their way out, uplifted and perhaps cured, they had left small offerings of food or coins for the monks.

Kuskov, with cameras rolling, pulled out a pocketknife and slit the sarcophagus all the way round, then ordered Theodosius to lift the lid. Inside, illuminated as never before, the gawking assemblage witnessed a shriveled figure fashioned of crumpled cardboard and glued goat's hair. As the monk pulled the artifact from its "ancient tomb," his face flushed, and in faltering words he muttered, "One must get by." He then signed a preprinted affidavit acknowledging that no sacrilege had occurred.

Weeks later a truck made a tour of nearby villages, and the antireligious agitators triumphantly showed the film in the evening. But somehow, the glee of exposure was diminished by all-too-frequent peasant remarks, all sounding faintly reminiscent of "One must get by."

Propaganda Dropped in the Bolsheviks' Lap

Bukharin wrote in 1919:

> An excellent weapon in the struggle against the church has been employed recently in many parts of the Republic, namely the opening of "incorruptible" relics. This has revealed to huge throngs of fervent believers the gross charlatanism, which is at the base of all religion and of Russian Orthodoxy in particular.[15]

Revealing the fraudulent nature of venerated relics was an early method of undermining clerical dignity and respect. The process lasted roughly from mid-1918 to December 1920 and involved sixty-five inspections.[16] The object was both exposure of monastic mendacity and demystification of religion. Alexander Solzhenitsyn described one of the earliest cases where Soviet officials visited Father Superior Ion at the Zvenigorod Monastery and ordered him to turn over the holy relics of Saint Savva. Not only did the officials smoke behind the iconostasis and refuse to remove their caps, one of them took Savva's skull in his hands and spit into it, demonstrating that its sanctity was an illusion. The monks rang the church bells and a popular uprising ensued, resulting in one of the officials being killed.[17] Why were relics of saints such a life-and-death matter?

The Second Council of Nicaea in 787 affirmed, and the Council of Trent in 1546 (respected by Catholics only) reaffirmed, that no church could be consecrated without the presence of saintly relics. In medieval Europe the prestige of a church had depended on the value of a sacred relic on or under the altar. Orthodox (and Catholic) theology taught—and still does teach—that the human body and the soul upon death are sanctified and transfigured. They believed the Grace of God was present in saints during their lives and remained active in their relics long after death, but apparently not indefinitely. God used these relics as channels of divine power and as an instrument of healing. Thus the bones or other mummified organs of long-deceased saints were venerated. The supporting biblical passage was "Nor wilt thou suffer thine Holy One to see corruption" (Acts 2:27).

From the example of Christ's bodily ascension to heaven, Orthodox fathers concluded that after the millennium God would lift the pure and uncorrupted forms of *all* his earthly creation—organic and inorganic, living or dead—to exist with him eternally. The Russian Orthodox Church took the position that a saint's relics were helpful in interceding with God whether they remained in their burial condition or turned to dust. It did not *officially* state that the relics of saints were incorruptible, and it did not officially endorse the practice of relic veneration. It did not have to, as the belief had deep roots in popular and traditional religion. (Readers of Dostoevsky's *The Brothers Karamazov* might remember the scandal that ensued when the saintly Father Zossima's remains began to smell within twenty-four hours of his death.)

Aside from cases of out-and-out fraud, the church did not interpret reverence for bodily remains as being based on ignorance or superstition but rather as coming from a highly developed theology of the body. Parish priests encouraged in their parishioners a deep sense of the sanctity of these relics, and these remains played a large role in the religious lives of the common people. Peasants made pilgrimages from many miles away to see them, to express their faith, and to receive whatever benefits each particular saint's remains were supposed to impart. The church gained a significant portion of its revenues from the monetary gifts these pilgrims offered.[18]

The popular belief in the incorruptibility of saints' bodies may have developed among ancient hermits at the Pechersky Monastery in Kiev. Due to the ascetic lives their owners led, bodies there were especially well preserved. Living alone in caves, sleeping in coffins, and taking little food until death were, they believed, sufficient for salvation. Some buried themselves alive, leaving only a small hole through which a little bread and water could be passed. Some lived this way for years, gradually reaching the limits of emaciation and expiring of starvation and in filth. When several days passed and nothing was heard from such an ascetic, the other monks sealed the opening, declared him to be a saint, and consoled themselves with the knowledge that he had passed to his heavenly rest and joy. Because these bodies so gradually shriveled from undernourishment and were so desiccated, they decayed slowly after death. Their remaining flesh was mummified, and they were labeled the "incorruptible ones." Practices of this sort were still going on in the early years of the twentieth century.[19]

After the success of the Pechersky Monastery, other monasteries sought to acquire mummy-saints and to benefit from the huge crowds—and contributions—they attracted. Pechersky, however, had a limited supply. Monasteries all over Russia then resorted to the next best thing; they manufactured their own mummified saints out of whatever materials were available: wax, plaster, cardboard, and cotton stuffing. The practice grew, partly motivated no doubt by the unchristian trait of envy. *Their* saints were no less saintly than those of the Pechersky Monastery and therefore ought to be equally incorruptible. If remains were stolen from others, no shame was felt, as obviously the spirit of the departed saint would not allow the theft unless he or she desired to move.

Russian Protestants, of course, were disdainful of this practice. The Evangelical missionary Ivan Prokhanov wrote:

> The priests fostered the idea among the people that they could receive healing, blessing, and even forgiveness of sins by such acts of worship. Really it was a kind of fetishism, or idol worship, and a great tragedy in many lives. Millions of people, called Christians, were worshipers of these relics. . . . This was a great barrier to the acceptance of the Gospel.[20]

The first government inkling of this centuries-old manufacturing process was in October 1918 during a routine inventory of the Alexander Svirsky Monastery in Olonetsk province. Authorities discovered that the massive silver sarcophagus of Saint Alexander Svirsky contained not an incorruptible body but a wax effigy. The exposure of this hoax caused great consternation and indignation among priests and the public.[21] One priest left the church after addressing this letter to his bishop:

> The relics of Alexander Svirsky, which were disclosed to be a figure of wax, showed a blasphemous exploitation of the common people by a group of selfish monks. You, the high clergy, could not be ignorant of this deception, but you hid it from us, the common priests, and the people in general. You allowed the worship of idols in place of saints, encouraging it by your own example and preaching. You intentionally darkened the eyes and minds of the people and deceived trusting Russia. Woe to you when the enlightened people rise and move on you in their terrible anger, demanding an answer and an accounting which you will be unable to give.[22]

On March 1, 1919, the government issued a decree that all containers holding relics of saints be opened, with the stipulation that exposures not be carried out during church services. In the process, more examples of the monasteries' handiwork were uncovered. At Voronezh, Bolsheviks accompanied by church officials and lay observers opened the relics of Saint Mitrofan, a contemporary of Peter the Great. Inside the sarcophagus was an imitation body stuffed with cotton. When confronted with the evidence, the local archbishop is said to have commented, "It is, of course, very sad to look at such a thing."[23] One of the observers lamented:

> Until the examination of the relics I, as a believer, stood in the church feeling fear in my heart. When the relics were opened and the deception was revealed all my faith vanished and gave way to a sense of disgust and contempt for this brazen deception.[24]

The St. Sergius-Trinity Monastery, forty-four miles north of Moscow in Zagorsk, was one of the most popular and hence one of the richest monasteries in Russia. It featured two cathedrals, six churches, and the highest bell tower in Russia. Within its walls were buried the "uncorrupted" remains of Saint Sergius of Radonezh and several other saints. When news leaked out that government authorities were planning a visit, Patriarch Tikhon asked for an appointment with Mikhail Kalinin. Since the church was now separate from the state, and the law protected the "religious conscience of the believers," he hoped to persuade the government not to touch the holy relics that lay there. The chairman was "busy," however, and the meeting never took place.[25]

When the authorities arrived in April 1919—after working their way through protective crowds—their investigation led to the greatest of church scandals. The relics of St. Sergius, along with those of St. Tikhon of Zadonsk, were proven to be another hoax. The authorities, anticipating what they might find, made a full-scale show of the exposure. To prove their "impartiality" they brought along monks, doctors, and archaeologists to witness the proceedings. Although the crowds deterred them from removing the "bodies," they filmed the opening of the sarcophagus. This film, once again, was used to demonstrate the perfidy of the church—with the (unrealistic) hope that ignorant peasants would quickly be turned into unbelievers. The monastery itself was promptly turned into an antireligious museum. Authorities continued on, revealing the fraudulent relics of Sts. Michael the Pious and Arseny the Miracle Worker in Tver, of Sts. Vasily and Constantine in Yaroslavl, and scores of others.[26]

The journalist Louis Fischer, writing from Russia at the time, added this anecdote to the litany of church sins:

> In 1619 a boy named Gabriel had been found dead in a hamlet near the Polish town of Bialistok. It was alleged that he had been killed by Jews who wanted Christian blood for ritual purposes. The body, it was said, had been cast into the open field and had lain there for ten days, while dogs guarded it against the

Constantine Pobedonostsev
Championing Peasant Ignorance
(Credit: The David King Collection, London)

Grigory Rasputin
Giving Orthodoxy a Bad Name

John of Kronstadt
Sainthood in the Eyes of the Beholder
(Credit: The David King Collection, London)

Grigory Zinoviev
Petrograd Party Boss

Patriarch Tikhon (Belavin)
Resisting through Humility

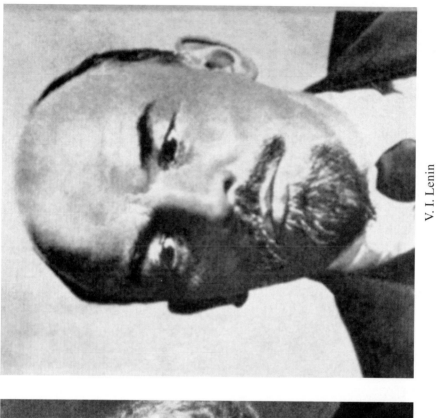

V. I. Lenin
A Pragmatic Atheist
(Credit: Library of Congress [LC-USZ62-1018771])

Karl Marx
Religion as the Opium of the People
(Credit: The David King Collection, London)

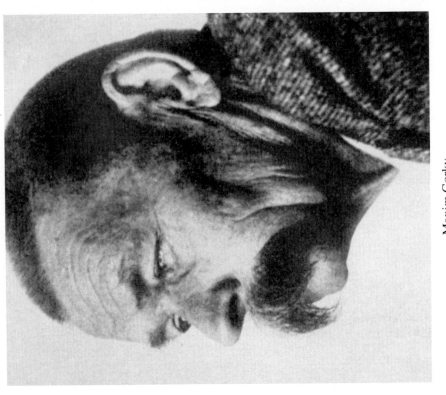

Maxim Gorky
Fighting Religion through Godbuilding

Leon Trotsky
Supporting Simplistic Solutions

Nikolai Bukharin
Bolshevik Theoretician
(Credit: The David King Collection, London)

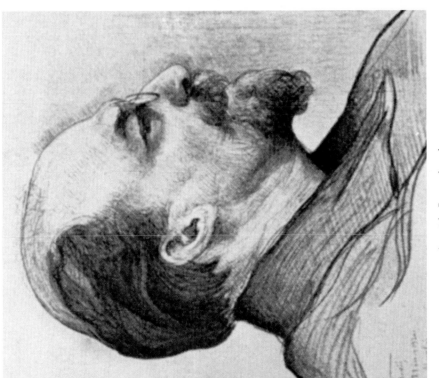

Anatoly Lunacharsky
Creating God-free Schools

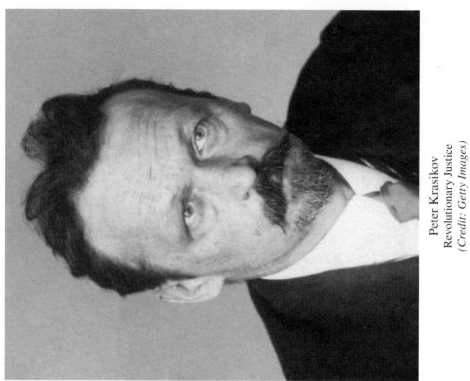

Peter Krasikov
Revolutionary Justice
(Credit: Getty Images)

Joseph Stalin in 1919
Continuing the Assault on Churches
(Credit: The David King Collection, London)

Mikhail Kalinin
Head of State
(Credit: The David King Collection, London)

Nikolai Krylenko
Atheist Prosecutor
(Credit: The David King Collection, London)

Nadezhda Krupskaya
Lenin's Revolutionary Partner
(Credit: The David King Collection, London)

George Chicherin
Representing Atheism Abroad
(Credit: The David King Collection, London)

attacks of hungry wolves. Gabriel was made a saint. In 1755 the body was removed to a convent in the nearby town of Slutzk.

In 1916 it was brought to Moscow and placed in a niche in the great St. Basil's Cathedral. Peasants came from all parts of Russia to see it and worship before it. Men and women laid gifts before it and asked for happiness. The priest who accompanied visitors always made it a point to state that although originally the body had not been given proper burial, it had nevertheless miraculously remained intact through all the centuries.

In October 1919 the coffin was opened by the Bolsheviks in the presence of a professor of anatomy of the Moscow University and of a number of church dignitaries. It was found to contain only a board on which was fastened the leg bone of some animal.[27]

The propaganda value of these exposures was a windfall. Cardinal Gasparri in Rome had written to the Soviet government complaining of the ill treatment of the Orthodox Church, but Foreign Affairs Commissar Chicherin must have relished the task of replying. Much of his letter was devoted to the issue of relics:

> You inform us that the Supreme Head of the Roman Catholic Church implores us to change our attitude toward the Orthodox clergy. This sign of solicitude for them, however, arrives at the moment when an open and determined action of our popular authorities has nullified the frauds through which the clergy deceived the masses and on which they based their ascendancy.
>
> Golden sepulchers glittering with precious stones, containing what the clergy called incorruptible saintly relics, were opened, and in the place where supposedly should be present the relics of Tikhon of Zadonsk [and a long list of saints] there were discovered some rotting bones crumbling into dust, a lot of cotton wool, cushions, dresses, and even women's stockings.[28]

If some might think it unfair to throw Orthodox failings in the face of the papal leadership, Catholic relics were uncovered as well. In August 1919 authorities decided to expose the remains of St. Andrew Bobola in Polock (in White Russia, near Vitebsk). Protests by the Catholic archbishop and, even more importantly, by Catholic workers at the nearby Putilov Factory caused postponement of this project until 1922.[29]

In a 1919 letter to Peter Krasikov, Lenin championed the cause of relic exposure and urged that films of these events be shown all over Moscow.[30] In that same year, the Commissariat of Justice issued this statement:

> In all cases disclosing charlatanry, trickery, falsification, and other criminal acts, intended for the exploitation of ignorance, . . . [the government] shall start criminal proceedings against all guilty persons.[31]

In some of the more egregious cases priests were charged with criminal fraud, and a few trials actually took place. One was in November 1920 in Novgorod where a Bishop Aleksy was convicted of sneaking homemade "remains" out of a coffin just before a scheduled inspection. The authorities mercifully suspended his sentence of five years' imprisonment. In many instances the monks claimed that the interred saints *themselves* knew that the Bolsheviks were coming and, to avoid meeting the Devil's agents, hastened their incorruptible bodies to heaven, leaving their bones behind.[32]

While the unveiling of relics certainly had an impact on the Russian religious mind (though its extent is difficult to measure), the party and the state should not have expected a nation of instant unbelievers. The church expressed a naive fear and the party expressed a naive hope that the exposures would turn the world upside down. Yet, when films were shown and lectures delivered explaining how the effigies of saints had been constructed, this knowledge failed to affect many pilgrims' devotion and actually further alienated many from the Soviet regime. They continued to flock to the "relics" as before.[33] In late May 1919 Krasikov in the Commissariat of Justice wrote, "It is impossible to make the old women . . . cease believing" in the miracles of these relics. But it was not just the women.[34] The enthusiasm of crowds was too contagious for undisciplined minds to resist. After the dreariness and monotony of village life, all restless souls longed for a pilgrimage.

On August 25, 1920, Krasikov ordered local authorities to proceed "to the complete liquidation of the cult of corpses and mummies." All such objects were to be transferred to state antireligious museums.[35] But there were myriad "relics"—the government could never expose and destroy them all. Even if it were possible, success would remain incomplete as new holy places, where miracles or holy visions had taken place, were cropping up all over the country. Stories circulated that a miraculous crucifix had appeared in Podolsk Province, and a great procession of pilgrims traveled there to erect holy crosses on the site. In the village of Kolomenskoe, near Moscow, there were reports of a vision of the Virgin Mary's ikon. Looking through it one could see how Mary had received the crown of Nicholas II. By 1921 the government concluded that in all sixty-five relic investigations no relics were genuine.[36]

More Fraud

It was not just relics that needed exposure; there were other fraudulent "miracles" as well. Priests were urging pilgrims to leave a donation so that ikons would "weep"—that is, until Bolshevik agents revealed the hookup to a rubber squeezer filled with water. Priests and monks claimed that lamps would burn indefinitely without oil and that ancient ikons would instantly appear in glowing freshness. Then the Bolsheviks uncovered a factory in Ekaterinoslav where entrepreneurs were using gold foil to achieve the rejuvenating effect (they were shot for their efforts). In another instance monks were secretly washing ikons with alcohol and ammonia, then claiming their sparkling condition was due to a miracle for which the priest deserved some credit and a fee.[37] A 1928 antireligious pamphlet told of this exposure in Yaroslavl:

> According to Comrade Ivanov's report an old ikon of Christ was shown to the audience. The lecturer said with a smile: "You will not, of course, pray to this ikon. We will simply ask it, 'Christ, are you for or against the League of the Godless?'" Suddenly a "miracle" was wrought before the eyes of the entire audience. The old ikon began to shine like a newly minted coin, and around the crown writing appeared in all the colors of the rainbow: "Join the league of the Godless without delay." . . .
>
> For a moment the audience gazed, spellbound, then broke into loud laughter. A little later the face of Christ puckered up and tears began to flow from the eyes. Christ was weeping. When the laughter quieted down, the lecturer explained the "miracle." The ikon had been prepared by treatment in the laboratory of the chemical factory. Little tubes and vessels full of chemicals had been inserted in it. Artificial fat had been employed for the tears.[38]

Then there was the "barometer trick," discussed in chapter 2. The white and the black clergy had long defrauded believers, but now antireligious propagandists were exposing the science behind the fakery to make *their* point. When local populations heard or read of these frauds, they would often retaliate against the accused priest or monk.

GODBUILDING: THE "SPIRITUAL REVOLUTION"

The best type of Communist, that is to say the man who is completely in the grip of the service of an idea and is capable of enormous sacrifices and disinterested enthusiasm, is a possibility only as a result of the Christian training of the human spirit. . . . If it were granted that antireligious propaganda were finally to destroy all traces of Christianity in the soul of the Russian people, and annihilate all religious feeling, then the actual realization of communism would become impossible, for no one would be willing to make sacrifices, and no one would interpret life as a service of a higher purpose.[39]

—Nicolas Berdyaev, 1960

Fifteen years before the Revolution, a coterie of Bolsheviks in European exile (not including Lenin) began the Godbuilding process—finding Communist-compatible replacements for the spiritual void left by the imposition of materialist philosophy. The movement was founded on the assumption that people needed spiritual stimulation to become enthusiastic and committed to societal projects. If organized religion was not going to provide it, then organized communism would have to. Some have said that there was a remnant of religiosity

among those Communists who espoused Godbuilding, but it was more complicated than that. It was certainly not a concern for the inner peace of individual
Russian citizens; rather, it was a calculated attempt to mobilize them.

The stark fact was that for 99 percent of the population Marxism was too
dry. There was little pleasure in reading Plekhanov, one of the main vehicles for
introducing Marxism to Russia. Something was needed to *attract* the people to
materialism without actually deviating (much) from materialism. The solution
for the Godbuilding group was to explain the Revolution in a religious idiom. An
example of that idiom is the story in the Bolshevik *Journal for Young Peasants*,
where a village librarian explained to his neighbors, "The Revolution, as we all
know, brought us to the heavenly kingdom and opened our eyes, showing us how
to walk the well-lit path."[40] If Godbuilding were successful, its proponents reasoned, the clergy would be further undermined because those who had turned to
the church for spirituality could now turn to "Communism-with-a-soul."

Godbuilders were fond of finding parallels between early Christianity and
the proletarian movement, as we saw in chapter 2 in the discussion of Engels.
One Godbuilder asserted that Christ and the Apostles must have been oppressed
workers and that early Christianity was a politically progressive (socialist) and
revolutionary movement.[41] He even cited Jesus's denunciation of private property, though nothing of the sort is to be found in the Gospels. Anatoly
Lunacharsky, Godbuilder extraordinaire, wrote in 1911:

> The Communist spirit of early, popular Christianity is not in doubt. But was it
> revolutionary? Of course it was. It's a negation of the cultural world of the
> time—radical, merciless negation—and in its posing in its place a completely
> new way of life, it was revolutionary. Any ideology that truly mirrors the mood
> of the oppressed masses is revolutionary.[42]*

He mirrored Engels in his insistence that priests and the upper classes had hijacked
true Christianity in the early fourth century to become an instrument of their oppression of the laboring masses. To pull this off, the church fathers had metamorphosed
the revolutionary Jesus into a model of meekness, humility, and forgiveness. Thus
for Lunacharsky, the early promise of Christianity had resulted in failure.

And who were the remaining Godbuilders? At various times and with
varying degrees of commitment the groups included Commissar of Foreign
Trade Leonid Krassin, Russian "president" Mikhail Kalinin, the writer Maxim
Gorky, the poet Vladimir Mayakovsky, and the scientist/philosopher Alexander
Bogdanov. They believed—in blatant contradiction to Marx's teaching—that the

---

*Of course, Lunacharsky was mistaken. Early Christianity did not advocate freeing
slaves. Paul, in Ephesians 6:5, wrote, "Servants, be obedient to them that are your masters according to the flesh, with fear and trembling, in singleness of your heart, as unto
Christ." Nowhere in the Old Testament or New Testament was slavery in the abstract condemned.

Russian people needed something mystical, sacred, ritualistic, colorful, and emotional to tide them over until materialism took root. Gorky, to the end of his life, believed that Communist ethics should be based on the ethics of Jesus. Mayakovsky wrote a play identifying the November Revolution with the Second Coming of Christ.

Lunacharsky, though, took the Godbuilding concept to its highest level, having written a two-volume book on the subject while in prerevolutionary Italian exile. For him this was not a mere tactical program but a genuine spiritual experience conducted without God or superstition but with poetry, beauty, and hope. He realized that reading Marx and Engels failed to set the heart aflutter and preferred to think of man filled with "dreams, myths, sounds, and rituals who would elevate humanity to the status of divinity and bring collective [though not individual] immortality." He had faith in the future of a Marxist "perfected organism," but he was certain that it could not be achieved without the enthusiasm of the religious impulse.[43]

Of course, Bolsheviks could generate some passion by hyperbolizing the building of the New Soviet Man and appealing to love of country (also completely un-Marxist), but by substituting *party* mystique and ceremony for what the church had to offer they could further stimulate the people's need for reverence and do it through a more productive outlet. Party heroes would replace church martyrs, and a new party liturgy would obviate the need for any other. So, in the greatest of ironies, some Bolsheviks wanted to save Marxism in Russia by infusing it with a religious element. This, of course, could never be openly proclaimed, yet it subtly underlay much of the leadership's thoughts and actions.

Not long after the end of the Civil War, prerevolutionary Godbuilding proposals began to poke their heads above the surface again. The experimental period of the New Economic Policy (NEP) from 1921 to 1928 was perfect for it. Even Leon Trotsky, though not a true Godbuilder, expressed a fleeting interest. He wrote in *Questions of Social Custom*:

> The need of an outer expression of feeling is most powerful and legitimate. . . .
> The creation of a revolutionary social cult, . . . placing it in opposition to the cult of the church, is possible not only in social and state celebrations but also in family events.

He observed that factory workers were already creating their own rites, and in effect he said that the vanguard of the proletariat had better get out in front and lead.

Also included in the Godbuilding venture was the physician V. Veresaev, who understood the importance of emotion in ritual and the need to leave no spiritual void in the countryside unfilled. He argued that substitute ritual was not capitulation to religion but instead peaceful competition with it.[44] He envisioned ceremonies centered on birth, marriage, death, and holidays—marking passage through the stages of life (to be discussed in the next chapter). Government authorities began an ongoing campaign to remove these ceremonies from church control and to reduce opportunities for contact between clergy and individuals. Priests would be cut off from the entire life process in Russia.

Godbuilders were sure that "party rites" could be substituted for soon-to-be-marginalized church rites. After all, the Soviet writer D. Balashov defined rites in a nonreligious sense:

> A rite is the symbolic and aesthetic expression . . . of collective social relations, of the collective essence of man, and the bonds linking him not only with his contemporaries but also with his ancestors. A rite is the thread of time by holding onto which people form a nation. A rite is created as the expression of the spirit, traditions, and way of life of a society.[45]

Rites enabled people participating in them to tangibly feel that there was a higher meaning to life, perhaps similar to the worship of the Goddess Reason during the French Revolution. This concept could just as well be applied to the party.

Lenin, however, was the dampening influence on this project. Neither God nor Godbuilding, he insisted, served any useful social function, as both were inherently oppressive and impoverishing. In a series of mildly polemical letters addressed to Gorky in November 1913, he wrote:

> Isn't Godbuilding the worst form of self-humiliation? Everyone who sets about building up a God, or even merely tolerates such activity, humiliates himself in the worst possible way. . . . All Godbuilding is precisely the fond self-contemplation of the thick-witted philistine, the frail man in the street, the dreamy self-humiliation of the vulgar petty bourgeois, exhausted by despair.[46]

It may seem in this quotation that he was referring to another ideological fad, Godseeking, but he went on to describe the difference between Godseeking and Godbuilding as amounting to nothing more than the difference between a yellow devil and a blue devil.[47]

Even when Godbuilding's supporters sidestepped Lenin's objections, it was a difficult task to magically create new rites for birth, marriage, or death or to establish new state holidays to replace traditional ones that were tainted with Christian associations. Still, what was the Communist Party to do? To abolish the old without replacement would be to leave a hollow place in the Russian heart. Not to abolish the old would be a concession to faith. To create new holidays that merely paralleled but did not supplant the old would be futile. Pride in modernity and rationality constrained its choice to the creation of a rational, sober, and traditionless replacement party "church." But what could the people see on the gray streets of Petrograd or Moscow that would replace the mystery of the candle-lit, incense-filled interior of an Orthodox house of worship?

Well, there was *one* thing. When Lenin died in January 1924, Leonid

Krassin, with the backing of the Central Committee—but over the objections of Trotsky, Bukharin, Kamenev, Krupskaya, and the deceased Lenin himself—ordered that the Great Leader's body be handled in such a way as to subtly undercut (if not mock) the clerical function. Krassin ordered that symbolic palm branches be laid around the coffin and that the "saint" be permanently embalmed. The church, recently embarrassed over the exposure of fraudulent relics, was now slapped in its reddened face. A "true saint," an incorruptible saint, the saint of communism and an earthly paradise, was presented for public veneration. Many were certain that Lenin's body would become a *real* relic to which the faithful would make pilgrimages.[48]

But there was more: Beyond incorruptibility came resurrection. Konstantin Melnikov, designer of the sarcophagus, called his creation a "sleeping chamber for a sleeping prince."[49] Krassin and others seemed to be waiting for a "kiss" from the people to wake him up. Godbuilders and many others in the party saw parallels between the deaths of Jesus and of Lenin. If Jesus was the Messiah, then Lenin was the prototype of the New Soviet Man. In this case, not faith but a strong belief in science led some to anticipate Lenin's physical resurrection; thus great care was taken in preserving the body. Admittedly it was a period of great grief, but it is still amazing to behold the director of the Agitprop Department, clearly acquainted with the early Christian docetic heresy,* writing in *Pravda* that there were *two* Lenins—one had died but the other was divine and would live forever! The chairman of the Soviet Supreme Court claimed that Lenin was comparable to Buddha, Jesus, and Mohammed, except that he was superior to them collectively.[50]

Several Russian scientists were certain that immortality was inherent in all life and began planning for Soviet Man's *individual* eternal existence. They influenced Krassin, Gorky, Mayakovsky, and Bogdanov. A manifesto was even published, ending with the words: "DEAD OF ALL LANDS, UNITE!" Lunacharsky later explained that resurrection-like comments he had recently made concerning the deceased Lenin were purely symbolic. Maybe so, but Bogdanov was serious. He became obsessed with blood transfusions, even convincing Stalin to build for him a special blood transfusion institute. Bogdanov believed that regular blood exchanges between random people would achieve both "physiological collectivism" and the prolongation of life. He explained it all in his book, *The Struggle for Viability: Collectivism through Blood Exchange*. However, in 1928 when he endeavored to prolong his own life in this manner, he ended up accidentally killing himself.[51]

---

*Docetism is the belief, accepted by many early Christian Gnostics, that there were *two* Christs: the flesh-and-blood one who felt pain on the cross and the spiritual one who had flown off just before the nails were pounded in.

CHURCHES TO CLUBS; PRAYERS TO PESTICIDES

Before concluding this chapter, we should take a brief look at two additional attempts at sapping the priestly establishment: Komsomol Clubs and agricultural science. Both were severely resisted.

Kalinin advised in the May 26, 1923, issue of *Izvestia*, "The organization of theaters, concerts, parties, different games, and interesting conferences creates an intercourse outside the church." Komsomol rose to the challenge with the overt intention of creating substitute churches for the young—antireligious youth clubs situated throughout the country. Sometimes these clubs took over abandoned mansions, sometimes they occupied newly constructed "medieval cathedrals" or "grand theaters," but the vast majority of clubs were rather stark and dismal buildings. Their interior designs varied little: an auditorium, a small movie theater, an antireligious library, a kitchen, a dining room, and recreational facilities. Every club also contained a Komsomol Corner devoted to mocking religion and meant to replace the religious corners in most homes that were crowded with ikons and other Christian symbols. A cartoon displayed in one of these corners showed Christ walking ahead of the cross, the burden of which was borne by the toiling masses. Sitting astride the cross was a grinning capitalist loaded down with moneybags.[52]

For obvious reasons, all were especially active on Sundays—some even staging antireligious "services."[53] But standard fare seriously lacked the mystery of the church and was often downright boring. A Soviet specialist on rituals visited numerous clubs and was frustrated when he observed decorations mostly consisting of red bunting hung on the walls, red cloths covering the tabletops, and a prominently displayed bust of Lenin. A brass band might play, but it knew few pieces besides the "Internationale." Meetings were nearly identical from place to place and time to time. Party functionaries made long and tiresome speeches and then awarded prizes to outstanding workers who were awkwardly ushered up to the front to accept. The band then played the same tune again.[54]

*   *   *

If youth clubs were substitutes for churches, agricultural instruction was a substitute for village priests. In the chapter 2 story "The Forbidding" we saw how peasants depended on the priest to bless their crops and repel pests. Weaning the people from protective prayers was part of the new agricultural training program spreading across the countryside. Modern agricultural methods were needed to increase yields and feed a growing population. Insecticides were introduced to kill snails and caterpillars. Even schoolchildren tried to help by demonstrating to their parents that darkness, not demons, caused calf blindness and that more outside light, not God's intervention, was the cure.[55]

To make an impact on the peasantry, propagandists would lay out two growing plots—one blessed by God and one run by the godless. The first was sprinkled with holy water and the second was doused with chemical fertilizers.[56] When the godless ground yielded higher and healthier crops the lesson should have been clear, but journalist Henry Noel Brailsford wrote as late as 1930 of the difficulty involved:

> It is hardly an exaggeration to say that in every typical village every advance in the technique and organization of agriculture has been made against the fierce resistance of priests, whose anger could doom these simple peasants to hellfire.[57]

A Soviet newspaper published this morality poem in 1925. It involved two peasants, Timofei and Eremei, who greet each other on the road to market:

Timofei: Well, what can I say,
I almost died.
What could have angered God?
How many candles I lit!
How many times did I bow?
In thanksgiving I gave
Ten hens and a heifer,
Oh, but I lost all my grain,
And I am quite confused,
Clearly I have sinned much!

Eremei: These are not sins, Timofei,
Obviously, I'm a greater sinner than you:
I don't believe in God, the miracle worker,
To save my life!
My grain grew excellently
Yet I did not bow down.[58]

The next venture for the Bolsheviks was the invention of tradition.

10

WHO KNOWS THAT I'M MARRIED?

Reinventing the Religious Calendar

Marx wrote, "Destroy the social world of which religion is the spiritual aroma and you destroy religion." Bolsheviks took this dictum to heart. Much of the social world of the Russian people, especially among the peasantry, was involved in ceremonies concerned with the milestones of life: birth, marriage, and death. Bolsheviks dealt with these matters in the flurry of decrees emanating from their headquarters at the Smolny Institute in Petrograd during the first weeks of their rule. They were part of the separation decrees.

In this chapter we will see how the Soviets offered substitutes for Christian ceremonies and how they had as much difficulty in this process as they did trying to get citizens to use the French *merci* for "thank you" instead of the tainted *spasibo*, which translates as "God save."[1]

MILESTONES OF LIFE

You are showing the way to others who are not party members. I am certain that the time is not far off when people will be happy and without priests.[2]

—testimonial at a Red Wedding, 1924

Baptism

Children born after December 20, 1917, and whose births had not been officially registered, were regarded as noncitizens. No food ration cards were issued to them, and anyone who gave or sold such cards to these children's parents would be arrested. Birth registration became just a matter of vital statistics handled by the *zags* office (a Russian acronym for the Registry of Births, Marriages, and Deaths).[3]

Baptism, however, was a separate issue. In July 1922 the government decided that Christian baptism of infants should be abolished, though those over eighteen could be baptized if they wished.[4] Apparently this decree was the straw that broke the camel's back, as there was deep resentment over, and widespread resistance to, the abolition of such an important aspect of the people's social lives. There was a conviction among the peasantry that christened children lived longer—how could the government deny them this opportunity?

Godbuilders rushed in to fill the gap, creating "Octobering" (*Oktyabrina*), a waterless Communist baptism named after the October 1917 (old calendar) Bolshevik coup. This "baptism" was conducted at a local party facility or in the clubroom of a factory instead of a church, and the child was consecrated to the Revolution and to communism instead of to God. Many urban workers were caught up in the new ideology, and during the early 1920s ceremonies of this type became a vehicle for the expression of their zeal.

The following account is based, in part, on a description by the traveler and journalist Louis Fischer, who witnessed an Octobering in the mid-1920s. When one of the factory workers had a son he informed the party committee, which then arranged for entertainment and invited a speaker from party headquarters. Announcements were plastered all over the factory walls: "Come to the Octobering." When the special evening arrived, workers decorated the clubroom with red bunting and revolutionary banners and hung up placards with Leninist slogans on them. The factory orchestra struck up the new national anthem—the "Internationale." Rising and pounding his gavel, the chairman asked all attending not to smoke. "Comrades, we are here to enroll a new member in the ranks of our international proletarian army. Comrade Ivanov of Furnace #2 desires to consecrate his son to the cause of communism." There was a great round of applause.

The chairman asked the mother of the infant to come forward to the platform. With cheeks glowing red, she approached with the child held up on a white cushion. The women in the audience could not contain themselves and rushed forward to peek at the child. The chairman finally persuaded them to take their seats. (The Orthodox Church had refused to allow mothers into the church until forty days after childbirth. Giving the mother a prominent role in the workers' ceremony stressed the equality of women and was meant to subtly ridicule the church.)[5]

Then the party speaker—a burly, blond Slav—rose. His arms looked more fitted for swinging a sledgehammer than for cradling a kicking ten-day-old infant. As the new recruit was mustered into the proletarian army, the father stood proudly beside his wife and swore, "I give my son to the cause for which our dear Ilyich [Lenin] lived and died." Alternately, the mother might say, "The child belongs to me only physically. Spiritually, I present him to society."[6] Or, if the father were at all eloquent, he would give a short speech on the glorious future under communism in which his son would live. He then lifted the cushion with the infant from his wife's arms and handed it to the party representative. While everybody smiled and applauded, the baby bawled.

Near the end of the ceremony the baby's name was announced. In tsarist times, all Orthodox children were named from a list prepared by the church, and the name was actually chosen by the male head of household (perhaps the grandfather). Commonly, the child was named for the calendar saint-day on which he or she was born. But in September 1920, the Commissariat of Justice ruled that "any name may be given to new-born children who are registered in the Department of Marriage and Birth," and the parents were legally allowed to choose the name. (A 1917 law had even permitted adults to change their saint names, and many did so.)[7]

Those more zealous for social change frequently chose a name that would either celebrate older revolutions or emphasize the beginning of the new Soviet Era. Some were named after Spartacus or Robespierre or dubbed Parizhkommuna, while others were endowed with Komintern (Communist International), Krasarm (Red Army), Revolyutsiya, Rem (an acronym for revolution, electrification, and peace), or Ninel (Lenin spelled backwards). The last two mentioned were Trotsky's suggestions. Girls were often given Krasnaya (red or beautiful), Borba (struggle), Barrikada, Avangarda, Marxina, or Engelina. One child, for reasons unknown, was forced to grow up with the name Embryo. Those who were named after Trotsky or Grigory Zinoviev (the party chief in Petrograd) would live to rue the day of their Octobering when, under Stalin, these names became synonymous with counterrevolution and treason.[8]

In the final ceremonial act, a delegate from the women workers rose and none-too-subtly provided a moral to the story. After presenting the baby with a small gift, she said:

> You see comrades, when you baptize your children after the old, prerevolutionary fashion, you have to pay the priest for murmuring a few unknown words over them. Here you pay nothing. What's more, Vladimir even gets a present from his father's co-workers.[9]

Occasionally, Octobering backfired. In one village the Octobered infant died, and the villagers decided it was an omen telling them to go back to the old ways.[10] In any case, by the end of the 1920s the *Oktyabrina* fad and revolutionary naming petered out.

Marriage and Divorce

Weaning the bride and groom from having a church wedding was more difficult than substituting Octobering for baptism. On December 31, 1917, Sovnarkom issued the decree "On Civil Marriages, Children, and Civil Acts Registry," stating that only civil marriages would be legally valid.[11] Church marriage ceremonies were still permissible, though legally superfluous.

Beginning in 1918, the government provided alternative civil ceremonies—Red Weddings—at the aforementioned *zags* office, but these were far from acceptable. The historian Richard Stites explained why church weddings were so desirable: "The civil office remained a cramped, crowded bureau where couples got married in twenty minutes without so much as a rose or a ring."[12] As one young woman protested:

> If I marry Soviet style, I simply go to a clerk with my man and register . . . then who knows that I'm married? But if I go to a church, a crowd comes. The whole neighborhood talks about me. The girls see my dress and my husband. It becomes a great holiday.[13]

Many brides and grooms still wanted the pomp and tradition of a church wedding.

In September 1921 the Party Central Committee decided that new party members could be forgiven for capitulating to their brides on the issue of church weddings, but established and responsible party members could be expelled for such an offense.[14] Other compromises were required, but it still seems strange to read this article written by a Communist and published in the February 1922 issue of *Izvestia*:

> Here are the facts. A Communist gets married in a village. All the wedding procession goes to church. In front is the red flag with the inscription, "Workers of the world, unite!" Next come the ikons and then the bridegroom with a red sash on his chest. Such marriages are frequent in the villages. Religion and communism make an excellent household together. In his fashion the peasant understands communism and Soviet power.[15]

The government finally began to make concessions to romantic attitudes, figuring out ways to create civil marriages outside of the *zags* office in so-called Wedding Palaces. Plenty of color and ceremony was offered with no obvious religious overtones. Sometimes several couples would be married in a joint ceremony to make it seem more extravagant. The Godbuilder Veresaev, however, thought the Red Weddings banal. He described one in a leatherworking plant in December 1924: A portrait of Lenin hung over a red-covered table, the bride and groom vowed to each other and then to communism, officials offered reports and speeches and a gift of Lenin's works to the couple, and a small band played the "Internationale."[16] This may have sufficed for some in the cities, but in the villages the wedding was the central event of the bride and groom's entire life. A wedding should include singing, wailing, joking, feasting, dancing, and drinking, and it should last for several days. A Red Wedding did convey the Bolshevik virtues of brevity, economy, equality, and sobriety, but as substitute ritual it was largely in vain.

The Trend in Moscow Marriages
Source: Hecker, *Religion and Communism*, p. 229

1927   33%   60%

1928   38%   58%

■ Religious Ceremony ※ NO Religious Ceremony

This lack of acceptance was partially explained by the more conservative and traditional inclinations of Russian women and the likelihood that, as mentioned above, grooms would defer to their brides' wishes concerning the wedding ceremony. For the marriage to be valid, the law required civil registration no matter where the ceremony was performed, but 75 to 80 percent of nationwide weddings were additionally performed in churches during the mid- to late 1920s. Maurice Hindus, as he traveled through the countryside during the late 1920s, put the number at 90 percent.[17]

As for divorce, in June 1918 the church sobor decreed that only diocesan church councils could grant them. This aroused the ire of the Commissariat of Justice, which charged that the church was thereby assuming the rights of a "juridical person" explicitly denied to it by the separation decree four months earlier. Divorce, the state maintained, was a legal issue, not a religious one. In late December 1917 Sovnarkom had already issued orders empowering local judges to grant divorces regardless of a citizen's religion. The Family Code of October 1918 even provided for "postcard divorces," whereby one party to the marriage could inform the Registration Office of the wish to dissolve the union, and the other party would be informed of the divorce by postcard.[18]

After losing a case before the Revolutionary Tribunal in Novgorod in February 1921, Patriarch Tikhon caved in. Divorce would henceforth be completely a civil matter, and the church would abandon its historic role.[19]

Funerals

Yaroslavsky had written that "religion can lead only in carrying the dead to the grave,"[20] but even funerals were to be lured away from church control. In late

1917 all cemeteries and morgues passed into the hands of soviets, which were now obliged to pay burial fees. Generally, religious funeral processions were still allowed, but the cost was billed to the deceased's relatives.[21] By early 1918 soldiers who died in combat were being buried with no religious services at all.

Maurice Hindus described replacement soviet funerals for party members as *more* impressive than church funerals, featuring "flowers, red bunting, red flags, a red canopy over the hearse, a band, a choir, and speeches by members of the party and friends of the deceased."[22] He found them solemn and moving. But the perpetual critic Veresaev, perhaps viewing ceremonies for nonparty members, portrayed Red Funerals as arid and sterile, leaving mourners standing around emotionless as they listened to formulaic eulogies; when they left, the empty space inside them had not been filled.[23]

The Orthodox Church had disallowed cremation, and no crematoria existed in Russia at the time of the Revolution.[24] A modern-day American archbishop explained:

> A person's body is not waste or an old rag! A believer's body anointed by the Holy Spirit, which has received the Holy Spirit, is God's temple, a vessel of eternal life. A temple can fall apart or cease to be used for prayer, but it is not burned. Both the living and the dead body of a person who believes in the Resurrection, is a seed for the Resurrection. . . . "You are dust, and to dust you shall return" (Genesis 3:19).[25]

The League of the Godless then spitefully proclaimed cremation as one of its aims. The League was not in the business of conserving cemetery space; it hoped to eliminate yet another function of priests and at the same time make death more democratic. Revolutionary heroes had been receiving "martyr's funerals," full of pomp and glory, but not all who died were heroes, revolutionaries, or even party members. Cremation would be not only a slap in the face of the church but would be consistent with the communist values of equality, standardization, and efficiency. Trotsky proposed that cremation ceremonies be quick, with a few red flags, a short funeral march, a brief eulogy, and a rifle salute. By 1919 architects were busy designing crematoria, but it was not until 1927 that the first of these was actually constructed—in Moscow, in the cellars of the vacated Donskoy Monastery. Within a year, 4,000 bodies had been consumed. The Communist economist and propagandist Ivan Skvortsov-Stepanov became a role model by stipulating cremation in his will.[26]

While either civil burial or cremation may have worked effectively to undercut the priest's role (and income), in the end the utopian aim of spreading communality and equality did not work out. Upon death, party higher-ups still received orchestral accompaniments (compared with the common man's lone guitar), larger and longer ceremonies, and prestigious internment sites. Yaroslavsky once told the no-doubt apocryphal story of a party comrade who, unable to retrogress to a church funeral and unable to stomach a Red Burial, willed his remains to a soap factory.[27]

In August 1918 the government ordered that all prerevolutionary records for births, marriages, and burials be turned over by the churches to the civil records office within two months—though it took at least a year to get this accomplished. Keeping church copies was allowed, but no fees could be charged for recording or viewing them. Priests were forced to acknowledge that these records no longer had legal validity.[28]

HOLIDAYS, REST DAYS, AND THE CALENDAR ITSELF

We must bear in mind that there is nothing holy in religious holidays. They have been established not by God, nor even by religion, but by primitive, ignorant, semiwild men. To combat religious festivals means to combat slavery, barbarity, ignorance; it means to fight against economic backwardness, against the blind, incomprehensible forces of nature enslaving man.[29]

—party member V. Rojitsyn

For Bolsheviks all religious holidays were troublesome, and some ideologues suggested that all such holidays simply be abolished with secular ones substituted, but separating holidays from priests and churches would not be easy.

Easter and the Christian Holidays

Earlier we saw something of the Bolshevik handling of Christmas, but Easter had been the most significant Russian holiday for a thousand years. The English traveler Bernard Pares observed Easter in Moscow in 1905 when the belfry atop the Church of Ivan the Great rang out "the promise of a new life to all the faithful people." When the first note sounded, the people turned to each other with the words "Christ is risen."

> To Russians [he continued] resurrection still means more than it does to us Westerners. The winter is long and hopeless, and the return of spring, when one has almost despaired of it, comes each year with a sudden beneficence, which gives it the aspect of a miracle.[30]

It was an ancient Russian custom on Easter Eve for the faithful to take portions of everything that was to be eaten the next day to the church for blessing. In the area around the Ukrainian city of Odessa during the final week of Lent

1919, groups of party members felt compelled to trek through city streets and country paths, forbidding this tradition. Priests were warned against even showing up at the church on the evening before Easter.[31] For the Bolsheviks, Easter promised nothing but annoyance.

A kind of duel took place in Petrograd when in 1921 Easter (old calendar) fell on May 1, or Labor Day. On Easter Sunday the Petrograd soviet organized a labor procession through the city and allowed a religious procession as well, hoping that the vast labor turnout would put the "dying church's" turnout to shame. When believers boycotted the Labor Day festivities, 200,000 cross-carrying Christians joined the Easter procession, the church was joyful. The soviet-conceived duel had backfired.[32]

Soon denunciations of Easter came fast and furious. The March 1922 issue of *Bezbozhnik* complained about legal laxity:

> [Celebrators were] clad in wild dresses, with flags and rags, with their idols, with pieces of the rotten bodies of some old "saints" who were usually merchants or landlords, to walk about and sing their counterrevolutionary hymns.[33]

After the counterproductive Christmas demonstrations in January 1923, however, Yaroslavsky resolved that for the upcoming Easter Sunday he would replace antagonism with alternative activities. He recommended sober but joyous celebrations of Soviet life, with revolutionary songs, poetry, fun, and enlightenment. The newspaper *Trud* (*Labor*) on April 4, 1923, discussed these plans:

> During the Easter holidays it is proposed to arrange lectures and discussions on the origin of Easter and organize, for the stage, plays antireligious in character. To keep children away from religious exercises during the Easter holidays it is proposed to cooperate with the Russian Union of Communist Youth [Komsomol] in order to arrange children's festivities in the schools, children's homes, and clubs.[34]

The government advised against using the term "Komsomol Easter," since some workers had taken this to mean that Komsomol was creating its own Easter! But Komsomol did circulate the pamphlet *Christ Did Not Rise* in 1923. Its first chapter described Easter as having originated thousands of years ago when man first noticed springtime growth and the renewal of life. He decided that God was offering him another chance at life; the resurrection of Christ was nothing but a legend based on this ancient understanding. The third chapter was titled "Jesus and Slaves Created the Tale of the Resurrection of Christ" and was an attempt to apply Marxist theory to the core tale of Easter. The resurrection myth was born, the pamphlet explained, out of the misery and despair of oppressed peoples. The priests created Christ's return to life ostensibly to spread hope among them, but actually to take money from them. Ever since the invention of this miraculous tale, Easter has been "at the service of the landlords and capitalists."

> [The third chapter continued:] At Easter the priests walked out among the people, saying that Christ had suffered and that, in consequence, they should be willing to suffer. "All power," said the priests, "comes from God. Therefore do not turn against the landlord. If he smites you on one cheek, turn to him the other. Love your enemies. Forgive your landlords!" Thus the representatives of the landlords' Easter went about, in white robes, to quiet the people with superstitions. . . .
>
> There is a new Easter. It is a very sad Easter for the priests and those who oppose the Revolution. . . . The proletariat hears the church bells ringing the funeral of the dying old world. The springtime now has become the humanity holiday. Oppressed peoples are fighting for the future. Looking back on the burning remains of the slave world that has been damned, they are asking: "Is the suppressed world risen?" And the answer already has come: "Yes, it is really risen. This is Easter."[35]

An observer of Leningrad's counter-Easter demonstration in 1924 described Young Pioneers singing "materialist songs," marchers displaying slogans such as "The Smoke of the Factory Is Better than the Smoke of Incense," and actors performing a new atheist play. The hitch was that these activities easily escalated to mockery and insult as before, but if ridicule of the religious was strictly curtailed, then the demonstrations became dull.[36] These new Easter efforts met with temporary and limited success.

Tver newspapers between 1925 and 1927 revealed the logical line now adopted by government propagandists against all Christian holidays. They claimed the Feast of St. Elias (Elijah), associated with thunder, had been carried over from Russian pagan belief in Perun, the god of thunder and lightning. Christmas had originated with pagan midwinter celebrations, and no one really knew the date of Christ's birth. The significance of his birth was related to the reappearance of the sun, which was worshiped in ancient societies for agricultural reasons. The Feast of the Circumcision of Jesus, just after Christmas, was a relic of human sacrifice.[37]

The Virgin Mary was widely worshiped in Russia, and holidays were set aside for her, but she, too, was explained away as just one of many stories of female bearers of god. The Christian virgin birth was founded on Egyptian legends going back to 2000 BCE when (presumably) the source of pregnancy was unknown to women—hence impregnation by the Holy Spirit. The story of Mary's presentation in the temple came from the apocryphal Book of Jacob. Tver newspapers appealed to the peasants' (also presumed) logical minds with the argument that if Mary had ever lived her bones would have been discovered by now—and they had not. Priests, to cover up this discrepancy, invented the story of her bodily Assumption.[38]

Although literacy had been on the rise in peasant villages since the late nineteenth century, and newspapers had a good readership, one has to wonder just how effective this "explanatory" type of propaganda could be. And how Lenin, who spent the early years of World War I in Zurich reading newspapers, could have missed the difference between British emotional propaganda, stressing mutilated corpses and bayoneted babies, and German logical responses explaining why the alleged wartime atrocities could never have occurred. The former was persuasive; the latter was not. The historian Helmut Altrichter noted:

> Criticism of Christ's circumcision or of Mary's presentation in the temple . . . presupposed a certain level of knowledge about theology that most peasants probably did not possess. It is equally doubtful that readers understood the references to sun worship and natural religion, to the ancient Slavic god Perun and the ancient Egyptian god Osiris, to biblical tradition, and to the demythologizing of the Gospel of Jacob, not to mention the extreme capacity for abstraction required to understand the transition from history to the criticism of religion.[39]

Between 1924 and 1927 Yaroslavsky's spectacles were less in evidence, but they resumed in 1928 with the theme slightly altered to associate religion with drunkenness; both were enemies of socialism. It was true, of course, that religious holidays and excessive drinking went hand in hand, but in most cases workers were more willing to give up religion than to have their drinking habits curtailed!

An April 1928 *Komsomolskaya Pravda* was still trying to eliminate any fun associated with Easter:

> No festive preparations for Easter are to be made in the family; no new dresses, no extra cooking, no shopping; no special Easter food, such as Easter cakes, ham, painted eggs, etc., are to be allowed. The custom of Easter greetings ["Christ is risen"] must be abolished.[40]

The article suggested rival activities. In every factory "friendly social gatherings" should begin at 9:30 on Easter Eve, and Komsomol should arrange that cinemas reduce their prices and show extra films. Ice-skating parties and chess competitions should be organized, and concerts should be presented in big-city squares—anything to keep the people out of church.[41] Komsomol leaders suggested that in the villages Easter be connected to the traditional—and somewhat secular—festival of First Plowing.

The Commissariat of Education, Komsomol, and the League of the Godless conducted surveys that showed the persistence of religious sentiment among students of all ages. Despite Lunacharsky's order that schools be kept open on religious holidays, many local school administrators closed them anyway. If schools were left open on holy days they often suffered absentee rates of 50 to 70 percent.[42]

Days of Rest and Feasting

There were constant debates over when the worker should get his weekly day off and whether or not religious feast days could be celebrated. Religious connections to Sunday made it vulnerable. During the spring of 1918, the government declared the last Sunday of April a workday; factories and businesses were ordered to carry on as usual. The following Tuesday, May 1, was declared the substitute rest day—the "Day of Holy Revolution"—and all factories and businesses were ordered closed.[43] This ploy, as might be imagined, failed miserably. For the time being, alternative rest days were abandoned.

But it was not just the "religiousness" of religious holidays but the loss of productivity they entailed. In a collection of *Bezbozhnik* articles, N. Amosov wrote "On Drunken Holidays," in which he decried such events:

> Religious holidays harm the working people enormously. For each celebration, gigantic resources are wasted in order to organize massive, festive gluttony and collective drunkenness. Peasants will often sell their last sheep, heifer, piglet, firewood, etc. . . . What could be done with this money, were it spent strategically![44]

The Bolsheviks were unrelenting in their attempts to replace days of religious inefficiency (church holidays) with days of scientific effectiveness (labor). As mentioned in chapter 2, these days provided relief from tedium, opportunity for socialization, and excuses to get drunk. Peasants lived from holiday to holiday, never having to wait long. Between Sundays, Easter, Christmas, New Year's Day, feast days for almost every major event in the lives of Mary and Jesus (Annunciation, Transfiguration, etc.), feast days for major Russian saints, feast days for powerful ikons, and celebrations of ancient battles won, there were more than 100 days a year of nonproduction. (There were hundreds of saints, but not all deserved a feast, and some were remembered more in one region than another.) Some feast days fit between agricultural cycles and so were less disruptive, but many interrupted planting, haymaking, or harvesting.[45]

Considering religious feast days "orgiastic"—not far from the truth in many instances—the government, as it had with its Red Weddings, tried to "create tradition" by inventing new holidays. In 1922 the Code of Work strove to gain state control over workers' days off, declaring March 8 as International Women's Day, May 1 as International Labor Day, a day later in May as Journalism Day, a day in early July as International Cooperation Day, and November 7 as the Day of the Revolution. Electric Day replaced Elijah Day, and Forest Day replaced Trinity

Sunday; Harvest Day substituted for the Feast of the Intercession, and the Day of Industry replaced the Feast of Transfiguration. Also celebrated were the Day of the First Revolution (the 1905 uprising) and the Day of the Paris Commune (1871), as if many peasants had ever heard of the latter.[46]

In July 1923, in an effort to increase worker productivity, all government holidays—which heretofore had coincided with church holidays on the old calendar—were switched to the new calendar, advancing them by thirteen days and leaving church holidays as government workdays.* Patriarch Tikhon tried to move the church holidays to coincide with the new official holidays, but parishioners would not follow his lead, and the scheme was abandoned. In July 1924 the Politburo ordered the Commissariat of Labor to cut the myriad holidays in half, but this took at least five years to accomplish. In 1927, out of sixteen *official* holidays, ten were still church feast days. (The League of the Godless, at its Congress in 1929, resolved that *no* work or school days off should correspond to church feast days and that Christmas and the day after should be declared Days of Industrialization, with attendance at work mandatory.)[47]

"New traditions" never caught on. They were primarily concerned with the interests of the state and had little to do with the deep sociality of the truly traditional celebrations. Many government holidays dealt with rational economics and agricultural techniques, and peasants were expected to play a receptive role. This was unlikely to go over well. The Soviet filmmaker Vitaly Zhemchuzhny wrote in 1927, "The spreading or propagation of some sort of novel, invented ritual is an absurd utopia." Although he opposed reactionary church ritual, he held that artificial ritual was worse, as it was "inorganic" and lacked links to popular psychology.[48]† Artificially induced rites and holidays were unconsciously and consciously resisted. They were seen as bureaucratic measures imposed from above, having no history, no ancient and unknowable origin. They added nothing to the meaning of life.

For a while Moscow had left the weekly day of rest to the soviets. They could choose Sunday or any other day of the week. Then, in August 1929—mainly for economic reasons but with purposeful antireligious effects—Sovnarkom attempted another assault on tradition: Henceforth there would be a continuous seven-day workweek in factories and offices, with one day of rest occurring on

---

*Apparently, when the calendar switch had occurred on February 1, 1918, church and official holidays had remained on the same *dates*.

†This insight could well have formed the basis for a comment made decades later. In the Khrushchev era, D. Balashov wrote: "So far it is possible to name only one successful experiment in transplanting an old rite onto the soil of new social relations. That is the New Year Tree." And this festival was primarily secular in the first place. Lenin Commemoration Day, January 22—perhaps not truly artificial—survived until 1952, and May Day, twisted into a day of military parades and saber rattling, as well as November 7, made it to the fall of Communism.[49]

different weekdays rotated in order through the week. The plan alternated the workers' one day of rest by assigning one-sixth off on Monday, one-sixth off on Tuesday, and so on. Thus six-sevenths of the workers labored on Sundays, and church attendance suffered correspondingly. The staggered six-day workweek never affected rural areas, but in the cities it managed to survive until 1940, when Sunday was reinstated. Christmas Eve 1929 in Leningrad was turned into the "night of struggle against religion," during which a large portion of the believing intelligentsia was locked up and had no holiday at all.[50]

A Revolutionary Calendar

Muslims had called 622 anno domini the year 1, and eighteenth-century French revolutionaries had attempted to start the counting of years over again, even changing (for a while) the names of years and months. By the end of the 1920s it occurred to Russian Communists that any respectable revolution should do the same. Why should atheists count the years from the birth of Christ? In 1929 the League of Militant Atheists asked the public for input: Perhaps count 1890, the year that the European working class began celebrating May Day, as the year 1 and begin the year on May 1? Perhaps begin counting years on November 7, 1917?

It was seriously suggested that the days of the week be renamed as follows: Trade Union Day, Culture Day, Party Day, Soviet Day, Day of Godlessness, and so on. A simpler proposal was First Working Day, Second Working Day, until the Day of Rest. At the very least the names Saturday and Sunday had to be changed, for the Russian *subbota* meant the biblical sabbath and *voskresenie* meant the day of Christ's resurrection.[51]

None of these proposals were ever implemented, however, most likely due to remembrance of the short life of the French experiment and to awareness that the Russian people, too, would never accept anything so drastic.

TACTICAL NICETIES

Although the Soviet government in no way wished the Orthodox Church or any other church well, it did come to realize that for tactical reasons it could not accomplish its goals overnight and that crude methods only drove the faithful deeper into their superstitions. The Commissariat of Justice seems to have spent much of its time and energy reining in wild-eyed atheists who believed that busting up churches and beating up priests was furthering the cause. In January 1919 it felt compelled to remind party members that "free performance of religious rituals is guaranteed insofar as they do not violate public order and are not accompanied by violations of the rights of citizens." It also refreshed the memory of subordinates that arrests of priests were not to be made during church services and that searches were to be conducted only when a member of the congregation or clergy was present.[52] It admonished:

> [In respect to the clergy, officials] should in no way permit their acts to show a feeling of hostility and scorn for the eternal assistant of all exploitation, which the clergy have been throughout history; it is necessary to avoid all treatment of individual persons which is unworthy of the Workers' Power and is in any way similar to abuse.[53]

The circular went on to explain that officials should not confiscate clerical clothing and church paraphernalia to use for antireligious purposes—apparently zealots had been making atheist banners out of clerical vestments and mantles—because "no general order about removing religious objects from churches . . . has yet been published" (though it would be a few years later). It was entirely inappropriate to force clergy in clerical garb to do manual labor in the streets for the purpose of humiliation.[54] The reason, again, was not sympathy for clerics but the counterproductivity of the exercise. Citizens glimpsing the priest cleaning the streets would feel the insult and become more resistant to Bolshevik propaganda.

At the end of the Civil War, Mother Nature handed the Bolsheviks a great opportunity to further assail the Orthodox Church and further undermine its clergy. It came with the famine that spread across the land.

11

THE MOUNTAIN
BRINGS FORTH A MOUSE

Bolshevik Uses of the 1922 Famine

In late 1921, on the tail of the bloody Civil War, famine struck the southern provinces of Russia. By early 1922—as people ate grass and the soles of their shoes—the suffering became difficult for the government to ignore. Cannibalism broke out, with reported cases of parents consuming their own deceased children—quietly rationalized by the belief that, since the soul had already fled the body, what remained would otherwise go to the worms. In Orenburg a police report described peasants digging up bodies to consume them, and the city government imposed a 9:00 PM curfew to prevent late-night murders for meals. The local Board of Health recommended that animal bones be mixed with the little flour available to make it stretch further (actually more nutritious than rye bread, the peasant staple), but the American Relief Administration reported that the starving mixed weeds, tree bark, clay, and manure for food, which was especially lethal for children. Then there were the epidemics, spread by soldiers returning from wars and peasants fleeing from famine. Typhus was the worst, but plague, dysentery, relapsing fever, malaria, cholera, and scurvy were almost as bad.[1]

The Bolsheviks were slow to show concern (except for feeding party supporters in the cities); instead they plotted to use the famine for antireligious ends. It was not only the hungry who would suffer.

A MAN-MADE FAMINE

We find ourselves in the presence of one of the most terrifying catastrophes known to history. An incalculable number of human beings, stricken with famine, exposed to typhus and cholera, are wandering in desperation across an arid country, hoping to find bread, and they are driven away by armed force. From the Volga basin thousands of human beings, doomed to a most cruel death, are calling upon humanity for aid.[2]

—Pope Benedict XV, August 1921

The famine scoured the land throughout the Volga River Valley and into the Ukraine, Crimea, and Western Siberia. Why now? The rural population, doubled in Russia's Black Earth regions since the 1861 emancipation of the serfs, struggled to survive during the 1920s with smaller and less efficient farm holdings. Then came two successive years of drought, alone causing crop failures on 20 percent of all Soviet farmland. Droughts were cyclical and common in Russia, the last serious one having hit in 1891–1892, but tsarist officials had arranged for government and private food supplies to be shipped to famine-stricken areas, and deaths by starvation and disease had been kept under a half million.[3] The 1920s drought by itself would also have caused "bearable damage," however, combining natural disaster with *man-made* disaster let loose a catastrophe of biblical proportions. In the final year of World War I, the Allied blockade had prevented importation of farm equipment from the West, then the drought hit hardest in areas already devastated by the man-made Civil War. During back-and-forth fighting, peasant villages experienced military requisitions of grain and livestock by both Reds and Whites. At first peasants coped by planting only enough for their family's immediate needs, but then men needed for sowing and reaping were dragooned into one or the other of the armies. Soon there was no planting at all in some areas, and existing food reserves had already been turned over to the government as taxes-in-kind.

The American anarchist Emma Goldman traveled through southern Russia during this period and claimed in *My Disillusionment in Russia* (1923) that, in addition to war, man-made causes of suffering included bureaucratic bungling in seed distribution and widespread government corruption.[4] Although most peasants believed the famine to be God's punishment for allowing godless Bolshevik rule, the government (with some accuracy) claimed it was caused by agricultural practices governed far more by religious superstition than by science. Whoever was correct, during 1921–1922 food production nationwide fell to only half of prewar levels, and the number of cattle fell to 30 percent. There were no food reserves in the afflicted areas and no surpluses elsewhere that could be brought to the region—at least this is what the government asserted.[5]

Thus, at least partially, the cause of hunger was to be found in the lack of its alleviation. The Allied naval blockade had been lifted in January 1920, but the "financial blockade"—that is, the refusal of European banks to lend to Russia—was not lifted until mid-1921. Still, major responsibility for the slow response to the growing tragedy must be laid in Lenin's lap. Top Bolsheviks, unwilling to admit to a catastrophe in the young "workers' paradise," ignored the people's privation until it was too late. Finally, on June 26, 1921, *Pravda* admitted that there was indeed hunger in the south and that it was affecting 25 million people, though the true number was more like 35 million. (Eventually, the Soviet government would admit to a death toll of 5.1 million, but the actual figure easily could have been twice as high.)[6]

No doubt there was a conflict within the Communist Party between those who refused to beg for help from the "capitalists, exploiters, and bourgeois hypocrites" of the West and those who put saving the nation before pure ideology. Thus it was not until July 11 that Lenin approved an appeal for help, and only then if Patriarch Tikhon and Maxim Gorky did the asking unofficially. Lenin sent Gorky to persuade Tikhon to appeal not only to foreign church leaders for aid but to write to the heads of their states. The hope was to open the door slightly to diplomatic recognition of the "underrecognized" Soviet state. Tikhon, perhaps wise to the ploy, refused to go beyond his church appeals, and the government had to settle for what it could get.[7] Gorky's appeal was published in the Soviet press on July 23, reading in part:

> Russia's misfortune offers . . . a splendid opportunity to demonstrate the vitality of humanitarianism. . . . I ask all honest European and American people for prompt aid to the Russian people. Give bread and medicine.[8]

In the late spring of 1921 the government had ordered food purchases abroad, but upon arrival during the summer—politics prevailing—most of these imports were transported to cities instead of to starving peasants in the countryside. The leadership never even visited areas at the height of their hunger. Then, incredibly and tragically, long railway trains of wheat were exported to Germany to fulfill the terms of the 1918 Brest-Litovsk Treaty.[9]

Continuing its efforts to avoid official involvement with foreign aid, the government created the nominally private All-Russian Public Committee to Aid the Hungry (*Pomgol*). According to Goldman, Pomgol was composed of right-wing Constitutional Democrats and other conservatives (excellent propaganda for foreign consumption) and, at Trotsky's insistence, pro-Soviet clergy (excellent for fomenting church dissension). Once the famine had run its course, most of the conservatives were deported, imprisoned, or shot.[10]

In typical Bolshevik fashion, Pomgol was overcentralized, and it actually served as a *restraint* on worldwide religious and secular efforts to relieve the suffering. Finally—and reluctantly—Pomgol requested food aid from the newly formed American Relief Administration (ARA), run by Secretary of Commerce Herbert Hoover and administered in Russia by Col. William Haskell. Although the United States had not yet recognized the Soviet regime, the ARA shipped $61.5 million worth of food, seed, clothing, and medical supplies to famine-stricken areas and dispatched hundreds of American volunteers to operate the program.[11] At its height it was feeding 10.5 million people a day.

In spite of the expressed concern of church hierarchs, hardly any priests remained active in the afflicted areas, excepting a few who were hired by foreign relief agencies. Even this was difficult, as local soviets intervened to prevent active clerical participation in relief programs.[12] When the ARA tried to include priests in the village committees for food distribution, an official objection was made:

> According to the laws of our constitution, the ecclesiastical element is harmful to the younger generation, and by the principles of the Soviet Government this element is deprived of all active or passive participation in our work.[13]

Many of the clergy who stayed in the villages refused to help because of frustration with the church's refusal to sell consecrated objects to raise relief money (see below). The rest fled with the exodus of refugees.

CONFISCATION AND CONFLICT

It is necessary that all honorable ministers of religion, who do not transform their God into a golden calf, who do not turn the work of helping the starving into a monarchist plot, should help in the struggle against the inhuman men of violence [the Orthodox hierarchy], who in the name of Christ bless cannibalism.[14]

—Pravda, May 7, 1922

Feeding the Hungry: Early Efforts

In the summer of 1921 Tikhon made the aforementioned appeals to Western church leaders and set up a church charity for the hungry—the Fund in Aid to the Famine Stricken—before Pomgol was even created. But by autumn the government still had not made a clear decision as to who would collect and administer whatever famine relief was available. Trying to keep the process under its centralized control, it originally demanded that all foreign relief be handed over to the government for distribution to the hungry. When English contributors and the ARA refused to allow this, the Soviets relented. As contributions at home steadily declined, it gradually became apparent to the Bolshevik leadership that they could not avoid a direct church role. In early December, Kalinin issued a statement permitting ecclesiastical authorities to make collections from church members for the relief program and directed Pomgol to enter into agreements with religious societies about methods of making these collections, "having in view the wishes of the donors." The government, suspecting churches of holding back, now tried to stimulate them to greater generosity. Anxious about the possible concealment of treasures that could be sold to finance the effort, it quickly took an inventory of churches, synagogues, and mosques to catalog what was available.[15]

During the winter of 1921–1922 the government finally focused on the problem, but its efforts were not entirely high-minded. Concern for the physical succor of its citizens was trumped by fear of food riots toppling their vulnerable regime, anxiety that famine was turning more citizens to the church, and embarrassment abroad. Any evidence of religious revival jolted the leadership, and if disaster was somehow fueling faith then the disaster must be alleviated. Since the Orthodox Church, the Catholic Church, and several Protestant denominations were *necessarily* involved in any proposed solution, the government had to find a way to relieve suffering without granting them any advantage in the process. This was difficult to accomplish, as churches were sincere in their efforts to save lives, and of course any success would be to their credit.

Another problem was that revolutionary ardor was cooling, and a continuing revolution could not be a lukewarm revolution. Not only the broad masses but also the lower and middle echelons of the party were tired of uprisings and war. Many simply wanted a chance to make a little money. What could the vanguard of the "vanguard of the proletariat" do to maintain the heat of revolution? The antireligious program—at least the enforcement of it—had been neglected during the Civil War, but now might be the time to renew it with vigor. In addition, the New Economic Policy's concessions to private enterprise seemed positively un-Marxist—as indeed they were—and there were those who worried that Lenin was abandoning the founding philosophy. The concessions caused divisions within the theoretically unified party and had to be propitiated. What better way to fire up the boilers within the tepid and divided ranks of Bolshevism than a rousing attack on the church?

The ARA shipped food directly to Tikhon early in the spring of 1922, but when it attempted this again in late April the government denied the ARA permission to move the goods. Then it forced the dissolution of the patriarch's fund and ordered all money previously collected to be handed over to central authorities. When Tikhon approached Colonel Haskell about selling donated church treasures in America and then using the funds for famine relief, Haskell refused; if he helped, it would appear that he was interfering in the internal affairs of a sovereign country.[16]

Several foreign-based churches sent relief missions to Russia, among them the Papal Relief Mission, an American Jewish mission, and American and English Quaker missions. The pope set aside ten million lire for Russian relief, and the Catholic mission, arriving in mid-August 1922, began the distribution of food and clothing in early October. Later, when typhus and malaria rampaged through the stricken countryside, the Vatican spent an additional 1 million lire on medicine. Catholic relief reached its peak during the spring and summer of 1923, at which point it was feeding 160,000 people a day, mostly children.[17] (Catholic relief efforts and Bolshevik responses will be discussed in more detail in chapter 20.) Most of these missions demanded a physical presence on Russian soil to ensure that money was not being misspent and that contributions were not being mixed in with those of other churches.

Although recipients of aid welcomed these missions, the government was suspicious of foreigners who were a little too anxious to assist. Bolshevik leaders considered foreign missions to be nests of spies and resented—as countering their propaganda—these living examples of Christian charity. Any public impression of church generosity ran directly counter to the carefully created image of greedy, self-serving priests, indifferent to suffering. For this reason, Soviet officials offered cold receptions to faith-based missions upon their arrival in Soviet territory. The Papal Commission on Relief for Russian Children received an especially frigid welcome.[18]

At the same time, the government was hostile to émigré clergy who were *opposed* to famine relief. The Karlovtzy clergy resented the missions, willing to see more Russians die to expose government incompetence in the people's eyes. They addressed a letter to Baron Wrangel hoping that the famine would lead to government collapse and appealed to the delegates at Genoa urging a military crusade against the Bolsheviks as a substitute for food assistance.[19] There may have been a direct cause-and-effect relationship between Karlovtzy pronouncements and the pending Soviet crackdown.

Desperate Need or Devious Opportunism?

The government, pushed to the point of wanting to look like it cared, cast its own hungry eyes on church treasures—chalices, vestments, gold and silver plating, precious stones—that could be sold to raise funds for famine relief. All ecclesiastical property, it argued, had been nationalized during the first year of Soviet rule, and this included not only church buildings but also the "equipment" inside. The buildings and the objects therein had been leased back to local congregations as a concession to the church, "voluntarily made by the Soviet people." Ornaments, vessels, and ikons were not the patriarch's to dispose of, and he should stop acting as if they were. Until now, the state had no need for "its property," but with the advent of famine the situation had drastically changed. Now citizens needed their property for more useful purposes. The government regarded itself as having an airtight legal case, not that it needed proof of its correctness to proceed with confiscations. Planning, however, must be secret and action swift. Trotsky persuaded Lenin to put him in charge of a covert commission with the task of stripping valuables from the churches before organized internal opposition could be mounted and before the foreign press could get wind of it.[20] Government propaganda, as Trotsky anticipated, put all churches in an awkward position. Any hesitation in relinquishing treasures would make churches appear avaricious and more concerned with church decorations than people's diets.

Church hierarchs pointed to the resolution passed in the final days of the First Church Sobor: "Concerning the Protection of the Church's Holy Things from Sacrilegious Seizure and Blasphemy." It described the churches' contents as "the property of God."[21] They might not have minded handing over *some* of their valuables if they had been assured that the government had exhausted every *kopeck* of its own funds and if the church could have counted on its contributions going directly to buy bread for the hungry and not into the pockets of the commissars. Concern was justified, as Cheka agents—popularly known as "pearl divers"—were already notorious for ripping jewels out of ikons and trying to sell them in foreign markets. (The gems that parishioners donated to their churches, however, were of such poor quality that buyers could seldom be found.)[22]*

Just as the government was suspicious of the church, the church did not trust the government. When requested guarantees were not forthcoming, Tikhon entered into negotiations. Finally he was able to inform the faithful that an agreement had been reached with civil authorities: The church would be allowed to contribute its valuables *directly* for relief without first having to turn them over to the state. Similar agreements were negotiated by other relief organizations.[23]

Francis McCullagh, writing from the scene, speculated that Tikhon (and his church) would have been far better off if he had handed over every church treasure without complaint and chosen instead another battlefield. His suggestion was a firm and consistent stand against the Soviet denial of religious education to children. While Europeans and Americans could not rouse themselves over church valuables during a famine, they would have been incensed—and let the Soviets know it—over denial of the basic parental right of educating their children as they saw fit.[24] Tikhon could have responded as did Exarch Fyodorov, leader of the small group of Catholics of the Eastern Rite in Russia:

> If the Soviet government orders me to act against my conscience, I do not obey. As for teaching the Catechism, the Catholic Church lays it down that children must be taught their religion, no matter what the law says. Conscience is above the law. No law that is against the conscience can bind.[25]

The patriarch, however, was naive as to the relative foreign propaganda values of the two issues (or perhaps he was totally focused on the situation in Russia).

On February 19, 1922, Tikhon issued a proclamation urging churches to be generous and make sacrifices on behalf of the starving, but he specifically described as uncanonical the donation of *any consecrated item*, whether or not it was used in the service. Unconsecrated items would mostly be adornments of ikons (not the ikons themselves), which Tikhon estimated to be of relatively little value. The government allowed Tikhon's statement to be printed in the newspapers,[26] but at the same time it maintained that any item left to facilitate worship

---

*The December 7, 1917, mandate creating the Cheka nowhere mentioned antireligious work, but over the next few years it practiced a little self-aggrandizement by establishing a Secret Department in charge of religious affairs. Before long it was organizing the confiscations described in this chapter.

was a result of government generosity; the patriarch had no power to dispose or not dispose of anything.

Tikhon's concessions and offers seemed to have pleased no one. Many in the church hierarchy grumbled that Tikhon had capitulated too easily. Moderates in the government regarded the church proposal as adequate, but firebrands such as Mikhail Gorev scoffed. He wrote an article in *Pravda* titled "The Mountain Brings Forth a Mouse," asking about all the pearls, precious stones, and precious metals that were embedded in ikons[27] (which, of course, most likely had already been removed). And Commissar Krasikov ordered a 50,000-issue press run of a new journal, *Church Gold to the Starving*. The press called the patriarch "Bloody Tikhon,"[28] and its campaign for confiscation of *all* valuables mounted in intensity. Meanwhile, Trotsky's commission pressed furiously ahead.

Kalinin's Central Executive Committee decreed on February 23 that "all valuable objects of gold, silver, and precious stones . . . which cannot actually interfere with the interests of the cult itself" be confiscated, and he made it clear that this would apply to all Russian faiths. He deliberately ignored Tikhon's distinction between consecrated and unconsecrated items, focusing on the issue of actual *use* in the service instead—presumably this would leave more valuables available for confiscation. (Apparently the government honored this rule, as there is no record during this period of any church complaint that it was deprived of instruments essential for the divine service.) The confiscation decree did promise that removals would take place in the presence of believers, that all resulting funds would be used exclusively for famine relief, and that detailed reports listing church-by-church confiscations would be published periodically in the newspapers. It also contained provisions—not always honored in the field—to protect valuables of historic or artistic significance. Treasures were to be delivered to the Commissariat of Finance within one month, where they would be sold on world markets and the proceeds delivered to Pomgol. Kalinin's decree countermanded the decree issued earlier in the month that had allowed the church to make direct donations; church charity was now forcibly closed.[29]

Tikhon wrote to Kalinin on February 25—the day before the confiscation decree was actually published in *Izvestia*—asking again that the church be allowed to voluntarily contribute the valuables instead of having them forcibly seized. He also wanted congregational consent prior to donations and the bitter press attack on "church greed" discontinued. Kalinin never replied; Tikhon could read about it in the newspapers.[30]

On February 28 Tikhon issued a circular letter explaining the church's position. He recited in some detail the church's efforts to collect money for the starving and described how the government had obstructed all its endeavors. He reiterated the distinction between consecrated ornaments that must be retained and unconsecrated items of no liturgical value that could be donated. Chalices, altar crosses, Bible covers, and the small vessels where the sacred bread of the

Eucharist was kept must be retained. If the government's motives were purely to raise money, making an exception for consecrated vessels should make no appreciable difference. Very few such vessels were gold, and those made of silver represented an insignificant portion of all silver treasures within the churches. The patriarch reminded all priests that laymen were not even to *touch* consecrated objects on pain of excommunication and that—as the canon required—any priest cooperating with government confiscations was in danger of losing his sacerdotal rank. Cautiously, he did not specifically instruct them to resist. His letter also called for continuing collections among parishioners, "desiring only that these offerings should be the response of a loving heart to the needs of their neighbors."[31] When, a week later, the government got wind of this internal communication, it sent an *Izvestia* reporter to interview Tikhon, who responded:

> Remember the words of Christ, if you have two shirts give your shirt to your neighbor. The church cannot remain indifferent to those great sufferings that the starving are experiencing.[32]

Strangely, Trotsky wrote to the Politburo a month after Kalinin's decree had been published: "I repeat—this commission is a complete secret." The Politburo responded two days later, urging him to be harsh in the completion of his task. Trotsky put his lieutenant, Sapronov, in charge of the physical confiscations and ordered him to work with local soviets and under the cover of the famine relief committee.[33] The only way to make sense of this is to assume that the work of local soviets (and perhaps the Cheka) was general knowledge but that Trotsky's commission was still a deep secret. A clue may be gleaned, however, from Lenin's request to Trotsky not to speak out publicly on this issue to avoid charges that the Jewish Trotsky was heading a Jewish conspiracy to destroy the Russian Orthodox Church. Plenty of anti-Soviet propaganda had already zeroed in on the relatively high percentage of Jews in the Bolshevik high command. Nonetheless, Trotsky was also put in charge of the commission to *sell* the valuables and convert them into cash, which was not an easy task; many foreign brokers refused to touch the treasures once they learned of their origin.[34]

   In spite of confidence in its legal position, the government also sought virtue. It claimed that only "accumulated treasures" were taken, nothing that would infringe on cult practices. As its agents sacked the churches, Kalinin asserted in *Pravda* that confiscations were never intended to be an attack on religion itself. But another article in *Pravda* belied his point, stating that the confiscations "should serve to sunder the crumbling body of the former state church."[35] And a Moscow publication was even more explicit, stating that the confiscations were meant as a "blow aimed at the complete disorganization of religion."[36]

   Saying "a crust of bread is better than a cross, especially when there is an excess of crosses,"[37] the Soviet press ran a campaign to bring the extent and value of church treasures to the people's attention. One newspaper calculated that the sale of church silver alone could purchase 525 million pounds of bread, enough to feed every starving peasant in Russia (for how long was not mentioned).[38]

For church hierarchs, however, it was not just a matter of bread calculations; there were canonical calculations to be made as well. Apostolic Canon 73 read:

> Let no one convert to his own use any vessel of gold or silver, or any veil which has been sanctified, for it is contrary to law; and if anyone be detected doing so, let him be excommunicated.[39]

But attitudes toward the Apostolic Canons were similar to attitudes toward the US Constitution in that some favored judicial restraint and others supported judicial activism. Progressive clergy argued that the intent of this canon was to prevent the theft of church vessels for personal gain; with the famine spreading this was hardly the issue now. After all, the ancient church had exercised the right to regulate itself in accordance with the exigencies of the times (activism). There were, for example, numerous instances where church treasures had been melted down and sold to purchase the freedom of hostages or prisoners of war. St. Ambrose had sold the treasures of Milan to rescue prisoners taken by the Goths. The government press noted that in tsarist times church valuables had been sold to relieve natural calamities and even to finance wars, and there were reports that some tsars had ravaged these treasures for their own personal collections. The government claimed that church treasures had happily been handed over to General Denikin. Tikhon's retort: "The tsars took but they also gave."[40]*

A different patriarch might have followed this reasoning to justify full compliance with government demands. But Tikhon was conservative and legalistically minded, and from his point of view (restraint) the government's plan was full-scale plunder that offered him little room to maneuver. It was clear in his mind that consecrated items could not be released. Laws handed down from ancient church councils were immutable and binding; they were to be observed under all conditions and for all time. Yet if this were so, argued progressive professor B. Titlinov, what about the ancient church canon that states: "The church estate is the estate of the paupers and beggars." So much more then, he continued, is it the property of the famine-stricken starving people.[41]

Soon other progressive (and pro-Soviet) priests began supporting the government's position. In the March 23 issue of *Izvestia*, Bishop Polycarp of Lukyanov wrote, "It is sinful to hold in our sanctuaries treasures for which we have no use, while in the meantime people are suffering agonies of hunger." Over

---

*Anthony Khrapovitsky and the émigré hierarchs in Yugoslavia also supported the sale of church treasures in national emergencies, but for them the "emergency" was overthrowing the Bolsheviks.

the next several days, twelve progressive priests wrote in *Krasnaya Gazeta* and *Petrogradskaya Pravda* that Tikhon had displayed "unchristian feelings"; was motivated by "malice, heartlessness, and slander"; and was "playing politics." They extolled the "apostolic zeal" of progressive clergy (themselves) in coming to the aid of the starving.[42]

Adding to the pressure on the hierarchy, on March 23 *Izvestia* printed an appeal and petition from a group of "believing workers" at the Moscow Dynamo Factory:

> The only escape from our suffering is to buy bread for the starving with the church gold and silver. That gold and silver was collected through the ages and is national property. Is it not possible now to turn a portion of that wealth into bread? Most holy patriarch, remember that millions of people who are now about to perish will die of hunger with a curse upon their lips against God and the church, which was unwilling to exchange golden goblets for wooden ones. ... Faith without works is dead. ... Convert the gold, silver, and precious stones into bread, and save from death those who are starving![43]

While such polemics may have emboldened the government to go further with its confiscation program, there remains the problem that the government itself had written some of these letters (though the Dynamo appeal was possibly genuine). When the church investigated, it found that parishes complaining about lack of Christian charity did not even exist.[44]

Under intense pressure from Communist authorities, Tikhon officially condemned violent resistance, yet his influence over the Orthodox masses was not so great that he could simply issue instructions to be obeyed. In March and April congregations across the country—including Moscow, Petrograd, and Smolensk—resisted church looting on their own, with violence and bloodshed ensuing. As mentioned above, much of their fury was based on the priest-fueled, but fully justified, belief that the treasures from their churches would be used to fund Communist propaganda abroad or go directly into commissars' pockets rather than be used for their intended purpose. In Vitebsk a rumor spread that gold taken from the churches would be made into gold teeth to replace the rotten teeth of the commissars. In Roslavl the people were convinced that all collected funds were being distributed to local Jews.[45] Suspicion of government intentions and violence against church looters even had a gender bias. According to a police report: "Discontent over the seizure of church valuables is noticeable chiefly among women."[46] Since the First Church Sobor, women's role in the church had grown; they had full voting rights at the parish level and could serve as church elders. They expressed their newfound strength in the protection of their churches.

As resistance stiffened, a frustrated government agent in Smolensk wrote to GPU headquarters in Moscow:

The attempt to achieve the practical removal of valuables from Smolensk Cathedral was not successful. Day and night the crowd of believers remains in the cathedral and does not allow the commission to set to work. All talks with representatives of the believers lead to nothing. We have spoken on this question with Trotsky and have received from him directions that we are putting into effect. Report whether it is necessary to act decisively.[47]

Three days later, on March 20, the Politburo met to discuss the crisis. It suggested that confiscations take place first in rich city churches, followed by poor city churches, and then the countryside. In the provinces a full week of (unannounced) agitation should precede any actual confiscations, and the best agitators would be soldiers; any Jews on confiscation committees must be kept in the background. Concealing its duplicitous aims, the party leaders suggested, "Give the agitation a character far removed from any struggle with religion and the church, and [keep it] completely directed at helping the starving." If protests were organized, the local government should empty any nearby garrison and parade the soldiers around the church carrying placards reading, "Church valuables to save the lives of the starving." The Politburo actually recommended dragging starving peasants from the lower Volga to northern churches and presenting them to confiscation resisters. Its rationale for all this was "the criminal, stingy attitude to the valuables on the part of the inhuman and avaricious lords of the church."[48]

But the Politburo realized it also had to placate. It permitted representatives of the "loyal clergy" to be present at any counting of confiscated treasures and announced that the population would have plenty of opportunities to see that the money gained would go nowhere but to the starving. But it also warned confiscators not to take seriously any local offers to pay cash in lieu of treasures.[49]

Izvestia published this account of turbulence occurring on March 28, 1922, in the town of Shuya, just northeast of Moscow:

Monday, March 13, was appointed as the day of requisition in the Cathedral of Shuya. The Commission arrived at the spot at noon, after the service. It was met with hostile shouts of the crowd. Wishing to avoid a collision, the Commission decided to postpone its work till Wednesday and quitted the church. When it was leaving some swearwords were uttered by the crowd, and the members of the Commission received several kicks and blows.

On Wednesday, March 28, a large crowd began to assemble at the Cathedral Square before the service. It consisted mainly of women and youth. The detachment of mounted militia was stoned as soon as it approached. The tocsin resounded from the belfry of the church and lasted an hour and a half, attracting an enormous crowd. A detachment of infantry and two lorries with machine guns were ordered to the spot. They were met by a gale of stones and revolver shots. Four soldiers were swept away by the crowd and severely injured. After the first volley in the air, the second was charged at the crowd. Four people were killed and ten seriously injured, after which the crowd dispersed. In the evening many arrests were made and the Commission continued to work. [Over one hundred pounds] of silver were requisitioned.[50]

Although Shuya was a textile-manufacturing town, its "proletariat" was made up of workers who had recently migrated from the countryside, and the majority of these workers were women. The government felt, though, that it was not their gender but their inadequate class-consciousness that accounted for their vehemence in defending the church. Obviously bourgeois elements (mainly merchants) in the town had stirred up "the very darkest elements of the population" by spreading rumors that money from the sale of the valuables was going to make payments to Poland or support the Red Army rather than feed the hungry. Another rumor was that the Communist leadership knew that their days were numbered and were planning to stash the money in European banks for their forced retirement.[51] On the same day as the Shuya incident, Smolensk factory workers laid down their tools and rushed to protect their church. In both Shuya and Smolensk, *proletarian* defense of church valuables must have been especially galling for local Bolsheviks.

Then angry crowds in Petrograd killed six party members and eleven militiamen. Eventually government authorities admitted to 1,414 bloody encounters in front of churches, which, between 1921 and 1923, led to the deaths of around 2,700 priests, 2,000 monks, 3,500 nuns, and an untold number of laity.[52] The government did not mention how many of its own had been killed.

What tactics were available to the government? In many of these confrontations spies would circulate within the crowds, jotting down the names of the least restrained of resisters and occasionally provoking angry responses just so that they could record them.[53] Those whose names ended up on notepads were labeled counterrevolutionaries who had been driven to extremes by the clergy's reactionary propaganda. But Lenin urged stronger action and pushed for a violent confrontation over the church valuables issue. Aggravated by the mayhem at Shuya, he wrote a top-secret note to Viacheslav Molotov on April 2, asking him to circulate it among Politburo members but to make no copies. He would be unable to attend the meeting the next day, but he wanted his views known. Lenin's note is presented at length for what it reveals:

> It becomes perfectly clear that the Black Hundreds clergy, headed by its leader [Patriarch Tikhon], with full deliberation is carrying out a plan at this very moment to destroy us decisively. . . . I think that here our opponent is making a huge strategic error by attempting to draw us into a decisive struggle now when it is especially hopeless and especially disadvantageous to him. For us, on the other hand, precisely at the present moment we are presented with an exceptionally favorable, even unique, opportunity when we can in ninety-nine out of a hundred chances utterly defeat our enemy with complete success and guarantee for ourselves the position we require for decades.

Now and only now, when people are being eaten in famine-stricken areas, and hundreds, if not thousands, of corpses lie on the roads, we can (and therefore must) pursue the removal of church property with the most frenzied and ruthless energy, and not hesitate to put down the least opposition. We must pursue the removal of church property by any means necessary in order to secure for ourselves a fund of several hundred million gold rubles (do not forget the immense wealth of some monasteries). Without this fund any government work in general, any economic buildup in particular, and the defense of our positions in Genoa are absolutely unthinkable. . . .

With success we can do this only now, . . . for no other opportunity but the current terrible famine will give us such a mood among the masses that would provide us with their sympathies or at least neutrality. . . . Now our victory over the reactionary clergy is guaranteed. Moreover the main part of our enemies among the Russian émigrés . . . will find it very hard to carry on their struggle against us. . . .

One clever writer on statecraft [Machiavelli] correctly said that if it is necessary for the realization of a well-known political goal to perform a series of brutal actions then it is necessary to do them in the most energetic manner and in the shortest time, because masses of people will not tolerate the protracted use of brutality. . . . The campaign itself for carrying out this plan I envision in the following manner. . . . In Shuya [a government agent] must arrest more if possible but not less than several dozen representatives of the local clergy . . . and the local bourgeoisie on suspicion of direct or indirect participation in the forcible resistance to the decree on the removal of property of value from churches. . . . Immediately on his return he makes an oral report to the Politburo which in turn will give a detailed directive to the judicial authorities, also verbal, that the trial of the insurrectionists from Shuya, for opposing aid to the starving, should be carried out in utmost haste and *should end not other than with the shooting of the very largest number of the most influential and dangerous.* If possible, similar executions should be carried out in Moscow and other spiritual centers of the country.

I think we should not touch Patriarch Tikhon, although he is at the head of this rebellion of slaveowners. At the [next] party congress a secret session should be organized jointly with leading members of the GPU, the Commissariat of Justice, and the Revolutionary Tribunal. A secret decision of the Congress should approve a mercilessly decisive confiscation of church valuables. The more members of the reactionary bourgeoisie we manage to shoot the better.[54]

Notice how Lenin explicitly says what the funds raised from the sale of church valuables will be spent on.

It is difficult to ascertain the number of executions and imprisonments that resulted from the Shuya incident, as it depends upon the length of time afterward that is being considered. There may have been as few as three executions or as many as eleven (in the latter case, eight priests, two laymen, and one laywoman), and the government imprisoned twenty-five believers.[55] In his note to Molotov, Lenin authorized the full-fledged attack on the Orthodox Church that would soon lead to three major trials: two Orthodox (chapter 12) and one Catholic (chapter 21).

Although church scholars had searched the historical record and found many ancient precedents for church opposition to civil authority, on April 11, 1922, Tikhon nonetheless circulated a letter to his bishops again urging them to discourage violence in preventing the confiscation of church treasures. In the end, however, the patriarch's efforts were inadequate. When conflict continued, the government, not about to tolerate open revolt against its orders, raised the stakes in its offensive. The press began to list resisters by name, placing blame all the way to the top of the church hierarchy. Lenin ordered the GPU to closely monitor Tikhon and discover the contents of all his communications. *Pravda* demanded that the clergy face "the revolutionary tribunal just as murderers do. Let the punishment be speedy and ruthless."[56] At a meeting of Sovnarkom in April, Trotsky pushed through a resolution calling for a still more aggressive policy, antireligious motivations trumping any genuine concern for the plight of the hungry.

Government agents were now stripping the ikons and other treasures from the churches more thoroughly than had the French during the invasion of 1812. Paul Scheffer, a correspondent for the *Berliner Tageblatt* (sympathetic to the Communists) described what he had seen as of December 1922. Silver and gold had been peeled from the vestments and coats-of-mail of statues of saints. Even the silver badges from the brass cases that covered the tombs of the patriarchs had been ripped away. All the tapers, censers, and silver candleholders had been sent somewhere to be melted down. Brocade coverings had been thrown in piles on the floor to be packed in boxes for transport. Sometimes, Scheffer reported, historical items of little monetary value were left behind, and frequently the authorities would leave one large valuable item in the church as a "specimen," so people might be reminded of the treasures that used to be.[57]

Francis McCullagh, in his book *The Bolshevik Persecution of Christianity* (1924), offered this perspective:

> The Bolsheviks have certainly some reason to say that they were victorious in this, their first serious encounter with the greatest organized force in Russia apart from Bolshevism itself. History must record the fact that in 1922 Russian Orthodox soldiers plundered churches at the bidding of a government consisting wholly of atheists and anticlericals. They threw into sacks the chalices to which, ten years ago, [these same men] attributed supernatural powers. They tied up priests whom they looked upon ten years ago as wonder-workers who could blast them with a curse. They shot down fellow Christians for attempting to defend their churches; and, lastly, they executed ordained priests of God. . . . The men who did this were, unfortunately, Russians, and furthermore the country as a whole did not express its displeasure by the general insurrection that one would have expected.[58]

The confiscation campaign informally ended in September 1922, though the famine continued through the coming winter. Deputy Sovnarkom Chairman Aleksy Rykov decreed that all church property, even of a nonsacred nature (bells, furniture, etc.), that had "fallen into the hands of soviets" could be sold. All proceeds from these sales, of course, were to be turned over to the national treasury in Moscow. There is not a single piece of evidence that any of this money ever went to famine relief.[59]*

Throughout 1922 and 1923 the government sold Russian (mainly Ukrainian) grain in Europe to earn hard currencies for Lenin's high-priority industrialization projects, and some Ukrainian Communist Party members had the nerve to protest this policy. For example, at a Party Central Committee session in Moscow on November 15, 1922, a Ukrainian worker-delegate named Romanchuk condemned the party's grain export policy:

> The villages demand from their delegates that they prevent the export of even one pood [thirty-six pounds] of grain. . . . The workers and the sailors of [my village] condemn this project as robbery of the last piece of bread snatched from starving workers. This, comrades, is the authentic voice of the people.[60]

In January 1923 citizens of Odessa watched in puzzlement as the SS *Manitowac* discharged a cargo of ARA relief supplies in their port while right next to it the SS *Vladimir* was loading a cargo of Ukrainian grain bound for Hamburg. When the ARA discovered that, rather than feeding its own people, the Soviet Union was exporting millions of tons of cereal grains to Germany, Italy, and Finland, it terminated its relief efforts.[61]

With the famine subsiding in 1923, Kalinin—accompanied by a large retinue of staff, foreign correspondents, and piles of propaganda—made a "triumphal march" through the stricken areas on the Volga to congratulate his government for the effective work it had done.[62]

CHURCH LOSSES

When the confiscations ended, assessments of material losses varied widely. No official and complete record of the cash realized from the sale of church treas-

---

*The 1970 edition of the *Great Soviet Encyclopedia* described the American Relief Administration as follows: "The food products, medicine, and other goods shipped by the ARA were of some help in fighting the famine. At the same time the ruling circles of the USA tried to use it to support counterrevolutionary elements, espionage, and sabotage, to fight the revolutionary movement and to strengthen the position of American imperialism in Europe." It should also be noted that by 1924 Soviet agriculture was well on its way to recovery. The 1925 grain harvest was the highest in Russian history.

ures was ever published by the government, nor was any accounting ever offered of how this revenue was used. On September 3, 1922, *Izvestia* reported the following figures, which did not include confiscations in Petrograd and Siberia: 291 pounds of gold, 610,440 of silver, 3,071 pounds of copper, 57 pounds of pearls, 166 carats of diamonds, 3,265 gold ruble coins, and 41 gold watches. In Petrograd, St. Isaak's Cathedral and the Kazan Cathedral lost 180 pounds of gold and 9,570 pounds of silver between them, and there must have been much more from the other city churches.[63]

There was also an interim (and partial) report from Pomgol in October, putting the total value of gold, silver, and gems taken at 19.3 million gold rubles. As the government had originally estimated a haul of 800 million gold rubles, *Izvestia* characterized the total as "ridiculously insignificant" in comparison with the confiscation effort and the magnitude of the crisis.[64] Of course, at the risk of being charged with "theft of government property," priests and laymen had hidden much of the treasure. In January 1925 *Izvestia* carried the story of fifteen clergy members at Kiev's Pechersky Monastery—closed and sacked several years before—who were arrested after authorities discovered a cache of gold, silver, and precious stones in the cellar. Tikhon denied any knowledge of the concealment.[65]

Another way of measuring the church's losses is by counting personnel. There were many more local trials of clergy than the three major ones discussed in upcoming chapters, and consequently there was a drastic reduction in the population of Russian priests. During the summer of 1920, Tikhon announced that 320 Orthodox bishops and priests had been executed. Later, the Soviet writer (and ex-priest) I. Brikhnichev offered incomplete statistics for sentences handed down by 55 tribunals: Of those found guilty, 181 were ecclesiastics and 408 were laity; out of the whole group, 33 had been shot. But this pales in comparison to the Soviet *admission* in April 1922 that 28 bishops and 1,200 priests had been executed (and they were not even finished yet). Others have put the figure at around 8,100 clerics, monks, and nuns killed one way or another during 1922.[66] The clerical structure of the church was essential for its survival; without it the sacramental needs of parishioners could not be met. This was, of course, the plan.

For Paul Scheffer, writing from Russia in December 1922, the hardest loss to measure was that of the inner mystery of the church:

> Formerly, thousands of big and tiny candles used to shine here out of the darkness (only above, near the cupola, some light broke through). Their light shone and showed reflections upon silver and gold, upon the rich cloths and dark faces of the saints, and the massive outlines of censers and the heavy splendor of the vestments. From the eighteenth century on the custom was established to leave open only the faces, the hands, and the feet of the saints, and to cover all the rest with gold or silver; it was mostly these dusky coats-of-mail on the walls and columns and at the altars, upon which the light of wax candles played its reflec-

tions, that filled the churches with solemn flowing life, which came no one knows where from.[67]

Now, with the confiscations, the bare wooden bodies of the saints were exposed. The light no longer shimmered on precious metals, and the churches were truly dark.

If the point of the confiscations was famine relief, other opportunities to raise funds were certainly open to the Bolsheviks; they were not explored because of the lack of political gain they would provide. For example, in March 1922, Archbishop Nikander appealed to authorities to exclude consecrated items from the list of items to be taken. He proposed substituting unconsecrated items of the same metal and equal worth, but no attention was paid to his offer.

Before taking the treasures of the church, could Soviet authorities have sold the Russian crown jewels, worth 1 billion gold rubles, or the jewels in the Kremlin Museum, worth 300 million gold rubles?[68] Herbert Hoover asked this question in a telegram to Politburo member Lev Kamenev in October 1922, when the confiscations had already ended. Kamenev replied that the government would pledge the crown jewels as collateral for a loan if there were a guarantee that foreign claimants against Russia would not attach the jewels as payment. He knew full well that, since there were many claimants in many lands, such a guarantee, in a practical sense, could never be arranged. The crown jewels remained in storage.[69]

And one last revealing fact: Nikolai Bukharin reported to the party in May 1923 that the Soviets had spent the ruble equivalent of $13.75 million on foreign propaganda during the famine period.[70]

It was not just the confiscations that interested the government; it was also the clergy members and how they could be made to pay for their obstreperous attitude. 1922 and 1923 were the years of the major church trials.

12

THE FOULEST, BLACKEST FOE OF THE WORKING PEOPLE

Trials of the Orthodox Clergy

In 1922 the Bolsheviks were a small minority of the population who saw conspiracies everywhere and imagined them easily. Power may have been used harshly, but it was also fragile—indeed, it may have been harsh *because* it was fragile. Internationally, Russia was still an outlaw nation, diplomatically recognized by no European nation (except Germany after the April 1922 Treaty of Rapallo). *Any* challenge to Bolshevik power, no matter how objectively inconsequential, was automatically an attack on the Revolution.

One perceived attack came from clergy members who were less than generous in their contributions to famine relief. They were rounded up and tried in bunches. The purpose of their trials was not justice in the Western sense; it was victory over Bolshevism's enemies with the least amount of negative foreign reaction possible.

A DIGRESSION ON SOVIET LAW

In drawing up evidence, do not look for incriminating material to prove that the person under prosecution acted by deed or word against the Soviet power. The first question that you must ask of him is, what is his ancestry, education, and profession. These questions must determine the fate of the accused. Therein lies the meaning and the essence of the Red Terror.[1]

—a leading member of the Cheka

Lenin abolished the entire tsarist court system and replaced "bourgeois courts" with Revolutionary Tribunals in mid-December 1917. These courts were handed extraordinary powers to root out the enemies of the Revolution or even those suspected or being capable of counterrevolutionary acts. In March 1919 the Communist Party Program stated that in cases where the law was absent or incomplete, "socialist conscience" should guide judges. By this time the Cheka had accumulated such extraordinary powers that it could arrest without warrant, try without publicity, and execute with only a *subsequent* notification to the Commissariat of Justice.

On June 1, 1922, the government finally adopted the RSFSR Criminal Code.* It contained nothing like an ex post facto law to prevent people from being charged with "crimes" that were not against the law when committed. Instead, Article 57 made it clear that any action at any time that *tended* to overthrow the revolutionary government was by definition the crime of "counterrevolutionary action." Articles 62, 63, and 77 further elaborated on this theme, providing penalties for any hindrance of the legal actions or demands of Russian authorities. Articles 119 through 125 and 227 dealt with violations of the separation of church and state.[2] Their salient points included some prohibitions that had appeared in earlier decrees and some new ones:

- no arousing "the religious superstitions of the masses" to plot against the government or encourage "resistance to its laws and decrees."[3]
- no using "fraudulent devices to excite the superstitious spirit of the masses" for personal profit.
- no celebrating religious rites or exhibiting religious images on state property. (Otherwise the performance of religious rites was legal so long as it did not "offend against public order" and was not "accompanied by attacks on the rights of citizens.")
- no celebrating religious rites in such a manner that they violated the traffic laws in local jurisdictions. (Of course, this last article exists in modern Western countries as well—the devil is in the implementation.)
- no teaching religious doctrines to persons under age eighteen in public and private schools.
- no exerting pressure "in the collection of funds for ecclesiastical or religious organizations."

Each of these banned activities carried with it very specific penalties, usually a certain number of months at hard labor and/or a fine in gold rubles. But in October 1922 Nikolai Krylenko, Deputy Commissar of Justice and chief prosecutor at the Supreme Court, further clarified this aspect of the law, "If a sentence does not correspond to the spirit of Bolshevik legislation, it can always be cancelled"—meaning that the penalty could be increased administratively.

It would be a mistake to call these proceedings trials in the Western sense. They were really an amalgamation of the trappings of Western legal procedures

---

*Henceforth, there were no jury trials in Russia until 1993.

and the quick certitude of kangaroo courts. Independence of the judiciary and separation of powers were considered "false theories," part of the capitalistic superstructure. Here is a sampling of early Soviet legal theory, most excerpted from prosecutor Krylenko's writings and speeches (obtained by Solzhenitsyn from an obscure Soviet publication):

- Defense was constrained: Defense attorneys were employees of the state and were expected to cooperate with the prosecution (or at least not to struggle too hard against it) to achieve "revolutionary justice."
- Law was concocted: Tribunals were "at one and the same time both the creator of the law . . . and a political weapon." This was true because for at least four years there was no law outside of Lenin's multifarious decrees. Tsarist legal codes had been thrown out and little had formally been written to replace them. The new law was similar to English Common Law in that it was based on court decisions and precedent. Krylenko made this clear: "Don't tell me our criminal courts ought to act exclusively on the basis of existing written norms. We live in the process of Revolution."
- Guilt lost its meaning: "Guilty" and "not guilty" were worn-out bourgeois concepts, irrelevant because the court was not really a court at all. "A tribunal is an organ of the class struggle of the workers directed against their enemies." It must act "from the point of view of the interests of the Revolution . . . having in mind the most desirable results for the masses of workers and peasants." No matter what the individual qualities of the defendant, "only one method of evaluating him is to be applied: evaluation from the point of view of class expediency." Neither the law nor extenuating circumstances really mattered.
- Truth was irrelevant: There was no concept of objective Truth and therefore no interest in it. The function of the courts was to "defend the socialist state of workers and peasants."
- Courts were proactive: Tribunals protected the people not only from what the defendant did but also from what he had not yet done but might do if he was not shot right now. "We protect ourselves not only against the past but also against the future."[4]
- Innocents were condemned: Collective justice was reasonable; the family of a traitor could legally be shipped off to Siberian work camps.
- Offenses were ill defined: Analogous penalties were applied. Western countries followed the Roman practice of *nullum crimen sine lege* (if there is no law, then there can be no crime), but Revolutionary Tribunals, when unable to find a legal basis for prosecution, simply punished its citizens for violation of whatever law was "most similar."[5]
- Mitigation was rare: The Bolsheviks, ironically, took a page out of the New Testament in the interpretation of the law. James 2:10 stated, "For

whosoever shall keep the whole law, and yet offend in one point, he is guilty of all." For the Soviets, you were guilty of counterrevolutionary activity no matter how many Soviet laws you had obeyed, as long as you had offended on one.[6] In other words, your overall record of law-abiding citizenship would not be used to lessen your sentence.

On the first day of religious trials, the prosecutor would read a "Statement of Accusation" to the court, pointing out that the Revolution had destroyed the *political* power of the capitalists and landowners but had failed to suppress completely the *moral and intellectual pressure* this class could bring to bear on the conscience of the masses. Much of this pressure was exerted through the church, which was defined as "a social organization for the special benefit of the exploiting classes" and an "instrument for the exploitation of the workers." The statement went on to explain that the clergy of all denominations belonged to this exploiting class, and it was therefore inevitable that they would view the Revolution "as something wholly hostile."

Revolutionary justice overrode any religious freedoms guaranteed in the 1918 Constitution. In that sense, the Constitution was not a constitution at all. Michael Bourdeaux described a hypothetical situation:

> It is not impossible that at the height of some Soviet antireligious campaign a prosecution counsel might stand up in court and claim that the celebration of Holy Communion in a Russian Orthodox church contained precisely the intention of "arousing religious superstitions." . . . There would be no legal mechanism in the Soviet system for asserting at this point the technically superior guarantee of the "right to hold religious services" contained in the Constitution.[7]

THE MOSCOW CHURCH TRIAL

Judge: "Do you consider the state's laws obligatory or not?"
Tikhon: "Yes, I recognize them, to the extent that they do not contradict the rules of piety."[8]

Tikhon had been living in three rooms in what was called the "town residence" of the St. Sergius-Trinity Monastery. Police guarded his rooms and regularly searched his possessions and his visitors, and each evening they took his guest book to the GPU office for inspection. His followers, fearing for his safety, daily crowded around his residence to watch him wave from his window. Yes, he was still alive. He could continue his habits of handing out candy and apples to children who climbed over the back wall, and he could still take walks around the small adjoining garden late at night. The house contained its own chapel where he would occasionally hold small services. The government insisted that other rooms in the residence be filled with orphaned children from the famine area, perhaps as punishment for Tikhon's resistance to the confiscation decree.[9]

Then in April 1922 the arrests began. Early in the month the GPU learned of a secret meeting held two months earlier among Tikhon, Archbishop Nikander (Fanomenov), and several others at which, it was alleged, they had conspired to obstruct the confiscation of church treasures. Using this information, the Commissariat of Justice decided to crack down on "the nest of reaction—the Tikhonites," taking Nikander and virtually every church administrator in the Moscow diocese into custody. A nationwide sweep of deacons and priests led to 231 trials, resulting in forty-four death sentences, though not all were carried out. The most notorious of these trials was the Moscow Church Trial of April 26–May 6, 1922, also referred to as "The Trial of the Fifty-Four."[10]

The Moscow Revolutionary Tribunal met in the Polytechnic Museum, with Judge Bek (and two other judges) presiding. The original defendants were divided into three groups according to the charges. The first was composed of deacons, who were charged merely with participating in the general disturbances. Eventually they were released on the grounds that they were simply following the orders of their priests. The second group included the priests who had allegedly given those orders; they were charged with "resisting the authority of the Soviet Government." The third group consisted of seven archdeacons; they were accused of having taken part in the Tikhon–Nikander conference.[11] The patriarch himself was not a defendant.

When the trial began there were no longer fifty-four defendants due to the pretrial releases. For those who were held over, part of the indictment read:

> [Soviet decrees] called forth a violent protest from that section of the clergy that, having been deprived during the preceding four years of its previous greatness, had already entered several times into strife with Soviet Russia. . . . Taking advantage of the famine on the Volga, relying on old people, fanatics, weak-minded persons, and hooligans, and concealing their selfish objects under the cloak of religion, they are again trying to enter into conflict with Soviet Russia.[12]

The indictment further asserted that the accused clergy had encouraged violence and had aided landowners and capitalists at the expense of peasants and workers.

Nikolai Krylenko led the prosecution. A schoolmaster until 1914, he briefly headed the Red Army after the Revolution. He was about forty-five years old, of ordinary appearance, medium height, and light build. With graying and receding hair, he wore a small mustache of military cut. Although his manner was quick and decisive, he frequently adopted the odd posture of standing upright behind his table with his head thrown back and a cruel, sneering expression on his face. (British agent Bruce Lockhart belittled him as a "degenerate epileptic.") In his opening statement Krylenko claimed that the clergy's motives were entirely materialistic and political. He was unable or unwilling to admit that any of their actions could have been spurred by religious and spiritual intentions.

The prosecutor accused Tikhon, who was not yet under arrest, of refusing assistance to the starving as part of a counterrevolutionary plot "in order that he may regain his own lost rights and privileges as well as the abundant wealth which the Soviet power is at present giving to the starving with the object of saving their lives." Then, in a surprise move just two days before the trial ended, and at 11:00 PM, Krylenko called Tikhon as a prosecution witness! His presence in the courtroom caused quite a stir, with over half the packed room (in both senses of the term) rising in respect when he entered and blessed the spectators.[13] Officials seemed impressed with their power to compel him to appear, and the press gloated at this show of Soviet power. Although he was only a witness, he was described in *Pravda* as follows:

> The patriarch has been called to make a legal deposition. He has been called to the red table where three atheists are sitting in judgment. Still worse: he, the patriarch of all Russia, is being brought to trial as simple citizen Belavin on the charge of spreading counterrevolutionary proclamations. Isn't it something unheard of?[14]

Tikhon would not answer questions when called by his secular name and, when finally referred to correctly, remained aloof. He spoke in a firm but nondefiant voice and smiled occasionally at the impertinence of the young judges. A sympathetic eyewitness described his countenance:

> When the noble figure, all adorned in black, came through the door of the hall escorted by two armed guards, everyone automatically stood up. . . . All heads were bent low in a deep, respectful bow. The most holy patriarch quietly, majestically . . . turned toward the judges, standing straight, stately, and gravely, leaning on his staff, awaited their questions.[15]

His testimony was what one might have expected. He took full responsibility for the circular he had issued a little over two months earlier, calmly stating:

> The authorities know very well that in my proclamation there is no summons to resist the authorities, only a call to preserve the holy relics [church treasures], and in order to preserve them to ask the authorities for permission to pay in money for their value. While rendering help to their starving brothers, [the churches could] preserve their sacred treasures.[16]

He explained that there was no sacrilege if the church *voluntarily* surrendered its valuables but there was if those valuables were seized against the church's will. Tikhon then turned to bless the accused, who fell to their knees: "I bless the true servants of the Lord Jesus Christ [who endure] torture and death for him."[17]

Some observers were worried that Tikhon, by testifying, had recognized the legitimacy of the Soviet government and had thus compromised his earlier, more defiant position. What had happened to the government as Antichrist? But under increasing pressure Tikhon and other Orthodox hierarchs were coming to accept the government, just as early Christians had learned to accept Caesar. Render unto the government that which was its due.

Tikhon realized that his role in the trial went beyond being a mere witness; in a very real (but not yet physical) sense he and his hierarchy were being prosecuted. One of the themes that Krylenko hammered home was that the *very existence of any church hierarchy* was illegal under the February 5, 1918, separation decree. The fact that Tikhon, Nikander, and the other archbishops had met, combined with other evidence, established a "special hierarchy" and constituted something in the nature of an independent state within the boundaries of Soviet Russia. The separation decree permitted only individual—and isolated—religious congregations, not a joining together under unified administrative authority. Since each community freely elected its clergy, confirmation by episcopal councils and, by extension, any higher authority was unnecessary.[18]

Even though this argument was brought up at the Trial of the Fifty-Four and other trials, it never became the basis for a concerted effort to destroy the church. The reason may have been that destruction of the entire church hierarchy would have too obviously exposed the government to criticism from abroad at a time when it was trying to appear reasonable and civilized to the international community. In addition, this argument would have logically required the government to attack the hierarchies of *all* Russia's organized religions at the same time. This it was unprepared to do in 1922. Tikhon would be handled in other ways.

On the morning after his testimony the patriarch made a bold attempt to take the sting out of the prosecution's case and possibly mitigate the verdicts. As mentioned in chapter 6, he announced that the Higher Church Administration Abroad, which had called the Karlovtzy Sobor, had no legal jurisdiction over anything. He put Metropolitan Evlogy in charge of the entire church outside of Russia, declared Karlovtzy resolutions invalid, and considered bringing its leaders to justice. The government, however, was not impressed. It demanded that, minimally, Tikhon should excommunicate all who had participated in the illegal Yugoslavian sobor.[19]

Judge Bek pronounced all defendants guilty and condemned eleven of them to death (eight priests and three deacons). Beyond the death sentences, he ordered four to serve five-year prison terms, thirteen to serve three-year terms, and ten to spend one year in jail. Apparently the government was worried about popular reaction to the severity of the sentences, as Soviet newspapers downplayed them or omitted them altogether.

On learning of the death sentences, Tikhon wrote three letters to government officials protesting the miscarriage of justice. He argued that the condemned prisoners had merely been following the rules of their religion and the orders of their ecclesiastical superiors. All responsibility was his, and his life should be taken instead.

Two days after the sentences were announced, Stalin wrote to all members of the Politburo:

> Kamenev proposes to limit the execution to two priests. I ask for votes, "yes" or "no," on comrade Kamenev's proposal. I am personally voting against a change in the decision of the court.

Lenin, Trotsky, Stalin, and Zinoviev voted against any change; Rykov and Tomsky supported Kamenev.[20] Nonetheless, Kalinin eventually commuted six of the death sentences. Even Trotsky and the other extremists failed to object, so pleased were they with their overall victory. As for those whose sentences were not reduced, the priests Zaozersky, Sokolov, Nadejdin, and Telegin, and the deacon Tikhomirov, were shot. Father Zaozersky had surrendered all the valuables in his own church but had dared to defend the patriarch in principle.[21]

Outside of the Orthodox hierarchy, only a few Tolstoyans and a few Jews protested the sentences. The Orthodox clergy were intimidated and justifiably fearful that the more they expressed their outrage the more it would appear to judicial authorities that the church hierarchy had immense influence over the faithful masses. The more the government believed that there was a rival center of power in Soviet Russia, the more severely it would crack down on church leaders.[22]

In a sense there was a second verdict, as Krylenko demanded that Tikhon and Nikander (who also was not among the original fifty-four) be held over for trial as the principal culprits. He wanted them charged with "inciting the masses of the people to engage in civil war." On May 6 a *Pravda* editorial tried once again to tie Tikhon to the Karlovtzy Council:

> [The struggle over church property] was not for golden vestments—it was for the tsar's crown, for returning their holdings to the landlords. . . . Under the black cassocks of the higher clergy were hidden the foulest, blackest foes of the working people and the revolution.[23]

THE PETROGRAD CHURCH TRIAL

Regardless of what my sentence will be, no matter what you decide, life or death, I will lift up my eyes reverently to God, cross myself, and affirm: "Glory to Thee my Lord; glory to Thee for everything."[24]

—Metropolitan Benjamin at his trial

While Tikhon languished under house arrest in his monastery residence, another major trial of Orthodox clergy was being acted out in Petrograd. On May 28, 1922, the police arrested Metropolitan Benjamin (Kazansky), the hierarchs of most of Petrograd's Orthodox churches, some professors at the Theological Academy, and all the lower clergy and laity who had been involved in the recent anticonfiscation demonstrations. These eighty-seven persons were charged with resisting confiscations and inciting the masses to overthrow the government, though, as in the Moscow Trial, many were released before or during the upcoming trial.[25]

How did it come to this? After Tikhon's rejection of Kalinin's February 23 confiscation decree, Benjamin expressed willingness to bend further than the patriarch, agreeing to submit even *consecrated* chalices that had contained the body and blood of Christ on the condition that church authorities first melt them down, thus preventing them from being handled in their sacred state by laity or nonbelievers. Benjamin affirmed that the treasure under his jurisdiction actually belonged to God, but "we will give all of it by ourselves."[26] At the Petrograd Pomgol session of March 5, 1922, hoping that he was not blatantly contradicting the patriarch, he announced:

[As long as it can be done voluntarily] the Orthodox Church is prepared to give everything to help the starving. . . . I myself, at the head of the worshippers, will remove the cover [of precious metals and precious stones] from the ikon of the Holy Virgin of Kazan. I will shed sweet tears on it and give it away.[27]

The Petrograd soviet accepted his condition, and local newspapers reported the following day, "Church vessels and ikon coverings would be melted down into ingots in the presence of the believers."[28] Locally, Benjamin was praised for finding a peaceful solution to the problem. He immediately wrote to Lenin to inform him of the church's charitable contributions.[29]

Lenin was not pleased. Solzhenitsyn described the government's reaction to the Petrograd soviets' attempt at compromise:

The noxious fumes of Christianity were poisoning the revolutionary will. *That kind* of unity and *that way* of handing over the valuables *were not* what the starving people of the Volga needed! The spineless membership of the Petrograd Pomgol was changed. The newspapers began to howl about the "evil pastors" and "princes of the church," and the representatives of the church were told: "We don't need your *donations*! And there won't be any negotiations with you! *Everything belongs to the government*—and the government will take whatever it considers necessary."[30]

Benjamin, however, was looking for a two-way street. He presented Pomgol with a three-point ultimatum:

- Provide proof that the government had exhausted all other sources of revenues before confiscating church valuables.
- Guarantee that any money collected from the church would go only to feed the starving.
- Obtain Patriarch Tikhon's consent before proceeding with confiscations.

Pomgol failed to answer, but the Petrograd soviet (before being replaced) agreed to an exchange of views. Apparently the metropolitan agreed to drop the first and last demands in exchange for three church representatives being allowed to oversee Pomgol activities in the area. On March 12, however, Benjamin made new and stricter demands on the soviet, and this led to the collapse of the talks. Thus the government charged Benjamin with "entering with evil intent into an agreement with . . . the Soviet government . . . and thereby obtaining a relaxation of the decree on the requisition of valuables," even though the "relaxation" never took effect.[31]

Benjamin also made arrangements with the Petrograd soviet to allow his parishioners to collect funds and distribute them to the hungry. This was subsequently overridden by Moscow when top leaders realized that the church would receive the credit. Both temporary arrangements with the local soviet (or "plots" against it) were allegedly inspired by Patriarch Tikhon and the Karlovtzy Sobor. (Benjamin was also accused of obstructing the government-backed progressive clergy's attempt to take over the Orthodox administration, but this will have to wait until the next chapter.) Although offered numerous chances to save himself at the expense of others, Benjamin steadfastly refused.

The trial got under way on June 9. The prosecutor was archatheist Peter Krasikov, who, like Krylenko in the Moscow Trial, saw conspiracy rather than genuine religious passion as the cause of the violence surrounding churches. He had orders from Moscow to discredit the church, and the verdicts were foregone conclusions. At one point in the trial he shouted that the entire church was a subversive organization and everybody in it should be thrown in prison.[32]

The defendants, as before, cited the power of church canons. They also argued that priests had actually attempted to *calm* the angry crowds that were surrounding and protecting the churches. But when three witnesses came forward to testify for Benjamin they were promptly arrested, thus effectively ending the defense's case. When Benjamin spoke in his own defense, he only offered that he had always acted alone and was never an enemy of the people.[33] He had dedicated his whole life to them, and they had repaid him with love.

In his closing statement defense attorney S. Gurovich cautioned the government:

If the metropolitan [Benjamin] perishes for his faith, for his limitless devotion to the believing masses, he will become more dangerous for Soviet power than now. . . . The unfailing historical law warns us that faith grows, strengthens, and increases on the blood of martyrs.[34]

The judge, ignoring the warning, announced his verdicts on July 6: Ten defendants, including Metropolitan Benjamin, were declared "dangerous and uncompromising foes of the republic" and condemned to be shot; the others received prison terms ranging from three years down to seven days. On appeal, the Central Executive Committee commuted six of the death sentences, but Benjamin, Yury Novitsky (a law professor and president of the Administration of the Parochial Councils), abbot Sergei Shein, and a lawyer named Kovsharov remained on the executioner's list.[35]

After the trial Gurovich lamented: "There are no proofs of guilt. There are no facts. There is not even an indictment. . . . What will history say?"[36] Constantin de Grunwald met Gurovich in Paris years later, where the defense attorney said of Benjamin, "I felt that I had a genuine saint sitting behind me on the accused's bench."[37]

Carrying out the death sentence against Benjamin proved to be more difficult than expected, as he was extremely popular with the masses. Metropolitan Nicholas (Benjamin's replacement), the Petrograd clergy, and the Higher Church Administration presented petitions for a review of his case, but Kalinin, uncharacteristically hardhearted this time, refused to defy the Petrograd Tribunal. On August 6 *Izvestia* reported Kalinin's conclusion: "The heads of the church have declared civil war against the government . . . [and] there cannot and will not be mercy for those princes of the church."[38] Well after the trial was over, Kalinin even added the charge that Benjamin had corresponded with counterrevolutionaries abroad.

A rumor circulated that Benjamin had already been executed. When a crowd gathered around the prison where he was being held, demanding he be shown to them if he were still alive, GPU agents fired into the assemblage and it disbanded. When it formed again, the warden was forced to make a deal: He allowed three members of the gathering to come inside, where they ascertained that Benjamin indeed was still among the living.

In late August time had finally run out for the metropolitan. He wrote a last letter, wondering why some had advised him to save himself by cooperation with the authorities. If he had compromised his conscience, he said, "What would be the use of Christ?"[39] The authorities announced, as a diversion, that the execution would take place in Moscow. Then on the night of August 25–26 they shaved off his beard, dressed him and the other condemned prisoners in rags, and dragged them off to the Porokhovye Railway Station to be shot.[40] Benjamin was not even recognized by his executioner.

FOREIGN REACTION: FROM NAIVITE TO HYPERBOLE

News of the Moscow and Petrograd clerical executions was squelched inside Russia for several years, mainly so that foreign journalists would not get wind of them and embarrass the nation abroad. This, along with the "progressive" ideological blinders of many British and American journalists, led to some incredibly naive reporting abroad:

- John Haynes Holmes wrote in the *Nation* in May 1923 about the "alleged" seizure of church treasures and the perfect condition of Russia's churches, except for a little dirt on the floors. He emphasized the instances where Red soldiers were called out to protect church buildings from hoodlums. Atrocity stories were "pieces of cloth cut from the same artificial weave of calumny and falsehood" as propaganda against the Germans during World War I. (There was some truth to this—see below.) "As a matter of fact," he wrote, "there is no persecution, only stern governmental action against conspiracy and treason." He concluded that the tumultuous situation in Russia was a force "working out to some ultimate pattern of beauty and beneficence."[41]
- Henry Noel Brailsford wrote in the *New Republic* in May 1930 that "belief is not an offense for which any man has ever suffered punishment" and that "there is no attempt to suppress the church, nothing indeed that could compare with the much more ruthless struggle in Mexico." He seemed completely unaware of Bolshevik ideological opposition to religion, attributing what he called the government's "unfriendly attitude" solely to the Orthodox Church having been "a prop of tsardom." He did concede that religion in Russia was being "handicapped," though not persecuted.[42]

"No persecution" stories were certainly, in part, a reaction to extreme rhetoric from the Western churches and from others who had a political ax to grind with Russia. Holmes was correct in the sense that Lenin was being demonized just as the kaiser had been during the war. Atrocity stories were being circulated about priests who were forced to drink molten lead, were scalped, or were broken on the wheel. And, just as during the war, Americans seemed especially attracted to tales of the mass rape of nuns. Many Americans swallowed the calumny that only avowed atheists were allowed any bread in the Soviet Union.[43] None of these stories could be verified.

In spite of (or because of) the confusion, Moscow's difficulties in foreign capitals were on the rise—in direct relation to the level of confiscations of church valuables and the continuing trials of "resisters." The more the government looted the churches, the more it threatened access to foreign funds for famine relief. When news of trials and sentences of church leaders leaked to Europe and America, private charitable organizations began pressuring their governments to file protests with the Soviets, and Western governments hinted that relief shipments were linked to Soviet good behavior.

For this reason the Russian government always justified its actions in terms of the overall benefit to its people and the counterrevolutionary nature of the clergy. Thus, when the Anglican Archbishop of Canterbury wrote to Lenin during the trials to complain of the attack on Patriarch Tikhon and his church, the Soviet ambassador to England, Leonid Krassin, replied that no attack had been made on the church and that the government had tried to "save the lives of millions of human beings, including children." Krassin supported government policy toward the church on the grounds that "public opinion" and a majority of Russian clergy supported it. Those who did not were obviously connected to tsarists and capitalists.

Then Krassin put a logical question to the British archbishop: Why had no protests been made by the English church when the British fleet had blockaded Russian ports during European intervention in the Russian Civil War, thereby strangling the lifeblood of workers, peasants, and children? Ignoring the question, the archbishop again wrote to Lenin, requesting permission to send a small body of representatives of various English churches to examine the condition of Russian churches. A month later a reply was dispatched from Lev Karakhan, Assistant Commissar for Foreign Affairs:

> The suggestion made by the Archbishop of Canterbury . . . constitutes a claim even less justifiable than would be a suggestion made by the Soviet Government to send to England a small Commission to investigate to what extent the laboring masses are exploited materially and spiritually by the hierarchy of the various English churches in order to maintain the domination of the exploiting classes.[44]

A small piece of evidence that the Bolsheviks might have been winning the propaganda war came in a report dated May 26, 1922, from the US Commissioner in Riga, Latvia, to his superiors in the State Department. He referred to the "clever maneuvering" of government leaders compared with the "vacillating policy" of higher church officials. He also acknowledged the growing resentment by the people toward the church.[45]

In 1922 another opportunity presented itself to the party and the government—a chance, paradoxically, to weaken the Orthodox Church by supporting those whose aim was to renew and invigorate it.

13

AN UNFORTUNATE MISUNDERSTANDING

The Emergence of the Living Church Movement

The Bolsheviks were certainly not above betrayal of their long-term principles to gain short-term advantages. In this chapter we will see how they championed one branch of the Orthodox Church against another, hoping that this wedge would divide and destroy church institutions. The wedge was a group of partly sincere, partly opportunistic clergy who had recently turned from reaction to reform. They were liberal, progressive—even Communist—and they had an agenda that would serve the government's interests. They were the renovationists.

STIRRINGS OF REFORM

Interviewer: Considering the present situation in Russia, is the church called upon to bring a new interpretation of Christianity?

Patriarch Tikhon: How can there be any change in that which is already wholly true and all truth?[1]

During the late nineteenth century, a divergence of thought had emerged within the Orthodox Church. The parish priests and those close to them hoped to draw the peasantry—the "dark people"—closer to the church and not lose them to revolution and anarchy. One way to do this was to alter the point of contact with the people: the church services and the liturgy. Underestimating peasant traditionalism, clerical progressives hoped to make ritual more accessible by making it more understandable and by involving more parishioners in its practices.

As might be expected, progressivism appealed more to the better-educated clergy. In December 1904, Metropolitan Antony of St. Petersburg (not to be confused with Bishop Antonin, a main character in the following narrative) appointed a group of liberal professors from the Theological Academy to help free the church from state dependence. This "Group of Thirty-Two" priests, along with the Christian Socialist Labor Movement, worked to rid the Holy Synod of "bureaucratic Caesaro-papism" and to bring the church nearer to the needs of the people. The tsarist government and the reactionary Black Hundred Party, however, soon trampled on these little sprigs of change. The Group of Thirty-Two was temporarily buried, and the progressive movement as a whole did not break the surface again until the overthrow of the tsar. At that time a group of progressive priests formed the All-Russian Society of Democratic Orthodox Clergy and Laity, an organization pushing for democracy and socialism in Russian life.[2] This society urged that noble rank be abolished, women receive equal rights, words remain uncensored, peasants own the land, and workers own the factories. Christian socialism would blaze a path parallel to state socialism. These ideas held a certain dialectical appeal and attracted radicals from the left and the right. Their beliefs gained traction five years later in the renovationist movement.

Renovationists reacted against the conservative resolutions of the 1917–18 church sobor. Boris Titlinov—who had resigned from the sobor in disgust—proudly called progressive efforts "not a reforming but a revolutionary movement."[3] As if to prove this point, some neophyte priests tested the boundaries of Orthodoxy by wearing shorter hair and beards, symbolizing their modern approach to theology. A British correspondent interviewed one of these priests who had introduced evangelical preaching, congregational singing, and weeknight Bible study courses. This priest even abandoned his clerical attire during the week so that he could work more closely with the people.[4]

Progressive clergy condemned asceticism as decadent, rejecting all monastic teachings of salvation through denial of the world and scorning of human nature. The conception of God as a wrathful avenger and chastiser of sinners also had to go. Gospel descriptions of the subterranean pits of hell "where the worm dieth not, and the fire is not quenched" (Mark 9:44) were replaced by an angelic heaven where the saved lived face-to-face with God. Heaven and hell were to be thought of ethically, not physically. These priests offered a God of compassion and love—a more comradely and less monarchical God—and emphasized the *human* and immanent attributes of Christ the Savior, almost to the exclusion of his divinity. Salvation was now defined as a reawakening of man's sense of brotherhood, realized through God's love for man. Labor was joyous and an expression of the fullness of life. All toilers were to be equal, women included, and the family would be the foundation of ethical and moral life. Soon progressives would be purging the church calendar of saints of bourgeois origin.[5]

Protestant ministers abroad were excited about Russia's relinquishing of "Byzantine thinking" and its grasping of "true Christianity"—except, perhaps, the part about skipping hell. Patriarch Tikhon, however, was not so excited. Immediately after his election, he spread the word that he could not bless innovations in ritual and insisted that the entire process be put on hold, at least until the next sobor.[6] There were other critics, both contemporaneously and among modern scholars and churchmen. In 1946 the historian Robert Pierce Casey, for example, referred to the various factions of progressives as "united only by a common trust in expediency rather than precedent, experimentation rather than discipline, and opinion rather than dogma."[7] Church critics saw a more insinuating danger. Russian Orthodoxy had always promised only spiritual solace in cases of misfortune, but progressives were crossing the line into the area of material succor. They railed against poverty and crime and promised to do something about these societal ills. They were stepping onto the treacherously shifting ground of politics and policy.[8] Although some were opportunists, many in the movement genuinely hoped to revitalize their church and supposed that they could make it compatible with Bolshevism—in spite of the latter's atheism!

Clergy members who were tilting toward reform were appalled at the monarchist resolutions and pronouncements now pouring into Russia from the recently concluded Karlovtzy Sobor. Since those clergy who supported White Army causes had for the most part fled Russia by this time (or had been imprisoned or exiled), those who remained were not the sort to undo the revolutionary work of March 1917 in favor of a Romanov return. Antipathy toward the Karlovtzy "right" pushed many into the arms of the progressive "left."

Those priests who supported liturgical and practical change were the same ones who most harshly criticized the hierarchy's reluctance to permit confiscations of church valuables to ameliorate the famine. Twelve progressive clergy members condemned the church hierarchy's approach to the famine in a March 1922 newspaper story (space happily provided by the government):

> Churchmen! An unfortunate misunderstanding . . . has separated us. We must, with mutual love, with mutual respect, and burning love for those of our brethren who are perishing of starvation, help them all, even to the surrender of our lives. That is what Christ expects of us! [We oppose] that number of ecclesiastics among whom the feeling of malice exists, and they plainly witness to the absence of Christ. One's heart is pained by it, and the soul weeps. Brethren and sisters in the Lord! People are dying! Old men are dying; children are dying. Millions are doomed to perish. Have not your hearts been moved yet?[9]

The Bolsheviks sensed an opening.

DIVIDE AND CONQUER

We cannot deprive ourselves of the pleasure of seeing the views of one part of the clergy opposed by those of the other. But we cannot stop at that and will make use of the splitting among the clergy in order to lead the masses away from any religion whatever.

—Ivan Skvortsov-Stepanov,
The Tasks and Methods of Antireligious Propaganda, 1923

The first church schism that Bolsheviks encouraged and exploited was led by a former Penza archbishop, Vladimir Putyata. At the First Church Sobor he had been discharged from his duties for moral turpitude, but that did not stop him from founding the Free People's Church in 1919 to oppose the patriarchal church. The Cheka saw its chance for mischief and backed his (renamed) Independent Soviet Orthodox Church for over two years. By the end of 1920, however, the secret police felt Putyata was no longer useful and arrested him for anti-Soviet activity. There were a few other such ventures, but at a meeting held on December 4, 1920, the Commission to Establish Separation of Church and State condemned them all as fiascoes.[10]

But the idea of splitting the Orthodox Church into factions was running along other underground currents within the Soviet state. In 1919 Petrograd party chief Grigory Zinoviev held unofficial talks with the progressive archpriest Alexander Vedensky concerning a concordat that would provide government support for Vedensky's followers against more conservative elements in the church—those whom a Cheka leader termed "the old church wolves."[11] T. Samsonov, head of the Secret Department of the Cheka, wrote in a December 1920 letter to his boss, Felix Dzerzhinsky:

> The lowest clergy, preaching our line, will bring destruction right to the heart of the believers, and then that will be it.[12]

Commissar of Education Lunacharsky also swam in schismatic currents,[13] as he sought subtler and less confrontational methods in the antireligious struggle than the hooliganism that had so far prevailed. Pushing the usefulness of wedges, he telegrammed Lenin in May 1921:

> A significant part of the clergy, undoubtedly sensing the stability of the Soviet regime, wants to be reconciled with it. Of course, this renovated Orthodoxy with a Christian-socialist lining is not at all desired and, finally, . . . will be eliminated and disappear. But as an active opposition to the reactionary patriarch and his supporters . . . it can play its role because it is based mainly on the peasant masses, the backward merchant class, and the more backward part of the proletariat. For these groups, such a temporary center of clerical unity [renovationism] is a great shift to the left of the one that they still hold in the reactionary Orthodox Church. . . .
> We cannot, of course, support the activity of Russian Orthodoxy. It might, however, be most advantageous to render aid secretly and to create in the religious arena several transitional stages [on the way to atheism] for the peasant masses.[14]

During the spring of 1922, with the Civil War over and confiscations of buildings and valuables in full swing, the party and the government decided to implement this policy and administer what they hoped would be the coup de grâce to the church. Leon Trotsky, at the peak of his power, hoped to be in on the kill. His approach to the religious question was both dismissive and extremist. At one point he seriously proposed abolishing the patriarchate, shooting the patriarch, and closing a few major cathedrals as a method of quickly resolving the religious issue in Russia. (This folly was nixed by Lenin.) He then proposed "an ecclesiastical NEP"—the promotion of church schism in the sense that, as the NEP temporarily tolerated petty bourgeoisie and kulaks for economic reasons, it could also temporarily accept a progressive priesthood for antireligious reasons. Another way of looking at it was, since the government actively sought sectarian Protestant support as a way of weakening the far more dangerous Orthodox Church, why not consider Orthodox renovationists as "honorary Protestants"?[15] Trotsky's impression that religion was of minor importance in the lives of both peasants and workers, and that it could easily be purged, caused him to greatly underestimate the people's resistance to party manipulation of their faith.

Trotsky attended a March 20, 1922, Politburo meeting that called for a "decisive initiative" in protecting clergy who spoke out in favor of the ongoing confiscation of church valuables.[16] On March 24 he wrote to the Politburo:

> Our whole strategy at this time must be aimed at a schism in the clergy over the concrete question of the requisitioning of valuables from the churches. Since the question is a burning one, the schism on this basis can and must acquire a very burning character, and that part of the clergy that will support the requisitioning, and aid it, will no longer be able to return to Patriarch Tikhon's clique.[17]

On April 2 the Politburo met, with Stalin, Trotsky, Kamenev, and Molotov present, but Lenin absent. It was here that the strategy of church schism was finally adopted. Ten days later, Trotsky issued a memo calling for a short-term alliance with the renovationists. He would keep them occupied with the confiscation issue, preventing their development into a modern movement that could threaten Soviet power:

> This change-of-signposts [renovationist] clergy is our most dangerous enemy of tomorrow. . . . But today we must bring down the counterrevolutionary ecclesiastics . . . with the support of the change-of-signposts clergy. We ought to permit them, even convince them, to start a weekly publication for the preparation of a church council, setting a concrete date for it. Simultaneously, using Cheka methods, we shall be getting rid of the counterrevolutionary clergy.[18]

Lenin quickly agreed, writing that the Politburo ought "to impose a schism onto the clergy's ranks [by taking] a decisive initiative in this matter, taking under government protection those priests who openly support the confiscations."[19] Although breaking promises and switching tactics was no problem for Lenin, it is worth noting that using the better-educated and more progressive clergy for his own ends did violate his earlier admonitions against allowing a more refined— and harder to combat—faith to develop.[20]

Trotsky was deadly serious in his comment about the "counterrevolutionary clergy." The coincidence in time between the confiscation of church valuables and support for the renovationists indicates the level of danger that the Bolsheviks felt they were facing. Bolshevik popularity was waning, the church was still wealthy, and émigrés were screaming for an overthrow of Soviet power. In the minds of many party leaders these were the ingredients of a much-dreaded (but nonexistent) conspiracy. So "counterrevolution" seemed palpable; the use of this term was not just propagandistic posturing. To head off the imagined church-financed coup, the Bolsheviks hoped to co-opt progressive clergy and manipulate them into the forefront of the confiscation process.[21] As we saw in the previous two chapters, these were the men who first spoke out about using church treasures for famine relief and the men who tried to publicly embarrass those church hierarchs who hesitated or resisted.

But the splitters were also split. There was a rift within the party leadership as to whether encouraging a church schism was the correct path. Some took Marx's aphorism about religion being the opium of the people as a literal truth and resisted attempts to manipulate the church—they simply wanted to destroy it. In December 1920 Felix Dzerzhinsky, head of the Cheka, wrote to a comrade:

> My opinion is that the church is disintegrating, and we must help this process, but we must by no means regenerate it in a renovationist form. That is why the church politics of disintegration must be carried out by the Cheka and by no one else. . . . We are counting on communism and not on religion.[22]

Actually, he was counting on the Red Terror to do the trick.

Others took a less "principled" and more opportunistic tack: fight fire with fire and religion with religion. The state could make use of religious prejudices to hasten the church's demise. These manipulators won and the reason is clear. Even though "counterrevolutionary forces" hid within the church, a direct assault on them would embarrass the government abroad where it wanted to avoid the onus of persecution. Direct action would also stiffen internal resistance. Therefore the most effective method of driving counterrevolutionaries from the church would be to let reformist church groups do the job for them.

Keeping up his barrage, Trotsky wrote a top-secret letter to Lenin, the Politburo, *Pravda*, and *Izvestia* on May 14, 1922, pushing his plan. He complained that party and government newspapers were not giving enough play to renovationists. In the following excerpt from his letter, Trotsky was trying to have it all his way:

> It goes without saying that we now have a complete and total interest in supporting the reformed church group against the monarchists, of course deviating not one iota from our proclaimed principle of the separation of the church from the state or, even more, from our philosophical, materialist attitude to religion.[23]

He went on to assert that the state was actually *protecting* "loyal and progressive elements of the opposition clergy" from the "machinations and material repressions" of Tikhonites. To prevent a rapprochement between the two church factions, he advised that materialist philosophy should be kept in the background. That way the struggle between them would "turn most bitter and decisive."[24]

Perhaps fear of foreign reaction was what drove Lenin to ignore the lessons of his own hard experience and approve Trotsky's schismatic plans. It does seem odd that the tactics that had propelled his success would not be applied—or at least appreciated—here. Lenin was the leader of the Bolshevik faction that broke with the Mensheviks at the 1903 Russian Social Democratic Labor Party Conference, and he had won power by sloughing off all those who deviated from his "perfectly correct" interpretation of Marx. Although he appropriated for his followers the label "Bolshevik" (majority), he was actually in the minority when the split occurred and was well satisfied with that position. Better to lead a small band of zealous and dedicated revolutionaries than an amorphous grouping based on the unity principle. Had Lenin forgotten this, however, when he approved the idea of separating out Tikhon and his loyal supporters from those who would renovate the church? What if this process allowed Lenin-like fanatics to rise to positions of power within either branch of the church and undermine his long-range goals?

On the other hand, the patriarch, already in custody since mid-May 1922, could not be shot without offering him martyrdom, as Lenin had earlier warned Trotsky. The schismatic approach, less stringent and potentially more effective, could isolate Tikhon and split the church into warring factions. Those among the clergy cooperating with the Bolshevik plan—the renovationists—now loosely called their movement the "Living Church" (presumably intended to be juxtaposed with Tikhon's "Dead Church"). Handling of the Living Church schism was transferred from the Commissariat of Justice to the Secret Department of the Cheka/GPU, now headed by agent Evgeny Tuchkov, a garrulous and overbearing peasant of mediocre intelligence.[25] (At the end of the year, Tuchkov would be made secretary of the powerful Commission to Establish Separation of Church and State, soon to be renamed the Antireligious Commission.)

No attempt was made to conceal divide-and-conquer tactics. To the contrary, government officials publicly gloated over successes when particularly bitter dissension between church factions broke out.

RENOVATIONIST LEADERS

While the Marxists, Communists, and Soviet authorities do not follow Christ, they work to fulfill Christ's precepts.

—Alexander Vedensky, 1923

The stalwart hierarchs of the Orthodox Church saw renovationists as vile heretics, unworthy of the cassocks they wore. The progressive American journalist John Haynes Holmes, who attended some of their meetings, called them "reformers of true apostolic courage, zeal, and sincerity."[26]* The Bolsheviks called them useful.

Antonin

Bishop Antonin (Granovsky) was the most fascinating and enigmatic of the renovationist leaders. Strongly built, with a booming voice, he exuded charisma but also instability. A *New York World* reporter described him as "a mountain of a man. An enormous head rests upon great hunched shoulders. His hands are big, his eyes wide and blazing."[27] He was born in Poltava Province in 1859, which would have made him sixty-three in 1922, the year he emerged on the renovationist stage. He was educated at the Poltava Seminary and then the Ecclesiastical Seminary in Kiev, where he became a proficient preacher and a good linguist. His theological erudition was considerable, having written a highly praised commentary on the Prophet Isaiah. His views, however, were heterodox and rebellious, which cost him standing among his fellow clergy (who referred to him as a "turkey") and among the people. Twice he underwent treatment for mild mental illness. Nonetheless, in 1905 he rose to become bishop of Narva in the St. Petersburg diocese. He quickly lost his position (but not his rank), however, when he took up antimonarchism and insisted on reading the liturgy without using the term "autocrat" in connection with the tsar's name. He was retired to the Voskresensky Monastery near the capital "for a rest," then transferred again. His new avocation was writing pamphlets denouncing bishops and describing the tsarist regime as "Satanic." He scandalized the office he held by walking through the streets of the city instead of riding in a carriage.[28]

After other appointments and more rest, Antonin surfaced in Moscow in 1917, still a church member in good standing but a man consumed by ambition and a bitter personal hatred for the new patriarch. In 1920–21 Antonin had a chance to assert himself in a series of public debates against another adversary: Anatoly Lunacharsky. Ably defending the church against Soviet authority, he gained some favor within the hierarchy, but, ironically, he also became friendly with Lunacharsky and other government leaders. Since Antonin was in active opposition to Tikhon, he was clearly a man to be cultivated. Tikhon, however, retired him once again.[29]

In April and May 1922 Antonin wrote articles in the Soviet press condemning Tikhon's reluctance to offer church treasures for famine relief. As a

---

*Holmes, however, was rather naive, stating in the same article that it was ridiculous to believe that the Bolsheviks were atheists out to exterminate religion in Russia.

reward for his efforts, Kalinin invited him to serve on Pomgol—that is, to supervise the stripping of church treasures. Then, during the Moscow Trial in May, testifying for the prosecution as an expert on canon law, he argued that Tikhon's opposition to "contributions" had no religious authority. Tikhon's decree on the subject was, Antonin implied, political and counterrevolutionary. Trying to establish himself a head above the other renovationists, he derisively referred to them as "the sewer of the Orthodox Church."[30]

Antonin was unpopular among the people, and, as conflict within the church heated up, citizens on the street hurled insults of "Antichrist" and "Satan" as he passed by, and others sent him death threats. One renovationist leader called him "a fool and a clown," especially after Antonin began inserting modern poetry into the ancient liturgy. Anatoly Levitin, who was close to Antonin, presented a more appealing picture of an ascetic dedicated to purity and truth, a man who exposed hypocrisy with "crude peasant humor."[31]

Vedensky

The other leading renovationist was the previously mentioned archpriest Alexander Vedensky, described variously as attractive, charismatic to women, intelligent, scholastic, eloquent, theatrical, and idealistic. He was a true believer in his faith but too romantic in its application; many of those who knew him well went further and described him as "morally and politically unscrupulous."[32] In tsarist times he had been a member of the fascistic Black Hundred Party in St. Petersburg, but as revolution approached he became increasingly liberal. Although he had begun with suggestions for mild reform—rearranging the position of the altar and introducing new hymns and prayers—he soon developed wilder ideas that incurred the wrath of the church hierarchy. After the abdication of the tsar in March 1917, Vedensky served as chaplain under Metropolitan Benjamin in Petrograd and secretary of the Society of the Democratic Orthodox Clergy and Laity. He preached vigorously against the Bolshevik coup in its early days but soon changed his views.[33] In the early 1920s he served as dean of two of Petrograd's Orthodox churches.

Maurice Hindus was in the audience of one of Vedensky's lectures in Moscow, where the priest explained the disintegration of the Orthodox Church:

> The extraordinary Byzantine glitter of our Orthodox services has been our greatest curse. Our church has striven after external gorgeousness at the expense of inner virtue, after showy splendor at the cost of spiritual perfection. It acquired pomp, power, riches, but lost its soul. Only now are we beginning to realize what a feeble spiritual infant our Orthodoxy has been.[34]

Vedensky often entered into public debates with atheist leaders such as Lunacharsky and, like Antonin, just as often emerged victorious, due not to the logic of his ideas but to the passion with which he delivered them.[35]

Levitin, who was once Vedensky's student, offered this appraisal:

> [He had] a sense of the inescapable senselessness of everyday life. His passion for truth was flooded by his immense oratorical talent, and this produced tremendous sermons, which galvanized his listeners. At the same time the confusion of his thought and the mixture of moral values in him, typical of decadence, promoted a shocking lack of principle.[36]

When he left the podium or the pulpit, Vedensky was overcome by "vulgar, petty and vainglorious interests," chief among them an obsession with personal success. Antonin saw him as a "great sinner"—he married, divorced, remarried, and kept several mistresses on the side (leading another critic to call him an "erotomaniac")—and thought that he should reform himself before taking on reformation of the Orthodox Church.[37]

In 1922 Vedensky justified the death sentences handed down in the Moscow Trial and testified against Benjamin at the Petrograd Trial. For this a woman threw a stone at him while he was leaving church, which put him in the hospital for two months. His trial testimony (and his frequent visits to Communist Party headquarters) may also have been the source of rumors that he was a police collaborator. His authorship of a booklet titled *The Church and Patriarch Tikhon*, in which he accused the top hierarch of all sorts of counterrevolutionary crimes, invigorated those rumors.[38] A man who espoused compassion and equality through church linkage with communism, Vedensky was as full of contradictions as the renovationist movement he represented.

Krasnitsky

Father Vladimir Krasnitsky came from Ekaterinoslav, studied in St. Petersburg, and rose there to become a junior priest at St. Vladimir's Cathedral. He, like Vedensky, signed up with the Black Hundred Party in reaction to the 1905 uprisings, even becoming chaplain to the St. Petersburg group.[39]* In 1911 he lost his church position due to involvement in intrigue for a higher office, but a year later he accepted the position of archdeacon of the St. Petersburg District. The Theosophical Society was then fashionable among the aristocracy and clergy, and Krasnitsky joined. His turn toward progressivism seems to have resulted more

---

*Krasnitsky was also accused of having written articles about Jews drinking Christian blood. Though speculative, it is possible that former admirers of autocracy were attracted to renovationism due to its potential, with the help of the Cheka/GPU, to be equally autocratic within Russian Christianity.

from personal animosity than from ideological conviction. In 1918 an old rival of his was appointed dean of St. Isaak's Cathedral, and Krasnitsky blamed both Patriarch Tikhon and Metropolitan Benjamin for his failure to win the post. He began a campaign against both superiors, which led him also to testify against Benjamin at his trial.[40]

Krasnitsky used the above-mentioned stone-throwing incident to lay out his revolutionary credentials:

> Let those who aimed the stone at the head of Father Vedensky remember that this preacher of love who is so indulgent to his enemies will be replaced by men who will crush their counterrevolutionary plans with an iron rod. The stone thrown at Father Alexander will rebound on the heads of those who directed the arm of this dark, fanatical woman.[41]

He adopted the role of church reformer and played it well. By 1923 he was appointed dean of the Cathedral of Christ the Savior in Moscow (where he himself was later beaten into unconsciousness for his renovationist views). Krasnitsky's interests were not mainly spiritual or even liturgical—they were clerical. He wanted power for the priesthood, from whence he came, at the expense of the bishops, and he wanted state protection of the interests of priests, as we will see below. Although called a careerist by some, Krasnitsky showed a true Christian spirit when his time of influence was over (in 1924) by accepting a position, involving some hardship, as a priest at a Leningrad cemetery chapel.[42]

Vedensky said of Krasnitsky: "I'd like to know where this fellow has sprung from. He's never been a member of any renovationist group. None of us know him, but he suddenly appears at one of our meetings. Why? What for? He's clearly up to something."[43] The implication was that Krasnitsky worked for the GPU. He admitted to an American reporter that he had been a candidate for Communist Party membership. When asked about the obvious contradiction, he responded that he hoped to destroy the "bourgeois church," not religion. He added:

> The Communists are wrong in believing that they can destroy religion. Otherwise their program is immaculate and unquestionable.[44]

As for Krasnitsky's relations with Antonin, the former once tried to place the latter in a lunatic asylum, and Antonin was not very happy about it.[45]

Kalinovsky

Father Sergei Kalinovsky also emerged from the Black Hundred Party, his ordination having been achieved through Rasputin's influence. He was a chaplain to the troops during World War I but made sure he stayed well away from actual danger.

When soldiers elected him a delegate to the Petrograd soviet anyway, he journeyed to the capital only to find himself excommunicated by Metropolitan Benjamin for his revolutionary sympathies. Wandering intellectually, he tried to form a Worker-Peasant Christian Socialist Party in 1919. Although he had no ties to the prerevolutionary progressive movement, somehow by 1922 he was one of its leaders. In May he was entrusted with editing the first issue of the renovationist newsletter, *The Living Church* (*Zhivaya Tserkov*), but a few days later, for unknown reasons, he left the church and became a freelance antireligious propagandist.[46]

*   *   *

Other progressive leaders of consequence were Bishop Evdokim of Nizhny-Novgorod; Father Evgeny Belkov (who would leave the priesthood in 1925); psalm-reader Stephan Stadnik; professor N. Kuznetsov, a lay teacher of canon law; and Father Bogoliubsky, a professor of theology at the University of Moscow. Boris Titlinov was a lay professor of history at the Petrograd Theological Academy and the renovationists' ideological leader. He edited the popular journal *The Church and Social Messenger* which in March 1918 relentlessly criticized Tikhon for his anathema of the Bolsheviks.[47]

All of these leaders opposed a patriarchal style of church administration, favored the liturgy read in modern Russian, and pushed to involve the laity and lower clergy more closely in church decision making. And all had socialist or pro-Communist tendencies but were in denial concerning the atheist government's fundamental antagonism to religion. They convinced themselves that Bolshevik antireligious policies were the simple result of historical conditions in nineteenth-century Russia or specific church abuses; in other words, it was just a matter of reform.

THE COUP

The Renovated Church began its existence by breaking with Patriarch Tikhon. Intellectually dishonest scholastics who mumble something about a canonical succession from Patriarch Tikhon and are sometimes believed by some of the Renovated, are, it seems to me, mistaken and harmful.[48]

—Alexander Vedensky, 1927

Frustrated by traditionalists and conservatives in the seats of power, the renovationists ached to reform both church organization—with themselves in charge—and doctrine. One renovationist said that their planned changes would make Luther's reforms seem as "child's play."[49]

With government favor, the embryonic Living Church developed quickly toward its goals. Renovationists were given access to major Soviet organs of news and propaganda, and government newspapers began carrying stories on the Living Church's goals and aspirations. Soon it was given permission to publish its own newsletter, a privilege not granted to the patriarchal church. An article by Krasnitsky urged personnel changes in the highest church offices and called for a new sobor, which he hoped would iron out differences within the church and smooth relations with the state.

During the first few days of May 1922, the Petrograd priests Vedensky and Belkov arrived in Moscow and joined the Muscovite Kalinovsky. Events were moving quickly now. Antonin wrote an open letter in *The Living Church* accusing the Orthodox hierarchy of being "aloof from the great struggle for truth and the wellbeing of humanity" and of siding with the enemies of the people. He concluded:

> We consider it necessary that a sobor be called without delay for a trial of those who are guilty of the ruin of the church, to order the ecclesiastical government, and to establish normal relations with the Soviet authorities. The civil war that is carried on by the Tikhonite Higher Church Administration against the government must be stopped.[50]

On May 5 Tikhon finished one of a series of grueling sessions with the GPU, and, upon his return home, one of his attendants inquired about his treatment. The following exchange took place:

Tikhon:	They were very strict today.
Attendant:	So what will happen to you?
Tikhon:	They promised to cut off my little head.[51]

The next day, May 6, the secret police placed Tikhon under house arrest.

Six days later the guards surrounding his residence allowed the progressive leaders Vedensky, Krasnitsky, Kalinovsky, Belkov, and Stadnik through their lines.* Waking the patriarch from his evening slumber, they entered a spacious mid-Victorian drawing room and pulled the ancient carved and upholstered chairs into a circle for a planned and prolonged "conversation." To the still-drowsy old churchman, Krasnitsky read off the familiar list of counterrevolutionary acts that he had allegedly committed, finishing by claiming that the patriarch had left the church in anarchy.[52] Since the government restricted his movements, the visitors suggested that he was unable to lead the church and urged Tikhon to appoint Bishop Antonin—who was not present—as locum tenens. Francis McCullagh painted the scene:

---

*Although a year later Tikhon remembered only three renovationists at the meeting, omitting Krasnitsky and Stadnik, the following day *Izvestia* announced that there were five visitors, and this is most likely correct. Kalinovsky had already renounced his priestly vows by the date of the meeting.

On the one side the old patriarch, pious, gentle, simpleminded, unworldly, rather weak. On the other side a group of debauched communist priests, some of whom had been police spies, urging the patriarch to appoint as his successor, with unlimited power over the ancient church of Russia, a degenerate bishop who was secretly associated with the Bolshevik leaders and who suffered so much from neurasthenia that at times he could hardly be regarded as sane.[53]

Tikhon considered the general proposal but absolutely refused to consider Antonin. Krasnitsky then threatened Tikhon with responsibility for the fate of the eleven prisoners who had been condemned to death in the recent Moscow Trial. Some of their sentences had already been commuted, but Tikhon may not have known this. If he did know, Krasnitsky may have told Tikhon that they would nonetheless be shot and their blood would be on Tikhon's hands unless he stepped down.[54] According to Vedensky's later rendition of events, Tikhon then acknowledged:

> I never wanted to be patriarch; the patriarchate is burning me like a cross—this you know well. I shall gladly accept, if the church sobor relieves me altogether from the patriarchate, and I shall transfer the power to one of the oldest hier-archs and go away from the administration of the church.[55]

Next they handed Tikhon a document for him to sign, which included requests that he bless their efforts to reopen the chancery (so that church business might continue) and call a new sobor as soon as possible and then abdicate.[56] To the request for a sobor, Tikhon could hardly protest. The ordinances of the First Church Sobor (1917–18) called for succeeding convocations at least every three years, which meant that the second sobor should have been held no later than the summer of 1921—almost a year before. (Of course, the holdup was the government's refusal to sanction a sobor until it suited its interests.)

At the end of this discussion, which lasted until the sun was well up the next morning, a bleary-eyed Tikhon wrote to Kalinin:

> In view of the extremely difficult position of the Church Administration, which is the result of my being summoned before a civil court, I consider it in the interests of the church for me to place temporarily—that is, until the Church Sobor has been summoned—at the head of the Church Administration, either Agath-angel, Metropolitan of Yaroslavl, or Benjamin, Metropolitan of Petrograd.[57]

The five visitors then left.

Pleased with their success—except on the matter of Antonin's appointment—the renovationist conspirators carried Tikhon's letter to Kalinin. A few days later they obtained from Tikhon a letter written to Agathangel, informing the latter of his appointment and asking him to come to Moscow to assume his duties as head of the Higher Church Administration. They made sure that it was delivered. Kalinin accepted the patriarch's decision, probably because Agathangel was seventy years old and thought to be no longer dangerous, and because several others that Tikhon insisted be included in a reconstructed Higher Church Administration were also too feeble for active participation. *Izvestia* inaccurately announced, "Patriarch Tikhon Has of His Own Accord Temporarily Resigned."[58] A few days later Antonin wrote an article titled "Bring Tikhon to Justice,"[59] and his associates began asserting that Tikhon had *permanently* relinquished his office at the May 12 meeting. When the renovationists announced that the Communist Revolution was "the will of God," pressure on the ageing patriarch became barely tolerable.

Meanwhile, there was no one to administer the church, as Soviet authorities had purposefully delayed Agathangel's departure from Yaroslavl and refused to permit Tikhon to leave the monastery residence. Vedensky, Belkov, and Kalinovsky returned to Tikhon for a second time on the evening of May 18 and implored him to sign a paper blessing them and a few other bishops in their administration of the church until Agathangel arrived. After almost two hours of discussion, Tikhon capitulated; the progressive priests glimpsed an opening. At first they hinted that Tikhon should fully and permanently abdicate (as newspapers had prematurely stated), then they switched to the interpretation that he had already done so.

The next day, May 19, troops swept into the Patriarchal Palace and arrested most of Tikhon's supporters on the Higher Church Administration and the Moscow Diocesan Administration. So which body was in control of the church: the patriarch himself or the rapidly forming renovationist Higher Church Administration? The renovationists and the government took the position that the former had bowed to the latter. Confusion reigned. Either Tikhon had permanently resigned, appointing Agathangel locum tenens, or he had temporarily resigned, turning over authority to a new Higher Church Administration only until Agathangel arrived. Of course, Agathangel might never arrive, thereby making the new administration's authority permanent. Or perhaps Tikhon had not resigned at all, the term being too strong for the limited action he had taken.

A year later, after his release from confinement, Tikhon gave his version of events. When Vedensky, Belkov, and Kalinovsky had visited him at the monastery residence for the last time, he claimed that they had tricked him into relinquishing control of the church. Their ruse was feigned anxiety about correspondence piling up in his absence that desperately needed attention. He had agreed to permit the three renovationists to join the Higher Church Administration and to reopen the chancery *only until Agathangel arrived*. He thought of Agathangel as locum tenens only during the period of his own confinement, and it never occurred to him to abandon the patriarchate. He explained that the note he had written and signed at the May 18 meeting had specifically stated:

The persons named below [the three renovationist priests] are charged to take over and *transmit* to the Most Rev. Agathangel, upon his arrival in Moscow, the archives of the Synod. . . . [emphasis added] We gave [the three priests] no instructions as to how to deal with the entrusted affairs in case Metropolitan Agathangel should not come to Moscow at all, as we could not at that time foresee that eventuality; moreover, there could be no approval in the [signed document] for their replacing, in such eventuality, the metropolitan and of placing themselves at the head of the church administration, because the full-ness of power inherent in the episcopal office cannot be transferred to priests.[60]

When (and if) Agathangel entered Moscow, the renovationists were to retire from their duties; however, due to the close relationship between the renovation-ists and the government, Agathangel was *never* able to leave Yaroslavl. Antonin thus took over the Higher Church Administration with Krasnitsky as his deputy.[61]

On May 19, 1922, the day the renovationists took over the Patriarchal Palace, Tikhon was seized from the St. Sergius-Trinity Monastery town resi-dence (where he had spent several weeks under house arrest) and was transported through Moscow in an ordinary carriage to the Donskoy Monastery on the edge of the city, which had been converted to a holding facility for political prisoners. There he was taken up a narrow stone staircase against the monastery wall into a converted storehouse that consisted of two low-vaulted, simply furnished, and badly heated rooms. Although he could order his own food and was treated well by the guards, he was kept from the monastery church and was not allowed to visit with or write to anybody.[62]

The renovationist Titlinov frankly discussed these changes in leadership as a "coup" when he wrote in *The New Church*:

There can be no doubt that the group that organized the Higher Church Admin-istration after the abdication of Patriarch Tikhon was never authorized by the patriarch to do so. . . . The leaders of the Living Church usurped authority in a revolutionary, noncanonical manner, even in an anticanonical manner.[63]

The press now referred to Tikhon—reminiscent of French revolutionary attacks on the aristocracy—as "Citizen Belavin," denying him any privileges of rank. He was an ordinary mortal in a nation of ordinary mortals, having no legal public voice. Although he gradually became aware of his inability to effectively lead the church, he was unaware of any solution to his dilemma. On August 5, 1922, the GPU came to his Donskoy residence and escorted him to its more cen-tralized Taganka Prison for an indefinite period.

In the meantime, the Living Church was not allowed to run amok. Mikhail Gorev issued veiled threats in *Krasnaya Gazeta* on September 14, 1922, as to what would happen if it did not "fulfill the hopes which have been centered upon it."[64] Eight months later Antonin admitted to a *New York World* reporter, "We are bound hand and foot by the control of the secret service men, who use us as a political institution or weapon."[65]

PROGRESSIVES AND THE CHURCH TRIALS

At the Moscow trial, Antonin, Kalinovsky, and a few other progressive priests testified that Tikhon had misinterpreted the canons regarding church property. Even sacred items were not inviolate, they claimed, if the purpose of their sale was one of mercy, and prohibitions in canon law had been placed there only to prevent items being taken for private use (which apparently at one time had been a serious problem). Donating treasures to relieve starvation was not a sacrilege.[66]

During the final days of Metropolitan Benjamin's freedom, Vedensky and Krasnitsky traveled from Moscow to Petrograd to convert him to their cause. Benjamin, with mind made up and confident of the outcome, offered to put the issue to his congregation at the St. Alexander Nevsky Monastery. The next Sunday, May 28, the renovationists were allowed to speak first, then Benjamin would make his points and the people would vote. According to modern Orthodox sources, Vedensky spoke as follows:

> Brothers and sisters, up to now we have been subject to the tsar and the metro-politans. But now we are free, and we ourselves must rule the people and the church. More than 1,900 years have already passed since it was written for us that the Lord Jesus Christ was born from the Virgin Mary and is the Son of God.
>
> But that is not true. We recognize the existence of the God of Sabaoth [Sabbath], about whom our whole Bible and all the prophets have written. . . . But Jesus Christ is not God. He was simply a very clever man. And it is impos-sible to call Mary—who was born of a Jewish tribe and herself gave birth to Jesus—the Mother of God and Virgin. And so now we have all recognized the existence of God, that is the God of Sabaoth, and we must all be united; both Jews and Catholics must be a living people's church.[67]

Krasnitsky then spoke against the practice of infant baptism, arguing that baptism should occur only when the child has grown to sufficient age that he or she understands the meaning of the ceremony and the extent of the commitment. He explained the Living Church's rejection of saints and relics and acceptance of married bishops and remarried priests.[68]

It is not hard to imagine the appalled reaction of the worshipers and the strength of their vocal rejection of the speakers. Benjamin calmed them down and then accused the renovationists of the fourth-century Arian heresy of not including Jesus in the Godhead. He then anathematized the Living Church—leaders and followers alike—viewing the renovationists not just as schismatics but also as heretics. As he spoke, Vedensky slipped out a side door and informed

GPU agents of what had transpired. The secret police then entered the building and arrested the metropolitan. A crowd of many thousands surrounded the police and their prisoner, but armed cavalry eventually broke up the demonstration.[69]

The next day Benjamin excommunicated both Vedensky and Krasnitsky, and this no doubt did not sit well with them. Vedensky made a point of being present when the secret police went to Benjamin's home to arrest him, and he may have instigated the action. And, as we have seen, he testified in support of the prosecutor's case. Before Benjamin was shot in August, the new renovationist-controlled Church Administration passed its own sentence, stripping Benjamin, Novitsky, and, Kovsharov (three of the four condemned) of their priestly and monastic ranks.[70]

The following year, the renovationists would receive their very own sobor. And schisms would continue in the Communist Party as well.

14

A CHRISTIAN BY NATURE

The Second (Renovationist) Sobor

T he Living Church craved legitimacy, and the way to get it was to hold a sobor. Both the renovationists and the Communist Party planned for this overdue event, and their interests *seemed* to coincide.

PRE-SOBOR MACHINATIONS

Friends of Tikhon advised me to ask for his blessings on my reforms, but I considered that it would be as impossible for me to ask for Tikhon's blessings as it would have been for Christ to ask for the blessings of Caiaphas, the High Priest.[1]

—Antonin complaining in *Izvestia*, November 1922

A renovationist Legislative Assembly met in Moscow on May 29, 1922, with 146 delegates attending. Its purpose was to formally create what in fact already existed—the Living (or New) Church Party; however, only thirty-six of these delegates voted to adopt the assembly's platform and ended up as founding fathers of the organization. The platform was relatively apolitical, concerning itself mainly with the rejection of tsarist innovations and a return to the presumed purity of the early Christian Church. For example, priests were now to be elected by their parishes, and episcopal authority was now to be shared equally among the bishops, the priests, and the laity.[2] (Technically, the Living Church as an organization or as a party should not have existed. The separation decree had made it clear that churches could be organized *only* on the local or parish level, not as national entities. Only the parishes had "juridical status." Selective enforcement was the key here.)

The schism was developing according to government plans—while some still considered Tikhon head of the church, others looked to Antonin, Vedensky, and Krasnitsky for leadership. Instead of simply reopening the chancery, these three renovationists conceived a more ambitious task; they cobbled together a reconstituted Church Administration with themselves, Kalinovsky, and Belkov in charge. As might be expected, hierarchs critical of the government were expelled from office and those sympathetic to their cause were offered positions. Antonin and his followers met on June 2 at the St. Sergius-Trinity Monastery and began preparations for a Second (Renovationist) Church Sobor. At a meeting on June 12, Antonin was asked whether they would need Tikhon's approval for a certain measure; he replied:

> As Patriarch Tikhon has transmitted his authority to the [Higher Church Administration] without reservations, we have no need to run after him to receive from him what he no longer possesses.[3]

By early summer personnel changes were well under way. Archbishop Nikander was expelled from his see in Moscow. In June all twenty-two archdeacons and deans in Moscow were summoned to renovationist High Church Administration headquarters and asked whether they would recognize the reformed church. Police paddy wagons with motors idling were parked outside the door, and young men with guns in holsters waited inside, making it clear what a negative answer might mean. At two o'clock in the morning, after seven hours of soul searching, all answered affirmatively.[4]

As mentioned earlier, the government was under the impression that the aged Agathangel would be putty in their hands and for this reason did not initially oppose the transfer to him of "temporary" locum tenens power. Krasnitsky, Vedensky, and GPU agent Tuchkov traveled to Yaroslavl to negotiate with Agathangel immediately after his appointment, attempting to get him to accept renovationist guidance. But one quality of old age is obstinacy, and Agathangel refused their gesture. The two renovationists then returned to Moscow, spreading rumors that the locum tenens was busy with his own affairs and had no interest in hurrying to the capital to assume his duties.[5]

Still in Yaroslavl, Agathangel spent the next month in secret negotiations with Tuchkov, who actually wanted Agathangel immediately "in charge" (but not in Moscow). His negotiating position was that, in exchange for government support, the locum tenens would have to renounce Tikhon's "line." Meanwhile, the government was making Agathangel's life difficult. GPU agents searched his rooms at the Tolgsky Monastery and seized his letter of appointment from the patriarch, but no incriminating evidence was found.[6] (This monastery, a short distance up the Volga from Yaroslavl, was closed in 1926 and turned into a penal colony for young offenders.)

Suddenly on June 18, with negotiations going nowhere and Tuchkov caught by surprise, Agathangel penned a dispatch to all Orthodox clergy. Printed on an underground press and distributed in Moscow, Petrograd, and other major cities, it described his acceptance of the locum tenency and scorn for the renovationists. He was appalled at attempts to revise the services that "were given to us by the great ascetics of Christian piety." Since bishops were temporarily without leadership, he urged them, "Govern your dioceses now in independence according to the Holy Scriptures, the Holy Canons." In difficult or doubtful cases bishops were to "apply to our humility." He asked them to remain close to the people and to increase their "holy zeal."[7] Frustrated in his attempts to reach Moscow, Agathangel continued:

> Against my will, and under circumstances for which I am not responsible, I have been unable up to the present time to go to the place of my service. At the same time, as is officially known to me, other people have arrived at Moscow and have taken over the administration of the Russian Church. I have no knowledge of what authority they have received, or from whom, and therefore I regard the powers they have assumed, and their acts, as unlawful.
>
> They have declared their intention to revise the dogmas and the moral teachings of our Orthodox Church, the canons of the Holy Ecumenical Councils, the Orthodox Church discipline given to us by holy men and champions of Christian piety, and to organize in this manner a "New Church," called by them the "Living Church."[8]

He asked the dioceses to henceforth operate independently of central church administration, in accordance with Tikhon's earlier orders.

Reaction came quickly. On June 28, as soon as Agathangel had printed and distributed his letter, he was placed under house arrest in Yaroslavl's Spassky Monastery. Then in August he was placed in isolation in the city's main prison. Later in the fall the authorities brought him to Moscow and incarcerated him in the Taganka prison. In December the court condemned him to three years of hard labor in the Narym region of Western Siberia. (Remember that Tikhon's second choice as locum tenens, Metropolitan Benjamin, would soon be shot.)

Renovationists held a small organizational conference on July 4, then an All-Russian Conference during the second week of August 1922. Within the Cathedral of Christ the Savior in Moscow, 190 delegates from twenty-four dioceses tried to assess and then strengthen their position. On opening day the conference president, Krasnitsky, implored delegates to abandon attempts to use the church for "temporal political schemes," meaning that they should keep their attention on God and renounce counterrevolutionary plots. The nation's problems were placed squarely in the lap of Tikhon:

> Five years of civil war, the heavy sacrifices made by our fatherland, the dreadful economic crisis, millions of Russia's sons killed and maimed during the war [World War I]; all this is the fruit of criminal treachery towards the Russian

laboring people—a treachery of which the Orthodox bishops were guilty when they sided with the people's foes.

Our bishops, headed by Patriarch Tikhon, preferred to keep gold, silver, and jewels in the Orthodox temples, and for this sake they falsified the canons, they sowed dissension among their flock and they called forth troubles, local revolts, and bloodshed.[9]

Krasnitsky stated that his purpose was to guarantee to the parish clergy "pastoral creativity" in carrying out their duties. To this end, he immediately ejected from the chamber all monks, including Antonin.[10] Krasnitsky's antimonastic views were clear-cut:

The Revolution drove the landowners off their estates and the capitalists out of their palaces, and it is going to drive the monks out of their bishops' residences too. It is time to settle accounts for all the suffering the white clergy has undergone at the hands of the despots—the monastic bishops.[11]

There were at the time 143 active Orthodox bishops; whom could they count on? They tallied thirty-seven bishops solidly for the Living Church, thirty-six firmly opposed, and the remainder undeclared. Krasnitsky announced that the conference should "clear away all the reactionary bishops and fill their places with the rank and file of the white clergy." The conference then resolved that their thirty-six enemies plus twenty-four of the undecided should be "retired" to monasteries, and the rest should be forced to state their allegiances. Most of the sixty bishops who lost their sees were, or soon would be, under arrest and headed for prison, exile, or execution.[12] If he thought he could have gotten away with it, Krasnitsky would have asked for abolition of the episcopate as an institution and left the Orthodox Church entirely in the hands of priests (but not the pro-Tikhon laity).

The conference became entangled in a bitter dispute over the role of the (married) white clergy and (unmarried) monks, but no conclusion was reached. Consensus was much easier to achieve on the final recommendation:

The Living Church group should demand at the next sobor that Patriarch Tikhon be deprived of his clerical orders, because he bears the chief guilt for the present disorganization of the church.[13]

He was denounced for his alleged earlier support of the White Army and the Karlovtzy clergy and for his resistance to the contribution of church treasures for famine relief.[14]

Krasnitsky promised financial and administrative independence for the white clergy, from both the laity below and the bishops above, and this led to the defection of a dozen of the diocesan delegations, which now turned to the previously ejected Antonin for support. From the government's perspective, what was better than a church schism? Answer: a schism within a schism. Although Krasnitsky had been certain that the government would assist him in keeping the progressive movement intact, it had its own plans. When he tried to get the GPU to escort Antonin out of Moscow, he was told that separation of church and state prevented the secret police from interfering in church affairs![15]

On August 20, a few days after the conference adjourned, Antonin bolted and formed a splinter group, the Union of Church Regeneration. In his eyes the Patriarchal Church was too conservative and was incapable of adjusting to modern conditions, but the Living Church was too radical. He had hoped to clean and purify the Patriarchal Church from within, but now he feared that the Living Church would fill the role of the Protestants during the Reformation and permanently split the church. Yet in the same breath he complained that the Living Church was not active enough in reforming time-hardened practices. His Church Regeneration party simplified the hierarchy, switched to vernacular Russian, and adopted the Gregorian calendar. But, as a believer in monasticism, he contested Krasnitsky's support for white clerical promotions to higher church office. Devoted to his new group of "spiritually pure" believers, he became more isolated from mainstream renovationism, which was more city- and town-focused, and turned his attention to the villages. "I don't need priests," he said. "I need people." (He remained the movement's figurehead, though, for the next ten months.)[16]

To the certain amusement of government leaders, Antonin and Krasnitsky proceeded to relate in the press every gory detail of their personal antagonism. Antonin publicly recalled how Krasnitsky had come to visit him one Sunday at the Strastnoy Monastery. During the recitation of the credo, Krasnitsky had uttered the customary words "Christ is among us." Instead of answering, "He is and shall be," Antonin had replied, "Between us there is no Christ."[17] Antonin begged the government to recognize his Church Regeneration party as the true leadership of Orthodoxy, but the government obviously took much more pleasure in letting the various factions fight it out. The Bolshevik Jacob Okunev, speaking in Kharkov, noted:

> Were the church to apply to the Soviet Government with a request that it help it to decompose, we should gladly, I think, help it. But if they were to ask us to help them unite, they would hardly find response among us.[18]

In October 1922 the renovationists finally pasted together a new Higher Church Administration (HCA), including members of all splinter parties that the government would officially recognize—but no Tikhon supporters. The Patriarchal Church charged that the new administration had become a subsection of the Agitprop Department of the Communist Party and that it received orders directly from the party's Central Committee. Avoiding the watchful eye of the GPU, secret Tikhonite meetings had already convened in major cities two months earlier to oppose the new Church Administration (before it was even officially formed).[19]

In December, Vedensky announced to an audience at Moscow's Zimin Theater that he, too, was no longer a member of the broader Living Church. He organized a group of parish priests into the Union of Congregations of the Ancient Apostolic Church, with the goal of returning to what he believed was first-century Christianity's pure communism. This second Living Church splinter planned for "the spiritualization and simplification of liturgy, the reduction of superfluous verbosity, . . . [and] a defense of the liturgy against deviation into ritual-faith and mechanical ritual performance."[20] For a while, the Ancient Apostolic Church had strong support among the peasantry, and it became a formidable rival to its parent body. Splintering, once begun, was hard to stop; soon the Union of Religious Communal Societies and the Free Labor Church went off on their own. The term "Living Church" thus developed two meanings: one covering the entire renovationist movement and the other a faction within it led by Krasnitsky. Despite this internal cleavage, the Patriarchal Church and the Soviet press continued referring to the whole conglomeration as the Living Church.

Yet these subchurches had a lot in common, and it was frequently difficult to tell where one left off and the other began. They all recognized the Soviet government, desired simplified church ritual, wanted married clergy as bishops (except for Antonin), and hoped to return to "a democratic state of original Christianity," whatever that might have been. They also had no scruples about compelling patriarchal churches to submit to their authority. In December renovationists in Vladimir resolved to purge "counterrevolutionary" clergy and parish councils. Their plan was to report recalcitrant churches to the civil authorities, requesting that their lease contracts be annulled. The renovationists manipulated the police to do their dirty work for them (and vice versa).[21]

THE SECOND (RENOVATIONIST) CHURCH SOBOR

The sobor declares capitalism a deadly sin and to fight it a sacred duty of the Christian. In the Soviet power, the sobor sees a world leader for brotherhood, equality, and, peace among nations.[22]

—Krasnitsky at the sobor

Progressives Assemble

Parish priests supported the calling of a new church sobor, and in principle Patriarch Tikhon did not oppose it. Many reforms had already begun that only a sobor could sanction, and by early 1923 such an assembly was already a year and a half overdue. The government had been the stumbling block to an earlier meeting, but now it was changing its tactics. Both the progressive clergy and the Communist Party expected these "positive" achievements from a sobor: depose the patriarch, legitimize the new HCA, and subordinate the Tikhonite Church to the civil government. They also had to be careful about foreign reaction. Once permission was granted to convene the sobor, *Bezbozhnik* asserted: "From now on no one dares to say that the Soviet government persecutes the church, persecutes religion."[23]

When the patriarch finally got wind of how this sobor would be used to destroy himself and his supporters, he moved quickly and decisively against it. He called the upcoming "Sobor of the Living Church" a sham, denounced it as uncanonical, and forbade any member of the church to attend it. Only a patriarch or his locum tenens could convene a sobor.[24] Beyond recriminations, however, the real issue was who was going to attend.

Back in August 1922, Vladimir Lvov, chief procurator of the Holy Synod during the Provisional Government and now a member of the renovationist HCA, had written in *Izvestia* that the Second Church Sobor should not convene until all reactionary elements had been purged from the hierarchy. (This tactic was reminiscent of the Bolshevik's mid-1917 hesitation in proclaiming the revolutionary slogan "All Power to the Soviets!" until they were in complete control of those soviets.) The sobor was originally scheduled to meet on February 2, 1923, but the renovationists were still not ready, needing more time to ensure that friendly priests and bishops—what the Soviets called the "left clergy"—dominated the gathering. Tikhon's followers, the "right clergy," would have tried to preserve the church's rituals and traditions intact and would have blocked any pro-Soviet resolutions.

On February 27 the Antireligious Commission handed the GPU the task of taking the "most decisive measures" against any Tikhonite clergy who still had plans to attend the already-postponed sobor. Bishops hostile to the renovationists were arrested on various pretexts. In Kiev, for example, the local soviet arrested the Tikhonite metropolitan, along with four other bishops and numerous priests, when he refused to submit to his "replacement" sent by the renovationist-controlled HCA. The GPU pressured some Tikhonites into signing statements that they would not leave their dioceses and denied others permission to ride on state-controlled railroads. Given the abominable conditions of Russian roads, this meant that they stayed home. At the same time the government granted renovationist delegates travel subsidies and transferred the boarded-up Zaikonospassky Monastery to them for their headquarters. And the progressive clergy had full access to *Izvestia* to make their accusations against the patriarch and his followers, while the latter had no access to the government press to make their rebuttals.[25]

The renovationists used other tactics to stack the delegations in their favor; for example, no one was allowed to attend who had been censured by the renovationist HCA or who had been tried and sentenced by the civil courts. This in itself disqualified virtually all the patriarchal party leadership.[26]

Even the Tikhonites "helped." Aware of widespread rumors that all the delegates had been chosen ahead of time and the elections were just a sham, many patriarchal parishes simply refused to hold elections, in effect boycotting the second sobor altogether. (The truth of these rumors was corroborated by a recently discovered internal GPU report written in mid-April 1923.)[27] Then, as delegates assembled in Moscow, renovationist leaders further attempted to weed out dissidents by circulating intimidating questionnaires. Delegates were asked:

- What is your attitude toward the Soviet government?
- What do you think about Patriarch Tikhon's attempt to block the sale of church treasures?
- Should the patriarch be deprived of his office?
- How do you regard the First Church Sobor of 1917–18?
- Do you support the patriarch's anathema of the Bolsheviks?
- What church party do you belong to?[28]

Sixty-six of the elected delegates claimed no party allegiance and demanded that, if Tikhon were brought to trial before the sobor, it be an open trial with Tikhon present to defend himself. Since they answered "wrong" on the questionnaire, they never got in the door.[29]

By the end of April 1923, in the whole of Russia only fifteen bishops remained who had attended the First Church Sobor of 1917–18; 84 had been dismissed or arrested in the meantime.[30] Evlogy, metropolitan of the Russian Orthodox Churches in Western Europe, claimed that *no* Tikhon loyalists remained at their posts. Clearly, neither the Bolsheviks nor the progressive clergy were interested in accurate representation of the actual church.

When the sobor—referred to by Francis McCullagh and other critics of this meeting as the "Red Sobor"—finally convened on April 29, 1923, there were 466 delegates in attendance; 430 of them with voting rights. Of those voting, 308 were clerics and 122 were laity. Two hundred fifty represented Krasnitsky's Living Church (a majority all by itself), 110 stood for Vedensky's Union of Ancient Apostolic Churches, and 25 belonged to Antonin's Union of Church Regeneration. Out of the remaining 45, most were Tikhonites (fifteen elderly bishops and thirty laymen—all of whom had violated Tikhon's boycott). This meant that 385 out of 430 delegates (90 percent) represented various renovationist programs, explaining, in turn, why the stated purpose of the gathering was "transforming the Russian Orthodox Church into conformity with the new conditions."[31]

At a time when the vast majority of nationwide clergy and laity supported Tikhon, the vast majority of delegates in Moscow were progressives and reformists. Aware of the dangers ahead, Tikhon's minuscule delegation protested the illegality of this sobor. It was not a right that could be arbitrarily assumed by a church administration *created by civil authorities*. But, given their numbers, the protest was drowned out. (Two months later, Tikhon objected: "The composition of the bishops seems to be strange. Out of sixty-seven bishops who were present at the sobor, I know only ten or fifteen persons. Where are the others?")[32]

Opening and closing ceremonies were held in the Cathedral of Christ the Savior, while working sessions were held nearby in what had been the Graduate Theological Seminary. Antonin, president of the HCA and bishop of Moscow, opened the ceremonies with a prayer: "Christ is risen and today the grace of God hath gathered us." He finished with a toastlike effusion: "To the Russian Republic and its government, long life!"[33] After that the delegates quickly passed a resolution expressing loyalty to the current regime and enthusiastically endorsing the separation of church and state. Krasnitsky, fulfilling another duty, handed a draft of all resolutions to GPU agent Tuchkov for his approval prior to their introduction.[34]

At the second session on May 2, Vedensky stepped onto the speaker's platform. Behind him hung an unframed portrait of Christ; in front of him, across the hall, hung a poster of Lenin. With powerful eloquence he gave—in the form of a resolution—a clear sense of where the sobor was heading:

> The Second Sobor of the Russian Orthodox Church, having begun its labors, expresses its gratitude to the All Russian Central Executive Committee for the permission granted to the elected sons of the church to meet in order to deliberate upon current problems. At the same time . . . the sobor presents its respects to the supreme executive of the Workers' and Peasants' Government and the world leader, V. Lenin.
>
> The great November Revolution has carried into life the great principles of equality in labor that are found in Christian teaching. All the world over the strong strangle the weak. Only in Soviet Russia has war begun against that social lie. The sobor affirms that every honorable Christian should take his place among these warriors for humanitarian truth and use all means to realize in life the grand principles of the November Revolution.
>
> To Vladimir Ilyich Lenin the sobor wishes a speedy recovery [from his recent stroke] so that he may again become the leader of the warriors for the great social truth.[35]

According to the sobor's secretary, this resolution was passed unanimously, but it is hard to see how the small group of Tikhonite delegates could have supported it. Perhaps, in a voice vote, their negative votes were never heard or counted.

There seemed no end to Vedensky's gushing over the virtues of communism:

> The sun of social truth shone out on the world on [November 7]. The Soviet government does not persecute the church, but punishes individual ecclesiastics

for counterrevolutionary activities. The government, though not believing, does the work of love that we, though believing, do not carry out. . . . [We are grateful] also to the leader of Soviet Russia, V. I. Lenin, *who must be dear also to church people.* . . . We must bear witness before the world that political truth exists only in Soviet Russia. I do not blaspheme; I feel that at this moment Christ is with us.[36] [emphasis added]

Another delegate referred to the November Revolution as a "Christian creation."[37] The sobor also urged every loyal citizen to "fight by every means, in common with the Soviet power, for the realization of the ideals of the Kingdom of God upon Earth."[38] It was almost as if communism had become an official doctrine of the church!

When (rarely) allowed to speak, Tikhon's supporters presented a starkly clear position:

One may ask how the Bolsheviks, enemies of religion, are able to tolerate the Living Church and to patronize it. The answer is easy. The Living Church is in the service of the Bolsheviks, being allowed to show a concern for the religious sentiment of the Russian people, and at the same time serving to establish in the life of the people Bolshevik principles which are contrary to those of Christianity—principles of hatred and violence opposed to the principles of the love and sweetness of Christ.

The rulers of the Living Church do not offer a single reproach or one word of blame against the Soviets. On the contrary, they not only proclaim their praises but justify all their violence and their murders; and they chant prayers for the prolongation of their days. Does not the complacency with which the [Orthodox Church's] rulers turn the churches over to the Bolsheviks, who make them places of blasphemy and orgy, reveal the secret work of the Living Church as tending to the destruction of the true Church of Christ in Russia?[39]

The vast majority of the nation's clergy and laity insisted that Tikhon had only temporarily handed over authority to the senior metropolitan, Agathangel. But both the government and the renovationists had contended over the past year that Tikhon had renounced his post as patriarch, and power had devolved to the new HCA. The progressive periodical *Living Church* expressed its view of the whole patriarchal institution:

We wish to do away with all possibility of the patriarchate existing any longer. The patriarchate is an institution of recent growth, foreign to ancient church history and deeply impregnated with the monarchical principle. We propose to create a collegiate body, or small assembly, responsive to the newly born spirit of union; this collegiate body will be more successful than the patriarchate, with its individual character.[40]

On May 3 Vedensky, Krasnitsky, and Antonin made impassioned speeches denouncing Tikhon for everything from capitalism to counterrevolution and declared his earlier anathema against Soviet power to be without force. Tikhon was still under house arrest and not present at the sobor, nor (uncanonically) was there counsel for his defense. Anyway, no evidence was ever presented against him. After Vedensky spoke for two and a half hours declaring the First Church Sobor to have been "reactionary" and "counterrevolutionary," the current sobor misused provisions of the first sobor to defrock and dethrone the patriarch, stripping away his status as a monk in the process. The resolution declared Tikhon to be "a transgressor against the true commandments of Christ and a traitor to the church."[41] According to some sources, Krasnitsky threatened to arrange for the arrest of all sixty-seven bishops present if they refused to sign the anti-Tikhon resolution; fifty-four signed it, so there may have been as many as thirteen who were carted off to prison.[42] After the deed was done, the sobor abolished the "undemocratic" institution of the patriarchate in favor of a more conciliar governing body.

The sobor performed a real service to the government. Apparently unwilling to bring Tikhon to trial while he remained patriarch for fear of creating a martyr, the government now felt free to make its move. Officially reduced to the status of a layman of the church, Citizen Belavin was now as vulnerable to Soviet authority as any other Russian. Still in custody, he was relentlessly interrogated, threatened, and bribed.[43]

On May 4 a motion was presented to abolish all sacred relics, as they tended to perpetuate rank superstition. The original proposal was vetoed by Antonin, who argued that a saintly life could indeed help to preserve the body in death. A compromise was finally agreed upon whereby the bodies of saints were declared to be incorruptible only for a limited—but unspecified—time, and relic veneration would be allowed as long as the remains were either deeply and permanently buried or kept in the open, uncamouflaged, and not concealed in caskets.[44] This prompted the Soviet apologist M. Sheinman to write (ten years later for foreign consumption):

> These "reformers" had not courage enough to dispense with relics altogether. They decided that the relics should remain in the churches in the future as before. This fact, as well as the entire activity of the "live" church clergy shows how timid the church "reformers" proved to be in the matter of "purifying" religion.[45]

On May 5 the calendar issue appeared on the agenda. The sobor voted for the substitution of the Gregorian for the Julian calendar, to take effect on June 12, 1923—a change made in the secular sphere within three months of the Bolshevik takeover (but among many in the Tikhonite Orthodox Church would not be made even to this day). On May 7 the delegates voted to excommunicate each individual member of the Karlovtzy Synod. On May 8 the sobor resolved to abandon the old HCA and replace it with a new High Church Council. Power would be shared between Krasnitsky's group (ten seats), Vedensky's group (six), and Antonin's group (two).[46] Also on this day the sobor refused to accept the autocephaly of the Ukrainian Orthodox Church.

Two other major issues occupied the delegates' time: proposals for liturgical change and efforts to alter the marital status of the white and black clergy. As for the first, the sobor voted to excise all pagan remnants and tsarist additions to the liturgy; the idea was to go back to the early Christian Church, before corruptions had set in. (This was an even more radical retrogression than that adopted by the Old Believers in the seventeenth century.) As mentioned earlier, progressive leaders wanted to abandon the use of Old Slavonic—superstitiously revered but not understood by the people—and require the liturgy to be spoken in the vernacular. (Church Slavonic is to modern Russian as the language of Chaucer is to modern English.)[47] The Gospels should be read directly to the congregation, and priests should cease their prayerful mumblings and speak audibly. Renovationist priests had already begun leaving the altar and—like Jesus among his flock—moving into the midst of the congregation, and many churches had already switched to modern Russian, but the sobor passed all these proposals anyway. The sobor then lifted the ban on reading the works of Leo Tolstoy.

There were even more radical proposals that failed to pass, most interestingly the suggestion that priests be allowed to wear secular clothes and have short hair and shaven faces. The sobor supported exchanging ancient ikons for ones painted in a modernist—even futurist—style, though it is unclear if any such ikons were actually produced.[48] Some delegates even ventured into trivialities, such as printing the first letter of the deity in a lowercase letter, while still capitalizing "Bolshevik."

The second major issue that occupied the delegates' minds involved improvement in the priests' position relative to that of the bishops. Although canon law was silent on the subject, traditionally bishops were chosen from among the black clergy (unmarried monks) while white clergy (married) were denied promotion. Under existing rules priests were allowed—actually expected—to marry *before* ordination, but not afterwards, nor could they remarry if their wife died. Even if their wife died, because of their previous marital status it was exceedingly rare for priests to become monks, which was a prerequisite for becoming bishops.

The long-standing feud between these two clerical ranks was compounded during the Civil War period by the black clergy's general support for the patriarch, White Armies, and foreign interventionists. The white clergy suffered for the black clergy's alleged acts of counterrevolution. When renovationists spoke out in defense of the white clergy, many priests rallied to their position. Over the past year they had been denouncing monks, claiming they had been fostering superstitions among the ignorant masses and exploiting their credulity. Now the sobor resolved to shut down monasteries all across Russia and turn the buildings into hospitals for aged priests or into almshouses.[49]

But there was an ulterior motive for allowing married priests to rise to the episcopacy. The sobor's "reforms" could not last unless renovationist support came from the bishops as well as the priesthood. Power was at the top. The reformers had to have strength among the bishops, and this could be done only be removing the older, traditionalist hierarchy and bringing in new blood. As a start, the sobor allowed monks to renounce their monastic vows yet retain their ecclesiastical (priestly) positions. Then it argued that the earlier Bolshevik confiscation of monastic property had led to a decrease in the ranks of monks so that now white clergy should be allowed to make up the deficit by filling episcopal offices. Vedensky supported married bishops on the grounds that this arrangement existed in the early Christian Church. Krasnitsky placed the problem in a Marxist perspective by referring to white, toiling clergy oppressed by black, non-toiling exploiters. (This analysis accorded well with the now deeply ingrained habit of viewing all change as the result of resolving dialectical contradictions.)

The previous June (1922), right after the renovationist coup, Archbishop Leonid had already ordained as bishops the Moscow priest John Chancev and the Petrograd priest John Albinsky, both of whom were married, thus breaking a thousand-year-old precedent. During the previous year Krasnitsky had elevated fifty-three priests to the episcopacy, but it is not known how many, if any, were married. At the sobor he proposed that widowed priests be allowed to remarry (and to marry divorcees, if desired)—allowing greater opportunity and greater freedom for priests. The sobor passed this resolution overwhelmingly, as the feeble opposition was drowned out in roars of approval. Vladimir Bonch-Bruevich commented that the white seemed to have replaced the black, but in his view, "the white is no less black than the black."[50]

In its last session, the sobor promoted Krasnitsky to the rank of protopresbyter, or chief priest, and Vedensky, though married, to the office of metropolitan of Krutitsa—the vicar of Moscow. (Later Tikhon would appoint Peter Polyansky, whom we will meet in the next chapter, to the same post.) It also raised Antonin to the office of "Metropolitan of Moscow and All Russia"—virtually making him a replacement patriarch. Then the sobor officially closed on May 9, 1923. Fifty bishops signed the sobor's summary resolution, which was then taken to Tikhon for his signature.[51] He simply remarked that he had read it and wrote:

> The sobor did not summon me; I do not know its competence and for that reason cannot consider its decisions lawful.[52]

Some sources say that he merely scrawled "Unlawful" across the face of the document and signed his name. Either way, the government kept Tikhon's rejection quiet.

The Meaning of the Sobor

For a while, the renovationists and the state became allies, though officially and theoretically each was separated from the other. Being allies implied not mutual friendship but mutual benefits. For its part the state supported, either tacitly or directly, every action the renovationists took against the Tikhonites, from denying them transportation to arresting priests who refused to join the progressive movement. The Living Church was allowed to maintain a nationwide organization, operate theological seminaries in Moscow and Petrograd, and publish church newspapers, while Tikhon's supporters were denied these privileges. (Their theological academy in Moscow, however, was an impoverished operation run in the St. Sergius-Trinity Monastery residence where Tikhon had once lived.)[53]

But renovationists were deluding themselves as to their future, and the government clearly got the best of the bargain. Renovationists supported the government in its charitable efforts, including programs for widows, orphans, and invalids. They fought against inequality and exploitation (of course, with the help of the state, which had the resources to carry out such programs). They helped suppress the Karlovtzy clergy, who were embarrassing Russian diplomats abroad. After excommunicating its entire synod, the new HCA declared that the émigré church had no connection with the "true" Orthodox Church in Russia. Renovationists supported worldwide revolution against capitalism. At one Moscow May Day parade, they marched down the street carrying banners depicting Jesus among the heroes of the Revolution.[54] Completely separating itself from the tsarist church and those who still clung to it, the Living Church drove a wedge into the Orthodox world. Vedensky exemplified this wedge in a speech on August 5, 1923:

> The leaders of the church, the bishops in monastic orders, members of the Union of the Russian People [Black Hundred Party], mobilized the church for the strengthening of the autocracy. Upon the assassination of Alexander II [1881], the church ordered the believers to pray for the prosperity of the imperial family, and one of the bishops declared . . . that the autocracy was a dogma of the church.[55]

And the very existence of the renovationists gave weight to the Communist argument abroad that there was no religious persecution in Soviet Russia.

During 1922 and 1923, the new Church Administration (and Council) organized programs across the country aimed at persuading clergy and laity to recognize the legitimacy of the Soviet government. The Living Church Conference of August 1922 sent a letter to the faithful that urged them to cease referring to the Soviet state as the Antichrist and that reminded them that the constitution protected the rights of both religious and antireligious propaganda. If they wanted to defend their beliefs they should do so with meritorious arguments. The letter concluded that the Soviet authority was "the only one throughout the world which will realize, by governmental methods [on Earth], the ideals of the Kingdom of God."[56]

The Second Church Sobor confirmed this position, continuing to educate the Russian people as to the virtues of communism. Lenin had suffered his first of several strokes one year before and had returned to work only the previous October, so the sobor sent him a copy of its resolution along with a get-well message urging that he recover to "stand among the fighters for the great social truth." (This was nothing, however, compared with the words of one of the renovationists who gave a requiem oration at Lenin's funeral in January 1924, when he called Lenin "a Christian by nature," or "essentially Christian."[57] It is a wonder the great leader did not rise out of his grave!)

The Monastery (1923)

Father Theophilus had called the meeting. The leader of Krasnitsky's Living Church renovationists in the overcrowded Simonov District of Moscow needed unity, at least among the white clergy against the black. In a back room of the Church of the Blessed Virgin's Nativity on Simon Street, the twenty-seven clerical and lay attendees vented their pent-up hostility against the monks of the nearby Simonov Monastery. Mostly they expressed their feelings in Christian terms and without raised voices, but the resentment could not be entirely concealed. And why should they conceal it? Their career paths had been blocked by their marriages, and they who dealt most directly with the people had been relegated to an inferior status within the body of Christ's church.

After half an hour of discussion, Father Theophilus asked for silence and then a prayer. His supplication, he thought, was a generous one—that the Lord grant the light of Truth to the Tikhonites in his district and show them the path to reform. Having set the stage nicely, he then slipped in his proposal. Why not ask the local soviet, which had already arranged for the shuttering of several of the district's smaller churches, to close the offending monastery as well. Wasn't it a haven for the least progressive elements among the Orthodox, perhaps even a sanctuary for counterrevolutionaries? All agreed that the monastery could best serve the people as a regular parish church. Resident monks could rejoin the priesthood or move elsewhere.

Negotiations were expanded to include Communist leaders at the nearby Dynamo Factory and were conducted by courier, as a public meeting would be unseemly. But negotiations were short; after a few rounds of notes between the workers, the soviet, and the renovationist group, Theophilus received this message:

The workingmen of Moscow care not at all about the squabbling between the white and black clergy. During the Civil War we had to fight against both hues, without distinction. Why should we care about a simple competition for parishioners and a contest for the contents of collection plates? The white clergy is just seeking to monopolize the fooling and robbing of Simonov residents. As Communists, let us recommend this solution to the alleged problem: We will close both the Simonov Monastery and the Nativity Church. The workers of our district know how to put both of these buildings to better use and at the same time save the people's hard-earned money.

—The Red Workmen of Moscow

And the "people's will" was done.[58]*

DISSENSION WITHIN BOTH CAMPS

The six months or so after the Second Church Sobor was one of internal difficulties for both the Bolshevik Party and the renovationist leadership. Consensus was hard to come by.

Bolshevik Disarray

As mentioned above, Lenin had suffered the first of several strokes on May 26, 1922 (a week after the progressive coup). His right side was partially paralyzed, speech was difficult, and recovery was slow. As Stalin, Kamenev, and Bukharin began jostling for position in the succession struggle, they increasingly isolated Lenin at his residence in Gorky. For the remaining period of his life (less than two years) he would be held virtually incommunicado, given little or no political news, and allowed to dictate through his secretaries for only a few minutes a day. Partly due to his affliction and partly due to his isolation, he grew irritable, frustrated, suspicious, and angry, while at the same time he became obsessed with detail and capricious of opinion. Then, in December, he suffered two additional minor strokes and the following March another major one.[59]

Feuding within the Politburo regarding antireligious policy (and nearly everything else) now resurfaced. While many still supported the schismatic program, many others now became impatient for results. Okunev wrote in *Pravda*:

---

*This story is based on an (unverified) article Arthur Ruhl discovered in *Pravda*. The Simonov Monastery, built in 1371, still exists. Five of the six churches within its walls were blown up in 1935, but the clergy holds signed Orthodox services for deaf believers in the remaining church.

The time has gone when the social protest of the suffering masses can take the form of religious reform. Religion cannot stand for universal ideas in an epoch of steam and electricity, of airplanes, and radium. A horse and a timid deer cannot be yoked to the same cart.

If the progressive clergy is planning a serious reform, really corresponding to the spirit of the present time, it will have to suppress religion altogether. . . . God himself must be eliminated, just as a stone is gradually destroyed by the influence of the atmosphere.[60]

Trotsky, who had initially championed the schism, now felt that the rate of stone erosion was too slow and became more impatient than Okunev. He charged that the Living Church (in the larger sense) was merely an attempt by the clergy to put on protective coloration while pursuing essentially bourgeois aims. At the December 1922 Ninth Congress of Soviets, delegate Alypov threatened: "What we need now is not a reform of the church, but the entire liquidation of it. We don't need any Soviet Church at all. . . . [Renovationists] only change color and try to adapt themselves to the present life." Bonch-Bruevich wrote that neither the proletariat nor the peasantry needed a living church or a dead one, a new one or an old one.[61]

Ivan Skvortsov-Stepanov wrote in his pamphlet *A Summary of the Argument of the Living Church* that Marxists among the renovationists misunderstood their historical role, as they blamed all their problems on Patriarch Tikhon and on the black clergy without realizing that *all* religion was by definition part of the exploiting class and therefore had to be eliminated. He was disdainful of renovationist attempts to form an ideological rapprochement with communism and characterized them as naive if they thought they could save themselves by casting the monastic body from the sinking ship and then attempting to struggle to port under the banner of revolution. Thus he recommended that the government take neither side in the church schism, that it should instead concentrate on revolutionizing the masses.[62] Okunev penned this exposé in 1923:

The Living Church has declared that from now on it is going to struggle against capitalists and oppressors, that it is ranking its forces with the laboring masses, that it is on the side of revolutionary authority, that it is on the side of the workmen and the peasants. Fine words! The declarations issued by it are so beautiful that really some of the less experienced workmen may believe that Communists have donned priestly robes and are preaching communism from the church pulpit. But how is it that the counterrevolutionists of yesterday are publishing such revolutionary declarations today? It seems to me that this revolutionary dye has been adopted to save their own skins and their material interests.[63]

Renovationist Disarray

Personality conflicts continued to weaken the renovationists. Although Antonin was the president of the postsobor High Church Council, Krasnitsky's Living Church faction dominated it. For a time, though, Antonin felt obliged to remain administratively, but not spiritually, in this organization in order, as he said, to keep the Krasnitsky's faction within certain boundaries and check its impetuousness.

In an interview with an *Izvestia* reporter, Antonin claimed to have received complaints against the Living Church faction from all over Russia: "The threats, oppression, arrests, and exiles which the Living Church inflicts cause great exasperation against it."[64] Living Church leaders retorted that Antonin had compromised progressive principles and that many of his followers had gone over to the Patriarchal Church. In July 1923, the High Church Council stripped Antonin of his "Metropolitan of Moscow and All Russia" title as well as his council seat. He claimed he could no longer sit in that body with a clear conscience because to do so would mean remaining "in intercourse with those who have broken the church canons," but most likely he was eased out by those within the movement who could no longer stomach his eccentricities. Bishop—soon to be Metropolitan—Evdokim (Meshchersky) of Nizhny-Novgorod (Gorky) was invited to preside in his place, where he served until his OGPU-forced retirement in February 1925.[65]

WERE THE RENOVATIONISTS REALLY COMMUNISTS?

[A socialistic government] being hostile to all religion would be untrue to itself if it made use of any religion for its own aims.

—professor and renovationist leader B. Titlinov

Although recently turning more temperate, renovationists still accepted the Marxist analysis of history (except for that bothersome part about the role of religion in society). They were, of course, perverting the philosopher's intent, which, in turn, led to many progressive statements sounding neither fully Marxist nor fully religious. For example, Vedensky's communism was really the presumed communalism of the first-century Christian Church. He told foreign clergymen that the church should live in harmony with communism.

Krasnitsky's communism, however, was more overtly Marxist, as is seen in this excerpt from one of his resolutions, overwhelmingly passed by the sobor on its second day:

At present the whole world is divided into two classes: capitalist exploiters and proletarians upon whose toil and blood the capitalist world is building its welfare.

In the whole world the Soviet government of Russia has ventured to struggle with this social evil. Christians cannot be indifferent spectators in this struggle.[66]

Many in the Patriarchal Church took the position that the origins of the Living Church were grounded in a legitimate yearning for reform. Many priests, after all, had been working for church reform well before the Bolshevik uprising. Progressivism, they said, had risen in response to a real need that was felt by a significant minority of the Orthodox priesthood who admitted that the church had stagnated and was ripe for religious revival.[67] The Cheka/GPU had opportunistically twisted reformist zeal into a tool of state policy. Sincere efforts had been co-opted.

Harsher critics believed that the Living Church movement was an original *creation of* the government and that from the beginning the progressive clergy were willing tools of their makers. The historian of Christianity W. C. Emhardt charged that there had been no spontaneous reform movement. He found it to be more than coincidence that in 1922 control over religious policy was transferred from the Commissariat of Justice to Tuchkov in the Cheka/GPU, and in that same year the Living Church suddenly appeared on the scene. Tuchkov's job description was to destroy the church by whatever means available. (Tikhon called him "the angel of Satan.")[68]

A *London Times* reporter obtained the original of a renovationist petition submitted to the government just before their coup; it was an application for permission to establish Communist cells in every center of the Orthodox Church. The petitioners even offered to spy on Orthodox leaders and report to the government.[69] Emelyan Yaroslavsky wrote in late 1923, "Frequently [renovationist] priests called on committees of the party requesting that they enlist them, . . . and sometimes they even wanted to organize special groups of Communist priests." He added that "our ways were far apart" and claimed that all contacts were rebuffed, but it is the application that is revealing.

The progressive Titlinov partially supported the theory of the Communist origins of renovationism when he wrote, "External conditions made our move possible, for precisely at that time the revolutionary authorities were ready to support a new movement within the church." And Krasnitsky seemed to support the claim of Soviet control when he stated in August 1922 that during the previous spring "the state authorities suggested . . . that the church change its policy" and that he and his followers had agreed.[70]

The confluence of Soviet and renovationist goals may have simply been due to their mutual rejection of a backward past. Progressives were certain they had found a path to transforming the Russian people while guaranteeing church survival. The government took advantage of their naiveté, but it demonstrated its own naiveté when it supposed that through devious and conspiratorial techniques—or even direct techniques—it could eliminate religious faith in the entire country.

Meanwhile, the Bolsheviks still had Patriarch Tikhon scheduled for trial. It would not be an easy thing to accomplish.

15

THE NIGHT WILL BE LONG AND VERY DARK

Patriarch Tikhon's Confession, Release, Death, and Will

Tikhon was increasingly enfeebled, both physically and in terms of his freedom to act. Yet in 1923 and 1924 the Bolsheviks were still afraid of him.

A TRIAL?

After Tikhon's "abdication" and arrest, the press vilified him with renewed ferocity. In June 1922, *Pravda* announced that the Moscow Revolutionary Tribunal had decided to bring him to formal trial. There was some nervousness about trying Tikhon, however—some of it due to fear of endangering Russia's already shaky relations with Great Britain. The Archbishop of Canterbury had maintained a keen interest in the fate of the patriarch and the Orthodox Church. On the other hand, after their military interventions in Russia's Civil War, the British were hardly in a position to protest too loudly. Had they done so, it could be construed as more evidence that Tikhon was in collusion with foreign, capitalist, and counterrevolutionary powers. The result was that European powers voiced their protests in vague and diplomatic ways, which the Soviets interpreted as a "go-ahead" for Tikhon's trial. The patriarch, in his rooms at the Donskoy Monastery and still under arrest, awaited his fate.[1]*

The original trial date was set for November 1922 but was then postponed, most likely due to debates within the state Central Executive Committee as to timing. Apparently the left wing won out, as the trial date was reset for mid-April

---

*After Tikhon was transferred from the Donskoy Monastery to the Taganka Prison on August 5, 1922, it is not clear how long he remained there before being allowed to return to his monastery rooms. It appears that he had returned at least by the period of the Second (Renovationist) Church Sobor in the spring of 1923.

1923. On April 6 the government announced the following charges against him: "Dealing with foreign powers, counterrevolutionary work directed toward over-throwing the Soviet order, opposition to decrees of the authorities, and using religious beliefs and prejudices for creating a disobedient and rebellious attitude among the masses." The government specifically accused Tikhon of communicating with the Karlovtzy Sobor and leading the violent opposition to the use of church valuables for famine relief. Then, on April 24, when admission tickets had already been printed, the date was again put off.[2] *Pravda* explained that new evidence had recently been obtained linking Tikhon with other accused priests, including Archbishop Nafanail in Archangel, who had allegedly informed the patriarch of his efforts to get the Archbishop of Canterbury to influence the British government to leave its Arctic forces in place.[3] Another date would soon be set.

The press continued to berate Tikhon for "meddling in politics" and "collusion with foreign powers." In the spring of 1923 Soviet newspapers blasted the patriarch—who was, after all, a citizen of the Soviet Republic—for communicating with foreign countries through their diplomatic and religious missions in Moscow without seeking permission from the authorities. Party and government leaders remembered his earlier denunciation of the February 1918 Brest-Litovsk Treaty, and they now presented it to the public as evidence of counterrevolutionary tendencies. It is doubtful that Tikhon ever understood how impossible it was to remain outside of politics. The Soviets interpreted any move Tikhon made to preserve the sanctity and privileges of his church as political—as moves counter to *their* political goals. Tikhon remained frustrated in his attempts to avoid the counterrevolutionary charge, but the simple fact that he was the patriarch labeled him as such in Communist Party eyes.

Plans for the oft-postponed trial continued. The prosecutor would be Nikolai Krylenko, and his approach would be harsh. He remarked to a provincial party delegation: "The fate of citizen Tikhon is in our hands and you may be sure that we shall not be merciful." The government's scathing antipatriarchal rhetoric fed rumors spreading throughout Moscow that Tikhon had already been killed in prison.[4]

But there were also pressures—especially from those concerned with foreign reaction—to be merciful to the patriarch. George Chicherin wrote to Stalin on April 10, 1923:

> The commissariat proposes that the Politburo adopt in advance a decision not to pronounce the death sentence on Tikhon. The facts have shown how much damage we brought on ourselves by the execution of Budkiewicz [a Catholic leader shot a week and a half earlier]. . . . Anyone who knows even a little of what is happening beyond the border posts will confirm that our position in all our relations has grown much worse as a result of this case. . . . [Because Tikhon cannot be accused of being a Polish spy, as Budkiewicz was] all other countries view his sentence as nothing other than naked religious persecution.[5]

CONFESSION AND RELEASE

We declare that there is no earthly power strong enough to inhibit our conscience as head of the church or restrict the liberty of our patriarchal utterance.[6]

—Patriarch Tikhon, June 1923

Confession

In January 1923 the government was still planning to prosecute Tikhon, and a meeting of the Antireligious Commission held at the end of the month set a deadline of March 25 for preparation of the legal case. At the end of February the Commission issued orders to begin "suitable agitation measures" to get ready for the trial.[7] But by March a trial of Catholic clergy was under way (to be discussed in chapter 21), and it was causing quite a stir abroad. There was already talk of Tikhon's possible release.

In early May 1923, the British diplomat Lord Curzon used not-so-veiled threats in an attempt to further postpone diplomatic recognition of Moscow if Tikhon were tried. Although not presented as such, the Soviets called it the Curzon Ultimatum and bitterly resented it. Chicherin replied with a diatribe against British atrocities committed against the Irish. Nonetheless, the Soviets could not afford to ignore the threat.[8]

Then, on June 1 after five o'clock tea, Tikhon suffered a bout of vomiting and fainting spells; he remained unconscious for an hour and a half. Some said he ate some bad fish. The patriarch's friends, however, believed that he had been poisoned, and, ironically, Soviet authorities were worried about the same thing; they were not about to create a martyr of such international standing. They quickly moved him from the Donskoy Monastery to the GPU's Taganka Prison.[9]

Events During Patriarch Tikhon's Final Years

Moscow Church Trial April 26 – May 6, 1922	"Abdication" Meetings May 12 & May 18, 1922
Taken to Donskoy Monastery May 19, 1922	First Taken to GPU Prison August 5, 1922
Second Church Sobor April 29 – May 9, 1923	Confession & Release Late June 1923
Krasnitsky Repents Mid–May 1924	Death April 7, 1925

After this scare, it became increasingly clear that the patriarch was ageing faster than the passing of years; he appeared pale, weak, and thin. In prison he was further isolated, being allowed to read only the government press, which exaggerated the strength of the renovationists.

Over several weeks, GPU agents proposed that Tikhon recognize Soviet authority, repent of his "crimes" against the Russian people, and distance himself from counterrevolutionary organizations.[10] If he would do so, freedom would soon await him as well as other imprisoned priests. Yaroslavsky, representing the Commission, presented conditions for Tikhon's release to the Politburo, which approved them on June 14. The patriarch must:

- repent of his crimes against the Soviet power and the people and admit that his prosecution was just.
- declare his loyalty to the Soviet state.
- cut off all relations with anti-Soviet exiles and other counterrevolutionary organizations.
- make negative statements about the "machinations of the Catholic clergy."
- denounce the efforts of the Archbishop of Canterbury and the patriarch in Constantinople.
- consent to certain progressive religious reforms.[11]

Unwilling to be the cause of further suffering and hoping to at last bring peace to the church, Tikhon capitulated.

On June 16 the patriarch wrote a confession and recantation, which was presented to the Supreme Court nine days later. This led to his release the following day, though the promise to free other clergy was callously broken.[12] His followers believed that release revealed the Hand of God in play. Due to its controversial nature, the confession is presented here in full:

> In addressing myself to the Supreme Court of the RSFSR I deem it my pastoral duty to declare the following: Having been brought up in monarchist surroundings, and being up to my arrest under the influence of anti-Soviet persons, I had indeed hostile feelings toward the Soviet Power, and those hostile feelings sometimes changed from a passive state into overt acts, such as the declaration in connection with the Brest-Litovsk Treaty in 1918, the anathematizing of the authorities in the same year, and finally an appeal against the decree ordering the requisition of church valuables in 1922.
>
> All my anti-Soviet activities are formulated, with the exception of a few inaccuracies, in the indictment of the Supreme Court. Recognizing the correctness of the decision of the court to bring me to trial according to the articles of the Criminal Code enumerated in the indictment, for my anti-Soviet activities, I regret my actions against the state regime and request the court to do away with my detention; that is to release me from arrest. I also declare to the

Supreme Court that I am no longer an enemy of the Soviet Power. I am finally and positively breaking all relations with the monarchist and White Guard counterrevolution at home and abroad.

Patriarch Tikhon (Vasily Belavin)[13]

When the confession was released to the press, an uproar immediately arose as to why Tikhon had written it, as did skepticism as to whether he actually had done so. Some Orthodox clergy abroad said they had received a communication from Tikhon in the spring of 1922 warning that papers bearing his name might be forgeries. A GPU agent reported at the time that contradictory rumors were circulating in a desperate attempt to explain Tikhon's inexplicable behavior. Possibilities: he had gone mad, the Bolsheviks had paid him off, or the "Tikhon" who signed the confession was an impostor—with no word on where the real Tikhon had gone.[14]

After the confession's publication, a correspondent for the Soviet Telegraph Agency claimed that Tikhon had told him:

While kept in custody I suffered no restraint except, of course, the prohibition to conduct services. Communications in the foreign press alleging that I was tortured are absurd; my treatment was of the best. I have completely adopted the Soviet platform and consider that the church must be nonpolitical. If the news that the prelates who have gone abroad [Karlovtzy clergy] are engaged in counterrevolutionary activity proves true, I propose that they cease such work as incompatible with the pastoral office. I think that they will listen to me.[15]

Julius Hecker, in Moscow as an appointed member of the second sobor's Educational Committee, also visited Tikhon and confirmed that he had indeed written the confession and that he had been neither forced nor threatened.[16]

The historian John Shelton Curtiss felt the most likely explanation was that "the weight of the evidence shown to him during his imprisonment was so convincing that he, fearing to suffer the fate of Metropolitan Benjamin, listened to the arguments of his captors and secured release by admitting guilt." Curtiss also argued that people around him easily swayed Tikhon and that, while in confinement, isolated from conservative advisers, he became convinced that perhaps he *was* guilty.[17] Yet it is doubtful that his own freedom was foremost in his mind. He was very concerned about the survival of the True Church in Russia and, fueled by what he read in Soviet newspapers—his only source of news while in prison—may have come to think of the Living Church and its new Church Administration as more dangerous than Soviet power.

He appears to have begun rationalizing that he was not so much opposed to the Soviet system of government as he was to a particular few of its laws, as he explained in an interview with the *Manchester Guardian*: "In 1918, I stood openly against some of its decrees."[18] Refusing to implicate the Patriarchal

Church in any of his "crimes," he decided to accept full personal blame. Soviet sources insisted that Tikhon had a change of heart and had sincerely adopted a moderate position. They claimed that, in custody, he had come to realize that his monarchist, Orthodox upbringing had prejudiced him against the Soviet regime. They had shown him articles in the foreign press where statements made by him had been distorted and slanted to bring discredit on his country, thus gradually convincing him that all the calumnies heaped upon the government were not necessarily true. A fair conclusion would be that the confession was genuine enough—the only dubious aspect of it being its journalistic style. It was written in Bolshevik phraseology, not that of an Orthodox churchman. Most likely *they* wrote it and *he* signed it.

In spite of Tikhon's rationalizations, controversy lingered. Half a century later Father Gleb Yakunin, typical of many in the church, wrote of his continuing disgust at Tikhon's bending to the will of the GPU. What had happened to the patriarch's "righteous indignation" at Bolshevik brutality? His earlier "calling of men to heed their consciences" seemed hypocritical now. Yakunin concluded:

> In spite of the greatness of the personality and exploits of Patriarch Tikhon, we must with great sorrow admit that the principle of the use of lies and false witness for the sake of "the salvation of the church" was applied in the Moscow Patriarchate for the first time by him.[19]

Release

Surely to Krylenko's great disappointment, he never got the chance to make his case. Tikhon's trial was never held, and the whole subject was simply dropped from mention in the press without explanation. Jane Swan described eyewitness accounts of his June 26 prison release:

> Soon the entire [Taganka Prison] square was filled, and then the people quietly waited. A door opened and there, surrounded by guards, walked out a disheveled old man with uncombed gray hair and a tangled beard. Only his deep eyes were alive in a face aged and blank with a set expression. Over his naked body he wore an old soldier's coat. His feet were bare. When he saw the enormous crowd, tears ran down his face. All knelt before him, and so emotional was the atmosphere that even the guards bowed their heads.[20]

The crowd then escorted him back to his old rooms at the Donskoy Monastery, where he was no longer in government custody. He would now be allowed to celebrate mass in the chapel, receive visitors, and come and go as he pleased (though he was always closely watched, and Tuchkov interrogated him on a regular basis).

Tikhon seemed not to have connected his release with his confession, convincing himself instead that the government had finally come to understand him. This is an excerpt from the same interview with the *Manchester Guardian* mentioned above:

Tikhon:	We, the members of the old clergy, are not now struggling against the Soviets, but against the Living Church.
Guardian:	What were the causes of your liberation and the change in the attitude of the Soviet government toward you?
Tikhon:	I am persuaded that, having studied my case, the government has convinced itself that I am no counterrevolutionary. It was suggested that I should make a public declaration of the fact, and I wrote a letter to say so.[21]

On Sunday, July 1, the patriarch twice led services at the monastery, once inside and again to the masses outside who had been unable to enter the crowded chapel. A "lady of eminence in the church" rejoiced:

> When he makes his appearance flowers are strewn under his feet, and in one church he walked literally upon a carpet of flowers. A whiff of fresh air seems to have entered our church life; the bells seem to ring more joyfully.[22]

He pledged once again to refrain from political utterances. To his close associates, he confided that he would work for a *"modus vivendi* with the government" and seek permission for the calling of a new sobor that would vindicate his actions.[23]

> I decisively condemn any attack upon the Soviet government, no matter from where it comes. Let it be known to all foreign and domestic monarchists that I am not an enemy of the Soviet government.[24]

When criticized for the "I am not an enemy" statement, he replied that he had never said he was the government's *friend* either. He still rejected registration of churches with the government and official approval of episcopal appointments. He was still the patriarch and rejected all renovationist actions (not the least of which was his unfrocking).

The government was satisfied for the time being. It now had a signed statement binding Tikhon to political neutrality. If he ever stepped out of line and began a new political offensive, his rearrest would be all the easier. By his confession, the government received a windfall on the antireligious front. The entire first page of the July 1 issue of *Bezbozhnik* was devoted to a reproduction of the document. Newspapers ran numerous articles stressing these three themes:

- There was now proof of what the government had been saying all along—Tikhon had been an active agent of the "manorial landlords and capitalists abroad."

- The foreign bourgeois press, which had been defending Tikhon as a victim of Soviet persecution, was now placed in a "silly and ridiculous position."
- The Soviets were merciful and understanding when an enemy of the worker-peasant revolution showed that he was repentant.

On July 4 an article in *Izvestia* concluded: "The church is dead,"[25] then two days later it printed another Tikhon proclamation confirming his loyalty to the state. He blamed his errors on "the milieu that trained us" and "evil-minded persons" who, unable to overthrow the Bolsheviks on their own, used him and his church to do their dirty work. He reiterated his nonpolitical position, calling the Orthodox Church neither a Red Church nor a White Church, and warned the Karlovtzy clergy to submit to Soviet power or he would—quite unrealistically— drag them to Moscow for trial.[26]

The government was profiting not only by Tikhon's confession but also by his release, which had the advantage of aggravating the church schism. The July 15 issue of the *Workman's Moscow* (*Rabochaya Moskva*) carried a cartoon depicting Tikhon in a violent hand-to-hand struggle with another clergyman— possibly Antonin or Krasnitsky—while a grinning worker stood by with his hands in his pockets. The caption read: "While two are engaged in a struggle, the hands of the third are free."[27]

Another indication of internal conflict occurred during the summer in what came to be known as the "Scandal of St. Isaak's Cathedral." The priest Chuev, pastor of the cathedral, and Stepanovich, the keeper of the keys, supported the Living Church. The three remaining priests and the Archdeacon Dmitriev favored Tikhon. At a Saturday evening service Dmitriev publicly prayed for the patriarch, whereupon the priest Chuev, acting within his power as pastor, forbade Dmitriev to perform any further services. As the parishioners became aware of the squabble, they demanded an explanation of the pastor. The conversation became heated, and Chuev had to flee out the back door amid the shouting of the excited crowd. The result: Both halves of the congregation condemned the other. During this especially bitter season, *Krasnaya Gazeta* summed up the situation from the government's perspective:

> [The fight against religious opium] is carried on most effectually by the church servitors themselves, who are persons without any convictions and are lacking the most simple human conscience.

Although Tikhon's release deepened the religious divide, it also spelled the beginning of the end for the government's ally. All but five of Moscow's churches had gone over to the renovationists, but one by one they expressed their desire to return to the fold. Tikhon officiated in and reblessed each recanting church. News of Moscow's repentance soon reached down to the village level, in spite of renovationist attempts to block it. Parishioners replaced many village priests, and the Living Church began sliding down the slope of obsolescence.[28]

A month after Tikhon gained his freedom, the government tried to push its advantage by asking GPU agent and Commission secretary Tuchkov to persuade Tikhon to write to the Archbishop of Canterbury verifying his confession and declaration of loyalty.[29] There is no evidence, however, that Tikhon ever complied. He was too busy trying to undo the damage he had done and reestablish traditionalism and conservatism within the Orthodox community. On July 15 he solemnly read aloud from the Donskoy Monastery's pulpit a statement anathematizing the Living Church and excommunicating its members. He referred to its leaders as "usurpers" and to their having gained control of the Church Administration the previous year as "nothing else but lies and fraud."[30] He also claimed that his removal from the patriarchate at the recent sobor was a violation of canon law:

> All arrangement made during our absence by those ruling the church, since they had neither legal right nor canonical authority, are nonvalid and void, and all actions and sacraments performed by bishops and clergymen who have forsaken the church are devoid of God's grace and power; the faithful taking part in such prayers and sacraments shall receive no sanctification thereby and are subject to condemnation for participating in their sin.[31]

Tikhon presented a convincing case that had he known how weak the Living Church was he would never have signed the confession in the first place, preferring to remain in custody. A certain Father Mikhail, who spoke with Tikhon during his confinement, offered corroboration, saying that Tikhon relented only because he thought, in his isolation, that the renovationists were making great inroads into the church.[32] It is not clear, though, why "renovationist inroads" should have caused him to cave in unless at the time he had simply decided to ride what he thought was the wave of church reform rather than allow it to break over him.

Both Tikhonites, not wanting to see weakness in their leader, and renovationists, not wanting the government to trust the patriarch, argued that the confession had been insincere. In spite of Tikhon's apparent verification, his followers thought it to be a forgery. And the renovationists challenged that if Tikhon were truly repentant, let him demonstrate it by admitting not only his political errors but his mistakes in church policy as well. This, of course, he would not do.

Tikhon's return to freedom did not mean a complete return to power. He told visitors:

> I'm only considered to be free, but in fact I can do nothing. I send a hierarch to the south and he turns up in the north; I send him to the west and they take him to the east.[33]

And the charges had not actually been dropped; the case against him was still pending. The Antireligious Commission decided on August 14, 1923, to keep the fear of a trial hanging over his head.[34] While the government permitted him to retain the rank and vestments of patriarch, the press referred to him as "citizen Belavin," showing that it recognized the actions of the 1923 Renovationist Sobor.

Government and Renovationist Pressure

Although Tikhon was nominally free, Tuchkov kept on squeezing him. During the summer and autumn of 1923 the GPU agent tried to wring out of the patriarch three additional concessions:

- Church services should honor the government (or at least Tikhon should not voice opposition if they did).
- Tikhon should adopt the Gregorian calendar, as the government and the Living Church had done. (This was a part of the progressive reforms mentioned earlier, but apparently it was not explicitly stated in the earlier conditions for release.)
- Tikhon should reconcile with the renovationists.

It is difficult to see why the government cared about any of these issues, other than to make more trouble for the church. Perhaps Tuchkov and the government were not reading from the same page. For a while Tikhon accepted the insertion into the service of a blessing "for the Russian land and its authorities"—an obvious compromise—but some clergy rejected even this innocuous phrase and substituted another word that in Russian rhymed with "authorities," hoping no one would notice. It was not long, though, before the entire insertion fell into disuse.[35]

As for the second of Tuchkov's demands, the changeover from the Julian to the Gregorian calendar, the government set a high priority on achieving church compliance, even refusing to authorize the much-loved ikon processions through the streets unless they were timed according to the state calendar. Tikhon wrote:

> This demand [for change] was repeated many times and was reinforced by the promise of a more benevolent attitude on the part of the government towards the Orthodox Church and her institutions in the case of our agreement, and the threat of deterioration in these relations in the case of our refusal.[36]

The advantages of moving to the Gregorian calendar might seem obvious:

- Synchronization: The West and the rest of the world had made the switch centuries ago, the Russian government had complied on February 1, 1918,

and the renovationists had changed their calendars a few months after the Second Church Sobor. (Of course, the latter change could be considered by the Patriarchal Church to be a reason *not* to change.)
* Accuracy: The old calendar was falling further and further behind, based as it was on miscalculations of the Earth's orbit.
* Consideration: Orthodox factory employees had to work according to the Gregorian calendar, which did not allow for Julian calendar feast days. Tikhon had repeatedly been petitioned by workers who had been fined for missing work to attend Orthodox celebrations.[37]

Yet from a religious perspective, the advantages were outweighed by the disadvantages. As the historian Gregory Freeze has pointed out: "Calendar reform . . . had a transparent political aim of marginalizing the Orthodox Church and, especially, its liturgical life."[38] Tikhon warned:

> [The government seeks calendar "reforms"] for the sake of combating the faith of the majority of the population and with the intent of limiting the influence of the Orthodox Church on the people.[39]

Many in the church understood this and clung to control of their calendar so as to preserve the church's "specialness" and its rule over the rhythm of life.

Under great pressure, Tikhon was ambivalent and inconsistent on the subject. On July 30, 1923, he actually ordered that the change take place. Then, according to some observers, Soviet agents provocateurs circulated through the capital's churches spreading rumors that only a senile patriarch would overturn centuries of church tradition. Parishioners believed that this was an omen of a Living Church coup and raised an uproar. Tikhon then annulled his own decree. Finally, on October 15, Tikhon consulted with a small council of bishops that had been meeting since summer in St. Michael's Church within the Donskoy Monastery. After much discussion—and without much enthusiasm—he again offered an endorsement of the change and ordered it put into effect, with the exception of Easter, whose date would be calculated as before. There was, however, no specific timetable for implementation.[40]

No sooner had he made this decision than he came to realize how repugnant this reform was to the patriarchs of other autocephalous Orthodox Churches, the Russian Orthodox Church in exile, and especially the domestic laity. The chief lay objection was that major religious holidays would have to be shifted by thirteen days, causing what were perceived to be drastic disruptions in the seasonal flow of life. One priest commented sadly: "It is difficult to part with the old calendar, to which the believer's heart is so attached."[41] Laity had been gaining strength relative to the clergy for over a century, a trend encouraged by the Bolsheviks when they arrested the hierarchy, removed the surviving clergys' state income, and wrote Committee of Twenty requirements for church leases. This meant that many priests, either because of pressure from the renovationist-controlled Church Council or to opportunism, sided with the reformers, while the laity, having become a power to be reckoned with, resisted drastic social change.[42] The Bolshevik strategy had backfired. The bishop of Tambov, a Tikhonite, described the attitude of the parishioners:

> In this province the faithful—who until now have stood aside from events in church since the "renovation" did not directly affect them—have begun to voice opposition to the renovationists. The transition to the new calendar woke the people up and caused them to discern here a precedent for the encroachment on their "holy of holies."[43]

Tikhon also realized that the renovationists' switch to the Gregorian calendar had already caused them to lose influence among the masses. In addition, the Orthodox Church was already split by the seventeenth-century breakaway of the Old Believers (discussed in chapter 22), and calendar change would just force more irreconcilables in the villages into their fold, where the calendar remained the same. Once he fully grasped what he had done, Tikhon again rescinded his earlier order.

On November 20, 1923, the Antireligious Commission once again urged Tuchkov to get the new calendar implemented within the Tikhonite Church. Wracked by indecision, Tikhon announced just before Christmas that the new calendar, though acceptable, was not mandatory for 1924 due to the confusion it would cause in the liturgy and the celebration of Lent—as if any more confusion were possible. When he received a telegram asking about the celebration of this year's Christmas, he responded: "Maintain the old [calendar], or, if the parishioners desire, perform services according to the new calendar."[44] There the issue remained until his death.

Tuchkov's third demand may seem counterintuitive. Why would the GPU hope for reconciliation between the Tikhonites and the renovationists only two years after the Communist Party had approved support of the schism? Would not union imply strength? The government side did not explicitly offer an answer, but we can surmise that reconciliation was meant to exacerbate the schism! Pressuring the two sides, which now saw each other as enemies, to make up would only serve to highlight their differences and emphasize their irreconcilability. Still, various hierarchs met in Moscow during the fall of 1923 hoping to actually achieve peace in the church. One almost-agreed-upon scenario was to convene a sobor during which Tikhon would offer his resignation, and then renovationists would vote for his reinstallation (or would they?).[45] As the Soviets no doubt anticipated, all scenarios were met with distrust and all the meetings came to nothing.

Undoubtedly the government realized that renovationism had no appeal to the masses, so the push for reconciliation may have been simply an example of making the best out of a bad situation. Tuchkov hoped that some of the high-level "reconcilers" could work effectively within the patriarchal hierarchy as infiltrators and spies, especially Evdokim and Krasnitsky (as we will see below.)[46]

Unrelated to party or government tactics, in the spring of 1924 Patriarch Gregory IV in Constantinople—who had caused a schism in his own church by introducing the new calendar—tried to broker a peace between Russia's Patriarchal Church and the Living Church. From Tikhon's perspective, however, the cure was worse than the disease, as the suggested compromise would this time entail his permanent resignation. Tikhon decisively rejected Gregory's "offer," indignantly accusing him of uncanonically sticking his nose into Russian affairs. If the renovationists wanted peace, they could submit and repent.[47]

Tikhon's own followers were also split on the issue. The "left wing" Tikhonites urged compromise with the renovationists for the sake of unity, while the "right wing" remained intransigent. Thus Bishop Illarion (on the left) wrote in August 1923:

> A change of landmarks is taking place. The church is also changing the landmarks. She has definitely cut herself away from the counterrevolution and welcomes the new forms of Soviet construction.[48]

But Archbishop Theodore (on the right) expressed total distrust of the Soviets and their renovationist cronies. Theodore suggested that Tikhon must be assured of an *absolutely free church* before even talking to the Soviets or the renovationists—otherwise, if need be, he was obliged to rot in prison until death. A few bishops in the St. Michael's Church group charged that Tikhon had already compromised his leadership beyond repair, as he had failed to head off the renovationist schism before it had gained strength. Eventually, though, dissent was sufficiently suppressed, and the bishops voted to stick with Tikhon and support him.[49]

Tikhon's June release and the enthusiastic welcome he had received aggravated divisiveness within the renovationist movement as well and dragged it further into disrepute. After months of acrimony, more levelheaded reformist leaders stepped in to restore a semblance of unity, hastily calling a second All-Russian Conference in August 1923 to include all the warring factions. The conference decided to abandon the separate-group form of organization in favor of a single progressive, democratic, and synodical New Church Party. All of Vedensky's Ancient Apostolic Church and most of Krasnitsky's Living Church and Antonin's Church Regeneration united under the new banner. Krasnitsky and Antonin, however, refused to join. (On June 30, 1924, Antonin organized his own Church Regeneration Sobor in Moscow, attended by two bishops, three priests, and one hundred twenty laity.)[50]

Delegates to the August 1923 conference, well aware of the emptiness of their churches, decided to discontinue use of the term "renovated" and simply call itself the Russian Orthodox Church. It created a new Holy Synod, based upon the assumptions that the masses had forgotten about the patriarchate between its abolition under Peter the Great and its revival at the First Church Sobor in 1917–18 and that the term "synod" would convey a sense of regularity of succession between the Old Regime and the new Soviet one, thus imparting legitimacy. The Synod superseded both the renovationist Higher Church Administration created after the May 1922 coup and the High Church Council created during the 1923 sobor. The government supported synodal administration all along, seeing eye-to-eye with Tsar Peter that a synod was easier to control than a patriarch, as power would not be concentrated in a single person who could become beloved by the people. In early June 1924, a Moscow church conference gave the stamp of approval to this reorganization and began planning for a Third Church Sobor for some time in 1925. It issued a statement that the Holy Synod was "recognized by the People's Commissariat of Justice as the organ of the Orthodox Church."[51] Both the renovationists and the government, however, underestimated the personal popularity of Patriarch Tikhon, who stubbornly remained on the scene.

Under the new organization, renovationist bishops began moderating the radicalism of only the year before. They used the now-departed and far-too-radical Krasnitsky as a scapegoat for the excesses of the recent past and allowed Vedensky to remain only after he agreed to tame his rhetoric. Acknowledging earlier intemperance by the splinter groups, the renovationist leadership emphasized synodal conciliarity and political loyalty. The new Synod announced recognition of both the first and the second sobors—while the Tikhonite Church recognized only the first—and deemphasized liturgical reform; many of the more radical reforms agreed upon at the second sobor were postponed or forgotten. The progressives now acted as if the only bone of contention between themselves and the Tikhonites was the former's praise of Soviet authority.

More pressure was applied on December 8, 1923, when the Commissariat of Justice ruled that church prayers for "citizen Belavin" could be considered "political demonstrations" and evidence of disloyal conduct, warranting reconsideration of contracts for the religious use of government property—that is, church buildings.[52] But some pressure was released as well when three months later, in March 1924, the government finally dropped its official investigation of Tikhon, claiming this step was possible only because of evidence that the masses were turning away from superstitions toward "science and enlightenment" (or perhaps it was because Tikhon had been thoughtful enough to send condolences after Lenin's recent death). Whichever it was, *Izvestia* declared Tikhon no longer socially dangerous. Perhaps he was no longer a threat, but he was still popular; the Soviet press reported that *Te Deums* were sung in all Moscow churches in gratitude.[53]

As mentioned, for several months various renovationist clergy had been migrating back to the patriarchal fold, many of them sincere when they cited intimidation to explain their earlier apostasy. Then on May 19, 1924, Tikhon received a letter from Krasnitsky, the most Marxist of the renovationist leaders. It was an appeal—no doubt instigated by Tuchkov—to be allowed back into the Patriarchal Church and to serve under the man whom the year before he had been so instrumental in defrocking:

> I beg your Holiness to receive my brethren and me . . . and to cover with your archpastoral love all that in which I have sinned during the period of the church reform movement.[54]

Apparently penitent—but much more likely an agent of the government's new "reconcile and infiltrate" policy—he even wrote to the renovationist Synod, entreating its members to place themselves under patriarchal control.[55]

Replying the same day, Tikhon not only accepted Krasnitsky but also offered him a position in the patriarchal Higher Church Administration, without even imposing terms of atonement. Why? His stated reason was "for the sake of peace and weal of the church, in manifestation of my patriarchal clemency,"[56] but there was more to it. At this time Tikhon was appealing to the authorities for permission to call his own sobor and to form a government for that part of the church that still recognized him as its leader. Tuchkov had advised him that to proceed he would have to not only give up connections with the Revolution's enemies but also surround himself with men whom the Soviets could trust. Reconciliation with Krasnitsky offered a practical solution. From the Soviet perspective, the GPU no doubt wanted Krasnitsky inside the Tikhonite Church as a Trojan horse.[57]

As might be expected, after Krasnitsky and a few other progressives rejoined the Patriarchal Church its divisiveness increased. Conservative Tikhonites who had stood by the patriarch through many struggles now refused to sit at the same table with the "repentant" newcomers. When Krasnitsky, uninvited, moved into the patriarch's residence at the Donskoy Monastery and insisted on retaining a title granted him by the Renovationist Sobor, Tikhon had to choose. He stuck with his old friends. On June 26 Krasnitsky and his associates withdrew; reconciliation with the progressives foundered, as did any hope for a Patriarchal Church sobor. The infiltration tactic—at least on the hierarchical level—also failed.

Tacitly acknowledging the comedy of the second sobor's defrocking of the patriarch, Tuchkov pushed Tikhon to make four more concessions: Condemn Poland for meddling in Russian affairs, remove Metropolitan Platon from his duties as head of the Orthodox Church in America, write to the Archbishop of Canterbury testifying to the absence of religious persecution in the Soviet Union and—amazingly—sign the whole Orthodox Church over to Soviet control. On this last point, Tuchkov had the papers already drawn up and repeatedly presented them to the patriarch. Reportedly, Tikhon trembled and suffered fainting spells every time Tuchkov approached him on the subject. He never signed, nor did he capitulate on any of the additional demands, though he may have allowed a secret police agent into the Higher Church Administration.[58]

As a final, but minor, insult the Antireligious Commission decreed in July 1924 that Tikhon could no longer refer to himself as the patriarch of all Russia—a designation too tsarist in its connotation—but only as the patriarch of the whole of the Union of Soviet Socialist Republics.[59]

DEATH AND WILL

Patriarch Tikhon suffered from asthma, kidney disease, angina pectoris, dental infections, "nerves," and possibly several small strokes, but, to his physical if not spiritual detriment, he considered his work more important than his health and did not adequately rest.

Death of the Patriarch

Anticipating his own demise, Tikhon feared that his successor would be a renovationist, so in a preemptive move he sent an epistle to all clergy:

> Whoever was in the administration of the Living Church in the HCA [renovationist Higher Church Administration] cannot take up any further administrative position in our church. And not only can he not be an administrator, he cannot have a vote during a sobor.[60]

(This decree will have later importance, as in the eyes of the Patriarchal Church it would disqualify Metropolitan Sergei of Nizhny-Novgorod from becoming the next patriarch.)

In his waning years, weakened by the stress of confinement, Tikhon still endured renovationist attacks, but the government press eased up a little. Peter Smidovich, deputy chairman (or vice president) of the USSR and a member of the Antireligious Commission, talked with Tikhon and testified to his honesty in refraining from involvement in political activities. He also noted that the patriarch, at this point in his life, was too weak to impose his will on associates and that he frequently allowed those around him to thwart goals that he had set for himself.[61]

Tikhon became seriously ill in December 1924, but GPU agents—not as considerate as Smidovich—continued to wake him in the middle of the night to answer questions or sign documents that could easily have been taken care of in the morning, the implication being that stress on his frail constitution was deliberate.[62]

There is some evidence that more drastic measures were taken to hasten the patriarch's death, for his life was certainly an impediment to Soviet plans. Any such measure, of course, would have to be completely deniable by the government. The present-day independent Russian Orthodox Church in America and other Orthodox sources strongly hint that the patriarch was fired upon and, when that failed, poisoned by government agents. According to their scenario, on the evening of December 9, 1924, Tikhon, while praying in front of his bedroom ikons, heard a shot. He crossed himself and then tried to open the door to the outer room, which was stuck. When it gave way, he saw his faithful servant Jacob Ostrumov slumped against it, covered in blood. Two men stood there, but on seeing the patriarch they turned and ran. Jacob opened his eyes and looked at Tikhon, then died. The police were called immediately, but no investigation was ever made. The next day *Izvestia* carried a story of two men entering the patriarch's rooms to steal a fur coat; no mention was made of Jacob's death. Later, as Tikhon knelt at Jacob's grave, someone fired two more shots in Tikhon's direction, but both missed.[63]

Continuing with this version of events, Tikhon's kidney inflammation and angina attacks subsequently became more severe, and on January 13, 1925, he was admitted under his secular name to a small private hospital. After a few weeks of rest and some improvement in his health, he decided to resume his duties: receiving visitors, celebrating mass on Sundays, and attending sessions of the patriarchal Holy Synod. He received morphine injections for an aching tooth and later had it extracted, weakening him still more. Although he would go out to perform his duties, apparently he returned to the hospital each evening and slept there. Before he retired for the night he would read Russian literature and Pobedonostsev's letters. Visitors described him in his nightclothes as "a small, shrunken old man." Tuchkov and other OGPU agents regularly visited him there, sometimes spending hours in private conversations.[64]

Using direct revelations from Tikhon's new attendants, Mark and Stratonicus, Bishop Peter (Ladygin) completed this scenario. The patriarch celebrated the liturgy on the Day of the Annunciation, April 7, and was in "good health." Then, after 8:00 PM there was a ring at the door of his monastery apartment. (Apparently he felt well enough not to return to the hospital.) A doctor whom Tikhon had never met entered the room, claiming that Tikhon had summoned him. He asked to examine the patient and then prescribe some medicines. Tikhon protested that he felt fine and had not called for a doctor. "All right," the doctor insisted, "but just allow me to examine you. Your pulse is weak. You must drink some medicine." Tikhon asked for his personal physician, Michael Zhizhilenko, but was told he was unavailable. The doctor then said he would send the medicines in an hour.

Later, when his attendant returned with the medicine, Tikhon obediently took a spoonful. Immediately he began to vomit. The attendant called Dr. Zhizhilenko, who, upon arrival, demanded to see what his patient had been given. Inspecting the medicine, he threw up his hands and ordered Tikhon rushed to the hospital, but it was futile; an hour and a half later, at 11:45 PM, the patriarch died. According to attendant Constantine Pashkevich, his final words were: "I shall now go to sleep . . . deeply and for a long time. The night will be long and very dark."[65] Metropolitan Anastasy described Tikhon's face at death as extremely careworn and lined with suffering. He appeared ninety, not the mere sixty years that he had lived.

Tuchkov appeared at the hospital immediately, probably aware of Tikhon's passing due to tapped hospital phone lines. When he arrived—in a very fine mood—he announced: "[Tikhon] was a good old man. We must bury him rather solemnly." But he also helped himself to 4,000 rubles in a basket by the bedside, money that had been collected by parishioners to build Tikhon a proper house at the Donskoy Monastery. He then sealed the room for two days, later returning to make a detailed inventory of its contents.[66]

The next morning the Donskoy's bell tolled forty times, signifying the passing of a patriarch. Observers recounted that at the exact moment Tikhon's body was laid in his oak coffin the sun disappeared behind clouds, creating a profound effect. Fifty-eight bishops attended the funeral, with crowds so immense that it took all day for the procession to file past his casket. The eleventh Russian patriarch was buried on April 12 under the pavement in the Winter Chapel of the Donskoy Monastery, one of the most ancient buildings in Russia. Even Vladimir Bonch-Bruevich, in his memoirs, admitted a grudging admiration for the patriarch's courage.[67]

The Will

There were at least two contradictory stories concerning the origin of what came to be called Tikhon's will. The first was eyewitness testimony that Metropolitan Peter (Polyansky) of Krutitsa*—who one Russian historian called "tall, well-fed, and somewhat insolent"—visited Tikhon's hospital room on the evening of his death.[68] When he left he carried with him several written pages held close to his body, showing them to no one. This may have been the will. The second was that, when Tikhon's hospital room was reopened after several days, Tuchkov handed Peter of Krutitsa a document he had not previously seen. Tuchkov represented this as being the will. These seemingly insignificant discrepancies actually make quite a difference when we consider that Tikhon may not have written (or signed) a will at all.

---

*Not to be confused with Bishop Peter (Ladygin), who related the story of Tikhon's death.

Metropolitan Anthony (at Karlovtzy) later called Tikhon's signature on the will a forgery, on the grounds that it was too legible for such a sick man to have written. But since 1924 Anthony had been *selectively* accepting patriarchal declarations: If he liked them, they were genuine, and if not they must have resulted from Communist pressure and were therefore unenforceable. This would render Anthony's opinion on the subject less than credible. In the summer of 1925, Peter, now locum tenens, officially verified the signature.[69] Both opinions, however, are suspect, as Anthony had reason to reject the will, and Peter had reason to accept it.

The Politburo certainly had good reason to publish the will two days after Tikhon's death, as it was accusatory toward the Karlovtzy Synod and conciliatory toward the Soviet government. It blamed the émigré clergy in Yugoslavia for acting without ecclesiastical authority and pursuing counterrevolutionary activities. "We positively declare," the will read, "that we have no connection with them, as our enemies affirm; they are strangers to us, and we condemn their harmful activity." The will even called for creation of a special commission to investigate "the activities of the pastors and archpastors who have run away from Russia, in particular Metropolitan Anthony, formerly of Kiev." Here are some other highlights from the document:

> It is time that the believers understand the Christian point of view that "the destiny of nations is directed by the Lord," and to accept all that has come to pass as the expression of the will of God [Romans 13:1]. Without sinning against our faith or church, without permitting any compromises or concessions in the realm of belief, in our relations as citizens we must be sincere in our attitude toward the Soviet government and the labors of the USSR for general welfare, conforming the outward form of church life and activity to the new government order, condemning all association with the enemies of the Soviet government and all open or secret agitation against it. . . .
>
> We call upon the parochial societies . . . not to admit any individuals of antigovernment inclinations, nor to nurture hopes for the restoration of the monarchical system, but to become convinced that the Soviet government is actually the government of workers and peasants, and hence durable and stable.[70]

Since conciliation of the government would have made Peter's job as locum tenens (and Tikhon's possible successor) much easier, there was speculation that Peter had written the will, perhaps pressuring Tikhon to sign it on his deathbed. Priest Vasily Vinogradov, who was standing just outside the hospital room door as Peter and Tikhon had their last words, swore that he heard Tikhon in a pleading but firm voice state: "I cannot do that." Dr. Bakunina, who was in attendance during Tikhon's final hours, also testified that a loud and stormy session between Peter and Tikhon raged behind closed doors, with Peter eventually emerging holding a paper in his hand. Peter was a strong Tikhonite, but he had to look out for his own—and the church's—future. He hoped that some accommodation with the government would persuade it to terminate its support for the renovationists, and he may have feared that without the will the government would see a glaring omission interpretable as hostility. There is some evidence that Peter threatened not to accept his locum tenens duties if Tikhon refused to accept conciliation.[71]

This, of course, does not square with the alternative version of the death-room story, where Tuchkov later handed the will to Peter. It may be that Tuchkov himself wrote the document during the period when the death room was sealed and that he forged the signature—a vindication for Anthony. The monk Epiphanius (Chernov) pointed out that the wording of the will was lifted almost word-for-word from a renovationist appeal made on May 25, 1922, titled "To All the Believing Sons of the Orthodox Church of Russia."[72] If this were true, Peter could not have written it, as he loathed the progressive clergy.

It is highly unlikely that Tikhon wrote the will and signed it by himself. Reasons for this conclusion abound:

- He was far too sick and in pain. A severe toothache, kidney infection, and blocked arteries would make composing a four-page document such as this difficult.
- There was a slight, but significant, error in the will's opening greeting— the kind of mistake that a forger could easily make. The document began: "By the grace of God, humble Tikhon, the patriarch of Moscow and of all the Russian Church." But patriarchs had always assumed that all Russia was Orthodox and had begun their proclamations with the phrase ". . . and of all Russia."
- The author of the document declared the "enemies of Holy Orthodoxy" to be Catholics, Protestants, sectarians, new-churchmen [renovationists], and atheists (this last perhaps being thrown in to provide authenticity). It was not Tikhon's style to characterize other churches in this way.
- *Izvestia* claimed that it had received a message from Peter and another hierarch on April 14, imploring that the will be printed in the newspaper. The note said, "signed by him on April 7," which was Tikhon's last day of life. Yet halfway through the document we read the words, "Now we by grace of God, having regained health, again entering upon the services of the church of God. . . ." This may indicate that whoever wrote the "will" did so much *earlier.*
- The final signature read: "Patriarch Tikhon, Donskoy Monastery, April 7, 1925." He never signed documents flaunting his title but always ended with "the humble Tikhon," and he always dated his signature according to the Julian calendar. To sign with the April 7 (Gregorian) date would have

infuriated his followers, who would conclude that he had gone over to the Living Church. In addition, he died in the hospital, not at the monastery.

• And last, Tikhon had little motivation to write such a pro-Soviet document, unless it was out of concern for Peter's position.[73]

THE THIRD (RENOVATIONIST) SOBOR

The [renovationist] Holy Synod presumes that it is time to forget the very words of "Tikhonites" and "new-church men" and solely to remember that we are all Orthodox children of one Mother Church.[74]

—invitation to the sobor, 1925

Upon Tikhon's death, there were developments on two schismatic fronts. First, the Synodal Church—as the renovationists were now styling themselves—pursued reconciliation with its patriarchal rival. Since personal loyalty to Tikhon had previously blocked attempts at reunion, the prospects now appeared improved. On April 30, 1925, the renovationists extended a sincere invitation to the Tikhonites, asking them to join in the Third Church Sobor planned for the coming fall.[75] But a single offer, no matter how conciliatory, could not heal a wound so deep. A July 1925 OGPU report gauged the mood of a parish in Leningrad Province:

> Members of the parish council in the village of Begunitsa vigorously agitated against the renovationist movement, saying: "Renovationist priests are commissars in cassocks. They support Soviet power because it pays them. They betray the people. They don't believe in God; they burn ikons and rob churches. God has sent Soviet power to punish us for our sins. If people will pray as they did in the past, then the Lord God will deliver us all from this evil."[76]

On July 28 Peter sent a rejection letter to the renovationist Holy Synod, saying that the "new-church men" should not talk of reunion until they showed "sincere repentance of their errors." He was sure that the synod only wanted a token delegation of Tikhonites, enough to legitimize the proposed sobor but not enough to have any influence within it.[77]

The Third (Renovationist) Sobor convened on October 1, 1925, in the Cathedral of Christ the Savior in Moscow, with 345 delegates representing 17,000 parishes. Although only forty-two delegates favored reconciliation with the Tikhonites, the tone of this sobor was much subdued compared with the previous one, and reformist leaders were more temperate in their pronouncements. Gone were lavish praises of the Communist Party. The leaders extended a hand to both Metropolitan Peter and to Metropolitan Sergei (a onetime progressive who had returned to the patriarchal fold), but Peter called this convocation "a false sobor," and Sergei refused to talk to those who approached him.[78]

Perhaps to show their change of heart, the delegates disassociated themselves from the "irresponsible groups" led by Krasnitsky and Antonin, and condemned "the dishonor they brought upon the dignity of the ecclesiastical order."[79]* However, the sobor would not move one iota on any issues of substance, except to postpone implementation of second sobor decisions on the white clergy/black clergy marriage controversy.[80]

The second schismatic development was an attempt, orchestrated by either Metropolitan Anthony or his followers, to reject Peter as locum tenens and run the Russian Orthodox Church from Yugoslavia. They were worried—with good reason—that Peter might follow Tikhon's anti-Karlovtzy policies. Anthony justified this move by claiming that no meaningful elections for a new patriarch could occur inside Russia, and, after all, Anthony had received more votes than Tikhon in the *first* balloting for patriarch during the 1917–18 sobor. By late December 1925, however, after Peter was safely in prison, the Karlovtzy Synod changed its mind and accepted him.[81]

During this period, the Patriarchal Church operated at a distinct disadvantage. The government denied permission for it to organize into diocesan units—a privilege generously granted to the renovationist Synodal Church—and its members lived in constant fear of arrest and imprisonment. In the summer of 1926, for example, ten bishops were evicted from Moscow simply because they aroused the suspicions of authorities. All were extremely hesitant to talk with foreigners, lest they be accused of connections with émigré clergy, monarchical groups, or foreign capitalists. Confining bishops to Moscow and then punishing them by evicting them from the capital is indicative of the Soviet Union's schizophrenic antireligious policy. Presumably they were not allowed to return to their dioceses, however.

Just as with secular kings, after Tikhon's death there was a struggle for the succession. Although this fight was not a bloody one, it was bitter and extremely complex.

---

*In August 1926 Antonin and his followers would be readmitted to the Synodal Church, but five months later Antonin died, and his Union of Church Regeneration died with him.

16

OUR JOYS AND SUCCESSES

The Decline of the Living Church and the Rise of the Soviet Church

The Living Church had a limited usefulness to the Communists and an air of artificiality among the people, so the government decided to coerce and manipulate the splintered Orthodox Church into creating a replacement more to its long-term liking. After Tikhon's passing, this would be done by splitting the Tikhonites themselves. In the midst of all this, the renovationists were desperately clinging to the power they once knew, and the traditional church was struggling to provide an orderly succession to the patriarchate.

DECLINE OF THE RENOVATIONIST CAUSE

May you be accursed, Judas, for your attacks on the Orthodox Faith and its priests! Your place is in Hell, together with your inspirers, the Devils, and you will not escape the fate of your teacher, Judas Iscariot. He sold Christ for thirty pieces of silver, and you, who sell your Christian conscience for an even smaller price, will not escape the wrath of God.[1]

—letter handed to a renovationist leader after his sermon, 1922

Skirmishes between the Patriarchal Church and the renovationists were fought out in parishes throughout Russia, mostly between 1922 and 1925.

Opposition

Renovationist influence peaked immediately after the 1923 sobor, when out of the myriad churches in Moscow only a handful remained loyal to the patriarch. There were so many arrests of Tikhonite clergy that priests' wives hectored their husbands to join one of the Living Church organizations for the sake of their families. But already pressure was welling up from the overwhelmingly traditionalist laity. Archpriest Vedensky in Petrograd had been stoned, and others would have been dealt with in the same way if the militia had not protected them. When renovationist bishops and priests appeared in church or on the streets, they were met with reproach and profanity. People began to talk about the coming of Antichrist. Gossip in Petrograd had it that Vedensky was using an automobile with "the number of the Beast" (Revelation 13:18) upon it—the mystic number 666—as his car had a license plate numbered 999, or 666 inverted.[2]

Although progressives briefly had the advantage in Moscow and Petrograd, they were the recipients of abuse in provincial towns and villages. From the Vologda Cathedral (about 250 miles north of Moscow) church authorities filed this report in September 1922:

> Unfortunately, among those present there were many people who were drawn to the meeting not by a thirst for the living water of Christ's truth, but by malice and a desire to insult the church renovation activists. When the latter began to speak of establishing loyal relations of the church toward the government, the audience began to hiss, stomp its feet, scream insults at the speakers, and even to use the most vulgar obscenities in a holy place.[3]

A December GPU report from the same city continued this theme: "The renovationist church has affected only the city; . . . as far as the countryside is concerned, the revolution in the church has had virtually no impact. The believers do not agree with the reforms of the renovationist movement."[4] Renovationist strength in larger cities was no doubt due to the higher educational level of the clergy there and the extent to which renovationists could count on police support in more tightly controlled urban areas. But in rural areas, worshipers could not get used to the priest officiating not from the altar but from the middle of the congregation, and they resented the translation of hallowed Old Slavonic liturgical phrases into the vernacular—tradition trumped comprehension.[5]

Boris Titlinov wrote a pamphlet titled *The New Church* (1923) in which he expressed amazement at how much opposition to the Living Church existed in the country:

> The large majority of the clergy and of the church communities refused to recognize the new ecclesiastical administration created under the auspices of the "Living Church." The names of the leaders soon became odious.

And Joseph, the bishop of Kazan, reported in the fall of 1923:

> There were cases when peasants wanted to drown priests who adopted the new calendar and drove them from their churches.[6]

A year later the trend back toward the traditional church was still going strong. Emelyan Yaroslavsky noted in late 1924:

As for the renovationist movement, it must be noted that it has practically ceased to exist. It has an organization, but for the most part it is of no consequence. The renovationists play virtually no role at all in the villages; they have absolutely no organization there. In the larger cities the Tikhonites have a rather significant influence. They are succeeding in re-establishing their former power there.[7]

By the October 1925 Third (Renovationist) Sobor, the renovationists conceded their own decline. Archimandrite Avraamy lamented:

Many of our [renovationist] churches are positively vacant. I personally attended the holiday services at the Church of the Three Holy Bishops . . . and I saw for myself that the church was [virtually] empty—ten people. . . . We all remember when this church, prior to our split, was . . . filled with people praying.[8]

An understated sobor resolution read, "The immediate adoption of the new calendar often evokes unfavorable complications."[9] The sobor agreed to accept *either* calendar, whichever local communities preferred, until an ecumenical council of all Eastern Orthodox autocephalous churches could decide the issue. This, of course, had been the de facto situation for several years, leading to massive confusion and anomalies. Neighboring parishes often celebrated religious holidays at different times, so that one parish would be preparing for the New Year, while next door Christmas had not yet begun. In Vladimir diocese, a parish attempted to conduct services according to *both* calendars, but the people filled the church only for services based on old calendar dates.[10]

Confusion also reigned in the reckoning of parishes held by one side or the other, most figures coming from either the Living/Synodal Church or the avowedly neutral, but in fact strongly anti-Communist, Patriarchal Church. Each would obviously exaggerate its membership at the expense of the other. Many of the cathedrals technically held by renovationists were empty of worshipers, and even in well-attended churches, since the clergy tended toward liberalism and the congregations tended toward traditionalism, how should one count the church? Public discussions within the parishes frequently had to be broken up by the authorities when they got out of control. Since the decree separating church and state had put effective church power in the hands of the lay Twenties, this group often made the decision as to which way to go. A priest with leanings toward the Living Church would often have to find a pretext for dissolving the existing Twenty to elect a new one. The practical result was frequently the closing of the church.

By 1926 many renovationist priests had lost their revolutionary zeal and preached mostly obedience to civil power "as ordained by God." They calculated that out of all Orthodox believers in Moscow, only about 20 percent supported the New Church against the Old Church.[11] By 1929 an internal party directive contained this understated observation:

The internecine church struggle, which disintegrates the church from within and contributes to a decrease of religiosity, has reached a very low ebb.[12]

In reality the progressives were in full rout and had abandoned as premature and ill-conceived the vast majority of their liturgical innovations. The main difference between the Tikhonites and the anti-Tikhonites had become one of personality; simply put, they hated each other.

Reasons

What were the deeper causes of the renovationists' gradual descent into irrelevance? Here are twelve possibilities:

- Lack of unity: There really was no concerted renovationist movement; instead there were at least half a dozen movements all at loggerheads with one another. Most laity considered renovationism a patchwork of upstart factions and held it responsible for the schism(s), while viewing the Patriarchal Church as a unifying force.
- Renovationism as communism: Repressed (and often not-so-repressed) hostility to the Communist regime remained strong outside of cities, and renovationists were bound in people's minds to their new and unwelcome masters. Most Russians saw the renovators as Soviet agents (which many were, according to recently uncovered Soviet documents).[13]
- Inefficiency: Renovationists were hampered by their lack of preparation and organization; there was no clear theological structure. All was emotion without much thought. At the 1925 sobor, Vedensky commented that their badly translated texts violated the aesthetics of the service and elicited opposition. By 1927, partly because of disorganization and disunity but also because of lack of funds, the renovationists still had not put together and distributed a decent, standardized, reformist liturgical text.[14]
- Weak fieldwork: Tikhonite efforts in the parishes were stronger and more effective than government and renovationist commitments to root out "reactionary" priests. Sometimes, as renovationist hierarchs moved about the country on missionary work, Tikhonite monks would precede them, warning the people not to receive the "Communist impostors." Often conservative clergy would invade church services conducted by left-leaning priests, with the result that congregations would side with the invaders against their own priests, whose protests were shouted down. In other cases the priest was forced to conceal his true beliefs to such an extent that the congregation never suspected him of being a renovationist.[15]
- Victims of ignorance: Tikhonites used peasant superstitions to their benefit. In 1925 "ikon illumination" became a favorite ruse. Tikhon's fol-

lowers claimed that they possessed ikons that lighted up as soon as they were carried into patriarchal churches but darkened upon entry into renovationist ones. The ikons always performed on cue. Tikhon's supporters also spread rumors that Living Church ikons were unholy and incapable of working miracles.[16]

- Victims of distance: People in remote areas (that is, most of Russia) heard little or nothing of the schism within the Orthodox Church and hence remained with the beliefs they knew and were comfortable with.

- Victims of tradition: While many priests saw adoption of the progressive program as an opening of opportunities, there were no corresponding opportunities for lay congregations. Although progressives did offer such advantages as a vernacular liturgy, most rural congregations were too tradition-bound to accept these changes. Even Vedensky soon conceded. "I am afraid that nothing good will come of abolishing the liturgy in Slavonic."[17]

- Unpopular antimonasticism: The peasantry had a deeply rooted reverence for monasticism—the renovationists' chief target. The Russian historian I. Shabatin wrote, "[Renovationists] considered monasticism an 'unnatural institution,' monasteries 'hotbeds of obscurantism and sloth,' and the monastic clergy as endowed with all the fancied vices."[18] Attacks on monks were thinly disguised attacks on bishops whose positions were well entrenched within the Orthodox scheme of things. In the end, renovationists had unwisely chosen an adversary still revered by the common people. When monasteries were closed, they released into the countryside itinerant monks who began preaching apocalyptic notions—usually including the Living Church as Antichrist.

- Democratization: Ironically, the force of democratization turned against the very progressives who advocated it. Because the government had decimated the church hierarchy, more decisions were being made at the parish level. Whereas before 1917 bishops had been appointed from above, now diocesan councils of clergy and laity frequently elected them. Parishes of *elected* bishops tended to be more loyal to the patriarch and more resistant to the entreaties of the renovationists.[19]

- Illegitimacy: Renovationists bore the stigma of illegitimacy, as major changes could be made only by a sobor. When the renovationists seized power within the Church Administration in May 1922, they immediately set out to implement their innovations without waiting for the next sobor. A year passed before the Second (Renovationist) Church Sobor met, and when it did it was widely perceived among the laity as not representative of the church—which indeed it was not. Some referred to it as the "counterfeit council" and, as such, it was lacking in Divine Grace.[20]

- Income gaps: Massive boycotts of renovationist churches led to income inequalities between Tikhonite and anti-Tikhonite priests. Tikhonite laity often cut off monetary and food contributions to unduly idealistic priests.

In Tatarstan, parishioners adopted the slogan "Let the Living Church give firewood to the priests if they decide to join it."[21] Thus at the 1925 sobor, Vedensky expressed sympathy for renovationist priests who had a decent meal only one out of three days and who were forced to live on a mere ten rubles a month. Many left their parishes but, as former priests, could find no other work, especially during the NEP, with its high unemployment rate. Some, as we shall see later, turned against religion altogether.[22]

• Government apathy: Although the antireligious front was plowing straight ahead, Soviet enthusiasm for the strategy of church schism wavered; party leaders were tiring of it, not all of them having backed this policy in the first place. Besides, it did not seem to be doing much good. Despite its lip service to socialism, renovationism *was religion*, an ideology that should have been on its way to perdition by this point. Ivan Skvortsov-Stepanov wrote, "These days 'religious communism' is an incident of little importance in the larger movement under the hoisted scientific Communist flag."[23] And Evgeny Tuchkov added, "[Renovationism is a mere] figure on the chessboard of the struggle against the church."[24]

The Twelfth Communist Party Congress met in April 1923, just before the second sobor, and stressed the need for worker-peasant unity; church schism did not fit well into this picture. A comparison of two government proclamations illustrates the change of heart. In October 1922 the Antireligious Commission urged a "relentless struggle" against the Tikhonite Church and overwhelming support for the renovationists. Parish and diocesan councils were to be purged. Yet by June 19, 1923—eight months later—the Commissariat of Justice decreed that local authorities should no longer favor one church over another; they were ordered to distribute church buildings according to the relative memberships of each of the church factions. Cleverly, if there was only one church and a divided population, the church was itself partitioned, leaving warring sides in proximity. Insurance payments and taxes were apportioned according to the relative sizes of each group. The beauty of this, from the government's perspective, was that it was easily defended as an evenhanded approach to a problem that was not its fault, though its actual effect on religious communities was easy enough to predict. By the end of June the party reassessed the effectiveness of the schism and decided to withdraw its support.[25]

Tikhon's release from custody during the same month was a nail in the progressives' coffin; it caused believers to pour out of renovationist churches and return to those still favoring the patriarch. A year later, in July 1924, the Antireligious Commission recommended that the OGPU avoid "overt support of renovationists by state agencies and trampling on the rights of the Tikhonites." Charges by renovationists against Tikhonites were required to be carefully verified before any arrests were carried out.[26]

Gregory Freeze summarized the reasons for renovationist decline: "Buoyed by a deep hostility to mere 'ritualism' and determined to raise the peoples' religious consciousness, the renovationists were remarkably insensitive to the power and vitality of popular religion."[27] A gulf had developed between the progressives and the people, who simply wanted to pray and be saved, as had their ancestors. Renovationists never fully understood the *inherent* gulf between themselves and the government. Like Ulysses sailing between the wandering rocks, they were being squeezed from both sides. The broad mass of the Orthodox considered them to be Bolsheviks in disguise, while the Bolsheviks thought of them as an enemy organization that was easy to manipulate but was only temporarily useful.

From the government's perspective, the schism had been a *partial* success. Although it failed to kill off the Orthodox Church, it had mightily embarrassed it. Mutual recriminations between church hierarchs did not seem very Christian—though, of course, clerical bickering had a long and colorful history. Episcopal authority had been weakened, and individual parishes had withdrawn inside themselves, not knowing whom to trust.

At this point, another group of Orthodox churchmen interjected their opinions on communism and renovationism.

FROM THE SOLOVETSKY ISLANDS (1926)

The church bases its own relationship with the state on the full and consistent application of the principle of the separation of the church and state. It does not aim to overthrow the existing order and does not participate in actions directed to this end. It never calls people to arms and political struggle, it recognizes all laws and measures of a civil nature, but it wishes to preserve fully its spiritual freedom and independence offered to it in the Constitution and cannot become a servant of the state.

—"To the Government of the USSR," from the Solovetsky Islands, 1926

In the northwest of Russia is the White Sea. In the southern section of this sea is the beautiful but isolated archipelago of the Solovetsky Islands, and on the main island is the Solovky Monastery. The various religious buildings on these islands had been used to incarcerate small numbers of the tsars' prisoners since the sixteenth century, and the Bolsheviks starting using the monastery for the same purpose in 1920. For much of the decade that followed it was a disorganized secret police "camp of special significance" for criminal, political, and religious prisoners. (During the 1930s its mission would become more focused, using prison labor to construct a canal between the White Sea and the Baltic.)[28]

As late as 1926 priests, monks, and church hierarchs at the camp were allowed special privileges such as living together, celebrating Easter, and using pen and paper.[29] This enabled a group of imprisoned bishops in May of that year to compose a lengthy letter to the government explaining their position in relation to the state. It was not a complaint about their personal suffering but rather a candid statement that, no matter what their degree of suffering, the church would persevere. They asked for cordial relations—but not reconciliation—with the state based on *true* separation of church and state, a condition where the state would be neutral in deed as well as word and take no actions favoring atheism:

> The church does not involve itself in the political organization of the state because it is loyal to the governments of all countries within the borders of which its members reside. The church can live with all kinds of state structures, from the eastern despotism of Turkey of a past age to the Republic of the North American States.[30]

The bishops castigated the government for violating its own laws. Was forcibly preventing duly consecrated bishops from residing in their dioceses part of church-state separation? How consistent with their own principles was the Bolshevik practice of granting favors to the Renovationist Church at the expense of the Patriarchal Church? They logically asked, "If censuring the acts of government is prohibited, then praising them [as the renovationists had done] should equally be prohibited, for that too is interfering with politics."[31] The bishops contended that it was the church that was making every effort to remain apolitical, while the government meddled in every aspect of church life.[32]

The letter contained an admission that in the past the church had involved itself in politics, but that was when the country was torn by war and famine, and the government had not been able to maintain civil order. Now that stability had been restored, the church desired only to be left alone. The bishops noted with pride that since 1923 not a single Orthodox cleric had been tried and convicted of anti-Soviet activities. (This was true for two reasons: because the most obstreperous clergy had already been arrested and because all actions against the clergy since 1923 had been administrative actions, bypassing the courts.)[33]

Finally, the letter pointed to the irreconcilability of the church's teaching with materialism. The bishops noted that the church:

- recognized the existence of a spiritual principle, which communism denied.
- believed in the Living God . . . who guides human life and destiny, but communism did not accept his existence.
- saw the purpose of human life in the divine call of the spirit. Communism, in contrast, did not recognize any purpose in human life except that of earthly gratification.
- preached love and compassion, whereas communism preached comradeship and a ruthless struggle against its enemies.

Patriarchal Church Succession During the 1920s

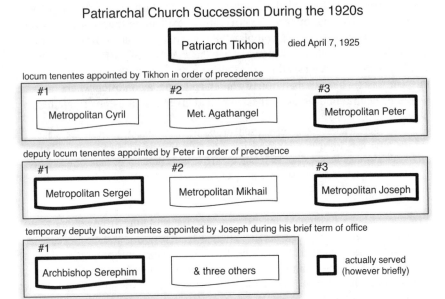

Metropolitan Joseph (uncanonically) appointed Archbishop Seraphim, who served from November 30, 1926, to March 27, 1927. Both Joseph and Seraphim served while Sergei was in prison. After Sergei's release from prison in the spring of 1927, he resumed the locum tenancy until, during World War II, he briefly became patriarch.

- inspired believers to show humility, which ennobled. Communism encouraged pride, which degraded human nature.
- defended sexual purity and the sacredness of human fertility, whereas communism saw no more than the gratification of instinct in marital relations.

The bishops could conceive of no coming together between such deeply divergent worldviews—any more than there could be between "yes" and "no"—because "it is the very soul of the church, the condition of its being and the meaning of its existence, that communism categorically rejects."[34] They scoffed at the renovationists' claim that there was no country where the church enjoyed such complete freedom, calling such a statement "a despicable falsehood that could only have been inspired either by hypocrisy or servility, or total indifference to the fate of religion."[35] They concluded:

> The Orthodox Church will never stand upon this unworthy path [of compromise] and will never, either in whole or in part, renounce her teaching of the faith that has been winnowed through the holiness of the past centuries [in exchange] for one of the eternally shifting moods of society.[36]

In addition to the issue of religious freedom—which was essentially uncomplicated—the church in the mid-1920s had to confront the much thornier issue of who would replace Tikhon. There were several volunteers, and of course the government had its own stake in the outcome.

THE SUCCESSION

Realizing that the patriarchal office was the strongest force for church unity and fearing that Orthodoxy in Russia could not long survive without it, Patriarchal Church hierarchs hoped to elect Tikhon's successor as soon as possible. The government, however, saw its interests best served by disallowing a Patriarchal Church Sobor and effectively blocked any such election.* A locum tenens would have to serve in the meantime. Anticipating this problem precisely three months before his death, Tikhon had named, in order of succession: Metropolitan Cyril (Smirnov) of Kazan, who was promptly exiled; Agathangel (Preobrazhensky) of Yaroslavl, who was prohibited from traveling to Moscow and then, after a run-in with authorities, was exiled to Narym in Siberia; and Metropolitan Peter (Polyansky) of Krutitsa—the only choice still free. It is not known if these were the same three locum tenens candidates chosen at the First Church Sobor seven years earlier, as those names had been kept sealed in an envelope. Tikhon may also have chosen locum tenens candidates immediately after his release from prison in June 1923, but these names as well are not known.[37]

Born in 1862, Peter, the third in line, was raised within a priest's family in Voronezh Province. When he graduated from the Moscow Theological Academy at the age of thirty, his mentors considered him a bright and promising theologian. For a while he was secretary to the Grand Duchess Elizabeth, the tsarina's sister.[38] As a delegate to the First Church Sobor, he was noticed by Tikhon and quickly raised through the ecclesiastical ranks. When Tikhon asked him to assist in administration, Peter mused at home that evening: "I cannot refuse. If I refuse then I will be a traitor to the church. But when I agree, I know that I will thereby be signing my death warrant."[39] He accepted and took the vows of a monk in 1917. The government first arrested Peter in August 1921 but then released him in late 1923, despite his denunciation of that year's "Living Church Sobor." Tikhon raised him to archbishop and then, in 1924, to metropolitan of Krutitsa (Moscow). When Tikhon died in April 1925, a gathering of fifty-nine hierarchs confirmed Peter in the locum tenency with the admonition that he "cannot decline from the obedience given him."[40]

As discussed in the previous chapter, Peter now had to deal with renewed ren-

---

*As it turned out, it was Stalin's need for national unity during World War II that led to the election of the next patriarch in 1943, eighteen years after Tikhon's death.

ovationist overtures for unity between the two church factions. This was in preparation for the third sobor, still approved for the autumn of 1925. The government wanted Tikhonite concessions to the renovationists so that it could control the sobor, but Peter rejected any compromise by proclaiming such a meeting uncanonical and illegal. Peter dreamed of a return to the "purer orthodoxy of the Middle Ages."[41]

In November 1925, after reading Tuchkov's report on recommended post-Tikhon policy, Yaroslavsky and Skvortsov-Stepanov decided to exacerbate frictions within the Patriarchal Church. Tuchkov was quoted as advising, "We need another schism among the Tikhonites."[42] During the following month, government newspapers accused Peter of disloyal conduct toward the state. Skvortsov-Stepanov, Tuchkov, and Peter Krasikov then manufactured or obtained evidence against Peter, which they turned over to Vedensky. With this material in hand, Vedensky charged Peter with involvement with an "émigré-monarchist plot." Prosecutors claimed that they had evidence of both Tikhon and Peter blessing the claims of Grand Duke Cyril, a cousin of the late tsar and one of several pretenders to the throne. Peter, perhaps a little too proudly, refused to either confirm or deny the charges, which some took as evidence of guilt.[43]

With the pressure on, Tuchkov approached Peter with a promise of Soviet recognition of the Patriarchal Church, but there were strings attached. Peter would have to:

- exclude from the hierarchy any bishops displeasing to the government.
- condemn the émigré clergy (one more time).
- endorse a certain document written by the government (without prior knowledge of its contents).
- allow Tuchkov (or another OGPU agent) to participate in all future church activities.

It is not difficult to visualize Peter's reaction; telling Tuchkov to leave the room, he shouted after him, "You're all liars."[44]

Anticipating arrest, Peter wrote his own will on December 6, naming Sergei (Stragorodsky), metropolitan of Nizhny-Novgorod, as his deputy locum tenens and entrusting him with carrying out the day-to-day affairs of the church. Peter was indeed arrested on December 10 and two days later was incarcerated in Moscow's Butyrka Prison. A dozen or so other Moscow bishops sympathetic to Peter's position were also rounded up. The following June, without trial, he was moved to the political isolation cell in the Spaso-Efimiev Monastery in Suzdal. Through fellow prisoners, Peter smuggled out a letter pledging that he would "never under any circumstances leave his [locum tenens] post" and that he would remain faithful to the Orthodox Church "until death itself."[45]

All these hierarchs were tried during the summer of 1926. Matthew Spinka interviewed Peter Smidovich in late August and inquired into the charges against

Metropolitan Peter. Smidovich told Spinka that the government had been gathering evidence against Peter for years, but, unable to get the government's story straight, he now claimed that Peter had supported Grand Duke Nicholas Nicholayevich's claim to the throne. Smidovich claimed that Peter had already confessed to being in contact with monarchist groups, repented at the trial, and pleaded for mercy and that a full record of trial testimony would soon be printed in the papers, though it never was. In any case, the court found Peter guilty and ordered him exiled to a small town at the mouth of the River Ob on the Arctic Sea. (In 1928 he was transferred to a monastery in Tobolsk Province in northern Siberia.)[46]

Peter never did relinquish the locum tenency. Therefore, from his perspective, there was never any need for his "deputy" to assume any responsibilities. Sergei, however, was willing to assume the office anyway.[47] Church historian Vladimir Moss explained the controversial nature of the appointment:

> A chief hierarch [especially a locum tenens] does not have the right to transfer the fullness of his power to another hierarch as if it were a personal inheritance; only a sobor representing the whole local [Russian] church can elect a leader to replace him.

There was no provision in canon law, or precedent in the church, for the office of deputy to the locum tenens. Metropolitan Cyril pointed out at the time that, at the very least, any deputy that Peter appointed should lose all power with Peter's death. Possibly suspecting that Sergei might want to usurp his power, Peter included in Sergei's confirmation the statement that "the raising of my name as patriarchal locum tenens remains obligatory during divine services."[48]

Sergei had broad experience in leadership and diplomacy. Born in 1867, he graduated from the St. Petersburg Theological Academy at age twenty-eight. After serving the Orthodox Church in both Japan and Greece, he entered the episcopacy and rose swiftly within the hierarchy. From 1901 to 1903, he presided over a religious philosophical circle in St. Petersburg, holding debates with the secular intelligentsia—a group that Lenin disdainfully called the "god-seekers."[49] In 1905 he became archbishop of Finland and in 1907 joined the Holy Synod, serving as chairman of its Educational Committee. Under the Provisional Government he ascended to the Archbishopric of Vladimir, and after Tikhon's election he served as metropolitan of Nizhny-Novgorod.

Early in his career he had been sympathetic toward the Socialist Revolutionary Party and had harbored some of its members in his home. This may have fueled the tsarina's motive in trying to drive him from the Holy Synod in 1915. Later, in 1922, he continued his experiment with liberal views and joined the Living Church, but in March 1924 he accepted Tikhon's appeal to all clergy who had left the fold to return. He went down on his knees, saying that he was "making a public repentance as a simple monk before the patriarch." Tikhon raised him up and placed upon him his former metropolitan's white cowl. Paradoxically, some among the émigré clergy later charged Sergei with having had ties to Rasputin and the reactionary officials he supported, but by this time the émigrés detested Sergei (see the next chapter) and may have been willing to hurl any charges easy to make and difficult to disprove.[50]

Assuming the incarcerated Peter's position of locum tenens—at least for those who accepted him—and pending a new church sobor, Sergei's early administration was threatened by arrest and more schisms. The authorities took him into custody as soon as he assumed his office, holding him for two months. On his release he enjoyed a few weeks of freedom before being imprisoned again for another month. These arrests were part of the intimidation process resulting from Sergei's repeated efforts to register the Tikhonite branch of the Orthodox Church as a legal entity. In the autumn, police discovered that he had secretly been arranging for a patriarchal election through clandestine correspondence. By November 1926 Sergei had collected the signatures of seventy-two bishops supporting the aged Metropolitan Cyril of Kazan—still in exile—who had also been Tikhon's first choice as successor. (A rival, but unverified, story is that Archbishop Illarion in the Solovky prison camp had begun the campaign for Cyril and that Sergei had given this information to the OGPU to strengthen his own campaign for power.) Either way, Sergei was arrested a third time on December 3 and remained in prison through the following March.[51] Clearly the government wanted something out of him.

During this period of arrest and release, Sergei had to face another attempted splintering of his church. On December 22, 1925—a few weeks after Peter's arrest—Archbishop Grigory (Yakovetsky) of Ekaterinburg (Sverdlovsk) set up a rival Temporary Higher Church Administration at the Donskoy Monastery in Moscow. Later Grigory wrote concerning Peter:

> It was not pleasing to the Lord to bless the labors of this hierarch. During his [eight-month] rule disorders and woes only deepened in the Holy Church. . . .
> We consider it our duty to witness to our complete legal obedience to the government of the USSR.[52]

Grigory also pointed out that Peter had been in prison since December 10 and could not administer the church. It is difficult to tell if Grigory was motivated by sincere concern for the future of the church or by personal ambition.

Rumors spread that Grigory's administration was sponsored by the OGPU, and, as if to lend credence to this charge, the government—ever vigilant to foster dissension—recognized and legalized Grigory's Administration on January 2, 1926, while refusing this status to the Patriarchal Church. Sergei was not even allowed into the capital. The government saw the advantage of Grigory's organization being canonically and liturgically conservative (thus acceptable to church laity), while (possibly) being under secret police management.[53] Letters flew back and forth, with Peter denouncing Sergei as a usurper (since Peter had not relinquished the locum tenancy) and Sergei impeaching Grigory and his fellow bishops (invalidating their recent promotions). Grigory also raised the issue of Sergei's earlier ties to Rasputin and suggested that Sergei might harbor support for the Living Church—two not very compatible charges.

Meanwhile Tuchkov, while pretending to facilitate each claimant's cause, was using various deceptions to manipulate all three into more irreconcilable conflict, including promising to send letters or telegrams and then not doing so.[54] To put pressure on Sergei, in office only for a few weeks, Grigory was permitted access to Peter in prison. There, through a series of deceptions, he persuaded Peter—in spite of his prior commitment to Sergei—to hand over the "keys of the church" to him.

> [Peter wrote that] in order to pacify believers and help the church, and in the interest of peace and church unity, we recognize the usefulness of temporarily transferring our prerogatives to the [Grigorian Administration] until our case is cleared.[55]

But, upon being informed of the true situation within the church, Peter revoked the transfer to Grigory. If this did not put enough pressure on Sergei, Tuchkov also arranged for the arrest of 117 out of the 160 patriarchal bishops and threatened to shoot them.[56]

At the peak of Grigory's power he claimed the loyalty of twenty-six minor bishops, but it was not long before a slow avalanche of defections began. To prop up the Grigorians, the government whisked the well-respected Illarion (Troitsky) from the Solovky Camp to Yaroslavl, where Tuchkov exhorted him to join the archbishop's organization. When Illarion refused, however, he was sent straight back to the prison camp (where he died in 1929 at the age of forty-four). Finally Sergei, during one of his brief sojourns out of prison, managed to overcome the rival group; with the support of Peter in early June, Sergei placed an official ban on Grigory's activities. (Nonetheless, the Grigorians struggled along until final liquidation in 1943—when the government saw church *unity* as paramount.)[57]

In 1926 the government was still stoking the fires of trouble. After Sergei's ban on Grigory, the Soviets decided to release Agathangel from prison. On his way back from his Siberian exile, Agathangel was briefly imprisoned in Perm where, on May 1, 1926, he stated that he was once again taking up his locum tenens duties—that is, reinstating himself in the position that Sergei now believed he de facto held. Since Agathangel was higher in Tikhon's line of succession than Peter (and the elder of the two) and since Peter had appointed Sergei deputy locum tenens, there ensued a predictable *four*-way power struggle with byzantine intrigues. Sergei met with Agathangel, and they agreed to let the status quo ride for a while. Tuchkov pressured Agathangel to resign in favor of Sergei, which the former was reluctant to do. Sergei may have been a power seeker, but he also may have had legitimate concerns over Agathangel's doddering naiveté—the aged metropolitan was sure that Tuchkov respected him—and his isolation from church affairs after spending three years in prison.[58]

Finally Agathangel caved in. "For the sake of the peace of the church" (as well as poor health) he agreed to abdicate his position and return to Yaroslavl. On June 9 he telegraphed Sergei: "Continue to administer the Church. I will refrain from all contrary steps." Three days later, he informed Peter who, true to his word, refused to give up his title, presumably not for personal pride but to maintain the concept of the patriarchate in the minds of the people and to sustain the distinction between the Patriarchal Church and the Living Church. Since Peter was not free, Sergei took over all leadership duties and characterized advice or instructions from the incarcerated Peter as "coming from a person without responsibility."[59]

On June 10, soon after his second release, Sergei sent a letter to "the bishops, priests, and the faithful" of Moscow, reminding them of Tikhon's nonpolitical stance (with the implication that toeing this line was all that stood between them and Siberia):

> We promise freely that to the degree to which it depends upon our authority, we will not henceforth permit the church to find itself involved in any political adventure whatever.[60]

But he was not yet a full cooperator, as his letter made a clear distinction between the Orthodox faith and communism. He instructed the bishops to take no extraordinary steps to demonstrate their loyalty to the Soviet regime: "We cannot accept the duty of watching over the political tendencies of our co-religionists." The church would not "become an agent of Soviet policy"—it would remain true to itself:

> Far from promising reconciliation of that which is irreconcilable and from pretending to adapt our faith to communism, we will remain from the religious point of view what we are—members of the traditional church or, as they call us, Tikhonites.[61]

Apparently Sergei allowed himself to believe that his June 10 statement—combined with the Solovetsky letter that said pretty much the same thing—would be acceptable, but the government was still dissatisfied with his performance. He had not yet reached the requisite stage of capitulation. Arrests of church leaders intensified during the rest of the year, including Sergei's third arrest. Doubting his ability to continue in office, he appointed Metropolitan Joseph of Nizhny-Novgorod to take over for him, but Joseph was quickly snatched by the OGPU. Then came Cornelius of Ekaterinburg, who was also arrested; then Archbishop Thaddeus of Astrakhan, who was taken into custody as well. The policy of political neutrality was not having the hoped-for effect, these arrests amounting to a purge of the country's hierarchy. The émigré clergy claimed that over a hundred bishops were exiled during the fall and winter of 1926–27, and the whereabouts of many others was unknown. As mentioned earlier, ten bishops had been ejected from the capital "merely on suspicion of disloyalty." This meant that Soviet authorities had weeded out all Orthodox hierarchs who had the moral courage to stand up to them, leaving only the most pliable behind.[62] It would be next to impossible for Sergei, even if he so intended, to lean on the shoulders of his weak-kneed coreligionists.

As he sat in prison—this time for three and a half months—Sergei pondered the church's position and its strategies for survival. He was unwilling to follow the path of the Living Church, not so much because of its rapprochement with the government as its alterations of canon law, the very basis of Orthodoxy. He realized that the government was no longer satisfied with political neutrality and that the mere *existence* of the church was considered a counterrevolutionary act and politically criminal.

As he searched his soul, an act abroad jolted him. An Orthodox youth had assassinated the Russian ambassador to Warsaw, apparently in retaliation for the diplomat having converted a church into a dance hall.[63] The church as a whole was innocent, but individual acts of defiance were making it hard for its leaders to remain politically aloof. Although he anticipated popular resentment to this move, Sergei, like Tikhon before him, began to consider recognition of the political dominance of the Soviet government as the only means to ensure his church's continued existence. The question was: How far would he go?

THE "SOVIET CHURCH"

Vladyka! At the time of my consecration you told me that I should be faithful to the Orthodox Church and, in case of necessity, that I should also be prepared to lay down my own life for Christ. And now such a time of confession has come, and I wish to suffer for Christ. But you, by your Declaration, instead of a path to Golgotha propose that we stand on the path of collaboration with a God-fighting regime that persecutes and blasphemes Christ.[64]

—Bishop Dimitry, falling on his knees before Sergei, December 1927

An unintended consequence of Soviet repression of the church from 1922 through 1925 was that, having weakened, exiled, or eliminated the hierarchy, the parishes had become necessarily more self-sufficient. Between 1925 and 1927 parishes actually had a little breathing room. As parishioners flexed their muscles, the government found that its control mechanisms via the church hierarchy were ineffective or nonexistent. It was crucial to get its hands on the handles of the church once again. In a memo, Tuchkov grumbled:

We have terribly complicated the work of the OGPU, which will have to work with a multitude of communities [parishes], which will hardly make it possible to establish correct control over them.[65]

But the steady downhill slide of the renovationists provided an opportunity for normalization of relations between the state and the Patriarchal Church. Sergei, still in prison, continued his soul-searching concerning the church's relations with the Communist state. Realistically, he knew close communication with the new social and political order was essential for church survival. Finally, it appears, he accepted a government deal and came to terms. On March 30, 1927, he was released from prison with no explanation, and a month and a half later the government quietly recognized him as locum tenens, dropping the "deputy" designation.

On July 14 Sergei ordered all Russian Orthodox clergy abroad to cease their criticism of the Soviet government, otherwise they would be ejected from the Moscow Patriarchate. He even wrote out a pledge for them to sign. This was a reversal of his order ten months earlier that allowed independent administration abroad, and it was a transparent political act. Evlogy in Paris agreed to sign as long as the word "loyalty" was interpreted as an aversion to politics, not an embracing of the atheist state. Since he no longer considered himself a citizen of the Soviet Union, no loyalty to that state should be expected from him. Anthony Khrapovitsky was outraged that his two former students, Sergei and Evlogy, had bound themselves to "the disgusting, blaspheming Bolsheviks."[66]

Then came Sergei's July 29 bombshell—the fulfillment of the terms of his release. He announced the government's recognition of the Patriarchal Church's Synod, making it "not only a canonically legal central administration, but a central administration that is legal also according to the law of the state of the Soviet Union," and he revealed his earlier recognition as locum tenens. Declaring his submission to Soviet power, he contradicted the apolitical statements he had made to the Moscow clergy on June 10 of the previous year. Now he promised political cooperation and even active participation in the Soviet program:

We must show that not only in words but also in deeds, we can be true citizens of the Soviet Union, as loyal to the Soviet power as nonbelievers. We wish to be Orthodox, and at the same time to recognize the Soviet Union as our civil fatherland, *whose joys and successes are our joys and successes, and whose failures are our failures.** Every

---

*Although most sources translate "the Soviet Union as our civil *fatherland*," several historians of the church (Fletcher, *Orthodox Church Underground*, pp. 54–55; and Pospielovsky, *Russian Church*, p. 109) translate the term as *motherland*, and say that the pronoun "which," as in "the joys and successes of which," is feminine. According to this line of thinking, Sergei's intended meaning was that "joys and successes" referred not to the Soviet Union, which takes a masculine pronoun, but to the motherland, which takes a feminine pronoun. Therefore he wished the nation—not the government—joy and success. However, this subtle distinction was lost on almost everybody.

blow directed against the Union, be it war, boycott, or any other common disaster . . . we regard as a blow directed against us. [We offer the church's] gratitude to the Soviet government for its attention to the spiritual needs of the Orthodox population.[67] [emphasis added]

He proclaimed spiritual solidarity with the government and, as it turned out, granted permission to the state to actively intervene in church affairs. The government, for example, could now require the transfer of bishops for reasons of political expediency and could give or withhold approval for all clerical appointments.[68]

Although by this time Sergei was more theologically and liturgically conservative, and no longer a renovationist sympathizer, he, like the renovationists, now granted full recognition to the Soviet government. His desperate hope was that he could maintain a strict separation of church and state at the same time as he admitted subservience to that state. A year before, he had preached about the irreconcilability of the church and communism, but nothing was heard of this now. A year before, he had said that church hierarchs could not be held responsible for the beliefs of their followers; now he demanded their promise of loyalty to the Soviet government, even for hierarchs living abroad.[69] He justified this approach with the words:

Only impractical dreamers could think that such an immense and organized society as our Orthodox Church might exist peacefully in the state while refusing to have any contact with the authorities.[70]

Most controversial of all, Sergei now avowed that all Soviet actions taken in the past against his church's clergy were "just." This supported the fiction, perpetuated until the fall of communism, that the government had *never* been at fault in its thousands of arrests, imprisonments, exiles, and executions; punishment of the Russian clergy had *always* been justified as those charged had fallen under the evil influence of the émigrés and other counterrevolutionary forces.[71] Some in the church felt that Sergei had gone much further than necessary if his goal was simply to ensure the continued existence of an Orthodox Church administration in Russia.

Why did Sergei do it? One explanation involves the benefits of synodal registration and recognition of his person as head of the church (though registration was for the Synod only, not the entire church under his jurisdiction, and the right of juridical person was not granted). Synodal registration may sound like a mere legal nicety, but it was significant for a church that since the 1918 separation decree had been operating with only a de facto administration. Sergei was also granted permission to live in Moscow, though he elected to remain in Nizhny-Novgorod for the time being. (Sergei stayed away from Moscow until 1934, perhaps fearing the intense opposition of the capital's clergy.)[72]

Another explanation is that there were at least twenty Sergei supporters in the Solovetsky camps, and the OGPU may have threatened to execute them if he resisted coming to an agreement with the state. Or perhaps Sergei had been "brainwashed" in prison—persuaded, like Tikhon before him, that his "wrong thinking" was due to his upbringing within the tsarist system. An account accepted by many of his apologists was that his concessions were a tactical move to gain time for Orthodoxy until Bolshevism fell, or to gain respite and relief from persecution so the church could build up its strength for future resistance. According to this line of thinking, he deserved sainthood for avoiding the destruction of the entire church. There were even those who speculated that Sergei was anxious lest the Bolsheviks come to an understanding with the papacy about "a final eradication of Orthodoxy." By declaring his cooperation, Sergei could ironically "keep the Bolsheviks on his side." (More on possible Catholic conspiracies in chapter 20.) Sergei never explained, other than asserting that if Tikhon had lived longer he would have done exactly the same thing.[73] And perhaps he would have. Although stubborn, Tikhon was also a man of practicality and a man dedicated to the long-term survival of his church. And had not Tikhon already "confessed"?

Sergei reckoned that the obeisance he offered should earn further concessions from the state. He asked for permission to call a new patriarchal sobor to ratify his Declaration and to open church schools for those over eighteen, but a sobor was not permitted until 1943 and church schools never opened during the reign of communism. The Soviets did, however, allow him to publish the *Journal of the Moscow Patriarchate*, as long as it was sold within the church and not publicly.[74]

Why did the Soviets do it? Possibly because it allowed the government to stress the legal standing of the Orthodox Church to critics abroad—saying, in effect, "If you will please notice, organized religion is well protected by our constitution." Perhaps the government accepted Sergei because the church was now so weak that it no longer posed a threat. Or it may simply have been that the government, gearing up for industrialization, needed some measure of domestic peace. The government certainly gained because the Sergei-Soviet deal included permission to place secret police agents (or their appointees) in key positions within the church, including the Synod itself. Sergei may not have been working hand-in-glove with the secret police, but police agents enjoyed interrogating recalcitrant priests and purposefully referring to Sergei as "our man" (with obvious later consequences).[75]

Reconciliation with the Revolution deeply troubled Orthodox clergy and laity alike, though the majority resigned themselves to the situation. According to Sergei's enemies within the church, the only reason for church-state reconciliation was that the government realized its failed policy. The blood of martrys has always been the "seeds of Christianity." A persecuted church could only grow stronger, while a co-opted church would wake up one morning and find itself irredeemably enfeebled. Thus resistance must continue. And clergy in opposition to Sergei were well aware of infiltration by OGPU agents.

Once again, splinter groups formed, led by hierarchs of many persuasions. Seventeen active hierarchs resigned rather than accept Sergei's capitulation, and all seventeen were quickly arrested. Ninety percent of the parishes in the Ural Mountain region sent Sergei's Declaration back in protest. Indeed, the clergy returned so many copies that *Izvestia* had to publish the Declaration in its entirety just to be sure its contents were known.[76]

When prayers for the Soviet government began to be heard in the churches, the laity revolted. The bishop of Serpukhov slipped the offending prayer into his service and found himself dragged from the altar, roughed up, and dumped in the snow outside his church. Sergei's critics pointed out that the trappings of the Orthodox heritage had been retained while the essential presence of the Holy Spirit of God had been lost. Just as with the renovationists, conservative church members held that Divine Grace did not enter churches where Sergei and his followers presided. Bishop Illarion of Smolensk went so far as to "rebaptize" and "remarry" those whose sacraments had previously been performed in a "Soviet Church."[77]

From Siberian exile, Peter immediately wrote to Sergei, regretful of his mistaken trust. "If you yourself lack the strength to protect the church," he challenged, "you should step aside and turn over your office to a stronger person."[78] Although it is doubtful that Sergei's July Declaration had canonical legitimacy— since Peter condemned it and Sergei was technically Peter's deputy—it is, of course, the fait accompli that history recognizes. Quoting 2 Corinthians 4:14–15, the self-exiled Metropolitan Anthony sent Sergei a scathing letter of protest: "Can light consort with darkness? Can Christ agree with Belial [a pagan god], or a believer with an unbeliever?" The Russian Orthodox Church Abroad then ceased all contact with the Moscow Patriarchate.[79]

In 1927 there were around one hundred bishops imprisoned on Solovetsky Island, not all of them in agreement with each other. When news of Sergei's Declaration reached them, sixty or so decided to break with the "deputy" locum tenens. On September 27 they wrote another carefully crafted open letter, surprisingly moderate considering the injustice that they believed had been applied to them. They reiterated the crucial distinctions between Christianity and communism and noted that Sergei seemed to be allowing the church to shoulder all the blame for church-state discord. They wholeheartedly supported Sergei's written acceptance of separation between church and state but felt that he had already violated it by allowing state interference in church affairs. Sarcastically, they wondered what Sergei meant in the Declaration. If the government were joyous in its complete eradication of religious sentiment, would Sergei also be joyous with success? If the government failed and the League of the Godless had to be dissolved, would Sergei feel the blow struck against him? They concluded by noting Sergei's expression of gratitude to the Soviet state "for its understanding of the religious needs of the Orthodox population," and they protested the syrupy-sweet tenderness with which Sergei thanked the Soviet authorities for their "attention." Their letter then listed many of the atrocities against the church that this attention had brought down on their heads. "Such kind words," the bishops scolded, "on the lips of the head of the Russian Orthodox Church cannot be sincere and therefore do not correspond to the dignity of the church."[80]

Although Sergei had proposed no liturgical innovations, in his critics' eyes he was barely a step above the renovationist Synodal Church. Deputations from all over Russia journeyed to Moscow, imploring Sergei to renounce his collaboration with the government. In December 1927 Bishop Dimitry (Lyubimov) of Gdov led a delegation of Leningrad priests and laity to Moscow to try to "bring Sergei to his senses." He directly asked the "deputy" locum tenens, "As the Soviet authority is Antichrist, can the Orthodox Church be in union with an Antichrist authority and pray for her successes and be joyful with her joys?" According to Ivan Andreyev, who attended the meeting, Sergei began laughing and brushed off the question with, "Well, what Antichrist is here?"[81] For Andreyev, this was when the rent in the garment of the Orthodox Church became irreparable. Some began to argue that Sergei and his supporters had fallen under Tikhon's anathema of 1918, which included all the confederates of communism.[82]

Bishop Victor of Glazov wrote a pastoral letter castigating Sergei for worrying more about the organization of the church in the material world than about welcoming the Holy Spirit into each believer's soul:

> In his action of destruction against the church, in addition to his treason, Metropolitan Sergei has affected also a heavy blasphemy against the Holy Spirit, which by the unlying word of Christ will never be forgiven him, neither in this life nor the one to come. . . .
>
> Being in all his activities as an antichurch heretic, as one who turns the Holy Church from a house of grace for the salvation of the believing into a graceless worldly organization, deprived of the Spirit of life, Metropolitan Sergei, at the same time, due to his deliberate renunciation of truth and in his mindless treason to Christ, is an open departer from the God of truth.[83]

He saw Sergei as worse than a heretic or schismatic, certain that the "deputy" locum tenens had plunged himself into "the abyss of destruction." Having no other recourse, he and the other signatories delivered Sergei "up to God's judgment."[84]

There were physical demonstrations and uprisings against Sergei as well, which must have amused the heads of government antireligious agencies. Some congregations attacked their priests and bishops inside the churches, and thousands of anonymous anti-Sergeiite pamphlets circulated throughout the major cities.[85]

As the year 1927 ended, Agathangel wrote a letter to a fellow bishop that described Sergei as "a usurper of ecclesiastical power." On February 6, 1928, he broke communion with Sergei and formed a separate "Yaroslavl Group." Tuchkov traveled to Yaroslavl to persuade Agathangel to accept the new reality, but the metropolitan maintained his independence there until his death in October. The two Orthodox leaders never fully reconciled.[86]

In July 1928 Sergei finally felt compelled to eject the Russian Orthodox Church Abroad from the Moscow Patriarchate. Later he wrote to Metropolitan Cyril of Kazan defending his use of excommunication as a patriarchal weapon:

> You are deeply grieved that we call them departed ones and schismatics. But they call our church, led by me, "the kingdom of Antichrist," our temples "the den of Satan," . . . the Holy Eucharist "demon food." They spit on our holy things.[87]

Then in December, Peter (still in exile) sent a new letter clothing his harsh criticism of Sergei in courtesy:

> Your Eminence, forgive me magnanimously if by the present letter I disturb the peace of your Eminence's soul. People inform me about the difficult circumstances that have formed for the church in connection with the exceeding of the limits of the ecclesiastical authority entrusted to you. . . . I have not accorded you any constituent right as long as I retain the locum tenency. . . . It is burdensome for me to number all the details of negative evaluations of your administration: the resounding protests and cries from believers, hierarchs, and laypeople. The picture of ecclesiastical division that has been painted is shocking.[88]

He went on to blame Sergei for placing the church "in a humiliating position," causing "quarrels and divisions" within it, and "blackening the reputations of its leaders."[89] Sergei defended himself by pointing to the words in the Declaration where he left all his decisions to be ratified by a future sobor. By this time, however, Sergei really did not need to defend himself, as most of the church opposition inside Russia had been rendered ineffective by exile or silenced by imprisonment or execution.

Metropolitan Anastasy, writing from France, produced arguably the most scathing attack of all:

> Our descendants will be ashamed when they compare the language of our chief hierarchs at the present day, when addressing those in power, with the language of the first Christians to the Emperors of Rome and their representatives. . . . To please the Soviet power, the chief hierarchs are not ashamed to propagate a flagrant lie, by saying that there have never been religious persecutions in Russia under the Soviets. In this way they commit sacrilege, by turning to derision the multitude of Russian martyrs, openly calling them political criminals.[90]

Why was Sergei so castigated for what was essentially an extension of Tikhon's policies in relation to the government? If Tikhon had lived until the end of the decade, he might well have found himself where Sergei did—seeing no other way out. Sergei was more obsequious (maybe more necessary as two more years had passed), but it may have been Tikhon's more beloved nature—and his martyrdom—that allowed for his forgiveness by the faithful. Also, Tikhon had been patriarch.

But it was also because deep in the Russian religious mind there was suspicion of organization, and Sergei seemed to have assigned the physical, hierarchical, organizational aspect of the church a higher priority than the spiritual, otherworldly aspect. He had saved its structure but not its soul. Or, put even more simply, he had denied the church its right to suffer. Reflecting from the perspective of the fall of communism, Patriarch Aleksy II said in 1991:

> Metropolitan Sergei wanted to save the church. I know that many people, hearing these words, protest that it is Christ who saves the church and not people. This is true. But it is also true that, without human efforts, God's help does not save. The Ecumenical Church is indestructible. But where is the celebrated Church of Carthage? Are there Orthodox believers today in New Caledonia, in Asia Minor, where Gregory the Illuminator and Basil the Great earned their renown? Before our eyes the church in Albania was destroyed . . . and in Russia there were powers wishing to do the same thing.[91]

But there were many in the church during the late 1920s who would much rather have had no structural church at all, if it could be maintained only by compromise, and instead have allowed the church to persevere within the hearts of the people. The church Sergei now led became known as the Soviet Church, the Red Church, or the "Fall-Down-and-Worship-Me-Church," after Satan's temptation of Christ—"All these things will I give thee, if thou wilt fall down and worship me" (Matthew 4:9).[92]

Having won some measure of cooperation from the Patriarchal Church did not mean that Soviet antireligious policy could rest on its laurels. Antireligious propaganda, carried out by two major organizations, could now become more sophisticated and focused.

17

THE ABYSS OF CONDEMNATION

Antireligious Organizations, a New Crackdown, and the Catacombs

The Thirteenth Party Congress in May 1924 passed a resolution to cease fighting religious prejudice by administrative means and to use only the services of Agitprop and education.[1] The congress pushed for a switch from negative to positive propaganda: Instead of explaining how religious obscurantism had harmed you in the past, explain how atheism and science will benefit you in the future. One resolution read:

> Antireligious propaganda in the village must have exclusively the character of a materialistic interpretation of the conditions that the peasant is familiar with. To explain the origin of hail, rain, storm, drought, the appearance of harmful insects, the character of the soil, the role of fertilizers, and so forth, is the best kind of antireligious propaganda. . . . [A victory] can be obtained only through a long period of years of persistent educational work.[2]

In October the Party Central Committee emphasized caution in the antireligious struggle, demanding "revolutionary legality" and denouncing hooliganism and frivolity.

In this chapter we will look at the two major organizations charged with carrying out this program: Komsomol and the League of the Godless. Emelyan Yaroslavsky was involved in controversies within and between these agencies. From 1924 through 1927, following the above-mentioned guidelines, antireligious efforts were less vicious than before, but in 1928 and 1929 they heated up again, driving "noncooperating" Orthodox groups underground.

THE VANGUARD OF THE ANTIRELIGIOUS FRONT

If we cast even a cursory glance at the immense task that has been set before antireligious propaganda as a result of the educational revolution, we shall immediately see how very insignificant the work [completed so far] is.

—Fyodor Oleshchuk, *Revolution and Culture*, 1928

Upon the not-so-broad shoulders of Komsomol and the League of the Godless (later renamed the League of Militant Atheists) was placed the task of getting the antireligious message out to the people. Komsomol, whose task went beyond spreading atheism, was the earliest of these groups, but the League of the Godless, beginning in mid-decade, was soon given primary responsibility for antireligious propaganda. There was always an overlap and a rivalry, however.

Komsomol

"Komsomol" is short for the Communist Youth League formed in 1918 for men and women between eighteen and twenty-six. Four years later the party set up the Young Pioneers as an alternative to international scouting and as a feeder group for Komsomol. Communist training was thus pushed into childhood to include nine- to fourteen-year-olds, and education in atheism became a major part of their curriculum. The Young Pioneers' emblem showed a child in the uniform of a Red Army soldier brandishing a flag with the motto "Long live the world movement of the Godless."[3]

During the mid-1920s, half of the rural population was composed of children and teenagers, so the Young Pioneers and Komsomol had plenty of recruiting opportunities. Although the Young Pioneers accepted the sons and daughters of the bourgeoisie, Komsomol took only the children of workers and peasants. Since both organizations were completely financed by dues, membership numbers were important. Statistics are not always reliable, but in 1923 Komsomol reported a membership of 300,000. By 1924 it claimed 700,000 members, by 1925 almost 1 million, and by 1928 its rolls had purportedly swollen to just under 2 million. In 1924 there was a "turn to the village" campaign to increase peasant membership relative to the cities, and by 1928 *Komsomolskaya Pravda*, the organization's newspaper, boasted that out of 67,700 local branches, almost 73 percent were from rural areas. But, to look at this issue another way, only 5 to 10 percent of eligible peasants had joined.[4]

Komsomol's theme was "youth striving to establish a socialist state." Although it worked on other projects—for example, improving agricultural techniques—everything seemed to come back to religion as the essence of culture. If villagers would not stop paying priests to say prayers over their crops, there was no way for modern agriculture to take root. The organization used the negative strategy of making young people with religious sentiments feel ostracized, making no meaningful contribution to their country's progress, but it also appealed to youth in a positive way by portraying atheism as daring, thrilling, and adventurous, in a word, "revolutionary." It also used amateur theatrics and colorful spectacles—an "antidullness campaign"—to attract the younger generation.[5]

Although this might seem like a recipe for success, Komsomol cadres in the field had four interrelated impediments to overcome:

- Membership and atheism were not synonymous. During the height of NEP, peasant recruits often brought their religious preconceptions with them and later retained them.[6] Weeding out the religious from the antireligious organization was a constant challenge.
- The organization had begun in the cities where youth was already less tied to the church and freer to come and go. When it made tentative ventures into rural areas it caused family conflict. "Why is our son, whose young hands are needed on the farm, idling away his time talking with those unbelievers from the city?" When recruitment was successful, though, it weakened bonds within the home and rendered instruction in Communist values easier. Often children grew up ridiculing their parents for attending church—a behavior that was often encouraged—and this, of course, led to further family alienation. Yaroslavsky resisted pushing this too far, however, saying, "We urge the godless workers to exercise tact and patience in such cases and not to break up their family life with quarrels on the question of religion."[7]
- Komsomol youth were seen as aliens in the villages. Some Komsomol agents had been fighters in the Red Army and retained their militarist, even bossy and overbearing, behavior. Others were too bookish for the peasantry, too involved in unfathomable theories and the latest news in periodicals. Some Komsomol teenagers disrupted church services and vandalized gravestones, which did not endear them to the rural populace, and "antireligious circles" were consequently poorly attended.[8] As the Komsomol presence in the countryside was greater than the party presence, these young people were taken as representative of Bolshevism, and the poor impression they made weakened the regime's already anemic popularity. Stalin complained in the spring of 1924, "[Komsomol] hooliganish escapades under the guise of so-called antireligious propaganda—all this should be cast off and liquidated immediately."[9]
- Young men in the villages turned to atheism more quickly and easily than young women. In 1923 in rural areas only *one percent* of Komsomol members were female,[10] though by 1928 about a quarter of its members were girls or young women. Still, it was aiming for female percentages

much higher than for males, for this was where religious "stubbornness" resided. (In 1921 the Party Central Committee explained this phenomenon, "Economically, women have still not been freed to the extent that men have by the Revolution." A woman's backward existence "survives from a time when hardly any ideology other than a religious one was available to her.")[11]

By 1926 the Komsomol Central Committee decided to rein in its branches, and it began scripting every detail of antireligious activities in advance. It delivered model lectures to the provinces with specific requirements for presentation. Every lecture had to include an explanation of how the world and human beings began, a slide presentation (perhaps on the same subject), a question-and-answer period, and entertainment that satirized the Bible by a skit or by playing charades. Komsomol headquarters even dispatched suggestions for the antireligious subject to be guessed.[12]

Nikolai Bukharin addressed Komsomol's Eighth Congress in May 1928 in a speech titled "Let Us Pin Our Colors to Our Youth." He bore an unhappy message, reporting on the difficult times that had befallen the antireligious organizations. Churches were modernizing, and *their* propaganda was increasingly successful. He estimated that Christian youth organizations held as many members as did Komsomol. New methods were needed to confront them, and Komsomol must work with renewed vigor, as many earlier zealots were ageing and had graduated into the Communist Party.[13]

The author of "Militant Religion Is Attacking Us" in the June 6, 1928, issue of *Komsomolskaya Pravda* berated its own members in the North Caucasus region for slovenly work and indifference. Out of 69,000 members in his survey, only 6,000 had joined the League of the Godless as well. He pleaded:

> We are hanging back in an unpardonable manner instead of withstanding the religious attack. This front of our class struggle is quite unprotected. Komsomol must immediately mobilize all its strength for a widespread, steady, and competent counterattack.[14]

By late 1928 Komsomol's newspaper was fiercely attacking the "remnants of religion." Whole pages were devoted to the atheistic cause, and no issue skipped the topic.[15]

The League of the Godless/Militant Atheists

From the realization that the average worker was too exhausted after his shift to indulge in propaganda grew the idea of forming a special organization whose *sole* mission was on the antireligious front. There was also a need to coordinate the antireligious work of Komsomol, trade unions, and the party itself. In the autumn of 1924 some Moscow atheists organized the Society of the Friends of the Newspaper *Bezbozhnik*, but by 1925 it (mercifully) shortened its name to the League of the Godless. It was formally launched at Easter 1925, nominally independent but in fact controlled by the party.[16] The chain of command ran from the party Politburo down through its Agitprop Department to the League. By 1926 membership was open to party members and nonparty members alike, as long as the applicant was willing to renounce all religion.

Financing, as with Komsomol, came from dues alone, but dues were very cheap—initially five kopecks a year for urban members and two for rural members. Red Army soldiers, students, and the unemployed were exempt from any dues. This arrangement put a premium on boosting the number of dues-paying members, whether or not new recruits were active in League projects. Those who joined would typically be party members, Komsomols, war veterans, young working men, and orphans. Just as with Komsomol, there was a young godless organization, the Junior Sector, set up to capture schoolchildren before someone else got to them. One of the Junior Sector's major campaigns was to reduce drunkenness associated with Orthodox feast days—children reprimanding their fathers.[17]

In the first year of the League's existence the regular party organization and the Soviet press de-emphasized its significance, reflecting a feeling that its leaders were eccentrics and fanatics who would push too hard and excite religious fervor. The party claimed that these radical intellectuals were out of touch with the real problems of the workers and peasants, which was no doubt true. These League "fanatics" included F. Putintsev, an editor of *Bezbozhnik*; Maria Kostelovskaya, editor of *Godless at the Workbench*; Alexander Lukachevsky, head of the antireligious department of the Communist Academy; and Mikhail Gorev. The League's Executive Committee included the Old Bolsheviks Ivan Skvortsov-Stepanov, the editor of *Izvestia*, and Peter Krasikov. Above them all stood the chairman, Emelyan Yaroslavsky.[18]

One of the League's first projects involved the contemporaneous Tennessee trial of John Scopes, who was accused of teaching Darwin's theory of evolution in a biology classroom. When Scopes was found guilty, the League began collecting money for a John Scopes Fund, the proceeds of which would be used to circulate books on evolution among Russia's peasantry. It even offered to pay Scopes's $100 fine.[19] But its main project, run out of its headquarters on Tverskaya Street in central Moscow, was providing antireligious speakers for the whole country. On the wall hung a large map of Russia that showed the League's thirty-six provincial branches, with red dots placed where atheistic propaganda programs were in place.

William Henry Chamberlin visited the League's new and improved headquarters in 1926 and got an earful of accomplishments. A zealous young staffer claimed 600,000 members in 12,000 local branches; no doubt a wild exaggeration, as the League's official membership figures for that year were only 114,000 and, by 1928, 123,000. With both Komsomol and the League, friends were prone to exaggerate membership figures upwards, and rivals tended to exaggerate them downwards. Julius Hecker, sympathetic with the Communist cause, claimed 465,500 people on League rolls in 1928 and 2 million in 1930, but he acknowledged that not more than 10 percent were active agitators, the rest being satisfied with simply paying their dues (much like Americans might contribute to the United Way charity at work without becoming directly involved in charitable activities). Yaroslavsky feared that many members were actually believers who were attempting to protect themselves and their careers and that some were infiltrators from the churches.[20]

League executive secretary Fyodor Oleshchuk lamented in 1928 that the League had enrolled so *few*—he claimed 250,000—at a time when fanatical boosters were claiming millions! At the end of the decade, the League itself claimed 2.5 million, but that was only after it had lowered the minimum membership age to six and signed up entire schools at the stroke of a pen. Oleshchuk acknowledged that there were only around 6,000 local branches, that many were poorly organized and attended, and that 80 percent of the membership that showed up was male when it was women they needed to convert. By the end of the decade interest in the antireligious crusade was lagging. Nearly half of the "members" had not paid their dues but were counted anyway. Both government and party press printed numerous articles complaining about the inactivity of many godless cells and revealing that some of the League's highly touted successes had been the results of someone's too fertile imagination. Yaroslavsky noted in 1930 that whole villages in rural and backward regions had been declared "godless" although no antireligious agitator had ever visited there. He called it "a joke." One reason for the League's dismal showing was that it concentrated too much on its publishing empire and too little on agitation in the field.[21]

YAROSLAVSKY AND HIS CRITICS

Yar-os-lav-sky? Don't you know what Yar-os-lav-sky is? Why, it would make a hen chuckle. He will never be able to manage this work.[22]

—Lenin at a Politburo meeting, after hearing that during his (Lenin's) convalescence Stalin had replaced Trotsky with Yaroslavsky as head of the antireligious campaign, 1923

The terms "Left" and "Right" were bandied about during the mid-1920s, and before we delve into Yaroslavsky's problems in this regard it will be helpful to consider what these terms meant. The Left—the "priest-eaters"—were crude, impatient, and militant along their path to atheist victory. Fighting religion, as the name implied, meant war, and the soldiers of this war needed no particular intellectual qualifications to do the job. The Left had no qualms about using force to close churches or insulting the feelings of believers with tactless articles and cartoons. Although they supported science, they were intolerant of science education as a means to achieve universal atheism. Russian society was seen exclusively through the spectacles of class-consciousness and class warfare. Religion had been invented by the exploiting classes to maintain power, and believers were tools of those classes; simply put, the priests had to be destroyed. With these tactics they could quickly remold society. Maria Kostelovskaya was of this persuasion.[23]

The Right was centered in the Ukraine, but this position was also supported by schoolteachers throughout the Soviet Union. They took the "liquidationist" or "mechanicist" view that aggressive antireligious propaganda was counterproductive and should be replaced by "enlightenment"—the simple dissemination of knowledge from the natural sciences. As socialism and communism were being built, as a classless society became a reality, religion would gradually disappear and no longer be of concern—Lenin's "revolution first" argument. The only appropriate method of hurrying along the process would be more and better science and history education.[24] The Old Bolshevik Ivan Skvortsov-Stepanov was of this persuasion. Both Kostelovskaya and Skvortsov-Stepanov were strong atheists, but their approaches differed markedly.

So how did Yaroslavsky fit into this picture? Emelyan Yaroslavsky rose to membership in the Party Central Committee Secretariat in 1921 and to the office of Secretary of the Central Control Commission (the party's disciplinary organ) in 1923, but his real passion was advancing atheism through science, especially anthropology and archaeology. *Officially* his goals were pacific, such as teaching agricultural workers how the principles of materialism would improve crop yields (as no doubt they would), but he also urged children to fight for atheism within their families and was known to incite workers to violence when they encountered recalcitrant believers. He was zealous and creative but not a true intellectual. His books tended toward the crudest and most primitive of arguments against God. Refusing to see allegory in the Bible, he took each statement literally and tried to demolish it with arguments from science and nature. Yaroslavsky was a cautious politician—in other words, a survivor—and dialectically proclaimed both the Left and Right deviations "equally harmful," while embodying aspects of both. Whatever his position on a particular issue, he claimed it as the center, and he moved as if he owned a coach on Stalin's train.

The centralization and bureaucratization of the antireligious struggle was a perfect microcosm of Stalin's political maneuvering during the same period. During Lenin's convalescence from his first stroke (May 1922), it was Stalin who pushed Yaroslavsky into the propaganda business to remove Trotsky from it. Trotsky, as we have seen, took a harsh view on religion, but he also took an apathetic approach toward antireligious propaganda, arguing in his one public pro-nouncement on the subject that the working class was virtually atheistic already, as the ritualistic peasantry had never truly absorbed a religious consciousness.[25] Stalin also made sure that Yaroslavsky was appointed as the first head of the League of the Godless when it was created in 1925.

Although he had Stalin's backing—probably because he was perceived as no threat—Yaroslavsky found himself enmeshed in controversy with many others. In 1923 he wrangled with the Swedish Communist Party leader Zeth Höglund, who felt deeply that Communists *should* be unbelievers but that believers must be admitted to the party, and the party itself must take no action against those whose religious beliefs lingered too long. Höglund supported the struggle against counterrevolutionary church activities but not against individual belief. Yaroslavsky fired back that Communists could not be indifferent to religion; it made a difference whether one fought in the name of humanity or in the name of God. A truly Marxist revolutionary must be a materialist.[26]

With the struggle over Lenin's succession—even while he still breathed—and bitter rivalries within the antireligious movement, the years 1923 through 1926 saw more controversy. By 1924 Stalin was in the process of decoupling Trotsky's coach from his train, and antireligious policy would soon become the least of the latter's concerns. Yaroslavsky slid past Trotsky without much trouble. Maria Kostelovskaya, however, offered serious ideological and personal opposi-tion. She took aim at Yaroslavsky through the pages of *Godless at the Work-bench*, and her attacks on him were persistent. She and her fellow priest-eating editors made the newspaper into a rude mouthpiece for their views.

Animosity came to a head in January 1925 when Kostelovskaya wrote an article in *Pravda* titled "On Mistakes in Antireligious Propaganda," accusing Yaroslavsky and his periodical *Bezbozhnik* of mere anticlericalism and unequal treatment for all churches. Why, for example, had he supported the Living Church and opposed the Tikhonites? True atheists, she scolded, should denounce religion no matter what the politics of its practitioners. She additionally objected to Yaroslavsky's historical approach—studying the minutiae of obscure and dead religions to better understand the origins of all religions—and she revived Lenin's admonition about the cruder religion being easier to fight and the subtler religion being more dangerous. Her fear was that instead of undermining reli-gion, Yaroslavsky's approach would enable religious thinkers to refine their faiths by accommodating the science, thus making them stronger. Yaroslavsky's use of religious terminology and employment of turncoat ex-priests in League programs led to the charge of Godbuilding. She demanded that *class struggle* be the basis of propaganda and that all efforts be turned over to working-class agi-tators. Religion was such a primitive and shallow phenomenon that it could easily be defeated by an all-out, militantly repressive effort. The party, she was convinced, should be in total control of this campaign.[27]

Assuming a position slightly to the right of center, Yaroslavsky responded to his rival in the *Pravda* article "On Methods of Antireligious Propaganda." He answered the charge of mere anticlericalism by describing it as an integral part of godlessness, and he claimed no favoritism toward any faith. It was, he retorted, foolhardy and counterproductive to attack religious peasants and workers as "class enemies"—most were loyal Soviet citizens who were simply in need of re-education through agitation in the countryside. He cited Lenin's 1909 opinion that, due to the low level of sophistication among the masses, they must be *taught* the materialist explanation of where religion came from. He made the case for studying religion's past so as to arrive at more convincing explanations of the origin of the universe and of human beings. Admitting that religion was a part of an economic superstructure, he also felt that some of it was due to plain and simple ignorance—an ignorance that he intended to rectify.

Yaroslavsky believed that Kostelovskaya's mockery of priests and their churches did more harm than good, driving people away from identification with the party. He also opposed coercive methods of shutting down religion; for example, he condoned church closures only when local citizens *genuinely* desired it—that was, after all, the law. Kostelovskaya, he contended, was so obsessed with the "class enemy" aspect of the struggle that she viewed her fellow man too narrowly. Believers were not merely "tools of class exploitation," they were people with an entire worldview of emotions, ethics, and complex behaviors. All these had to be taken into account while persuading them to give up their faith.[28]

Both party *and nonparty* agitators should guide the antireligious struggle, Yaroslavsky continued, as this would draw more people into the party. He defended his Godbuilding methods as both Marxist and effective. Lenin's actual prerevolutionary views on this point were surprisingly flexible and dependent on the historical and social context, as when he explained that if a dedicated socialist were to adopt the view that communism is a religion, then it would be harmful to the advancement of the class struggle, but if a religious proletarian were to adopt the same view, then it might help to pull him into the socialist movement. In the latter case, Yaroslavsky argued, Godbuilding would be useful and it should be temporarily supported.[29] He saw religion as a deeply rooted phenomenon, one that would take decades and decades of relentless scientific education to dig up and destroy. He denounced Kostelovskaya's impatience and her neglect of rational study and science.

In February 1925 the Antireligious Commission deprived Kostelovskaya of her seat, a sure indication of declining influence.[30] Finally, the Central Committee stepped in to clarify official policy and to settle personality conflicts. It called a Party Conference on Antireligious Propaganda in April 1926 that produced a series of eleven theses. They (more or less) resolved the Kostelovskaya-Yaroslavsky dispute and offered specific instructions for atheistic propaganda nationwide. Propagandists were reminded to speak against *every* existing religion and thus convince each church that it was not the sole focus of attention. The first thesis established three basic conditions for the proper organization of propaganda:

- The propagandist must understand the class basis of religious organizations and how they serve capital. He had to expose the antiscientific nature of religion. He needed to know that capitalists imposed religious morals such as meekness, silence, patience, and passivity on workers to keep them docile. Similarly, emotions such as awe and reverence worked against workers' interests. And when churches preached love, brotherhood, and cooperation, he needed to expose the class nature of these pronouncements.
- While it was objectively true that religion was a manifestation of the class struggle, there was a subjective aspect to religion as well. There was the "philosophy of life and the universe," the "emotion and mystic sentiment," and the system of morality. Propagandists must be aware of the distinctions between these two roles if they were to be effective.
- The propagandist must relate atheism to the political and economic problems of the particular period. "Antireligious propaganda must be construed upon an exact computation and scientific Marxian grasp of all the peculiarities of the given moment." Otherwise the growth of atheism in one time and place, and the growth of religion in another, would be incomprehensible.

The theses went on to say that people had to individually "work through" the role of religion in the class struggle in order for the atheistic conclusion to be valid; anything less would be superficial and a violation of Marxist principles.

For May Day celebrations—coinciding with Easter Eve—the conference issued an order to all party branches forbidding parodies of the holy day. Bukharin, spouting the new party line, publicly proclaimed, "Let no one think that because he defiles the doorstep of a priest, he is leading an antireligious propaganda." In the villages, financial persecution of priests was (temporarily) given up as bad policy.[31] Party members were now to more directly control local atheist organizations. By early 1927 teaching manuals on nature, the history of man, and biblical criticism were ready for propagandists to take into the field.

Although Lenin had been gone for over three years, the theses and other pronouncements attempted to bring the antireligious struggle back to Leninist principles and to find a middle position between the hard-line Left and the more moderate, or patient, Right. This was a victory for Yaroslavsky; now his position was vindicated and he could gather the reins of power on the antireligious front firmly in his hands. He was careful in the celebration of his success, though, continuing to criticize both the Left and the Right.[32]

But perhaps this was a false dichotomy: In a sense the Left and the Right were *linked*. If religion were truly a mere matter of social class (Left), then, as economic changes led to a classless society, religion would have no basis and would die (Right).[33] The "building of socialism" would take care of everything.

There was, however, one major ideological contradiction in this period. The 1926 theses were produced five years into the New Economic Policy, a period of concessions made to private enterprise in agriculture and industry to boost production to prewar levels. The theses claimed, however, that what progress had been made on the atheistic front was due not to propaganda alone but to the people's increasing participation in the socialist economic system: "The drift from religion to atheism is the ideological expression of the gigantic material changes taking place at this moment in our country." In other words, reliance on the antireligious effects of true socialism was being advocated at a time when, since the Revolution, the country was the *least* socialist.

But theoretical issues would soon lose their importance. As the decade drew to a close, Stalin's (thus Yaroslavsky's) strategy moved toward the eradication of both extremes and a return to violence.[34] It was Kostelovskaya's turn for vindication.

1928 AND 1929

It may have been a sense of desperation, or sensitivity to pressure from above, that drove atheist propagandists to abandon the moderating advice of the 1926 theses. During the Christmas season of 1927–28, the tenth anniversary of the Revolution, the Communists staged over seven hundred anti-Christmas demonstrations in Leningrad alone. Easter 1929 reminded one observer of the period of mockery of religion that had occurred in 1923. Antireligious parades and effigy burning spread through the cities of Russia.[35]

There were still meager signs of moderation to be found, if one sought them out. The June 11, 1928, issue of *Krasnaya Gazeta* carried the full text of "The New Law Regarding Religious Communities," which included such hopeful provisions as a guarantee that "new houses of prayer could be erected without hindrance" and a promise that old houses of prayer would not be closed if "such an action would be prejudicial for the further practice of the cult in the given community." But the new law also contained plenty of exceptions, and it reiterated the harsher terms of earlier laws.[36]

Yaroslavsky announced an Antireligious Five-Year Plan in late 1928.[37] *Pravda*'s yearlong campaign of criticism of the atheistic front was a prelude to and buildup for a major regeneration of the antireligious struggle planned for 1929. With the advent of long-term economic planning and the collectivization of agriculture came a renewed radicalism within the Soviet leadership. Collectivization became a heavy-duty antireligious weapon, which could be expressed as a syllogism:

Peasants will be forced onto collective farms.
No religiosity will be allowed on the collectives.
Religion will die.

Although Komsomol and League membership rolls (apparently) skyrocketed during this period, both organizations were actually marginalized—administrative measures were making a comeback.[38]

On the Rights and Obligations of Religious Associations

Just as an alien invasion would unite the world's quarreling peoples, the onslaught against all religions that Stalin initiated in the spring of 1929 put at least a temporary end to bickering among what was left of Tikhonite, Sergeiite, Grigorian, and renovationist factions. The government's April 8, 1929, "Decree on Religious Associations"—supplemented and clarified on October 1 by the Commissariat of the Interior's "On the Rights and Obligations of Religious Associations"—aimed at plugging loopholes that had become apparent in the 1918 law separating church and state. It was therefore more extensive and detailed than its predecessor.[39]

The new law reiterated, "Religious unions and executive organs elected by them do not have the rights of a legal [juridical] person." All centralized control and church hierarchy was once again pronounced illegal—the point being repeated as the 1918 stipulation had never been effectively enforced. (Paradoxically, the government's rationale for forcefully eliminating the church hierarchy was that rank was inherently "coercive.") It was still a crime for any centralized church body to give instructions to diocesan bishops, for bishops to govern priests, and even for priests to pretend to any role of authority in parish communities. The local church was defined as "a group of communicants above the age of eighteen who voluntarily associated together for purely ceremonial and devotional purposes."[40]

But the April law was also elaborated and expanded. Article 17 prohibited these church activities: material or medical aid to members, mutual-aid funds, children's groups, children's playgrounds, children's excursions, children in the choir, youth groups, women's groups, religious study groups, and libraries. Religious societies now were required to submit agendas to local government "committees for religious affairs" before meetings could be held, and they were subject to surveillance and inspection at any time. Deviation from the agenda would be considered a violation of the lease and could mean closing of the church. The law included broad language—such as "protecting public order"—that local committees were allowed to interpret and were therefore allowed to abuse. All that was legally left to the faithful was quiet worship within the church building, holding only such books as were necessary for prayer. The law did contain a punishment of up to six months of hard labor for anyone disrupting a church service, but it was rarely enforced. As if this were not enough, at the end of the year the government banned Christmas trees and declared that Santa Claus was an ally of the priests and the kulaks.[41]

Many churches had been closed, but all were now silenced. The April Law—and the following month's Fourteenth Congress of Soviets—retracted the 1918 guarantee of the right of religious propaganda. The Constitution now read, "Freedom for religious worship and freedom for antireligious propaganda is recognized for all citizens," leaving the field wide open to Komsomol and the League. It was an admission of governmental failure. It would no longer be—if it ever was—a fair fight.[42]*

The Polish historian Wladyslaw Kania summed up the situation this way:

> The tolerated religious hierarchy, after the removal and the extermination of the men of independence, became an inert proponent of state authority, incapable of defending itself against anti-God propaganda, and a controlled body of the government unable to protest against atheism.[43]

To top it all off, Metropolitan Sergei agreed, in exchange for a government promise to end the eviction of priests from their homes, to utter again the preposterous assertion—for foreign consumption—that no persecution of religion existed now or in the past under Soviet power. In an interview with Western reporters he never blinked when he stated, "The confession of any faith is completely free." He added that the aspirations of the church and of the government were identical.[44]

Feeling that his interview had done yeoman's work for the government, Sergei was once again emboldened to ask Peter Smidovich for more favors. Could the government stop taxing priests for things that had no relationship to their work (for example, agricultural taxes on their little gardens)? Could the government once again permit priests to live within the boundaries of the villages they served? How about ending the practice of labeling priests as "unproductive workers" and denying their children educational opportunities? But either he received no answer or he got a negative reply to every request.[45]

When criticized again by the émigré church, Sergei was clearly irritated. Archpriest V. Vinogradov remembered hearing him grumble:

> Is it really possible that the West does not understand that an Orthodox bishop in Russia could not possibly say freely what I said in my interview? Is it pos-

---

*The 1936 Constitution retained the 1929 wording.

sible that they cannot infer from this statement the difficult position in which the Higher Church Administration finds itself in the Soviet Union?[46]

The 1929 League Congress

On June 10, 1929, the League of the Godless opened its Second Congress—also known as the All-Union Conference of Antireligious Societies—in Moscow. For the moment, the party was looking more kindly on this organization than it had in 1925, and it allowed Bukharin, Lunacharsky, and Gorky to address the two thousand delegates. Although this was the largest atheistic gathering before or since, it was still a tiny island of atheism in a sea of faith. There was a reminder of the surrounding waters when one of those attending wrote a note on a scrap of paper and had it passed up to the main podium. The speaker opened it and read aloud the words, "Woe to him who goes against his Creator." Although this incident caused uproarious laughter, it might also have given some reason to pause and consider what the delegates were up against.[47]

The main business of the congress was a rehash of the battle fought out in the press during 1925–26 between the Left and the Right and presumably resolved with the 1926 theses. Yaroslavsky, Lunacharsky (at the end of his career), and their supporters argued that the major roadblock to a materialist worldview was the lack of culture among the peasantry. They were willing to condemn the leaders of organized religion as subversive elements, but their greater goal was to change the consciousness of the rural population.

Top Komsomol leaders, anticipating attack, refused to attend the congress. Moderates attacked anyway with a hodgepodge of charges: becoming interested in the stuggle for materialism only at Christmas and Easter, using aggressive and uncompromising tactics, being too fond of military metaphors, making no distinctions among diverse faiths, and seeing no difference between leaders and followers of a particular faith. Although there was plenty of infighting and personal denunciation, the diplomatic language of congressional debate took the form of, Who was the most loyal disciple of Lenin? Both sides found plenty of ammunition in the departed leader's often-contradictory writings on religion.

To emphasize its new commitment, a name change was in order. The League of the Godless became the League of Militant Atheists—though it was no more militant than before—and it adopted the slogan: "The fight for godlessness is a fight for socialism." The government gave the League nominal control over all atheistic efforts in the Soviet Union, and the party fully backed a massive recruitment drive that boosted membership—at least on paper—dramatically. In the fall, the League persuaded the Printers' Union to refuse to print religious materials and the Construction Workers' Union to erect no more edifices for religious associations. Quickly following in step, the transport workers refused to carry any materials destined for religious ceremonies, and the Post and Telegraph

Workers Union stopped carrying religious mail and answering religious calls.[48] With party support, the League now *seemed* to be coming into its own, and churches seemed increasingly isolated.

But Yaroslavsky, despite his tolerance of Godbuilding, had never fully comprehended the central truth of religion in Russia. Being scientific-minded, he was sure that science would triumph. He criticized Christian dogma, biblical tradition, and the catechism as if religiosity were a matter of form, only partially grasping the social nature of faith. After listening to logical or historical explanations as to why they should abandon their silly superstitions, the people went right back to them. And even if propaganda, in rare instances, caused a peasant to probe the deeper, more critical aspects of religion, this would not necessarily lead him to agnosticism or atheism. He would simply turn to the Protestant sects—the Lutherans, the Baptists, or the Adventists—that were thriving during the 1920s.[49]

Stalin was becoming impatient, and Yaroslavsky, resting on his laurels, was not able to move quickly enough. Stalin's support for the radical-leftist position left him and the League's *relatively* moderate position behind. His coach—like Trotsky's—became detached from the train and soon would be shunted aside.[50] Although League membership was still on the rise and press runs of *Bezbozhnik* increased, its actual power decreased. Membership had been dramatically inflated, as millions of urban and rural workers were enrolled in atheistic organizations without their consent (and sometimes even without their knowledge.) More copies of *Bezbozhnik* were printed as fewer were paid for and read. Stalin's turn to violence and forceful administrative measures against the churches would render the cultural and educational approach that Yaroslavsky favored irrelevant and unnecessary. There would never be another League congress.

Churches that had weathered the storm of closings in the early 1920s found themselves subject to the same pressures once again in 1929. The justification this time was that the country was moving so rapidly toward socialism that it no longer had any need for churches. Local soviets began closing them without consulting parishioners—so much for "socialist legality"—then calling out troops to enforce their decisions. The doors of 1,100 churches were slammed shut and locked tight in 1929.

JOSEPHITES, CATACOMBS, AND ANTICHRIST

Not only did we not leave, we are not leaving and never shall leave the bosom of the True Orthodox Church. Her enemies, traitors, and murderers are those who are not with us and for us, but against us. It is not we who enter schism by not submitting to Metropolitan Sergei. Rather it is you, those obedient to him, who are following him into the abyss of condemnation.[51]

—Metropolitan Joseph in a letter to Archimandrite Lev (Egorov), February 1928

Clerical opposition to Sergei's "approved" Orthodox Church took many forms and involved many personalities, and there were many degrees of opposition. Metropolitans Agathangel and Cyril—both senior to Sergei in Tikhon's will—were simply "noncommemorators," meaning that, while they condemned Sergei's declaration of loyalty to the government and refused to pray for him or the government, they recognized his position as canonically legal and the sacraments he presided over as valid.[52]

When Peter chose Sergei as his deputy locum tenens in December 1925, he also appointed Joseph (Petrovykh), archbishop of Rostov, as his second, or alternate, deputy in case Sergei could not serve. Then in August 1926 Sergei elevated Joseph to be metropolitan of Leningrad. In September, however, the same government that Sergei championed denied Joseph a residence permit for the city, and Joseph bitterly turned against his superior. Despite his acceptance of promotion from Sergei, Joseph now saw him as being in bed with the "godless Communists."

In October, while Joseph was hidden away in the Modensky Monastery in Novgorod Province, Sergei transferred him to Odessa, most likely to rid himself of a hierarch he now considered a troublemaker and a liability. Sergei justified the transfer by pointing out that Joseph could not effectively administer his Leningrad diocese if he did not live there, though many bishops were in the same predicament. The possibility exists, of course, that the *government* initiated the transfer from such an important city; this would leave the see vacant and available to be filled with someone the authorities could more easily deal with. Joseph, however, refused to leave, and, rather than accept Sergei's charge of fostering a church schism, he bounced the charge back by accusing Sergei of "plunging a knife into the church's very heart."[53]

Ages of Orthodox Clergy at the End of the 1920s

Source: Miliukov, *Russia and the Church*, p. 204

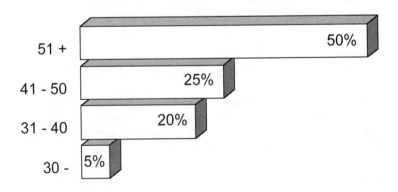

- 51 + : 50%
- 41 - 50 : 25%
- 31 - 40 : 20%
- 30 - : 5%

While Sergei was in prison in December 1926, Joseph briefly filled his appointed position and in the process secretly appointed three others as "*temporary* deputy locum tenentes." Concern for the preservation of hierarchical command was being taken to ridiculous—and uncanonical—extremes.[54] The "Josephites" included several hierarchs: Archbishop Dimitry of Gdov, Metropolitan Peter (from exile), Metropolitan Cyril of Tambov, and Metropolitan Agathangel of Yaroslavl (briefly). There may have been as many as forty bishops who were loosely associated with Joseph, as a part of the larger resistance to Sergei. The heart of Josephite territory was the Church of the Resurrection on the Blood—built in St. Petersburg on the exact spot where Tsar Alexander II had been assassinated in 1881—but there were a half dozen other Josephite sites in the region.

Josephites were diverse in their hatred for Sergei. Some saw him only as a bishop who had gone astray and who had exceeded his power. At the other extreme, however, were denunciations such as this:

> If all churches were taken away from us we would then pray secretly in cellars. If we are persecuted for our faith in Christ, then we, in imitation of first century Christians, shall go joyously to the fires and to prisons. But we shall not willingly allow the landlord of the Church of God to be the Antichrist, Communist Tuchkov.[55]

Josephites traveled far and wide and tried to "electrify" the people by dressing in the garb of ascetics and claiming mystical inner relationships with God. Under the leadership of Bishop Aleksy Bui, the rebellion against Sergei and the godless government spread in 1928 and 1929 into the provinces of Voronezh, Tambov, and Kursk. Voronezh may have been the seedbed of the True Orthodox Church, of which Joseph considered himself a founder. The True Orthodox Church was an extreme form of the Catacombs Church (see below), though later Soviet sociologists claimed that it was made up of "religious monarchists" rather than the heirs of Tikhon.[56]

Joseph did not consider himself a member of any underground church. He was not endeavoring to establish a new church but rather an independent alternative to attending the state-sanctioned church on the one hand and going underground in the catacombs on the other. To emphasize this point, the Josephites spurned offers of union with the exiled Karlovtzy Synod.[57] Joseph explained:

> I am not at all schismatic, and I call not to a schism, but to the purification of the Church from those who sow real schism and provoke it. To indicate [to] another his errors and wrongs is not schism, but to speak simply it is putting an unbridled horse back into harness.[58]

Responding in August 1929, Sergei declared sacraments performed by Josephite priests to be ineffective.[59]

The Josephite movement did shield some members whose interests could easily have fit into the Communists' definition of counterrevolutionary, and this doomed it from the start. The government press denounced its members as "Black Hundreds." By 1930 all Josephite churches had been closed (except for one shut down in 1936), and all prominent Josephite clergy had been imprisoned, exiled, or shot. Joseph himself was exiled in late 1929 to the shores of the Aral Sea in Kazakhstan. This did not mean, however, that the movement died out.[60]

It was becoming clear to the Orthodox faithful that their only chance to worship outside of the officially sanctioned Soviet Church—and outside of Siberian exile—was underground, in secret, in what was known as the catacombs. The term "catacombs" (literally a network of underground burial vaults or sepulchers) is evocative of the plight of the early Christians in the Roman Empire, who hid out of sight in cemeteries to avoid capture, torture, and death. Referring to the Orthodox Church in the 1920s and 1930s, it simply means the church that the authorities did not know about or, as was the case with Sergei, knew about but denied. Some consider this church to have begun as soon as Tikhon hurled his anathema at the Bolsheviks early in 1918, and for this reason they called it the Tikhon Church. Others place the beginning of the movement in 1922, with the emergence of the schismatic renovationists. Archbishop Fyodor (Pozdeevsky) was preparing extremists at the Danilov Monastery in Moscow—Danilovites—for the catacombs as early as Tikhon's 1923 confession.[61] But the major impetus for the "catacombniks" was Sergei's 1927 Declaration.

Michael Zhizhilenko, the tall, gray-bearded doctor who had been present at Patriarch Tikhon's death, became a leader of the Catacombs Church under the name Maxim. He claimed that Tikhon on his deathbed had prophesied increased religious persecution and had urged him to help organize the catacombs.[62] Michael became the monk Maxim and then bishop of Serpukhov—the first bishop of the Catacombs Church—in 1928. He may have been involved in a secret 1928 Catacomb Council called to anathematize Sergei's Church.

The Catacombs Church differed from the Josephites on two points: The Catacombs did not recognize the locum tenency of Metropolitan Peter (most likely because of his appointment of Sergei as deputy locum tenens), and it refused to accept *any* Soviet laws governing religious organizations (while Joseph had at least attempted to work within the governmental framework).[63]

As for practical Catacombs operations, priests often worked in the world by day and held clandestine services in private homes at night or in the wee hours of morning. They would quietly leave their official parishes and disappear, only to reappear later at a small chapel on the outskirts of a nearby town. Sometimes more extreme—literally underground—measures were employed. An issue of *Orthodox Life* magazine, published in 1959, described this 1920s scene:

In the village there is a chapel dug deep beneath the Earth, its entrance carefully camouflaged. When a secret priest visits the village, it is here that he celebrates the liturgy and the other services. If the villagers for once believe themselves safe from police observation, the whole population gathers in the chapel, except for the guards who remain outside and give warnings if strangers appear.[64]

The Catacombs Church made liberal use of Antichrist, not opposing Bolshevism as merely the cruelest possible form of government but as the *embodiment* of Antichrist (Mark 13:22—"false prophets shall rise" and 2 Thessalonians 2:3—"the son of perdition"). Thus professor Ivan Andreyev, a Catacombs member, ascribed a mystical quality to the Bolsheviks that the rest of the world, seeing Bolshevism as a mere politico-economic abomination, failed to grasp. He wrote, "If the Orthodox Christian Church is mystically the 'Body of Christ,' then the Bolshevik Communist Party is mystically the body of Antichrist." Those who submitted to Bolshevism submitted to Antichrist; one bishop even interpreted Revelation 13:16 to mean that the stamp of Antichrist on a Russian's forehead meant voluntary submission, while a stamp on the hand—a lesser mark—meant one had given in only out of fear.[65]

As collectivization of agriculture began, it, too, was labeled the work of Antichrist. Protest against the violence of the government's program was often expressed in these terms. In some villages tractors were labeled as "Satanic forces." Letters from God or from the Virgin Mary—many with revealingly poor penmanship—mysteriously appeared in villages, damning Soviet collectivization and modernization efforts and warning of the imminence of the end of the world.[66]

The government denied the existence of a Catacombs Church (and, of course, of Antichrist), citing as evidence overflowing attendance in officially sanctioned churches. One could easily rebut, however, that overflowing attendance was the inevitable result of the scarcity of churches to attend. And at the same time that the government denied the catacombs, it was arresting and harshly punishing people for belonging to it. (Just before World War II, Ivan Andreyev said that he knew of two hundred places to clandestinely worship in the Leningrad area alone.)[67]

Percent of All Orthodox Parishes Loyal to Various Groups in 1928

Source: Shkarovsky, "The Russian Church vs. the State," p. 374

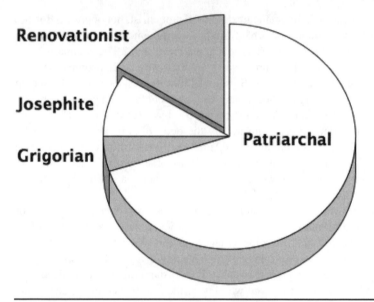

Renovationist

Josephite

Grigorian

Patriarchal

Millions had left the Orthodox Church for agnosticism, atheism, or sectarianism, but Evgeny Tuchkov's plan of achieving mass atheism through manipulation *of* the church was having only partial success; the party and the government would have to turn to antireligious propaganda techniques used *against* the church. Propaganda supplemented administrative methods, such as church closures and confiscation of valuables, and it was aimed not so much at the church hierarchy as at the common people and their "prejudices."

18

ABOLISHING GOD

Reassessing Propaganda

In November 1918 enthusiasts placarded public places with "Religion is the opium of the people" slogans. Antireligious lectures were delivered on street corners, and wild-eyed zealots predicted a quick victory. One young revolutionary informed a visiting British minister, "We have now overthrown the crown and monarchy; in a few years we will abolish God also from Russia." He explained to the visitor that he was in the process of training twenty-eight young propagandists to go out to the villages to undermine loyalty to the monarchy and eradicate religious convictions. Others were doing the same, and soon there would be enough propagandists that every village in Russia would be visited at least twice.[1]

But the euphoria quickly faded. From late 1917 through late 1922 the Bolsheviks concentrated on a direct assault on the institution of the church and paid little attention to the minds of the people. They separated church and state, closed places of worship, confiscated church valuables, exacerbated church schisms, and staged clerical trials. Although these techniques grievously wounded the physical church, they did little to affect the habits and the hearts of the great masses of the Russian people. Nikolai Bukharin wrote in 1919:

> It has been comparatively easy for the proletarian authority to effect the separation of the church from the state and of the school from the church, and these changes have been almost painlessly achieved. It is enormously more difficult to fight the religious prejudices which are already deeply rooted in the consciousness of the masses and which cling so stubbornly to life.[2]

To the party's disgust, religious sentiment actually *rose* during these years. A new approach was needed, one that was aimed directly at individual believers but that would also change the ancient and collective religious mind. Concern with the political threat to the new regime now turned to the cultural threat.

The new approach would be propaganda. In the early years of Bolshevik rule propaganda was conceived of as exposing the lies and falsehoods of the church, with the assurance that once believers' eyes were opened they would simply cease believing. An example of this naiveté was the exposure of fraudulent relics and the widespread use of cinema in their uncovering. The people's unwillingness to cooperate in unbelief was seen as "their failure." This chapter and the next are about the turn to antireligious propaganda *in earnest*, a process commencing in early 1923. Since the process was now conceived on a much vaster scale—but in a country with poor transportation and few telephones and radios—it would have to be accomplished by trained cadres on a person-to-person basis. This, in turn, would require creation of new antireligious bureaucracies.

A note on terminology: "Propaganda" as used here does not imply the spreading of false ideas—only that certain beliefs were propagated, true or not. *Everything* the Communists did on the antireligious front had a propaganda value.

THE ANNULMENT OF CHURCH PROPAGANDA

The government had one advantage not available to the churches—the power to thwart. It could make more room for the propagation of its own views by closing churches and arresting clergy, but it could also deny the religious side the constitutional right to its own propaganda by tossing prerevolutionary religious books out of public libraries, banning their sale (to remove, as it said, "their pernicious influence"),[3] and censoring sermons. As if to demonstrate where religion stood, book-banning orders were included within larger decrees against pornography. The law allowed citizens to *own* and *read* religious books, but the government did all in its power to make sure that none were available to beg, borrow, or steal, much less purchase legitimately. There were even cases in the villages where teachers told students to bring their Bibles from home; as soon as the Bibles were collected they were thrown in a pile and burned.

In early 1918 the state confiscated church presses and type, making it nearly impossible for churches to rebut malicious calumnies against them. This preemptive censorship ended the publication and distribution of all patriarchal letters, academic religious works, and even simple church news—unless, of course, they were carried by hand or, as was the case when it was to the government's advantage, carried in the state-run media. The acts of the First Church Sobor of 1917–18, for example, were only partially known across the country. Rural priests were groping in the dark. It became extremely difficult to publish even church calendars.[4]

When Donald Lowrie interviewed Patriarch Tikhon in 1921, he asked about the church's "most urgent need." Tikhon answered:

Send us Bibles. Never before in history has there been such a hunger for Scripture in the Russian people. They clamor for the whole book—not only the Gospels but the Old Testament as well—and we have no Bibles to give them. Our slender stocks were exhausted long ago.[5]

The British and Foreign Bible Society complained that before the war they sold 500,000 copies of the Scriptures in Russia, but in 1923 they managed to sell only 1,800. Domestic Bible publication was not reauthorized until 1926, when 25,000 copies were to be printed from American Bible Society (Baptist) plates. There is some evidence, however, that this number may have been reduced to 2,500, if they were ever printed at all. (Bible publishing would not reappear until 1956, when a mere 50,000 were printed, many of which were then sold abroad.)[6]

The government placed restrictions not only on the written word but also on oral propaganda. During the Civil War, sermons were not subject to censorship, though priests knew they had to watch carefully what they said. On June 26, 1921, however, the state decreed that sermons must be restricted to purely religious subjects essential for the service. It would not tolerate hostility toward the government disguised as religious worship and would consider any such statements indictable and criminal. The government never offered more definitive guidelines—probably a purposeful ambiguity.[7] Then, on December 26, Anatoly Lunacharsky issued a decree obliging all priests to submit their sermons to the censor *in advance*, declaring: "Religion is a brutalization of the people. Education must be so directed as to efface from the people's minds this humiliation and this idiocy."[8] Religious leaders had no corresponding power to prevent the government from teaching atheism in the schools and to the public.

Hours/Year Spent on Prayers & Church Attendance in 1922

Source: S. Strumilin, in Pethybridge, *One Step Backwards Two Steps Forward,* p. 38

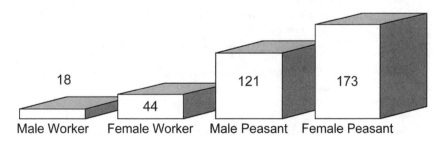

Male Worker	Female Worker	Male Peasant	Female Peasant
18	44	121	173

THE FRACTURING OF SOCIETY

It is hard even to imagine how deeply rooted are the prejudices even in the large indus-
trial centers. Only two miles separate Novo-Belitsa from Gomel [in Byelorussia], but if
you touch in Novo-Belitsa upon the questions of religion you will see in what depths of
darkness and ignorance you are. They don't want to listen to any arguments and are easily
carried—especially the women—to fits of hysterics.

—*Izvestia* on April 12, 1923

The Bolsheviks had to deal with the religious issue as a divisive force in society. Town and countryside were split, households were rent both by gender and by age, and the party itself was far from monolithic in its atheist creed. On March 18, 1923, *Pravda* carried a commentary about lingering faith within the workers' households:

> The women, especially, are intractable; they worship before the Holy Ikons and impede the progress of the war on religion. They insist on having their children christened and obstruct the removal of ikons. Our campaign is proceeding nervously. It is necessary to move slowly, word by word, drop by drop, to worm our way and convince the stubborn that by the unwritten decrees of the victorious proletariat the inhabitants of heaven and all their attributes have been abolished. With an iron sweeper the workmen must clear their homes of the last vestige of all that is holy.

The press was well aware of generational differences within families and often ran concocted, stereotyped conversations, usually pitting a young, well-trained atheist son against his parents and the old folks. Here is an example from *Pravda*, April 14, 1923:

> The parents are asking their (adult) son's permission to hang an ikon on the wall.

> **Parents:**   No, no. Whatever you say, we must hang it. It's a holiday, and the priest will come to hold a thanksgiving service. We can't do without ikons.
> **Son:**   I have nothing to do with the priest. And all your gods have flown away. They saw that something was wrong down here and departed hastily.
> **Parents:**   Oh, you wretched Nicholas. [The mother wipes the tears from her skirt.] Didn't your friends go to the Holy Communion today?
> **Son:**   Those are no friends of mine that go to the Communion. You are mistaken.
> **Parents:**   And if you die, what shall we do? Just bury you like a dog? Perhaps your wife wants to pray?
> **Son:**   Let her, but not before the ikons.

Parents: Both you and your wife are lost sheep, I see. She doesn't go to church either. [They continue to wail.]

The son hangs a portrait of Lenin where the ikons once were.

Of course, what the government preferred was a monolithically atheist society. Short of that, a fractured society was preferable to a monolithically religious one. Theoretically, society should have been divided only along class lines—and that only temporarily—so great efforts were made to understand family divisions dialectically.

But the party, contrary to theory, was also divided; members were leaving for religious reasons or being ejected as religiously unreliable. A Leningrad party official—after rejecting fifty party candidates in 1926—noted the setback and complained that the situation was not getting any better.[9]

RELIGIOUS REVIVAL

The opposition of the Bolsheviks to religion has probably done more to help the Orthodox Church than the active cooperation of the tsar's government has done in the past fifty years. The persecution has helped to weed out the less consecrated and more corrupt from among the priesthood and has brought to the front the more earnest of the religious leaders.[10]

—Jerome Davis, a sociologist from Dartmouth College, visiting Russia in 1921

Monolithic atheism was quickly turning into a utopian dream. In the cities, religious feelings were stirring during the half decade after the Bolshevik takeover, and according to many observers church attendance was actually *rising* during the early 1920s. After the turmoil of the Civil War, the indifferent educated classes began returning to their forsaken faith, some even joining the priesthood. Part of the resurgence was due to the simple fact that no other non-Soviet institution remained for those with a protesting spirit.

A Petrograd sociologist noted that many more believers were coming into the churches to pray in front of the ikons, even when no services were scheduled. Although church attendance dropped during the middle 1920s, due to both the closing of churches and the people's rejection of the Living Church, religious *sentiment* seems to have continued its surge. Eugene Trubetzkoy observed in 1919 that the "blood of the new martyrs" was winning the people's hearts.[11]

The people's focus on religious themes went well beyond church attendance. Increasingly, peasants across the land saw heavenly apparitions, witnessed miracles, and feared portents of the Apocalypse. When a meteorite fell on December 5, 1922, peasants claimed that it was made of gold, had fallen from Jupiter, and was a sign of the end of the world. Thousands of peasants slaughtered their animals, reckoning that they might as well gorge themselves now. God came to speak personally to some peasants, as he had to Moses in the desert. He revealed the number of years to the End Times or led the way to buried treasure; occasionally he killed a peasant's enemies. In many regions ancient ikons suddenly appeared shiny and new, causing masses of pilgrims to descend on the site. Rumors spread of the miraculous appearance of crosses, holy flames, and sacred springs. The historian Lynne Viola noted this event:

> At a spring outside of a village in 1924, an elderly peasant woman stopped for a drink and saw "holy figures." News of the sighting spread, and peasants flocked to the area to pray and to seek healing powers from the spring. It was reported that people were still making pilgrimages to the spring as late as 1928.[12]

MOVING TOWARD A GENTLER TOUCH

The campaign against the backwardness of the masses in this matter of religion must be conducted with patience and considerateness, as well as with energy and perseverance. The credulous crowd is extremely sensitive to anything that hurts its feelings.

—Bukharin, *The ABC of Communism*, 1922

So, with an increasingly polarized society and manifestations of faith on the rise, what propagandistic tactic should the party recommend? Lenin, as we have seen, was initially opposed to staging a specifically atheistic propaganda campaign. His theoretical reason was that too heavy a reliance on propaganda was the mark of an anarchist or of a socialist who did not understand the intricacies—or even the basics—of dialectical materialism. Only those who considered the world of ideas as being primary and independent could undertake such a campaign against religion. A pure materialist should comprehend that religion flowed from economic causes, thus early antireligious efforts should be devoted to forming class-consciousness among workers and peasants. When the trappings of the capitalist regime were finally shed, the world of religious ideas would be discarded with them. As Lenin put it:

> It would be absurd to believe that in a society founded on the continual oppression and degradation of the working masses, religious prejudices can be dissipated by means that are of a purely propagandistic character. It would take bourgeois mediocrity to forget that the religious yoke on humanity is only an effect and a reflection of the economic yoke existing in a society.[13]

Beyond theory, there was the practical problem of not raising the hackles of the workers by pushing too hard too soon. Beginning the struggle against personal religious feelings too quickly would only sow discord and dissension within the targeted population. In November 1918, after a year in power, Lenin admonished:

> Religious prejudices must be fought against with the utmost prudence, so as not to offend the sensibilities of believers; one must carry on the battle with propaganda and education. To go into the struggle headlong and without restraint would be to risk the hatred of the masses and their alienation on religious grounds.[14]

This does not mean that Lenin found antireligious propaganda to be useless; it was simply that this could not be the first line of attack. It should be employed only with workers who were sufficiently class-conscious and who had already gravitated toward class struggle. Once that stage had been reached, antireligious propaganda would reinforce class struggle: "Antireligious propaganda should be subordinated to the class struggle and not vice versa."[15]

This could be one of the reasons that little propaganda was produced at first, and what was produced got off to a bumpy start. To move the process along, the Commissariat of Justice set up a special section ominously called the Liquidation Commission, headed by Peter Krasikov, to handle antireligious propaganda. Among its other duties it published a limited number of books and pamphlets, though few of these actually reached the masses. Mikhail Gorev, Krasikov's colleague and the party's "theological expert," suggested that the Commissariat of Justice publish an atheistic journal. His brainchild, *Revolution and the Church*, pushed for acceptance of church and state separation and urged an anticlerical attitude by offering examples of church collusion with the White Armies. Krasikov took Lenin's "moderate" line in the first issue, arguing that the excesses of the French Revolution proved that creating priestly martyrs was inimical to long-term success. This periodical, though, was targeted more at those who would spread the propaganda than at those on the receiving end. Only twelve issues in small print-runs appeared over the next several years.[16] It was more useful to historians in understanding the government's intentions than it was in directly converting the masses.

Another sign of initial propaganda weakness was the tendency to resort to crude and transparent newspaper stories, such as the one in a 1919 issue of the Red Army's *Krasnaya Gazeta* titled "Christ—the Bolshevik." Christ was portrayed as complaining that the people were no longer listening to him, so he was going to turn the people over to the Bolsheviks for their moral lessons. It is difficult to understand how anyone could have been swindled out of his faith with such cheap tricks, yet it is even more difficult to understand how anyone within the party could have thought this effective.

The government would have to do better than this, as propaganda coming from the other side—in spite of efforts against it—was formidable. The churches were arguably better at this craft than the relatively neophyte Bolsheviks. Nikolai Krylenko acknowledged this while condemning Catholic priests (see chapter 21). He accused the clergy of ramming Catholic ideas into the heads of children from the age of seven—children "who are incapable of forming a reasoned judgment on the subject in which they are instructed." They "catch them fast from tender years in tentacles from which not everyone has the strength to free himself afterwards."[17] Other Communists were also sure that the church had the upper hand in this contest. The 1922 antireligious pamphlet *Summary of the Argument in the Living Church* explained:

> The discipline of the church can be compared only with the most severe discipline of an army. The Christian Church, through its bishops, clergymen, and deacons, has a large opportunity for propaganda, not only among the large groups present at sermons, but also for individual propaganda, through permanent contacts with communicants. Our agitators and organizers have nothing of the kind because they have not the daily close connections with the people that the church has.[18]

Recognition of the party's second-rate capability was a stimulus toward improvement, as was the controversy over the New Economic Policy. As mentioned earlier, not all party members were happy about Lenin's "blasphemous" emphasis on profit incentives to boost production, and many argued that easing up on the bourgeoisie would—given the bourgeois nature of religion—set the stage for a religious comeback (as was occurring). Thus the March 1921 Tenth Party Congress resolved to launch a vigorous antireligious crusade to counterbalance and placate the NEP's critics.

> [We should] make accessible to the broadest masses knowledge of natural history by publishing newspapers, books, and textbooks, by a systematic series of lectures, and [by] the utilization of all modern means of mass communication.[19]

The congress did urge some subtlety and common sense in this utilization though, as the country was still in great turmoil. A resolution stated that antireligious workers should avoid any action that would give citizens at home or critics abroad any excuse to say that the Soviet government persecuted religion.[20]

During the church-valuables confiscation crisis of 1922 and the trials of clerical resisters, propaganda moved to a higher position on the party's priority list, and Lenin offered advice on how to carry it out. In his March 1922 article "On the Significance of Militant Materialism"—his last writing on religion—he castigated party and state agencies for their "extremely inept and unsatisfactory" methods and the bureaucratization of the entire antireligious campaign. He urged getting beyond "the boring, dry, nonillustrated expositions of Marxism" and creating materials more accessible to the masses.[21] Let's not put the audience to sleep!

During 1922 and 1923 Communist propagandists were still clarifying their position. It was important not to make the cause seem in any way amenable to or consistent with any theology or faith. The November 5, 1922, issue of *Pravda* elaborated:

> We must bear in mind that the Russian Communist Party has nothing whatever in common with any religious denomination. Communism, if it wants to be consequential and true to itself, that is really scientific communism, can be as little fitted to the most liberal Protestantism as to the most hidebound Orthodoxy.[22]

In April 1923 Lunacharsky explained to the Twelfth Party Congress that it was of no consequence if religion in general, or any particular religion, was true or false. Even if it were proven that a particular religion was rooted in fact, and God had truly inspired its founder, Communists would still need to scrutinize it. If its goals were found to be antagonistic to those of the new Soviet society, then antireligious propaganda would be used against it. He used a reptilian metaphor to make his point more striking: "We do not consider a snake innocuous because its bite is a fact, not a fiction."[23]

Soviet publications kept coming back to the theme that efforts to discredit religion often ended up strengthening it and giving ammunition to village priests. Once, for example, a young Communist climbed into a belfry to steal the clapper— a common and counterproductive prank—and in the process fell to the ground. The congregation considered his descent a miracle and their faith was buoyed.[24] Some antireligious policies were likewise having a counterproductive effect.

Something new and more effective was needed. The challenge of refining antireligious propaganda while keeping it effective came up at the 1923 congress. One resolution read, "Deliberately coarse methods do not hasten but instead hamper the liberation of the laboring masses from religious prejudices"[25]— enough offense had been given to the villagers. But crude and unsophisticated methods had the upside of being comprehensible to simple and unsophisticated minds. Besides, propagandists could be quite sophisticated in their use of crude methods. Their techniques often played upon social prejudices, vanities, and quirks of the peasant mentality. Clever slogans had their place in the countryside.

One technique, both crude and subtle, was to publish the prices priests charged for their services. For example, Soviet newspapers revealed that in the village of Medveditsa the priest collected a half pood* of rye for each christening and funeral and charged seven poods for each wedding. When one mother had no grain with which to pay, the priest refused to baptize her child.[26]

Any new approach would have to emphasize holding the interest of youth. If they could be won over to atheism, what difference would it make if the elderly

---

*One pood equals thirty-six pounds.

went to their graves confident in their faith? On May 15, 1923, *Pravda* advised lecturers to know their audience and adapt their presentations to it. Red Guards, youth, workers, and peasants should all be spoken to differently. Propagandists should avoid disputes and be careful not to hurt the religious feelings of the people they addressed. Lectures should be serious, not mocking or humiliating.

The party now discouraged spectacular displays of antireligious fervor, such as counter-Christmas and counter-Easter parades, and outlawed the burning of God in effigy, though it took a few years for this message to filter into rural regions where rebellious teenagers took the attitude of "any excuse for a party." Grigory Zinoviev warned:

> We shall pursue our attacks on Almighty God in due time and in an appropriate manner. We are confident that we shall subdue him in his empyrean [heaven]. We shall fight him wherever he hides himself, but we must go about such a question as antireligious propaganda more carefully in the future. Our campaign against God and religion must be carried out only in a pedagogic way, not by violence or force.[27]

More and more professional lecturers were trained, equipped, and inspired, then shipped off to rural areas to do slow, painstaking propaganda work on the village and individual level. They were expected to approach their audiences very carefully, not directly attacking God at all. Simple lessons in science and natural history would imperceptibly erode former superstitions. Formerly destructive propaganda would now become constructive.

By 1923 these lecturers frequently found themselves, upon arrival in a village, welcomed by a small group of atheists formed by the local soviet. The hosts would discuss with the visitors the appropriate techniques for use with this particular community. Where religious missionary work had been recent, as that conducted by Catholics around Smolensk in early 1923, Moscow would send out the best propagandists available. Occasionally progress exceeded expectations and the priest was driven out of the village. But there was at least one case in 1923 (and possibly more at other times) where the villagers turned on the lecturer and killed him. Such embarrassing incidents were never reported in the press.

DEBATES: LOGIC DID NOT MEAN VICTORY

We must not forget that the religious standpoint is for many, many peasants the very basis of their whole ideology. If you pull one screw, one stone, one brick out of this edifice, the whole building will become unstable. The believer begins to ask other questions which are connected with his religious viewpoint.

—Yaroslavsky, *Revolution and Culture*, 1928

Although the antireligious campaign had a theoretically high priority, in practice the party reserved its best workers for more urgent needs and sent agents of lesser abilities into the countryside to preach against God. The historian Robert Conquest called the propagandists in the field "thoroughly second-rate people, not thought suitable for more concrete work and qualifying only by adequate fanaticism and willingness to intrude."[28] In 1922, 93 percent of party members had only a primary-school education; a mere six-tenths of 1 percent had any university or other higher-educational training.[29] It was the second-raters from this pool who became antireligious propagandists. Although only a small percentage was illiterate, internal party surveys showed that large majorities of antireligious workers were "politically illiterate," having only a "slogan-level" understanding of basic party tenets.[30] Many had narrow, parochial outlooks and were only dimly aware of events outside their own country. They had seen backwardness and corruption at the parish level and had been instructed that Christianity was evil; now they attributed sinister motives to every Christian with whom they came in contact. Yet these people were explaining religion and atheism to a generally hostile audience.

Antireligious workers in cities and towns across Russia had little stomach for the tedious and time-consuming—but necessary—job of sitting with individual believers in reading rooms and slowly picking away at their well-encrusted faith. Instead they did little between "events" (remember criticisms of Komsomol laziness discussed in the previous chapter).

The premier event was a debate on religion, attended by a large audience in a concert hall, university auditorium, or even an open field. Some debates lasted six hours a day and went on for two days, with thousands of people in attendance.[31] The Bolsheviks tried to pack the audience with their supporters, and there was initial booing of the Christian apologists, but—according to religious observers—the audience would often turn to the side of the church, especially when the quality of church speakers was high and atheist agitators low. The historian Glennys Young described these events as "a face-to-face confrontation between an often motley contingent of *bezbozhniki* on the one hand and clergy and lay activists on the other."[32] The few high-quality debates were between Yaroslavsky, Lunacharsky, or Krasikov on the state's side and Archpriest Vedensky, Professor Pavel Florensky, or V. Martinskovsky on the church side.[33] It was in a debate between Lunacharsky and Vedensky that the latter uttered his famous phrase: "Marxism is simply the Gospel rewritten in atheist script."[34]

What attracted the government to debates was the opportunity for direct confrontation with religious "class enemies." The usual procedure was a series of rapid-fire questions addressed to the priest or a lay member of the audience designed to show that the church advocate could not provide empirical and scientific evidence supporting religious claims. Provocative banners were carried around the stage with slogans extolling science and challenging whether Christ had ever lived.[35]

What party and government speakers were not interested in was subjecting themselves to debates in the Western sense of a fair exchange of ideas with equal time for both sides. A propaganda circular, written for party members' eyes only, advised:

> In many a case the comrades had proposed to our opponents to arrange disputes on equal footing. This tendency to regard the priests as an equal party in the dispute is nothing short of democratic vomiting, betraying an opportunist inclination towards freedom: we give no freedom to obscurants and never acknowledge their right to obscure the conscience of the masses.
>
> We allow them to speak at the "workers" meetings not in order to "seek the truth," but merely in order to divulge their lies. "Dispute for the sake of dispute" is a foreign, democratic formula. We go to the disputes only on the condition that they serve as an instrument for our class objects, helping to strengthen the class conscience of the proletariat.
>
> Otherwise we must not give in; we must not give to our enemies, for the sake of "abstract" justice, the opportunity to fight about the truth. We know on whose side the truth is, and in this matter we want no assistance from the priestcraft.[36]

In spite of their efforts to stack the cards in their favor, the party did not always "win" debates when the criterion for victory was crowd reaction. Donald Lowrie witnessed a Bolshevik-instigated face-off in Yaroslavl during Easter Week, 1919. A Communist orator spoke of the "Christ Myth," explaining that, though Jesus was indeed the first communist, he was still but a man and could perform no miracles. The audience politely applauded. The second speaker was a Jewish woman who debunked the story of Christ's birth from the Virgin Mary, claiming that she was merely a "woman of the streets." Applause was more subdued for this presentation. Then a senior priest of the town rose to speak and uttered only the words, "Christ is risen." The crowd responded in thunderous applause, surging toward the priest, repeating the holy words. After three repetitions, the priest quieted the crowd and asked: "What more is there to say? Let us go to our homes." The debate adjourned.[37]

Often the government's contestants were amateurs who were either unduly sophisticated or unduly crude. When they read philosophical passages, the audience was left in confusion. When they demanded that the priest produce a miracle on the spot, they were ridiculed. When poorly educated and ill-prepared government debaters could not answer questions posed by priests, the audience would erupt in raucous laughter, leaving the antireligious spokesman humiliated. Maurice Hindus met a priest who described one such embarrassment: The party speaker was describing the strength of man to build and create. The priest then asked him why, if man was so powerful, he had not invented sunshine and rain and the stars in the sky. Nature created them, replied the party man. The priest then challenged him as to who made nature, since all things must have a maker. His opponent could only answer "Nature made nature," which evoked hilarity among the audience.[38]

Lunacharsky arranged for an exchange with Father Hotovitsky of the Church of the Savior in Moscow in 1921. (This was an anecdote circulating in the capital whose veracity cannot be confirmed.) Hotovitsky had asserted the omnipresence of God, and Lunacharsky challenged him: "You say that God is everywhere. Now you will surely admit that one could imagine a small box somewhere without God being in the box." The priest retorted, "Why suppose an imaginary box when we have you, Mr. Commissar?"[39]

When he scheduled a series of debates with Professor Martinskovsky, an Orthodox lecturer in ethics at the University of Samara, Lunacharsky seemed to tolerate "an equal footing," but when he lost the first debate he canceled those remaining. Martinskovsky was arrested (for the second time) in late 1922 and, with the following words from his prosecutor, was expelled from the country:

> We know you are not a political enemy. . . . We know you as a sincere man dedicated to your ideas of God. But your work is harmful to us. You attract the intelligentsia. . . . In about three years, when our workers have become wiser, you may return to Russia with your religious preaching.[40]

But he was never allowed to come back.

Regardless of audience reaction, the Soviet press usually claimed victory in these debates and often alleged that after being oratorically trounced the outclassed priests abandoned their calling. Internally, however, there was criticism. The Central Committee's Agitprop Department complained in October 1923, "Debates . . . are transforming our battle with religion into a sport."[41] Nonetheless, they continued; in 1929 Yaroslavsky was still complaining to the League of Militant Atheists that government debaters needed better preparation.[42]

What other propaganda techniques did the government utilize? And how did believers resist?

A BANDAGE OVER THE EYES OF MAN

Propaganda Vehicles and Techniques

In September 1928, as he was turning to increased administrative violence, Joseph Stalin met with a group of visiting American workers and, in response to a question, issued this implied complaint about slow progress:

> Have we suppressed reactionary clergy? Yes, we have suppressed them. The trouble is that they are not yet completely liquidated. Antireligious propaganda is the means that ought to bring to a head the liquidation of the reactionary clergy.[1]

What were the propaganda techniques that were apparently having such little success?

THE USES OF FINE ARTS

Theater, concerts, moving pictures, radio, visits to museums, richly illustrated scientific and especially antireligious lectures, well-arranged periodical and nonperiodical children's literature—all this must be set in motion, developed, completed, or created for the great objective of most quickly transforming the whole growing generation into an absolutely atheistic one.[2]

—Lunacharsky, *Pravda*, March 26, 1929

Theater: The Trials of God

George Plekhanov thought that religion was a simple matter of ignorance and believed it could be eliminated by aesthetics—especially music, theater, and painting. Well before the actual administrative closing of church buildings, he urged that churches be transformed into theaters for the edification of the people.

346

It was fitting, he said, because religion was created through ample use of the imagination and was itself a form of art. As for Lenin, he enjoyed some plays and thought others a waste of time, but he once told Kalinin that no single institution except the theater could replace religion in Russia.[3]

In his mid-1920s travels through Russia, Maurice Hindus observed the love of the people for theater, though the facilities might be primitive and the staging crude. In 1914 there had been only 210 theaters in the whole country, but by 1920 there were 6,000, with more on the way. Many theaters became vehicles for atheistic propaganda. The government opened the Atheist Theater in Moscow in November 1923, its avowed mission being to expose as shams all religion from the pagans to the present. Its manager boasted that it was "the only one in the world" to produce solely antireligious plays, but it showed only two plays—*Tarquin the High Priest* and *Torquemada the Inquisitor*—before it folded six months later from lack of attendance. (The government, understandably, enjoyed retelling stories of the Inquisition through any media.) Mikhail Gorev attended opening night of *Tarquin* and was somewhat embarrassed by the awkward amateurishness of the performers.[4] In the excerpt that follows, the cast includes a priest, an old woman, the prophet Moses, God, the Devil, two Jews, a Young Pioneer, a Komsomol officer, and a chorus of angels.

The old woman speaks coarsely and is depicted as ignorant in her acceptance of God, yet she asks the priest how the world could have been created in six days, as stated in Scripture. The priest responds by quoting from the Book of Genesis. Then the scene shifts to Mt. Sinai, where Moses stands with the Tablets of the Law, facing two Jews who have been sent to find him. Moses claims to be preparing to converse with God, but when the Jews ask if they, too, might talk with God, Moses replies that all others must cover their faces or they will be blinded. Once he is sure that they cannot see, Moses improvises a conversation by changing his voice to play both parts. The next scene (not in very good order) is in Heaven, where God performs the successive acts of creation. He is made to appear as blundering and stupid, while the Devil has a little more common sense. Then the following conversation takes place:

Komsomol officer: It appears from this play that God created everything at the suggestion of the Devil, for some reason or other. He created the grass because there was nowhere to sit down. He created the stars to decorate the old wooden firmament, and finally he tried to create man to rule over the beasts. There's nothing like this in the Bible, comrades. According to the Bible, comrades, God created everything for no purpose at all, visible or invisible, except that you might live well. And it couldn't be otherwise, for primitive imagination created God. Yes, comrades, God didn't create man, but man, primitive man, created God. But swindling priests like Moses or this priest here used all these facts to oppress the illiterate, ignorant workers. The world was created quite differently. The world was created not in six or seven days, but in many, many millions of years.

Priest (angry): But tell me, sir comrade, whatever created itself? And you say man descended from a monkey [winking at the audience].

Old woman: Holy Mother of God!

Komsomol officer: The world and life on Earth and man, all these are parts of one whole. This whole is called: the eternal cosmic motion in space. But let us see, father priest, how your God created man?

God (morosely): Let us create man in our image and likeness. . . . [From an opening emerges an almost naked, hairy man.]

Chorus of Angels: Man, O man, immortal never, be our willing slave forever.

Komsomol officer: What's this? A man or a woman?

God: I don't know.

Komsomol officer: Yes, comrades. In the first chapter of the Bible nothing is said of this. Most likely this creature was sexless. But in the second chapter of the Book of Genesis, it is said that man was created first and then woman from his rib. The one piece of nonsense contradicts the other.

And this is quite intelligible. Moses did not write the Bible by himself. He may never even have existed. The learned representatives of the classes in power wrote the Bible from one tribe to another. They added one thing to another, inventing combinations of folk tales and fables. . . .

But the really offensive thing, comrades, is the fact that among us now in the Soviet Union are people who believe in this nonsense. They have before their eyes the splendid achievements created by the liberated proletariat. The proletariat says, "Let there be light," and electric light shines not only in the towns but in the dark, downtrodden villages. The proletariat says, "Let there be plants in the dusty villages," and on the squares rise green paths and garden plots. The proletariat says "We shall create a warrior equipped from head to foot with science," and this man already exists; he is already growing up, he is around us.

[During this extensive speech God, the Devil, and the Angels disappear from the scene. The Young Pioneer comes out from behind the lectern and stands behind the Komsomol officer.]

And the proletariat says, "Be ready to take our places, to destroy the old world, to break the accursed yoke of capital, and to build a new world for a new, free humanity. Be prepared, comrade, eventually to subdue nature to yourself, to dominate it and compel it to serve your aims. Be prepared to conquer blind destiny, fate, and providence. Be prepared to conquer death itself, to subject the movements of the Earth to your control and after that all motion in universal space." And now what does the young comrade have to say in reply?

Young Pioneer: Always prepared.

Komsomol officer: And you, black face [priest], when will you perish from our city? Only when there shall be no more illiterates in our towns and villages; then you will flee to Hell along with your [God] and Devil.[5]

Whatever appeal these plays may have had, it was certainly not their literary style. Some attended for entertainment value (enjoying their iconoclasm) or for the allusions to the real accomplishments of the Soviet people, of which they were proud. Their biblical criticism was very crude but, as has been mentioned earlier, was on an appropriate level for the viewers. Overall, though, antireligious theater never caught on.

Films

During the early to mid-1920s, motion pictures were also milked for their propaganda value. The government's Cinema Department produced *The Miracle Maker* (1922), *Holy Griasnov, The Feast of St. Georgeus, Behind the Convent Walls*, and *The Cross and the Mauser.* The latter was directed against Catholics by depicting their murderous pogroms and a degenerate, foreign Catholic priest whipping a Russian woman. Nowhere near enough antireligious films were available, however, and early efforts, as with plays, were crude, with protagonists and antagonists utterly unconvincing on the screen. Monks and nuns were portrayed as depraved or idiotic, and priests did little but plot counterrevolution. In other words, these films were anticlerical rather than exposing the social roots of religion.[6]

Nonetheless, Trotsky championed the cinema as the proper propaganda vehicle for an "unthinking peasantry," not so much because of its potential for a powerful message but because of its diversionary capacity:

Meaningless ritual, which lies on the consciousness like an inert burden, cannot be destroyed by criticism alone; it can be supplanted by new forms of life, new amusements, new and more cultured theaters. Thoughts go naturally to the most powerful—because it is the most democratic—instrument of the theater: the cinema. . . . The cinema amuses, educates, strikes the imagination by images, and liberates you from the need of crossing the church door.[7]

Before the complexity of the problem began to dawn on him, Trotsky seemed to think that moving pictures were *all* that was needed to solve the "peasant religious problem." (He also believed they might bring in much-needed revenue.) The 1928 party conference, however, disparaged these early efforts and asked screenwriters to opt for a subtler approach. Then the Cinema Department rolled out less entertaining but more edifying films, such as *Man and the Ape* and *The Mechanism of the Brain.*[8]

Graphic Arts

Soviet art was carefully positioned to replace church art—and the ikons in the home. The dark interiors of Russian churches sparkled mysteriously with light and color. Candles reflected off vestments, gilded crosses, and draperies. So, too, ikons in the home contrasted with the dull and bare walls of the average peasant's dwelling. The new art of "Soviet realism" provided replacement color and a new moral message. With vivid hues and large splashes of color, Soviet posters in the new style proudly portrayed Bolshevik leaders and the Red Army in action. One poster merged two themes: "Guard Your Children against Religion and Alcohol" and featured an obviously inebriated priest. Science penetrated these corners too, with pictures of dinosaurs emphasizing the Earth's age and illustrations of great apes, early man, and modern man to demonstrate humanity's origins. Many workers' homes actually had two devotional corners—the religious corner for the wife and the Lenin corner for the husband. Sometimes perplexed wives crossed themselves in front of "ikons" of Lenin or Bukharin. Unfortunately for the propagandists, two ikon corners often meant not that the husband had replaced his faith but rather that he had added to it. Pagan, then Christian, and now Communist symbols simply accumulated in his mind.[9]

Even with its bold colors, antireligious art was often crude in content. One portrayed the Virgin Mary obviously on the point of delivery, staring at a billboard on the subject of abortion. The poster's caption had her saying, "Oh, why didn't I know that before!"[10] An article in *Bezbozhnik* in May 1928 pleaded: "We are in want of antireligious pictures. They must be cheap, amusing, clear, and not uselessly complicated."[11] But there was no call for decency.

Music

This category of antireligious propaganda is included only because of the frustration in achieving it. Religion had Mozart's "Requiem," Bach's "Mattheus Passion," and the symphonies of Tchaikovsky, but antireligion had nothing.[12] The reason, of course, is that emotion is translatable into music while rationality is not. No modern composers, whether in Russia or elsewhere, have been able to compose atheistic music. This was a great disappointment.

THE USES OF SCIENCE

Science is the rapier with which they hope to cut through the intellectual fabric of religion. . . . They are spreading science with the zeal of missionaries distributing Bibles in heathen lands.[13]

—Maurice Hindus, 1929

The Application of Science

The Orthodox Church never developed the antipathy toward science that was characteristic of Catholicism. Although it harbored in its recesses a vast number of very unscientific notions, no member of the Orthodox Church, as long as he actually *attended church*, was ever harassed as a heretic merely because he held scientific views contrary to church dogma. There was no Russian Galileo.

For the Communist Party the active teaching of science was both highly educational in its own right and a surefire path to secularization, not to mention that it was true. Stalin told visiting American workers:

> The party . . . conducts antireligious propaganda against all religious prejudices because it stands for science, whereas religious prejudices run counter to science. . . . We have no need for the hypothesis of God. We are 100 percent for science, and science requires no faith.[14]

Nikolai Bukharin wrote in the *ABC of Communism* that scientific knowledge "slowly but surely undermines the authority of all religions."[15] If the falsehood of superstition could be demonstrated, then the whole structure of faith would crumble. There were two scientific approaches: anthropological science, which explained the origins of and similarities between religions, and natural science, whose mission was to explain everything about the mystery and meaning of life. Although emphasized for the first four years of Bolshevik rule, the anthropological approach was not going so well. The author of an *Izvestia* article in November 1922 summed up the problem:

[Many antireligious] agitators have been historical specialists who absolutely failed to realize that an audience in this country is anything but inclined to regard religion as a fit object for scientific examination.[16]

Regarding natural science, Komsomol village reading rooms were filled with leaflets, pamphlets, newspapers, and books on the simple principles of electricity, the working of tractor motors, the dangers of germs, and the source of weather. All this was antireligious propaganda. So, too, were pictures of gestation in the womb, the evolution of man, and the strata of rocks. History properly taught was also included in the category of science. Lenin was convinced that the propagation of science would overwhelm the propaganda of superstition. Information logically applied would turn the workers and peasants into materialists without them being aware of the incremental changes involved. When a new planetarium was built in Samara, the precise detail of the stars made the priest's mysterious description of the heavens look primitive.[17] Yaroslavsky wrote:

Religion acts as a bandage over the eyes of man, preventing him from seeing the world as it is. It is our task to tear off this bandage and to teach the masses of workers and peasants to see things correctly, to understand what does exist and what does not.[18]

An All-Russian Exposition was held in Moscow in 1923, highlighting the nation's products, but especially its applied science. Model irrigation systems were laid out for farmers to inspect, and plenty of the newest tractors were displayed.[19] Applied science was an unspoken indictment of the church's teachings. The introduction of tractors in the fields gave the tiller of the soil a sense of control that he had not known that he lacked. Mikhail Gorev explained in 1925 that modern agricultural techniques "would attract the sympathies of peasants to us one hundred times faster than ten disputes with priests."[20]

It was not just Christian teachings that applied science was to replace but also the pagan superstitions that had long ago merged with Christianity. In many regions of Russia a peasant would bury an effigy of a penis with his crops to ensure fertility. Once the peasant realized what *really* led to higher crop yields, he would no longer need the village priest or the village sorcerer. It must be mentioned, however, that there were some priests who worked with the government in trying to introduce modern agronomy into the villages. A few cases exist where antireligious activists were even willing to acknowledge this cooperation.[21]

In 1926 the government initiated radio propaganda, broadcasting from the Comintern station and provincial transmission facilities. Programs were of two types: current political and social events with antireligious morals, and short stories and popular songs broadcast on Sunday mornings to lure citizens away from church attendance.[22] But the mere fact that there was a radio—regardless of the message—was itself antireligious propaganda, as it projected the power of science. Even God could not talk to them in that way.

The government then pressed tractors and trains into atheistic service. Posters showed tractors in mortal combat with the cross, and at the start of the Five-Year Plan propagandists distributed the pamphlet *Prayers or Tractors?* (as if one could not have both). Perhaps some kind of crude dialectical synthesis was achieved when peasants began painting crosses on their tractors, and, when a new tractor arrived in a village, the priest held a thanksgiving service.[23] As for locomotives, the government sent "Agit-trains" like the Godless Express speeding across the expanses of Russia carrying the "Gospel" of an atheistic world.

Sometimes godless airplanes buzzed church bell towers during services. When one such plane was forced down by bad weather on a Sunday morning, causing the church to empty so that worshipers could see it, an antireligious propagandist boasted, "The aeroplane stopped the service."[24] But airplanes had an additional mission, revealed in the League's 1928 project to collect money to purchase an airplane to be named "The Godless."[25]

The Flight (1928)

As the plane's engine sputtered and then hummed, the poor muzhik was beside himself with terror. His fellow villagers watched with anticipation and some glee as Semyon Alexandrovich climbed into the rear seat of the Bolshoi Baltisky B, a biplane used as a trainer during the Great War. Once strapped in, he cupped his hands over his eyes. This flight was to be a first in aviation history.

Semyon didn't understand the full import of what was happening; all he knew was that the pilot had appeared in his village with two government agents and instructed him, as village elder, to take this ride. He had seen planes soaring overhead, of course, and knew that people flew in them, but no one from his village near Voronezh had ever been inside one or even known anyone who had. The pilot and his assistants informed these peasants that the purpose of this little adventure was to "discredit superstition."

As the plane taxied down a well-worn dirt road, Semyon managed a feeble wave to his friends and family, unsure if he would ever see them again. The plane circled like a rising hawk on a thermal, since to fly away would remove the desired impression on those below. Semyon felt the queasiness of vertigo as his village receded below. He had been instructed to observe everything carefully, and his natural leadership abilities now called him to duty.

The pilot knew why the flight had been postponed for several days, but the passenger did not. They needed clouds, and now they were about to penetrate one.

The plane disappeared into the white mist and then emerged above. With his head in his hands, Semyon watched carefully, having no idea what he was supposed to see. After about ten minutes at maximum altitude there was a slow descent to the ground and a rough landing.

Every single one of the 143 villagers old enough or young enough to walk surrounded the two adventurers. Although a little unsteady, Semyon radiated pride in accomplishment. The two antireligious propagandists jostled their way through the crowd, then one, in a voice loud enough for all to hear, asked Semyon if he had spied any angels up there. He had to admit that he hadn't. Did you see the prophet Elijah? Semyon shook his suddenly confused head. Heaven? No. Your Christian God himself? Not really.

Then, the propagandist inquired, where could all these so-called heavenly personages possibly be? The villagers, though always having looked skyward in their prayers and imagination, were hardly convinced. One speculated that God may be invisible to the human eye, another offered that perhaps he had hidden from that monstrous contraption rudely sent into his sphere. A discussion followed with distribution of some pamphlets. Perhaps that was all the propagandists could hope for. Food and tea were served to the strangers and lodging provided for the night; then they flew off to the next village.

One might think that the Communist agitators would have had a more sophisticated sense of religion, even if they were denying it. But their propaganda was heavily influenced by their recent experiences in their own villages or the stories that grandmother had told in their childhood. Their antireligious sense was just as primitive as the peasants' religious one, and demonstrating that God was *not* hiding behind the clouds seemed perfectly reasonable. Flights such as these continued well into the 1930s.[26]

A danger inherent in the peeking-behind-the-clouds tactic was plane crashes. The Soviets were about to exploit their first stratospheric flight in October 1933, when the experimental plane suddenly crashed. Many ordinary citizens considered the death of the three pilots to have been divine punishment for invading God's space.[27] (The launching of *Sputnik* in October 1957 also had a partial antireligious purpose in exposing the religious emptiness of the heavens. How well this worked is hard to say. One post-*Sputnik* visitor to the Moscow Planetarium said, "Well, well, who would have believed how wisely God has organized the world."[28] But Soviet scholars also reported this comment made by a peasant during the early 1960s: "For a long time I was religious, but now I don't know what to be. They launched the *Sputnik*, and they did not find God.")[29]

THE USES OF HEALTH

The ikon on Barricade Street is kissed by thousands of passersby, the sick, the syphilitic, the consumptive, and the healthy.[30]

—Yaroslavsky, *Trud*, September 18, 1927

Soviet propaganda placed a heavy emphasis on the association between communism and health and between religion and disease. A rudimentary understanding of medicine and bodily functions would go a long way toward eliminating dependence on that aspect of Christianity that was still rooted in sorcery, especially concerning the birth of a baby. Thus teaching hygiene was propaganda against the church. Agitators would ask: "Why have hundreds of you used the same communion spoon? Don't you realize that you may be spreading typhoid, diphtheria, tuberculosis, or syphilis?"[31] Yaroslavsky tore into the unhygienic aspects of the christening ceremony:

> Not only are we prepared to prove that the mortality and diseases among baptized children are no less than among the unbaptized, we further maintain that where ignorant priests baptize, where the font is not kept clean and the priest himself has insufficient regard for personal cleanliness, the font is actually a source of disease and infection.[32]

Another more specious claim was the ill effects of contact with stagnant holy water (though it was not drunk).

Religious fasting, it was repeatedly pointed out, would weaken the body and the ability to fight off sickness. There were six-week fasts before Easter (Lent) and Christmas, a four-week Fast of the Holy Apostles, several weeklong fasts, and a one-day fast every Wednesday and Friday. Among an already undernourished population, such privation could lead to malnutrition, anemia, night blindness, and, of course, the primary concern: lost productivity.[33]

Soviet efforts to vaccinate the population against smallpox, diphtheria, and other communicable diseases, though intended purely as a public health service, became antireligious propaganda when health workers had to confront ignorant religious leaders who spread rumors far and wide that "vaccination was the seal of Antichrist." In 1919 Bishop Viktor of Ufa told believers that a typhus epidemic raging through the area was God's punishment for the sins of the Bolsheviks. When a smallpox epidemic broke out in the Ural Mountain region, Old Believers refused inoculations on these grounds.[34]

There existed, however, a weakness in the argument. Many Communist-run facilities were filthy, and some churches, especially Protestant ones, were way ahead of the government in the campaign for clean living. Many factories operated workers' housing that was not far removed from sardines in a can, and in their dormitories the younger, presumably more "proletarian," workers lived in drunken filth while older, religious workers practiced sobriety and cleaned up after themselves. Many churches had small medical clinics attached to them, and many priests and ministers counseled against smoking, drinking, and casual sex while nagging their congregations about washing their hands before eating.[35]

Nonetheless, a cartoon in *Godless at the Workbench* offered a kind of reverse exorcism by picturing a peasant sneezing out of his nose not only devils but also priests and saints. A party man standing next to him shouts, "Good health."[36]

THE USES OF CAPITALISM

No number of pamphlets and no amount of preaching can enlighten the proletariat if it is not enlightened by its own struggle against the dark forces of capitalism.

—Lenin, 1905

Antireligious agitators made heavy use of the "capitalistic nature" of the Orthodox Church, citing not only the church's wealth but also the source of that wealth. Bukharin claimed that in 1903, St. Petersburg churches and monasteries owned 266 rent-producing properties in the form of houses and shops, and Moscow churches owned 1,054 rent-producing houses plus 32 hotels. And then there was the land, which amounted to somewhere between 5 million and 7 million acres. The church also made money from the sale of ikons and candles. The government informed its citizens that the *real* trinity in tsarist times, though less mysterious than the original, had been the collusion between state, church, and the capitalist class, each supporting the other and each benefiting from the other.

Antireligious lecturers relied heavily on the fundamental Marxist argument that religion was a tool of capitalists in their suppression of workers and peasants. Since it was true that the Orthodox Church had been funded by the tsarist state, had worked hand-in-glove with the state in beating down any progressive or liberating reforms, and had been subservient to state interests, this argument was an easy sell to any mildly receptive audience. The journalist Louis Fischer observed, "All Communist antireligious propaganda rests on the premise that . . . the machinery of the church is a tool created and maintained by the capitalists in order to further enslave the peasants and workers."[37]

THE USES OF CHESS

Yes, chess! Since at least the time of Peter the Great, chess had been a pastime for the educated class. Both Marx and Lenin were players. The Bolsheviks recognized chess's usefulness early, seeing it as a political weapon to raise the intellectual and cultural level of workers' minds. Due to the complete rationality of play, it was also useful in the struggle against superstition—"a living piece of propaganda against religious delusion." Nikolai Krylenko, the notorious prosecutor, became the game's most enthusiastic promoter and was appointed chairman of the All-Union Chess Section in 1924. In Leningrad alone, registered players rose from 1,000 in 1923 to 140,000 in 1928. There was a slight setback, however, when Alexander Alekhine became Russia's first world champion in 1927, then proceeded to denounce the Soviet regime.[38]

ANTIRELIGIOUS MUSEUMS

After 1924 antireligious museums were springing up in closed churches and monasteries all over Russia. Fyodor Oleshchuk claimed that by 1928 there were such museums in twenty provinces, and St. Isaak's Cathedral and the Kazan Cathedral in Leningrad, the St. Sergius-Trinity Monastery in Zagorsk, and the Pechora Monastery in Kiev were now serving this purpose. When St. Isaak's became an antireligious museum, the curator had an immense Foucault pendulum hung from the dome to convince science-starved Russians that the Earth rotated on its axis.[39]

The pinkish church of the Strastnoy Monastery in central Moscow opened in November 1929 as the Central Antireligious Museum. It emphasized the conflict between science and religion, the common origin of all religions, and the hand-in-glove relationship between the Orthodox Church and the monarchy. Well-trained guides took visitors to the Science Room, where they could examine detailed yet clear models of human embryology and anatomy. Then they were ushered to a room full of copies of old manuscripts, illustrations, and charts demonstrating different faiths' common origins. The room also contained examples of idols, totems, and crosses from Africa, the South Seas, and Babylon. Church-state connections were demonstrated by exhibitions revealing the wealth of the tsars and the monasteries: photographs of the tsarina's precious fur robes, monastic land inventories, church collection plates, and candles sold to poor pilgrims. The museum laid out the "relics" of ancient saints side-by-side with mummified cats, dogs, and rabbits, showing how the mummification process could preserve any living thing, not just those that God protected. The guide then led visitors to the sectarian section (in a back room), which featured purloined correspondence with foreign capitalists and appeals for money from Western sources. During its first year this museum claimed 235,000 visitors.[40]

By the end of the decade there were forty-four antireligious museums spanning the whole of the Soviet Union.[41]

INFORMERS AND TURNCOAT PRIESTS

As we have seen, neither the party nor the government interpreted the separation of church and state to mean keeping their noses out of church affairs—quite the contrary. Separation was pushed aside when it came to obtaining useful information from within the churches, the government busily recruited and cultivated informers from within the ranks of the clergy. The Cheka and its successor secret police agencies played upon the weaknesses of the priests—and sometimes their physical hunger—to search out information that would not be voluntarily turned over. But it was not just fear and hunger that turned the priests; often it was an appeal to their vanity or their ambition; career advancement could be facilitated or favorite projects implemented.

Cheka agents were encouraged to get close to the religious world to uncover the idiosyncrasies and character (or lack of it) of each "servitor of the cult." They handed out bribes, opened their mail, and searched their residences. A secret police report called bribes "subsidies" and concluded that this "will tie [the priest] to us and to a new relationship, indeed a relationship where he becomes an eternal slave of the Cheka, fearing the unmasking of his activity."[42]

An October 1924 OGPU top-secret internal circular ordered district executive committees around Moscow to bring priests whose names were on a list to a covert meeting at its counterintelligence department. The order was followed by the comment "True, we trust these insurgents in cassocks little, but for mutual control their information is extremely necessary." Ordinary believers were also recruited to spy on their churches and monitor sermons, and the circular called for an increase in the number of these secret informants.[43]

There were some, however, who voluntarily transcended the role of mere informer. Some Living Church priests sought Communist Party membership *as members of the clergy*. Yaroslavsky thought it bizarre that they should have troubled to apply and declared that they had all been turned away.[44] There were others who were not priests but came from clerical families, including Fyodor Oleshchuk and Peter Krasikov, who maintained party membership in good standing. But our concern here is with those who shed their cassocks and then sought membership in the Communist Party (or perhaps the League of the Godless). The government was willing to accommodate—or use—them, just as during the early 1920s it needed to rely on tsarist army officers and prerevolutionary factory managers ("bourgeois specialists") to keep the military and the economy functional. But, while former army officers and managers were nonideological, priests were not, and employing them endangered ideological purity. It seemed hypocritical to many.

It soon became clear, however, that employing city-bred antireligious workers to rant and rave against the church in the countryside was not going to suffice. The party was incapable of running an antireligious operation without the expertise of former priests; propagandists with insight into both biblical teaching and the intricacies of church ritual were indispensable. It was not only the former clergy's inside knowledge of the enemy but also their literacy and public speaking abilities. Turncoat priests could make antireligious propaganda plausible,[45] and they would be needed until the Bolsheviks had recruited and trained sufficient working-class and peasant cadres to competently handle these jobs, which would take a decade or more. (Bolshevik utilization of converted clergy is reminiscent of Lenin's comment about hanging Western capitalists with their own rope.)

Why would a priest become not just an informer but also a propagandist for atheism? Part of the answer lay in the undercurrent of disbelief that ran through the church's major theological academies at the turn of the century. Many young men who had entered these schools in tsarist times had come from clerical families and were legacies to the church—their occupations virtually hereditary. But their ideological commitment to the church was tenuous at best—a religious surface but a core full of doubt. Many were easily swayed by Communist ideology, which seemed full of great intentions. Other persuasive pressures were their need for personal safety and the chance to work. By the early 1920s, remaining in the priesthood was bad for one's long-term health. Many, as we have seen, were arrested, exiled, or shot—and in some cases all three. Although former priests would always be suspect, at least cooperation was a step in the direction of longevity. As priests they were considered social and economic parasites; giving *anti*religious lectures was at least considered an honest day's work (and deserving of a food ration card). And, as with the informers, the self-importance of being chosen played a role.

The most influential ex-priest in the antireligious campaign was Mikhail Gorev. He never experienced a socialist epiphany but rather moved gradually from disillusionment with religion toward expanding radicalism, leading to a final break and apostasy. Gorev had been ordained in St. Petersburg in 1913, and by 1914 he was already denouncing Russia's participation in the Great War. During the First Church Sobor, which spanned the November Revolution, he remained outside the convocation, berating the delegates for not going far enough in separating church and state. The government was gracious enough to print his antisobor tirades in *Pravda* and invited him to work on the government commission drafting the separation decree, where he provided valuable assistance. He then published the newspaper *The Banner of Christ* (*Znamia Khrista*), in which he harshly criticized the new Patriarch and his policies.[46]

Gorev anguished, however, over how far he should go. He wrote to his mentor Vladimir Bonch-Bruevich in May 1918 lamenting the violence and extremism he had witnessed in the implementation of the separation decree. At this stage in his development he was hoping for a smaller and simpler apostolic Orthodox Church far removed from politics. In June he took the position of deputy director of the Commissariat of Justice's church-state relations department, and in January 1919 he defrocked himself and joined the Communist Party. Between 1918 and 1921 he traveled through rural areas resolving issues over compliance with the separation decree as well as participating in the exposure of church relics. He also headed the editorial board of *Revolution and the Church* until 1924.[47]

In 1922, at the height of his career, Gorev was appointed to the party commission handling the confiscation of church valuables for famine relief, and *Izvestia* carried his attack on "counterrevolutionary" church leaders who seemed reluctant to contribute. He edited the twenty-four issues of *Science and Religion* (*Nauka i Religiya*) that appeared in major cities during 1922 and in December became coeditor (with Yaroslavsky) of *Bezbozhnik*. Between 1924 and 1926 he served as deputy chairman of the League of the Godless, but in April 1926 he was removed from his position for reasons unknown; little was heard of him again.[48] Nonetheless, it remains a remarkable career for a former priest in an atheistic state.

Gorev was not the only turncoat; Ivan Brikhnichev, the ex-renovationist Sergei Kalinovsky, and dozens of lesser-known former priests rose to positions of influence in the Soviet antireligious establishment. Kalinovsky petitioned the Thirteenth Party Congress in 1924:

> No one can be as useful in this work as one who was a *pop* [derogatory term for a village priest], who knows all of religion's weak points, who is familiar with all of the underhanded work of churchmen.[49]

The party accepted the contributions of both, but Brikhnichev was removed from his duties on the League's staff in October 1925 for Judeophobic outbursts against Yaroslavsky, and Kalinovsky was booted out in 1927, possibly for the sexually explicit examples he used in an antireligious lecture in Uglich.

Turncoat priests were in a delicate position, barely tolerated by either side. N. Voinov, a priest turned antireligious propagandist from the Ukraine, was bitter:

> No matter how much antireligious literature I have read, I have never seen one line even obliquely defending those who had broken with religion. . . . This situation is extremely insulting for those who have sincerely broken with religion and who have explained the full absurdity of it to the masses. . . . Even if a former "servitor of the cult" actively conducts antireligious work, he feels shunned.[50]

Concern for ideological purity and worry about class background was turning away people who should have been given a red-carpet treatment.

Later, when more time could be devoted to antireligious propaganda and it became a higher priority, all Orthodox apostates were swallowed up. Already in the summer of 1927 Anton Loginov, the League's deputy chairman, roundly reprimanded the lower echelons for continuing the practice of employing former priests, writing that he had "no sympathy towards priests defrocking themselves and offering their services for godlessness." By 1929 this practice was officially dead, though isolated instances of ex-priestly participation continued unofficially into the 1930s.[51]

ATHEIST PUBLISHING AND PRESS

With all my heart I wish Bezbozhnik *new victories in the coming year—victories over the hideous specter of god, who has in truth inflicted diabolical evil on mankind throughout the whole course of history.*

—Lunacharsky

The Bolsheviks had been publishing antireligious literature since at least 1906; this included *The Ten Commandments of a Social Democrat* in that year and Yaroslavsky's *The Catechism of a Soldier* the following year. The latter tore into the tsarist army's use of chaplains to convince troops that God was on their side and the tsarist government's manipulation of Christ's teaching to suppress worker uprisings.[52]

Postrevolutionary publishing got off to a resounding start when Bukharin's *Program of the Communists (Bolsheviks)* sold a million copies in Russia within three months of its 1918 publication.[53] But many early antireligious publications were tentative in the extreme, which seems odd in light of the passions of the times. A book published in Moscow in 1919 spouted the Godbuilders' message that, while the government opposed the church, communism had much in common with the teachings of Jesus:

> Jesus devoted his time directly to the workingmen and the poor, grouping them about himself. We know how he loved the children. When they came to him and the Apostles forbade them, he said, "Suffer the little children to come unto me and forbid them not." In the same way in the Soviet Republic we say that the children are our best friends. They are the first in our thoughts and plans. We find ourselves also in agreement with Jesus in his attitude toward women.[54]

Well into 1922 even this type of literature was in short supply, though Lenin pushed and prodded to have something done about it.

The answer was *Ateist*, a nonparty publishing house created right after the Tenth Party Congress in the spring of 1921, which specialized in translations of bourgeois atheists and free thinkers. At great expense during a time of economic crisis, it completely rewrote and published new school texts with all references to religion excised.[55] At about this time *Ateist* translated Sinclair Lewis's *Elmer Gantry* and John Steinbeck's *Grapes of Wrath* into Russian, along with other Western books that reflected badly on religion or capitalism. Lenin, however, was highly critical of the lack of Marxist commentary in the new publications—strange for a leader who often said that his people should read widely and that man could not live by Marx alone. Reiterating advice that he had offered since at least 1905, he suggested in 1922 that the eighteenth-century materialist writers were far more fascinating and would be a thousand times as effective as the "dull and dry paraphrases of Marxism" that were currently being printed.[56] Although in the West few besides historians read this material, he urged that it be translated, printed, and distributed cheaply for the benefit of the Russian people.

Russians themselves produced no antireligious works of scholarly value during the 1920s, but by the end of the decade they were producing plenty of bulk. By 1929 there were 1,200 antireligious book and pamphlet titles to choose from. The problem was not the printing—perhaps 40 million copies rolled off the presses—but the reading. Most of these publications were not purchased in bookstores but were sent out through government institutions to be placed on local agency bookshelves, where they sat without their covers ever being cracked.[57]

In the final months of 1922 came the first issue of the weekly newspaper *Bezbozhnik*, cited many times above. This mouthpiece for the League of the Godless was written to appeal to the peasant masses. Its early lack of sophistication was exemplified by its advertisements, one of which read: "Is there a God? Then whence came the Earth and the men and animals that dwell on it? Read *Bezbozhnik* and find out."[58] It targeted the peasantry and stressed natural science and milder criticism of religion so as not to offend its audience.

A bimonthly periodical, also named *Bezbozhnik*, was illustrated in color and was harsher. Mimicking the French Revolution, it dated its issues in terms of months and years since the November Revolution—the beginning of the New World. One of its cartoons depicted a young Communist telling a priest, "We live after Lenin." Editors instructed their correspondents to write in plain and simple language, include only one idea in an article, write positively of success stories, and include a hand-drawn picture or a photograph. On the full-page cover of (periodical) *Bezbozhnik*'s first issue was drawn a muscular worker climbing a ladder to heaven; below him lay destroyed churches and above him in the clouds hid various gods, fearful of his mighty hammer. He was out to destroy "the tsars of heaven" (see photo insert). A typical cartoon showed a grotesque monster labeled "Capital" being protected by a group of priests from attacks by workers. Another portrayed a priest blessing soldiers as they fired into a crowd of striking workers. Some graphics were grisly, such as a caricature of Christ being lowered from the cross and disemboweled. Ravenous men gnawed on his flesh, and one held a cup to catch his draining blood; the caption mocked the Eucharist: "This is my body; this is my blood."[59]

Bezbozhnik devoted a lot of space to satirizing the foibles of the clergy and pointing out how the Old Regime had degraded women. It also provided scientific explanations for all the forms of weather, which priests had claimed were the "will of God." Here are a few scenes from the newspaper in the spring of 1923:

- A front piece representing the Jewish, Christian, and Muslim deities sitting idly together—the first with one cyclopean eye and a vulgar combination of three fingers instead of a nose.
- A picture titled "The Miracle of Cana of Galilee" that showed Jesus making home brew instead of wine with a samovar still.
- A picture of angels stealing eggs, chickens, pigs, milk, and grain from peasants and conveying the loot to priests.

A single 1926 copy of *Bezbozhnik* revealed wide-ranging propaganda techniques:

- The horrendous tale of the "ikon of death," which the masses insisted on kissing during the plague of 1771, thus spreading the disease.
- A cartoon showing two fat kulaks supporting a church sobor.
- A word game that, when solved, revealed an atheistic moral.
- A hostile article about the Salvation Army operating in the Odessa area.
- Photographs of priests participating in the funeral of Grand Duke Nikolai.[60]

In 1924 the government set up the State Publishing House for Antireligious Literature, which complemented the League of the Godless's publishing efforts. Books such as *God and the Stock Exchange* (arguing that God was a tool of the capitalist class) and pamphlets such as *Did Christ Live?* (casting doubt on Jesus's historical existence) rolled off the presses. Anton Loginov wrote *The Godless: The Best Friend of the Peasant* in 1925. In this work a peasant is expected to give up religion and asks, "What do we replace it with?" The author replies, "Evil does not have to be replaced, but simply rooted out." The state also published home-study courses, such as *Teach Yourself to Be Godless*, and even printed atheistic playing cards.[61]

The League of the Godless published the first issue of *Antireligioznik* in January 1926. This was a monthly journal on propaganda techniques, model antireligious lectures, and so on, for rural agitators; it was not to be read by peasants.

An interesting side note is that from the beginning (through the late 1980s) the Soviet atheistic press practiced "orthographic atheism"—spelling "God" with a lowercase "g." This was true as well for objects of religious veneration and for the names of organized churches. It abandoned church titles of rank as well, preferring the egalitarian "servant of the cult."[62]

THE RED ARMY: MORE THAN MILITARY SKILLS

The Red Army alone has become a mighty propagator of education.[63]

—Nadezhda Krupskaya, "A Nation at School," 1923

The Red Army's Political Administration carried out extensive antireligious propaganda with the aid of special textbooks prepared by the Commissariat of Education.[64] This effort was blessed with many advantages, foremost among them being accessibility to large numbers of men. The services inducted 500,000 to 600,000 men each year,[65] most young, many illiterate, and all primed for training in obedience. Another advantage was the Red Army's service against the White Army during the Civil War. The Whites were riddled with religion, and many soldiers no doubt adhered to the aphorism: The friend of my enemy is also my enemy.

Serious teaching of atheism within army ranks began immediately after the Civil War. Soldiers received seven hours of training a day, two of which were composed of antireligious lectures or study. At the Moscow garrison's clubhouse the Agitprop conducted a trial of God, with Trotsky, Lunacharsky, and 5,000 troops attending the performance. Since the defendant had declined to attend, the "jury" found him guilty in absentia.[66]

Despite these efforts, Mikhail Kalinin grumbled during the spring of 1923 about insufficient indoctrination in the armed forces. He worried that whatever indoctrination soldiers received while in uniform was lost as soon as they returned to their villages—they easily succumbed to the embrace of the local church. Western observers also noticed that indoctrinated soldiers quickly returned to their old ways upon returning home. If antireligious propaganda did not stick, it was worthless.

Figures are scarce, but a survey of one army unit in 1925 produced these results: Of the 60 percent of recruits who were believers when they joined, 28 percent (of the total surveyed) were still religious when they left the military, while 32 percent had rejected God by the end of their service.[67]

The Red Army was initially reluctant to accept a branch of the League of the Godless because of the fear that it would drive religiously minded troops to mutiny. By 1927, however, the League had gotten its way and its cells were popping up in every branch and unit of the armed forces. Since many sectarians served in noncombatant roles, special programs were created to talk them out of their pacifism (see chapter 22). The success rate, however, is unknown. At its second congress in 1929, the League issued a fourteen-page resolution, "On the Work in the Red Army," critical of the military's inattention to antireligious work.[68] Apparently there was still a long way to go.

Julius Hecker, writing in 1933, claimed that 75 percent of Russian soldiers avowed atheism when they were released from the Red Army, but the accuracy of this polling is questionable. Respondents would try to appease their officers and, as mentioned above, would backslide after returning the the villages, seriously downgrading this figure. Hecker also claimed that the Red Army trained 10,000 antireligious agitators as part of the Five-Year Plan, destined to spread their message throughout the countryside.[69]

RESISTANCE AND PROPAGANDA'S INADEQUACY

In order to liberate the common masses from ritual and the ecclesiasticism acquired by habit, antireligious propaganda alone is not enough. Of course, it is necessary, but its direct practical influence is limited to a small minority of the more courageous in spirit. The bulk of the people are not affected by antireligious propaganda.[70]

—Leon Trotsky, July 1923

How could peasants in the villages and workers in the cities avoid drowning in a tidal wave of propaganda against their faith? Surprisingly, there were many ways to keep one's head above water. But first it must be understood that a tidal wave that spread over the whole of Russia would not be very deep. In Ivanovo-Voznesensk Province in 1928, for example, there were 660 active Christian communities with 175,000 members and only 13 antireligious groups with 200 members.[71] *Bezbozhnik* complained on May 6:

> The Church members do all they can to creep in through every crack; first tentatively pushing through a finger and after that getting the whole hand through.[72]

During the early 1920s one of the most effective forms of resistance was for clergy and believers to infiltrate and then take over the discussion circles that Komsomol and other propagandists organized in towns and villages.[73] When the government speaker would bring up an embarrassing quotation from the Bible, they would demand that the Christian side of the story be told as well.

Besides infiltration, there were many small ways of opposing government influence. Some priests risked arrest by including in their sermons a warning to parents to keep their children away from Komsomol Clubs and reading rooms. And many exaggerated the evil nature of the godless agitators in the community. Village priests who were literate often read *Bezbozhnik* to better understand their foes and sometimes gave lectures contradicting point-by-point what the government's propagandist had earlier asserted. All priests were ready to blame any village misfortune on too much listening to the godless. Since the government allowed teaching of religion to three children at a time, a church would dragoon every knowledgeable member of its congregation to instruct children in groups of three, so eventually they all were taught. Thousands of men and women joined the growing Eucharist Movement, promising to receive Holy Communion at least once a month. Parishioners cleaned and repaired their churches without payment, provided food and fuel to their priests, and took roles in the divine services. And the people saw through many of the League's campaigns, such as its denunciation of the cutting of Christmas trees as a way to save Russian forests. After over six years of propaganda, the Communist author of the manual *To the Atheistic Youth* complained that its impact was barely measurable—most peasants were still praying to God for rain and good harvests, and there had been little lessening of superstitious practices.[74]

A more indirect and ill-defined method of resistance was the spreading of rumors, though by their nature it is nearly impossible to tell if they were intentionally started as counterpropaganda or if they just sprang out of fertile imaginations. Besides the "mega-rumors" of the coming Antichrist and Armageddon, stories of Lenin's impending death abounded (until the actual event) along with more stories that his death would instigate mass conversions of church buildings to movie theaters. Rumors were not just anti-Soviet; they were also pro-church. Many involved miracles, such as the widely believed Civil War story that when a Jewish commissar fired at an Orthodox ikon, the image deflected the bullet back and killed him. (The church's acceptance of this story contributed to anti-Semitic sentiment along the Civil War's southern front.) It was also prophesied that Yaroslavl Province, as punishment for acceptance of atheism, would be inundated with rain.[75]

In the second half of the 1920s, out of frustration and despair, many in both towns and villages resorted to violence—actually terrorism—against atheist propagandists. In the Donbas region on Easter Eve of 1929 there were threats against a Komsomol musical ensemble if they played during the holiday, and a Komsomol member was murdered for his atheist agitation. In the Sredensk region some clergy helped to organize the Union of Michael the Archangel to physically assault traveling atheist lecturers. Elsewhere a gang of workers beat a schoolteacher who had dared to enter a religious debate on the government's side.[76]

By the late 1920s, in spite of all the efforts of propagandists and the clever projects they conceived, Komsomol's and the League's antireligious fronts were in trouble. The campaign to turn villagers against their priests did not always have the intended effect. One propagandist described his frustration in an antireligious magazine. He had given the village an eloquent description of the unworthiness of priests and then accepted questions from the audience. One woman wanted to know more details of priestly failings, and the speaker gladly obliged. When he was finished the woman thanked the speaker and added, "Now we know better how many difficulties and temptations hinder their work, and we'll pray more warmly to God to pardon and help our pastors."[77]

Pravda ran a grievance series throughout 1928 about lack of progress on the antireligious front. On April 13 it scolded propagandists for spending too much time in the big cities, especially Moscow. Religious missionaries, the article claimed, traveled far and wide visiting villages and provincial monasteries. They reached a larger audience and one that was less affected by the views of unbelievers. When they arrived the children would shout, "The bishop is coming!" and games and singing would ensue.[78] Antireligious lecturers were neglecting the public relations aspects of their work. On April 19 *Pravda* complained that state-run bookstalls failed to keep antireligious literature on their shelves. When queried on this, one worker replied, "There's little demand for that rubbish, so we don't keep it."

Komsomolskaya Pravda, in its May 13 edition, admitted that Komsomol was not winning the propaganda war. Religious organizations were using sewing circles for women as a means to lecture against smoking and drinking, and this was raising their political capital. Various sectarian churches established "Christomol" (Christian Youth Movement) groups to rival Komsomol, and membership in the two organizations was about equal.[79] On September 11 *Pravda* carried a report that sectarians had managed to sell 25,000 copies of their hymnal, while the League was having difficulty selling antireligious literature even at reduced prices. One of the League's representatives flatly stated that they were losing ground to the people's religious prejudices. *Bezbozhnik*, on November 17, carried a report by Comrade Krinitzky, director of the party's Agitprop Department, revealing respect for the abilities of priests and preachers. He noted that Christian missionaries carefully studied the godless literature available to the masses so as to better refute it. In Tula Province the priests were even ordered to read Marx's *Capital*,[80] though it is unlikely that they actually slogged their way through it. *Dawn of the East* (*Zarya Vostoka*) reported on December 12 about the situation in Tiflis. In three workingmen's libraries there existed 35,500 books, yet only 230 of these were antireligious. Out of a total circulation of 20,000 (over a three-month period) only 120 of the antireligious books had been checked out.[81]

All through the 1920s (and into the 1930s) there was a constant barrage of criticism that antireligious propagandists in rural areas still kept ikons in their homes, still were married in church, and still had their babies baptized. The inherent contradictions apparently had not dawned on them. In 1923 the Central Committee checked on party members in twenty-nine provinces of European Russia and was appalled by the number of believers lurking within.[82]

Until around 1929, when the antireligious front began gearing up again, the cause of most of these problems was, as mentioned earlier, the lack of qualified personnel. The Yaroslavl League complained of a chronic shortage and reported to the central office in Moscow in 1927 that this was its "number one problem." The party acknowledged the difficulty and passed endless resolutions to rectify it, but little was accomplished.[83]

Perhaps out of frustration, the Soviet press began showing great sensitivity to any remark or comment in religious literature that could possibly be interpreted as antigovernment. *Bezbozhnik*, on May 6, 1928, nitpicked that a Ukrainian article, "Talks on Morality," was going beyond religious instruction, Bible interpretation, and hymns, venturing into thinly disguised anti-Soviet propaganda:

> The author of this article gives us a description of well-known priestly discus-
> sions "on the great importance of humility and gentleness," but behind these
> explanations we seem to hear more contemporary words. The author says,
> "When he is poor, a moral man does not try to compete with others." What does
> this word "compete" mean? Perhaps the author wanted to say, "does not want
> to struggle against the oppressors."[84]

The same article protested against the sectarians who, it said, "bite in a more underhanded manner." They published seemingly innocent remarks and then slipped in a few words aimed directly at the Soviets. It cited one of their articles on a sectarian assembly in Leningrad:

> Sister Andreevna gave a short report on the work in the family and among the
> children, because Satan is trying to take away from us what is dearest to our
> hearts—our children.[85]

Bezbozhnik was certain that "Satan" was a reference to Soviet schools. This kind of cryptic criticism is about as far as religious publications could go, but, in retrospect, it seems hardly likely that statements of this type were a danger to the Soviet state. It is a measure of the antireligious forces' lack of confidence that they would have spent this much time and energy worrying about such trifles.

*   *   *

A final note and a word of caution: As much as the Russian people had legitimate complaints of religious persecution, they were not above taking advantage of the situation. In many cases, deep down, it was not specifically a religious issue that concerned them; it was a disturbance in their way of life, their routine, and their tradition. Or it was a primeval objection to outsiders telling them what to do and how to live. They framed these issues in a religious manner with the knowledge that they could make a better case for themselves, appear more persecuted than they actually were, and be more likely to find redress for their grievances.

The Orthodox Church was not the only Christian church barraged with church closings and antireligious propaganda. The Catholic Church, though relatively small in membership, presented a special problem for the Bolsheviks because of its connections to the Vatican and international politics. The next two chapters will deal with its particular difficulties.

20

THE BLACK INTERNATIONAL

The Catholic Church and Alleged Conspiracies

In what ways were the problems of the Catholic Church similar to or divergent from those of the Orthodox Church? Catholicism was not native to Russia, and this became the major source of differential treatment by Bolsheviks, who were foreign in ideology but were native Russian in culture. The Bolsheviks always argued that they were not persecuting religion but only arresting counter-revolutionaries, but with the Catholics this argument falls apart; it was not likely that a single one of them wanted to return to the era of tsarist repression.

As for Patriarch Tikhon, he at first adopted a conciliatory tone toward Catholics in his country, but eventually, under pressure from the Bolsheviks, he renounced any concordance with the Vatican.[1]

RUSSIAN ANTI-CATHOLICISM

The hatred of the Russians toward the Latin Church is primordial and somehow inborn; their ancestors took it over from the Greeks and passed it on as a heritage to their off-spring.

—a seventeenth-century German living in Russia

Catholics came to Russia early in its history, but they were few and far between, and the tsars restricted them to localities where they could be controlled. They lived in Kiev as early as the twelfth century, and a papal bull established a Catholic diocese in the Caucasian city of Tiflis in 1328. When Ivan III captured Novgorod he found Catholics there, and nineteen years later he closed their church. With the rise of Muscovy, the tsars gained experience with Catholics from contact with foreign embassies. Soon foreign Catholics were being recruited to help administer the Russian state.

During the sixteenth century some Protestants made inroads in Russia and experienced a degree of tolerance there. This infuriated Catholic Jesuits who were determined to extirpate the Orthodox "heresy" by bringing their own missions to Moscow. In the early eighteenth century Peter the Great had little interest in religion except as it affected his political, military, social, and economic plans for the modernization of Russia. As he imported Western talent and ideas, he no doubt saw Catholics as an effective counterbalance to the Orthodox Church, which he blamed for much of Russia's backwardness. Thus in 1705, Peter granted Catholics the right to build churches in his land and live in freedom. They soon extended missionary work as far south and east as Astrakhan on the Caspian Sea. Franciscan and Carthusian orders then entered Russia, but in 1724, at the end of Peter's reign, they were accused of overambitious proselytizing and were expelled. The Dominicans then moved in, but in 1730 all Catholic missionary work was officially—but ineffectively—banned.

Catholic parishes in the nineteenth and twentieth centuries were impoverished—the exception being St. Catherine's in St. Petersburg, worth several million rubles. Most churches were small and were built in slum areas of the cities, some even constructed of corrugated iron. As an institution, the Russian Catholic Church had nowhere near the accumulated wealth of the Russian Orthodox Church.[2] Its poverty made the church appealing to the working poor, but because the hierarchy espoused a conservative social policy the church was also attractive to the upper classes. Priests, though multilingual and cultured, lived in one-room or two-room apartments on meager salaries. Most were Poles with Russian citizenship, holding strong sentimental ties to their ancestral homeland.

Despite the church's attraction for some, most Russians subscribed to the anti-Catholicism that had permeated the country for centuries. In 1819 Joseph de Maistre explained why Tsar Alexander I felt such hostility toward Rome and its Russian extensions:

> There is in the teaching of the Catholic Church hauteur, an assurance and an inflexibility that displeases temporal rulers, who cannot believe that they are master where there exists a power with which they cannot do as they please.[3]

And Dostoevsky wrote in *The Idiot* (1868):

> Roman Catholicism is more dangerous than atheism, since it presents to us a profane and desecrated Christ usurping the earthly throne.

The Orthodox Church jealously guarded its prerogatives. If Catholic bishops ever became established on Russian soil they would certainly put the interests of the pope in Rome before the interests of the tsar in Moscow, to the detriment of Orthodoxy. From the tsar's perspective, nurturing—even milking—the schism between the Eastern and Western churches was to his advantage if the "Autocrat of all the Russias" intended to maintain the meaningfulness of his title; he needed to keep the ambitions of the Orthodox Church in check.

From the days of Peter onward, some degree of tolerance was granted to Catholics *of non-Russian nationalities*, but much less to Russian subjects who had converted from Orthodoxy. When Catherine the Great (reign: 1762–96) acquired a chunk of eastern Poland, she carefully considered the political and diplomatic advantages that state control over such a concentration of Catholics would give her. She attempted to form a strong Catholic hierarchy, loyal to her person and as independent as possible from Rome. To that end she issued a 1772 decree stating that all communications between the Roman Curia and the Russian Catholic Church must travel first through the Ministry of the Interior. Near the end of the Romanov monarchy, this requirement was again laid out in Article 17 of the Code for Ecclesiastical Affairs Respecting Foreign Religions. These restrictions spoiled the effect of Article 1 of the very same code, which stated that non-Orthodox churches "enjoy everywhere liberty of faith and of worship according to their own rite." But Catholic children could go to Catholic schools and diocesan seminaries, and there was even an Ecclesiastical Academy in St. Petersburg. Priests were "permitted" to do charitable work among the poor, the sick, the aged, and orphans. The church could own property (with certain restrictions) and could receive gifts (but could not send money out of the country without authorization).[4]

Until 1905, Catholic students were forbidden to study outside Russia, further isolating them from the spiritual center of their faith. This not only kept them out of touch with the Vatican but also denied them access to the more vigorous intellectual climate of the West. Catholic literature—including even the canon law—was so rare in Russia that the hierarchy had to arrange for it to be smuggled in from Latvia and then laboriously copied by hand, reminiscent of Irish monastic textual copying in the Middle Ages.

With the 1905 reforms, Catholics for the first time in two centuries saw an opportunity to grow and spread under the cover of official "freedom of conscience," though it would still be "as difficult for an Englishman to proselytize in Ireland as for a Pole in Russia."[5] An indication of the force of earlier tsarist oppression was the sudden appearance after 1905 of at least a quarter-million "new" Catholics—those who, for reasons of personal safety, had previously claimed Orthodox membership but now could worship in the open. Official toleration was not always the *people's* policy, however, and during the late nineteenth and early twentieth centuries there were incidents of hangings of Catholic priests and rapes of nuns, some of whom were forced into Orthodox convents. There were even instances of entire Catholic villages being burned down.[6]

Nicholas I (reign: 1825–55) once expressed a hatred for Russians who embraced the "Polish religion," and he observed accurately that the overwhelming majority of Catholics were of foreign nationality. The 1913 census put the number of Catholics under Russian control (including Poland) at eleven million. Almost every Catholic within the empire's borders was of Polish descent or had emigrated from another Catholic European country.[7] However, after the 1919 re-creation of independent Polish, Estonian, Latvian, and Lithuanian states and the March 1921 Treaty of Riga, the Catholic population was reduced to around 1.5 million.

There were 38,000 Armenian Catholics and 150,000 Catholics in Asiatic Russia. Siberian Catholics were mostly Poles and Ruthenians, or their descendants, who had been banished by Nicholas I or had been internally exiled after the failed Polish Uprising of 1863. In the southern and central regions of European Russia, Catholic communities were overwhelmingly of German origin. They were well represented in the Ukraine and the Crimea, with a heavy concentration in Odessa.[8]

On the eve of World War I, there were five Catholic churches in St. Petersburg, two (or possibly three) in Moscow, and at least one in every large town in European Russia.[9] Considering only areas that would be within Soviet borders after the 1921 Treaty of Riga, in 1915 there were 237 Catholic churches and 143 chapels, served by 246 priests.

THE RED AND THE BLACK INTERNATIONALS

In direct opposition to the International of Moscow stands the International of Rome, which has its agents everywhere and its adherents in all lands. Even in Soviet Russia it has an organization, and the head of that organization is the Archbishop of Petrograd.

—*Bezbozhnik*, April 3, 1923

With the overthrow of the tsarist autocracy and the coming of democracy in March 1917, Catholic hopes soared that liberalization would follow. The church even drew up a list of past grievances: restrictions on correspondence with the Vatican, obstacles placed in the way of religious orders, regulations making school construction nearly impossible, and hindrances to religious instruction outside of the church building.[10] Although they were confident of satisfaction, the November coup forced them to face a new reality.

Bolsheviks may have inherited the national "primordial aversion" to the Latin Church, but because of diplomatic concerns during the 1920s they could not acknowledge it. Internally, though, Lenin and other Bolshevik leaders often spoke of the irreconcilability of Catholicism with the Russian national character. Catholic hierarchs exuded a sense of independence and authority, and they presented an inflexible front to their unseasoned Bolshevik opposition. By early 1918 Grigory Zinoviev, the party leader in Petrograd, became infuriated with the "iron rigidity" of the Catholic community in his city. From his perspective,

Catholics were trying to run their own state within the presumably monolithic Soviet state—an entirely unacceptable proposition. Emelyan Yaroslavsky wrote in 1934 (after the Catholic Church had given up on diplomacy and the United States had granted diplomatic recognition to Moscow):

> The history of the Catholic Church is replete with deception and the mockery of the masses. It is a chronicle of [unparalleled] villainy and of crimes perpetrated against the people. [He then provided a long list of Catholic "sins."][11]

Indeed, proportional to its numbers, the Catholic Church in Russia presented a graver problem for the Bolsheviks than did the Orthodox Church. There were four reasons for this:

- Catholic hierarchs were reluctant to compromise with the Soviet regime and openly stood up to its atheist policies. There was no Catholic "Living Church" (though the government briefly tried to establish one).[12] Catholic priests had tighter spiritual authority over their flocks than did Orthodox priests, making conversion to the Communist way of thinking much less likely.
- The Catholic connection with ethnic minorities—especially the Poles—turned religious problems into nationalities problems. Catholicism seemingly threatened Russian national traditions.
- The Vatican in the international arena stood staunchly opposed to formal diplomatic recognition of the Soviet regime. As a result, the Soviets portrayed Catholicism as pro-capitalist—even pro-fascist—and antisocialist. It was blamed for military interventions at the end of World War I and during the Civil War that had sought to rid the world of the young Bolshevik state.
- Unlike the Russian Orthodox Church, which was Russian and had no pretensions to a worldwide mission (except to exiled or emigrated members), the Catholic Church saw itself as universal and borderless. All Catholics everywhere had to remain in communication with the pope in Rome. It thus became a rival of Communist internationalism.

Every attempt to "Sovietize" and revolutionize Russia's Poles, Germans, Latvians, and Lithuanians was thwarted by their allegiance to the Roman Church. It was an embarrassment to the Soviet government that the international movement of communism, which intended to sweep the world, could not even sweep the international peoples within its own political borders. To convince itself of the power of its movement, the government began publishing unprecedented amounts of anti-Catholic literature in the Polish language. The Communist Party's Twelfth Congress in April 1923 adopted a resolution that called attention to the "growth of nationalist-clerical influence among the Polish minority in the USSR," and the congress denounced Catholic priests for attempting to sway schoolchildren. Bolsheviks also worried about German Catholics living in their midst. They were seen as more dangerous than German Protestants because they were more conservative and more numerous, most Lutheran pastors having fled to Germany during the 1917 uprising or soon thereafter.

In the early days of Communist power, idealistic party leaders and followers took internationalism quite seriously. Catholicism was resented not only because it blocked the spread of communism but also because it represented an alternate internationalism already in place. Not only that, it was *truly* worldwide, while communism lingered at the stage of potentialities. The Catholic Church was a supranational enemy power, and "Christian universalism" had to be fought. The Bolsheviks saw to it that papal bulls were not promulgated in Russia and that Catholic communications leaving the country, as under Catherine II, were censored.[13] Fearing any rival, the Bolsheviks would have attacked the Catholic Church even if not a single Catholic had lived on Russian soil.

That having been said, the actual state of affairs for Catholics in Russia—aside from issues directly related to the Civil War and some church closings—was reasonably comfortable from 1918 until 1922. The papacy initially sought cordial relations with the Bolshevik leadership, sensing that its coreligionists' role as a persecuted minority in tsarist times might create some political capital in the present. Indeed, Polish Catholic leaders in Russia who had been imprisoned by Nicholas II were released, and all tsarist restrictions against Catholics were removed. In the summer of 1918, Catholics went unmolested on their solemn Corpus Christi procession through the streets of Petrograd, though the second such procession, in nearby Kolpino parish in 1921, would be the last in all Russia.[14] One reason for early leniency was that during the first years of Bolshevik rule Lenin was counting on a proletarian uprising in Germany, which was heavily Catholic in the South. Rude treatment of Catholics in Russia, especially German Catholics, would dampen any prospects for German revolution. But there was another reason that extended into 1921 and 1922. This involved complicated conspiracy theories and will be discussed later in this chapter.

CATHOLICS AS POLES

In Russia the Roman Catholics are mainly Poles, and the feud between Russia and Poland has been too intense not to react with some vehemence on as patriotically minded a body of Poles as are the Polish clergymen on Soviet territory and especially along the Polish frontier.[15]

—Maurice Hindus, 1929

During the first four years of Bolshevik rule, Catholics followed the leadership of Pope Benedict XV, but he passed away in January 1922 and was succeeded by Pius XI. Inside Russia, Archbishop Edward Ropp led the church until he was imprisoned in April 1919 and was succeeded by John Cieplak.[16] Ropp was allowed to return to Poland in November. The new archbishop was born into a mining family in Poland in 1857 and studied at St. Petersburg to receive his doctorate in theology in 1901. He was assigned to the archdiocese of Moghilev and was stationed on the eastern edge of White Russia until his ascension to the leadership position.

Just as Patriarch Tikhon wavered in his last years and the locum tenens Peter proved to be the stronger man, Archbishop Ropp grew more accommodating near the end of his rule and was bolstered by Monsignor Constantine Budkiewicz. Born in Poland in 1867, Budkiewicz was ordained in 1893 and made vicar of St. Catherine's Church in St. Petersburg in 1908. During the war he served as vice president of the Polish Relief Committee and afterward sponsored innumerable Polish charities, but he was especially known for his firmness and business acumen. When he became monsignor in 1918, he established schools in Petrograd that raised children to be *Polish* Catholics—not Russians. Only very slowly did he come to admit that Russians might have a place within the predominantly Polish Catholic Church in Russia. In September 1922 Budkiewicz wrote *The Condition of the Church in Russia*, a document that is crucial to an understanding of what went on between Petrograd Catholics and the Soviet government. This document, written in Latin, was addressed to Archbishop Lorenzo Lauri, the papal nuncio in Warsaw, but was lost when the Primate's Palace was bombed during World War II. Historian James Zatko obtained a rough draft of the document from another Polish clergyman and published it in 1960. Details from it will be incorporated into the narrative that follows.[17]

From the government's perspective, the "Polish problem" was essentially the "Catholic problem" and vice versa, in spite of the clergy's insistence that they were members of an "international church" without borders. In 1917, in addition to Poles in (Russian-occupied) Poland, there were 476,000 Poles in the Ukraine and 100,000 in White Russia (Byelorussia). The Polish Executive Committee in Ukraine and Byelorussia operated along the western and southern borderlands, and by 1918 it had established over 1,300 schools with 85,000 students, teaching the Polish mother tongue and the "Catholic spirit." Bolshevik extension into these areas was hindered by this obstruction, thus when the Red Army finally entered Kiev in early 1919, it shot the chairman of the Polish Executive Committee and forced its members to flee with the retreating Polish Army. Very few Catholics were amenable to Communist propaganda or "re-education." By 1926 only 3,000 Ukrainian Poles had joined the Communist Party, and only 8,200 had joined Komsomol.

After unexpected military reverses the Red Army was forced to abandon its advance on Warsaw, and the Bolsheviks meekly signed the March 1921 Treaty of Riga. The terms of this pact—for what they were worth—"guaranteed" Poles caught behind Russian borders the free use of their language and the right to educate their youth as they saw fit. Article VII contained provisions on religious rights:

> The churches and the religious associations to which persons of Polish nationality belong in Russia, the Ukraine and White Russia have the right, *within the limits of internal legislation*, to organize their internal ecclesiastical affairs independently. The abovementioned churches and religious associations have the right, *within the limits of internal legislation*, to hold and to acquire such movable and immovable property as is indispensable for religious practices and for the maintenance of the clergy and of the ecclesiastical institutions. [emphasis added][18]

From exile Archbishop Ropp wrote a letter to the Catholic leadership in Russia describing the Treaty of Riga as "so infinitely stupid that I think we can expect little from it."[19] He must have anticipated the complaints that came pouring in. The Polish chargé d' affaires sent a protest note to the Soviet Deputy Commissar for Foreign Affairs in late April 1922 listing his grievances. He insisted that both the coerced signing of church contracts and the confiscation of valuables (see below) violated Article VII, but the voice of the Polish government carried little weight in Moscow, and the gaping loophole—emphasized above—was quickly exploited by the Soviet side. Guarantees of religious freedom for Polish Catholics in Russia were meaningless in practice. Two months later George Chicherin replied to the original protest, but his answer was so discourteous that the government in Warsaw refused to officially accept it.[20] The unaccepted letter nonetheless made these points:

- All Catholics in Russia remained subject to the laws of the Soviet state.
- Catholic churches in Russia were at the disposal of their membership (the Twenties) on the same terms as other churches.
- The Catholic Church, through the treaty, did not acquire the status of a juridical person.
- Article VII dealt only with goods and property that originated in Poland.[21]

In summary, the fate of Catholics in Russia was an internal Soviet matter, and Article VII had to squeeze itself into the confines of Soviet law.

During the Civil War, Polish Russians were unsure whether they would even be allowed to remain in Russia. From the Soviet perspective, every Pole on the western frontier could potentially give aid and comfort to the enemy. Bolshevik propaganda accused the Catholic clergy of treasonous Polish nationalism, a charge denied by many Catholics living in Russia at the time.[22] Close to the western border, however, the accusation was no doubt true. In 1918 the Bolsheviks put the question directly to the clergy in Petrograd: Either become Russian citizens and remain in Russia or keep your Polish citizenship and leave the country for good. Cieplak had urged the Polish clergy to stay and, at that time, most did.

In 1919 the Civil War on the western front was fought against Pilsudski's Polish Army, which was welcomed as a liberator by the Catholic clergy of the Byelorussian capital of Minsk. As the pressures of the Civil War increased, Catholic laity began to defect, vast numbers returning to their homeland. By 1922 Budkiewicz reported that parishioners of St. Catherine's in Petrograd had fallen from 30,000 to 5,000 faithful. Part of this disaffection, however, was because many Polish Russians felt neglected, as the Catholic clergy concentrated its efforts on converting the Orthodox.[23]

In 1925 there were 1.2 million Catholics in Russia, and over 95 percent of them were Poles (the remainder being mostly Germans). Ninety-two percent of the priests were of Polish nationality,[24] but many of these came from families that had lived in Russia for generations and spoke fluent Russian.

TO SIGN OR NOT TO SIGN

Sooner than give way to the Bolsheviks, we will close our schools and teach the children in defiance of the law, for every concession we make only strengthens the enemy of God and of our country.[25]

—Sigismund Lozinsky, Catholic bishop of Minsk, 1918

As mentioned, Catholics initially saw opportunities in the immediate postrevolutionary period. The February 1918 separation decree seemed a blessing, as it could be aimed only at the Orthodox Church. Since Catholics had never been connected to the Russian government, how could they be separated from it? Now, Russian Catholics supposed, both churches would stand equal before the law. Archbishop Ropp, while still in Petrograd, endorsed the decree with a sigh of relief.[26] (As late as the Genoa Conference in 1922, Chicherin disingenuously explained to the Italian Archbishop Signori that separation would make for a more virile Catholic Church with greater "moral fiber." Signori rose and clinked his wine glass with Chicherin's, effusing, "I thoroughly agree with you.")[27]

Catholics could not foresee that the separation decree would have as drastic an impact on them as it had on Orthodox Christians. Their church was now placed in the category of a mere "religious association," with even fewer rights than cultural or professional associations, and was stripped of over 11 million rubles in confiscated property, investments, and other funds, with no hope of acquiring any in the future. Catholic teaching, including the catechism, was ban-

ished from schools, and no means were allowed to counteract anti-Catholic propaganda. In Petrograd even instruction in the speaking, reading, and writing of
Latin was prohibited, lest Catholic religious content slip into it (or perhaps
because the Bolshevik leadership did not understand it). Catholics were bitter
due to their inability to instruct their young. Archbishop Cieplak tried to cope by
organizing secret schools for Catholic youth in Petrograd as well as secret theological courses in Moscow.[28]

Another consequence of separation was even greater poverty among the
clergy. When church buildings and property were nationalized, the already-
inadequate incomes associated with these properties were denied to them. Many
priests abandoned their parishes for lack of financial support and returned to
Poland—part of the continuing exodus. Then, of course, the abandoned churches
were turned into clubhouses.

To more closely control church buildings and the affairs of each parish, the
government, just as it had with the Orthodox Church, relied on local soviets
signing contracts with Committees of Twenty; no contract meant no access to
"their own" churches. The contracts mandated that heavy taxes (euphemized as
"rent") be paid and that buildings be kept in good repair. Accepting Soviet law
as a premise, the contracts were eminently reasonable and logical conclusions; if
you rent a rowboat you have to leave a deposit until you return it in good condition. But Catholics stubbornly refused to accept the premise. In any case, the
church had no way to pay the rent except through what it could collect in the
offering plate each Sunday. Hierarchs strongly resisted any arrangement that
undermined discipline among believers and limited control over what they
regarded—contrary to Soviet law—as their own property. Cieplak issued instructions to subordinates to resist local soviets by whatever means possible.

In the spring of 1918 Petrograd Catholics actually signed some contracts on the
grounds that Bolshevik power would soon be overthrown and the contracts voided.
By autumn, however, most Catholic clergy in Petrograd were resolved never to sign.
Symbolic of their desperation was their agreement to join together in protest with
Orthodox and Eastern Rite Catholic leaders (in some instances Orthodox laity even
volunteered to sign the Catholic contracts, but this was not numerically necessary).
Chosen as the group's delegate, Budkiewicz traveled to Moscow to negotiate, but
Peter Krasikov in the Commissariat of Justice made no concessions.[29]

By December, as the likelihood of Bolshevik demise became increasingly
remote, Budkiewicz adopted tactics of stalling and obstruction. At first he urged
priests and parishioners to ignore contracts as contrary to canon law. Then, when
pressure mounted, he urged procrastination and protest, much as a condemned
prisoner might file every possible appeal to forestall the end. Apparently this
tactic met with some success, as later, when he faced trial, obstructionism was
one of the charges against him. He even suggested to the government an alternate form for the contract: Parishioners would "retain custody" of church prop-

erty and paraphernalia, not signing leases but conceding that it all belonged to "the people." When these tactics failed, Budkiewicz gave reluctant permission for priests to sign, as long as they made it clear that they were doing so tentatively and under duress.[30]

In April 1919 Archbishop Ropp adopted a marginally more conciliatory position, publishing in the Moghilev *Chronicle* a circular letter that backed off from Budkiewicz's more obstreperous approach. He capitulated on the signing of contracts but instructed parish Twenties to protect the churches and their liturgical treasures. He also arranged for each Twenty to send two delegates to a central committee, which would coordinate what resistance was still possible and be authorized to negotiate with the government. Budkiewicz, of course, took exception to Ropp's stray from stringency, especially as Ropp had not sought prior papal approval. Budkiewicz considered every contractual signature obtained under these circumstances as "fictitious." He was also sure that Bolsheviks would not deal with a church that had already given in; refusal to sign would strengthen the Catholic bargaining position.[31]

Conciliatory or not, Ropp was arrested and imprisoned on April 19, a few weeks after his letter's publication. Catholic laity in Petrograd marched to the place where he was being held on Gorochovaya Street, but to no avail. Later, Cieplak led marches to the Cheka building, protesting in vain against those who had made the arrest and offering to take Ropp's place in prison. Although some hotheaded Bolsheviks wanted Ropp immediately shot, he was more valuable either as a hostage or as a trade commodity. Since Ropp's arrest followed immediately on the Polish Army's expulsion of the Red Army from Vilna, there was some speculation that the archbishop was indeed a war hostage. But a few months later a swap was arranged; Ropp was released into Poland in November, and the Marxist Karl Radek, held in a German prison, was handed over to Russian authorities. Interestingly, the Bolsheviks would not make any exchanges as long as Ropp remained a citizen of Poland, a country with whom they were at war. Only when Benedict XV agreed to make Ropp a subject of the Vatican could the deal go through.[32] As mentioned above, with Ropp's departure John Cieplak became the new archbishop and head of Russia's Catholics.

After Ropp's deportation, more Catholic priests were rounded up, and rumors spread of large-scale executions. Floods of Catholic clergy and laity now poured out of Russia into Poland and Lithuania, but Cieplak labored on.[33] In September he issued a circular letter to his clergy stating the case for the inviolability of church property:

> To take possession of these things, to hand them over to persons having no legal right to them, to execute agreements or other civil documents about them without the permission of the ecclesiastical authorities, is not only to violate the rights of the church in respect to these things but is a profanation of sacred objects in which Catholics can take no part.[34]

Attempts to remove the temporal possessions of churches should be resisted as well, he continued, for they were gifts to the church and not the belongings of the state. Although this letter may have bolstered the spirits of the clergy, it gave no practical advice as to what to do when Red Guards appeared at the church door.

There were those among the Catholic hierarchy who thought the archbishop poorly suited for his new job. After Cieplak had served for two years, Father John Troigo wrote to Ropp in Poland complaining that Cieplak was without principle and will and had hardly enough talent for rule in normal times, let alone the present. Troigo claimed that the archbishop had to be pushed to take action at critical junctures in the struggle with the Bolsheviks.[35]

Cieplak did arrange for two Catholic conferences to be held in January 1920 to further clarify relations with the Communist Party, and two resolutions resulted:

- Being a member of the Catholic Church was completely incompatible with membership in the Communist Party.
- Communist publications should be purchased by priests and read in church so as to better understand their opponents and instruct their listeners.[36]

By late 1922 conditions had changed; the major Orthodox trials were over, and the wrath of Europe had proven bearable. Now the Catholic Church was sighted in the government's scope. On December 2 a church in Petrograd was closed, and a few days later ten more were closed. The reasons given were lack of compliance with the decree on the use of nationalized property—the contracts had not been signed.[37] In *Pravda* a high Petrograd official described a typical scene:

When the [government] Commission entered, Gritzko and another priest kneeled and began to sing psalms. They were joined by the parishioners. After they were repeatedly asked to desist and leave the church, it proved necessary to apply force and lead out those who opposed the sealing of the church. The crowd was in extreme exaltation and one could hear voices like the following: "The Soviet Government is not everlasting, but the Church will abide."[38]

The government tried to break the standoff by asking the clergy to sign "receipts" for the churches and their contents, but the receipts looked suspiciously like contracts, and the priests refused to sign them.[39]

The clergy needed help, even outside intervention. The Reverend Edmund Walsh was a Jesuit priest from Boston University and Georgetown University, as well as director of the Papal Famine Relief Mission and the Roman Curia's official delegate to Moscow. On December 6 Cieplak sent him a letter complaining about church closures and threats made against priests if they attempted to hold services in private homes. Implicitly, he was asking for papal intervention. Six weeks later the Reverend M. Amoudru, pastor of the Church of Our Lady of France, wrote a similar letter to Walsh informing him that his was the last Catholic church remaining open in Petrograd. It was Amoudru's opinion that the government aimed to wear down the laity by allowing them no place to legally worship. When the laity protested to the clergy, a wedge would be driven between them by the government's "innocent" revelation that their priests had refused to comply with "very reasonable demands." Meanwhile, Ropp in Warsaw was sending letters to Cieplak to go ahead with the signing before it was too late (meaning impending arrests and trials), but Catholics inside Russia still refused.[40]

An article in *Izvestia* in late March 1923 suggested that if Cieplak truly wished to obey canon law, he should solicit the pope to order compliance with the contract requirement—then it *would* be canonical to sign. Otherwise, the article warned, all the Roman Catholic churches in Russia could be closed.

CONSPIRACY AND THE GENOA CONFERENCE

Never was there a more favorable moment for Catholic imperialism, and Catholicism is only making use of the openings presented to it.[41]

—Moise Beilinson, September 1922

The years 1922 and 1923 saw accusations flying left and right concerning the Catholic Church in Russia and papal intentions. More accurately, there was a triangle of conspiracy theories involving the Bolsheviks, the Orthodox Church, and the Catholic Church.

Conspiracies

With only a slight oversimplification, Vatican foreign policy toward Moscow can be divided into two periods: Prior to 1924 the hope was to exploit the situation to the advantage of Catholic expansion in Russia; after 1924 the hope was to diplomatically isolate the Bolsheviks and, if possible, overthrow them. The "expanders" followed Pope Pius X, who before World War I had declared Russian Orthodoxy to be the "greatest enemy of the Roman Church."[42] Edmund Walsh favored the overthrow of Soviet power and, mincing no words, explained this directly to Chicherin.

Recall from chapter 11 the extent of suffering caused by the post–Civil War famine in southern Russia. In August 1921 the pope sent a message to Cardinal Gasparri, the papal secretary of state, explaining the extent of the famine, the hunger of the Russian people, and the need to send aid. He instructed that money be sent through the relief mission in Geneva and that a Papal Relief Mission be organized so that the Holy See might more effectively administer (and control) this aid.

During the same month Cieplak appealed for Catholic relief, and fifty train carloads of food were already in Russia by December, before negotiations for the entry of Catholic relief workers were even complete. After Benedict's death, Pius XI continued pushing for humanitarian aid. Both popes were no doubt genuinely concerned with the plight of starving Russians and no doubt also anxious that their church be perceived as playing an active role in relief efforts. In March 1922 the Soviets agreed to admit the mission, and in mid-July a group of nine priests and three laymen left Rome for the Crimea, and one thousand Catholic famine relief workers left Poland for Russia. Members of the Congregation of the Most Holy Redeemer (Redemptionists) headed for northern Russia, Jesuits moved into central Russia, and the Society of the Divine Word ("Brothers of the Word of God") turned to the South. The Catholic Organization for Famine Relief (Papal Relief Mission) officially employed them all, but, revealingly, a Catholic bishop in Poland referred to them as "missionaries."[43]

By early October the mission was at work. By its own accounts it established hundreds of food kitchens in the Crimea and many more reaching as far north as Moscow and Petrograd. Eventually it gave a daily food ration to over 160,000 people in over 400 localities and employed 2,500 Russians as workers at the stations. At its peak in the summer of 1923, it had created clothing and boot-making factories, donated money to sanatoria for children with tuberculosis, and imported medical supplies to combat typhus and malaria, ultimately spending the equivalent of $1.5 million on all programs.[44] This effort can, of course, be construed as magnanimity or opportunism—the latter interpretation favored by many Orthodox Church hierarchs and clergy.

All conspiracy theories boiled down to three possibilities: The Vatican wanted to seize the opportunity to proselytize Russian Orthodoxy, the Bolsheviks planned to use Catholics against all of Russia's Christian churches, or the Bolsheviks granted concessions to the Vatican to accelerate their own diplomatic recognition (or some combination of these three, as they were not mutually exclusive.)

Although no document in the words of Pope Benedict XV exists clearly attesting to expansionist plans, it is difficult to believe that he did not at least contemplate the chance of converting close to 100 million Orthodox Christians to the Universal Faith. If the Orthodox Church was the paragon of evil in Bolshevik eyes, and the plan was to destroy it as a national institution, a religious power vacuum would be created that needed filling. Sarcastic cartoons appeared in the Italian press that showed the pope blessing the Bolsheviks in their assault on Russian Orthodoxy.[45] Thus the first of our conspiracy theories is that this was the long-awaited opportunity for the Catholic Church to overwhelm Orthodoxy in Russia and unite the ancient schism under papal rule.

The Vatican may indeed have been excited about the possibilities of this venture; allegedly many internal conferences were devoted to the topic. What a coup it would have been for any pope who could achieve Catholic ascendancy in Russia! There was even speculation that the Vatican had pushed the idea of deposing Patriarch Tikhon as part of an arrangement with the Communists. This was at the same time as the most likely government-inspired "visit of the priests" to Tikhon's monastery cell, where Vedensky claimed to have obtained the patriarch's abdication. Tikhon's removal may have been a precondition for a Vatican-Moscow concordat. In a game of tit-for-tat, the Soviets may then have insisted that the Vatican drop support for the Polish Catholic clergy already in Russia and send in new, non-Polish relief missions. This speculation is plausible as there is evidence that Poles (in Poland) had been attempting to block papal initiatives in Russia because they knew any agreement would be at their expense.[46]

Immediately after his release from custody in June 1923, Tikhon bitterly attacked the Vatican for what he saw as a chipping away at the Orthodox Church. He called on all Russians to stand firm against the "Catholic invasion." Outside observers considered Tikhon's assault as rather ungrateful, for they believed that Pius XI had been working ceaselessly to obtain Tikhon's release.[47] Catholic historian James Zatko was critical of those who spread rumors of plots against the Orthodox Church. After all, Benedict XV in 1919 had sent a message to Lenin protesting against the persecution of Orthodox clergy. And Walsh had said publicly that the Papal Relief Mission was to scrupulously avoid religious propaganda; the mission was under explicit orders from both the Bolsheviks and the Vatican *not* to proselytize. Even communion for relief workers was to be held behind closed doors. On the basis of available evidence, Zatko concluded that:

> The documents do not show that the Vatican ever attempted to take advantage
> of the Orthodox Church, but rather had used its high position in the world, both
> of religion and diplomacy, to intervene on behalf of the Orthodox Church.[48]

Many observers claimed the mission stuck to the terms of agreement, but others wrote that missionaries brought along colored photographs of the pope to hang in plain view in relief centers as the hungry were being fed.[49] In October 1923 some Catholics connected to the mission were forced out of the country, allegedly for proselytizing. The very word "missionary" was obviously ambiguous. In any case, they provided food for the hungry and medical aid for the sick of *all* religions and nationalities on a nondiscriminatory basis. (Of course, dedicated conspiracy theorists would just see nondiscrimination as a greater opportunity for religious imperialism.)

Looked at from the Bolshevik perspective, very soon after the November coup the idea must have also popped into Lenin's head that Catholics could be used against the Orthodox. Every Catholic gain would entail an Orthodox loss— a zero-sum game. Later, when the Bolsheviks were stronger, the still-weak Catholics and the recently weakened Orthodox could be easily crushed. Thus a second theory was espoused by, among others, the Orthodox Archbishop John of Latvia. He saw the Catholic Relief Mission not so much as a papal initiative but as a *Bolshevik* initiative to infiltrate the Russian countryside and insidiously convert ignorant peasants, who would surely be grateful to the Holy Father for relief from years of suffering and might not understand doctrinal differences.[50] They might even join the Catholic Church without realizing that they had done so. Martha Almedingen, a devout Catholic living in Russia at the time, backed up this theory when she wrote in her book, *The Catholic Church in Russia Today* (1923):

> [Aside from the issue of acceptance of the papacy] the only difference in doctrine was one that not one Russian in 100,000 could comprehend. . . . A little pressure from the Soviet authorities would help these millions (mostly illiterate) to see that the Catholic pope was a far holier person than the Orthodox patriarch.[51]

This would be a Bolshevik double-barreled shot: The Orthodox Church would be split and weakened by both the Catholic Church and the Living Church, whose operations were just getting under way.

Evan Young, the United States Commissioner in Riga (Latvia), claimed that the Soviets sent an emissary to the Vatican in November 1921 carrying an offer to introduce proselytizing Catholics into Russia in a tactical attempt to destroy the dominance of the Orthodox Church. He wrote:

> A blow is now to be made at Orthodoxy by an agreement with the Vatican. If Roman Catholicism can be introduced into Russia the last mainstay of the old regime will have been uprooted, and further, the Soviet government will be in agreement with the [Catholic] church rather than antagonistic to it. The Communists . . . consider that Catholic propaganda will result eventually in causing the whole structure of the church to crumble.[52]

The Jesuit order was the traditional enemy of Orthodoxy, and credibility was lent to rumors of conspiracy by Archbishop Ropp's and Edmund Walsh's membership in this order, and by the new pope's prior membership. When Patriarch Tikhon was "coincidentally" arrested in May 1922, those of a conspiratorial persuasion needed no further proof—the Bolsheviks had fulfilled the precondition for Vatican cooperation.

The driver of the presumed papal assault vehicle was Walsh. As we saw above, he traveled to Russia to investigate the possibility of a food mission during the post–Civil War famine, but at least part of his assignment was to get firsthand information on the religious situation that would help the pope determine the feasibility of a massive Catholic *proselytizing* mission. He submitted his report in April 1922 and then returned to Russia for more "survey work." Seeming to corroborate Orthodox suspicions, Walsh at first insisted that Italian monks accompany all relief expeditions. The Bolsheviks put their foot down on this proposal (which casts some doubt on their likely participation in a conspiracy). Walsh then tried to arrange communications between the Russian Catholic Church and White Army émigrés, the purpose of which was transparent. Hoping to implement his aggressive views, he then misrepresented Soviet proposals to the Vatican to the Russian government's disadvantage. Referring to Walsh as "most objectionable, proud, and inclined to make a terrible scandal out of every little issue," the Soviets withdrew his welcome.[53] Despite rumors and speculation, this conspiracy theory is of doubtful validity. The Bolsheviks would just be asking for trouble if they purposefully encouraged such a powerful international organization to come into the country. It is mentioned here because of the *possibility* of its existence and what it shows about the perceptions and complexities of the time.

Bolshevik theorists were never concerned with Catholic theology or the spiritual content of missionary preaching. Instead they worried about clerical influence over foreign policy in capitalist countries or about the immense power of the Vatican in world affairs. In the tumultuous early 1920s, much of the contact between Rome and Moscow involved the issue of diplomatic recognition—specifically the intense desire of the Soviet government to be accepted as an equal among nations. In a word, the Bolsheviks wanted respect. But the attempt to achieve recognition was not straightforward; it involved manipulation, intrigue, and convoluted diplomacy. From the Vatican, the Soviets sought only de facto—not de jure—recognition: low-level talks and arrangements that would legitimize Bolshevik rule sufficiently to stimulate de jure recognition from European powers. Both the Vatican and Moscow were reluctant to accept an exchange of ambassadors because of fundamental philosophical differences. In addition, the Vatican did not want to be *seen* as pulling the rug out from underneath the Orthodox Church in its own struggle. Any contact would, for the time being, have to remain unofficial.

Thus the last conspiracy theory involves diplomatic recognition for the Soviet Union. The Bolsheviks were tempted to grant concessions and curry favor to get it. The international conference in session in Genoa, Italy, during the spring of 1922 was meant to handle issues of trade and repayment of war debts, but an ancillary purpose was to examine relations with the USSR. The Vatican could exert pressure on attending nations to grant the sought-after de jure recognition. In spite of Catholic claims that thousands of its clergy had been shot, and in spite of its revulsion at atheism in power, the pope did instruct the Archbishop of Genoa to court the goodwill of Chicherin, the head of the Russian delegation.[54]

Allegedly, there was a Bolshevik agreement with the Jesuits that in return for permitting entry for Italian monks as part of the Papal Relief Mission, the Jesuits would pressure the Italian, French, and Belgian governments to recognize Moscow. But if this was the arrangement the Soviet government, as we have just seen, nixed it, and the pope finally labeled the mission's purpose as relief and nothing more.[55] Still, on April 29, Pius XI wrote to the Genoa Conference expressing his hope that "normal relations" in Europe could be reestablished— diplomatic code for resolving the Russia Question. On May 14 he demanded conditions for any pact that included diplomatic recognition. The Soviet government must:

- grant full liberty of conscience to all Russians.
- permit public and private practice of all religions.
- allow all religious denominations to own property (including the return of already confiscated property).[56]

But the futility of making demands—even if agreed to—can be seen in the flouting of agreements already reached in the Treaty of Riga a little over a year earlier.

Émigrés connected to the Russian National Committee in Paris and the Karlovtzy clergy swallowed *all* conspiracy theories involving a Catholic-Communist "arrangement" to weaken or replace the Orthodox Church.[57] Thinking through the ways it served both sides' interests convinced them that such a concordat existed, though there was no documentation to support their claim. Some of their writings charged that secret meetings had been arranged at Genoa between Catholic leaders and Chicherin, though Pius XI himself never met with the Russian diplomat. Apprehensive about any such alliance, the Russian National Committee published in May an "Open Letter to the Pope," arguing against any Russian-Catholic religious agreements. The Vatican characterized the letter as extremely offensive.

Meanwhile, in all their diplomatic contacts with the Vatican and in the foreign press the Soviets heaped lavish praise on the Papal Relief Mission. Cagily, however, they downplayed Catholic contributions in the domestic press. Budkiewicz wrote in 1922:

> We had thought that the Russian government would be grateful for the Apostolic See's assistance in the famine, but this hope has deceived us. Russian officials endeavor to discount that aid both in their newspapers and in their conversations.[58]

As the famine slowly subsided, government authorities began imposing restrictions and minor harassments on Catholic (and all) relief workers. The intent may have been a last-ditch effort to force the Vatican to grant the mission diplomatic status; if so, the ploy failed. Soon more workers were forced to leave the country, most returning home by October 1923 and all by September 1924. It was then that Pius XI gave up hope for Catholic inroads in Russia and was forced to admit that atheism was its permanent policy. He turned to nurturing hopes of an overthrow of the Communists, but in that same year Walsh—that fiercest of anticommunists—left the country, and the British, French, and Italians granted de jure recognition to the Soviet Union.[59]

An Eastern Rite Catholic Conspiracy

The Eastern Rite Catholic Church originated at the Union of Brest in 1596, when the Polish king ordered the Orthodox in White Russia and the Ukraine to acknowledge papal leadership. Since they were allowed to continue in the Eastern Rite—including use of the Slavonic language and the Orthodox liturgy—they were dubbed the Catholic Church of the Greek (or Eastern) Rite.[60] They were severely persecuted by tsarist authorities (often rounded up by whip-wielding Cossacks and herded into Orthodox churches), so when Benedict XV named Leonid Fyodorov as Eastern Rite Exarch of Russia in March 1921 he led fewer than a dozen congregations with a mere 3,000 total members.*

In September 1922 the government exiled Eastern Rite Catholic Vladimar Abrikosov, arrested his wife (who had established the first Russian Dominican community) along with eighteen of her nuns, and closed her convent. Fyodorov, too, was arrested for "anti-Soviet activities."[61] The Soviet press in 1923 began a campaign that justified these arrests and closures by claiming that Eastern Rite Catholics were the tool that scheming Roman Catholics were using to gain control of the Orthodox Church; then all Russian Christians would be united in a giant conspiracy to overthrow Soviet power. Conspiracy theorists alleged that Soviet policy was transformed from one of welcoming Catholic influence as a divisive force to shunning Eastern Rite Catholic influence as a unifying force. Considering Eastern Rite Catholic influence a vanguard of Roman Catholic–Orthodox unification and charging that all liturgical and canonical differences were being submerged to expedite an anticommunist campaign, *Bezbozhnik* on April 23, 1923, carried the headline "The Approaching Union of the Black Internationalists." The newspaper affected fear of an even wider Christian Church conspiracy: "If the conversations at present taking place between Rome and the Americans, English, Greeks, and Russians meet with success, the 'Red International' will be in great peril."[62] Ecumenism of this sort had, of course, been unattainable for a millennium, but then these were extraordinary times.

In fact, there was some truth to the Communist accusation. Archbishop

---

*There had been another group of several million Catholics of the Greek Rite in Galicia, but it became part of reconstituted Poland at the end of World War I.

Ropp, Exarch Fyodorov, and Metropolitan Benjamin of Petrograd *had* met together in Budkiewicz's apartment in February 1919 to coordinate strategy—if not their churches—and had sent a joint protest to Moscow. Fyodorov *did* act as a liaison between the Latin and the Orthodox churches in coordinating strategy to resist confiscations of church buildings and liturgical treasures.[63] At his 1923 trial, Fyodorov testified:

> From the time that I gave myself to the Roman Catholic Church, my cherished dream has been to reconcile my homeland with this church, which for me is the only true one.[64]

CONFISCATION OF VALUABLES

In most cases [confiscation] raids were accompanied by wild outbursts of most abject and vulgar profanation, hardly ever checked by the higher officials who were invariably present at such proceedings.[65]

—Martha Almedingen (an eyewitness), 1923

The Soviet famine decree of February 1922 hit Catholics as hard as it did the Orthodox. Treasures were stripped from Catholic churches all across Great Russia, White Russia, and the Ukraine. The Catholic churches in Smolensk were plundered. In the Ukraine fifty-two out of sixty-eight churches were sacked,[66] the others spared as being too poor to bother with. Graves in church cemeteries were even opened as government agents hunted for jewels. The priest Rutkovsky in Yaroslavl appealed to Cieplak as to how he should handle the decree. On March 19 Cieplak sent this message by telegram: "Demand illegal; do not deliver inventory."[67] For dutifully following this advice Rutkowski spent one year in prison.

On April 9 Petrograd's Church of St. John the Baptist was stripped of all its valuables.[68] On May 2 agents removed valuables from the church in Kamenetz, near Lvov, and heaped them in a pile in the churchyard. When a crowd of parishioners tried to move them to safety, the Red Army was called in and soldiers with fixed bayonets drove these salvage teams away. Several priests were arrested. On the same day churches in Minsk were ordered to comply with the decree, and many resisters were arrested and imprisoned. In a church in the Moscow suburbs, the head of a government requisitioning party, arriving in the middle of the night, demanded the keys to the Tabernacle, which they had been told contained "the greatest treasure of the Catholics." When the aged priest refused, he was knocked to the floor and sent rolling down the aisle, while one of the raiders was sent to rouse a locksmith. The chalice inside turned out to be of little value, and the intruders left swearing. The congregation found the priest dead the next morning.[69]

Pius XI sent a message to the Soviet delegation at Genoa, appealing for an end to the confiscations of liturgical vessels and vestments. He took a distinctly Catholic position, arguing that treasures in Orthodox churches could reasonably be considered the common patrimony of the Russian people, for indeed that was their source. Therefore "the people" had a case for revoking their gifts and using them for famine relief. Treasures in Catholic churches, however, came from foreign sources and were never part of the Russian heritage.[70] We can imagine how well this distinction satisfied Chicherin.

Then Cardinal Gasparri thought of an idea that could have resolved the standoff. He contacted the Soviet diplomat Vladimir Vorovsky in Rome about the possibility of the Holy See paying the Soviets a price equivalent to the value of the sacred objects, thus avoiding the confiscations. When Vorovsky seemed reluctant to reply to this proposal, Monsignor Joseph Pizzardo, on May 14, wrote to Chicherin at the Genoa Conference with the same request: "The price agreed on will be immediately paid to any . . . whom the [Russian] government may nominate."[71] Again there was no reply, so Pizzardo wrote directly to Lenin. Again the letter was ignored. The Soviets were in a bit of a quandary, for if they agreed to this proposal they would lose an effective weapon against organized religion in Russia, but if they disagreed it would look to the world as if they were more concerned with church destruction than with famine relief.[72] Anyway, for the Vatican leadership to have even suggested such a proposal shows that they were still under the mistaken impression that money was the issue.

Accepting defeat, the Vatican agreed to turn over the required church valuables, but only on the condition that proceeds from their sale be used solely for famine relief and be administered directly by the Catholic Church (or in conjunction with the Orthodox Church). The government responded by labeling the conditions an "act of resistance" and arresting those Catholics in Russia responsible for promulgating it.

In his 1922 report Budkiewicz described his many unanswered appeals to the government regarding the confiscation issue and the arrests of priests who resisted the looting of their churches. At the very least, he argued, imprisoned priests should not be treated as if they disobeyed the law out of a spirit of counterrevolution, but rather it should be acknowledged that they were simply endeavoring to obey canon law. This time he got a reply from Krasikov declaring that the government would continue to punish the guilty "most severely."

Krasikov pointed out that the confiscation decree was not going to be changed and suggested that if the Vatican sincerely desired the recovery of appropriated church treasures the Soviet government would be willing to sell them back to the Holy See at the highest possible price, just as it was currently selling them to merchants—but it was still going to confiscate them. Oddly, the Vatican did not accept this offer. It is difficult to tell what the objection could have been, as earlier the Vatican had suggested an essentially similar arrangement. Perhaps the price was too high or they did not want to appear greedy in a quest to recover their own treasures. Or maybe it was Bolshevik handling (contamination) of sacred items that soured the deal. A more likely explanation is that the Soviets never intended this offer seriously.

In 1923 the Russian government turned its attention to the Catholic hierarchy—attention in the form of arrests, trials, and executions.

21

A STATESMAN OF THE CATHOLIC COUNTERREVOLUTION

Trials of the Catholic Clergy

In this chapter we shall begin with a few examples of the difficulties that Catholics faced under Soviet rule. Then we shall turn to the major trial of Catholic clergy in 1923 and follow the faith to the end of the decade.

HARROWING STORIES

A more bitter struggle is being waged against the Catholic clergy than against the Russian Church, because Catholic organization is more powerful than that of the Orthodox, and Catholic ideology is better adapted to the general conditions of life.

—*Bezbozhnik*, March 18, 1923

Father Klimaszewski

Reverend Xavier Klimaszewski had just been appointed vicar general of the diocese in Saratov on the middle Volga when Bolshevik repression of Catholics in this area began. In July 1919 he was arrested as a war hostage but was released a week later. The following January his apartment was searched for the fifth time, and for the fifth time a statement was drawn up that "nothing suspicious was found." The Cheka took him in for questioning anyway, and this time they took from him the keys to the cathedral. A search was made—with neither Klimaszewski nor any witnesses present. Klimaszewski claimed that Cheka agents tore up the boards under the cathedral altar and planted dynamite, bombs, and cartridges there. Then they called him to witness the "search" as they "discovered" the arsenal.

A confession was concocted, and Klimaszewski was given the choice of signing the document and receiving life in prison or refusing to sign and being shot on the spot. He chose neither, stating that he would sign only if the Cheka stipulated in writing that previous searches had found nothing suspicious, that his keys had been taken from him, and that no witnesses were present at the final search. He also insisted that he be allowed to sign each page of the confession. This was not acceptable, but the Cheka generously imprisoned him anyway.

While locked up, Klimaszewski was mocked, threatened, and cursed until his guards came to realize that he was too obstinate to comply with their wishes. They then agreed to his conditions and he signed the confession. His audacity earned him the worst possible treatment in prison: three months in a freezing cell, little food, and lice-infested clothes and mattress. Finally he was released— turned loose into the overcrowded city, destitute and in rags. Continually evading the police, who had decided to rearrest him, he eventually made his way to Poland, abandoning his Russian parish.[1]

A Nun's Story (1922)

Sister Helena wasn't exactly in hiding, but she wasn't going to show her face too easily either. Although Polish by extraction (her grandfather had come to Novgorod as a grain dealer), she no longer even spoke her ancestral language. She did, however, remember her ancestral faith. Along with six other sisters, ranging in age from 17 to 33, she lived in a third-floor, two-room flat in a run-down building on the north side of town. All were studying with the conflicted hope of being transferred to Petrograd as teachers, but only Helena was fully aware that Catholic schools had already been closed.

It was early September and already freezing in their heatless flat. Asleep under piles of blankets, they were awakened with a jolt just after midnight. Eleven people poured into the rooms. After her eyes adjusted to the single lightbulb's glare, she counted six soldiers and five GPU agents (one a woman) rousting the sisters out of bed with the barrels of their guns. With nothing but the blankets wrapped around their bodies, they were prodded into a corner of one room for a concentrated interrogation. Comrade Nogin, the GPU agent in charge, was relentless: "What are your connections to the Polish government? For whom are you spying? Where are the letters you have received from abroad? Have you connections with that Polish filth Budkiewicz? Why aren't you married like decent women? Haven't you heard that the virgin birth was an ancient myth resurrected by the early Christian fathers to prove their preposterous Jesus story? Who are the others in your sisterhood? All Catholics are part of the 'Black International' that is trying to overthrow the workers' government in liberated Russia."

Sister Helena and the others swore that they knew nothing of these things. They had heard good things of Monsignor Budkiewicz, but that was all. Two of the women spoke Polish as well as Russian, but this was never discovered, as none of the intruders were conversant in the enemy tongue. Nogin instructed the ten men in the room to hide their eyes, as the female GPU agent conducted a full body search of the seven women. Nothing was found, but Nogin found that unsurprising—who would sleep with incriminating documents? A search of the flat revealed only some suspicious small books written in some non-Slavic language that Nogin didn't recognize (or perhaps it was a cipher). The fruitless questioning went on for several more hours, imperceptibly switching its focus from espionage to antireligious invective. It was beyond Nogin's comprehension how seven apparently sane women could be so devoted to such nonsense. Finally, getting nowhere (but more frustrated) Nogin commanded that the nuns be ushered into the back of an awaiting truck and driven to the GPU facility downtown.

Since they had not been observed actually communicating with anyone outside of their third-floor "convent," even the usual charge of "inciting counterrevolutionary sentiments" could not be applied. After another day and night of incarceration, they were all released the following morning with a warning. The little books had turned out to be Latin catechisms.[2]

TRIALS AND PROTESTS

Thus we see today what was never before seen in history, the satanical banners of war against God and religion brazenly unfurled to the winds in the midst of every people and in all parts of the Earth.[3]

—Pope Pius XI

By 1922, sixty-eight Catholic priests (including Archbishop Ropp) had been ejected from Russia, and in the late winter of 1922–23 the government press stepped up its denunciations of those remaining.[4] An article in *Bezbozhnik* on March 18, 1923, asserted that Benito Mussolini had risen to power in Italy with the aid and support of the Vatican, implying that no more proof was needed to condemn all Catholics as fascists and anti-Communists.

Arrests and Trials

In Petrograd, Grigory Zinoviev was anxious to rid the city of its Catholic hierarchs, and prosecutor Nikolai Krylenko was equally in favor of trials. Other supporters may have been Trotsky, Lev Kamenev, Nikolai Bukharin, and GPU chief Felix Dzerzhinsky. Those who resisted (at least public) trials were those most concerned with the reaction of the world community: Mikhail Kalinin, George

Chicherin, Leonid Krassin, and Maxim Litvinov. Had he been in better health (and better informed), Lenin might have opposed the trials on tactical grounds.[5]

Initial arrests had begun in April 1920 when the Cheka searched the apartment of Monsignor Budkiewicz of St. Catherine's in Petrograd and found minutes of secret clerical meetings held from December 1918 to that date. According to the participants these thirteen conferences were held not to find ways to oppose the separation decree but to find ways to live with it. They wanted to know how the Catholic Church could accommodate itself to the Soviet system without sacrificing its essential beliefs. Cieplak, who had attended the meetings, was also accused of preaching a particularly anti-Soviet sermon, but after being interrogated by Dzerzhinsky for two weeks he was released.[6]

Amazingly, two years passed without further Soviet action on the matter. Then early in 1922 Krasikov ordered Archbishop Cieplak to appear in Petrograd for interrogation in regard to his attitude on the confiscation of church valuables. After a few days of intense questioning, he was ordered to write a letter to his clergy members ordering them not to resist. When he refused to cooperate, he was hauled in at least ten more times for increasingly harsh interrogations. Still he would not comply. The timing of these interrogations coincided with the height of the Catholic famine relief effort, and they may have been designed to counteract any favorable publicity the church gleaned as a result. The implicit question was: How could they be sincere in their relief work if they resisted the sale of church valuables to pay for famine relief?

Almost four years after the first meetings in Budkiewicz's apartment, government prosecutors finally decided there was enough evidence contained in the minutes of these meetings to justify a series of charges. In early November 1922 Cieplak was indicted for antireligious propaganda, inciting Catholics to subversion and arousing religious prejudices against the government.[7]

A trial of Petrograd Catholics was planned for the middle of that month but was postponed for four months with no reason given. One possibility was that the authorities wanted time to gather more evidence and widen the charges. A far more likely reason was revealed at the February 6, 1923, meeting of the Antireligious Commission. The Commission suggested to the Supreme Tribunal that any Catholic trial precede the planned Tikhon trial. If this were done, it could be used as a "trial balloon" calculated to gauge overseas reaction before tackling the larger and potentially more damaging case. Also, after failure at the Genoa Conference to achieve widespread European diplomatic recognition, the Bolshevik leadership had pretty much written off assistance from the Vatican; thus an insult to the Vatican was less of a concern. Another consideration was that the Anglican Church had a special affection for Russian Orthodoxy—primarily because it was anti-Catholic—and sentencing the patriarch to death would not be of much help in achieving British recognition. Better to try the least damaging case first.

On March 2, 1923, the government ordered sixteen Catholic leaders to report to the Supreme Revolutionary Tribunal in Moscow. Facing the wrath of the prosecution were Archbishop Cieplak, Monsignor Constantine Budkiewicz, Monsignor Anthony Malecki, Exarch Leonid Fyodorov, and the priests Edward Junievicz, Theophilus Matulanis, Stanislaus Ejsmont, Francis Rutkowski, Anthony Wasilewski, John Troigo, Paul Chodniewicz, Lucian Chwiecko, Peter Janukowicz, Dominic Ivanov, and Augustin Pronckietis. James Sharnas, a seventeen-year-old Lithuanian layman, was also charged.* Only one priest was left in Petrograd: Father Maurice Amoudru, a French Dominican who had a powerful state supporting him.[8]

Arriving by train on March 5, they enjoyed a few days of freedom. The GPU, however, interrogated Cieplak on March 9. He denied that he owed any allegiance to Warsaw—only to the Vatican—and he denied, since he had not yet been tried and sentenced, that he had appointed a successor as archbishop.[9] The next day the entire group was arrested and transported through the city in an open truck to the Butyrka Prison. There they were held in a single cell and were allowed no communication with their defense attorneys.

Rather than see a trial in Moscow, the pope demanded that the case be transferred to Rome, where he would act as an impartial judge. There, he promised, the Soviets could fairly present their case and justice would be served.[10] This must have led to some chuckling within the Kremlin walls. After the pope's demand was rejected, the trial finally got under way on Wednesday, March 21, in the Blue Room of the house of the Red Labor Unions (formerly the Club of the Nobility) near Opera Square in Moscow.[11] The chamber had been a ballroom in tsarist times; around it ran a frieze of dancing maidens and naked cupids trailing wreaths of roses. The sixteen accused were seated on wooden benches with straight backs, in five parallel rows—the most important in the front.

The higher the rank, the broader the brush with which the defendants were painted. The one archbishop, two monsignors, and one exarch were accused of many crimes—some added while the trial was in progress. Many of the lower clergy, however, were accused only of specific acts of resistance to government decrees, not grand conspiracies.

The accusations explained that there was only one line of action open to the clergy: elimination from their religious activities of "all suspicion of political action or of criticism of the government or of its laws." Anything beyond that was defined as a crime. Technically the Soviet constitution still guaranteed the "freedom of religious propaganda," but they were nonetheless charged with having published an anti-Bolshevik magazine in the Polish language. (It was very difficult even for an objective observer to distinguish between a proreligious publication and an anti-Bolshevik one, when almost any manifestation of positive views toward religion was, deep down, defined as counterrevolutionary.)

---

*For non-Polish-speaking readers, *j* is pronounced like an English *y*, *c* like an *s*, *w* like a *v*, and the ending *icz* like *ich*. Thus Monsignor Bood-key-e-vich.

Cieplak was specifically accused of issuing antigovernment propaganda, inciting Catholics to overthrow the Soviet government, and taking advantage of the religious superstitions of the people to bring about counterrevolution.[12] In addition to the charges filed against him the previous November, Cieplak (and most of the others) were accused of maintaining in Petrograd from late 1918 through late 1920 a counterrevolutionary organization (the above-mentioned meetings) designed to thwart the separation decrees of the Soviet government. It was something like a conspiracy charge in that it was their *intent* that was the violation of the law more than any actual *success* they achieved. In the middle of the trial, *Izvestia* claimed that these meetings were not just religious but *political* in nature. This charge was based on words Cieplak had written in a letter indicating that Catholic parochial committees needed to be established "pending the restoration of law and order in Russia." These words were a code, the newspaper charged (no doubt correctly), for "pending the overthrow of the Russian government."

All defendants were charged with resisting and violating three specific Soviet decrees:

- The obligation of twenty laymen of each parish to sign a contract with the local soviets acknowledging government ownership of church buildings and the conditions for using them.
- The requirement to turn over church treasures to the famine relief program.
- The prohibition against religious instruction of the young.[13]

In addition, many were charged with:

- continuing to hold services in private apartments after church buildings were closed in December 1922. All the priests admitted having done this, though none would admit to it being a crime.
- warning members of their parishes not to join the Communist Party.
- purchasing Communist publications so as to better equip themselves when teaching about the "insidious poison of Communism." At one such session Budkiewicz was accused of telling church members that the Communists, being socialists, shared their wives, as did the great apes. (At the trial he did not deny this, calling it only a "war of words.") Trying to get Catholics to leave the Communist Party, charged Krylenko, was a political act, though it is unclear why the Communists wanted Catholics in their party in the first place.

And Budkiewicz was specifically accused of trying to raise a loan for St. Catherine's Church by offering this already nationalized property as collateral.[14]

Captain Francis McCullagh,* who witnessed the trial—indeed, sat through every day of it—described Cieplak as a tall, upright, and spare man. His face was wrinkled, but he retained a full head of hair and bushy eyebrows. His mind was clear and he spoke distinctly. During the trial he wore his violet-red skullcap and cincture. A Bolshevik pamphlet published during the trial described him as "this episcopal director of the Russian branch of the Catholic Syndicate of Darkness and Profiteering."[15]

McCullagh described Budkiewicz as a man of medium height and stout build, with a ruddy face, a clear complexion, and very bright eyes. He was always cleanly shaven, and his small, white hands were indicative of his aristocratic origins. His neat-fitting cassock, bordered in red to denote his rank, made him so striking that he might have been mistaken for the secretary of state at the Vatican. He had the bearing of a man who could not be shaken from his beliefs and his chosen path. His manner was cold and impassive; he emitted no body language. But where McCullagh saw efficient virtue, the Bolsheviks saw a class enemy. It was his immovableness that made him so irritating to the Bolsheviks. Here he is portrayed in one of their pamphlets:

> There is among Catholics a special type of drawing-room prelate, and of this type Budkiewicz is a good example. He is rosy and fat, and strikingly elegant in a well-cut cassock. He wears pince-nez, and his shining bald head and clean-shaven jowl testify to years of a quiet life and to meticulous care of his own body. . . . He has an arrogant expression and a broad face, and he looks at the judges with an ill-concealed disgust. . . . He was a statesman of the Catholic counterrevolution.[16]

Leonid Fyodorov, exarch of the Eastern Rite Catholics was Russian, the son of a cook. He converted from the Orthodox Church and entered the Catholic Ecclesiastical Academy in St. Petersburg in 1905. He was ordained as a priest in Constantinople in 1911, later journeying to Lvov and then Kiev, all the time converting Russians and Ukrainians to the Greek Rite. After moving from Moscow to Petrograd, Benedict XV appointed him to his leadership post. He was thus under the control of the Vatican but not directly under Archbishop Cieplak. McCullagh pictured him at the trial:

> Fyodorov was in many respects the most picturesque figure in the court. A handsome, well-built man in the prime of life, with that strong, gentle, Christ-like face that is so often found among Russian peasants, with long, dark hair, a noble beard, and [the] ample flowing robes of the Russian ecclesiastic.[17]

---

*Though McCullagh was a highly respected foreign correspondent his Irish Catholicism inclined him toward sympathy for the accused. He saw no political activity among the defendants, only pure religious commitment.

A. V. Galkin, one of three judges in a trial without a jury, looked about forty-five years old. He was tall, with a broad, yellow, flabby face; a straggly mustache; and puffy eyes. McCullagh thought he looked Kyrgyz. While moderate in most matters of Bolshevik ideology, Galkin was fervent in his antireligious attitude. Earlier he had written scathing articles for *Pravda* attacking both the Orthodox and Catholic churches for withholding their treasures from famine relief. He was also a professor at the Bolshevik "Antireligious Seminary" that had opened just a few months earlier in Moscow. One of the other judges was presented as a worker and the other as a peasant. McCullagh was appalled by all three judges' abysmal ignorance of the basic tenets of the faith on trial. During the proceedings Galkin had to ask Fyodorov the meaning of the phrase "Graeco-Catholic," as he knew nothing of it. On occasion Cieplak ended up giving the judges and the prosecutor lectures on Catholic canon law, as they were ignorant not just of the details but of the origins and general scope of it. McCullagh thought he saw the judges lapse into an attitude of respect for the antiquity of this code, which had begun long before Russia even came into existence.

All judges, prosecutors, and prosecution witnesses were members of the Communist Party—Galkin asked each one to be sure—while the two defense attorneys, Bobrishchev-Pushkin and Kommodov, were both members of the Orthodox Church. Bobrishchev-Pushkin was a lawyer from the old regime, with a tall, noble bearing and a reputation for integrity. His lameness in one leg and long, white beard revealed his age. Kommodov was a large, plump man with a slight beard and mustache. He insisted on wearing a *rubashka*, a suit without collar or tie, in defiance of the judicial dress code of black Western suit and cuffs. Fyodorov, charged under Articles 62, 119, and 121, and with "maintaining a hostile spirit against the Soviet government," conducted his own defense.

Due to sensitivity about Western reaction, the government allowed these genuine defense attorneys to conduct their business as best they could, though they were not free to pursue a vigorous and aggressive case. While the prosecution called many witnesses, the defense was allowed none. Kommodov was arrested two weeks before the trial opened, while on his way to visit Cieplak in Petrograd. During his brief captivity he must have received a few "guidelines" as to courtroom conduct, as once the trial began both attorneys were reticent and apologetic and actually cringed when their clients took the stand to assert their positions with strong, uncompromising language. Krylenko, on the other hand, was overbearing and hostile, as befitted his knowledge of the outcome. (McCullagh also noticed a subtler sign of intimidation. There was a large and prominent sign in the courtroom reading "Smoking Strictly Prohibited," yet Galkin and Krylenko smoked whenever they pleased. No one else in the courtroom did.)

The refusal of the Petrograd clergy to sign the contracts and their encouragement of others around the country to follow their lead were the major charges.

Yet the hierarchs and priests never denied that they refused to sign; they simply said they could not do so without specific instructions from the Vatican, which were not initially forthcoming. Soviet authorities testified that they had attempted many times to negotiate the issue but had gotten nowhere. The obstinacy of the clergy on this issue was entirely predictable.

The prosecutors charged Budkiewicz with being the leader of the effort to resist the contracts, and they produced documents written in his hand showing him to have made these arguments to other clergy:

- Since signing the contracts violated canon law, those who did sign were subject to excommunication.
- "The nonsigning of the contracts had an advantage—we would not be bound by any obligations, and the Bolsheviks would have to pay more attention to the protesting Roman Catholics than to the yielding ones."

They also pointed out that when Budkiewicz had expected the imminent downfall of the Bolsheviks he had urged signing of the contracts, but when he finally realized that the regime was firmly entrenched he urged refusal. Thus it was not difficult for Krylenko to demonstrate to the judges' satisfaction that this defendant had committed crimes against the state.[18]

Strangely, at one point in the trial Krylenko, frustrated with the clergy's contention that only the pope could make decisions regarding Catholic churches in Russia, insisted that the churches belonged to those on trial. Apparently in the heat of argument he had forgotten government decrees on land and property nationalization. Another interesting twist on the contract issue was that several weeks before the trial opened the pope *did* send permission for the clergy to sign the contracts. On the fourth day of the trial Cieplak tried to argue that this charge against him was now out of date. Would this take the wind out of the prosecutor's sails? Not at all; Krylenko expressed his total disinterest in communications between the Vatican and the Russian clergy and in issues of canon law. He was interested only in political crimes transpiring within the borders of the USSR.[19]

The prosecutor accused Cieplak of sending out a pastoral letter in January 1922 protesting the confiscation of church valuables and containing the aforementioned injunction to his clergy about not delivering the inventory.[20] This was interpreted as violating Article 77 of the penal code, which prohibited "any participation in civil disorders," any "acts of disobedience to the legal demands of the civil authorities," or any hindrance of the authorities while carrying out their official duties. Then Krylenko violated his previous disinterest in external communications by charging that Cieplak had been ordered by the Vatican to purposely create incidents of resistance to compel the government to negotiate directly with the Holy See. (This seems unlikely, however, as it was the Soviets who were desirous of receiving diplomatic representation from the Vatican, not the other way around.)

The priests Rutkowski and Pronckietis were conducting services at the Church of the Assumption of the Blessed Virgin on December 5, 1922, when this church had already been officially closed. The authorities warned them of their transgression but they were ignored. When the authorities entered the church to take the valuables, the priests threw themselves upon their knees and asked that the congregation join them in prayer. The authorities interpreted this as passive resistance and charged the priests under Article 119 (utilizing the religious superstitions of the masses to plot against the government). When Rutkowski testified about this at the trial, Krylenko shouted, "That was a counterrevolutionary act!"[21] The following exchange then took place between prosecutor and witness:

Krylenko:	Did you know of the Soviet decree . . . ordering sacred vessels to be confiscated for famine relief purposes?
Rutkowski:	I did, in a general way. But there are other laws—those of God and of the Catholic Church.
Krylenko:	We care not about any other law. There is no law here but Soviet law. When that law comes into conflict with any other law, you must choose which you will obey.
Rutkowski:	I will obey the law of God and of my conscience.
Krylenko:	Your conscience does not interest me in the least.
Rutkowski:	But it is of very great importance to me.
Judge Galkin:	Your conscience has nothing to do with this trial.[22]

Were Russian Catholics morally bound to obey the laws of the state or the laws of the church when the two were mutually contradictory? Did an appeal to canon law justify refusal to obey Soviet law? From the perspective of the government, the press, the judges, and the prosecutors there was never any doubt about how these questions must be answered. Thus the defense argument that Catholic clergy were obeying the laws of God had no effect on Krylenko. He responded that canon law was a product of the Middle Ages, a time when the church claimed powers above temporal authority, and that it had no bearing on the Modern Age—and certainly none on the modern, atheistic state of the Soviet Union.[23] Outside the courtroom *Izvestia* offered historical arguments that canon law had been interpreted flexibly in other times and places. For example, it had adjusted to the separation of church and state in both France and the United States, so why could it not practice the same "opportunism"—for which the church was notorious—in the Soviet Union?

In response to the charge of illegally giving religious instruction to the young, many of the priests freely admitted holding secret educational sessions with the children of their parish, and some said they would continue to do it in the future.[24] This courtroom exchange took place between Krylenko and Cieplak:

Krylenko:	What is it that gives the Catholic clergy so strong an influence over the minds of the faithful? Are not the schools your principal means?
Cieplak:	Not only the schools, but, above all, our teachings of the truth, of the moral precepts of Christ, the influence of the faith and of divine grace.
Krylenko:	Let us talk of things a man can understand. We see clearly that by your teachings about torments in the other world you frighten and mystify the ignorant and the children. Now, the terrorization of the ignorant is political action.[25]

As the trial progressed, Krylenko seems to have developed an interest in "the Polish connection," though nothing concerning this was included in the original indictment. He accused both Cieplak and Budkiewicz of being agents for a foreign state—Poland—which only a few years before had been at war with the Red Army. Apparently Cieplak had received some Vatican letters that had been channeled through the papal nuncio in Warsaw, and Budkiewicz, had approached the Polish government for 400,000 rubles in loan guarantees (for expenses at St. Catherine's) and had expressed some loyalty to his country of ancestry. It looked somewhat worse for Budkiewicz, who, unlike Cieplak, was a Russian citizen—therefore more traitorous. The prosecutor had trouble, however, clinching these points and soon moved on to other charges.[26] Other than the Polish connection, there was never any question about the *facts* of the case; the priests freely admitted taking almost every action they were accused of.

The Vatican, the Russian Catholic Church, and the two Orthodox defense attorneys naively believed that if they played their cards right there was a chance to win—winning being defined as the survival of the Catholic Church in Russia (or perhaps just in Petrograd). Bobrishchev-Pushkin and Kommodov followed the strategy of giving no unnecessary offense to the judges, yet standing firm on matters of principle. Nonetheless, they myopically saw the courtroom struggle as being over alleged violations of specific laws and decrees. Thus early in the trial the defense entered as evidence letters the pope had sent to Chicherin offering to pay in one lump sum the value of all Catholic church treasures in Russia, and they described Chicherin's complete lack of response. But this evidence was just ignored by the judges and by the press as if it never entered their consciousness.

Although at times the defendants boldly stood up for their principles, at others they minimized the differences between themselves and the Soviets. Father Troigo repeated the argument that the clergy members were not trying to resist Soviet decrees but rather hoped to find ways of complying with them without doing violence to their consciences. For example, to avoid defying the decree separating church and state the clergy held family services in private homes. But Krylenko responded by showing that frequently 100 to 150 persons attended these services, hence they were public. In addition, full liturgical paraphernalia was being utilized—illegally obtained paraphernalia that should have been sealed up with the closed church buildings.

On March 23, after the trial's second day, *Pravda* carried an article titled "Christian Exploits—Trial of Roman Catholic Priests." It claimed that they had passed a resolution concerning "the struggle from the altar against the Bolshevik infection" and had excommunicated parishioners for joining the Communist Party. The article concluded: "Even a blind man could see that the case is purely political and has nothing to do with religion."[27] Inside the courtroom, the defense begged to differ:

- The meetings the clergy had attended dealt with purely ecclesiastical—not political—matters.
- The acts of noncompliance with decrees were isolated incidences, and no implication of conspiracy could be drawn from them.
- Article 57 defined counterrevolution as "intending to abolish the Soviet power," and surely the clergy had not set such a tremendous task for themselves.[28]

The defendants and their attorneys tried to convince the prosecutor and the judges of the distinction between the *religious* struggle against atheism and the *political* struggle against the state. Cieplak argued that fighting atheism was his sacred duty but agreed that he had no right whatsoever to fight against the government. Father Chodniewicz rose at one point to explain how Catholicism was concerned with Marxism only insofar as it affected religion, but Communists in the courtroom saw Marxism as a unity and refused to admit any such distinction. Kommodov proposed that semantics were at the root of the problem, as Communists had no term for ideas that were simply in opposition, other than the word "counterrevolutionary." Thus the conflict had been blown way out of proportion. He also pointed out that the clergy had been thoroughly trained in their beliefs, and it was too much to expect them to instantly accept the Soviet system.

At one point Cieplak brought up the Treaty of Riga's guarantee of immunity for the Catholic Church, but Krylenko jumped to his feet and pointed to the loophole phrase "within the limits of the internal legislation of the RSFSR." Bobrishchev-Pushkin suggested that even if the defendants were found guilty the proper punishment would be deportation to either Poland or Vatican City.

Only near the closing arguments did it begin to dawn on the defense attorneys that the trial was really concerned with fundamental ideological and political antagonisms and that details really did not matter. The government, of course, knew what was going on from the start, giving it the advantage. Yet *in public* the conflict was never allowed to seem ideological; it was always over the application of specific laws to specific activities. Knowing the world was watching, the government could thus avoid the onus of persecution and intolerance of religion.

In his speech to the court on the final day, Fyodorov stressed his great love for the Greek Rite Church and for Russia; these were the guiding principles of his life. Russian Catholics, he said, were as loyal as any other Russians, and he described how joyous they had been when hearing the news of the Revolution; now they would be free from tsarist oppression and free to live equally with other churches. He also congratulated the Bolsheviks for the decree separating church and state. Although these sounded like obsequious comments, Fyodorov was sincere and principled and went on to describe the wrenching difficulties that Catholics faced when they tried to obey Soviet law.[29]

Krylenko then began his two-hour-long closing arguments. Raising his voice, he stated that the purpose of the prosecution was to study the activities of the Catholic clergy under the actual conditions of life in Russia. The laws had been violated, the accused were the violators, and the crimes were "socially dangerous." Enraged, he shouted, "As for your religion—I spit on it, as I do on all religions: Orthodox, Jewish, Mohammedan, and the rest."[30]

Sentences and Protests

When Krylenko demanded that the clergy be sentenced under the new Criminal Code, Articles 69 and 199, the defense attorneys made a last-ditch argument that these laws had not even been written when some of the alleged crimes were perpetrated. "Revolutionary legality," however, prohibited consideration of this technicality. The *London Times* referred to this as "the Soviet's elastic system of justice."[31]

Under Soviet law all the defendants could have been sentenced to death, but Krylenko "mercifully" recommended it only for Cieplak, Budkiewicz, Ejsmont, and Chwiecko—the "instigators and organizers" and the ones deemed most likely to continue breaking the law. Concerning the deportation option, he rejected it with an inept analogy: "That would be like throwing the fish back in the water."[32] He spoke directly to the four condemned men:

All the Jesuitical duplicity with which you have defended yourself will not save you from the death penalty. No pope in the Vatican can save you now. . . . There is no law but the Soviet law, and by that law you must die. I demand the death penalty, not because we are bloodthirsty, but because it is necessary to make people understand that we will allow no one to attempt to overthrow the revolutionary people's government with impunity.[33]

For the others, Krylenko recommended sentences ranging from three to ten years in prison,[34] and for the seventeen-year-old boy, Sharnas, he recommended only six months.

As mentioned, the Soviets were sensitive on the issue of the sentences in relation to the world beyond their borders. Chicherin's deputy, Maxim Litvinov, constantly reassured the foreign press during the trial that there "would be no shooting." The Soviet representative in Rome gave similar assurances to the Vatican, as did the Soviet ambassador in Warsaw to the Polish government. Outgoing telegrams were carefully censored to avoid arousing foreign sympathy for the accused. When one reporter described how "the Polish women fell on their knees" at the sentencing, it was lined out before being sent.

At the stroke of midnight on Saturday, March 25 (Palm Sunday), the judge read the verdicts and sentences to the court. Not surprisingly, he declared the clergy guilty on every charge and every count. He accepted Krylenko's recommendations for sentencing, except that the two priests—Ejsmont and Chwiecko—were spared the death penalty. Cieplak and Budkiewicz were condemned to be shot in three days; Fyodorov, Chodniewicz, Chwiecko, Juniewicz, and Ejsmont received ten-year terms; Pronckietis, Rutkowski, Ivanov, Troigo, Matulanis, Janukowicz, Wasilewski, and Malecki received three-year terms; and Sharnas got his six months.[35] The next day, however, *Izvestia* announced that the two death sentences were to be postponed until further notice. Hesitation was due to fear of foreign reaction if the two hierarchs were actually shot, but it is also likely that they were being kept as bargaining chips in Soviet negotiations for diplomatic recognition.

Protests against these sentences emanated most strongly, of course, from Warsaw. The Polish newspaper *Gazette Poranna* blatantly accused the government of the bargaining-chip tactic:

> The "postponement" of death sentences has become a regular weapon in the hands of the Red tyrants with which they terrorize and blackmail the civilized world. In the meantime the wretched condemned will slowly die.[36]

Prime Minister Sikorsky spoke in the Polish Diet of the harshness of Soviet "justice," but the Soviets just turned this around and claimed Polish outrage proved that Catholics in Russia were "agents of foreign capital."

Protests followed from other countries. On March 29 the following telegram was sent from Bern, Switzerland, through Poland to the Soviet leadership:

> The entire press of Switzerland—Roman Catholic as well as Protestant—protests with indignation against the new crimes of the Soviets. The majority of the newspapers utter their hope that the Soviet government will at the last moment stop before committing a crime that would prove that it still adheres to its barbarous policy, thereby excluding Soviet Russia from the number of civilized powers.[37]

The British House of Commons was on the verge of expelling all Russian commercial agents, and the Catholic Irish sent vehement denunciations of the sentences.

The Soviet press responded by calling all such protests "a chorus of counterrevolutionary jackals and hyenas" and labeling the pope as the head of an international conspiracy of "counterfeit indignation." On March 30 *Izvestia* carried this tirade against British hypocrisy:

> Old Ben Turner [head of a British labor mission to Petrograd in May 1920] sent us the following wire: "Human life is valuable. Don't hang the archbishop." English labor press has not spent even one tenth of the sum paid for that telegram on a similar telegram of protest against the execution of South African strikers so brutally carried out at the orders of the idol of British liberalism, General Smuts. But when it comes to priests, the Labor Party remembers that human life is sacred.[38]

Karl Radek wrote an article in *Pravda* on April 15 threatening to concoct a history of the archbishops of Canterbury (who had spearheaded many protests), revealing all their sins—including their illegitimate children—and to circulate one million copies in England. And how, the Soviet press reasonably continued, could the current Archbishop of Canterbury assume the mantle of righteous indignation when his forebears had burnt such a large number of Catholics at the stake?[39]

We will never know for sure if these protests triggered a twinge of compassion in the Soviet heart or if the government's reaction was part of a cynical manipulation of international opinion. There is some evidence to suggest that Edmund Walsh had been asked by the Soviets to relay private assurances to the Vatican *before the trial had even begun* that if death sentences were imposed they would be later rescinded. Apparently Commissar Chicherin had told the German ambassador to Moscow the same thing.[40]

Either way, on March 29 the All-Russian Central Executive Committee, having reviewed the petitions of both Cieplak and Budkiewicz, commuted Cieplak's sentence to ten years imprisonment in strict isolation. It offered two explanations:

- Cieplak had misinterpreted the religious freedom granted to all citizens.
- "The carrying out of the punishment which he really deserves might be interpreted by the most backward elements of the Roman Catholic population . . . as directed primarily against their creed."[41]

A more plausible explanation is that the Soviets were concerned with the danger of creating martyrs. The execution of Cieplak would surely have hardened Catholic hearts toward the government. And how would the headline "Archbishop Shot" appear in foreign print? By sentencing Cieplak to death and then showing mercy the Soviets could hail the benign quality of their judicial system and further refute charges of religious persecution.

Domestically, however, they did not want "mercy" misconstrued. An *Izvestia* article on March 30 asked for understanding:

The mildness of the Soviet government must not be falsely interpreted. Let everyone know that under whatever banner the active counterrevolution might hide itself, it would be ruthlessly dealt with by the Soviet government.[42]

On this theme, Budkiewicz's petition for clemency was rejected, as the Soviets placed his case in a different category. The same issue of *Izvestia* wrote that mercy could not be applied in Budkiewicz's case, as he was "an agent of the Polish Government . . . whose counterrevolutionary actions were dictated not so much by religious fanaticism, as in the case of Cieplak, as by the interests of the foreign powers." High treason could not be forgiven, said the Central Executive Committee. Let international diplomats "howl as much as they like—that will not alter our decision."[43]

The details of Budkiewicz's execution are difficult to obtain. A few lines in *Pravda* on April 3 announced that the deed had been done three days earlier. McCullagh provided the following account, which he said he had obtained from a "reliable source." Budkiewicz was taken to the Lubyanka prison on the night of Good Friday and made to descend stairs into the cellar. There he was stripped naked and forced to walk through the corridors. At the end of one corridor he was told to enter a darkened room, where someone switched on a bright light, startling him; then he was shot in the back of the head by an experienced executioner. (Another account says that he blessed his executioner before being shot.) His body was wrapped in cloth and transported by truck to Sokolniki, near Moscow, where he was buried along with nine bandits.* The official announcement triggered new rounds of international protest, many countries referring to it as "judicial murder."[44] The extent of this protest may have been instrumental in Tikhon's release in late June.

The government was able to have it both ways: It had shown its merciful nature by granting clemency to Cieplak and shown its implacable determination to root out counterrevolution by executing Budkiewicz. A year after his sentencing, Cieplak was ordered out of prison and into an automobile, having had no idea whether he would be freed or shot. His Russian guards, without explanation, drove him to the Latvian border, handed him some bread and a fish, and put him (ticketless) onto the train bound for Riga. He had been traded for three Bolsheviks in Polish prisons and then expelled from Russia. In 1926 the convicted Polish priests were exchanged in the same manner, and Fyodorov was paroled (but banned from Russia's six major cities). When he resumed preaching his ecumenical ideas in Moghilev, he was rearrested and sent to the Solovetsky Island camp to finish his ten-year sentence.[45]

---

*The similarity of this story to that of Jesus being crucified along with two thieves should incline one to some suspicion concerning this detail.

Trying the Pope: An Exercise in Futility

Radical elements within the Soviet leadership saw the logical next step to be a direct attack on the pope himself. Had not all the defendants sworn that their first allegiance was to him? Were they not following his specific orders? Pius XI was the ringleader, and the clergy on trial had been mere accomplices.

Pravda, on March 31, 1923 (the day of Budkiewicz's scheduled execution), urged this measure, adding, "The recent trial and the sentence pronounced . . . have proven . . . that the Catholic clergy are the bitter enemy of the poor and of the Peasants' and Workers' Government." The article even accused Catholics of refusing aid to famine victims![46]

On April 3 *Pravda* carried an article titled "Why Have No Proceedings Been Instituted against the Pope?" Was it because he offered no direct resistance? No, as Patriarch Tikhon was facing trial and he had not resisted—at least recently. Was it fear of international complications? No, because those complications could arise only from "real and material economic causes," not the trial of a priest.

> Or perhaps [the article continued] it was thought that as the pope is outside Soviet Russia it would be impossible to carry the verdict out? . . . Yet we are firmly convinced, nay, more, we know that it will be carried out, for sooner or later bourgeois Italy will become a Soviet country, and then his holiness the pope will be in exactly as awkward a position as his colleague Patriarch Tikhon.
> . . .
> After all the pope is regarded by devout Catholics as being an infallible, saintly, almost supernatural being. Imagine this saint being tried and sentenced as an ordinary layman![47]

Trials of Pius XI were actually conducted in various localities throughout Russia in 1923, but these were by local soviets and never received Moscow's official sanction.

CATHOLICS AT THE END OF THE DECADE

Between 1924 and 1929 persecution of the Catholic Church in Russia abated somewhat. Anti-Catholic propaganda continued, however, and a few new martyrs were created. This was consistent with the new trend in antireligious propaganda described in an earlier chapter. There were no more *public* Catholic trials during the 1920s. There were more arrests of Catholic clergy between 1923 and 1925, but after short periods of imprisonment the accused were quietly escorted to the border and released—Bobrishchev-Pushkin got his way.[48]

There was, however, a *secret* trial of Monsignor Theophile Skalsky, apostolic administrator of the diocese of Zytomir and dean of the St. Alexander Church in Kiev. He was a champion of Ukrainian Poles who had been encouraging young people to abandon the USSR and travel to Poland for seminary training. For those who remained, he preached resistance to the Soviet way of life. His activities did not escape notice for long, and he was arrested in June 1926 and charged with counterrevolutionary activities ("paralyzing the efforts of the Soviets to educate Ukrainian Poles in the Communist spirit") and espionage, though there was no evidence to support the second charge. A year and a half later he was tried by the Military Collegium of the Supreme Soviet, which traveled to Kiev just for this purpose. Convicted and sentenced to ten years in prison, his punishment was widely publicized throughout the region as a deterrent to others. In 1929 the Soviets staged a massive roundup of Catholic clergy in the Ukraine.[49]

By the end of 1923 every episcopal see in Russia was leaderless. After the expulsion of Cieplak in 1924, the government refused to allow the appointment of any more bishops in Russia. Pius XI then, not wanting his Russian flock to wander leaderless, secretly consecrated Father Eugene Neveu, a French cleric who had been living in Russia for twenty years. The secret, however, must have slipped out, as the police quickly put him under surveillance and neutralized him.[50]

A Polish Catholic in Russia wrote to Archbishop Cieplak in Rome explaining the current problems of his church under Soviet control as of 1925. Authorities were concentrating on Poles in White Russia, he wrote, under the pretext of stamping out nationalist propaganda. (No doubt there was clerical nationalist propaganda along the borderlands, but Catholic priests in Petrograd at least had been scrupulous in avoiding it.) The 242 Catholic priests in White Russia in 1915 had been reduced to 67. He warned of the Soviet tactic of creating wholly autonomous parishes, which would then be infiltrated and taken over by local Communist groups and destroyed from within. And do not, he stressed to Cieplak, allow the Vatican to enter into any concordat with the Soviet government, which will break any agreement that it signs.[51]

Anti-Catholic sources made allegations that the Soviets were deeply involved in negotiations with the Vatican during 1925 and 1926. The theory was that the Living Church was increasingly perceived as a failed experiment—or at least one that had run its course—and new wedges had to be created to weaken the Orthodox Church. What better wedge than renewed and increased Catholic activity in Russia? (This may sound familiar, as it closely parallels conspiracy theories of the early 1920s discussed in the previous chapter.) According to the modern-day Orthodox deacon Herman Ivanov-Treenadzaty, secret documents have been uncovered within the bowels of French Foreign Ministry archives that confirmed accusations not so much against Communists as against Catholics. One February 1925 telegram from the French Embassy in Berlin claimed that the Soviet ambassador to Berlin offered Cardinal Pacelli—the future Pope Pius XII—

access to Russian territory for Catholic bishops and a metropolitan. Another telegram described an offer of a Catholic seminary with the very best of accouterments. Further discussions apparently took place during the autumn of 1926.[52]

The problem with these "revelations" was that the events they describe were not all that secret. It is widely known that in 1925 there were talks in Berlin between Chicherin and the papal nuncio regarding the appointment of Catholic bishops in Russia and about the handling of Vatican funds destined for Catholic clergy in Russia. Nothing came of these discussions, and in 1927 the pope indicated he was dissatisfied with Soviet concessions.

What nixed the venture from the Russian side was the conversion of Metropolitan Sergei to an attitude of cooperation with the government. Once the Soviet Church was in place, Orthodoxy was under control; there was no longer a need for wedges. As a loyal Tikhonite, Ivanov-Treenadzaty did not credit Sergei with ending the "Catholic threat"—it was merely a coincidental and fortunate result of his "ungodly act."[53]

Many Russian Catholics thought it was time to make administrative changes, due to borders that had changed since World War I and the decimation of the hierarchy. Now that the government was easing up on its attacks, perhaps the church would have time to rebuild. The reorganization mission was entrusted to the French Jesuit Michel d'Herbigny, president of the Pontifical Commission for Russia. D'Herbigny first arrived in Moscow in 1925 but then returned to Rome. In February 1926 Pius XI was "divinely inspired" to secretly ordain d'Herbigny as a bishop and send him back into Russia to lay his hands on the shoulders of others. As far as the Bolsheviks originally knew, his papal mandate was to "encourage the Catholics to be steadfast in their faith," but with far-reaching and clandestine authority he proceeded to rearrange the dioceses of Russia into nine new ecclesiastical administrative districts, four of them headed by bishops he himself secretly ordained.[54]

D'Herbigny, however, failed to cover his tracks. When word got out that there were French, Polish, German, and Latvian clergy among these bishops, their multinational character caused more consternation among Soviet leaders than if they had all been Polish. When two of the new bishops were packed off to Siberian work camps, the Vatican owned up to its undercover operations, and D'Herbigny was recalled and retired from service. The new administrators, once appointed, were one-by-one singled out for martyrdom. Monsignor Ilyin of Kharkov was arrested in December 1926, and Bishop Sloskans of Moghilev and Minsk and Monsignor Neveu of Moscow were arrested during the winter of 1927. Sloskans was sent to Siberia, then to Solovky, and then exiled. By 1932 all—except for Monsignor Neveu, who enjoyed French citizenship—had disappeared into the Soviet prison system, been shot, or been escorted to the border never to return.[55] The new church hierarchy was exterminated along with the old.

Edmund Walsh was later able to recite a long list of Catholic clergy who had been arrested during the years 1927–28, in spite of the apparent lull, and sent to prison camps on the Solovetsky Islands. Typical of these was Father Dominic Ivanov, vicar of St. Catherine's in Leningrad and one of the defendants in the 1923 trial. He was transferred to the islands in 1928, where he froze to death. Walsh estimated that by 1930, half of the Catholic clergy in Russia had been executed, imprisoned, exiled, or forced into starvation. The graph below demonstrates even more drastic reductions by 1934. On the other hand, the anti-Catholic Joseph McCabe accused Walsh of reporting with Jesuit fervor, wildly exaggerating these numbers and ignoring the treasonous activities (from the Bolshevik perspective) of some of the clergy. McCabe cited another instance of overzealous reporting aimed at foreign audiences: Lancelot Lawton, in *The Russian Revolution* (1927), claimed that 1,275 bishops had been shot, though there were actually nowhere near that number of bishops *and* archbishops in both the Catholic *and* Orthodox Churches combined.[56]

The Decline of Catholic Priests & Members of Catholic Religious Orders over 17 Years

Source: Gussoni and Brunello, *The Silent Church*, p. 19

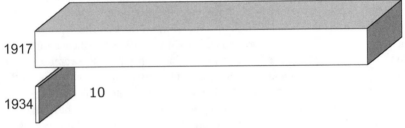

1917

1934   10

Most of the Catholic churches, monasteries, schools, orphanages, and poorhouses had been closed, and Pius XI was driven to the limit of his endurance. He despaired of any reconciliation with Moscow. In 1929 he established the *Russicum* in Rome, a Jesuit center for the study of Orthodoxy and future Catholic missions into Russia.[57] On February 2, 1930, he wrote to Cardinal Pompili:

> Since Christmas not only have several churches been closed, ikons burned, workers and schoolchildren forced to take part in the campaign, and the Sabbath rest abolished, but the factory workers, men and women, have been compelled to sign declarations of apostasy and of hatred against God under penalty of losing their bread cards and food and shelter, without which in that unhappy country they can only die of famine, misery, and cold.[58] [The part about the bread cards was a consequence of rumormongering, from which the pope was not immune.]

On March 19 the pope held a Mass of Expiation in St. Peter's Cathedral "for the salvation of so many souls put to such dire trials and for the release of our dear Russian people and that these great tribulations may cease." In a sense his prayers were an admission that his missionary probes into Communist Russia were a failed policy.[59] (It would take Pius XI until 1937, however, to issue the encyclical *Divini Redemptori* denouncing communism.)

Although he prayed for Orthodox as well as Catholic, it must not be assumed that tolerance was a value for him. Only the year before, this same pope had signed the Concordat with the Fascist Mussolini. The Holy Father had pressured Mussolini at that time to make Catholicism the sole religion of Italy, and restrictions on Protestants and apostates had become matters of law. The American Catholic Monsignor Ryan justified these policies as "truth having rights and error none."[60]

*   *   *

Earlier in the 1920s there existed a popular theory that Catholics were treated with leniency because they had been persecuted under the tsars, because they were a small minority in Russia, because they had powerful friends abroad, because the Soviets needed diplomatic relations with the Vatican, or because the Soviets hoped to use the Catholic Church against the Orthodox Church. But little leniency was actually shown. The plain fact is that the Catholic Church had always been vulnerable. Lacking the mass base of Orthodoxy and stigmatized by its foreignness, by the end of the decade it was virtually wiped out in Russia.[61]

Besides Catholics, there were numerous offshoots from the Orthodox Church that the Bolsheviks had to deal with. These, along with Protestants in Russia, were classified as sectarians, and, like Catholics, they posed special problems for the Bolshevik antireligious crusade.

22

GREATEST MENACE

Sectarians

W hile the great mass of Russians, White Russians, and Ukrainians worshiped within the Orthodox faith, other Christian denominations
existed within these areas as well. Here we will look at the conflict
between the Communists and the groups they called "sectarians." Soviet antireligious policy was theoretically nondiscriminatory—in itself an improvement
over tsarist days—but because of their historical experiences and particular the-
ologies, Soviet policy had different meanings for different denominations.
Because of the Civil War and because of early attempts to woo sectarians, serious
antireligious work among them did not get started until 1923.

A BRIEF INTRODUCTION TO THE SECTS

Most sectarians can conveniently be placed within two large groupings—offshoots
from Orthodoxy and Western imports—though, as we will see below, the Soviets
had an alternative way of defining the categories. Both the tsarist and the Soviet
governments described "sectarians" as non-Orthodox and non-Catholic Christians.
For the Orthodox Church the term sectarian had a strongly pejorative sense, but for
the Soviets there was a tilt in the opposite direction, at least for a while.

Offshoots from Orthodoxy

During the reign of Tsar Alexis, Patriarch Nikon (1605–81) endeavored to return
Russian Orthodox practices to consistency with the earliest Greek Byzantine
sources and in the process discarded "corruptions" in tradition, misrepresentations on ikons, and copying errors in texts that had slipped into his church largely
unnoticed. He antagonistically declared, "I am Russian, but my faith and religion

412

are Greek."[1] The Old Believers were those within Russian Orthodoxy who rebelled against this break with (corrupted) tradition. They were referred to as Raskolniki, meaning literally to "split asunder."*

The Dukhobors were an eighteenth- and nineteenth-century offshoot of the Russian Orthodox Church. Originally calling themselves Christians of the Universal Brotherhood, they eventually were stuck with the Dukhobors (Spirit Wrestlers) name, derisively assigned to them by their parent church. Doctrinally similar to the English and American Quakers, they rejected sacraments, church hierarchy, and most other outward symbols of Christianity. The soul, they believed, entered the body in stages between the ages of six and fifteen.[2] Dukhobors came from the lower, peasant level of society, living democratically and communally. As they worked hard, saved their money, and abstained from alcohol, they prospered in whatever environment they found themselves. Nonetheless, government persecution drove many to emigrate to Canada.

Molokans, or Spiritual Christians, were a utopian sect that split from the Dukhobors around 1770 but were also in rebellion against the Orthodox Church. The Russian term *molokane* (milk drinkers) was another example of derogative nicknames applied by Orthodox clergy, in this case because during religious fasts they permitted the drinking of milk. Believing that they knew best how to organize their lives without external government, they obeyed the tsars only out of necessity. Molokans emerged first in Tambov and Voronezh provinces, then proselytized their way southward into the Volga and Crimea regions. Tsarist persecution in the 1840s drove many eastward into the Caucasus and Central Asia. At their peak in the late nineteenth century they may well have numbered three-quarters of a million. As a group, they were cursed with internal dissension and schisms too numerous and complicated to delve into here. Some were ideological cousins of the American Pentecostals, feeling the Holy Spirit descending

---

*The points of discord may seem trifling to the modern Western mind—reminiscent of the proverbial debates in the Middle Ages over how many angels could dance on the head of a pin—but to those involved at the time they were taken quite seriously. Ancient Greek churchgoers had been tridactylous, crossing themselves with three fingers, while somewhere back in time the Russians had changed to the bipennate two fingers. A monk told Bernard Pares that it was absurd to cross oneself with three fingers, as three represented the Trinity, and the Holy Spirit was never on the Cross. Two fingers represented the dual nature of God and man, and both of these natures were crucified. The Greeks had recited three hallelujahs in the liturgy, while the Russians had dropped to two; there was a difference in the number of ritual prostrations performed before the altar; and Nikon had changed the spelling of Jesus's name from Isus to Iisus, robbing it of its magical potency. By 1656 Nikon had managed to institute the Greek procedures within the Russian Church, and in 1669 the law made membership in the Old Believers a capital crime. Many were tortured—ripping out of nostrils with pincers was common, as was herding people into barns and setting them ablaze.

Origins of Russian Sects

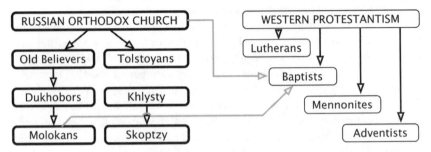

Dark-bordered sects are of Russian origin (though the vast majority of Baptists and Evangelicals were native Russians). Arrows indicate paths of conversions. Of course, this chart is simplified, as relationships were complex.

upon them and driving them into religious ecstasy and trancelike jumping about. Others adjusted themselves to surrounding secular life and became hardly distinguishable from the Orthodox. Their idealistic ethics were equality, brotherhood, and pacifism, and their practical ethics were no meat, no alcohol, no tobacco, and no foul language. Brotherhood was their greatest consistent virtue, as their communities allowed no exploitation of another's labor and tolerated no hunger or poverty.[3] Molokans had great confidence in human reason, which separated them from Russian Baptists, who believed that man's fate was entirely in God's hands. They stressed man's ability to shape his own environment through his own moral and intellectual efforts. Thus education, especially scientific education, was a high priority; if science conflicted with the Bible they went with science.

The mystical sect of the Khlysty (Flagellants) originated in Russia at the end of the seventeenth century. They believed in the "permanent incarnation of God in the individual" and the continuing reincarnation of Christ, Mary, and the Apostles. At their meetings they whipped themselves with birch saplings or belts into a religious fervor as they called forth the Holy Spirit, but instead of receiving it they often fell into orgiastic excesses. The lure of this sect was its mysticism and secrecy—much like the Gnostics in the ancient Middle East. And like the Gnostics they outwardly obeyed all the rules and practices of the established church to avoid detection, while secretly claiming that priests of the church had missed the true road to God. Only within the Khlysty could ordinary men communicate directly with their Heavenly Father. Though rejecting marriage, the movement spread horizontally among the peasant and merchant classes. During the reign of Alexander I it penetrated even the high society of St. Petersburg. This sect is perhaps most famous for its influence on Rasputin, who appreciated its teaching that it was necessary to yield to the temptations of the flesh to overcome them and achieve forgiveness.[4]

The Skoptzy—the sect of the castrated—began in 1757 as missionaries traveled through the countryside promising redemption and salvation if only a male convert would agree to amputation of first his testicles and later his penis. Apparently they rationalized self-mutilation by a contorted reading of Matthew 18:8–9. Sexuality, they claimed, led to damnation. This practice was also justified by the self-castration of Origen, one of the early church fathers, and by the seventy-two eunuchs found in the list of Christian saints. Boys were often castrated and then were escorted from village to village to be displayed as part of the conversion effort. Women were not excluded, often having clitoral and breast amputations as a sign of commitment and devotion.[5]

A brief mention should be made of the Tolstoyans. Leo Tolstoy had been excommunicated from the Orthodox Church for his unorthodox views—especially his pacifism. Although he died in 1910, his followers persevered.

Western Imports

Marx and Engels saw Catholicism and Orthodoxy as perfect expressions of feudalism and Protestantism as the perfect expression of capitalism. (For example, the Calvinist belief in predestination mirrored the proletarian's own inability to control the factors leading to his economic salvation.)[6]

Most Protestants who entered Russia in the sixteenth and seventeenth centuries were German, while during the eighteenth century many more came from France and Holland. They came for trade, were members of diplomatic missions, or were hired as tutors for the children of aristocrats. Peter the Great was the primary importer of Protestant talent. As he had spent time in Protestant countries and was overwhelmingly concerned with the economic and military development of his own country, toleration of foreign denominations came easily to him. He may even have delighted in it, as he perceived Orthodoxy as symbolic of his people's backwardness, and he reveled in impiety. Over Orthodox objections, there were approximately 3 million Protestants within the Russia Empire by 1917.[7]

Lutherans began building churches in Russia during the early seventeenth century. Their congregations grew quickly, both as a result of Peter's successful Swedish campaigns in Estonia and Latvia and through immigration. Later there were Lutherans in other Baltic provinces, in Finland, and in German colonies along the Volga River. Very small communities were scattered over the rest of Russia, extending into Siberia and the Caucasus; the pastor of the Lutheran church in Irkutsk had to travel 6,500 miles to visit his entire congregation. The church's strong Germanic overtones, however, appealed little to the Slavic mentality. On the eve of the Revolution there were 1.1 million Lutherans within the Russian Empire, 70 percent Germans by nationality and the rest Finns, Estonians, Latvians, or Swedes.

Baptist history in Russia goes back only to 1867, when a Lithuanian traveling minister baptized a former Molokan in the Kura River in the Caucasus. Soon small Baptist groups were popping up in the Ukraine—where they were called Stundists—and later in St. Petersburg, where they called themselves Evangelical Christians. A decade or so later the two groups learned of each other's existence and of their common belief in adult baptism, which was contrary to the Orthodox practice. The Russian Baptist Union arose during the 1880s to coordinate the various Baptist groups, mainly in the south of Russia and the Caucasus, but it remained underground and largely ineffective until the toleration decree of 1905. V. Pavlov was the pioneer of Russian Baptism; after his death his son Pavel Pavlov led the sect. Evangelicals in St. Petersburg formed the All-Russian Evangelical Christian Union in 1909, with Ivan Prokhanov at its head. There were few differences between the Baptists and Evangelicals beyond their leadership and the Russian Baptists' close connection with the World Baptist Alliance. Both groups absorbed large numbers of Molokans, which resulted in their ideology being Western but their membership being largely native Russian. Baptists taught that individually they had never sought God, but God had come to find them— they were chosen.[8]

Soviet historians considered Thomas Münzer (c. 1489–1525), the socialistic Anabaptist leader, to be one of the only truly progressive Protestant reformers. The Anabaptists themselves thought of Münzer as having had "a dim presentiment of communism." Among the larger group of Anabaptists were the Mennonites, who traced their ancestry to the Dutchman Menno Simonis (1496–1561), who split with the Catholic Church a few decades after Luther. They first entered Russia at the end of the eighteenth century, having fled Danzig when Frederick the Great refused to grant them an exemption from military service. Most settled along the Dnieper River; then in the first decade of the nineteenth century another group settled along the Molochna River in the Ukraine. A high birth rate and theological differences with neighboring communities led many to disperse farther into Russia. Some slid up and down the Volga, and one group called the "breadbreakers"—because they believed that the bread of the Eucharist should not be previously cut but broken by the communicant himself—traveled into the Crimea. During the 1880s there was alarm over the expected arrival of the Antichrist, and many groups fled deep into Central Asia where they could not be located. Tsarist authorities were relatively lenient with them, as they opened up vast new tracts of agricultural land and established compulsory schooling for their own children. Nonetheless, their aversion to military conscription caused some to flee to Canada at the end of the nineteenth century.

When American missionaries brought Seventh-Day Adventism to Russia in 1886, it became the most recent addition to Russia's sectarian mélange. Adventists strictly followed the Saturday Sabbath and awaited the millennium, when they could join Christ and his saints in heaven for a thousand years between the first and second resurrections. During this time the wicked dead would be judged, and the Earth would be utterly desolate, without living human inhabitants, occupied only by Satan and his angels. At its close, Christ would descend from heaven to Earth where the unrighteous dead would be resurrected. Fire from God would consume and cleanse the Earth. The universe would thus be freed of sin and sinners forever. Adventists had a minuscule influence until the 1905 declaration of toleration.[9]

The Salvation Army and the Christian Scientists were barely established in Russia during the period under consideration. And there were other, more difficult-to-categorize sects, such as those who awaited the Second Coming of Napoleon.

*   *   *

The degree to which Russians concerned themselves with heresy and apostasy depended upon nationality. To Russians it was in the nature of things that Russians should be Orthodox, Tatars should be Muslims, Poles should be Roman Catholics, and Germans should be Protestants. If Tatars, Poles, or Germans became Russian subjects it was not incumbent upon them to switch faiths, but woe unto the Russian who switched to any other faith or denomination. Public opinion regarded him as a renegade, and the law regarded him as a criminal.[10]

The Soviets claimed not to make distinctions on the basis of national origin, seeing all dissident groups as having their origins in the nature of Russian life itself. Following Marxist theory, they concluded that social contradictions within tsarist society led to the emergence of all Russian sects. The multiplicity of religious dissidence—that is, splinters from splinters—was interpreted as being "a unique expression of the class struggle" and as having developed due to social contradictions within the dissident groups themselves. Bending fact to fit theory, Soviet scholars concluded that some were essentially feudal and some essentially capitalistic. To elaborate, some were of democratic origin (those that arose on the basis of contradictions within the structure of serfdom and represented *political* protest under *religious* guise), and others were of bourgeois origin (those that arose subsequent to the liberation of the serfs in 1861 and were based on contradictions within the structure of capitalism).[11] This latter group was considered reactionary, as it dissipated the political and social protest of democratic elements into religious fervor. The first Soviet grouping included the Dukhobors, Molokans, Khlysty, and Skoptzy; the second included Lutherans, Baptists, Mennonites, and Seventh-Day Adventists—in other words, groups of Western origin. Implicit within this division was the idea that sects of feudal origin should have been long dead, as was the economic system upon which they were based, and that it was only the economic "step backward" of the NEP that was keeping the second group alive.

USES AND ABUSES OF SECTARIANS

Sectarians, by discarding superstitious practice and attempting to smuggle in the idea of God by contraband means, are a greater menace than Orthodox believers.

—Nadezhda Krupskaya (paraphrase)

The Easter Gift

All non-Orthodox faiths suffered mightily under tsarist rule, both from official government policy and from the simple fact of their historical minority positions in relation to the National Church. It was illegal in tsarist Russia for members of a schismatic group, sect, or minority faith to proselytize among the Orthodox faithful. Some who did so were locked in the dungeons of Orthodox monasteries. As a double safeguard, no one christened as Orthodox could legally become a member of any other church. Orthodox baptism was permanent under the law, Article 185 of the tsarist Criminal Code providing that all possessions of anyone who abandoned Orthodoxy were to be confiscated and the dissidents imprisoned. They would be released only when they demonstrated "due and convincing repentance" and were willing to return to the church of their heritage. Under Alexander I (reign: 1801–25) dissident denominations enjoyed some degree of toleration, but under his successors the heavy hand of persecution once again fell. Conformity to the state religion became the distinguishing mark of loyalty to the tsar and to the nation. Nevertheless, the tsars could never completely overcome the major attraction of the sects—their independence from the state.[12]

After "Bloody Sunday" 1905, Nicholas II grudgingly made concessions to religious dissenters. In April he issued what came to be known as the "Easter Gift," a decree titled "Regarding the Increase of Toleration." Although it reaffirmed the dominant position of the Orthodox Church, it also stated that all citizens and foreigners residing in the country were at liberty to worship according to their own rites and were allowed to transfer from one communion to another. Chapels of the Old Believers were now legally opened.

This newfound liberty was tempered, however, by the laxity of the law's enforcement and by the brevity of its existence. Not only that, but the millions of Jews in the empire received no relief whatever from their pitiful condition, and some of the more extreme native-Russian Christian sects were exempt from protection altogether. Nonconfessionalism remained illegal—every citizen was required to belong to *some* religious body—and civil marriages were still disallowed. Subsequent tsarist decrees began chipping away at what was left of the Easter Gift. By 1906 the tsar's reactionary bureaucracy was well on its way to a complete revocation of all that had been so recently granted, and the Orthodox Church was its able ally. For example, Nicholas's decree of February 7, 1912, gave his minister of the interior the right to be "kept fully and everywhere informed about the religious life of heterodox religions."

Supporting Any Revolutionary Movement

In 1903 Vladimir Bonch-Bruevich described how the sectarians were detached from the "advanced social movements of the day and were constrained by their belief in God." Being too concerned with the "revolution of the spirit," they had little room left for social revolution. They strove to perfect the inner man and tended to ignore the outside world, believing that the triumph of virtue in each individual automatically led to the uprooting of evil in society—rendering the Bolsheviks' social struggle superfluous. Consider how the words of the Baptist Pavel Pavlov, written in 1917, would have annoyed the dialectically minded Lenin (had he heard them):

> Socioeconomic problems are also close to the hearts of the Baptists, but their solution, in accordance with the teachings of the Gospels, must pass through a preliminary stage: revolution of the spirit. "Seek thou first the Kingdom of God, and all else will be given thee."[13]

But Bonch-Bruevich, downplaying the sectarians' own priorities, calculated that they should be approached with revolutionary propaganda to drive further wedges into Russian organized religion. He explained the sectarians' general opposition to the tsarist regime and called Lenin's attention to these opportunities. In spite of the membership of many sectarians in the merchant-industrial class, great masses of them were poor peasants on the verge of becoming urban workers. Close connections with these groups, Bonch-Bruevich insisted, would give the Bolsheviks more influence among the rising proletarian class.

Lenin had already professed his willingness to support "any revolutionary movement against the contemporary social order." During these prerevolutionary years he consistently, if disingenuously, took the side of oppressed religious minorities—even the Old Believers—against the established Orthodox Church. Posing as a champion of religious freedom, he wrote in his 1903 pamphlet, *To the Village Poor*, "Everyone should have full freedom not only to adhere to the faith of his choice, *but also to propagate any creed and change his confession.*" And all creeds and all churches, he continued, should be equal before the law.

The Second Congress of the Russian Social Democratic Labor Party, meeting in Belgium in 1903, passed the following resolution:

> Bearing in mind that in many of its aspects the sectarian movement in Russia represents one of the democratic trends in Russia, the Second Congress calls the attention of all party members to the necessity of working among members of sects so as to bring them under Social-Democratic influence.[14]

In 1904 Bonch-Bruevich reported to the party that many peasant sectarian groups demanded freedom of conscience, freedom of speech, abolition of private property and the present form of the family, and even the overthrow of the state. On the basis of this optimistic report, he was given permission to publish a monthly journal of 2,000 copies titled *Rassvet* (*Dawn*), directed at sectarians both in Russia and those who had emigrated to Canada. Articles were pro-sectarian but antireligious, designed to transform religious protest into revolutionary action under Social Democratic leadership. Nine issues of the journal were published in 1904 before it disappeared without explanation. At this early date Bonch-Bruevich was already espousing the tactical view that each religion should be treated differently—adjusting antireligious policy to fit the circumstance—in contrast to Lunacharsky's view that a consistent policy should be applied to all.

Lenin soon became disillusioned with the path sectarians had traveled to escape tsarist oppression. Between 1905 and 1907 he expressed his criticism by pointing to their antirevolutionary record and said that they impeded the class struggle rather than furthered it. Any propaganda that sectarians spread was full of bland platitudes accompanied by the claim that they were making a real contribution. During the 1905 uprisings and subsequent reforms, they seemed to have had complete faith in the government, Lenin complained, and had even appeared to curry imperial favor. He now concluded that the proletarian revolution would owe nothing to these groups.

Once they were in power, however, the Bolsheviks reverted to Bonch-Bruevich's earlier advice and again courted sectarians with the hope of weakening the cohesive power of the Orthodox Church. (Later the Living Church would take over this function.) The party made overtures to the Dukhobors (who returned in droves from Canada with the promise of freedom), the Molokans, the Baptists, the Evangelicals, the Mennonites, and the Adventists. Thus sectarians were relatively safe for a few years.

Besides the manipulation of sectarians for anti-Orthodox ends, there were other reasons for their early postrevolutionary immunity from persecution. Sectarians were widely scattered across the face of Russia and had no strong or united leadership; they posed no physical threat. Many sectarian groups had been pacifists during the Great War and had advocated Russian withdrawal from the conflict. Although Lenin's motives had been defeatist, not pacifist, there was at least a similarity of purpose on this one point. Among those who would fight, some joined the Red Army during the Civil War, helping to defeat Denikin, Wrangel, Yudenich, and Kolchak. And hundreds of years of communal living made their social organization seem compatible with communist theory. (Unfortunately, this "compatibility" would not save them from being forcefully herded into Stalin's collective farms at the end of the 1920s.)

Sectarian numbers actually *grew* during this period, both in church membership and proportional to the rest of the religious population, and Protestant churches originating in the West grew at an even faster rate than native-Russian sects. In the mid-nineteenth century the sectarian population was estimated at around 16 million, 11 million of these being Old Believers. This would have been about 10 percent of the entire Russian Empire. By the mid-1920s Soviet sources estimated there were between 27 million and 35 million sectarians of all persuasions, still the majority being Old Believers.[15]

What stimulated the postrevolutionary portion of this growth? War and revolution had shaken the traditional faith of many, turning some to indifference or atheism but others to that doubtful state that is conducive to seeking new faiths. Sectarians were not adversely affected by the fall of the monarchy because the tsarist government was no longer there to persecute them. Some even believed they had been *toughened* by tsarist repression, and this gave them the vigor to drive forward and expand their efforts. Many joined sectarian groups because it was politically prudent not to be closely associated with the Old Regime. There may have been a reaction against Bolshevik class-warfare propaganda—Protestants spread teachings of brotherly love among all men.[16] Finally, Baptist preaching about the coming End Times may have seemed entirely plausible to peasants whose economic and social lives were in such disarray.

Baptists/Evangelicals zealously proselytized. In one Moscow factory where several hundred evangelicals worked, each was expected to convert two other workers within the year and twelve by the following year. The Baptists developed an extensive network of clubs, recreational facilities, and mutual aid societies; they even offered classes in health and baby care. Some sects held dances and sponsored popular accordion-playing contests, winning many converts in the process. Funding that Protestants received from European or American headquarters, and the missionary work that was therefore affordable, stimulated expansion. Both Baptists and Methodists sent famine relief missions into Russia, attracting many converts. Evangelical missions stretched from Leningrad to Vladivostok.

A simpler and less idealistic explanation of the growth of Protestant sects in Russia was that belonging to one of these groups, especially the Baptists, was cheaper. In an Orthodox village a priest could extract a considerable amount of rubles during the passing of a year, and the ritual significance of vodka at life's every milestone could cost a small fortune (in relation to income). Protestant ministers were generally employed outside of their ministry and did not require fees for every sacramental act, and Protestant sects forswore alcohol.[17]

Within the party, sectarian growth caused mixed feelings. The success of Communist agricultural programs depended to a large extent on the party's attitude toward sectarians, as so many of them lived in rural villages. Disagreements came to a head at the Thirteenth Party Congress in May 1924, where a resolution was being composed on "Work in the Villages." This policy statement would need to be comprehensive, for they were dealing with a wide range of beliefs.

Bonch-Bruevich defended the sectarians, not, of course, for religious reasons but for economic ones. Having made detailed studies of sectarian agricultural communities, he concluded that their farmers were hardworking and efficient. In an article in *Pravda* he went so far as to suggest that decaying Soviet state farms be turned over to sectarians for regeneration! Since 99 percent of sectarian agriculture was in the hands of poor and middle-class peasants, he contended, they formed an economic and cultural vanguard in the countryside. It would be a crime not to use these assets in the revival and reconstruction of rural areas.[18] As a result of Bonch-Bruevich's influence with Mikhail Kalinin—who considered himself the peasant expert within the Supreme Soviet—Point 17 of the "Work in the Villages" resolution read:

> By assuming a reasonable attitude toward [sectarians], we must win over their most energetic and cultured elements to serve our purpose. Considering the great number of sectarians, this is a matter of the utmost importance.[19]

Kalinin reasoned that by this approach 10 million sectarians could be brought to the side of Soviet power with only a slight expense to the antireligious campaign. Other party members were not so sure that the expense was slight. Intransigent atheists such as Emelyan Yaroslavsky and Ivan Skvortsov-Stepanov retorted that Point 17 of the resolution was a breach of principle, as it was a concession to one religious group to the detriment of another. (The Living Church experiment was conveniently left unmentioned.) And Yaroslavsky characterized these peasants as "petty bourgeoisie," not proletarians in the making. Nonetheless, Point 17 was included among the congress's final resolutions.[20]

Sectarian anti-Soviet attitudes were based not solely on religious belief but also on the wealth that some sects had accumulated over decades and centuries. Principle and the fear of government persecution had caused them to band together into sober, strict, and hardworking communities, giving them a competitive edge over neighbors who were more often slothful and not imbued with the work ethic. Dukhobors, for example, had developed efficient, cooperative factories that sold dairy products at a healthy profit. By the beginning of the twentieth century sectarians had come to form the nucleus, if not the majority, of the merchant-industrial class, and many had indeed become bourgeois. So Yaroslavsky's point about the nonproletarian nature of *certain* sectarian groups was valid. In his work *The Political Role and Tactics of the Sects* (1935), F. Putintsev backed up Yaroslavsky by claiming that sectarian wealth was not just a hardworking, rags-to-riches story; sectarians had a head start, as they were drawn from the merchant class and even the nobility. Soviet official statistics, however, do not entirely support Putintsev's claims. A 1924 survey in rural areas of the Ukraine showed that 89 percent of the sectarians in that area (not including Old Believers) were born as poor or middle peasants. So sectarian wealth was in the eye of the beholder.

Either way, the sectarian "victory" at the Thirteenth Party Congress turned out to be a flimsy one, as, after a short respite, restriction after restriction was imposed on them. In 1927 Anatoly Lunacharsky assured a visiting American reporter that he actually preferred the Orthodox Church to the sectarians, as the former were disorganized and therefore more easily weakened. Well-organized sectarians were more resistant to Soviet propaganda, but he concluded that they would die out anyway, as "Russians will never be permanently satisfied with a religion that does not give them mystery and beauty."[21]

The year 1927 proved to be crucial in the gradual turning away from rapprochement with the sectarians. The demands of Communist dogma (ten years into the Revolution), the need to rapidly industrialize and make agriculture more efficient, and the fear that sectarian influence over young people was accelerating too quickly led Stalin to abandon Lenin's mollycoddling of dissident religious groups. There was an additional reason for the change in Communist attitudes toward the sectarians, especially the Baptists and the Evangelicals—jealousy. At a time of some apathy toward party enrollment and dedication, these sectarians seemed to have no trouble turning out clean, sober, moral, and enthusiastic cadres. They had a vitality that the party could only dream of; thus they became unwelcome rivals. On December 25, 1928, a *Pravda* editorial complained:

> [Sectarians] had particularly advanced since the Revolution in fooling the backward working masses and peasants; . . . making use of the freedom of religious preaching granted to them by the Revolution.[22]

And at the June 1929 League of the Godless Congress, Kalinin fretted over sectarian strength:

> An enormous mass of Orthodox Christians is going over to sectarianism. Sectarianism is a more complicated, more rational form of the idealistic worldview. This is a kind of narcotic that is not easy to get around. They have modest meetinghouses. If you destroy one, it doesn't matter to them; they create another. If we close the meetinghouse, they can pray under the open sky. . . . It is necessary to tear out religion by the roots, even the idealistic worldview that says, "If there is no God, then there is a higher intelligence."[23]

So the League congress passed its "On the Sectarian Movement" resolution, which proclaimed the end of preferential treatment for sectarians and the beginning of unremitting war against them.[24]

Kalinin no doubt underestimated the effects of Stalin's April 1929 law (discussed in chapter 17), which banned all church cooperative and welfare organizations: hospitals, nurseries, and other social pursuits. These services were a significant part of the appeal of Protestant denominations and were intertwined with their church life. The prohibition of circuit riding meant that there could be only one pastor for one congregation in one home, and missionary work was stifled.[25] These laws seriously undermined sectarian efforts.

ONE SECT AT A TIME

Is our freedom from sin, that freedom of the internally whole man, that freedom of the soul, really the same freedom that the revolutionaries summon us to? . . . Is that "brotherhood flying on the banners of the revolutionaries, that brotherhood without love, brotherhood without a father, brotherhood simply conjured up, really identical to our brotherhood in Christ?[26]

—the Baptist journal *Slovo Istiny* (*The Word of Truth*), August 1917

Each sect presented its own special problems for the Communist government, and, beyond a general overview, we, too, will have to look at them one by one.

Old Believers

Beginning with the largest of the "offshoots from Orthodoxy," the Old Believers rejected and refused to recognize the Bolshevik state, just as they had the tsarist state. Archbishop Melenty identified the Soviets as Antichrist, and even by 1926 many of the more stiff-necked Old Believers refused to cooperate with that year's census takers out of fear that the documents carried the mark of Antichrist. This view became even more widespread with the beginning of the Five-Year Plan at the end of the decade.[27]

Not much is known, however, of Communist propaganda efforts or administrative actions directed *specifically* at the Old Believers, probably because, in spite of their numbers, they lived unobtrusively, mostly deep in the northern woods, and made no efforts to foist their beliefs on others. They were left alone also for theoretical reasons; their break with the Orthodox Church could (with a little imagination) be interpreted as a struggle against the established tsarist system and a refutation of feudalism. In June 1923 the Antireligious Commission even permitted Old Believers to create a Higher Church Administration on the model of the renovationist one.[28] In 1929 Metropolitan Sergei and the Holy Synod attempted reconciliation, but to no avail.*

---

*The Russian Orthodox Church finally lifted its 1666 anathema against the Old Believers in 1971. Some cooperation between the two groups has since been achieved, but full communion has not.

Dukhobors

As rationalist religious sects, both the Dukhobors and the Molokans were tolerated through the mid-1920s. Some Bolsheviks were sympathetic with—one might even say admiring of—their communalism, self-sufficiency, and productivity, and during this period both sects flourished. As mentioned, Lenin encouraged émigrés in Canada to return to their Russian homes, and when they did he protected them as role models of Soviet production. They may have numbered as many as 300,000 at this time. By 1927, however, all Dukhobors were depicted as "reactionary servants of bourgeois hypocrisy" and by 1928 were subjected to the general antisectarian campaign.[29]

Molokans

It was hard for Lenin not to feel attracted to the rationalism, love of science, and communalism of the Molokans, and Soviet writers admitted that Molokans from the beginning had a positive attitude toward the revolutionary government. This sect saw socialism (but, of course, not atheism) as compatible with their religious beliefs and their pacifism. If they were just left alone, their notions of equality, brotherhood, and intellectual progress might have earned them a happy home within the Soviet state. They even donated money to Soviet causes and gave their villages socialist names ("Hammer and Sickle," "Red Banner," etc.). In September 1924, the All-Union Congress of Molokans met in Samara and passed resolutions supporting the separation of church and state, military service (if a man felt he could do so in good conscience), and partnership in the building of communism. In 1925, the high point of government-sectarian goodwill, there were around 2 million Molokans in the Soviet Union.[30]

By 1927, however, the government increasingly forced abandonment of sectarian communes, no matter how successful they might have been. Molokans who tried to set up their own collective farms on the Soviet model were denied permission. They were coerced in many cases to take up farming with people they did not know and to work side-by-side with peasants of differing faiths. Although most complied, some moved into towns to avoid collectivization, and some moved to the Russian periphery where the arrival of collectivization was delayed. In the Voronezh region, Molokan numbers fell by 90 percent between 1901 and 1928, and in the Tambov area they declined by almost 50 percent between 1915 and 1926.[31]

Schism was often their response to collectivization, as some tried to retain their traditions in isolated, introspective communities. This caused a further decline in the main body of membership. Geographic dislocation exposed others to a new, wider world of peoples and beliefs. In addition, atheistic propagandists had some success raising class-consciousness among poorer Molokan youth, and proselytizing Baptists pulled many from their faith. The major cause of decline, however, was that their reason for existence had disappeared. Molokans had arisen and prospered on protest against feudalism and Orthodoxy, but the former had disappeared and the latter had weakened. Communists co-opted much of their ethical program, as both supported the harnessing of human power to build a paradise here on Earth. There was little left to resist. As the older generation died off, the youth turned to new challenges. Molokanism became superfluous.[32]

Smaller and More Mystical "Offshoot" Sects

Perhaps due to the low level of the educational system and to isolation within the vast reaches of steppe and forest, other small, but not insignificant, religious groups emerged that both the tsarist government and the Soviets felt they had to contend with. These ascetic and mystic sectarians were represented mainly by the Khlysty and the Skoptzy. In the cities they were linked to "bourgeois-monarchists," but in the villages their members were poor and illiterate. A Soviet sociologist described the Khlysty as "constituting a foreign body within a socialist society," adding:

> Just as certain organisms, finding themselves in strange and unfavorable sur-
> roundings, cover themselves with a protective shell—a cyst—the Flagellants
> bury themselves ever deeper in their faith and preserve it virtually unchanged.[33]

After the Revolution, various articles of the Criminal Code continued the tsarist practice of outlawing their more extreme practices, though leaving out the part about their heresies. In 1928 Bonch-Bruevich called on the Skoptzy to end propaganda for religious mutilation because in the nation's new circumstances their energy and will was needed for socialist construction. In May 1929 the largest ever anti-Skoptzy trial took place in Leningrad, with 150 members being deported. In 1931 one of *Bezbozhnik*'s front-page stories ran under the headline "Rid Moscow of the Castrate Infection." The last "Castrati" communities were liquidated within a few years.[34]

Until Lenin's death Tolstoyan sects were tolerated, but afterwards they were mercilessly (and easily) crushed. Members were arrested and imprisoned or shipped off to Siberian work camps.[35]

Lutherans

Turning to the sects of Western derivation, head-to-head contact between Soviet authority and the Lutheran Church first came with the Red Army's short-lived occupation of Estonia and Latvia in 1917–18. With the enthusiasm of conquest came desecration of Lutheran churches and persecution of pastors; thirty-one pastors were shot in Latvia during 1918–19 alone.[36] Had the Red Army remained in the Baltic States throughout the 1920s, irreparable damage might have been done to the Lutheran Church there, but in March 1918 it was forced to retreat according to the terms of the Treaty of Brest-Litovsk.

Lutherans enjoyed some degree of toleration during the first few years of Bolshevik rule, at least in comparison with the Orthodox and Catholics. Several of the commissars even regarded Lutheran ministers as well-educated ideological opponents—as worthy enemies—and thus were less contemptuous of them. But overall they suffered along with every other faith. When they appealed for an exemption from the ruling against religious education for the young, it was denied. The government then cited this denial to prove that it was not showing favoritism toward the sects in the application of Soviet law.

Many Lutherans were well-to-do compared with their compatriots, especially during the Civil War period, and thus became targets of "revolutionary justice"—stripped of much that they held. Despite heavy losses, by 1921 there was a mood of optimism within their community. This was exemplified at the Lutheran General Synod in Moscow in June 1924, where they achieved synodal reorganization and the appointment of new bishops. In 1927 they were even allowed to publish a newspaper and in 1928 were allowed to hold their second and (unknown to them at the time) last synod.

Lutherans' major difficulty was a chronic shortage of pastors. In the Volga German Republic, for example, forty pastors in 1917 had dropped to fourteen by 1925. Socialist-leaning schoolteachers began taking over pastors' work in several congregations, and they even organized a pro-Soviet "German Living Church." During its brief lifetime it controlled Lutherans in the Volga and Ufa regions and even extended farther into Siberia. In 1925 traditional Lutherans finally managed to open a pastor's seminary in Leningrad to train church leaders who had been lost in the preceding period of turmoil.

Baptists and Evangelicals

[Peasants] are next called on to enter the [tsarist] military service, where they are hum-bugged to any extent; being first made to swear on the Gospel (in which swearing is pro-hibited) that they will do just what is forbidden in those Gospels and then taught that to kill people at the word of those in command is not a sin, but that to refuse to obey those in command is a sin. So that the fraud played off on soldiers when it is instilled into them that they may, without sin, kill people at the wish of those in command, is not an isolated fraud, but is bound up with a whole system of deception.

—Leo Tolstoy, *Letter to a Non-Commissioned Officer*, 1898

Baptists had some points of agreement with the Bolsheviks, but the points of disagreement eventually proved decisive. Civilly, they advocated withdrawal from the world war and development of a strong and stable state; religiously, they supported separation of church and state and equal treatment for all faiths. There were, however, two sticking points—one theoretical and one practical. Baptists opposed class warfare, calling it "a disintegrator of social order,"[37] and, as Christians, they obviously had a different dialectic. The practical difference had to do with Baptist opposition to service in the armed forces (to be discussed below).

Disagreements with the Bolsheviks grew more serious as the sect's numbers multiplied. Baptists probably had fewer than 100,000 adherents in 1917, but, as they took advantage of the Soviet Constitution's guarantee of religious propaganda, their numbers grew to about 250,000 by 1922 and 500,000 by 1926. An Orthodox observer writing in the latter year noted:

> Among the city poor, the Baptists and all kinds of "brethren" find many adherents. The simplicity of their moral preaching and often the severity of their personal life attract many to them.[38]

Some believers attracted to socialist and revolutionary religion might have remained in or joined the renovationist Living Church, except that by 1925 it had moderated itself to such a degree that it was no longer appealing. Many then migrated to the Baptists and Evangelicals, helping to account for their surge in membership. Including Evangelicals, there may have been as many as 1.5 million members by 1927.[39] (Official figures regarding the Baptists are notoriously unreliable, however, as Soviet authorities often used the term "Baptist" to denote any number of Protestant sects—as if they all looked the same in their eyes.)

Baptist prospects rose and fell during the 1920s—rising while Lenin lived and falling in direct proportion to Stalin's accumulation of power. Soviet toleration of the Baptists/Evangelicals may be attributed to their extreme persecution under tsarist rule, their egalitarianism and communalism, and their origins at the lower end of the lower class—many were recently "proletarianized" peasants. Some Old Bolsheviks publicly reflected that they had lived in Siberian exile with many of the Stundists and Evangelicals, and thus sympathized with them. Prokhanov related that when overzealous authorities closed one of his Evangelical meetings in Kazan, Lenin ordered the Commissariat of the Interior to reopen it and to punish those responsible for this inconsideration. In 1919 Baptists were even allowed to set up collective farms and to train their clergy in theological colleges. Until 1928 Baptists and Evangelicals were permitted to operate a religious press, and at one point the Soviet press published 175,000 books and pamphlets full of Protestant propaganda.[40]

Soviet antireligious decrees during the early 1920s had minimal effect on both denominations when compared with the Orthodox Church. For one thing, Baptists held little property to be confiscated—perhaps a few nondescript buildings in a few major cities—and they owned virtually no ornaments or treasures to be sold for famine relief. Matthew Spinka commented, "They have nothing to lose but their chains."[41] The classification of ministers as "nonproductive persons" and the corresponding reduction in civil rights was not troublesome either, as Baptist ministers were really laity; outside of their preaching and other church duties they had regular full-time jobs in the "productive" sector. The separation decree's provision of "loss of juridical person" might seem to have been felt as a slap in the face, but upon reflection Baptists realized that having the right of juridical person had brought them little or no advantage under the tsars.[42]

At first there were clear and specific benefits to living under Bolshevik rule. At least until 1922, they found it much easier to get Moscow's permission to hold national congresses and to get local soviet authorization for "under the open skies" baptisms. Proselytizing among the Orthodox was now legal, and it was easier due to the bewilderment of Orthodox believers whom neither the Holy Spirit nor priestly magic had spared from Bolshevism. Most Protestant sectarians had little sympathy for the plight of Russia's dominant religion.[43]

Of course, Baptists and Evangelicals were well aware of Bolshevik atheism and the imperative to spread it, and many withdrew their children from Soviet schools for as long as they could get away with it. But generally during the early 1920s they accepted what they could get, took the Bolshevik promise of "freedom of individual conscience" at face value, and adopted a wait-and-see approach. There was, however, that one practical problem. While they followed a literal interpretation of the Bible and eschewed smoking, drinking, and theater attendance—much as other Protestant sectarians—they were in the forefront of the Protestant pacifist movement.[44]

In the summer of 1918 Baptist/Evangelical Christians, Tolstoyans, Mennonites, and Adventists formed the United Council of Religious Societies and Groups (OSROG). In the fall, OSROG petitioned the government to bring some order to enforcement of conscientious objector laws and court rulings, as some pacifists had been excused from military duty on the basis of separation of church and state, while others had been executed. Thus the Revolutionary Military Soviet, chaired by Trotsky, issued Order #130 on October 9, 1918, exempting pacifists from military combat duty as long as they performed alternative armed forces medical duty that was presumably just as dangerous. After intercession by Bonch-Bruevich on behalf of noncompliant pacifists, Lenin, also in October, directed Sovnarkom to make protection of pacifists a national law. The resulting January 1919 legislation required sectarians to show that their objections were *purely* religious and to swear that they would not agitate against Russia's armed forces. Obviously, if they had fought with either the Reds or the Whites they would lose any exemption.

The burden of proof was placed on the sectarian inductee to demonstrate that "his religious convictions are not simply a cover for his cowardice or unscrupulousness."[45] (The "unscrupulous" part came from Soviet suspicions that the recent growth of sectarianism was primarily *due* to people joining to avoid conscription, or at least combat.) OSROG was nonetheless pleased with a provision granting it the power to certify conscientious objector eligibility—determined by level of sincerity—when cases went to court. Soon OSROG had 117 agents spread around the country working on these cases, and thousands of young men were spared military duty. Ordained Baptist clergy were generally exempted from alternative service as well, on the grounds that they were indispensable to their congregations.

What the Bolsheviks really sought, though, was voluntary rejection of pacifism by each of these sects. The plan was for secret police agent Tuchkov to manipulate each sectarian national conference to pass such a resolution, with the possibility of the sects breaking up into warring factions over this issue as icing on the cake. But the May 1920 Baptist Union Congress in Moscow elected the pacifist Pavel Pavlov as its president. Under his leadership the Union passed a resolution rejecting military service in all its forms and calling the shedding of human blood a "crime against conscience and [a violation of] the explicit teaching and spirit of Holy Scripture." One young Baptist, returning home after a prison term for his refusal to serve in the army, explained simply, "On the basis of the Word of God, I had the right to refuse to learn how to kill."[46]

But what did Scripture say? If the Old Testament had any validity, war was one of God's instruments. One Baptist writer countered, however, that biblical wars had God's approval, as they were part of his divine plan and were fought for his glory, whereas modern wars were fought only for earthly goals. Under these circumstances Christians could not participate, he concluded, and man should be at peace with everyone.

Baptist dissenters from southern Ukraine, who were not able to attend the congress due to being under White Army control at the time, believed that military service *was* a duty, and they showed no signs of anti-Soviet or anti–Red Army attitudes. And Evangelical leader Prokhanov, under pressure from Tuchkov, also abandoned the antimilitarist position for a short time.[47] Baptists were thus unable to present a unified pacifist front.

In spite of the new conscientious objector law, officials in the provinces, somewhat removed from Moscow's control, continued with the executions. Thirty-four pacifist Baptists were executed in Voronezh Province in August 1920, and at least thirty-two others were eliminated elsewhere in the country during that year. Bonch-Bruevich complained to the Commissariat of Justice, but he was appealing to the agency containing the nucleus of opposition to military exemptions, so nothing was done.

OSROG's brief period of effectiveness waned quickly with the end of the Civil War, the decline of Lenin's health, and the emergence of Stalin. It lost its exclusive right to offer expert advice in court cases, and in August 1921 the government decreed that exemption would be automatically denied to anyone who converted to the Baptist faith after 1919. This, as mentioned above, was based on the plausible suspicion that large numbers of potential draftees were "getting religion" to avoid conscription. Then, in November 1923, a clarifying decree stated that exemptions were available only to pacifists who could prove that this had been their conviction well before the Revolution, had refused all military service, and had actually been punished for it by the tsarist government. Other sects might still qualify, but most Baptists were excluded from exemption by this ruling.

By the fall of 1923 Bonch-Bruevich turned against the people he had previously protected, charging that Baptist refusal to serve could only be interpreted as hostility to the Soviet state. Quoting the Baptist Confession of Faith,* he showed that antimilitarism was "entirely unrelated to the very essence of their belief." He demanded that they either change their confession or accept military service immediately. Failure to do either would reveal the true bourgeois nature of their religion.

Planned congresses in 1921 and 1922 had never convened, as Yaroslavsky, supporting Bonch-Bruevich's new position, demanded prior assurance that they would abandon their pacifism. Finally two hundred Baptists were allowed to meet in November 1923, and Pavlov got his chance to answer Bonch-Bruevich. He delivered a brilliant speech to the congress, reminding delegates of Baptist aid during the famine and how much Russian citizens had appreciated it. He explained that Russian Baptists were "home grown" and a product of native Russian culture arising out of protest against oppression, not a foreign import. He claimed that they were not bourgeois but 95 percent peasant, and he heaped praise on the Bolshevik regime for its guarantee of religious freedom. The audience for this presentation was obviously not sitting in front of him but resided within the Kremlin walls.

But the military question was the centerpiece of the congress. Tired of the constant bickering on this issue, delegates unanimously hoped for a firm decision either way, but it was not to be. Only this compromise could be achieved:

> With respect to attitude toward military obligation and the means of its fulfillment, unity of views among Baptists has not been achieved. Recognizing war as the greatest evil and greeting the peaceful policy of the Soviet state and its call to the peoples of the world for universal disarmament, the congress leaves the determination of his own attitude toward the means of fulfilling his military obligation to the individual conscience of each Baptist.[48]

This resolution allowed the substitution of alternative service of a public or medical nature and condemned any "antimilitarist propaganda with the goal of weakening the Red Army." When twelve delegates refused to compromise their pacifist convictions, they were immediately arrested by the OGPU. A few months later Tuchkov twisted this resolution so that he could boast:

---

*The *German Baptist Confession of Faith* (1847), translated into Russian by V. Pavlov in 1906.

And so the Evangelicals and Baptists have recognized military service in Soviet Russia as compulsory for all their members and at the same time have caused a schism within themselves. This manifestation will without doubt help above all in curtailing the growth in sectarianism and will push them to a moral breakdown.[49]

The wording of this resolution papered over real differences within the Baptist leadership. Pavlov's faction, now known as the New Baptists, was stronger in the North and encouraged young men to take advantage of existing law and seek exemptions whenever possible. Pavel Ivanov-Klyshnikov led the Old Baptists, stronger in the South, who argued that when Baptists were called to the military they should serve without question. New Baptists held a slight membership edge over Old Baptists within the Baptist Union, but in February 1924 a compromise was reached in which Pavlov conceded that, though exemption was a right, Soviet courts also had the right to scrutinize the sincerity of any who applied.

The government, still dissatisfied, denied permission for a 1924 congress and for the publication of a proposed Baptist journal. At the end of the year there was a shake-up of the Union's leadership, resulting in Pavlov's ouster. The hand of the government could clearly be seen in this, for as soon as the deed was done permission to publish the journal was granted. Pavlov, though, continued to argue his case for exemptions, stressing how Baptists rejected private property, accepted building of the "new soviet-communist life," and obeyed all Soviet laws (including, of course, the one allowing Baptist military exemptions).

The government allowed no new congress until December 1926, at which time the military question again dominated debate. This time Old Baptists were in the majority, though some delegates still referred to members who became soldiers as "traitors and apostates." Ivanov-Klyshnikov delivered the main address, carefully tracing the recent historical development of this issue. He concluded that pacifism was not a Baptist principle but rather an aberration in Baptist history due to revulsion at the horrors of revolution and war; neither the Word of God nor past practice of the brotherhood required it.

After two days of vituperative debate within an almost evenly divided chamber, weary delegates hoped once again to decide the issue here, now, and forever. When a delegate moved that they simply revert to the wording of the Confession of Faith, the motion was carried overwhelmingly and with a huge sigh of relief—they could rely on precedent. The subsequent resolution stated:

Baptists always have recognized, and now recognize, the performance of military service on an equal basis with all citizens, which is expressed in the thirteenth article of our Confession of Faith, published in 1906.[50]

They then abrogated resolutions on this subject from recent meetings.

The congress then passed a resolution affirming that the government had "granted complete freedom of conscience" in all its laws and had "guaranteed the free observance of the obligations of our Christian faith."[51] Although Baptists were never allowed to hold another congress, they continued through 1927 praising Soviet power. They referred to socialism as "that form of human society that most corresponds to evangelical ideals" and railed against "the anti-God beast arising out of the abyss, called Capitalism in our era, which is armed with a war-making machine, called Militarism."[52]

This adoration does not seem to have done them much good, though, when the 1928 storm of repression against all sectarians was unloosed. Stalin perceived Baptists as being competitive with the party for the souls of workers and as being riddled with kulaks, Cossacks, and small shopkeepers—classes headed for extinction—and he saw them as being too connected to foreign capitalists.[53] Sixteen Russian Baptists who had fled to America after the Revolution, had trained in Philadelphia, and had smuggled themselves back into Russia in the early 1920s were arrested for "counterrevolutionary agitation" in White Russia during the winter of 1928–29. Others were picked up in the Ukraine and charged with espionage. Pavlov was arrested and exiled to Siberia, and his family was ejected from its Moscow apartment. The government arrested 100 more Baptist leaders during the fall of 1929, exiled them to work camps, and shut down all Baptist organizations and offices. Still, at the end of the decade Baptists maintained around 5,000 places of worship in Russia, either as chapels, leased buildings, or private homes.[54]

Mennonites

In 1917 there were around 110,000 Mennonites in Russia, spread over 365 villages—mostly in the Ukraine—and owning over 4 million acres of land. They were well educated and prosperous, dominating both the flour milling and agricultural machinery industries. But under the upheavals of early Bolshevik rule they suffered along with everybody else from war, banditry, typhoid, and starvation.[55]

The Soviets considered Mennonites a special problem and were at a loss as to how to handle them. At first the government tried to mold them into the structure of the class struggle by dividing them into the rich and the poor, hoping for propaganda purposes to side with the poor and thus gain a foothold within their communities. When this tactic broke down, they tried classifying the Mennonites as Germans to force them into the German Minority National District in the Ukraine. Mennonites, however, resented being moved and pigeonholed within the Soviet administrative structure. They claimed that their German mother tongue was inconsequential for this purpose and suspected other denominations within the German District of being agents of Communist influence. They then cleverly countered that they were really Dutch, formed an organization called

"The Association of Citizens of Dutch Origin in the Ukraine," and demanded that if the government wanted to propagandize among them they must send Dutch Communists. The government had no Dutch Communists and out of frustration decided in 1926 to forcibly disband the Mennonite "Dutch" organization.

Throughout the 1920s, Mennonites resisted Soviet attempts to destroy their communities and beliefs. Obedience to God came before obedience to man. When their Sunday schools were closed they opened smaller illegal ones in private homes, and their teachers completely disregarded instructions that they were to teach in an "atheist spirit." Some communities even refused to teach the history of the Bolshevik Revolution. Practicing nonresistance, virtually all refused induction into the Red Army, but they were hampered in their appeals to the state because small bands of Mennonites had been willing to fight against the anarchist bandit Makhno during the Civil War. Wealthy Crimean Mennonites, organized into special detachments, had also fought with Wrangel's soldiers against the Red Army.[56]

Insisting on their rights, Mennonites held a congress in Moscow in January 1925, where they drew up a list of minimum demands to be submitted to Soviet authorities:

- Freedom for religious meetings in both houses of prayer and private homes.
- Permission to teach the Scriptures and the faith to the young and to build children's homes for religious education.
- Freedom to print Bibles and other religious literature, including periodicals.
- Freedom to organize Bible courses to train teachers.
- Exemption from military service (only labor service would be acceptable).
- Exemption from the oath of loyalty to the government (instead they would make a "promise").[57]

The government regarded these demands as the height of impudence and rejected them all, though on a case-by-case basis some Mennonites were allowed alternative civil service in lieu of military duty.[58]

Even before rejection of their demands, Mennonites had begun to comprehend their impotence against the state and their dismal future in the Soviet Union. As with the generation of the 1870s, emigration became a solution. Waves of Mennonites left Russia for Canada—4,000 in 1925 and 6,000 in 1926—but by 1927 the government began to place obstacles in their way. It was diplomatically embarrassing for the world to watch droves of Soviet citizens desperately seeking to flee the "socialist paradise" (just as it would be in the 1970s to watch thousands of Russian Jews seeking exit visas for Israel). Only 900 Mennonites were allowed to leave in 1927 and a mere 300 in 1928. In 1929 the government ceased issuing passports altogether, which led to a demonstration in October by 6,000 to 10,000 German-speaking citizens on the outskirts of Moscow. Most were Mennonites, but some were Lutherans and Catholics (and some were Siberian farmers who refused to be herded into collective farms). They demanded to be allowed to leave the country; some were granted permission to go, but around 600 decided to flee eastward into Soviet Central Asia and beyond into Manchuria and China. By 1930, Canada had accepted 20,000 refugee Mennonites, and communities began to crop up in Brazil and Paraguay as well. Of the 8,000 or so Mennonites who could neither obtain exit visas nor escape, most ended up in forced labor camps in the far north and were never heard from again.[59]

Seventh-Day Adventists

One of the difficulties the government had with Adventists was that, given Russia's six-day workweek, they insisted on the Saturday Sabbath, thus eliminating fifty-two more workdays a year (assuming factories and shops were closed on Sundays). Soviet law did not tolerate putting religion ahead of civil duty, though some Adventists were allowed to work on Sunday instead of Saturday, where possible. Another difficulty was pacifism; as with Baptists, the worldwide Adventist organization decided to leave the matter to individual conscience. However, the True and Free Adventists, a splinter group led by D. Ostvald, stuck with the original pacifistic doctrine.[60]

A third difficulty may seem to have no practical consequences, but the threat to the economy seemed real to Soviet leaders at the time. Adventists expected the imminent end of the world, and this eschatology was inconsistent with the Communist view that citizens should labor hard to build a future earthly paradise. At any moment Adventist preachers might decide that the moment had come and urge their followers to lay down their tools and plows in anticipation of the glorious day. Even without such predictions, authorities were worried that a lack of belief in the Soviet future would lead to slackening and distraction.[61]

After the Thirteenth Party Congress in 1924, however, Russian Adventists declared their willingness to assist in Soviet cultural development:

> We are convinced that God, in his providence, has disposed the heart of our unforgettable V. I. Lenin and his closest associates and given them wisdom in the capable organization of the only progressive and up-to-date apparatus of government in the world. We delegates of the Fifth All-Union Congress of Seventh-Day Adventists express to the government of the USSR . . . our gratitude and sincere support for all the freedoms it has won.[62]

Perhaps as a reward, the authorities allowed publication of the Adventist periodical *The Voice of Faith* between 1925 and 1929.[63] But the sincerity of the 1924 declaration is suspect. A Soviet sociologist in the 1960s claimed to own a copy of a late 1920s Adventist letter that had circulated widely within the organization. It boasted of the 1924 declaration of loyalty as "a shrewd diplomatic maneuver" and "an agile and astute way out of the difficult situation which had arisen."[64]

*   *   *

As for the others, the Salvation Army ran into trouble in Moscow and Petrograd, where it was operating feeding stations for the homeless. In November 1922 they were shut down as a violation of an August 1918 decree against religious charity. The Antireligious Commission gave orders in 1923 to destroy their "anti-Soviet" church.[65] The tiny group of Christian Scientists in Leningrad and Moscow was disbanded in 1929. Jehovah's Witnesses did not enter Russia until World War II and are thus outside the scope of our study.

Thus we complete the narrative of the 1920s. But how did all the work laid down during this decade pay off during the succeeding five decades, that is, until the end of Communist rule? The short answer is that the imperative to remain in power trumped everything.

PART III
MEANING

23

YES, A MIRACLE!

Religious Persistence

T he time has come to find out what the details of this story mean for the present day. There are three aspects to this:

- Bolshevik efforts during the twelve years we have studied would have more significance for the present if the work continued successfully (if not, there are still many lessons to be learned). This aspect will be covered in this chapter, which is organized chronologically and will concentrate on two periods: the easing up on religion during World War II and Khrushchev's final crackdown during the early 1960s.
- The second aspect is critique. What mistakes did the Bolsheviks make in their antireligious campaigns? In chapter 24 I will evaluate both Bolshevik effectiveness and morality.
- In the final chapter in the book, chapter 25, I will try to place the Bolshevik experiment within the realm of possibilities. Is a religious sense part of human nature? If so, was Communist antireligious policy doomed from the start? Given the pervasiveness of religion, is there any way to create a moral society that is at the same time institutionally and psychologically secular? Will there ever be another opportunity?

1930 THROUGH WORLD WAR II

By May 1, 1937, not a single house of prayer shall remain in the territory of the USSR, and the very concept of God must be banished from the Soviet Union as a survival of the Middle Ages and an instrument for the oppression of the working masses.[1]

—prediction of the Five-Year Plan of Atheism, May 1932

The 1930s

During the first few years of collectivization of agriculture, 1929 into 1931, the government pressured—or more often forced—peasants to move out of traditional villages and into larger communal farms. Simultaneously, it made the relinquishing of church attendance a condition for admittance to the new collectives. Those who managed not to go—various tradesmen, kulaks, and so on—clustered for support around the old village church, and it became a gathering place for discontent. Stalin called these people the "rotting elements" and suggested that they "throw themselves under automobiles."[2] The existence of these malingerers convinced authorities, if they needed any more convincing, that the churches were bastions of counterrevolution and this justified further tightening of the screws on clerical thumbs.

At the Sixteenth Party Congress in 1930, Stalin called religion "a brake on the building of socialism."[3] Heeding his words, the ever-vacillating government and its bureaucracy virtually abandoned antireligious propaganda and resorted to force, which was quicker. In that same year, while there were 150 Orthodox bishops in prison (more than existed in freedom prior to 1917), the NKVD* set up a Commission on Cults whose assignment was to suppress the churches.[4] Resolutions favoring gradualism, passed at the 1929 League Congress, were ignored.

As for non-Orthodox churches, by 1931 there were barely fifty Catholic priests left in the whole of Russia. By 1934, out of 980 Catholic churches operating in 1917, only three still functioned outside of Siberia—one each in Moscow, Leningrad, and Odessa. There were no Catholic seminaries or religious academies open, no charities active, and no church presses operating. In 1935 the government shut down the Baptist Union and the chief Evangelical organization, as well as most of their churches. Baptist/Evangelical congregations fell from over 3,200 in 1928 to only 1,000 twelve years later.[5]

By 1936 Stalin felt that he had made progress on the antireligious front, but rumors still circulated that about 40 to 45 percent of the population was religious. Being well along in the process of wiping out all conceivable rivals to power, he was in a tolerant mood. Attending a meeting on the writing of the 1936 Constitution, he commented: "Why should the clergy be disenfranchised? Not all of them are disloyal."[6] However, the January 1937 nationwide census revealed a surprising endurance of religious sentiment (confirming the earlier rumors); apparently many dared to check the box "believer" as a silent protest, and many who were indifferent toward religion could not quite bring themselves to check the box "unbeliever." Stalin, who had expected the returns to demonstrate his solid antireligious achievement, could avoid embarrassment only by refusing to publish the exact numbers, though the figure of 50 million believers leaked out.

---

*The Commissariat of the Interior, now assuming the function of the secret police.

Another Western source claimed that 57 percent had claimed believer status, which if true would amount to some 80 million persons. These figures were astounding when we consider that respondents' names were on the forms! (The 1926 census had not asked about religion, as Yaroslavsky believed the question to be an invasion of conscience and therefore unconstitutional. Neither would the question be asked in all post-1937 censuses. Instead sociologists would circulate questionnaires, which were more easily manipulated.)[7]

On top of the census fiasco came Yaroslavsky's 1937 admission that, in spite of all the persecutions and propaganda, one-third of urban residents and two-thirds of villagers were still believers. Reportedly furious, Stalin ordered a renewed crackdown on church institutions. He pushed for more arrests, not only of clergy but also of census officials who had brought in such outrageous returns and League leaders who had botched the job of antireligious propaganda.[8] More churches were closed in 1937–38, with no partiality toward non-Orthodox faiths.

Yaroslavsky—perhaps to save himself—proposed a purge of "several hundred reactionary zealots of religion," but Stalin, not satisfied with this puny figure, sent 136,000 clerics of various faiths to Siberian labor camps or had them executed.[9] The Solovky Monastery/Prison Camp filled up again. This antireligious campaign, lasting sixteen months, was the most brutal since 1929. Stalin, who portrayed himself as the sole, true disciple of Lenin, was revealed—not that anyone was going to mention it—as being incapable of following Lenin's cautionary advice to avoid injuring the feelings of religious workers. Lenin had been impatient for revolution, but Stalin was impatient with the persistence of religion. In his 1927 Declaration, Metropolitan Sergei had said that the church would now enjoy "a peaceful and happy existence." It must have been difficult for the metropolitan to remain convinced that his earlier policy of capitulation to Soviet power had indeed saved the church from destruction.

Wartime Backpedaling

With the end of the purges and show trials, and with foreign policy concerns now paramount, Stalin switched gears and relaxed his grip around the neck of the churches. He began to place a higher priority on impressing foreign visitors with the benevolence of his reign than on further squeezing religious institutions. Nonetheless, 1939 was arguably the nadir of Russian Orthodox history; Stalin could relax his grip because the neck was already half broken. With a mere four to six active diocesan bishops left in all Russia, the church was in despair and close to collapse. The thinnest ray of sunshine was provided when *Pravda* announced on July 1 that a trial of several atheist "hooligans" had occurred. For raiding a village church at Easter, one was sentenced to eighteen months in prison and a few others to a year of compulsory labor without imprisonment.[10]

Then, on September 1, 1939, according to agreements reached in the previous month's secret Nazi-Soviet Pact, the German blitzkrieg rolled into western Poland, and the Red Army occupied eastern Poland, the Baltic States, and (after a brief war) Finland. Along with the Soviet annexations came an infusion of pre-existing (and unpersecuted) churches, clergy, and laity. Yet in 1940 in Russia proper the Soviet Press Bureau acknowledged only 4,225 open Orthodox churches with 5,665 priests—a huge reduction from pre-1917 levels. Although most churches were closed, the ranks of the religious held constant. In 1941 Fyodor Oleshchuk, mentioned earlier as a contributor to the antireligious campaigns of the 1920s, admitted that religion was still a major factor in Soviet life, with at least 50 percent of the people still clinging to some form of faith.[11]

Although Hitler had been Stalin's "ally" since mid-1939, on June 22, 1941, the Germans swarmed across the border in a three-pronged attack headed for Leningrad, Moscow, and Baku (seeking Caspian Sea oil). According to Nikita Khrushchev's later account, Stalin remained in shock and dismay at his "friend's" betrayal and at first did not understand the importance of the church for his country's defense. Rumors must have reached him, however, that occupying German armies were (cynically) proclaiming freedom of worship for all, opening closed churches, supplying vestments for clergy, and broadcasting Sunday mass over German Army transmitters.[12]

As a counterpoint to Stalin's temporary inability to deal with reality, Metropolitan Sergei responded quickly and effectively. Conjuring up images of Russia's military heroes and warning against any thought of going over to the enemy—that is, liberation from Stalin—Sergei issued a stirring statement the day after the attack, describing the patriotic role of the Orthodox Church:

> It will not abandon the people now. . . . In such a time as this when the fatherland calls everyone to the task, it will be unworthy of us, the pastors of the church, to look on in silence at what is going on all around and not to encourage the timid, not console the grief-stricken, nor remind the waverer about duty and God's will. . . . We shall lay down our lives alongside those of our flock . . . in defense of the sacred boundaries of our homeland.[13]

As in tsarist days, the church offered its full resources to the state in its time of emergency. It financed the creation of the Alexander Nevsky aircraft squadron and the Dimitry Donskoy tank column, and Sergei offered prayers for the country's "God-given leader."[14]

Of course, Orthodox believers in the catacombs and the Russian Orthodox Church Abroad were not as pleased as Stalin with what they had all along called Sergei's "adaptation." Boris Talantov, an anti-Sergeiite priest who had remained in Russia within the Moscow Patriarchate, described Sergei's wartime cooperation:

> All believers in Russia regard the Second World War as the wrath of God for the immense lawlessness, impiety, and persecution of Christians that occurred in

Russia from the beginning of the November Revolution. . . . Metropolitan
Sergei again revealed himself to be an obedient tool of the atheist regime.[15]

But Sergei was in charge and cooperation continued.

Yaroslavsky was one of the first to provide a new "unification" party line.
He now attacked the same antireligious propagandists that he had previously
spurred into action, calling them "simplifiers," "blind ignoramuses," and "pitiful
cowards." There were, he maintained, many believers who were loyal Soviet citizens and would fight for the national cause. Yaroslavsky must have been sad-
dened, however, by the League of Militant Atheists' decline in influence. In the
late 1930s it had already been under attack for "Trotskyite tendencies" and the
inflation of statistics showing its "successes." The rival NKVD had been criti-
cizing its naive internationalism (such as its championing of the international
language Esperanto). Now, with patriotism at its peak, the already moribund and
discredited League was allowed to die a painless death—sacrificed for the war
effort. (The government—at the same time that it was appealing for church assistance—rationalized that such organizations were no longer necessary, as the vast
majority of Russians had already abandoned their religious prejudices.)[16]

Millions of Orthodox and non-Orthodox believers gave unstintingly to the
war effort. They fought in trenches, in partisan bands, and in wartime industries.
Metropolitan Aleksy (who would become the next patriarch) was awarded the
Defense of Leningrad Medal for his efforts on behalf of the besieged city. The
Orthodox Church created a Fund for the Defense of the Country to which its
members donated 150 million rubles; even the much-abused Evangelicals, now
rebuilding their organization, offered 80,000 rubles. The Orthodox Church
altered its liturgy to reflect its patriotic attitude—praying for mercy from the
enemy, supporting the Russian military, and forgiving the sins of those who perished on the battlefield.[17]

Sergei, seventy-five years old and in poor health, was evacuated from
Moscow to Ulyanovsk (Simbirsk) in late October 1941. From there, urged on by
the Commission on Cults, he corresponded with the ecumenical patriarchs and
the leaders of other Christian churches around the world, pleading the Soviet
cause. He wrote to religious leaders in Czechoslovakia, Romania, and
Yugoslavia, entreating them to pressure their governments to refuse cooperation
with the Nazis. When he contacted his American counterpart, Metropolitan Benjamin, however, he received a cool response.[18]*

After the Battle of Stalingrad in the winter of 1942–43, as the front in
Russia's Great Patriotic War moved inexorably toward Germany, a grateful
Stalin made promises to the Orthodox hierarchy—promises that for the most part
he kept. On September 3, 1943, reasonably confident of ultimate victory and thus

---

*This was before Pearl Harbor.

(again) in a generous mood, Stalin, with Vyacheslav Molotov at his side, met with Sergei—just returned to Moscow—and two other metropolitans in an all-night negotiating session. The story goes that Molotov asked Sergei what the church needed. When Sergei began his list, Stalin interrupted by asking: "Why don't you have cadres? Where have they disappeared to?" Not wanting to seem rude by telling Stalin what he already knew—that the clergy had been filling up his gulag—Sergei answered: "There are all sorts of reasons. . . . One is that we train a person for the priesthood and he becomes a Marshal of the Soviet Union." Stalin replied that indeed he had been a seminarian as a youth in Tiflis, and he began a long reminiscence. In the wee hours of the morning they agreed on a new statute for the church, and the exhausted Sergei was satisfied. Stalin said he would not hinder the election of Sergei as patriarch of all Russia. His long locum tenency was over with his enthronement on September 12.[19]

Within a month of Sergei's elevation came a cascade of concessions to the church. The church appointed bishops (with government approval) for vacant dioceses, printed liturgical books, published the *Journal of the Moscow Patriarchate*, and opened a few seminaries. And the offices of the patriarchate were permitted to move from a log cabin on the edge of Moscow to the elaborate buildings of the former German Embassy. The government began liquidating the leftovers of the Living Church and its splinter groups. It also established a Council for the Affairs of the Russian Orthodox Church (CAROC), attached to Sovnarkom and headed by former NKVD agent G. Karpov. Its purported purpose was to facilitate communication between the church and the state and to resolve difficulties that might arise between them. Karpov took his mediator role seriously and in several cases tried to mitigate the harsh effects of government antireligious policy. When local CAROC officials were cooperative, church leaders had a rare chance to articulate their views.[20]

Sergei served as patriarch for eight months, until his death in May 1944. Karpov attended his funeral at the Patriarchal Cathedral of the Epiphany, and Sovnarkom sent a message of condolence—in effect, a message of official state approval of the now-cooperative church. Sergei had named Metropolitan Aleksy of Leningrad as his successor, but, for those who were never able to reconcile themselves to Sergei's accommodations, Aleksy was cut from the same poor cloth. He had been appointed by the renovationist-controlled Higher Church Administration to replace the executed Metropolitan Benjamin in Petrograd, and, in turn, he had been the first hierarch to recognize the renovationist coup.[21]

As locum tenens, Aleksy wrote a letter, published in *Izvestia* on May 21, praising Stalin as a leader appointed by God. Then he left on a tour of the ancient patriarchates of Antioch, Jerusalem, and Alexandria, which no doubt fit well into Stalin's foreign policy agenda. Aleksy was elected patriarch in January 1945, which was seen by many of those still in the catacombs as at least "more legal" than Sergei's 1927 usurpation of authority. Bishop Afanasy, a catacombs leader, sent out a circular letter to the underground churches urging them to come back into the fold. Any laity remaining in opposition could at least seek out good and sincere priests within the official church and serve under them.[22]

When Karpov addressed the 1945 Church Sobor, he uttered words of reconciliation that sounded almost tsarist in their gratitude:

> Bishops, priests, and delegates of the faithful of the Russian Orthodox Church! The government of the USSR has instructed me to greet in its name this exalted assembly and to convey its wishes for the success of your labors in organizing the higher administration of the church. . . .
>
> Throughout the sore trials to which our country has so often been subjected in the past, the Russian Orthodox Church has never broken its links with the people: it has shared their needs, wishes, and hopes and contributed its full measure to the common task. . . . Many eminent churchmen have given their lives for their country. . . . Without in any way interfering in the internal life of the church, the council [CAROC] promotes the normalization of relations between church and state.[23]

The sobor also adopted new "Statutes of the Russian Orthodox Church," but the lack of debate and the quickness of passage demonstrated to all observers that the entire content had been worked out with Soviet authorities before the sobor had even convened. These statutes subordinated the entire church administration to the patriarch's rule, though there remained a facade of conciliar authority. Aleksy, through agreements with Soviet authorities, held more power in relation to his church than Tikhon ever had, facilitating the government's lines of hierarchical control. This could be seen as an improvement in the church's institutional position, since before the war it had possessed no legal hierarchical and central administration—only dispersed parish communities.[24]

Although the hierarchy's position was now strengthened, the parish priest's position was weakened. Parish councils now replaced the former "groups of Twenty" and were given increased power, especially regarding finances.[25]

POSTWAR ADJUSTMENTS

Yes, a miracle! For the first time in thirty years they freed priests! They didn't actually go about seeking them out in camps, but whenever a priest was known to people in freedom, and whenever a name and exact location could be provided, the individual priests in question were sent out to freedom in order to strengthen the church, which at that time was being revived.[26]

—A. Solzhenitsyn, referring to events in 1947

Alexander Solzhenitsyn, quoted above, was not one to easily give the Communists credit, but the postwar "Soviet Church" was surely in a better institutional position than before, though many would say that it was spiritually corrupt. Stalin admitted the fiasco of the church closing campaigns. According to the Moscow Patriarchate, by 1949 the government allowed the reopening of 17,000 Orthodox churches, and 22,000 parishes were in full operation across the country. The number of operating dioceses rose to seventy-two and the number of monasteries to eighty-nine. Six thousand parishes had been added to Orthodox control due to postwar territorial adjustments in Russia's favor, mainly the relocation of Poland one hundred miles to the west.[27] So the modus vivendi worked out during the war extended for awhile into the late 1940s and early 1950s.

But there were ominous signs as well. Without any legal basis, the government closed all Eastern Rite Catholic churches and forced their members, if they wanted to worship at all, to attend Orthodox churches; again this was a matter of streamlining control.[28] To replace the defunct League, the Soviets created in 1947 the Society for the Dissemination of Scientific and Political Knowledge—the Knowledge Society—an elite organization of professionals in every field. By 1950 its 130,000 members were spreading technical know-how across the country and with it—both implicitly and explicitly—antireligious propaganda. Oleshchuk became the leader of the Society's "scientific-atheist section," and several other old League propagandists joined the new organization. Although membership in the Knowledge Society swelled, its antireligious propaganda efforts had no more effect than the League's efforts had before the war. The problem in this case was that the titles of its lectures and pamphlets ("The Reactionary Essence of Christianity," "Darwinism and Religion," "Religion, the Enemy of the Toilers," etc.) deterred people from listening or reading.[29] Its propagandists ended up preaching to the choir.

The Cold War brought renewed emphasis on Stalin's campaign of Russification. While the Orthodox Church—already sufficiently Russian—suffered relatively little in this regard, Catholics and Protestants paid dearly as both had connections abroad. Catholics were accused of acting at the behest of the pope and in the Vatican's interests; Baptists were vilified for association with the World Baptist Alliance.[30] Foreign "internationals" were always a threat.

In May 1952, during the height of the Korean War, the government convened a "Conference in Defense of Peace of All Churches and Religious Organizations in the USSR" in the St. Sergius-Trinity Monastery at Zagorsk.[31] Here religious faiths were turned to Soviet foreign policy goals, and the leader of each church was called upon to denounce countries participating in the United Nations effort to free Korea of Communists troops. Patriarch Aleksy, clearly under duress, labeled the Americans the aggressors:

> The Russian Orthodox Church decisively condemns this interference and the resulting annihilation of the peaceful population of Korea by American aviation.*[32]

---

*The same church endorsement of the "peace program" would be elicited during the Vietnam War.

Stalin died in March 1953. Initially, thousands of victims of earlier antireligious persecutions were released from labor camps—a gesture against the Stalinist "cult of personality" that rising star Nikita Khrushchev intended to reverse. A year and a half later, in November 1954, Khrushchev—not yet securely in power—set in motion the next swing of the policy pendulum by issuing a relatively innocuous statement titled "On Errors in the Conduct of Scientific and Atheistic Propaganda among the Populace." This document was almost kindly in its approach; what the errors boiled down to was a perceived lack of courtesy to believers. Khrushchev stressed that any offense to the church was not only unconstitutional but was "incompatible with the line of the party." He professed that "the party has always demanded and will continue to demand a tactful and attentive attitude toward believers," who were not to be considered "politically suspect."[33] This may seem a little hard to swallow in light of what had come before and what was soon to follow, but it makes sense in the context of the power struggle then taking place for Stalin's mantle. Khrushchev was less concerned with setting antireligious policy right than he was with distancing himself from Georgy Malenkov, his main rival. Between March and June 1953, Malenkov had carved out for himself a harsh line on religion, and Khrushchev meant to make him pay for it.

During the post-Stalin interregnum, when little of substance could be accomplished, progress was defined as dreaming up silly linguistic schemes—reminiscent of similar efforts in the 1920s—such as eliminating the word "God" from the Russian language and omitting it from the dictionary. Now parents were admonished to refrain from any references to the deity, angels, or the devil—including the ubiquitous expression "God preserve"—especially in the presence of children. (Oddly, both Stalin and Khrushchev, in their efforts to relate to the common people, often used such forbidden language.) The popular tongue unfortunately incorporated biblical terminology in much of its vocabulary, making it difficult to achieve an atheist mindset in this manner. Nothing came of these efforts; "God" had to remain in use, otherwise how could antireligious propagandists do their work?[34]

Along with the failure of linguistic reform, the party and the government were (very reluctantly) forced to admit to themselves that the class nature of religion was a myth. Or, to put it another way, if religion had served the class interests of the landowners and the wealthy during the tsarist era, this could hardly be claimed in the late 1950s. Neither had collectivization bred atheism. Since decades had passed—with many believers born in the Soviet era—and socialism was still under construction, some other non-Marxist explanation had to be found for the intransigence of faith. The resulting plethora of excuses will be discussed in chapter 25.

By 1958 the government was not merely seeking Patriarch Aleksy's silence, it sought his active complicity in erasing any persecution of the church from public memory. This was the theme of his book *The Russian Orthodox Church* and of interviews he granted to the domestic and foreign press. He persisted in arguing that all past clerical arrests had been for criminal or counterrevolutionary offenses, and in the present all Russians enjoyed "unhindered freedom of conscience under the Constitution." He asserted that socialism was God's vehicle for the proliferation of equality and justice throughout the land and professed that the government was pushing for Christian goals. At the behest of the government, Aleksy assailed the Vatican, the United States, and other Western countries for "warmongering," and he attempted to seize control of the patriarchate of Constantinople to advance Soviet interests in the Middle East.[35]

KHRUSHCHEV: ONE LAST TRY

How can I feel moved by a service that begins with a blessing for the Presidium of the Communist Party of the USSR? How can I confess to a priest who, for all I know, might report me to the secret police?

—a young professor of Russian literature in Kiev, 1959

During the postwar period, the harshest attack on religion—one might even say the death throes of the antireligious movement—was conducted by the Khrushchev regime. After his initial soft approach, staged to outmaneuver Malenkov, Khrushchev prepared to switch his position, as only a dictator can do. With his power consolidated around 1956, he began a policy of de-Stalinization that in the eyes of some old-timers put his Communist credentials in doubt, and an argument can be made that his launching of a vicious antireligious campaign in 1959 was designed to validate these credentials. The irony, though, is that many of those he persecuted after 1959 were the same clergy and religious activists that he had ordered released from the gulag a few years earlier.[36]

Rumors leaked from the 1959 Twenty-First Party Congress that a goal for the upcoming Seven-Year Plan would be the complete elimination of religion in the Soviet Union. A *Pravda* editorial in August explained why the renewed struggle was necessary (or, in other words, why the previous forty years of effort had been seriously lacking). It blamed failure on "the laxity of organizations called upon to supervise the strict observance of Soviet legislation on religious cults," the breaking of these laws, and a weakening of antireligious propaganda.[37] A more likely explanation for the renewed antireligious struggle—and one complementing the explanation given above—has to do with Khrushchev's embarrassment in front of his own party and worldwide Communist parties over the amount of time that had passed with religion's fruit still on the tree. The redness of his face can be sensed in his words to the Twenty-Second Party Congress in 1961:

The battle with survivals of capitalism [code for "religion"] in the consciousness of the people, the changing by our revolution of the habits and customs of
millions of people built up over the centuries, is a prolonged and not a simple
matter. Survivals of the past are a dreadful power, which, like a nightmare, prevail over the minds of living creatures. They are rooted in modes of life . . . long
after the economic conditions that gave birth to them have vanished.[38]

The predictions of Marx and Lenin seemed less and less applicable to Soviet
society in the 1960s, and Khrushchev planned to fix the situation. In so doing, he
tried to separate himself from Stalin's arbitrariness—the essence of his terror—
by portraying his antireligious efforts as following legal norms. Still thousands
of churches, synagogues, and mosques were closed against the will of the people
and against existing laws.

In January 1960 the Knowledge Society held an important meeting where its
members signed on to the renewed antireligious offensive and placed themselves
in the vanguard of accelerated propaganda efforts. In February Vladimir
Kuroedov replaced Karpov, who had been a little too chummy with the Orthodox
Church and had complained one too many times about administrative abuses of
power.[39] Under new leadership, CAROC abandoned its mediator role and moved
toward becoming an organ of control over the Moscow Patriarchate. Although
spreading atheism was not in its official job description, it began to assume that
role, too, through subtle means.

In 1961 CAROC blatantly violated separation of church and state by
pushing for new legislation that further removed the priest from control of his
parish, making him merely an employee of the parish council. Priests, choir
directors, and even the night watchman were not to be included in the councils.
This allowed the state to remove from these councils "fanatical" believers and
order their replacements with "nonfanatical persons who sincerely fulfill Soviet
laws." Sometimes these replacements were hostile to religion or out-and-out
atheists. CAROC also placed clerical income, received from employment by the
parish council, in the highest Soviet tax bracket—several times higher than ordinary income tax rates.[40]

In a country whose history was not open, lessons of the past were easily forgotten. The government now revived the same old tactics as antireligious agitators had employed in the 1920s: ridicule, misrepresentation, and insults to
believers. It also revived flights to inspect the heavens for deities, but now they
were much more impressive space flights. In these "cosmonautological proofs"
of atheism, Soviet crews flew to space and, seeing no God, declared his nonex-
istence. The government played up the antireligious aspects of these flights with
apparent sincerity. Old administrative measures against churches and monasteries continued as well. During 1961 CAROC oversaw the closure of 881
churches, and around 11,500 churches were closed during Khrushchev's entire
campaign. This could have been half of the functioning churches in the middle

1950s, which, of course, did not mean that half the people left Orthodoxy but that most just moved into unregistered congregations.[41]

The government stepped up its earlier campaign against infant baptism. After a fully immersed child died, the RSFSR made it illegal to endanger the health of children under the cover of religion. When grandparents—who had little to fear—began taking children to churches for baptism anyway, a follow-up law specified that the ceremony could be performed only with the written consent of both parents and that the father had to obtain a written police permit (and occasionally a workplace permit as well).

The government offered recycled "name-giving ceremonies" as baptismal replacements, only now the child received a medal with Lenin's portrait on one side and his or her name on the other. The name-giving certificate read:

> When you are grown, read these precepts and always follow them. Remember that you are a citizen of the great Motherland—the Union of Soviet Socialist Republics—the country of freedom and happiness, where man is a friend, comrade, and brother to man. Guard the Motherland as the "apple of your eye," and increase her wealth and glory.
>
> Walk firmly in the path of life indicated by the great Lenin. Be honorable, diligent, and orderly in great and small matters. Respect parents and elders. Support the honor of the collective, in which you learn and labor. Remember, man's fortune is in joyful labor for the glory of one's people, the battle for the beautiful future of mankind—communism![42]

All these restrictions and incentives, however, only marginally reduced the percentage of baptisms.

Some new laws went beyond anything seen during the 1920s or 1930s, including broadening the definitions of religious crimes and extending prison or exile sentences. In 1923 there was a three-year sentence for religious utterances that advocated overthrow of the government or resistance to its acts; forty years later there was a five-year sentence for any religious activity that endangered a citizen's health, prompted him not to fulfill his civic duty, or enticed the young into religious observances. In 1961 children were forbidden to attend Baptist worship, and in 1963 they were barred from Orthodox worship as well. Not even choirboys were allowed in.[43]

There were many cases of denial of parental "rights." Since these rights were given by the state they could be taken away, and parents who insisted, after a warning, on teaching religion to their children saw their sons and daughters hauled off to government boarding schools where they would receive a decent atheistic education with no home interference.[44] L. Ilichov, secretary of the Party Central Committee, justified these policies:

> We cannot and must not remain indifferent to the fate of children, upon whom fanatical religious parents are carrying out what is virtually spiritual rape.[45]

Komsomol operated patrols in major cities to follow citizens home from church. Once the patrollers identified their subject, it could mean eviction from living quarters, dismissal from work, or expulsion from school. Within the party itself there was renewed scrutiny of "religion in the family," and some senior party officials were removed from their positions due to their inability to maintain an atheistic home.[46]

Khrushchev's antireligious efforts also saw a return to the tsarist practice of using mental institutions as replacements for prisons.[47] A person who stubbornly retained religious faith this long into the building of communism clearly had some neurotic or psychotic difficulties. Besides, commitment to these institutions could be done administratively, without the messiness, publicity, and potential for protests that a trial might bring.

For the first time, the Soviet press encouraged all citizens, not just professional agitators, to engage in one-on-one atheistic persuasion. *Pravda* wrote in September 1962:

> The most important thing is to reach each man, to learn about his state of mind and his needs and demands, to show an attentive attitude toward him and to bring timely help to those people who are beset by troubles or those who fall into misery. It is necessary to go fearlessly to the believers, to help them to separate themselves from the inconclusiveness of religious ideas concerning nature and life.[48]

Another newspaper urged all Russians to leave their homes or apartments and make contacts with believers and their families wherever they might find them. They should drop words of doubt into their minds, slip Bible contradictions into conversations, and find things for them to do that isolated them from religious influences. Oleshchuk, in an article titled "Go to Each Believer," suggested that if this technique did not work then atheist agitators should barge into believers' homes and, in a kind of reverse exorcism, "drive out their belief in God."[49]

The government accelerated antireligious propaganda. Soviet publishers created high-quality atheist children's books in almost every language spoken in the Soviet Union and restarted the printing presses of atheist periodicals that had been dropped during the war. And now there was television, though in the mid-1960s godless programming reached only a small audience due to the lack of TV sets. The government provided schools with new or updated texts that integrated atheism into every curriculum; there was an atheistic way to teach agriculture, engineering, and math. Teachers were to turn their students not just into nonreligious citizens but antireligious propagandists. Already in 1959 there were two atheist universities pumping out ideologically pure atheist graduates, and "schools of atheism" were fitted into worker shifts in major factories.[50]

Just before his fall from grace (and employment) in 1964, Khrushchev boasted that finally a plan was in place that would fully and completely overcome

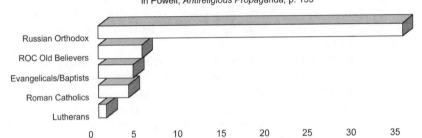

Christians in 1963 (in millions)
Source: Paul B. Anderson's Testimony Before Congress in January 1964,
in Powell, *Antireligious Propaganda*, p. 135

the religious prejudices of the Russian people. But soon after his replacement, the Party Central Committee issued a report demonstrating that the recent antireligious campaign had failed.[51]

TO THE COLLAPSE OF COMMUNISM

It seems that we are dealing here with a case of ideological atavism, whereby outdated concepts of militant atheism continue to motivate actions that not only do not benefit anybody, but are actually harmful from the point of view of the real-life interests of all sections of the population. The aims on which the present attitude of the state to religion is based were developed more than half a century ago, when the total destruction of faith in God was proclaimed as a realistic goal that could be attained in the near future. But life has demonstrated the illusory nature of these hopes.[52]

—an interdenominational *samizdat* (self-published) appeal, June 20, 1976

After Khrushchev's arrest and confinement to a home on the outskirts of Moscow, the nationwide administrative assault on religion eased. There were fewer church closings, but the legislation of the early 1960s remained on the books, and propaganda continued unabated. Religious policy became more centralized and regularized, with some laws being rewritten to specify more clearly which religious activity was a crime and which was not. Penalties, too, were standardized: a fifty-ruble fine for the first offense and three years in prison for subsequent violations. But a watershed had been reached—the government had given up on the idea of eradicating religion. Now the policy could best be described as "containment." Christian churches, however, refused to be contained, and from 1964 onward they began their recovery and resurgence. Much of the growth was Orthodox, but there was also that same trend away from Orthodoxy toward Baptists and fundamentalist Protestant groups that were observed in the 1920s.[53]

In 1965 the government replaced CAROC with the Council for Religious Affairs (CRA). With Kuroedov still in charge, the CRA continued his policy of spreading atheism. Clerical appointments had to be approved by the CRA, and only the compliant need apply. Solzhenitsyn charged in 1972 that the CRA purposely appointed unprincipled bishops to further divide the church. The CRA decided which applicants for the few theological academies would be admitted, which textbooks they would use, which religious literature would get printed, and which religious materials would be allowed into the country. It also made certain that all church activities abroad suited the aims of Soviet foreign policy.[54]

Sects, too, were under CRA control, and the trend in the post-Khrushchev era was toward their consolidation. The government forced small communities of Mennonites into abandonment of their pacifism and merger with the Baptists. (This led to a Mennonite exodus to West Germany during the 1970s, weakening the church in Russia.)[55] As many Protestant groups as could ideologically fit were lassoed into the All-Union Council of Evangelical Christians and Baptists, not out of Soviet concern for ecumenism but, as previously noted, to make administrative control more expedient. Of the 5,400 Baptist and Evangelical congregations registered before Khrushchev's offensive, less than half were still operating in 1965. One group called the Action Group—or Reformed Baptists— broke away from the All-Union Council over the issue of obedience to Soviet laws. Taking the position that Stalin's April 1929 law on religion violated the 1918 decree on separation of church and state, it refused to countenance any government interference in their religious practices, including education of their young. While registered Baptists were allowed to hold regular national congresses throughout the 1960s and 1970s, Reformed Baptists became the most persecuted of all Russian sects.[56]

Although Leonid Brezhnev's administration, from 1964 to 1982, initially tempered Khrushchev's antireligious campaign, it eventually saw the same vicissitudes of religious policy that characterized all earlier regimes. The government now began a period of introspection and historical investigation as to the causes of failure. Both the party and the government condemned Khrushchev for the sins of "subjectivism and administrationism."[57] Scholars went back to Yaroslavsky and studied his methods: What had worked and what had gone wrong? Why had Khrushchev not been more effective? Why were "Komsomol Christmas"–like activities, already discredited in the mid-1920s, being repeated in the 1960s?

G. Kelt was an atheist lecturer from Lvov. Writing in *Komsomolskaya Pravda* in 1965, she reminded her readers that religion was not born in a day; it had been around for thousands of years. She seemed on the verge of acknowledging that it would take another thousand years to get rid of it. Lambasting those who thought administrative church closures would do the job, she harked back to Lenin and to Engels, warning:

> We are deceiving ourselves again when we say that many believers have left the church and religion. Pure self-delusion. One thing is true, that in the greater part of the territory of the Soviet Union there are no churches and no servants of religion [priests]. But there are believers. If not Orthodox, then sectarians of all possible shades. Where do they come from? From the ranks of those who leave the church. The closing of a parish does not make atheists out of the believers. On the contrary, it intensifies the people's attraction towards religion and, in addition, embitters their hearts.[58]

She urged the creation of substitutes for the church that would avoid "a naked, purely negative, bookish-oratorical atheism." New rituals and liturgies should be invented that appealed to aesthetic and emotional senses.[59] *Oktyabrina* redux.

Both the government and the Christian churches were now taking a relatively tolerant tone. M. Morosov, writing in *Science and Religion*, discovered that "in their great majority the believers in our country are honest Soviet men, toilers just as we atheists are, and one should treat them with respect."[60] N. Bovtunov, representing the Evangelical Christian–Baptist community, explained in 1966 that he would never become a Communist, but:

> I travel hand-in-hand with sincere Communists because belief in God does not hinder us from traveling together toward desired goals. . . . [Religious belief] should not divide us. All who live on this Earth must live only for a single dream—how to construct communism throughout the world as quickly as possible.[61]

Metropolitan Philaret of Kiev continued the church's sanguine line in 1967:

> I do not have the atheistic point of view of the Communist Party. The party strives for the welfare of the people and for the just distribution of goods and the equality of all. There is nothing in this contradictory to Christian doctrine.[62]

On the surface this cozy relationship seemed like a budding love affair.

The government provided some protection for its believing citizens, so there were some practical results. A 1966 law forbade exclusion from jobs or denial of admission to educational institutions on the basis of faith. No one was to "deprive them of privileges or advantages guaranteed by law." Although the penalty for discrimination was up to three years' imprisonment, there are no known cases where the law was invoked and anybody was punished.

This is not to say that the entire Orthodox Church membership was pleased with its leaders and in an optimistic mood. Khrushchev's struggle against the church had not only frightened many clergymen but had also irritated them, mostly over restrictions imposed on the privileges they had become used to during World War II. Bishops, priests, and laymen all had difficulty keeping their mouths shut about the Khrushchev-era laws. Archbishop Ermogen of Kaluga

Nonreligious Belief in Voronezh Province in 1966

Source: Powell, *Antireligious Propaganda in the Soviet Union*, p. 11

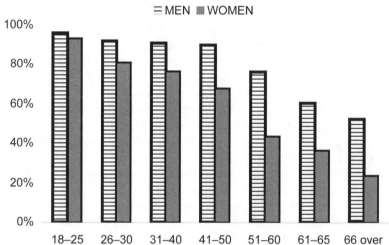

wrote to Patriarch Aleksy protesting the uncanonical nature of the agreements entered into by the Council of Bishops back in 1961 and their destructive effects on parish life. In November and December 1965 two Moscow priests, fathers Eshliman and Yakunin, courageously wrote letters to the patriarch, all the bishops, the chairman of the Supreme Soviet, and the chairman of Sovnarkom. They complained openly of the illegality of church and monastery closings, the abuses of priests, the forced registration of infant baptisms, the restrictions placed on children attending church services, and government interference in parish financial affairs. They accused Aleksy of total capitulation to secular authorities. For their efforts Ermogen was retired to a monastery and both priests were suspended from their positions. Although these protests continued into 1967, nothing changed.[63]

In the late 1960s the Orthodox Church had about 8,000 functioning places of worship, five seminaries, and two theological academies. Its strength was tending toward the countryside, while in urban centers, especially Moscow, it was losing members to Western Protestant sects, primarily Baptists. The missionary zeal and organizational flexibility of Baptist, Pentecostal, and Seventh-Day Adventist sects gave them an edge over other sects in both their raids on Orthodox membership and their resistance to atheistic incursions. In Stalin's time, protest was unthinkable, but during Khrushchev's crackdown Protestants tended to "not go quietly." Khrushchev's "socialist legality" created opportunities for speaking out and filing court appeals; going too far, however, still led to prison.[64] In 1979 Anatoly Levitin, a lifelong fighter for religious liberty in Russia, wrote, "The Soviet government is mortally afraid of sectarianism, because it is difficult to control and impossible to tame."[65]

Older Russian sects such as the Dukhobors and the Molokans were in steep decline. Isolated communal living had already become nearly impossible by the 1930s. They found it increasingly difficult to educate their young in church traditions, and they lacked the mentality to adapt to changing Soviet conditions. The average age of the devout grew steadily older. While Molokans were virtually nonexistent, Baptists—who had absorbed many Molokans—could boast of a larger membership than all other sects combined.[66]

In urban areas by the early 1970s, most citizens born after 1917 were probably indifferent to religion, though not necessarily accepting of militant atheism. Many wavered and many, as in America, went to church only on Christmas and Easter. But, taking the country as a whole, it is difficult to tell, as many of the truly religious kept a low profile. During the 1970s and even into the 1980s one still had to keep one's religion quiet; to discuss it openly could lead—in spite of the law—to expulsion from school or loss of a job.[67]

Middle-aged Russians had mostly left the Orthodox Church, but the young and the old attended—the young from disillusionment with the ruling ideology and a search for spiritual fulfillment. The Moscow priest Dimitry Dudko, already in trouble with authorities for his influence on the young, wrote in 1972:

> Many young people go to church now. [The government] should be grateful to me that I keep young people away from crime. People have a thirst for religion now. . . . You can't indoctrinate people with religion; you have to feel it. Young people are beginning to feel it.[68]

The old attended church out of habit and thoughts of death. Levitin wrote of the mid-1970s:

> [Now there are] no fewer churchgoers, there are more. Still old women [*babushki*] predominate. Most of them have had little education; they are cleaning women, domestic workers, and women who work in collective farms. Unlike in the 1920s, it cannot now be claimed that religion is a survival of the past, since 75 percent of the old women who go to church today were the Komsomol members of the past and went to Soviet schools. It cannot now be asserted that religion is the prop of the ruling classes of the past, since most of these old women come from worker or peasant backgrounds and can remember nothing of prerevolutionary ways.[69]

Fifty years after their split with Sergei over recognition of the Soviet regime, and in spite of calmer times, the government was still hunting down the remnants of the underground True Orthodox Church. Michael Bourdeaux told the story of a few of them:

Some True Orthodox prisoners are known of, including ten women, mostly eld-erly, who were arrested in the early 1970s and given sentences of between seven and thirteen years of camp and internal exile. The True Orthodox refuse to rec-ognize the existence of the Soviet state and to have any kind of official dealings with it. These women refused to accept bedding from the labor camp authori-ties, for which they had to sign a receipt, and slept on the bare floor until other prisoners took pity on them and signed the receipts for them.[70]

Bourdeaux went on to explain that True Orthodox believers were scattered all over the Soviet Union but that exact numbers were hard to come by as members operated in local cells and had no knowledge of the existence of others.

In response to persistent and renewed interest in religion, there were more efforts to contain it. In 1979 (corresponding to the Soviet invasion of Afghanistan), continuing in 1980 (corresponding to the boycott by many coun-tries of the Moscow Olympics), and persisting into 1983 the government arrested, interrogated, deported, and imprisoned religious leaders. Another stim-ulus for suppression was the late-1970s wave of Pentecostal petitions for emigra-tion to a country where they could freely raise their children in their faith. The names of thousands of these petitioners were smuggled out to the West, causing great embarrassment to the Soviet government. Seven members of two Pente-costal families from Chernogorsk managed to sneak into the American Embassy in Moscow in an appeal for emigration assistance. The "Siberian Seven" remained in the embassy basement for almost five years before international pressure persuaded the government to let them leave the country.[71]

By 1983 suppression relaxed somewhat, though it is doubtful that this was connected to growing worldwide awareness of George Orwell's *1984*. More likely it had to do with growing awareness of the nearing Millennium of Chris-tianity celebrations in 1988, an event that would also attract worldwide attention. Possibly for this reason, in 1984 Brezhnev—virtually on his deathbed—con-sented to restoration of the Danilov Monastery in Moscow, hoping to complete the work in time.[72]

By 1984 the number of Orthodox parishes had been reduced to around 6,800—less than 9 percent of the prerevolutionary total—and there were only sixteen monastic centers (including convents) left in the Soviet Union, most located in the Ukraine and none existing east of Moscow. This compares with well over 1,000 open in 1917 and 69 open in 1958, before the Khrushchev cam-paign. Genuine Russian monasticism existed only at Pskov and Zagorsk.[73]

With the election of John Paul II in 1978—a "Polish Pope"—morale among Russian Catholics was raised, but this did little to improve the physical plight of the church still behind Communist lines. By 1984 the only two functioning Catholic dioceses were in Latvia and Lithuania (these would be free of Russian control within half a decade). There was one Catholic Church in Moscow, one in

Leningrad, a few others scattered in European Russia, and a few in Siberia and Central Asia where German, Polish, or Lithuanian exiles had settled.[74]

Yuri Andropov's administration lasted only from 1982 to 1984, when he died. His successor Konstantin Chernenko was even less enduring but nonetheless made an effort to whip up some ideological fervor against religion. However, he ended up expending more effort explaining the campaign's failures and falling back on the worn-out excuse that the continuing war between Russian churches and the Soviet state was but a reflection of the ongoing conflict between capitalism and socialism. The implication was that worldwide conquest of capitalism was a precondition for the complete squelching of religion in Russia. He also blamed Western imperialism for spreading religious propaganda into his country.[75]

Next in line was Mikhail Gorbachev, who Westerners tend to view as the mellowest of leaders, yet in 1986 he called for a "decisive and uncompromising struggle against manifestations of religion and a strengthening of . . . atheistic propaganda."[76] To the extent that he tolerated religious expression at all, he channeled it into officially licensed and sanctioned organizations directed by the state. Underground Baptist groups and the Orthodox catacombs still refused to show their faces publicly.[77] Glasnost—the new openness in society and government— did not extend that far.

For recognized churches, however, glasnost did have an effect. Churches could now get away with changes that previously would have been stymied. Historian Jim Forest told the story of a December 1987 conversation he had with the red-bearded Orthodox priest Vladimir Makheev in the town of Maloyaraslavets, seventy-five miles from Moscow. The priest explained that since Khrushchev's time Orthodox believers had been stuck with unsympathetic parish council leaders. Recently the leader in his parish had been Brezhnev-appointee Vasily Osimin, an atheist who expected the priest to do nothing but "stand at the altar" and obey the council's orders; Father Vladimir was actually presiding over the death of his church. When his parish raised 18,000 rubles for church preservation, the money in the hands of Osimin simply disappeared. The bishop could not, and the local CRA would not, terminate the man, and he refused to resign. Finally in mid-December, due to new attitudes and new (unspecified) processes available to him, Father Vladimir was able to call a parish meeting where 200 out of 216 attendees voted to kick Osimin out:

> [It was] a day I will never forget. On that day a real believer was elected to head
> the parish council. And since then we have repaired the church and restored our
> parish community. It is a period of restoration, at least the beginning of it. Since
> that day in December, I feel I have wings on my back. We are celebrating not
> only our church's millennium, but also the resurrection of Christianity in the
> Kaluga region. There are many times in these months when I have cried for
> joy.[78]

By the late 1980s there were many public and samizdat calls for abolition of the CRA. "In a free country the church does not need regulation." As a consequence the Council adopted a more liberal posture, allowing the reopening of many churches.

By 1988 Gorbachev, too, adopted a more conciliatory stance, on April 29 agreeing to meet with Patriarch Pimen (served: 1971–90) and five Orthodox metropolitans in the Kremlin. This was only the second time that the head of the church had met with the head of the party since 1917, the first being Sergei's meeting with Stalin in September 1943. During the earlier meeting no photos had been allowed, but now television audiences watched Gorbachev welcome the Orthodox hierarchs, sit with them around a large conference table, and express regret for "mistakes made with regard to the church and believers." For his part, Pimen expressed hope for the future, but he also admonished Gorbachev that "not all the problems of church life are being resolved or duly attended to."[79] This was very different from Sergei's and his successor Aleksy's public contention that the church was perfectly happy and had no problems with the state.

In May and June 1988 both the government and the Orthodox Church celebrated one thousand years of Christianity in Russia. A millennium had passed since Vladimir I had accepted the faith in Kiev. Church dignitaries of all denominations from all over the world descended on Moscow for the event, and the government gave visitors the VIP treatment, including tours and speeches at the shrines of Russian Christianity. It also made concessions, such as the reopening of a part of the Pechersky Monastery in Kiev, closed since 1929. Gorbachev told party members that, though the party upheld its materialistic and scientific principles, "this is no reason for disrespect for those who believe in the spiritual world." He opposed all administrative means to achieve materialistic goals and affirmed that all believers were citizens of the USSR with full rights.[80]

In December, the chairman of the CRA referred to the 1929 law:

> I think as quickly as possible we must free ourselves of the [antireligious] legislation of 1929. . . . This legislation limits in a Stalinist and bureaucratic fashion all independent and democratic activity. . . . Practically every line of that law underlines the dependence of the church on the power of the state. All kinds of arbitrary actions are admissible under such conditions.[81]

He went on to suggest that all Russian Orthodox churches should be returned to the full control of the Moscow Patriarchate, and he pointed out that in 1988 over 500 new Orthodox parishes had been registered, compared with only sixteen in the previous year. The government also quietly dropped rules requiring the registration of baptisms. A church spokesman estimated that 50 million Soviet citizens were active in their faith, out of a population of 285 million (about 17.5 percent).[82]

Large-scale Bible shipments from foreign donors began to pour into Russia.

Over the next year and a half, almost a million full Bibles and 1.5 million New Testaments were legally imported, with several million more in the pipeline. In April 1989 the way was opened for Bible printing and the formation of a Soviet Bible Society! Yet minor harassments abounded. Although in the West much was made of the easing of controls on religious publishing in Russia, the publishers themselves had to pay the government—which still operated the presses—in hard currency, and, though individual Russians could legally subscribe to religious newsletters, the Russian postal service refused to handle such items and they seldom arrived.[83]

The Russian Orthodox Church canonized Patriarch Tikhon in October 1989, on the 400th anniversary of the Moscow Patriarchate.* No miracles were associated with the former patriarch; he was chosen for the purity and self-sacrifice of his life and for his humility ("Let my name perish in history if only this would benefit the church"). His remains at the Donskoy Monastery were declared to be holy relics, and the church commissioned ikons to be painted and hagiographies to be written. In the greatest of ironies, there is evidence that Tikhon's sainthood was instigated by Gorbachev rather than by the church! The Communist government was at the end of its rope, and, as during the Great Patriotic War, it sought religious support. Two months later Gorbachev met with Pope John Paul II at the Vatican and by this act recognized the Catholic Church.[84]

In June 1990 the church elected Aleksy II as patriarch, a clergyman with long-established ties to the KGB,[85] but on October 1 the Supreme Soviet passed a "freedom of conscience" law, containing these words in Section I:

> Every citizen shall have the right, individually or in conjunction with others, to profess any religion or not to profess any, and to express and disseminate convictions associated with his relationship to religion. . . . All religions and denominations are equal under the law, [there shall be separation of church and state], and clergy and religious organizations shall have the right to participate in political life on an equal footing with all citizens. . . . The state shall facilitate toleration and mutual respect between citizens who profess a religion and those who do not profess one. Registered religious organizations shall have the right to create institutions for the religious education of adults and children.[86]

Marxist-Leninist policy on religion was finally repudiated. Governmental antireligious policy was over.

The scope of this book is the Communist Era, thus we will leave the narrative at this point—the 1992 fall of the Communist Party from power. But there is still much to investigate.

---

*Metropolitan Benjamin of Petrograd was, in turn, raised to sainthood in 1992.

24

A PICTURE BADLY OUT OF FOCUS

Proximate Causes of Failure

In 988 CE, Vladimir I managed to convert his fellow Kievans from paganism to Christianity, and in 1555 the Treaty of Augsburg allowed German princes to choose among the various denominations of Christianity and impose their wills on their people. For the most part the system of compulsion has worked. But in the early twentieth century Lenin and his followers were not trying to convince pagans to become Christians or Catholics to accept Protestantism. They had taken on the far more challenging task of eliminating religion altogether, and their immediate problems were clear: They had no plan and their only weapon was hostility. Before the Bolsheviks' unexpected good fortune in March and November 1917, Lenin's writings had concentrated on why religion was undesirable, unscientific, and historically doomed. When Lenin woke up on the morning of November 8, mentally spent in the struggle for power, he had no idea of how he was actually going to rid the nation of its many faiths.

The Marxist Herbert Aptheker, writing in 1968, offered the only two possible outcomes:

> If Marxism is correct, and if the universal achievement of communism produces a world that is reasonable and controllable, and therefore a world in which religion, being unnecessary, will disappear, why, then, that is what will happen. If, on the other hand, this Marxian projection is wrong—and of course it may well be wrong—then religion will not and perhaps will never disappear. Very well, in either case the worst that can happen is that one of the two—the religious person or the Marxist—will have been proven in error. Then each will be wiser. Is this a calamity?[1]

In these final two chapters I will try to provide some meaningful commentary on the question that I asked in the introduction: Was it possible for the Bolsheviks to have won on the antireligious front? However, before presenting a specific and detailed critique—the proximate causes of failure—I would like to

461

offer a short review of the church's position and the government's tactics and to peruse the moral issues involved.

A REVIEW OF CHURCH WEAKNESSES AND STRENGTHS

Clericalist opposition to anticlericalist activity since the advent of the Bolsheviks has never been sufficiently general or sufficiently organized to give reason for supposing that any conflict between the two factions can arise in the near future.[2]

—Louis Fischer, 1923

Weaknesses: Why It Should Have Been Easy

The Orthodox Church was weak in ways that should have made it a pushover, even if the Bolsheviks restricted themselves to morally acceptable means (see below). Here were some of its vulnerabilities:

There was an undercurrent of atheism *already present* among peasantry, workers, and intelligentsia, so the Bolsheviks were hardly working from scratch. Both Western and Russian writers have commented for centuries about the thin veneer that was Russian religiosity. The historian N. Kostomarov called Russians "atheists without parallel in the history of Christian nations."[3] Sergei Bulgakov, writing of the intelligentsia in 1909, said that "with them atheism is a tradition, a thing which is taken for granted."[4] Thus by 1917, part of the Communist antireligious agenda had already been implemented. The following are three disparate testimonials to this proposition:

1) Nicolas Berdyaev, writing during the summer of 1917—

> Dostoevsky preached that the Russian nation is a bearer of God . . . but when the [March] revolution broke out it revealed a spiritual emptiness in the Russian people. . . . Since long ago the sacred has been exterminated from the people's soul.[5]

2) Leon Trotsky, writing in 1923—

> Religiousness among the Russian working classes practically does not exist. The Orthodox Church was a daily custom and a government institution. It never was successful in penetrating deeply into the consciousnesses of the masses, nor in blending its dogmas and canons with the inner emotions of the people. The reason for this is the uncultured condition of old Russia, including her church. Hence, when awakened for culture, the Russian

worker easily throws off his purely external relation to the church, a relation which grew on him by habit.[6]

3) Maurice Hindus, writing in 1928—

[To a monk at the Pechersky Monastery in Kiev] How do you account for the sudden [religious] apathy of the Russian *muzhik*? Ah, this *muzhik*, replied the monk. . . . He is a beast, that's what he is, this *muzhik* of ours. He is the ruination of our great country, he more than all the infidels and Bolsheviks and other Reds. He knows nothing. He never had God in his heart. That's the truth, my friend, the real truth. The *muzhik* never took Christ to his heart, because he never understood him. Oh, this damned *muzhik*, this human beast.[7]

There must have been failures on the part of *all* Russia's Christian churches because the full extent of outrages, blasphemies, and sacrileges cannot be accounted for merely by the efficacy of Marxist theory and Bolshevik antireligious propaganda. Anticlerical, if not fully atheistic, sentiment must have been pent up in the hearts of a large proportion of the Russian people for it to be acted upon so suddenly and viciously after November 1917. Two years into the Revolution, a British chaplain recorded this scene in Odessa:

Sunday afternoon I was passing through the town gardens when I saw a group of Bolshevik soldiers insulting an ikon of the thorn-crowned face of Christ. The soldier who held the ikon was spitting in the pictured face, while the others were standing around watching with loud guffaws of laughter. Presently they tore the sacred picture into fragments, danced on it, and trampled and stamped the pieces into the mud.[8]

This was not a quick turnaround of sentiment; it could have occurred only by building upon deep-seated disrespect.

The church was weak to the extent that it followed Christ and the Apostles' numerous teachings concerning the acceptance of existing government. St. Paul admonished: "Let every soul be subject unto the higher powers. For there is no power but of God. The powers that be are ordained of God" (Romans 13:1). How, then, could the Orthodox in the modern day do otherwise? And how could the passage "Submit yourselves to every ordinance of man" (I Peter 2:13) stiffen the modern church's backbone? Paul's very plain words meant that the 1917 Revolution had occurred with the sanction of God. Thus Tikhon addressed the faithful on the first anniversary of Communist rule with the words "It is not for us to judge earthly powers."[9]* He excommunicated Bolshevik sympathizers and

---

*Once, however, Tikhon remarked in frustration, "Any authority which God has permitted would receive our blessing if only it genuinely appeared as 'God's servant' for the good of its subjects and was a terror not for good deeds but for evil ones."

government, but he never specifically condemned the govern-
g Church, at least on this narrow point, could be considered more
Testament message. Acceptance of God's power implied acceptance ... power.

The church's political, though perhaps not spiritual, vulnerability increased
to the extent that it saw suffering as an unwelcome but nonetheless virtuous
human activity. Considering suffering holy—drawing the Holy Spirit to you—
tends to keep you off of the barricades. The Bolsheviks were correct about religion's, especially Orthodoxy's, tendency to sap human initiative. The Orthodox
Church provided proof of its passivity in its reaction to the Revolution. The historian Anne McCormick wrote:

> The tragedy of the church in the Revolution was that it was a slave church,
> untaught, unquickened, and too long schooled in the passive virtues of obedi-
> ence and resignation. It was better able to suffer than to resist. Thousands of its
> members, particularly the clergy, bore exile, imprisonment, and death with the
> courage of martyrs. The peculiar passion of the Russian soul for suffering, the
> belief that the divine design cannot be affected by human intervention, makes
> better martyrs than militants.[10]

Perhaps a healthy and vigorous church could have withstood the Bolshevik
onslaught, but the church was afflicted with osteoporosis. Not only were its
bones no longer growing; they had become rigid and riddled with holes. Its matu-
rity had been reached before the reign of Peter I, and by 1721 it had already
resigned itself to Peter's abolition of the patriarchate. Three hundred years later
it could manage only minor intransigence before capitulating to the Communists
in 1927; internal softness facilitated compromise.

Obsession with Apostolic Canon Law further sapped the church's vigor.
Admittedly, there was a certain sense to this—once the Truth was known it could
not change. But devotion to and pride in the ancientness of church theology carried over into matters of liturgy and ritual. Worship became traditional, mechanical, and a social obligation. It even became a peasant's excuse for getting out of
work. "Ancient" as a virtue had somehow been transformed into "archaic" as a
vice. Hindus wrote:

> The consequences of its mechanistic mysticism were doubly calamitous to the
> Orthodox Church. It failed to develop a reserve of vitality that would enable it
> to withstand with safety and effectiveness an outside onslaught such as the Rev-
> olution had launched on it, and it failed no less dismally to make the peasant, its
> chief pillar of support throughout the ages, loyal enough so that in a crisis he
> would rally to its rescue. It overawed him with its temporal power. It bewitched
> him with its grandiose magic. But it did not stir in him the fealty that comes
> from close fellowship, from a kinship of spirit, from a reciprocity of senti-
> ment.[11]

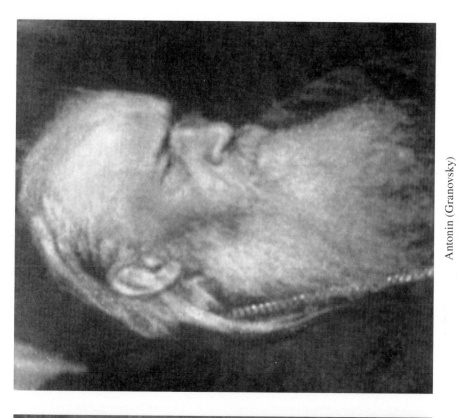

Antonin (Granovsky)
Renovationist Troublemaker
(Credit: The David King Collection, London)

Vladimir Krasnitsky
Merging Marxism and Christianity
(Credit: The David King Collection, London)

Alexander Vendensky
"Reforming" the Orthodox Church
(*Credit: The David King Collection, London*)

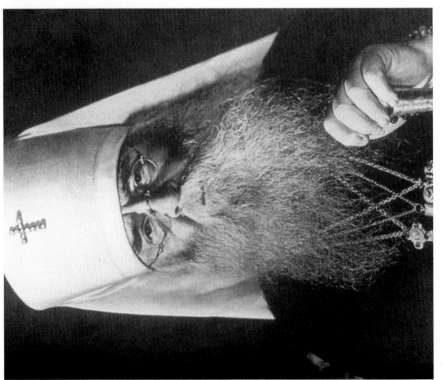

Sergei (Stragorodsky) in 1940s
Founding a "Soviet Church"

Emelyan Yaroslavsky
Propagandizing the Nation
(Credit: The David King Collection, London)

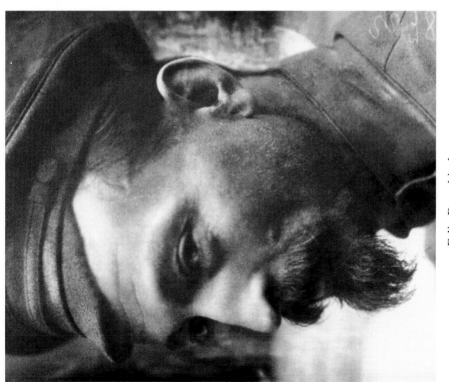

Felix Dzerzhinsky
Organizing the "Red Terror"

Archbishop John Cieplak
Leading the Roman Catholics

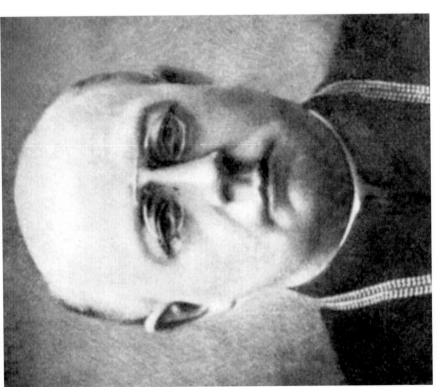

Monsignor Constantine Budkiewicz
Dying for the Catholic Cause

Edmund Walsh
Catholic "Missionary" in Russia

Exarch Leonid Fyodorov
Leading the Greek-rite Catholics

The Priest Says: "Easter Is Such a Profitable Affair! Forget about Your Ration Book. They Bring You Bread, Butter, and Eggs. Indeed, Christ Has Risen." (Credit: The David King Collection, London)

A Russian Orthodox Church Used by the Bolsheviks as a Grain Storage Warehouse (Credit: The David King Collection, London)

The Red Army Looting the St. Simonov Monastery in 1927
(Credit: The David King Collection, London)

Lenin in the Summer of 1923 after a Series of Strokes
(Credit: Photochronika Tass, Moscow)

"We got rid of the earthly tsars, now we'll storm the heavens."
(Credit: The David King Collection, London)

"Religion is poison. Protect your children."

An old hag tries to drag a young girl off to church, instead of allowing her to attend the new Soviet school. *(Credit: Hoover Institute Archives)*

Metropolitan Sergei clearly thought of himself as the proverbial willow, but many today wish he had been more oaken.

Church leaders, swathed in avowed humility, would never have acknowledged arrogance, but in a subtle form it was there. They overestimated their hold over believers and underestimated both the brutality and the staying power of their new enemy. Both age and ossification bred a kind of conceit—even complacency—that signaled decay, not vigor. It stands out in this period of great struggle that, in a land of many saints, no true candidates for canonization emerged directly from the masses during the 1920s. (Although, as you read in the previous chapter, some martyrs were granted the distinction in the 1990s, their primary qualification was that they had died at the hands of the Bolsheviks.) Where were the strong, courageous, and inspirational leaders who could have effectively *resisted* the Bolsheviks? Priests and parishioners were concerned mostly with salvaging their church buildings and treasures; blocking Red Guards as they approach the church door is usually not sufficient for sainthood.

Spirituality for the vast masses in European Russia had always been tied to magic—incantations to ward off evil or bless crops. The unwillingness or inability of the Orthodox Church to have long ago separated pagan nature worship and magic from its teachings meant that it became vulnerable to any campaign based on reason and science. Like all churches, it held dogma that transcended (or violated) the laws of science, but the violation was not just on the "high ground" of theology; it included the more earthly plane of holy water and relic veneration. The Catholic Church in the West had long ago turned against the "villains"—those in the villages who continued worshiping nature-gods—and had built a more intellectual faith. This never happened in Russia, and it weakened the Orthodox Church both in relation to the highly intellectualized Bolsheviks and the Bible-reading Protestant denominations.

One idea that Orthodoxy did have in common with Catholicism was that of considering its hierarchy above civil law, protected by God from worldly accountability. (In tsarist Russia the clergy had been accountable only to *ecclesiastical* courts.) Although this seemed to be an asset for many centuries, it became a liability when Tikhon was arrested in May 1922, placed under house arrest, and later imprisoned. Lightning bolts from heaven did not strike the blasphemous Bolsheviks, and neither hierarchy nor priests could invoke miracles to obtain his release. This introduced cracks in church credibility.

Church leaders made the mistake of believing that an apolitical approach would protect them. During the first three centuries of Christianity, there were long periods when the emperors did not interfere with Christians as long as they declared their political loyalty to the state, but nothing like this was possible in an ideologically driven Communist state. For the Bolsheviks, no compartmentalization was conceivable between politics and religion. When the state published its separation decree in February 1918, the latency of its antireligious tone was not immediately apparent to the church. When the church tried to protect itself behind the separation decree, Trotsky announced that the church had misunderstood it. Ideology required the state to pry into every nook and cranny of the land; there was no sanctuary into which the church could withdraw to ride out the storm. From a purely organizational point of view, Metropolitan Sergei should be congratulated for understanding this and, as he said, "saving the church." After all, he had written in his July 1927 Declaration:

> Only ivory-tower dreamers can think that such an enormous society as our Orthodox Church, with the whole of its organization, can have a peaceful existence within the state while hiding itself from the authorities.[12]

The church's only hope was *counter*-revolution, courageous, uncompromising, and consistent attacks on the entire Bolshevik program. If coordinated resistance had been the policy of all Russia's churches, they might have survived with their integrity intact—*mere* survival should not have been the goal. Another way to look at this issue is to ask the question: If the Bolsheviks had fought their antireligious struggle in Western Europe, how far would they have gotten? To be sure, social conditions were different on the two sides of Europe, but we must remember that Marx's theories for revolution and religion were supposed to be applicable *first* in the West, with its accelerated development of industry and advancement in the proletarian class struggle. So consider the question, just as a thought experiment. It is easy to believe that the Catholic Church with its militant aggressiveness and Protestants with their capitalistic investment and organized righteousness would have put up a much more direct and confrontational resistance.* The Orthodox Church, so long protected by the tsarist state, had never learned to fight.

Of course, it can be argued that in the short run both sides compromised and neither side won, and in the long run—the "run" that counts—Bolshevism is gone. The Communist Party is out of power and ideologically mutated, hanging on as a minority party in a more-or-less democratic country. At the same time the Orthodox Church and most other churches are still there; church attendance is even on the rise. But the church did not "win"—the demise of communism had much more to do with economics and geopolitics than with religious issues. Indeed, the church lost during the Communist period. Consider the level of vitality we might be seeing now had the church, anytime during the 1920s, led a popular revolt against the Bolsheviks and emerged victorious.

The point of this discussion is that, given the church's liabilities, it should have been easy to liquidate. After mentioning the contrary case, we will delve into the reasons why the Bolsheviks made such a mess of it.

---

*As a counterargument, one might cite the poor performance of Catholicism under the Nazis, but Nazi ideology was not overtly antireligious. The church was left alone to the extent that it stayed out of Hitler's way and did not preach against his movement.

Strengths: More Than Met the Eye

Perhaps—contrary to the earlier ossification hypothesis—Bolshevik failure was a simple consequence of religion's strength. After all, we are looking at over 900 years of Orthodoxy pitted against the Russian Social Democratic Labor Party that had seen the light of day only in 1903 (with few in Russia having heard of it until 1917). Vague ideological socialism, not to mention Marxism, was known to only a handful of the intelligentsia. How could these amateurish soldiers of antireligion win in such an unequal battle?

The latent power of the Orthodox Church can be seen in the outpouring of grief (and respect) for Tikhon upon his death in April 1925. The government was appalled at this display of love coming from *all classes* of Russian society. And Russia's Christian churches were more resilient than had been expected, as demonstrated by the religious revival during the early 1920s. The more these churches were suppressed, the more resourceful they became in their efforts to teach their young. The more churches were closed, the more unregistered congregations grew in number and membership. Government tactics were sighted on a determined and moving target.

In 1989 Aleksy II made the case for "Sergeian" flexibility as a virtue, arguing that the only alternative was exposing the church to destruction.

> The church with its many millions of members cannot descend into the catacombs in a totalitarian state. We sinned. But we sinned for the sake of the people, for the sake of preventing millions of people from departing this life for good. . . . The hierarchs of the church took a sin upon their souls, the sin of silence [in the face of evil], the sin of nontruth. And we have always done penance before God for this.
>
> Our refusal to take the church down into the catacombs bore an even more intense spiritual fruit. We members of the Russian Orthodox Church did not cultivate in ourselves hate and a thirst for revenge. I fear that a catacombs psychology would have driven us precisely to this.[13]

A REVIEW OF COMMUNIST TACTICS

As we have seen, there were two strategies, each in contradiction to the other. The first was Lenin's cherished idea of the gradual fading away of religious needs as the economy gained a solid socialist foothold. The complete destruction of religion required the complete construction of socialism, then communism. (He also believed crime and other social maladies would disappear in the same way.) This was completely based on Marxist "imperatives of history" and not on empirical information; it entailed no tactic except restraint. The second strategy was essentially the militant approach favored by Trotsky and Kostelovskaya: an all-out physical assault on the church and its priests, or at least the massive re-educational program favored by Yaroslavsky. Given changing personal ascendancies and political circumstances, neither held complete sway.

At this point it would seem useful to review Communist tactics in concise form and in no particular order: This will stimulate our thinking about which, if any, were justified (or at least morally acceptable):

- Persuading foreign governments and churches that no religious persecution occurred in Soviet Russia.
- Censoring sermons and spying on priests who delivered them.
- Fragmenting the church into independent parishes without any centralized organization.
- Shooting clergy, sending them to internal or external exile, and imprisoning them (sometimes with a trial but usually without).
- Setting tax rates for "nonproductive" clergy excessively high and denying them ration cards during periods of famine.
- Blaming the church for causing the famine of 1921–22 and stigmatizing it with greed for not happily relinquishing its sacred vessels for famine relief.
- Blaming the nation's public health problems on religious practices.
- Stimulating and supporting a "progressive" schism within the church for the purpose of weakening it.
- Abolishing religious schools and the religious curriculum within state-run schools. Restricting religious education to those over eighteen years of age.
- Taking the land from the monasteries, then closing the monasteries themselves. Converting many into prisons and labor camps.
- Holding carnival-atmosphere parades and demonstrations to ridicule Easter and Christmas.
- Writing and publishing thousands of antireligious tracts, posters, films, and plays to sway the minds of villagers.
- Participating in public debates with the clergy to show the logic of the atheistic position.
- Uncovering false relics to undermine the people's respect for priests and monks.
- Refusing to allow bishops to travel to or work in their dioceses and requiring priests to live outside of the villages they served.
- Educating children in atheism against their parents' wishes.
- Closing church access to printing presses and the newspaper press.
- Prohibiting the importation of Bibles.
- Blaming the domestic church for the extremist positions held by the émigré church.

- Suppressing seminaries so that the church could not instruct its next generation of leaders.
- Replacing the milestones of life, religious holidays, and rest days with secular ceremonies and artificial "traditions."
- Manipulating or denying dates for holding church councils or congresses.
- Denying the right of "juridical person" to church organizations.
- Manipulating workdays to keep people out of church on Sundays or organizing countersabbath rival activties.
- Promulgating natural science as a remedy for the malady of superstition.
- Creating and promoting antireligious museums.
- (Possibly) forging religious leaders' confessions and wills or pressuring them to sign what they had not written.
- Denying the right of religious propaganda that had been guaranteed in the 1918 Constitution.
- Putting ex-priests on the government payroll to better understand and combat the enemy.
- Using agents provocateurs in Russia and abroad to encourage anti-Soviet behavior, which then could be acted against.
- Enforcing the signing of contracts for church building use, the partial motive of which was to turn the laity against the priest.
- Requiring pacifist sectarians to serve in the Red Army.

PROXIMATE CAUSES

After eleven years of the Revolution, we are scarcely ahead of the priests.

—*Bezbozhnik*, May 6, 1928

So why did these tactics fail? If the Bolsheviks had played their cards more effectively, even to the extent of being more ideologically flexible (or perhaps more ruthless), could they have eliminated not just the institutionalized churches but also the personal faiths—even the need for faith—in Soviet Russia? Could they have done it in twelve years? Could they have done it in seventy-four years, the full span of the Communist experiment in Russia? Here we are dealing with proximate causes—ones that were controllable by the Bolsheviks. These failures were their own fault. In each of the follwing areas they should have been able to do better.

Russian Reality: Out of Touch with the People

The first of the Bolshevik problems was their distance from the Russian people, both physically and philosophically. Before assuming power, the leadership had spent so much time out of the country—"tainted" by Western Europe—that it had lost touch with the concerns of real Russian people. Even within the country the Old Bolsheviks traveled little, except for their prerevolutionary expeditions into exile and Trotsky's frenetic military maneuvers during the Civil War. White-collar revolutionary leaders were even out of touch with the lower echelons of their own party—none among the leadership had been serious proletarians. During the period of War Communism and well into the New Economic Policy, many were convinced that there could be a lightning-fast social revolution. They had only a dim concept of the pervasiveness of Russia's social backwardness, which led them to underestimate how much coercion would be needed to get anything done. Instead of change coming from Marx's historical necessity, it ended up being dictated to a people whose opinions were not sought and whose conditions were not seen.

Russian Marxists learned much of their philosophy either physically in Western Europe or from Western European writers. Consequently, they stressed the Western European dichotomy between science and faith—the two being incompatible. But native Russian atheism had long been built on the dichotomy between *misery* and faith in the sense that no conceivable god could tolerate the wretchedness of Russia. This meant that Marxist atheism had a difficult time fitting into, or even taking advantage of, the currents of preexisting, native Russian antagonism to God.

Michael Bakunin, Marx's greatest critic, understood Marx's vision of society as concrete and the individual as an abstraction:

> The government of science and of men of science, even if they be . . . disciples of the *doctrinaire* school of German Communism, cannot fail to be impotent, ridiculous, inhuman, cruel, oppressive, exploiting, maleficent. We may say of men of science what I have said of theologians and metaphysicians: They have neither sense nor heart for individual and living beings. We cannot even blame them for this, for it is the natural consequence of their profession.[14]

It was always the struggle for a socialist society, seldom "How can we help you to improve your life?" Thus antireligious propaganda never touched the real concerns of the peasantry.

Marx wrote:

> The mode of production of material life conditions the social, political, and intellectual life processes in general. It is not the consciousness of men that determines their being, but, on the contrary, their social being that determines their consciousness.

And "The real nature of man," he wrote elsewhere, "is the totality of social relations." Gorky exposed this point nicely, "The working classes are to Lenin what minerals are to a metallurgist"[15]—that is, something to be experimented with. And Nicolas Berdyaev observed:

> Lenin did not believe in man. . . . He had a boundless faith in the social regimentation of man. He believed that a compulsory social organization could create any sort of new man.[16]

This attitude, strong in the 1920s, developed to its logical conclusion in the forced labor camps of the 1930s and 1940s. Anne Applebaum, in her *Gulag: A History* (2003), described how everyone from Stalin down to the local camp commander referred to prisoners as "work units." Small increases in the prisoners' meager food rations were sometimes provided, not for humane reasons, but to raise production levels. The imprisoned clergy members had value only as clearers of the forests or builders of canals. Slave labor was, and was meant to be, the backbone of the Soviet economy.

Margaret Thatcher later saw the fascistic implications of Leninism when she commented: "There is no such thing as society. There are individual men and women, and there are families."[17] With their eyes over the horizon and not focused on individual believers and their families, the Bolshevik leadership had little chance of altering the religious mindset of the Russian populace.

Bad and Misapplied Theory

The historian Roger Pethybridge quipped, "The picture seen through Marxist eyes was often badly out of focus." As intelligent, knowledgeable, and dedicated as Marx was, his theories were riddled with error. Although he made contributions to economics, his reading of the "river of history"—flowing from the past, through the present, and into a presumably predictable future—was simply misguided. The past was nowhere near as simple as he saw it, divided neatly into exploiters and exploited. His present was viewed while wearing the blinders of socialism. And he grossly underestimated both the will of man and the effects of randomness on future development. His use of dialectics was clever, but it could not possibly explain all change and certainly could not explain "the end of change" in a perfect communist society.

Thus Lenin found himself saddled with a philosophy that, even if it were true for industrially developed Western Europe, was not applicable to a country scarcely removed from feudalism and overwhelmingly agricultural. Marxism was never meant for such a place at such a stage. When Lenin forced Marxism on Russia he was trying to cram a square peg into a round hole, rushing the dialectical process because he happened to be Russian, was alive at the time, and craved power. Thus a proximate cause of the antireligious campaign's failure was its basis in a flawed and unworkable theory applied by an overanxious revolutionary. If Marx was right, then Lenin misapplied his teachings; if Marx was wrong, materialism was not in history's destiny.

Although Lenin pushed for a premature revolution, both before and after the actual revolution he argued *against* launching a vigorous assault on Russian churches. These admonitions were both philosophical and tactical, and he certainly was not consistent (as no tactician could be). Marx had never pushed for rapid extermination of religion—the world had to be "put straight" first—and never predicted how long religious prejudices would last. What if the party had truly accepted the "liquidationist" position, which despite its ominous-sounding name was Lenin's gradualist position? It called for concentrating all efforts on the class struggle, industrialization, and electrification and simply ignoring the clergy. This would have been the true test—not that Lenin thought the theory needed testing. Would religion, based on the changing economic foundations of society, have faded over time into a historical footnote? Probably not, because, as the Communists would eventually admit, religion cannot be considered simply a part of an economic-based superstructure of society.

The tactical part of Lenin's concern was that initial brutality would be counterproductive. But, hoping to see victory over religion in his lifetime, he often contradicted his own advice, as in his brutal reaction to the disturbances at Shuya in 1922 and his sporadic calls for militant antireligious propaganda. In addition, he was not the only Bolshevik—others were even less patient—and he could not control the lower echelons of the party and hooligans in the cities. Except for the previous chapter, I have not ventured much outside of the 1917–29 time frame, but the following excerpt from the description of a trial of churchmen in Orel in 1937 is too good to pass up as an example of the impatience, frustration, and bitterness that Bolsheviks felt:

> The very fact of the existence of this counterrevolutionary fascist organization [the Russian Orthodox Church] proves that the stinking remnants of the rottenness of the past are making a last spasmodic effort to hold up the march of history, of the victorious socialist construction.[18]

Impatience is a portion of the reason for Bolshevik failure. These things just cannot be rushed.

I support the materialist core of Marxism, seen simply as the denial of supernatural entities, but there was nothing inevitable about others taking this view. Ludwig Feuerbach, Engels, and Marx provided great insight into the origins of religion (though they could not possibly have *known* how it developed 50,000 or 100,000 years ago), but they "got the cart before the horse" on the issue of alienation. It was not man's alienation from himself, his fellow man, or his work that engendered religious thoughts; it was religion based on nature worship that caused alienation. Religion most likely came first out of ignorance, and faith in higher beings impelled man on the course of self-abnegation and self-abasement. But, of course, I cannot *know* this either.

It is entirely possible that, as Joseph McCabe put it, "Soviet authorities were more deeply and sincerely convinced that religion is prejudicial to progress than democratic statesmen are that it is beneficial."[19] Yet, while it is true that the Bolshevik leadership was sincere, it is also true that it could at times be self-delusional. There was a strong tendency to attribute minor successes to the dialectical processes of history worked out as Marx had predicted, when the real cause of success was administrative suppression of organized religion. Economic determinism and the changing superstructure of socialist society were handy covers for the simple process of arresting, trying, convicting, imprisoning, and sometimes executing clergy.*

Theoreticians oversimplified when they insisted that religion was essentially the product of class-divided societies, a tool of the ruling class, without any usefulness in a classless society—indeed, without any possibility of existence. It was embarrassing in the extreme for both party and government when the "exploiting classes" had been effectively removed and alienation all but eliminated, but "religious prejudices" just kept rolling along.

Government as a Perpetual Dictatorship

Emma Goldman, after being deported from the United States for her anarchist views, toured Russia during the early 1920s. She amplified the theme that Leninism was a perversion of Marxism, writing in *My Disillusionment in Russia*:

> Lenin possessed clarity of vision and an iron will. He knew how to make his comrades in Russia and outside of it believe that his scheme was true Socialism and his methods the Revolution. No wonder that Lenin felt such contempt for his flock, which he never hesitated to fling in their faces. "Only fools can believe that communism is possible in Russia now," was Lenin's reply to opponents of the New Economic Policy.[20]

Her meaning was that Lenin had already realized that "the game was up."

Goldman went on to describe how Lenin had systematically eliminated factions and parties, Communist and non-Communist, on both the left and the right, and then crushed the soviets, the cooperatives, and the trade unions until he and

---

*While economic determinism is a gross oversimplification, there is little doubt that vastly improved economies *are* correlated with a slight reduction in religious belief and a slightly larger reduction in church attendance. This, however, is the result of social disruption, industrialization, globalization, and better education and would have occurred in Russia eventually even with continued tsarist rule. And it would have occurred more quickly with the advent of *any* revolution. All Europe is more secular now than it was during the eighteenth or nineteenth centuries.

his followers were the only power—and the only voice—left in Russia. (Although she failed to mention it, the church had to be added to this list.) None of this power-grabbing had much to do with Marx and his theories. Goldman said that Marxism had been changed into "fanatical governmentalism."[21] So one might argue that Marx was badly served and that, had dictatorship not been so brutal, faith might have withered away on its own. But dictatorships cannot be anything other than brutal, and all ideologues in power spend most of their time denouncing and destroying those who offer even a breath of opposition.

The plain fact is that Marx would have done the same as Lenin had he achieved power. As crucial as materialism was to Marxism, the whole ideological structure was bent so as to perpetuate itself. Even if Lenin had realized that Marxism was flawed in relation to religion, he hardly would have exclaimed: "Oops! The basis for Bolshevik rule is no longer valid. We abdicate." He was willing to live with religion to retain power. Goldman wrote:

> The political power of the party, organized and centralized in the state, sought to maintain itself by all means at hand. The central authorities attempted to force the activities of the people into forms corresponding with the purposes of the party. The sole aim of the latter was to strengthen the state and monopolize all economic, political, and social activities—even all cultural manifestations. . . . Revolution is indeed a violent process. But if it is to result only in a change of dictatorship, in a shifting of names and political personalities, then it is hardly worthwhile.[22]

The implication of this view is that the assault upon religion was never as important as it was stated to be; it was being pursued only because the church was a rival power base. Framing the struggle as, in effect, lip service to Marxism meant that the government was fighting the church with weapons inappropriate for its real purpose. It was never pursued with the dogged determination and commitment of resources that would be necessary to prevail; thus it did not prevail.

The Foibles of Human Implementation

The primary fact of human endeavor is that lack of time and money are hardly ever the essential problem; rather it is the failure to assign the problem a high enough priority. That funding the army or rural electrification projects was more important than antireligious work was a decision made at the very top. If the government had preferred, it could easily have had a more atheistic population that was poorly protected and sitting in their homes next to candlelight—that is, the way Russians had always lived. The antireligious campaign failed due to wavering commitment.

Human endeavor on a massive scale requires direction. Almost everything that Lenin said or wrote on religion was produced between 1905 and 1909 and was intended to resolve squabbles within the Social Democratic movement. Once in power, Lenin had no more idea of what to do about religion than anyone else in the party, except to continue loathing it. This confusion led to personnel problems: mediocre talent, lack of preparation, and more confusion. The most highly qualified Bolshevik agents were channeled into military and economic programs; leftovers were assigned to antireligious agitation. This worked the other way around as well; if a propagandist against religion showed real talent, he was promoted or transferred to a more important assignment.

In many districts the majority of Komsomol members had only an elementary school education, leading T. Samsonov, then head of the Cheka's Secret Department, to grouse in an internal December 1920 memo:

> The work of dispelling the religious darkness is extremely difficult . . . and for this reason one must not rely on speedy success. Strong and capable people are needed in this work that, unfortunately, we do not have, as the [Party] Central Committee does not give them to us.[23]

Reports poured in from the provinces with complaints such as "Antireligious work is not being conducted because there are no cadres to do it" and "New propaganda techniques cannot be tried because we have no trained personnel."

By the late 1920s *Pravda*, the party's own newspaper, brought these complaints to the public. Where was the funding? Where was the staff?

> The fundamental defect of antireligious propaganda is that its contents and the forms it adopts are very primitive; that the antireligious propaganda and the political, educational, and scientific work do not stand in sufficiently close contact [to the people]; that there is very little popular literature; and that the work is not carried on among the masses.[24]

When the 1923 Party Congress called for a relaxing of administrative measures, many workers in the field were all too ready to misunderstand. They concluded that they should ease up on their work or shut down altogether. Perhaps "caution" was a code word for "retreat." In Samara the League had 1,500 members and had just purchased new tractors with proceeds from confiscated church bells, but now, fearful that they had overstepped their bounds, they disbanded altogether. In some areas local atheist organizations interpreted the new directives to mean that only schoolteachers would spread atheist propaganda in the future.[25]

At the 1929 League Congress, Emelyan Yaroslavsky complained that his agency was grossly underfunded, which, in turn, led to a dearth of League branches across the country. He also rationalized the League's weak showing by pointing to lack of support from both the party and Komsomol.[26] On paper the League's position was vastly improved after the Second Congress, but only on paper. In 1930 Mikhail Kalinin was still complaining, "In the local areas there reigns complete arbitrary rule and a lack of understanding of the policy of the party in this politically important [antireligious] process."[27]

On top (or bottom) of all that, there was a general lack of interest in the entire project, or, to put it another way: laziness. An article in *Komsomolskaya Pravda* in June 1928 whined:

> What, then, is made by our antireligious groups and our educational organizations to counterbalance the influence of the church members? Neither the party nor the Komsomol groups, neither the factory nor the local committees, take any interest in the antireligious movement. [The common attitude is:] "Let those whose business it is think about those matters."[28]

One Moscow newspaper cartoon showed a League worker getting in bed on the day after Easter, mumbling, "Well, nothing to do until Christmas." Another showed a worker awakened by church bells, swearing, "Confound those bells— they won't let me sleep."[29]

Symptoms of bureaucratization appeared: overcentralization (with poor lines of communication to agencies in the provinces), overlapping bureaucracies, divisions within a single bureaucracy, jealousy among competing politicians, and lack of agreement on a single plan of operation. Although Lenin soon began railing against this process, it seems there was little he could do. The Politburo's Agitprop Department (created in June 1920), the Antireligious Commission (created under Agitprop in October 1922), the Commissariat of Justice, the Commissariat of Education, the Commissariat of the Interior (NKVD), Komsomol, the League of the Godless, various trade unions, the Cheka/GPU, and even the Moscow Party Committee's Special Commission all maneuvered for dominance in this area, or at least for a larger piece of the shrinking antireligious pie. Finally, the Antireligious Commission was given responsibility for coordinating the other organizations until, in 1925, the League of the Godless assumed the task. But all this was theoretical; it never worked out in practice. Lines of authority were far from clear, and there were often huge gaps between the central government's intentions and local implementation.[30]

A Misunderstanding of Religion

The Bolsheviks, obsessed with science, approached the Orthodox Church and the other Christian churches of Russia as if they were a product of some type of malformed science. They believed that if they could simply educate the populace in "correct science," religion would go away. Hence they scratched along the surface of religion, exposing internal contradictions, revealing the origin of gods in early man's fear of natural forces, and ridiculing the existence of miracles. This method, coming from a lack of appreciation of the deeper psychological aspects of religion, did have an effect on some individuals but did not penetrate very far into the entire social psychology. Robert Pierce Casey, writing in 1946, used a different metaphor:

> The Soviets accomplished little more than the pruner who cuts the leaves and surplus branches from the treetops. The result in the long run was to encourage a more healthy growth.[31]

One might argue that the Communists did have a (highly theoretical) deeper understanding of the withering away of religion with the development of the economic foundation of socialism/communism, but this "understanding" was unlikely to be true and was of no practical consequence.

Capitulation to the Spiritual

All the examples of Godbuilding that were discussed in chapter 9 are mud in the water as far as establishing a clear test of the implementation of Marxist theory. How will we ever know if Russian citizens could have lived with an atheistic "emptiness in the heart" if Lunacharsky, Bogdanov, Gorky, and others were attempting to fill this space with Bolshevik religiosity? Red Baptisms, Red Weddings, Red Funerals, and Lenin ikons in the corner should not have been necessary, and they were against Lenin's wishes. (On the other hand, if they were necessary, they are an indication of how difficult the job really was.) In 1949 Arthur Koestler used the phrase "the God that failed," but it was a mistake for any Bolshevik to ever have allowed conditions to exist where the implementation of atheism could have been considered "godlike."

Violence: A Lesson in Counterproductivity

Lenin once said (or is supposed to have said), "To make an omelet you have to break some eggs," but violence created martyrs and sympathy for the church. This was a lesson that Lenin already knew well and preached often. Yet he often argued, "The more executions of the clergy the better." He seemed psychologically driven toward counterproductive behavior.

Deference to Foreign Considerations

The reader will have noticed in the preceding chapters how many times fear of offending the Archbishop of Canterbury or the pope, or worry about derailing efforts to achieve diplomatic recognition at the Genoa Conference, prevented a clerical execution or ameliorated conditions in general for Russia's churches. The release of Patriarch Tikhon from prison in June 1923 and the release of Archbishop Cieplak a year later are two examples that come to mind.

In the introduction I wrote of the power of ideologies, but compromises for the benefit of better foreign relations also compromised the Bolshevik ideology. It might be argued that the Bolsheviks never *believed* in the compromises they made, that they were thinking only in tactical terms. But concessions do not leave an ideology unscathed; an accretion of compromises eventually saps its strength. The usual result is paying lip service to the anemic ideology for a few decades until it finally collapses. It takes time for man's natural self-deception and self-righteousness to come to terms with the ideology's subtle but inexorable demise. And this is exactly what happened.

Of course, if the Bolsheviks had not been executing clergy on trumped-up counterrevolutionary charges, they would not have had to worry about the reactions of foreign churches and governments.

*   *   *

Although I cannot claim to know what Lenin was thinking as he sat in his garden in Gorky recuperating from his strokes, I imagine him spending half his time ruminating over things that went wrong—not just on the antireligious front, of course—and the other half in denial. He must have missed the adrenalin rush of taking and holding power. He must have felt helpless. But we also know that he threw whatever mental resources he could still command into the minutiae of administration—work that could have easily have been left to others. This was the form of his denial.

WHAT WAS MORALLY ACCEPTABLE?

After describing Bolshevik mistakes (or at least actions with unforseen consequences), I would like to present seven retroactive suggestions as to how they might have acted against religion so as to avoid Western reprobation while at the same time remaining roughly consistent with their Marxist philosophy. These methods were a part of the Bolshevik program, but my point is that if handled well they would have been enough. The Bolsheviks had plenty of morally legitimate weapons available to them and did not need to resort to physical attacks on the clergy and their churches. These methods, applied fairly and in unison, could even qualify as revolutionary.*

---

*The enactment of these policies assumes that they are the "will of the people" (whatever that may mean) and not the ideology of a dictatorial elite imposed from above by military force. And there is this paradox: If moral policies encouraging nonreligion truly are the will of the people, it would seem that the nonreligious base already exists, and there would be little point in implementing these measures (except, perhaps, to discourage backsliding).

Separating Church and State

If the party had been completely separate from the state—that is, a private political organization—then there would have been no problem with party antireligious propaganda in the cities and villages of Russia. But the party, in fact, was even closer to the state in the USSR than the church had been to the state under tsarist autocracy. And the government acted as a prosecutor of religion for its own sake, becoming deeply involved in the antireligious campaign. The Commissariat of Justice, the Commissariat of Education, and the secret police all had special departments devoted to this task.

The government should have followed its own constitution in allowing religious propaganda, and it should have restrained itself. If the government had prosecuted only those members of religious communities who were truly engaged in physically counterrevolutionary acts—at the level of treason, not at the level of "spreading anti-Soviet ideas"—then its actions would have been supportable, but in their zealotry the party and the government clearly crossed the line into hypocrisy, the very sin with which they charged the church.

Being stuck with a bourgeois respect for private property, it is difficult for me to accept the nationalization of church buildings, many of which had been constructed from funds voluntarily contributed through thousands of individuals' meager donations. Church and monastic lands, a legacy of tsarist-supported feudalism, were another matter, however. Returning them to the people was justified.

The problem was that Lenin conceived of the separation of church and state not as a method of protecting the state from religious incursions but as a weapon aimed at the destruction of the church itself. If he had settled for the Western conception, however, he could have removed religion from public schools (while allowing religious schools to remain open), denied state subsidies to the church, required civil marriage and divorce, kept chaplains out of the armed forces, and made great progress toward secularizing Russian society.

Promoting Science

A legitimate function of government is the promotion of scientific and technological advancement, if for no other reason than because of their public health and military applications. Convincing medieval-minded villages that vaccinations were more effective than sorcery in preventing the spread of smallpox and other contagious diseases was a fully justified antireligious assault. Scientific methods of plowing, fertilization, and crop rotation deserved to be pushed by the government, which was held responsible for keeping the people fed. At one point Lenin was so obsessed with rural electrification that he equated it with communism itself. Any attempt to substitute the power of men's minds for the power of

God's was by definition antireligious, but no developing nation's government could be faulted for the effort.

Exposing Fraud

Exposing deliberately falsified relics and "weeping" ikons comes under the heading of consumer protection. When the church had lied, especially when prevarication was motivated by money, it was fraud—a crime in any country. Every such exposure was a blow struck against the church that the church fully deserved. If church hierarchs had instead told the masses that, of course, the bodies of saints disintegrate like those of any other mortal, but we still believe that the *spirit* of dead saints can intercede with God, it may still have been fraud, but certainly one much more difficult for the Bolsheviks to have nailed down. Consumer protection can only go so far, but it is a legitimate governmental function.

Improving the Calendar

Since there is a need for consistent rules over large areas, governments should be responsible for setting the calendar and determining holidays. Thus when the Bolsheviks, over church objections, abandoned the Julian calendar and advanced the date by thirteen days, they were within their rights. Attempts to eliminate labor-wasting feast days to increase economic production levels seem beyond reproach. One may question the wisdom of more obvious antireligious calendar manipulation, such as use of the rotating workweek to decrease Sunday church attendance, but it is still a legitimate governmental power.

Controlling the Borders

The Bolsheviks were reluctant to allow foreign clergy into the country and made exceptions only in such cases as the Catholic famine relief program. They banned the importation of Bibles and other religious literature. One may question the wisdom of these restrictions, but closing the borders to ideologically offensive people and materials was hardly new. During the 1920s the United States was, after all, furiously deporting anarchists and Communists.

Denying Faith-Based Military Exemptions

When the Bolsheviks were courting the sectarians, they made some provisions for true pacifists to avoid military combat as long as they provided alternative services, but this policy was brief and was soon replaced with universal conscription regardless of faith. There is no reason why governments must accept religious pacifism as an excuse for avoidance of full military service. The Soviet Union certainly had the right to protect itself.

Protecting Children

Remember the government's 1923 decree?

> Children who have not reached maturity (eighteen years) are regarded as belonging to no religion whatsoever, and the assertion of the parents that the child belongs to any particular church has absolutely no force.

Seven years later the journalist Henry Noel Brailsford voiced his approval:

> At the risk of horrifying my readers, I will confess that in principle this provision seems to me sound. It is an outrage on the immature mind of a child that any grown person should use his ascendancy to impose his dogmas upon it. Let it grow to ripeness and then choose for itself.[32]

This principle seems sound to me as well, though, admittedly, it is more problematic and less likely to be universally accepted than the ones discussed before. It is also much more difficult to implement. The geneticist Richard Dawkins explained: "A human child is shaped by evolution to soak up the culture of her people. . . . [Children] are likely to believe anything the grown-ups tell them, whether true or false, right or wrong."[33] Although Santa Claus, the Easter Bunny, and the Tooth Fairy are innocuous enough, I submit that religion is a special case due to its all-encompassing nature and the difficulty of escaping further indoctrination once the child gets started down that road. Children are simply too young to be branded with a religious name. Dawkins added that hearing that someone is a "Catholic child" or a "Lutheran child" should "clang furious bells of protest in the mind. . . . You should be free [at age eighteen] to choose your own cosmology and ethics without society's impertinent presumption that you will automatically inherit those of your parents."[34] Although parents have the right to teach their own moral values to their children, they should do so without religious context.

Therefore, it is reasonable for a government to discourage childhood religious indoctrination, and laws are justified that render it more difficult for parents to do so. As children grow older these injunctions can be eased, perhaps on a sliding scale, but young adults should reach that condition still capable of judgment. Soviet laws in the 1920s (and again in the 1960s) that tried to keep children away from the churches may have had a motive stronger than just the protection of children, but on their face they were merely allowing children to avoid the brainwashing effects of religious enthusiasm.

Unfortunately, the Communists reached the height of hypocrisy on this issue when they pressured elementary school children into the Young Pioneers with the goal—among others—of turning them into devoted materialists while their minds were still supple and receptive. As Dawkins saw, this process is simply irresistible to those who have a monopoly on Truth.

Finally—the ultimate reasons why the Bolsheviks were unable to carry out their mission. If they had thought deeply enough, they might never have begun in the first place.

25

AN ELEMENTAL IMPULSE

Ultimate Causes of Failure

ULTIMATE CAUSES

So long as man remains free he strives for nothing so incessantly and so painfully as to find someone to worship.

—the Grand Inquisitor in Dostoevsky's *The Brothers Karamazov*

The Bolsheviks must have noticed that as each day went by, with no divine retribution, it was more and more likely that they were right. If God had created Lenin, he could have uncreated him with a snap of his omnipotent fingers. And if God truly existed, why had he not done so? Surely the party had crossed any line that the Almighty might have drawn to limit the behavior of man. It would seem that it had exceeded even the transgression of Eve, yet its leaders were not banished from Eden, turned into pillars of salt, or consumed by fire.

Yet it must also have impinged upon their minds that Marx was wrong about the historical disappearance of religion in a socialist society. Just as the Jerusalem Christians waited daily for Christ's second coming and were disappointed, Bolsheviks, in moments of ideological frailty, must have experienced a similar disillusionment. Faith was not disappearing as Marx had predicted. There was even a church revival during the 1920s as many citizens—especially the intelligentsia—rediscovered what they had lost.

Over long periods of time—thousands or even tens of thousands of years—is such a thing as life without religion possible? It is, of course, for *individuals*, but what about the collectivity of individuals? And could society function in a civil manner under totally secular circumstances? In this final chapter we are going to look at the long-range, or ultimate, reasons why Bolshevism could not have succeeded in wiping religion from the map of Russia. Although these were reasons beyond their control, they were reasons that less ideologically blinkered leaders could reasonably have been expected to understand, or at least to notice.

A Religious Sense

The Protestant reformer John Calvin believed there was a *semen religionis*—a religious seed common to all humanity that, when expressed, could remain pure (as in his denomination) or be corrupted (as in Romanism). The German philosopher of religion Rudolph Otto called this the *sensus numinis*—an innate sense of awe and longing for the otherworldly that was the basis of all concepts of god. Julian Huxley argued that religion is "a function of human nature." And Leo Tolstoy upheld a universality of religious experience that had nothing in common with the forces of nature. It was based, instead, upon man's awareness of his insignificance, his isolation, and his sinfulness. No amount of education could affect this core of belief. Modern-day neuroscientists have even found that stimulation of certain neurons in the temporal/limbic system of the brain can produce intense sensations of joy and visions of being in the presence of God.[1]

My personal theory, which is as plausible and unprovable as any other, is that a religious sense exists as an end product of the evolutionary process. Over millions of years hominids with larger brains were favored due to their improved ability to interact socially, communicate linguistically, and obtain food. As computational power expanded, these same brains incidentally acquired the ability to grasp their loneliness and meaninglessness within the larger universe. Those who could not imagine a purpose for living turned to less purposeful lives and were less likely to survive to reproductive age or even to be interested in reproduction. As people without purpose were weeded out of the gene pool, increasingly large percentages of the surviving population were capable of turning their powerful minds to thoughts of gods, whose "existence" would itself become the purpose of life. Man became an animal that could no longer "live in a world it is unable to understand."[2]

If this is the case, there may be no specific *religious* human nature; scientists will never find a single gene for it. But there may be in man an adaptation—one not needed by plants and lower animals—very helpful to *Homo sapiens*. Man, who perhaps knows too much, may require a purpose in life. The neoconservative Irving Kristol observed:

> If there is one indisputable fact about the human condition it is that no community can survive if it is persuaded—or even if it suspects—that its members are leading meaningless lives in a meaningless universe.[3]

Religion, then, may simply be one of the brain's many ways of guaranteeing that the entire organism perseveres long enough to reproduce. In modern societies this habit of thinking may then continue into old age.

A similar explanation that I find attractive imagines religion as a forward extension of the gullibility or impressionability that a child needs to learn language and culture. The child must have the capacity to trust that whatever surrounding adults say is true and useful. It is similar in process to neoteny (the retention of juvenile features in adult animals). Just as over thousands of years wolves/dogs were selected by man for retention of their adorable juvenile features and for obedience, thus retaining them into adulthood, human childish acceptance—which provided "answers" to the seemingly unknowable—gradually extended into adulthood in the form of religion. Faith could be simply an extension of that adaptive trait, with priests (the "fathers" of the church) as guides.

Perhaps Stewart Elliott Guthrie is correct. In *Faces in the Clouds* (1993) he explained that religion comes from the universal tendency toward anthropomorphism. This is a survival adaptation in humans—when in doubt, unconsciously jump to the conclusion that both animate and inanimate objects are human, have human attributes, or pose a threat. When walking on a mountain trail and a boulderlike shape is seen ahead, it is safer to immediately assume it is a bear than to assume it is a boulder. Erring on the side of caution entails little cost. Animating the object ahead of time is safer, and people who have a genetic tendency toward this behavior are likely over time to out-reproduce those who do not. Hence trees and oceans have spirits, and religion is an artifact of adaptive anthropomorphism.[4]

Regardless of its anthropological origins—or even if there are no anthropological origins—the ubiquity of a religious sense cannot be denied. Every society known to man has been imbued with religious faith of one kind or another. Anatoly Levitin wrote from exile in Switzerland:

> Young intellectuals in the towns find their way to religion through conscious and prolonged searching, whereas workers and peasants in the provinces are drawn to faith because of an elemental impulse, which comes from the subconscious and is inspired [by God].[5]

Of course, there is a kind of circular reasoning here, as the impulse to believe in God is seen as coming from the God who wants to be believed in. Nonetheless, Levitin was sure that there was some "god-knowledge" in the minds of all people.

Michael Bakunin took up this issue in *God and the State* (1871), where he pointed out that universality is no more a proof of validity than was the commonly held belief that the sun revolved around the Earth proof that it was so. In the immediate post-Darwinian world, he saw this universality as a stage in man's development from the animals and supported the studying of religion only as a method of supplanting it as man's mind moved forward. Nonetheless, Bakunin did admit the pervasiveness and necessity of faith up to modern times. "Nothing," he wrote, "is as universal or as ancient as the iniquitous and absurd."[6]

Nicolas Berdyaev asserted that man was by nature a religious being and "the soul of man cannot live empty of religion." Nothing can take from him the urge to venerate and adore something higher than his mere self. There is an imperative toward the superhuman. More specifically, the Russian philosopher Soloviev asserted that his countrymen were "a God-seeking people."[7] All these writers detected universality. Writing in the 1930s, the anthropologist Ruth Benedict summarized:

> No matter how exotic a society the traveler has wandered, he still finds the distinction [between the religious and nonreligious] made. . . . And it is universal. There is no monograph in existence that does not group a certain class of facts as religion, and there are no records of travelers . . . that do not indicate this category.[8]

Universality within societies implies the inherent nature of a behavior or trait. Of course, what applies to societies does not necessarily apply to every individual within that society. There is a natural sexual desire that can (sometimes) be overcome by vows of abstinence; presumably there are some celibate monks and nuns, but I doubt that there is one who has never entertained (even enjoyed) a sexual fantasy from the day of his or her vows. An evolved biophilic love of pastoral lands with moving fresh water can be overcome by an individual's desire to live in the desert. In the same way individuals pledged to rationality and humanism can overcome a natural religious desire; modern societies contain a significant minority of nonbelievers. Years of pondering or wholesale subscription to ideologies contrary to any religious instinct might do it for a while, but what is suppressed lies latent in the mind.

Religious universality does not imply that a majority of the people within the society exhibits a very high level of devotion. Vacillations in the strength of religious sentiment have been great over time. Nathaniel Davis, in *A Long Walk to Church*, pointed to the thirteenth century in Western Europe as a period of powerful faith, but to Greece before Alexander the Great and to Arabia before Muhammad as periods of "vague and scanty" belief.[9] Although there might be an innate religious sense, church membership could still be minimal and church influence remain feeble.

If faith is inherent in the human condition, then the Bolsheviks were doomed from the start, for their goal was not just the destruction of religious institutions but the purging of minds. Marx, Engels, and Lenin, of course, rejected this premise, arguing that ever since separate social and economic classes emerged, religion was a product of the conflict between them. Their rejection of innateness is what enabled them to begin the engineering of society according to the Marxist-collectivist ideal.

The Blank Slate and Social Engineering

Aristotle wrote in *Politics*, "The citizen should be molded to suit the form of government under which he lives."[10] This is a more positive way of stating that human nature does not exist (beyond the basics of eating and reproducing). John Locke, in the same vein, asserted that the human mind is blank and is just waiting to be written upon. The Bolsheviks concurred and in their less theoretical moments considered religion a result of training in the home and church. Emelyan Yaroslavsky espoused the Communist approach, which was essentially the behaviorist approach popular in Europe and America at the time:

> If a person is brought up from the day of his birth in a way that precludes all contact with believers; if at the very onset he is taught a proper conception of the universe, and, when his mind is still in its plastic, its formative, and most receptive state, all the phenomena of nature and society are correctly explained to him; and if he is so circumstanced that he will not be socially oppressed by the classes that utilize religion in order to strengthen their power, he will not need any kind of religion whatsoever.[11]

It must be like language, the Communists believed: If one is raised in Spain, Spanish is spoken; in England, English is spoken; and if one is raised by deaf-mutes, the child will be mute. But the last example is valid only if the child never meets a speaking person. It is human nature to speak; only the particular language is determined by culture. So if atheists raised children, atheism would be the inevitable result only if the surrounding culture were already atheist—a condition it was virtually impossible to achieve starting from scratch.

Decisions are made by the mind—consciously or unconsciously—and the mind is the activity of the brain. The brain, in turn, is the result of millions of years of evolution, and what have evolved are adaptations to the environments in which we have evolved. This is where we *get* human nature. The cognitive psychologist Steven Pinker, rejecting the behaviorism of the 1920s, has recently reaffirmed the innateness of certain human behaviors:

> Human nature is the reason we do not surrender our freedom to behavioral engineers. Inborn human desires are a nuisance to those with utopian and totalitarian visions, which often amount to the same thing. What stands in the way of most utopias is not pestilence and drought, but human behavior. So utopias have to think of ways to control behavior, and when propaganda doesn't do the trick, more emphatic techniques are tried.[12]

Utopians were never advocates of freedom; they were social engineers.

It may seem that the issue of social engineering should lie in the realm of proximate causes, but that is not so because the reason for this engineering failure is *ultimately* the impossibility of success without physically reengineering the brain—a task somewhat beyond Bolshevik capabilities. The long-term failure of Lenin (as well as Mao Zedong, Pol Pot, and other social engineers) can be explained fairly simply by their mistaken assumption that ideology trumps mind. For these leaders, ideology was everything—common sense was useful tactically, only as a means to the end. Maxim Gorky was a Soviet ideologue who, like many others in Russia at the time, was fond of the phrase "the transformation of human nature"—usually meaning by prison camp labor—but to the extent that whatever the prisoners did "wrong" was human nature it was not all that transformable. A little *more* common sense might have led to the realization that humans are not infinitely malleable.

To deny the existence of universal human traits (or even to minimize their number and fortitude) is the essence of utopianism; it tempts certain men to imagine how receptive minds might be manipulated and theories vindicated. Lenin knew of Robert Owen's frustrations and failure with the utopian cooperative of New Harmony in Indiana. By 1828, within a few years of its founding, ambition and avarice bubbled to the surface, just as the impetus to religion would do in Russia. Of course, Lenin scoffed at Owen's pre-Marxist naiveté, crippled as Owen was without the "science of history."

Bakunin saw the problem, too (as anarchists are apt to do):

> Suppose a learned academy, composed of the most illustrious representatives of science [by which he meant, at least in part, "scientific" ideologies]; suppose this academy was charged with legislation for, and the organization of, society and that, inspired only by the purest love of truth, it framed none but laws in absolute harmony with the latest discoveries of science.
>
>   Well, I maintain, for my part, that such legislation and such organization would be a monstrosity and that for two reasons: First, human science is always and necessarily imperfect, and that, comparing what it has discovered with what remains to be discovered, we may say that it is still in its cradle. . . . Second, a society that should obey legislation emanating from a scientific academy, . . . imposed in the name of a science that it venerated without comprehending, would be a society not of men, but of brutes. It would be a second edition of those missions in Paraguay, which submitted so long to the government of the Jesuits. It would surely and rapidly descend to the lowest stage of idiocy.[13]

Despite their protestations, Marx and Lenin both harbored these utopian sentiments. They were like doctors forbidden to perform experiments on human bodies but somehow feeling justified in performing experiments on the social body. Had not Marx written that "the alteration of men on a mass scale is necessary"?[14] And had not Lenin, blinkered by pseudoscientific Marxist analysis, forced his atheistic vision of society upon reluctant recipients, perhaps even recipients who could not help but be reluctant? He seems not to have noticed how extremely small was the number of people voluntarily adopting his program.

Virginia Postrel in *The Future and Its Enemies* (1998) called social engineers "technocrats" and talked about their failure to control the future (for example, how cities just grew with little regard for the metropolitan plan). The twentieth-century Swiss/French architect Le Corbusier was the epitome of this type of technocratic social arrogance. But Lenin and his Bolshevik Party have to be the world's all-time champion technocrats, in the sense that they wanted to remold not just the structure and functioning of society but the way that its citizens *thought*. He could not see how futile his self-assigned task was. And even if technocratic change were in general possible—which it certainly is for brief periods—it may have eventually failed simply because of the impossibility in Russia at the time to overcome a thousand years of paganism and Christianity with a nonnative program introduced by revolution and based on rational premises. In any case, in the long run, all revolutions designed to rewrite the human program fail.

Or maybe the Bolsheviks did come to realize the futility of their efforts. In 1929, Maurice Hindus wrote:

[The Bolsheviks] realize that there are features in religion that appeal to man's sense of beauty, to his self-importance, his sense of superiority, his gregariousness, his search for a key to the mystery of life and the universe. So they [propose] to minister to these cravings with ideas, practices, institutions of their own.[15]

Lenin did worry from time to time, especially in his later years, about the emotional and aesthetic emptiness that he had helped to create. Science, though it might liberate man, might not completely fill the human vessel. Once he confided to Kalinin that perhaps the theater would provide a good substitute for lost faith, though he considered it mostly a waste of time. On another occasion he mused that the new Soviet ceremonies—the *Oktyabrina* and Red Marriages— might do, though, as was usually the case, he concentrated on form rather than substance. But he did seem to have a premonition of trouble; all that had been removed had not been replenished.

Lenin should have noticed from his reading of the Greeks how little human behavior, motives, and personality change over thousands of years. There can be no perfection of man; human beings are full of fallacies and foibles, and even if God does not exist men are still going to believe that he does. No imposition by government is going to change that. (Of course, if the Communists had stuck to the liquidationist approach there would have been no issue of imposition.) Marx's belief in the perfectibility of man (in the societal sense) is utopian despite his deprecation of that term. To believe—dialectics or no dialectics—that 100 percent of any society could achieve unanimity on anything is about as utopian as one can get. Marx's conception of society as an *entity* rather than as a collection of *individuals* was the fundamental error that drove him and his followers to ignore the constancy of human limitations.

From Purity to Compromise

Atheism was not tangential to communism; atheism was based on materialism—a doctrine central, even crucial, to Marxist theory. Article 13 of the Communist Party Program made this clear:

> It is impossible to be a Communist, a Leninist, and retain the belief that the conditions of life, of society, of industry, the weather, or an individual's health can be influenced by prayers, by sprinkling "holy water," by burning incense or by performing any other superstitious rites.

Yaroslavsky added:

> We must convince the masses that communism and religion cannot go together, that it is not possible to be a Communist and at the same time believe in devils or gods, in heavenly creatures, in the Virgin Mary, in the saints, in pious princes and princesses, bishops and landowners, who have been canonized by the priests.[16]

And Nikolai Bukharin clinched the case in *Pravda* in April 1923, "Religion and communism are incompatible both theoretically and practically."[17]

Bukharin, of course, was only half right. Theoretically communism and Christianity could not coexist, but in reality they had to do so because neither side was able to prevail. The third of the ultimate causes for failure is the overwhelming human propensity for compromise. In the process of compromise both sides always abandon the purity of their beliefs. Even such a "pure" ideologue as Hitler had to pretend that he was a socialist to garner working-class support. Eventually, the Communists grudgingly admitted that religion could not be exterminated, and Russian churches swore loyalty to an avowedly atheistic state. Pure, materialistic communism could not coexist with pure, spiritual Christianity, or any other religion in its unsullied state, but neither could long remain unsullied.

It is interesting to notice the timing of this particular compromise. The church began the conciliatory process first; Tikhon's confession in 1923 and Sergei's Declaration in 1927 were milestones along this road. At the end of the 1920s, when the party estimated that over 50 percent of Soviet youth—the principle target of its propaganda—remained believers,[18] it must have at least subliminally realized that the true cause was lost. But the party and the government probably did not *fully* understand the futility of their efforts until 1937, when Stalin read the returns from his nationwide census and discovered the minuscule effect of two decades of antireligious agitation. His turning to the church during the Great Patriotic War was a tacit admission of his failure. Khrushchev had to have conceived of his 1960s crackdown as a "politically necessary show." Amazingly, at the end of the 1980s Gorbachev was still making perfunctory efforts to suppress religion. But at no time during the entire history of the Soviet Union did either the party or the government claim success.

Thus the inquiry as to whether atheism could have triumphed if communism had survived for, say,150 years leads to a negative response, as the compromise was already deeply entrenched. There might have been slight gains and slight losses at various times for either side, consistent with the model of the yin and the yang discussed in the introduction, but at this late date such stability had been established that neither side could "win."

The Role of Science

Marxists, especially "mechanicists" among them, relied heavily upon instruction in science and the laws of nature to turn the heads of workers and peasants away from religion. Modern science should have run right over anachronistic superstitions. Old Believers were still obstructing demonstrably effective vaccinations, after all. But the story here is another one of movement from purity to compromise.

Science and religion, when they are considered at their cores, are truly incompatible and irreconcilable (though some like to claim each as a separate sphere of the Truth). There is nothing too complicated about this irreconcilability—science deals with what is natural and religion with the supernatural (or unnatural). Science has remained mostly true to its core, though there are many believing scientists and even some who argue that God created the Big Bang. Organized churches, however, have made many accommodations to the scientific age, allowing them to keep a modicum of credibility—enough to get by when not closely scrutinized. In 1992 Pope John Paul II lifted the Edict of Inquisition against Galileo and in the following year apologized for the church's persecution of the famed astronomer. In 1996 the same pope accepted Darwinism as "more than a hypothesis," with the stipulation that a soul must have entered the hominid line somewhere in its evolutionary progression.[19] Some Protestant leaders have argued against the existence of miracles since New Testament times. These and similar "flexibilities" have muddied the waters so that the science/faith dichotomy is more difficult to maintain.

Without these compromises organized religion would look increasingly foolish, but with these compromises it has been able to blunt the atheist agenda. The church has reconciled itself with some of the discoveries of the modern world, tolerating the compartmentalization of parishioners' beliefs in science and antiscience within the same brains. Communist reliance on the sword of science as the instrument of the death of faith has thus come to naught. It cannot find its target.

SOVIET EXCUSES

Religion is like a nail: the harder you hit it, the deeper it goes in. Our efforts should have been directed toward drawing it out.[20]

—Lunacharsky

So what did the Communist Party and the Soviet government have to say about *their* contributions to compromise? In the early days, failures on the antireligious front were attributed to practical difficulties with implementation: inadequately trained cadres, poor organization, lazy workers, and communications problems. Soviet apologists also pinned the survival of religion on carryovers from tsarist times. Marx had predicted that postrevolutionary life "would be stamped with the birthmarks of the old society from whose womb it had emerged."[21] This still seemed to be a reasonable explanation for religious persistence when Yaroslavsky used it in 1923:

> The human spirit is characterized by inertia. Although the body already finds itself in new relations of labor, the mind lags behind in grasping the new forms. Traditions, legends, have their hold on the brains of the living.[22]

Consciousness lagged behind reality.

At the 1928 Congress of Soviets, Aleksy Rykov admitted that harsh administrative measures had no doubt driven citizens potentially sympathetic to the government away from it. But as time moved on and embarrassment heightened, self-critical and philosophical evasions became harder to stomach.

Stalin's contribution to the Marxist excuse factory was his "surrounded by capitalism" theory, arguing that since the Revolution was supposed to be international it could not come to fruition while capitalist nations existed on the Soviet periphery. Thus, while the USSR was temporarily a mere enclave of socialism waiting for the ultimate result, religion within the country would still have some life left in it. He thus extended Marxism to fit the theory of what "should have happened" to the depressing reality surrounding him.[23]

During the height of Khrushchev's crackdown, two Soviet sociologists offered this rather tautological explanation:

> In our opinion two subjective factors, increased activity on the part of proponents of religion and current weakness in our atheist propaganda, are the prime factors explaining the existing religiosity of the backward section of the working people.[24]

By the 1970s and the 1980s the government became increasingly hard-pressed to account for the lingering of faith—indeed, the renewed interest in it.

By this time not only had a second generation arrived that was born after the Revolution, but a third generation was growing up never having known the tsarist autocracy. How could the economic conditions of those earlier times (presumably capitalism) still be affecting modern-day citizens? If religious faith were to be explained solely as part of the superstructure of a class-divided society, why was it hanging around in "nonexploitative" Soviet Russia?

Yaroslavsky's "lagging consciousness" theory, though still alluded to from time to time, was losing its punch. Everything else was a mass of contradictions. Pointing to the low cultural level of rural old women did nothing to explain the growth of religion among well-educated urban young men. When government spokesmen lamely declared that conditions were no longer appropriate for religion, they contradicted themselves by simultaneously claiming that the American threat of thermonuclear war caused insecurities in their country that were conducive to religion—the people still needed the consolations of the church *only* because of their fear of capitalist-instigated war.[25]

Some sense of reality finally penetrated Soviet governmental and academic life. Although they paid lip service to the old philosophy—for the sake of legitimizing power—leaders acknowledged that there were aspects of religion that could not be accounted for by economic theory. Soviet writers admitted the *emotional* quality of religion, as if this were somehow a discovery (meanwhile making no mention of Marx's contention that emotion of this type should no longer be necessary). The ideological component of religion was now pronounced dead, with believers merely seeking beauty, solemnity, and a place to calm their nerves inside of the church. The problem with this approach was that the surveys supporting it were conducted among the Orthodox, but among the growing numbers of sectarians ideology was paramount and the churches were anything but calm.[26]

Academics sometimes rationalized the situation by noting the ability of the church to adapt to modern life, presumably thus artificially extending its doomed existence for some small amount of time. And the church modernized its services—omitting some of its more obscure rituals—and offered vernacular sermons dealing with contemporary problems. There does not seem to be any evidence, however, that this "tactic" is the *cause* of religious revival; it might just as well be the result.[27] The ultimate excuse, however, was that the completeness of communism had not yet been achieved. When that remote date arrived, the world would see Marx's theories on religion vindicated.

But beyond excuses, religion may have survived—and even prospered—up to the end of communism simply because believers believed that it was a prerequisite for good behavior.

RELIGION AND MORALITY

When I do good, I feel good; when I do bad, I feel bad. That is my religion.

—Abraham Lincoln (attribution)

Human beings have social minds that create societies, and there is no doubt that morality is a necessity for societies. These are simply the rules for personal behavior that permit societies to function, and, as George Plekhanov had explained, these predated religion. Rules that worked effectively over significant periods of time came to be known as "good" and those that did not as "evil." Later, when the origin of these rules became obscure, morality was attributed to religion, either in the sense that the gods demanded it or in the sense that ancestors (or the spirits of the dead) expected it. It was not required that evil be punished in an afterlife; the punishment could come in the here-and-now, as it did for Jews in the time of Moses.

At the time of the Bolshevik suppression of religion, a common Western objection was that without religion man's baser instincts would be given free rein. Thus those who put forth the idea of an atheistic and moral society were often confronted with the argument nicely laid out by the French philosopher Pierre Bayle (1647–1706), though he personally rejected it:

> Man is naturally reasonable, he never desires without a conscious motive, he necessarily seeks happiness and flees unhappiness, and he gives his preference to the objects most agreeable to him. Therefore, if he is convinced that there is a Providence that governs the world, from whose workings nothing escapes, that rewards the virtuous with an infinite bliss and punishes the wicked with an eternal torment, he will infallibly follow after virtue and flee vice. . . .
>
> If he does not believe in Providence, he will regard his desires as his ultimate end and the rule of all his acts. He will scoff at what others call virtue and integrity, and will follow only the movements of his own lusts. If possible, he will do away with all those who displease him. He will perjure himself for the slightest gain, and if his position puts him above human laws, as he has already placed himself above the remorse of conscience, there is no crime that we should not expect of him.[28]

This theme pops up again in Dostoevsky's *The Brothers Karamazov*. As Dmitry languishes in prison awaiting trial the following day, he tells his brother Alyosha:

> It's God that's worrying me. That's the only thing that's worrying me. What if he doesn't exist? What if Rakitin's right—that it's an idea made up by men. Then, if he doesn't exist, man is the chief of the Earth, of the universe. Magnificent! Only how is he going to be good without God? That's the question. I always come back to that.[29]

Eugene Trubetzkoy applied this concept to the new rulers of Russia in 1919: "Religion has raised man above the savage state and made him *man* in the true sense of the word. The Bolsheviks have given a demonstration that irreligion ends in bestiality."[30] Yaroslavsky acknowledged that millions of workers and peasants were reluctant to join in the communist way of life because of "their belief that, without religion, without faith, without religious rites they will not know how to live right."[31] During the 1920s there seemed to be some evidence to support this view; many observers noted an increase in sexual promiscuity, prostitution, and venereal disease among village youth, and hooliganism and petty crime were also on the rise.[32] Of course it is difficult to tell if this trend should be attributed to the demise of religion, to disruptions in politics, to poverty caused by war and famine, or to "change in the air."

Lenin rejected all morality derived from superhumans, claiming a Communist morality "deduced from the facts and needs of the class struggle of the proletariat,"[33] or, in other words, a dialectically determined morality. This morality could be thought of in two ways: the behavior expected of a party member during the process of building communism and the refined, contradictionless purity that would be the natural result of the completion of the dialectic process. Party morality fluctuated along with the party line and consequently was never a reliable guide to behavior. In 1922 the Young Pioneers listed common decency, fairness, solidarity, and responsibility as virtues to strive for. In 1927 the Old Bolshevik Platon Kerzhentsev wrote an article lionizing Lenin's presumed qualities as models for future behavior: loyalty to class, daring, firmness, and superhuman energy, but it would be a stretch to call these pure morals.[34] A November 1961 issue of *Pravda* listed Communist moral precepts, some of which were:

- conscientious labor for the benefit of society
- a concern to protect and extend the nation's wealth
- a lofty sense of public duty, collectivism, and comradely mutual assistance
- humane relations and mutual respect among people
- honesty, unpretentiousness, and modesty in personal and public life
- respect for the family and concern for the upbringing of children
- disdain of parasitism, careerism, and profiteering
- rejection of racial and national prejudice
- hatred of the Soviet Union's enemies, but love of world peace.

(In 1968 the government legislated that all parents bring their children up according to these values.)[35] Morality *outside* of the party—that is, derived from any other source—was an issue unconsidered at any time in the Soviet period; indeed it was thought to be a logical impossibility. Nonparty members were to follow party morals, the morals of the vanguard of the proletariat.

Certainly there was some overlap between Communist and Christian values (honesty, mutual assistance, etc.), and Lenin would not have disputed the point. His assault on Christianity and all religions was only marginally based on the morals they held dear. Especially galling, though, were the Christian morals of silence, passivity, meekness, humility, and forbearance, which undermined the Communist values of pride in the work of the collective[36] and confidence in man's general ability to scientifically confront problems here on Earth. Lenin wrote:

> Being born from dull suppression, . . . religion teaches those who toil in poverty to be resigned and patient in this world, and consoles them with the hope of reward in heaven. As for those who live upon the labor of others, religion teaches them to be charitable, thus providing a justification for the exploiters to sympathize with religion.[37]

But a moral life should be possible without either religion or an oppressive, smothering party. In classical Greek religion the fickle and treacherous gods were certainly not looked up to for moral guidance (though certain gods may have *personified* virtues derived from earthly experience). More recently, Bakunin wrote that moral laws were real only if "they emanate from the needs of human society." He concluded that the idea of a god was not needed; in fact, thinking of a god as the source of moral law was degrading, demoralizing, and disturbing because it annulled man's capability of self-control.[38] There are millions of people in the modern world who do not base their personal morality upon religion and yet lead perfectly decent and law-abiding lives. (Admittedly, the laws that they obey may have religious underpinnings, but it is not fear of divine sanction that keeps them from committing crimes.)

Materialism and morality are perfectly consistent with each other. A society without God can perfectly well understand the difference between right and wrong because it was their prior understanding of this difference that led, thousands of years ago, to the attribution of virtue to God and sin to the Devil. Thus most religious prohibitions against sin are merely common sense, golden rule strictures co-opted by religions long ago. Every society on Earth values telling the truth and caring for children and condemns murder.[39] The last six of the Ten Commandments—the ones not dealing with a "jealous God"—could well have been thought up without the aid of priests and are universally honored regardless of faith (or lack of it). Marx was correct when he said that morality is more meaningful when you have to work it out yourself (or as a society), rather than have it handed to you on stone tablets. Even a Jesuit professor of moral philosophy understood the natural basis of moral law when he wrote in the 1909 *Catholic Encyclopedia*:

> Ethics takes its origin from the empirical fact that certain general principles and concepts of the moral order are common to all peoples at all times. . . . It is a

universally recognized principle that we should not do to others what we would not wish them to do to us. . . . The general practical judgments and principles: "Do good and avoid evil," "Lead a life according to reason," etc., from which [almost] all the Commandments of the Decalogue are derived, are the basis of the natural law, which St. Paul says is written in the hearts of all men, . . . made known to all men by nature herself (Romans 2:14).[40]

If one rejects the existence of natural law, morals can be founded on the word's root—"mores"—the social customs of a people. This line of thinking allows for some variety of morals worldwide and through time, perhaps determined by local economies and social conditions, but morals are still not based on the supernatural. The Soviet historian of religion A. Tokarev wrote in 1964:

In the sphere of morality, while people sometimes think that they act in accordance with the laws of God they are, in reality, obeying human laws without which society could not exist. . . . The roots of morality do not lie in religion, but in the real conditions of human beings as social animals, though even in primitive societies religion was utilized in the service of morality, thus sanctifying it.[41]

Religion may actually cause *immorality*. For Lenin, dependence upon "outside forces" for the rules and their enforcement meant that man was prevented from developing natural—and thus true—ethics. Religion was therefore a cause of less introspective behavior. Here he was in the good company of David Hume and Mark Twain, Hume arguing that increases in religious passion led to the worst of crimes[42] and Twain explaining himself as follows:

I believe that the world's moral laws are the outcome of the world's experience. . . . I have received moral laws *only* from man—none whatever from God. Consequently I do not see why I should be either punished or rewarded hereafter for the deeds I do here.[43]

Religion has often been the impetus to war—often with both sides invoking the same god—and war is difficult to defend as moral. In the Judeo-Christian Old Testament, God even *demanded* war, as when he ordered the destruction of Jericho and the Canaanites. Torture, death, and destruction are essential to war's conduct, while famine and disease follow in its wake. (Of course, I am not saying that a materialist society would shun war; after all materialists are human.)

Both the Christian and the Marxist analysis are flawed: Christianity because it depends upon supernatural beings to enforce moral rules and Marxism because the "laws of history" have not taken us to an earthly paradise where goodness would of necessity prevail.

The true measure of religionless virtue cannot be tested because of the pervasive influence of religion on the laws that states inculcate and enforce. That there are no religionless societies is not proof that religion is a prerequisite for civilized, ethical behavior, but rather a denial of the opportunity to find out otherwise.

HOW DID THE COMMUNISTS DO AS WELL AS THEY DID?

In spite of all the criticisms of Communist tactics that have been presented in the previous chapter and in spite of the "ultimate causes" over which they had no control, there has been a net decline of religious faith in Russia. Remember that I charged the Communists with failure only because they set their sights so high; they demanded and expected, at least in the early days, an annihilation of religion, not just a reduction.

What accounts for the limited success that they did have? The historian Walter Kolarz's term "indirect propaganda" is helpful. Direct propaganda—aggressive, noisy, ill informed, and rude—accomplished little. What did work was something not specifically planned: the milieu of Soviet times. During Stalin's and Khrushchev's rule, the core of the Soviet period, religion was not a part of what was going on; faith had nothing to do with the economic growth and development that was the focus of Soviet society. Most Russians today are not atheists in the sense of being materialists, but they have grown apathetic about faith because their energies have been channeled elsewhere, and the oldest sincere believers have died off. Since faith requires commitment, they could (with a stretch) be included in the category of unbelievers. When pressed, however, they would say that they believe in "something"—some higher force that directs earthly events.

Part of whatever success the Communists did achieve is the simple result of modernity. Just as Western ideas spread into Russia during the eighteenth century, during the reigns of Peter and Catherine, so, too, have twentieth-century rationalistic and technological approaches to society's problems. Religious belief has faded all across Europe, and in modern times it has faded in Russia as well. It would have faded even if the Communists had never held power there.

In the same vein, consumerism has deflected the Russian people's aim from a future paradise in heaven to—as the Communists (in a different sense) had hoped—earthly creature comforts. Kolarz wrote in 1961:

> In Russia, as in the capitalist world, many people cast off religion not because they embrace a nonreligious, philosophical concept but out of petty personal egotism. This Soviet egotism differs from capitalist egotism only in that its material objectives are less spectacular.[44]

Even those who return to the church often do so for the values of tradition, nationalism, beauty, and a warm feeling, and this lack of true devotion should count as half a point when we tally Communist accomplishments. Of course, even in the tsarist period "true devotion" was not pervasive.

WILL THERE BE ANOTHER CHANCE?

Religion, as Engels long ago predicted, will no doubt continue into the far distant future, yet I still hold out the slim hope that one day we shall see a decent, humane, rational, atheistic society somewhere on Earth—or beyond. Marxism will not lead the way; it had its chance. And no other revolutionary, dictatorial attempt at social engineering will succeed either. But aspects of Marxism—rationalism and materialism—may one day prevail, possibly through the recruitment of that minority in each society that has managed to suppress its *semen religionis* and finds a place to create a new society, though this is reminiscent of John Galt's efforts in Ayn Rand's *Atlas Shrugged* and about as probable.

If that future society ever comes, I would hope (against hope) that it would be allowed to live in peace with the majority of religious societies and that people could come and go between them as they pleased. Those in religious societies would be aware that nonreligious, yet civilized and viable, alternatives do exist. Those in atheistic societies would have a place to go in case the *semen religionis* could no longer be stifled. Although this would be reconciliation, it would not be compromise.

My dream of at least one free, secular society—won through moral means—is admittedly pretty remote. Man is not yet ready and perhaps will never be. The lessons of Russia during the 1920s teach that.

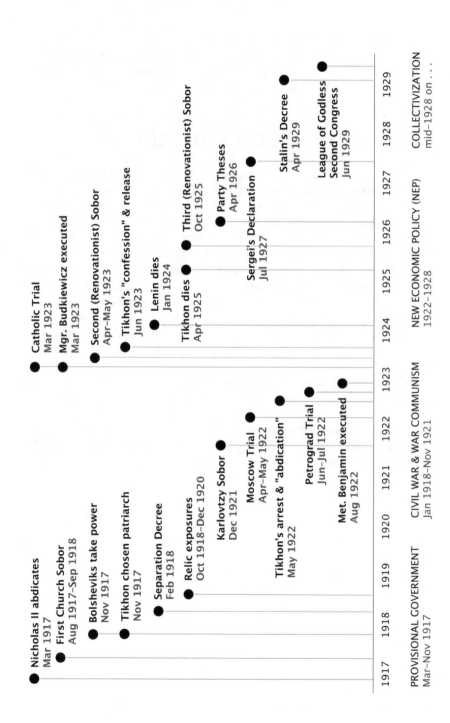

GLOSSARY OF PEOPLE

Note: All underlined terms or names are explained elsewhere in this glossary or the glossary of terms.

Agathangel (Preobrazhensky), Metropolitan (1854–1928): Agathangel was born in Tula Province. Ordained to the priesthood in 1885, he rose quickly through the church hierarchy. In 1889 he became a bishop, and in 1904 he rose to archbishop. In April 1917 he was promoted to the rank of metropolitan, and in March 1918 he was elected to the Higher Church Administration. During the Civil War the people of Yaroslavl (his home base) rose up against the Bolsheviks in bloody warfare, and Agathangel blessed the insurgents. Bolshevik retribution was quick and vicious, but Agathangel himself was left untouched. Patriarch Tikhon appointed him to be locum tenens, but the government made it impossible for Agathangel to serve. After years of conflict with the Sergeiites, Agathangel died of natural causes in Yaroslavl in October 1928.

Aleksy I (Simansky), Patriarch (1877–1970): Aleksy was the Russian Orthodox patriarch from 1945 to 1970 and heir to Sergei's capitulation to the state.

Anastasy (Gribanovsky), Metropolitan (1873–1965): Anastasy was a metropolitan of the Russian Orthodox Church and, after 1936, head of the Russian Orthodox Church Abroad (ROCA).

Anthony (Khrapovitsky), Metropolitan (1863–1936): Anthony led the Karlovtzy émigrés in Yugoslavia. The Bolsheviks used his staunch antirevolutionary stance and his toleration of monarchists against Patriarch Tikhon. Anthony passed away in August 1936 at Karlovtzy.

Antonin (Granovsky), Bishop (1859–1927): Antonin was a renovationist leader and member of Pomgol. He was a large man with an alleged but unspecified mental illness. He was often crude in his behavior and was not popular among the people. Support for the black clergy led him to break away from the Living Church to form the Union of Church Regeneration.

Bakunin, Michael (1814–76): Bakunin was a fiery atheist–anarchist–revolutionary who opposed Karl Marx in Europe. He wrote *God and the State*, among other works.

Belinsky, Vissarion (1811–48): Belinsky was an exiled literary critic who finally arrived at atheism. He died at a young age of tuberculosis.

Benjamin (Kazansky), Metropolitan (____–1922): Benjamin was metropolitan of Petrograd. Although he tried to negotiate with the Bolsheviks over confiscation of church valuables, he was arrested and tried as part of the Petrograd Trial of Orthodox clergy during the spring of 1922. The government had him shot at the end of August.

Bogdanov, Alexander (1873–1928): Bogdanov was an intriguing Russian scientist, philosopher, economist, novelist, poet, and Marxist revolutionary. He was a Godbuilder and wrote *The Struggle for Viability: Collectivism through Blood Exchange*.

Bonch-Bruevich, Vladimir (1873–1955): Bonch-Bruevich was Lenin's secretary and "one of Lenin's more illustrious cronies." He spent some time studying the Dukhobors—actually traveling with them to Canada in 1899—and thus considered himself an expert on sectarians. In Geneva before the Revolution he edited *Dawn* (*Rassvet*), a Social Democratic leaflet for sectarians. Between 1917 and 1920 he was the administrative secretary of Sovnarkom. He lost influence after Lenin's death and spent the last decade of his life as director of the Museum of the History of Religion and Atheism in Leningrad.

Budkiewicz, Monsignor Constantine (1867–1923): Budkiewicz was the Polish-Catholic vicar of St. Catherine's Church in Petrograd. His staunch opposition to every Bolshevik program led to his trial and execution in 1923.

Bukharin, Nikolai (1888–1938): Called by Lenin the "darling of the party," Bukharin joined the Bolsheviks in 1906 and rose to become its leading left-wing theorist, editing the party newspaper *Pravda*. Vacillating between support for and opposition to Lenin, he was the chief author of the party program adopted in 1919; eventually he reconciled himself to the NEP. After Lenin's death, he sided with Stalin against Trotsky, rose to Politburo membership, and was appointed head of the Communist International (Comintern) after Zinoviev. He wrote the *ABC of Communism* and was hugely popular among youth and workers. In 1928, though, he fell out of favor with Stalin and was removed from his Comintern position, though he remained on the Party Central Committee until 1936. He wound up another victim of the Great Purge and was executed in 1938.

Chernenko, Konstantin (1911–85): Chernenko was chairman of the Presidium of the Supreme Soviet of the USSR from April 1984 until March 1985.

Chernyshevsky, Nikolai (1828–89): Chernyshevsky was an ascetic, atheist, nihilist, and revolutionary who had a great influence on Lenin.

Chicherin, George (1872–1936): Chicherin was a Russian diplomat of noble origin. He entered the tsarist foreign office but resigned in 1904 after joining the Russian Social Democratic Labor Party. He was in London during the November 1917 revolution, was arrested for "enemy associations" after the Russian armistice with Germany, and was finally released by British authorities. He returned to Russia in January 1918 as Trotsky's aide and soon succeeded him as foreign commissar. He spoke fluent English, French, and German; had a keen knowledge of history and politics; and played the piano well. His workaholic habits led to illness, and he had to resign his foreign office post in 1930.

Cieplak, Archbishop John (1857–1926): Cieplak was appointed archbishop for Russian Catholics in 1919. He was arrested, tried, and condemned to death in 1923, but the Bolsheviks commuted his sentence. He died in Poland in 1926.

Cyril (Smirnov), Metropolitan of Kazan: Cyril was Tikhon's first choice as locum tenens. He was very popular among the clergy, refusing to support or condemn the Josephite "schism" during the early 1930s, but he hardened his position against Sergei during the middle of the decade. He had given Sergei extra time to see the errors of his ways and make changes, but in a letter of March 1937 he pronounced that time had run out: "The expectation that Metropolitan Sergei would correct himself has not been justified." The government exiled him to the far north in 1927, but there is some confusion about his death. He may have died in prison in 1936, been shot in 1937, died of snakebite in 1941, or died of natural causes (still in exile) in 1944—it depends on whom one asks.

Denikin, General Anton (1872–1947): Denikin was commander of the White Army in the South from late 1918. Defeated in his attempt to take Moscow in June 1919, he was forced to retreat. In 1920 he resigned his post and went into exile, where he wrote his memoirs.

Dostoevsky, Fyodor (1821–81): Dostoevsky wrote *Crime and Punishment* and *The Brothers Karamazov*. He spent time at hard labor in Siberia for his revolutionary activities but nonetheless possessed a deeply religious soul.

Dzerzhinsky, Felix (1877–1926): Born into Polish gentry, Dzerzhinsky joined the Russian Social Democratic Labor Party in 1895, leading to several episodes of imprisonment and banishment to Siberia. When the Provisional Government released him, he immediately joined the Bolsheviks and participated in the November coup. He organized the Cheka (later the GPU) and headed it until his death. He was extremely hardworking and ruthless in defense of the Revolution.

Evlogy (Georgievsky), Metropolitan (1868–1946): Evlogy was a member of the Karlovtzy Sobor but was nonetheless appointed by Patriarch Tikhon in

1922 to run Orthodox Church operations in Europe after Tikhon renounced the Yugoslavian exile organization. Evlogy opposed the succession of Sergei but finally submitted to the jurisdiction of the Moscow Patriarchate just before his death in August 1945 (or 1946).

Feuerbach, Ludwig (1804–72): Feuerbach was a German philosopher who supported a naturalistic and materialist approach. He wrote *The Essence of Christianity*, which influenced Marx and Engels in their atheism.

Fyodorov, Exarch Leonid (____–1935): Fyodorov was exarch of the Eastern Rite Catholics during the 1920s. He was tried with other Catholic hierarchs in Moscow in 1923 and was sentenced to imprisonment in the Solovetsky Islands. He finished his ten-year sentence there and died in Vyatka in 1935 at age fifty-four.

Goldman, Emma (1869–1940): Goldman was an American anarchist who toured Russia during the early 1920s, afterward writing *My Disillusionment with Russia*.

Gorbachev, Mikhail (1931–____): Gorbachev was Communist Party chairman (and a liberalizer) during the 1980s.

Gorev, Mikhail (____–1948:) Gorev was an influential ex-priest who joined the antireligious propaganda campaign. He moved gradually from disillusionment with religion toward expanding radicalism, leading to a final break and apostasy. The government invited him to work on its commission drafting church-state separation legislation. He took the position of deputy director of the Commissariat of Justice's church-state relations department and headed the editorial board of its mouthpiece, *Revolution and the Church*, between 1919 and 1924. In 1922, at the height of his career, Gorev was appointed to the party commission handling the confiscation of church valuables for famine relief and in December became coeditor (with Yaroslavsky) of *Bezbozhnik*. Between 1924 and 1926 he served as deputy chairman of the League of the Godless, but in April 1926 he was removed from his position for reasons unknown. His remaining years were spent in minor teaching and propagandist positions in various towns. He died in 1948 in Kharkov.

Gorky, Maxim (1868–1936): Gorky was born Aleksey Peshkov. After an orphaned and itinerant youth, he became a successful writer who financially supported the Bolsheviks during the 1905 revolutionary period. A restless soul, he spent many years in Italy, at times becoming despondent and grasping at religious solace, but quickly being reset on the atheistic path by letters from Lenin. After 1917 he was in and out of favor with the Soviet government but always Lenin's friend. He is credited with (or blamed for) founding the school of Social Realism in Soviet literature.

Herzen, Alexander (1812–70): Herzen was a writer, revolutionary, and eventual atheist who lived in self-imposed exile in Europe most of his adult life. He published *The Bell* and wrote extensively about the plight of the Russian people.

Joseph (Petrovykh), Metropolitan of Leningrad (___–1938): Metropolitan <u>Sergei</u> appointed Joseph to be Metropolitan of Leningrad at the end of the 1920s and then tried to move him to Odessa. Joseph led the Josephite Movement against Sergei in 1928–29. The government exiled Joseph to Alma Ata on the shores of the Aral in 1929, charging him with several crimes. In the waning days of 1938 he was executed by firing squad for the "crime" of giving encouragement to wandering priests.

Kalinin, Mikhail (1875–1946): Kalinin was a likable metalworker of peasant origin who joined the <u>Russian Social Democratic Labor Party</u> before the 1917 revolution. Though he opposed <u>Lenin</u>'s defeatist policy during World War I, he rose through the Party <u>Central Committee</u> and the <u>Politburo</u>, becoming the titular head of the Soviet state for many years. Peasants often brought their complaints directly to his office, and he became a link with the countryside, which was so little known by city-bred <u>Bolsheviks</u>. Emma <u>Goldman</u>, however, called him a "marionette."

Kamenev, Lev (1883–1936): Born Lev Rozenfeld, Kamenev joined the <u>Russian Social Democratic Labor Party</u> in 1901 and supported <u>Lenin</u> from the beginning. He directed the party from abroad during the prerevolutionary period, but when he returned to Russia in 1914 he was banished to Siberia. After the March 1917 revolution, he led the <u>Bolsheviks</u> until Lenin's return from Switzerland. Initially opposing the seizure of power, he nonetheless became chairman of the <u>Central Executive Committee</u> of the Soviets in the new Bolshevik government as well as president of the Moscow soviet. He was primarily involved in administrative and economic affairs, handling, for example, the delicate negotiations between his government and the <u>American Relief Administration</u> during the famine. After Lenin's death in January 1924, Kamenev at first supported Stalin and then opposed him, eventually winding up as another victim of the <u>Great Purge</u>.

Kerensky, Alexander (1881–1970:) During the final four months of the 1917 <u>Provisional Government</u>, Kerensky was prime minister and supreme commander of the Armed Forces. His basic policies were to remain in the war and postpone reforms until a <u>Constituent Assembly</u> could be formed. After losing power in November 1917, he fled to Paris and worked in opposition to the <u>Bolsheviks</u>. In 1940 he moved to the United States.

Khrushchev, Nikita (1894–1971): Khrushchev was Communist Party chairman from 1956 until 1964 and was responsible for a renewed wave of antireligious activity.

Kostelovskaya, Maria: Kostelovskaya edited *Bezbozhnik u Stanka* (*The Godless at the Workbench*) and was an antagonist of <u>Yaroslavsky</u> on the proper methods of antireligious propaganda. She downplayed the use of scientific education in exposing the origins of religion and advocated rougher tactics emphasizing the class struggle.

Krasikov, Peter (1870–1939): Krasikov prosecuted the Orthodox defendants in the 1922 Petrograd Church Trial. He headed the Commissariat of Justice's Eighth (Antireligious) Department from 1918 to 1924 and then became Commissar of Justice. He edited the government's *Revolution and the Church* periodical and served on both the presidium of the League of Militant Atheists and the party's Antireligious Commission. He also wrote *The Myth of Christ*. (Solzhenitsyn reported that Krasikov was a friend of Lenin's from their mutual prerevolutionary exile in Krasnoyarsk, where Lenin enjoyed listening to him play the violin.)

Krasnitsky, Vladimir (1880–1936): Raised in Ekaterinoslav, Krasnitsky rose to become a junior priest at St. Vladimir's Cathedral in St. Petersburg. At one time he was chaplain to the Black Hundred Party and was accused of writing articles about Jews drinking Christian blood. His turn toward progressivism seems to have resulted more from personal animosity than from ideological conviction. In 1918 an old rival of his was appointed dean of St. Isaak's Cathedral, and Krasnitsky blamed both Patriarch Tikhon and Metropolitan Benjamin for his failure to win the post. He began a campaign against both superiors, which led him also to testify against Benjamin at his Petrograd Trial. By 1923 he was appointed dean of the Cathedral of Christ Our Savior in Moscow. His interests were clerical; he wanted power for the priesthood, from whence he came, at the expense of bishops. He died a poor parish priest, regretting the harm that he had done to his church.

Krassin, Leonid (1870–1926): Krassin was an early member of the Russian Social Democratic Labor Party and was one of the Godbuilders. After 1917 he held various jobs relating to military supply, trade, and industry, rising in 1924 to the post of Commissar of Foreign Trade. He also served as ambassador to England and to France, working to reestablish commercial relations with Europe. He was a member of the Party Central Committee but not the Politburo.

Krupskaya, Nadezhda (1869–1939): Krupskaya was Lenin's wife and a major figure in the Commissariat of Education. She worked tirelessly for improvements in the lives of the peasantry, including better schools, teachers, and libraries.

Krylenko, Nikolai (1885–1940): Krylenko became prosecutor for the revolutionary tribunals in 1918 and tried the government's case against Orthodox clergy in Moscow in 1922. For a while he was Commissar for War in the Bolshevik government, then commander-in-chief of Russian Forces. In the early 1920s he became Deputy Commissar and then, in 1936, Commissar of Justice of the RSFSR. He prosecuted victims of Stalin's show trials before he was arrested himself in 1937. He died in a KGB prison.

Lenin, Vladimir Ilyich (1870–1924): Lenin was the leader of the Bolshevik faction of the Russian Social Democratic Labor Party; instigator of the

November 7, 1917, revolution in Petrograd; and chairman of <u>Sovnarkom</u>. He died after a series of strokes at the age of fifty-four.

Lunacharsky, Anatoly (1873–1933): Lunacharsky was a highly cultured literary critic and politician who joined the Bolshevik faction of the <u>Russian Social Democratic Labor Party</u>. From 1917 through 1929 he was Commissar for Education. His educational writings created for him a solid reputation abroad, but he was not successful in reforming the Russian educational system. His mind seems not to have been made for the nuts and bolts of improving the schools and the teacher corps. He died in Paris in 1933, on the way to an ambassadorship in Spain.

Lvov, Prince Georgy (1861–1925): Georgy Lvov was the head of the <u>Provisional Government</u> until <u>Kerensky</u> replaced him in July 1917.

Lvov, Vladimir (1872–1934): Vladimir Lvov was chief procurator of the Holy Synod during the first months of the <u>Provisional Government</u> and later became a member of the renovationist <u>Higher Church Administration</u>.

Marx, Karl (1818–83): Marx founded international communism, writing the *Communist Manifesto* in 1848 and *Capital* in 1867. He never entered Russia.

Maxim (____–1931): Michael Zhizhilenko, <u>Tikhon</u>'s personal doctor, joined the catacombs after the patriarch's death in 1925, taking the name Maxim. He was arrested in 1930 and executed at <u>Solovky</u> in July 1931, presumably for refusing to recognize <u>Sergei</u> as leader of the church.

Nicholas II, Tsar (1868–1918): Nicholas was the last tsar of the Romanov Dynasty. The <u>Bolsheviks</u> executed him and his family in July 1918 in Ekaterinburg.

Oleshchuk, Fyodor (____–1977): Oleshchuk's father was a priest, but the son learned to doubt religion at an early age. He joined the Communist Party in 1921 and in 1925 rose to the position of executive secretary of the <u>League of the Godless</u>. During World War II, he served in the Party <u>Agitprop</u>. He died in 1977 in Moscow.

Pavlov, Pavel (1883–1936): Pavlov was a pacifist Baptist leader and president of the Baptist Union during the early 1920s. In 1936 guards in the <u>gulag</u> executed him.

Peter (Polyansky), Metropolitan of Krutitsa (Moscow) (1862–1937?): Patriarch <u>Tikhon</u> appointed Peter third in the <u>locum tenens</u> line of succession, and Peter resolutely refused to relinquish his title. After he was arrested in December 1925, he was kept in Moscow's Lubyanka Prison for some time and then given a five-year sentence in a Siberian work camp. When, in 1927, he refused an offer of freedom in return for signing <u>Sergei</u>'s "Declaration," he had three more years tacked on to his sentence. Peter barely survived the bitter cold for twelve years, constantly being pressured by OGPU agent <u>Tuchkov</u> to give up his position and become a secret police agent, both of which he refused to do. Finally, in October 1937, patience running out, he was shot for being "an irreconcilable enemy of the Soviet Power." He died—most likely shot for recalcitrance—in the remote North Siberian village of Khe in October 1937. (Other renditions of his story have him shot in 1936 or in the Magnitogorsk Prison.)

Peter I (the Great) (reign 1682–1725): Peter was tsar of Russia during the early eighteenth century. He tried to westernize his country by, in part, opposing traditional church institutions.

Plekhanov, George (1856–1918): Plekhanov was a Russian philosopher, historian, and journalist who introduced Marxism to Russia and inspired Lenin.

Pobedonostsev, Constantine (1827–1907): Pobedonostsev was a professor of civil law at Moscow University who became chief procurator of the Holy Synod. He ran the government's religious bureaucracy from 1880 until 1905, when he was relieved of his duties as part of that year's reforms. His *Reflections of a Russian Statesman* was published in 1898. Reputedly, he served as the model for Dostoevsky's Grand Inquisitor.

Radek, Karl (1885–1939): Radek lived in Germany (1908–13) before working with Lenin in Switzerland. Radek joined Lenin and twenty-six other Bolsheviks in the German "sealed train" that took them to Russia in April 1917. After the November Revolution he became a member of the Bolshevik Central Committee. He organized a Communist uprising in Germany in 1918, for which he was arrested and later swapped for the Catholic Archbishop Ropp. Stalin had him executed in 1939.

Rykov, Aleksy (1881–1938): An early Bolshevik who urged conciliation with the Mensheviks. After the seizure of power he became chairman of the Supreme Economic Council but was never a popular leader (he often suffered fits of stammering when he spoke). He was chairman of Sovnarkom for a while and a member of the Politburo. He supported Stalin against Trotsky but was sentenced to death anyway in the final show trial of the Great Purge.

Sergei (Stragorodsky), Metropolitan (1867–1944): Sergei headed the Moscow Patriarchate after Tikhon's death and Peter's arrest in 1925. He issued the notorious Declaration of July 1927 that sent deep tremors through the church. In 1933 he proclaimed that, though not yet crowned as patriarch, he had full patriarchal authority. He finally attained the leadership position in September 1943 but died in May 1944.

Skvortsov-Stepanov, Ivan (1870–1928): The Old Bolshevik Skvortsov-Stepanov was a member of the Party Central Committee, a leading Bolshevik theorist, Commissar of the Treasury (Finance), head of Komsomol, and editor-in-chief of *Izvestia*. He played an important role as a prolific pamphleteer in the antireligious struggle's early years and wrote *Principles of Antireligious Propaganda*. Upon death, he was cremated as a final insult to the church.

Stalin, Joseph (1879–1953): Born Joseph Vissarionovich Djugashvili, Stalin was Commissar of Nationalities during the early 1920s, then he gradually assumed full power after <u>Lenin</u>'s death in January 1924. As Party Secretary, he was in a position to advance through manipulation of the party machinery and personnel. He was less ideological and more pragmatic than Lenin. He died, presumably of natural causes, in March 1953.

Tikhon (Belavin), Patriarch (1865–1925): Born Vasily Vasilyevich Belavin in the Pskov District of Russia, he rose to become the Russian Orthodox patriarch from November 1917 until his death in April 1925.

Titlinov, Boris: Titlinov was a lay professor of history at the Petrograd Theological Academy and the renovationists' ideological leader. He edited the popular journal *The Church and Social Messenger*, which in March 1918 relentlessly criticized <u>Tikhon</u> for his anathema of the <u>Bolsheviks</u>.

Tolstoy, Leo (1828–1910): Tolstoy was a Russian religious philosopher and author of *War and Peace*, among other works. After his death, many still followed his religious (but anti-Orthodox) teachings.

Trotsky, Leon (1879–1940): Born Leib (Lev) Bronstein, Trotsky was an early <u>Menshevik</u> who switched to <u>Lenin</u>'s side with the success of the Petrograd coup in 1917. He organized and ran the Red Army during the <u>Civil War</u> and later had a minor role in the antireligious movement, but he was squeezed out by <u>Stalin</u> after Lenin's death. Eventually he was exiled, at first internally and then out of the country, and was assassinated by one of Stalin's henchmen in Mexico City in 1940.

Trubetzkoy, Gregory, and Eugene: Both were delegates to the First Church <u>Sobor</u> and were <u>Tikhon</u> supporters.

Tuchkov, Evgeny: Tuchkov headed the antireligious struggle from within the Commissariat of Justice until 1922, and then with the creation of the GPU headed it there. He became the government "handler" of the <u>renovationists</u>.

Vedensky, Archpriest Alexander (____–1946): Vedensky (also spelled Vvedensky) was a progressive, <u>renovationist</u> priest with distinctly pro-Communist sympathies. He was described variously as charismatic, romantic, idealistic, vain, and unscrupulous. While dean of two Petrograd churches, he testified in government trials against fellow clergy. By the time he died in the mid-1940s, he had only a few parishes under his control, and even in these all signs of reform and innovation had disappeared.

Wrangel, Baron Peter (1878–1928): Wrangel led <u>White Army</u> forces on the southern front in 1920, after *Denikin*.

Yaroslavsky, Emelyan (1878–1943): Yaroslavsky was born Miney Izrailovich Gubelman to an exiled Jewish peasant family in Chita, near Lake Baikal. He began minor Social Democratic agitation along the local railway in 1898 and became a firm Lenin supporter. After a trip abroad where he met several European revolutionaries, he returned to Russia as a professional and full-time revolutionary himself. In 1907 he took up the cause of atheism. Work in Yaroslavl led him to incorporate this city's name into his revolutionary pseudonym. Prior to 1917 he spent many years in tsarist prisons or at Siberian hard labor. He helped organize the November 1917 takeover in Moscow and served on the editorial board of *Pravda*. Though suspicious of his talents, Lenin promoted him to secretary of the Party's Central Control Commission (authorized to conduct purges). He rose to become president of the League of the Godless (his proudest accomplishment) and editor of both *Bezbozhnik* and *Antireligioznik*. Briefly in 1921 he was secretary of the Party Central Committee and later chairman of the Commission on the Separation of Church and State. Although a dedicated antireligious propagandist, he posed as a moderate between extreme Left and Right factions, favoring science education and the historical study of religion's origins. His first antireligious book was *The Birth, Life and Death of the Gods and the Goddesses* (1923); then came *The Bible for Believers and Unbelievers* (1925), *Revolution and Culture* (1928), and *Religion in the USSR* (1934)—this last work produced for foreign consumption. After the demise of the League, he became a historian of the Stalinist regime. He died in 1943.

Zinoviev, Grigory Ovseyevich (1883–1936): Born Grigory Radomyslsky, Zinoviev joined the Bolshevik faction of the Russian Social Democratic Labor Party in 1903, and between 1909 and 1917 he was Lenin's chief lieutenant in the party organization. He was chairman of the Petrograd soviet after 1917, a full member of the Politburo from 1921 to 1926, and head of the Communist Third International (Comintern). An expert at arousing the emotions of the masses against capitalists, Mensheviks, or "deviants" of any kind, he excelled at manipulating party conferences to support his agenda. Like many others, though, he fell victim to Stalin's Great Purge and was executed in 1936.

GLOSSARY OF TERMS

Note: All underlined terms or names are explained elsewhere in this glossary or the glossary of people.

Agitprop: The Agitation-Propaganda Department of the Communist Party <u>Central Committee</u> Secretariat, created in June 1920.

American Relief Administration (ARA): Run by Secretary of Commerce Herbert Hoover and administered in Russia by Colonel William Haskell, the ARA provided food, clothing, and medicine during the 1922–1923 famine in Southern Russia.

Antireligious Commission: The successor to the Commission to Establish the Separation of Church and State, created by the party in 1922 and chaired by <u>Yaroslavsky</u>. Although responsible for coordinating all antireligious activities during the 1920s, it was dissolved in 1929.

Arian heresy: In the fourth century, Arians held that, within the Trinity, the Son was *of* the Father but *not equal* in essence to him. The Council of Nicaea in 325 CE ruled this view heretical.

atheism: The belief that there are no supernatural entities. There are no gods.

autocephalous: Orthodox churches headed by their own patriarch.

Bezbozhnik (*The Godless*): A Moscow weekly newspaper, created, written, and published by <u>Yaroslavsky</u> and the <u>League of the Godless</u> (later the League of Militant Atheists). Beginning publication just before Christmas, 1922, it aimed mainly at the peasantry and showed some restraint in dealing with age-old religious traditions in the countryside. A few weeks later, a magazine by the same name started up—illustrated, in color, and published every other week. The magazine, with press runs of around 60,000 in 1926, carried more virulent attacks on religion.

black clergy: Orthodox monks. Being a monk was a traditional requirement for becoming a bishop.

Black Hundreds: A reactionary organization, officially called the Union of the Russian People, founded in 1905 in opposition to the tsar's reforms. Its members were hostile to the intelligentsia, labor movements, and Jews and were intensely nationalistic—even protofascist. In the Soviet period the term became a code for counterrevolutionaries.

Bolsheviks: The followers of Lenin's branch of the Russian Social Democratic Labor Party. The name was changed to the Communist Party, but the older usage continued for a while.

bourgeoisie: A term used by Karl Marx denoting the city-dwelling middle class, often landowners or factory owners—controllers of the "means of production." Capitalists.

Brest-Litovsk, Treaty of: The March 1918 treaty Lenin felt he was forced to sign with the Germans if he was to retain power. Russia gave away one-third of its arable land and one-third of its population in return for peace on its western front. When Germany lost the war eight months later, most of the lost land was returned.

canon law: Orthodox or Catholic Church law, based on the Apostolic Canons.

Central Executive Committee of the All-Russian Congress of Soviets: The operative center of the government that oversaw day-to-day operations, known by its Russian initials as *VtsIK*.

Cheka: Lenin's secret police, administering the Red Terror, from December 1917 until 1922. The people called its agents the "peaked-heads" for their easily recognizable high-peaked caps. The full name of the Cheka was the All-Russian Extraordinary Commission for Fighting Counterrevolution, Sabotage, Speculation and Misconduct in Office. It was superseded by the GPU in February 1922.

Civil War: The war between the Reds (Bolsheviks) and the Whites (a coalition of anti-Bolsheviks including monarchists, democrats, ethnic nationalists, anarchists, and bandits). It was fought in the North, East, and South, and lasted until late 1921.

Comintern: The Third Communist International, founded by the Bolsheviks in March 1919 to spread communism worldwide and unite the international movement. Stalin dissolved it in 1943 as a gesture of conciliation toward the Allied powers.

commissar/commissariat: A minister of the Soviet government/a government department.

Constituent Assembly: Supposed to decide on Russia's new system of government. It presented an awkward situation as the Bolsheviks were already holding power—by their fingernails. Delegates were elected at the end of November 1917, but the Bolsheviks won only one-quarter of the total. They allowed it to meet in the Tauride Palace in Petrograd on January 18, 1918, but after one day Lenin ordered it dissolved by force, later offering many lame justifications.

cossacks: Free horsemen living on the southeastern edge of the Russian Empire. During the tsarist period many of these men were trained as a military caste to protect the emperor, and many served as an internal police force.

Decembrist Revolt: An 1825 revolt by army officers who had recently returned from "enlightened" France after the Napoleonic War. They tried to force the tsar to accept a constitutional government, but instead he executed five and sent many into exile in Siberia.

dialectics: A Hegelian/Marxist explanation of historical change based on the tension between thesis and antithesis, resulting in an advanced synthesis. In explaining economic history, Marx arbitrarily chose feudalism as the thesis and capitalism as the antithesis, thus forcing a synthesis of socialism (communism). Class conflict within the thesis and antithesis was the driving force of change. The synthesis would presumably retain the good, or progressive, elements of the thesis and antithesis and discard the rest; thus history would move forward.

Duma: The lower house of the Russian parliament after October 1905 and during the Provisional Government period.

Eastern Rite Catholics: Sometimes called Greek Rite Catholics, or Uniates. They followed the liturgy and ceremony of Orthodoxy but acknowledged the leadership of the pope. Since most of its members were native Russians, their apostasy infuriated the tsarist autocracy. In the 1839 Act of Polock, they were forced to merge with the Orthodox Church, as part of a policy of Russification. After the Revolution, some Orthodox hierarchs argued that recalcitrant Greek Rite Catholics were part of a papal conspiratorial wedge to destroy their church. The Bolsheviks, however, charged that they were part of a papal attempt to unify the three churches against the Soviet government.

First International: The International Working Men's Association, formed by Karl Marx in London in 1864. After the collapse of the Paris Commune in 1871, this organization, too, disintegrated.

Genoa Conference: An international conference held in Genoa, Italy, during April and May 1922, to handle issues of trade and repayment of war debts (and ex-officially to discuss the postrevolutionary status of Russia). The United States did not attend.

glasnost: Mikhail Gorbachev's late 1980s policy of openness, especially regarding knowledge of the country's real history.

Godbuilders: A loose group of Bolsheviks who tried to make Communism more palatable to the masses by portraying it as an alternate, or superior, religion. Lunacharsky was at its forefront.

GPU (and OGPU): A Russian abbreviation for the State Political Administration. It was the government security service existing from February 1922 to 1934, following Lenin's Cheka and preceding Stalin's NKVD. (Technically, it was called the GPU from 1922 to November 1923 and the OGPU from November 1923 to 1934.) It operated against the church, "socially alien" elements, kulaks, and party deviants and could convict and sentence without a public trial.

Great Purge: The show trials of the mid-1930s, whereby <u>Stalin</u> destroyed any Russian leader he perceived as a rival to power. Out of a sense of party loyalty, some defendants admitted to crimes they did not commit (and could not have committed).

Gregorian calendar: The calendar introduced during the sixteenth century by Pope Gregory XIII to bring the older Julian calendar into synchronization with the actual length of the day. It skipped eleven days ahead. By the time the <u>Bolsheviks</u> adopted it, they had to skip thirteen days ahead.

gulag: An acronym for the Soviet prison system—Main Directorate for Corrective Labor Camps—where prisoners, many political, were sentenced to hard labor in Siberia or the northern provinces. It was created in 1919 and saw hundreds of thousands of victims.

Higher Church Administration (HCA): The administrative body of the Russian Orthodox Church during the period of our study. For a while the <u>renovationists</u> controlled it.

Izvestia (News): A daily newspaper, originally published as the mouthpiece of the Petrograd <u>soviet</u> after the March 1917 overthrow of <u>Nicholas II</u>. When the <u>Bolsheviks</u> seized power in November, it moved to Moscow and became the organ of the governmental Presidium of the Supreme Soviet.

Julian calendar: See <u>Gregorian calendar</u>.

Karlovtzy Sobor: A council of émigré Russian Orthodox hierarchs and clergy that met in Karlovtzy, Yugoslavia, in 1921. It was overwhelmingly conservative, anti-Bolshevik, and monarchist and was a thorn in the side of both the <u>Bolsheviks</u> and Patriarch <u>Tikhon</u>.

Komsomol: The Communist Youth League, set up in 1918 to assist the Communist Party. Its members were from fourteen to twenty-six years old. It published the newspaper *Komsomolskaya Pravda*.

kulaks: Members of a village's economic elite; rich peasants. Often in Bolshevik usage they were any rural supporter of the church. Some said that a kulak was simply a peasant who had two cows instead of one.

League of the Godless/League of Militant Atheists: The leading antireligious organization, headed by Emelyan <u>Yaroslavsky</u>. The group adopted the latter name in 1929.

Liquidation Commission: Term used after 1924 for the Eighth Section (later the Fifth Section) of the Commissariat of Justice, entrusted with antireligious work. Peter <u>Krasikov</u> headed it.

Living Church: That branch of the Russian Orthodox Church, headed by liberal and progressive clergy (<u>renovationists</u>), that broke away from Patriarch

Tikhon and his followers in 1922. It desired to accommodate Soviet power and even praised it. Its critics charged that it was a schismatic tool of the Soviet antireligious front.

locum tenens: The man appointed to guard the Russian Orthodox Church in the absence of a patriarch. He was a temporary patriarch, serving until a sobor could be convened.

materialism/mechanism: Materialism is synonymous with atheism in the sense that all that exists is made of atoms—there are no supernatural phenomena or spirits. Mechanists maintain that the human body is solely a machine composed of interacting parts, or, in a more sophisticated version, chemical reactions.

Mensheviks: That faction of the Russian Social Democratic Labor Party that believed in waiting (as Marxism really required) until the full development of capitalism before attempting a revolution. They were rivals of Lenin's Bolshevik faction.

metropolitan: The Russian Orthodox office above the bishops.

muzhiks: A slightly pejorative term for common peasants.

New Economic Policy (NEP): A period beginning in 1921 when tactical concessions were made to private enterprise in agriculture and industry in order to boost production to prewar levels and overcome the deprivations of War Communism. Taxes in kind were once again allowed, wartime grain requisitions were ended, and peasants were encouraged to "get rich." This policy was already on the way out by 1928, when Stalin began his Five-Year Plans and the collectivization of agriculture.

NKVD: The Commissariat of the Interior; the secret police successor to the OGPU.

October Manifesto: A liberalization decree granted by Nicholas II in October 1905, creating a legislative Duma and looser regulations on religion.

patriarch: The canonically elected head of the Russian Orthodox Church.

Pechersky (Caves) Monastery in Kiev: *Lavra* is the term used by the Orthodox Church for its largest monasteries. Pechersky Lavra is one of the most famous monasteries in historical Kievan-Rus and the former Russian Empire. A site of pilgrimage for Orthodox Christians throughout Europe for centuries, it was Orthodox Christianity's "Rome." Founded in 1051, the primary goal of the monastery was to spread the newly adopted Christian religion. Monks worshiped and lived in the caves, and they were also buried there. The caves' mixture of cool temperatures and humid atmosphere allowed the bodies of the dead to mummify. The monks presented this natural process as a miracle, enhancing the monastery's prestige (and income).

Politburo: See Central Committee.

Pomgol: The State Commission for Famine Relief, or All-Russian Public Committee to Aid the Hungry. This was an ostensibly private, but in fact government-controlled, agency to distribute food and medicine during the 1921–23 famine on the lower Volga.

Pravda (*Truth*): The daily newspaper of the Central Committee of the Bolshevik/Communist Party. Beginning publication in 1912, it revealed the "party line" throughout the period under consideration here.

proletariat: A Marxist term for the oppressed, industrial working class. Those who have no capital.

Provisional Government: Russia's government between the overthrow of Nicholas II in March 1917 and the Bolshevik seizure of power in November 1917. It aspired to British-style democracy, remaining in World War I, and ending the domination of the Orthodox Church.

Red Guards: Armed, revolutionary factory workers (proletarians). They formed a sort of irregular army until Trotsky organized a regular one.

renovationists: A catchall term for members of the progressive clergy. Most were members of one of the three branches of the Living Church. For a while the Bolsheviks supported them as a divisive influence within the church.

Revolutionary Tribunals: Courts set up in December 1917 and given unlimited powers to try anyone even suspected of being an enemy of the Revolution.

RSFSR: Russian Soviet Federative Socialist Republic, instituted in 1918 and encompassing all of Great Russia.

Russian Social Democratic Labor Party: A revolutionary, socialist political party formed in 1898 in Minsk to unite various revolutionary organizations into one party. In 1903 in Belgium it split into Bolshevik and Menshevik factions, with the Bolsheviks eventually becoming the Russian Communist Party.

samizdat: Illegal self-publishing of dissident material, necessitated by the government's monopoly of copying and printing equipment.

sectarians: Non-Orthodox and non-Catholic members of religious groups derived from either Western Protestantism or offshoots of Orthodoxy.

Slavonic (Old Slavonic): The older language of the Russian Orthodox liturgy that renovationists wanted replaced with the vernacular. Twentieth-century parishioners did not understand it.

sobor: A canonically authorized council of the entire Russian Orthodox Church held in Moscow. Patriarch Tikhon's supporters did not recognize the two Renovationist Sobors.

Solovky/Solovetsky Islands: Solovky was a monastery that the government converted into a prison camp between 1923 and 1939. It was situated on the largest island in the Solovetsky Archipelago in the northern White Sea.

soviet: A council. Local soviets sent representatives to regional soviets, which sent representatives to the All-Russian Congress of Soviets (1917–22) in Moscow, or the All-Union Congress of Soviets (1922–36).

Sovnarkom: Abbreviated form (in Russian) for the state Council of People's Commissars, similar to a council of ministers or a cabinet.

ukaz: A government or church edict.

USSR: Union of Soviet Socialist Republics, the official name of the country since 1922.

War Communism: The political and economic condition in Russia during the Civil War. Its policies were harsh, including nationalization of property and militarization of society.

White Army: See Civil War.

white clergy: The priesthood of the Russian Orthodox Church. They were allowed to marry once but were effectively barred from the monastic life, which was the route to hierarchical advancement.

zemstvo: A semidemocratically elected institution of local self-government, established in 1864. It collected taxes in order to operate the public infrastructure.

NOTES

For reasons of space and clarity, I have not included Web site addresses in these notes. All listed sources that are not obviously books, periodicals, or interviews are most likely Web sites, and their addresses can be obtained in the bibliography.

INTRODUCTION

1. David Chidester, *Christianity: A Global History* (San Francisco: HarperSanFrancisco, 2000), pp. 131, 133; and Joseph Wheless, *Forgery in Christianity: A Documented Record of the Foundations of the Christian Religion* (New York: Knopf, 1930), p. 171.

2. Ivan M. Andreyev, *Is the Grace of God Present in the Soviet Church?* (Wildwood, Alberta, Canada: Monastery, 2000), p. 24.

3. Quoted in David E. Powell, *Antireligious Propaganda in the Soviet Union: A Study of Mass Persuasion* (Cambridge, MA: MIT, 1975), pp. 9–10.

4. Julius F. Hecker, *Religion and Communism: A Study of Religion and Atheism in Soviet Russia* (Westport, CT: Hyperion, 1973), p. 4.

5. Quoted in Powell, *Antireligious Propaganda*, p. 15.

6. Stewart Elliott Guthrie, *Faces in the Clouds: A New Theory of Religion* (New York: Oxford University Press, 1993), pp. 33–34.

7. John C. Bennett, *Christianity and Communism*, pp. 33–34, quoted in Nathaniel Davis, *A Long Walk to Church: A Contemporary History of Russian Orthodoxy* (San Francisco: Westview, 1995), p. xx.

8. Nicolas Berdyaev, *The Russian Revolution* (Ann Arbor: University of Michigan Press, 1961), pp. 83–84.

9. Quoted in William B. Stroyen, *Communist Russia and the Russian Orthodox Church, 1943–1962* (Washington, DC: Catholic University of America Press, 1967), p. 36.

10. Nikolai Bukharin and E. Preobrazhensky, *The ABC of Communism—A Popular Explanation of the Program of the Communist Party of Russia* (Ann Arbor: University of Michigan Press, 1966), p. 256.

11. Quoted in Elisabeth Achelis, "Russia's Difficulties," *Journal of Calendar Reform* (1954): 1.

12. Joseph McCabe, *Atheist Russia Shakes the World: How the Wicked Bolsheviks Save Our Christian World.*

CHAPTER 1

1. David Chidester, *Christianity: A Global History* (San Francisco: HarperSan-Francisco, 2000), p. 146.

2. Sergius Bulgakov, *The Orthodox Church* (Crestwood, NY: St. Vladimir's Seminary Press, 1988), p. 102; Rev. Thomas Fitzgerald, *Great Schism*; and Timothy Ware, *The Orthodox Church* (Baltimore: Penguin, 1963), pp. 58–59.

3. Ware, *Orthodox Church*, pp. 222–23.

4. Fitzgerald, *Great Schism*.

5. Roger Pethybridge, *One Step Backwards, Two Steps Forward: Soviet Society and Politics in the New Economic Policy* (Oxford: Clarendon Press, 1990), p. 36.

6. N. S. Timasheff, *Religion in Soviet Russia, 1917–1942* (London: Religious Book Club, 1943), p. 2.

7. Compiled from translations by Constantin de Grunwald, *The Churches and the Soviet Union* (New York: Macmillan, 1962), p. 25; Julius F. Hecker, *Religion and Communism: A Study of Religion and Atheism in Soviet Russia* (Westport, CT: Hyperion, 1934), p. 40; and Paul D. Steeves, *Keeping the Faiths: Religion and Ideology in the Soviet Union* (New York: Holmes and Meier, 1989), p. 37.

8. Hecker, *Religion and Communism*, pp. 42–43.

9. Quoted in Emelyan Yaroslavsky, *Religion in the USSR* (New York: International Publishers, 1934), p. 39.

10. Thornton Anderson, *Russian Political Thought* (Ithaca, NY: Cornell University Press, 1967), pp. 23–26, quoted in Steeves, *Keeping the Faiths*, p. 37.

11. Hecker, *Religion and Communism*, p. 44.

12. Joseph McCabe, *Atheist Russia Shakes the World: How the Wicked Bolsheviks Save Our Christian World.*

13. Dimitry Pospielovsky, *The Russian Church under the Soviet Regime: 1917–1982*, vol. 1 (Crestwood, NY: St. Vladimir's Seminary Press, 1984), p. 43; and Nicolas Zernov, *The Russians and Their Church* (Crestwood, NY: St. Vladimir's Seminary Press, 1994), p. 146.

14. De Grunwald, *Churches*, pp. 29–30.

15. Hecker, *Religion and Communism*, p. 50.

16. William C. Fletcher, *The Russian Orthodox Church Underground, 1917–1970* (London: Oxford University Press, 1971), p. 17.

17. Quoted in Louis Fischer, "Soviet Russia's Grim Battle against Religion," *Current History* 18, no. 4 (July 1923): 591.

18. Albert Galter, *The Red Book of the Persecuted Church* (Dublin, Ireland: M. H. Gill and Son, 1957), p. 37.

19. John Dewey, "Religion in the Soviet Union: II—An Interpretation of the Conflict," *Current History* 32, no. 1 (April 1930): 31.

20. Ware, *Orthodox Church*, pp. 263–64.

21. Bulgakov, *Orthodox Church*, p. 100.

22. Moshe Lewin, *The Making of the Soviet System: Essays in the Social History of Interwar Russia* (New York: Pantheon Books, 1985), p. 66.

23. Jim Forest, *Religion in the New Russia: The Impact of Perestroika on the Varieties of Religious Life in the Soviet Union* (New York: Crossroad, 1990), p. 17.

24. Edward E. Roslof, "The Heresy of 'Bolshevik' Christianity: Orthodox Rejection of Religious Reform during NEP," *Slavic Review* 55, no. 3 (Autumn 1996): 623–24.

25. Bulgakov, *Orthodox Church*, p. 102.

26. Father John Whiteford, *The Orthodox Approach to Truth/Sola Scriptura: In the Vanity of Their Minds/An Orthodox Examination of the Protestant Teaching.*

27. Bulgakov, *Orthodox Church*, p. 107.

28. Gerald Buss, *The Bear's Hug: Christian Belief and the Soviet State, 1917–1986* (Grand Rapids, MI: Eerdman, 1987), p. 17; John Shelton Curtiss, *The Russian Church and the Soviet State, 1917–1950* (Boston: Little, Brown, 1953), p. 9; Francis McCullagh, *The Bolshevik Persecution of Christianity* (New York: E. P. Dutton, 1924), p. 18; and Matthew Spinka, *Church in Soviet Russia* (New York: Oxford University, 1956), p. 17.

29. Hecker, *Religion and Communism*, p. 194; Sir Bernard Pares, *Russia between Reform and Revolution—Fundamentals of Russian History and Character* (New York: Schocken, 1962), p. 109; and Zernov, *Russians*, p. 141. Hecker actually puts the total number of monks and nuns at 95,259 in 1914.

30. Pares, *Reform*, p. 110.

31. De Grunwald, *Churches*, p. 27; Fletcher, *Church Underground*, p. 34; and Zernov, *Russians*, p. 143.

32. Pares, *Reform*, p. 116; and Zernov, *Russians*, pp. 143, 145n3.

33. Pospielovsky, *Russian Church*, pp. 44–45.

34. Zernov, *Russians*, p. 144.

CHAPTER 2

1. Quoted in John Haynes Holmes, "Religion in Revolutionary Russia," *Nation*, May 9, 1923, p. 544.

2. I have modeled this story very closely on one told, from his own experiences in

Russia, by Albert Rhys Williams, *The Russian Land* (New York: New Republic, 1928), pp. 92–102. Some of the prayers are quoted directly from his text.

3. Quoted in Julius F. Hecker, *Religion and Communism: A Study of Religion and Atheism in Soviet Russia* (Westport, CT: Hyperion, 1934), p. 119.

4. Moshe Lewin, *The Making of the Soviet System: Essays in the Social History of Interwar Russia* (New York: Pantheon, 1985), p. 59.

5. Stephen Graham, *Undiscovered Russia*, chap. XLIV (Holy Russia).

6. From an obscure 1920s publication, which can no longer be obtained for citation.

7. Maurice Hindus, *Humanity Uprooted* (New York: J. Cape and H. Smith, 1929), pp. 29–30.

8. G. P. Fedotov, *The Russian Church since the Revolution* (New York: Macmillan, 1928), p. 12.

9. Roger Pethybridge, *One Step Backwards, Two Steps Forward: Soviet Society and Politics in the New Economic Policy* (Oxford: Clarendon Press, 1990), p. 36.

10. Onyshkevych, *Folklore behind the Ivana Kupala Stamp.*

11. Hindus, *Humanity Uprooted*, p. 25; and Lewin, *Soviet System*, pp. 61–62.

12. Sir Donald Mackenzie Wallace, *Russia on the Eve of War and Revolution* (New York: Vintage, 1961), p. 13.

13. Sir Bernard Pares, *Russia between Reform and Revolution—Fundamentals of Russian History and Character* (New York: Schocken, 1962), p. 132.

14. William B. Husband, *Godless Communists: Atheism and Society in Soviet Russia, 1917–1932* (DeKalb: Northern Illinois University, 2000), p. 77.

15. Lewin, *Soviet System*, p. 60.

16. Ibid., p. 63.

17. Helmut Altrichter, "Insoluble Conflicts: Village Life between Revolution and Collectivization," in *Russia in the Era of NEP: Explorations in Soviet Society and Culture*, ed. Sheila Fitzpatrick (Bloomington: Indiana University Press, 1991), p. 205; and Hecker, *Religion and Communism*, p. 15.

18. Sula Benet, ed., *The Village of Viriatino: An Ethnographic Study of a Russian Village from before the Revolution to the Present* (Garden City, NY: Doubleday, 1970), p. 136.

19. Williams, *Russian Land*, pp. 90–91.

20. Lewin, *Soviet System*, pp. 63–64.

21. Hecker, *Religion and Communism*, p. 15.

22. Benet, *Viriatino*, p. 134.

23. Ibid., p. 135.

24. Altrichter, "Insoluble Conflicts," p. 202.

25. H. N. Brailsford, "Religion and the Soviets," *New Republic* 62, no. 805 (May 7, 1930): 322.

26. Pares, *Reform*, p. 112.

27. Hecker, *Religion and Communism*, pp. 21–23; Lewin, *Soviet System*, p. 61; and

Jane Swan, *A Biography of Patriarch Tikhon* (Jordanville, NY: Holy Trinity Russian Orthodox Monastery, 1964), p. 18n8.

28. Hecker, *Religion and Communism*, p. 24.

29. Graham, chap. XXXII ("The Ikon in the Home").

30. Benet, *Viriatino*, p. 272; Louis Fischer, "Soviet Russia's Grim Battle against Religion," *Current History* 18, no. 4 (July 1923): 596; and Hecker, *Religion and Communism*, p. 26.

31. David Chidester, *Christianity: A Global History* (San Francisco: HarperSanFrancisco, 2000), p. 198.

32. Hecker, *Religion and Communism*, p. 32; and Pares, *Reform*, p. 121.

33. Pethybridge, *One Step Backwards*, p. 37.

34. Quoted in Onyschuk, *Folklore*, p. 212.

35. Quoted in Hecker, *Religion and Communism*, p. 193.

36. From an obscure 1920s publication, which can no longer be obtained for citation.

37. R. O. G. Urch, "Bolshevism and Religion in Russia," *Atlantic Monthly*, March 1923, p. 396.

38. Quoted in *Hieromartyr Benjamin, Metropolitan of Petrograd, and Those with Him*, p. 1.

39. Ibid., pp. 6–7.

40. William Henry Chamberlin, "Russian Crusade against Belief in God," *Current History* 25, no. 1 (October 1926): 31.

41. Philip S. Bernstein, "Religion in Russia," *Harpers*, May 1930, p. 736; and William C. White, "The Triple-Barred Cross," *Scribner's*, July 1930, p. 78.

42. Onyschuk, *Folklore*; and Edward E. Roslof, "The Heresy of 'Bolshevik' Christianity: Orthodox Rejection of Religious Reform during NEP," *Slavic Review* 55, no. 3 (Autumn 1996): 625n30.

43. Quoted in Constantin de Grunwald, *The Churches and the Soviet Union* (New York: Macmillan, 1962), p. 27.

44. Norman J. Smith, "The Evangelical Christians in Russia," *Missionary Review of the World* 48, no. 7 (July 1925): 525.

45. De Grunwald, *Churches*, p. 27.

46. Quoted in Hecker, *Religion and Communism*, p. 16.

47. Stephen Batalden, "Modern Russian Bible Translation: Four Questions That Prevent Consensus," *East-West Church and Ministry Report* (Spring 1999): 9–10.

48. Hecker, *Religion and Communism*, p. 33.

49. Hindus, *Humanity Uprooted*, p. 27.

50. Francis McCullagh, *The Bolshevik Persecution of Christianity* (New York: E. P. Dutton, 1924), p. 54.

51. Quoted in Nicolas Zernov, *The Russians and Their Church*, 3rd ed. (Crestwood, NY: St. Vladimir's Seminary Press, 1994), p. 146.

52. Hecker, *Religion and Communism*, pp. 16, 29–30.

53. Quoted in Robert Pierce Casey, *Religion in Russia* (New York: Harper, 1946), p. 90.

54. N. S. Timasheff, *Religion in Soviet Russia, 1917–1942* (London: Religious Book Club, 1943), p. 4; and Emelyan Yaroslavsky, *Religion in the USSR* (New York: International Publishers, 1934), pp. 40–41. Estimates of prerevolutionary church and monastery land vary widely, ranging from less than 5 million acres to almost 19 million acres.

55. Quoted in Yaroslavsky, *Religion*, p. 42.

56. John Shelton Curtiss, *The Russian Church and the Soviet State, 1917–1950* (Boston: Little, Brown, 1953), p. 9; and Hecker, *Religion and Communism*, p. 194. Donald A. Lowrie, *The Light of Russia: An Introduction to the Russian Church* (Prague: YMCA, 1923), p. 206, states that just before 1917 the subsidy reached 50 million (1920s) *dollars*.

57. The first proverb is from McCullagh, *Bolshevik Persecution*, p. 64; and the second is from Pethybridge, *One Step Backwards*, p. 37.

58. I. S. Belliustin, *Description of the Clergy in Rural Russia: The Memoir of a Nineteenth-Century Parish Priest* (Ithaca, NY: Cornell University Press, 1985), pp. 122–23.

59. Benet, *Viriatino*, p. 128.

60. Hecker, *Religion and Communism*, pp. 32–33, 39.

61. Belliustin, *Clergy*, pp. 126–27.

62. De Grunwald, *Churches*, p. 31; William C. Fletcher, *The Russian Orthodox Church Underground, 1917–1970* (London: Oxford University Press, 1971), p. 34; and Zernov, *Russians*, p. 143.

63. Eugene Trubetzkoy, "The Bolshevist Utopia and the Religious Movement in Russia," *Hibbert Journal* 18, no. 2 (January 1920): 215.

64. Quoted in Saint John of Shanghai and San Francisco, *Holy Righteous John of Kronstadt: On the Occasion of his Glorification*.

65. Yaroslavsky, *Religion*, pp. 43–44.

66. Peter Kenez, "Pogroms and White Ideology in the Russian Civil War," in *Pogroms: Anti-Jewish Violence in Modern Russian History*, ed. John D. Klier and Shlomo Lambroza (New York: Cambridge University Press, 1992), p. 306

67. Bernstein, "Religion in Russia," p. 736.

68. Quoted in "Russians Standardize Religion," *Literary Digest*, March 13, 1920, p. 37.

69. Hecker, *Religion and Communism*, pp. 51–52; and Zernov, *Russians*, p. 142.

70. Quoted in Pares, *Reform*, p. 113.

71. Ibid., pp. 113, 115.

72. Ibid., p. 114.

73. Ibid., p. 117.

74. Zernov, *Russians and Their Church*, p. 149. Although Zernov argued that the Orthodox Church welcomed decoupling from the state, he failed to mention the church's continued demand for state subsidies. On p. 141 he began an argument that the Orthodox Church was not as corrupt as was commonly supposed in the West.

75. Quoted in Zernov, *Russians and Their Church*, p. 148.

76. Quoted in Pares, *Between Reform and Revolution*, pp. 113–14.

77. Andrew Q. Blane, "Protestant Sectarians in the First Year of Soviet Rule," in *Aspects of Religion in the Soviet Union: 1917–1967*, ed. Richard H. Marshall Jr. (Chicago: University of Chicago, 1971), p. 316.

78. Grigory Rasputin, *My Thoughts and Meditations* (Petrograd, 1915), included as an appendix in Maria Rasputin, *My Father* (Hyde Park, NY: University Books, 1970), p. 123.

CHAPTER 3

1. Stepniak, *Underground Russia: Revolutionary Profiles and Sketches from Life* (New York: Charles Scribner's Sons, 1885), p. 7.

2. Quoted in Hans Kohn, ed., *The Mind of Modern Russia: Historical and Political Thought of Russia's Great Age* (New York: Harper and Row, 1955), pp. 135–37.

3. Quoted in E. Lampert, *Studies in Rebellion* (London: Routledge and Kegan Paul, 1957), p. 173; and Edmund Taylor Weiant, *Sources of Modern Mass Atheism in Russia* (Mt. Vernon, OH: Printing Arts, 1953), p. 94.

4. Quoted in Weiant, *Sources*, p. 120.

5. Lampert, *Studies in Rebellion*, p. 218.

6. Michael Bakunin, *God or Labor: The Two Camps*.

7. Quoted in E. H. Carr, *Michael Bakunin* (London: Macmillan, 1937), p. 319.

8. Bakunin, *God or Labor*.

9. Stepniak, *Underground Russia*, pp. 3–4; and Weiant, *Sources*, p. 122.

10. Quoted in *Occult Roots of the Russian Revolution*.

11. Nikolai Chernyshevsky, *Selected Philosophical Essays* (Moscow: Foreign Language Publishing House, 1953), pp. 195–96, 505.

12. Ibid., pp. 19–21, 490.

13. Nicolas Berdyaev, *The Russian Revolution* (Ann Arbor: University of Michigan Press, 1961), pp. 28–29.

14. Nicholas Lobkowicz, "Karl Marx's Attitude toward Religion," *Review of Politics* 26, no. 3 (July 1964): 329–30.

15. Quoted in Edward Hulmes, "Marx and the Bible," in *The Oxford Companion to the Bible*, ed. Bruce M. Metzger and Michael D. Coogan (New York: Oxford University Press, 1993), p. 497.

16. Lobkowicz, "Attitude," p. 329.

17. Francis B. Randall, "Introduction to Karl Marx and Friedrich Engels," in *The Communist Manifesto* (New York: Washington Square, 1964), pp. 11–12, 15–16.

18. Quoted in Hulmes, "Marx," p. 497; and Marcus Bach, *God and the Soviets* (New York: Crowell, 1958), p. 102.

19. Randall, "Introduction," p. 15.

20. Quoted in Robert Pierce Casey, *Religion in Russia* (New York: Harper, 1946), p. 76.

21. Quoted in Lobkowicz, "Attitude," p. 329.

22. Quoted in Bach, *God and the Soviets*, pp. 104–105.

23. Casey, *Religion in Russia*, p. 82; and *Georgi Valentinovich Plekhanov*.

24. Bohdan Bociurkiw, "Lenin and Religion," in *Lenin: The Man, the Theorist, the Leader—A Reappraisal*, ed. Leonard Schapiro and Peter Reddaway (New York: Praeger, 1967), p. 110; and Adam B. Ulam, *The Bolsheviks: The Intellectual, Personal and Political History of the Origins of Russian Communism* (New York: Macmillan, 1965), pp. 11–13.

25. Quoted in Richard Stites, *Revolutionary Dreams: Utopian Vision and Experimental Life in the Russian Revolution* (New York: Oxford University Press, 1989), p. 122.

26. Quentin Lauer, "The Atheism of Karl Marx," in *Marxism and Christianity: A Symposium*, ed. Herbert Aptheker (New York: Humanities, 1968), pp. 48, 50–51.

27. Quoted in James Thrower, *Marxist-Leninist "Scientific Atheism" and the Study of Religion and Atheism in the USSR* (New York: Mouton, 1983), p. 117.

28. Quoted in Paul B. Anderson, *People, Church and State in Modern Russia* (London: Student Christian Movement Press, 1944), p. 45.

29. William B. Husband, *Godless Communists: Atheism and Society in Soviet Russia, 1917–1932* (DeKalb: Northern Illinois University Press, 2000), p. 70.

30. Quoted in Lauer, "Karl Marx," p. 42.

31. Quoted in Julius F. Hecker, *Religion and Communism: A Study of Religion and Atheism in Soviet Russia* (Westport, CT: Hyperion, 1973), p. 283.

32. Ibid., p. 7.

33. Two of my examples are paraphrases of Lobkowicz, "Attitude," pp. 321, 327.

34. Engels, *Anti-Duhring*, quoted in Karl Marx and Friedrich Engels, *On Religion* (New York: Schocken, 1964), p. 147.

35. Ludwig Feuerbach, *The Essence of Christianity* (Amherst, NY: Prometheus Books, 1989), quoted in Richard Lichtman, "The Marxian Critique of Christianity," in *Marxism and Christianity: A Symposium*, ed. Herbert Aptheker (New York: Humanities, 1968), p. 73.

36. Lobkowicz, "Attitude," p. 321; and Marx, *Critique*.

37. Feuerbach, *Essence of Christianity*, p. 99.

38. Ibid., p. 26.

39. Marx and Engels, *On Religion*, quoted in Lichtman, "Marxian Critique," p. 77.

40. Waldemar Gurian, *Bolshevism: Theory and Practice* (London: Sheed and Ward, 1933), pp. 223–24.

41. Quoted in Lichtman, "Marxian Critique," p. 94.

42. Emelyan Yaroslavsky, *Religion in the USSR* (New York: International Publishers, 1934), p. 33.

43. Quoted in Thrower, *"Scientific Atheism,"* p. 116.

44. Quoted in John Shelton Curtiss, *The Russian Church and the Soviet State, 1917–1950* (Boston: Little, Brown, 1953), pp. 44–45.

45. V. I. Lenin, *The Attitude of the Workers' Party to Religion*.

46. Ibid.

47. Dimitry Pospielovsky, *The Russian Church under the Soviet Regime: 1917–1982*, vol. 1 (Crestwood, NY: St. Vladimir's Seminary Press, 1984), p. 53.

48. Yaroslavsky, *Thoughts of Lenin on Religion* (Moscow, 1924), p. 58, quoted in Wladyslav Kania, *Bolshevism and Religion* (New York: Polish Library, 1946), p. 20.

49. Lenin's letter to Gorky, quoted in Casey, *Religion in Russia*, pp. 77–78.

50. Marx, *Capital*, vol. 1, quoted in Herbert Aptheker, "Marxism and Religion," in *Marxism and Christianity*, p. 30.

51. Lenin's letter to Gorky, early November 1913, quoted in Bociurkiw, "Lenin and Religion," p. 109.

52. Jay Bergman, "The Image of Jesus in the Russian Revolutionary Movement: The Case of Russian Marxism," *International Review of Social History* 35 (1990): 227.

53. Prince Eugene Trubetzkoy, "The Bolshevist Utopia and the Religious Movement in Russia," *Hibbert Journal* 18, no. 2 (January 1920): 218–19.

54. Feuerbach, *Essence of Christianity*, quoted in Lichtman, "Marxian Critique," p. 76.

55. Lichtman, "Marxian Critique," pp. 98–99.

56. Quoted in Conquest, *Religion in the USSR* (London: Bodley Head, 1968), p. 8.

CHAPTER 4

1. Quoted in Herbert Aptheker, "Marxism and Religion," in *Marxism and Christianity: A Symposium*, ed. Herbert Aptheker (New York: Humanities, 1968), p. 30.

2. Quoted in Richard Lichtman, "The Marxian Critique of Christianity," in Aptheker, *Marxism and Christianity*, p. 85.

3. Friedrich Engels, *Anti-Duhring*, quoted in Nicholas Lobkowicz, "Karl Marx's Attitude toward Religion," *Review of Politics* 26, no. 3 (July 1964): 325.

4. Quoted in Jay Bergman, "The Image of Jesus in the Russian Revolutionary Movement: The Case of Russian Marxism," *International Review of Social History* 35 (1990): 229–30.

5. Some ideas of Walter Rauschenbusch, discussed in Lichtman, "Marxian Critique," pp. 85, 95.

6. Lichtman, "Marxian Critique," p. 96.

7. Karl Marx and Friedrich Engels, *On Religion*, quoted in Lichtman, "Marxian Critique," p. 86.

8. Ibid., p. 91.

9. Lenin, *Socialism and Religion*, quoted in Emelyan Yaroslavsky, "Is the Communist Movement Antireligious? (An Answer to Höglund)," in William G. Rosenberg, *Bolshevik Visions: First Phase of the Cultural Revolution in Soviet Russia, Part I: The Culture of a New Society—Ethics, Gender, the Family, Law and Problems of Tradition* (Ann Arbor: University of Michigan Press, 1990), p. 241.

10. Quentin Lauer, "The Atheism of Karl Marx," in Aptheker, *Marxism and Christianity*, p. 53.

11. Marx, *Capital*, quoted in Lichtman, "Marxian Critique," pp. 87–88.

12. Ibid., p. 94.

13. Lichtman, "Marxian Critique," p. 87.

14. Bergman, "Image of Jesus," p. 227.

15. Lauer, "Karl Marx," pp. 48–49.

16. Engels, *Anti-Duhring*, quoted in Paul B. Anderson, *People, Church and State in Modern Russia* (London: Student Christian Movement, 1944), p. 47.

17. Quoted in Maurice Hindus, *Humanity Uprooted* (New York: J. Cape and H. Smith, 1929), p. 38.

18. Lobkowicz, "Attitude," p. 322; and N. S. Timasheff, *Religion in Soviet Russia, 1917–1942* (London: Religious Book Club, 1943), p. 21.

19. Quoted in James Thrower, *Marxist-Leninist "Scientific Atheism" and the Study of Religion and Atheism in the USSR* (New York: Mouton, 1983), p. 117.

20. Bohdan Bociurkiw, "Lenin and Religion," in *Lenin: The Man, the Theorist, the Leader—A Reappraisal*, ed. Leonard Schapiro and Peter Reddaway (New York: Praeger, 1967), p. 117; Robert Pierce Casey, *Religion in Russia* (New York: Harper, 1946), pp. 80–81; and Walter Kolarz, *Religion in the Soviet Union* (New York: St. Martin's, 1961), pp. 3–4.

21. V. I. Lenin, *Socialism and Religion*.

22. V. I. Lenin, *The Attitude of the Workers' Party to Religion*.

23. Ibid.

24. Camille M. Cianfarra, *The Vatican and the Kremlin* (New York: Dutton, 1950), p. 13.

25. Quoted in Robert Conquest, *Religion in the USSR* (London: Bodley Head, 1968), p. 9.

26. David E. Powell, *Antireligious Propaganda in the Soviet Union: A Study of Mass Persuasion* (Cambridge, MA: MIT Press, 1975), p. 14.

27. *The Program and Rules of the Communist Party of the Soviet Union*, pp. 20–21, quoted in Anderson, *People, Church and State*, p. 50; and Emelyan Yaroslavsky, *Religion in the USSR* (New York: International Publishers, 1934), p. 20.

28. From an obscure 1920s publication, which can no longer be obtained for citation.

29. Quoted in John Dewey, "Religion in the Soviet Union: II—An Interpretation of the Conflict," *Current History* 32, no. 1 (April 1930): 33.

30. Joseph Stalin, *Mastering Bolshevism* (New York: Workers Library, 1937).

31. Roger Pethybridge, *The Social Prelude to Stalinism* (London: Macmillan, 1974), p. 4.

32. Ibid., pp. 5–6.

33. Joseph Stalin, *The Foundations of Leninism*.

34. Bociurkiw, "Lenin and Religion," pp. 117–18; and Lenin, *Socialism and Religion*.

CHAPTER 5

1. Nicolas Zernov, *The Russians and Their Church*, 3rd ed. (Crestwood, NY: St. Vladimir's Seminary Press, 1994), p. 150.

2. Vladimir Moss, *The Orthodox Church at the Crossroads: From 1900 to the Present Day*, p. 5 (my pagination); Matthew Spinka, *Church and the Russian Revolution*

(New York: Macmillan, 1927), p. 8; and Jane Swan, *A Biography of Patriarch Tikhon* (Jordanville, NY: Holy Trinity Russian Orthodox Monastery, 1964), p. 13.

3. William C. Fletcher, *The Russian Orthodox Church Underground, 1917–1970* (London: Oxford University Press, 1971), pp. 16–17; and Moss, p. 5 (my pagination).

4. Moss, *Orthodox Church*, p. 8 (my pagination).

5. Donald A. Lowrie, *The Light of Russia: An Introduction to the Russian Church* (Prague: YMCA Press, 1923), pp. 200–201; and Paul Miliukov, *Outlines of Russian Culture, Part I: Religion and the Church* (Philadelphia: University of Pennsylvania Press, 1943), p. 153.

6. Catherine Evtuhov, "The Church in the Russian Revolution: Arguments for and against Restoring the Patriarchate at the Church Council of 1917–1918," *Slavic Review* 50, no. 3 (Fall 1991): 499–501.

7. Paul B. Anderson, *People, Church and State in Modern Russia* (London: Student Christian Movement Press, 1944), p. 41 (full text); Fletcher, *The Russian Orthodox Church*, pp. 17–18; Miliukov, *Outlines of Russian Culture*, pp. 153–54; and Moss, *Orthodox Church*, pp. 8–9 (my pagination).

8. Lowrie, *Light of Russia*, pp. 199–200; and David E. Powell, *Antireligious Propaganda in the Soviet Union: A Study of Mass Persuasion* (Cambridge, MA: MIT Press, 1975), p. 24.

9. Peter Kenez, *The Birth of the Propaganda State: Soviet Methods of Mass Mobilization, 1917–1929* (New York: Cambridge University Press, 1985), p. 66; Lowrie, *Light of Russia*, p. 201; Miliukov, *Outlines*, p. 153; and Matthew Spinka, *Church in Soviet Russia* (New York: Oxford University Press, 1956), p. 10.

10. Quoted in Moss, *Orthodox Church*, p. 9 (my pagination); and Dimitry Pospielovsky, *The Russian Church under the Soviet Regime: 1917–1982*, vol. 1 (Crestwood, NY: St. Vladimir's Seminary Press, 1984), p. 30.

11. I have given up trying to determine the *exact* breakdown of delegates at this sobor; almost every source describing this sobor offers a slightly different number. See M. M. Sheinman, *Religion and Church in the USSR* (Moscow: Cooperative Publishing Society of Foreign Workers in the USSR, 1933), pp. 13–14, for the "socialist" breakdown; and Spinka, *Church in Soviet Russia*, p. 9 (his source was one of the Trubetzkoy brothers, a delegate).

12. Serge Bolshakov, *Russian Nonconformity: The Story of "Unofficial" Religion in Russia* (Philadelphia: Westminster, 1950), p. 158; Moss, *Orthodox Church*, pp. 8–9 (my pagination); and Spinka, *Church in Soviet Russia*, pp. 9–10.

13. *Religion in Soviet Russia*, ed. William Chauncey Emhardt (London: Morehouse, 1929), p. 5; Spinka, *Church in Soviet Russia*, pp. 9–10; and Miliukov, *Outlines*, p. 155.

14. Thomas Whittemore, "The Rebirth of Religion in Russia," *National Geographic*, November 1918, p. 395.

15. Quoted in Evtuhov, "Church," p. 506.

16. Paul D. Steeves, *The Canonization of Patriarch Tikhon as a Reflection of New Thinking in the Glasnost Era.*

17. Evtuhov, "Church," p. 509; and Miliukov, *Outlines*, p. 156.

18. Lowrie, *Light of Russia*, pp. 207–209; Pospielovsky, *Russian Church*, p. 33; and Spinka, *Church in Soviet Russia*, pp. 11–12.

19. Swan, *Biography*, pp. 17–18: and Whittemore, "Rebirth of Religion," p. 3.

20. Quoted in *Tikhon: Saint, Enlightener of America, and Patriarch of Moscow*, p. 3 (my pagination).

21. From an obscure 1920s publication, which can no longer be obtained for citation.

22. Ibid.

23. Moss, *Orthodox Church*, p. 9 (my pagination). Richard J. Cooke, *Religion in Russia under the Soviets* (New York: Abingdon, 1924), pp. 66–67, quotes a description of this event from *Atlantic Monthly*.

24. Quoted in *Hieromartyr Tikhon, Patriarch of Moscow and All Russia*; and Swan, *Biography*, pp. 19–20.

25. Swan, *Biography*, p. 21.

26. Lowrie, *Light of Russia*, p. 212; and Whittemore, "Rebirth of Religion," p. 396.

27. Lowrie, *Light of Russia*, pp. 213, 227–28; and Pospielovsky, *Russian Church*, p. 34.

28. Quoted in Moss, *Orthodox Church*, p. 11 (my pagination); and Pospielovsky, *Russian Church*, p. 37.

29. Quoted in Lowrie, *Light of Russia*, p. 213.

30. Moss, *Orthodox Church*, pp. 11, 13 (my pagination); and Pospielovsky, *Russian Church*, p. 37.

31. Evtuhov, "Church," p. 511.

32. Spinka, *Church in Soviet Russia*, pp. 3–4; Swan, *Biography*, pp. 6–7; and Whittemore, "Rebirth of Religion," pp. 395–96.

33. Spinka, *Church in Soviet Russia*, p. 5.

34. Swan, *Biography*, pp. 9–12; and Whittemore, "Rebirth of Religion," p. 396.

35. Lowrie, *Light of Russia*, p. 218; Spinka, *Church in Soviet Russia*, pp. 5–7, 9; Steeves, *Canonization*; and Swan, *Biography*, p. 12.

36. Julius F. Hecker, *Religion and Communism: A Study of Religion and Atheism in Soviet Russia* (Westport, CT: Hyperion, 1973), p. 198; and Spinka, *Church in Soviet Russia*, p. 14.

37. Swan, *Biography*, p. 25.

38. Lowrie, *Light of Russia*, p. 219.

39. Quoted ibid., pp. 220–22.

40. Swan, *Biography*, pp. 108–109.

41. Francis McCullagh, *The Bolshevik Persecution of Christianity* (New York: Dutton, 1924), pp. 14, 75, 77.

42. Ibid., p. 75.

43. Prince Eugene Trubetzkoy, "The Bolshevist Utopia and the Religious Movement in Russia," *Hibbert Journal* 18, no. 2 (January 1920): 221–23.

44. Ibid.

45. Swan, *Biography*, p. 23.

46. Spinka, *Church in Soviet Russia*, p. 46.

47. Quoted in Kenez, *Propaganda State*, p. 66.

48. Ibid., p. 67.

49. Quoted in Moss, *Orthodox Church*, p. 10 (my pagination).

50. From an obscure 1920s publication, which can no longer be obtained for citation.

51. Hecker, *Religion and Communism*, p. 201.

52. Quoted in Constantin de Grunwald, *The Churches and the Soviet Union* (New York: Macmillan, 1962), pp. 44–45.

53. Marcus Bach, *God and the Soviets* (New York: Crowell, 1958), p. 93; James Bunyan and H. H. Fisher, *The Bolshevik Revolution, 1917–1918: Documents and Materials* (Palo Alto, CA: Stanford University Press, 1934), pp. 588–89; Fletcher, *Church Underground*, pp. 20–21; and Moss, *Orthodox Church*, p. 11 (my pagination).

54. Quoted in John Shelton Curtiss, *The Russian Church and the Soviet State, 1917–1950* (Boston: Little, Brown, 1953), p. 50.

55. *Acts of the Sobor*, vol. 6, p. 40, quoted in Hecker, *Religion and Communism*, p. 201.

56. Quoted in Swan, *Biography*, pp. 34–35.

57. Quoted in Miliukov, *Outlines*, p. 164.

58. Zernov, *Russians*, p. 158.

59. Moss, *Orthodox Church*, p. 11 (my pagination).

60. Curtiss, *Russian Church*, p. 47; Miliukov, *Outlines*, p. 163; Moss, *Orthodox Church*, p. 10 (my pagination); and Pospielovsky, *Russian Church*, p. 136.

61. Quoted in Swan, *Biography*, pp. 39–40.

62. Quoted in Curtiss, *Russian Church*, pp. 58–59.

63. Pospielovsky, *Russian Church*, p. 38; Swan, *Biography*, pp. 40–41; and Whittemore, "Rebirth of Religion," p. 383.

64. Swan, *Biography*, pp. 38, 50; and J. Zatko, *Descent into Darkness: The Destruction of the Roman Catholic Church in Russia, 1917–1923* (Notre Dame, IN: University of Notre Dame Press, 1965), p. 86.

65. Spinka, *Church in Soviet Russia*, p. 19; and quoted in Trubetzkoy, "Bolshevist Utopia," p. 222.

66. According to Metropolitan Anastasy, as told to Jane Swan. See Swan, *Biography*, p. 41n20.

67. Quoted in Moss, *Orthodox Church*, p. 15 (my pagination); and Swan, *Biography*, p. 50.

68. Quoted in Moss, *Orthodox Church*, p. 15 (my pagination).

69. Pospielovsky, *Russian Church*, pp. 33, 36; and Swan, *Biography*, p. 44.

70. Roger Pethybridge, *The Social Prelude to Stalinism* (London: Macmillan, 1974), p. 25.

71. Whittemore, "Rebirth of Religion," p. 389.

72. Ibid., p. 385. Many photographs of the destruction are included in this article.

73. *Revolution and the Church* 1 (1919), quoted in Curtiss, *Russian Church*, pp. 66–67.

74. From an obscure 1920s publication, which can no longer be obtained for citation.

75. Curtiss, *Russian Church*, p. 87; and Spinka, *Church in Soviet Russia*, p. 21.

76. Quoted in Gregory L. Freeze, "Counter-Reformation in Russian Orthodoxy: Popular Response to Religious Innovation, 1922–1925," *Slavic Review* 54, no. 2 (Summer 1995): 310n19; Kenez, *Propaganda State*, p. 68; Pospielovsky, *Russian Church*, p. 38; Spinka, *Church in Soviet Russia*, 21; and Trubetzkoy, "Bolshevist Utopia," p. 216.

77. V. I. Lenin, *Speech at the First All-Russia Congress of Working Women*.

78. Yaroslavsky, *Thoughts of Lenin on Religion* (Moscow, 1924), p. 25, quoted in Wladyslav Kania, *Bolshevism and Religion* (New York: Polish Library, 1946), p. 19.

79. Kania, *Bolshevism and Religion*, p. 18; and Yaroslavsky, *Thoughts of Lenin on Religion* (Moscow, 1924), p. 25, quoted in Kania, p. 19.

80. "Antireligious Propaganda in Ivanovo-Vosnesensk Governorship," *Pravda* 106 (May 15, 1923), in *The Russian Revolution and Religion: A Collection of Documents concerning the Suppression of Religion by the Communists, 1917–1925*, ed. Boleslav Szczesniak (Notre Dame, IN: University of Notre Dame Press, 1959), document 91.

81. Nikolai Bukharin and E. Preobrazhensky, *The ABC of Communism—A Popular Explanation of the Program of the Communist Party of Russia* (Ann Arbor: University of Michigan Press, 1966), pp. 248–49.

82. Quoted in Dimitry Pospielovsky, *A History of Marxist-Leninist Atheism and Soviet Antireligious Policies* (London: Macmillan, 1987), p. 30.

CHAPTER 6

1. Quoted in John Shelton Curtiss, *The Russian Church and the Soviet State, 1917–1950* (Boston: Little, Brown, 1953), p. 72.

2. Lynne Viola, "The Peasant Nightmare: Visions of Apocalypse in the Soviet Countryside," *Journal of Modern History* 62, no. 4 (December 1990): 751.

3. For some of this background material I relied on James Graham, *The Russian Civil War*.

4. Joshua Rothenberg, "The Legal Status of Religion in the Soviet Union," in *Aspects of Religion in the Soviet Union: 1917–1967*, ed. Richard H. Marshall Jr. (Chicago: University of Chicago Press, 1971), p. 65.

5. Ibid., p. 33.

6. Quoted in William Chauncey Emhardt, ed., *Religion in Soviet Russia* (London: Morehouse, 1929), pp. 30–31.

7. Marcus Bach, *God and the Soviets* (New York: Crowell, 1958), p. 46; and Dimitry Pospielovsky, *The Russian Church under the Soviet Regime: 1917–1982*, vol. 1 (Crestwood, NY: St. Vladimir's Seminary Press, 1984), p. 39.

8. Curtiss, *Russian Church*, p. 95; and Jane Swan, *A Biography of Patriarch Tikhon* (Jordanville, NY: Holy Trinity Russian Orthodox Monastery, 1964), p. 48.

9. William B. Husband, "Soviet Atheism and Russian Orthodox Strategies of Resistance, 1917–1932," *Journal of Modern History* 70 (March 1998): 80.

10. Peter Kenez, *The Defeat of the Whites: Civil War in South Russia, 1919–1920* (Berkeley and Los Angeles: University of California Press, 1977), p. 79.

11. Curtiss, *Russian Church*, p. 92; and Richard Stites, *Revolutionary Dreams: Utopian Vision and Experimental Life in the Russian Revolution* (New York: Oxford University Press, 1989), p. 105.

12. Quoted in Curtiss, *Russian Church*, p. 99; and M. M. Sheinman, *Religion and Church in the USSR* (Moscow: Cooperative Publishing Society of Foreign Workers in the USSR, 1933), p. 19.

13. Peter Kenez, *The Birth of the Propaganda State: Soviet Methods of Mass Mobilization, 1917–1929* (New York: Cambridge University Press, 1985), p. 67.

14. Ibid.

15. Curtiss, *Russian Church*, p. 95.

16. Quoted in Sheinman, *Religion and Church*, p. 22. See also Curtiss, *Russian Church*, p. 97.

17. Quoted in Boleslav Szczesniak, ed., *The Russian Revolution and Religion: A Collection of Documents concerning the Suppression of Religion by the Communists, 1917–1925* (Notre Dame, IN: University of Notre Dame Press, 1959), document 14.

18. Ibid., document 17.

19. Ibid.; and J. Zatko, *Descent into Darkness: The Destruction of the Roman Catholic Church in Russia, 1917–1923* (Notre Dame, IN: University of Notre Dame Press, 1965), pp. 85–86.

20. Curtiss, *Russian Church*, pp. 99–100.

21. Sheinman, *Religion and Church*, pp. 22–23; and *London Times*, September 9, 1919, quoted in Curtiss, *Russian Church*, pp. 99–101.

22. Quoted in Sheinman, *Religion and Church*, p. 23.

23. Edward Alsworth Ross, *The Russian Soviet Republic* (New York: Century, 1923), pp. 386–87.

24. Curtiss, *Russian Church*, pp. 99–100; and Peter Kenez, "Pogroms and White Ideology in the Russian Civil War," in *Pogroms: Anti-Jewish Violence in Modern Russian History*, ed. John D. Klier and Shlomo Lambroza (New York: Cambridge University Press, 1992), p. 306.

25. Maurice Hindus, *Humanity Uprooted* (New York: J. Cape and H. Smith, 1929), p. 31.

26. "Failure of Religion in Russia," *Literary Digest*, June 14, 1919, p. 32.

27. Quoted in Sheinman, *Religion and Church*, p. 23.

28. *A Historical Survey of the Parish of St. John the Baptist*; and Pospielovsky, *Russian Church*, p. 115.

29. Quoted in Curtiss, *Russian Church*, p. 98.

30. Ibid., p. 94.

31. Quoted in *Parish of St. John the Baptist*. See Swan, *Biography*, p. 49, for a different translation.

32. Pospielovsky, *Russian Church*, pp. 113–14, 120; and Matthew Spinka, *Church in Soviet Russia* (New York: Oxford University Press, 1956), p. 24.

33. Pospielovsky, *Russian Church*, pp. 113–14, 116; and Timothy Ware, *The Orthodox Church* (Baltimore: Penguin, 1963), p. 182.

34. Pospielovsky, *Russian Church*, p. 130.

35. Paul B. Anderson, "Reflections on Religion in Russia: 1917–1967," in Marshall, *Aspects of Religion*, p. 12; Vladimir Moss, *Orthodox Church at the Crossroads: From 1900 to the Present Day*, p. 2 (my pagination); and quoted in Pospielovsky, *Russian Church*, p. 128n30, 130.

36. *Compassionate Love—Metropolitan Anthony Khrapovitsky*; and Pospielovsky, *Russian Church*, p. 134.

37. Louis Fischer, "Soviet Russia's Grim Battle against Religion," *Current History* 18, no. 4 (July 1923): 592; Pospielovsky, *Russian Church*, p. 116; and Matthew Spinka, *Church and the Russian Revolution* (New York: Macmillan, 1927), p. 166.

38. Quoted in Spinka, *Church in Soviet Russia*, p. 25. For the full text of the December 3, 1921, Karlovtzy Sobor resolution, see Szczesniak, *Russian Revolution*, document 21.

39. Pospielovsky, *Russian Church*, p. 119.

40. William B. Stroyen, *Communist Russia and the Russian Orthodox Church, 1943–1962* (Washington, DC: Catholic University of America Press, 1967), p. 16; and Donald W. Treadgold, *Twentieth Century Russia*, 2nd ed. (Chicago: Rand McNally, 1964), pp. 234–35.

41. Quoted in Spinka, *Church and the Russian Revolution*, p. 168.

42. Quoted in Spinka, *Church in Soviet Russia*, p. 26.

43. "Epistle of the Holy Synod of the Russian Church to Metropolitan Anthony," May 5, 1922, in Szczesniak, *Russian Revolution*, document 29; and Spinka, *Church in Soviet Russia*, p. 26.

44. Quoted in Pospielovsky, *Russian Church*, p. 121.

45. Paul Miliukov, *Outlines of Russian Culture, Part I: Religion and the Church* (Philadelphia: University of Pennsylvania Press, 1943), p. 169.

46. Pospielovsky, *Russian Church*, p. 138.

47. *Vladimir, Metropolitan and Hieromartyr of Kiev*, pp. 1–2; and Thomas Whittemore, "The Rebirth of Religion in Russia," *National Geographic*, November 1918, p. 401.

48. Moss, *Orthodox Church*, p. 29 (my pagination); and *Vladimir*, p. 3.

49. *Vladimir*, pp. 3–6.

50. Walter Kolarz, *Religion in the Soviet Union* (New York: St. Martin's, 1961), p. 108.

51. Kolarz, *Religion*, pp. 109–10; and Archpriest Igor Kutash, *A Brief History of the Ukrainian Orthodox Church*.

52. Dimitry Pospielovsky, *A History of Marxist-Leninist Atheism and Soviet Anti-religious Policies* (London: Macmillan, 1987), p. 48.

53. Kolarz, *Religion*, pp. 108–109.

54. Quoted in Moss, *Orthodox Church*, p. 29 (my pagination).

55. Ibid.

56. Kolarz, *Religion*, pp. 111–12.

57. Moss, *Orthodox Church*, p. 30 (my pagination); and *Ukraine before World War II*.

CHAPTER 7

1. J. Zatko, *Descent into Darkness: The Destruction of the Roman Catholic Church in Russia, 1917–1923* (Notre Dame, IN: University of Notre Dame Press, 1965), p. 150n22.

2. V. I. Lenin, *Socialism and Religion*, p. 85.

3. Ibid.

4. Helmut Altrichter, "Insoluble Conflicts: Village Life between Revolution and Collectivization," in *Russia in the Era of NEP: Explorations in Soviet Society and Culture*, ed. Sheila Fitzpatrick (Bloomington: Indiana University Press, 1991), p. 200.

5. Trotsky's May 14, 1922, letter to the Politburo and Lenin, quoted in Felix Corley, *Religion in the Soviet Union: An Archival Reader* (New York: New York University Press, 1996), document 12.

6. *Izvestia*, May 6, 1922, quoted in William B. Stroyen, *Communist Russia and the Russian Orthodox Church, 1943–1962* (Washington, DC: Catholic University of America Press, 1967), p. 20.

7. Joseph McCabe, *Atheist Russia Shakes the World: How the Wicked Bolsheviks Save Our Christian World*.

8. "Decree on Land Nationalization, November 8, 1917," *Izvestia*, November 10, 1917, quoted in *The Russian Revolution and Religion: A Collection of Documents concerning the Suppression of Religion by the Communists, 1917–1925*, ed. Boleslav Szczesniak (Notre Dame, IN: University of Notre Dame Press, 1959), document 3.

9. Quoted in Julius F. Hecker, *Religion and Communism: A Study of Religion and Atheism in Soviet Russia* (Westport, CT: Hyperion, 1934), p. 231.

10. Joshua Rothenberg, "The Legal Status of Religion in the Soviet Union," in *Aspects of Religion in the Soviet Union: 1917–1967*, ed. Richard H. Marshall Jr. (Chicago: University of Chicago Press, 1971), p. 62.

11. William B. Husband, *Godless Communists: Atheism and Society in Soviet Russia, 1917–1932* (DeKalb: Northern Illinois University Press, 2000), p. 46.

12. John Shelton Curtiss, *The Russian Church and the Soviet State, 1917–1950* (Boston: Little, Brown, 1953), p. 48; Vladimir Moss, *The Orthodox Church at the Crossroads: From 1900 to the Present Day*, p. 11 (my pagination); and Jennifer Wynot, *Russian Orthodox Monasteries' Response to the Relics Exposing Campaign, 1917–1922*, p. 22 (my pagination).

13. Husband, *Godless Communists*, p. 49.

14. Rothenberg, "Legal Status," p. 63.

15. Husband, *Godless Communists*, pp. 47, 52; and Dimitry Pospielovsky, *The Russian*

Church under the Soviet Regime: 1917–1982, vol. 1 (Crestwood, NY: St. Vladimir's Seminary Press, 1984), p. 32; and Szczesniak, *Russian Revolution*, document 7.

16. Curtiss, *Russian Church*, p. 56; and Husband, *Godless Communists*, pp. 48, 54.

17. Joan Delaney, "The Origins of Soviet Antireligious Organizations," in Marshall, *Aspects of Religion*, p. 105; and Husband, *Godless Communists*, p. 53.

18. Quoted in James H. Meisel and Edward S. Kozera, eds., *Materials for the Study of the Soviet System: State and Party Constitutions, Laws, Decrees, Decisions and Official Statements of the Leaders in Translation*, 2nd ed. (Ann Arbor, MI: G. Wahr, 1953), p. 63.

19. Ibid.

20. Andrew Q. Blane, "Protestant Sectarians in the First Year of Soviet Rule," in Marshall, *Aspects of Religion*, p. 305.

21. John N. Hazard, *The Soviet System of Government*, rev. ed. (Chicago: University of Chicago Press, 1957), pp. 127–28; and "Decree of the Soviet Commissars concerning Separation of Church and State, and of School and Church," *Gazette of the Workmen and Peasant Government*, no. 15, February 1, 1918, quoted in Szczesniak, *Russian Revolution*, document 6.

22. Robert Conquest, *Religion in the USSR* (London: Bodley Head, 1968), p. 13; and N. S. Timasheff, *Religion in Soviet Russia, 1917–1942* (London: Religious Book Club, 1943), p. 22.

23. Constitution of the RSFSR, adopted by the Fifth All-Russian Congress of Soviets, July 10, 1918, Article 13.

24. Quoted in Bohdan Bociurkiw, "Lenin and Religion," in *Lenin: The Man, the Theorist, the Leader—A Reappraisal*, ed. Leonard Schapiro and Peter Reddaway (New York: Praeger, 1967), p. 125.

25. Rothenberg, "Legal Status," pp. 65–66; and "Resolution of the Commissariat of Justice Concerning Execution of the Decree of Separation of Church and State, and of School from Church," *Izvestia*, no. 186, August 30, 1918, quoted in Szczesniak, *Russian Revolution*, document 10.

26. Quoted in Dimitry Pospielovsky, *A History of Marxist-Leninist Atheism and Soviet Antireligious Policies* (London: Macmillan, 1987), p. 28.

27. Corley, *Religion*, pp. 50–51.

28. Alexander Solzhenitsyn, *The Gulag Archipelago, 1918–1956*, vol. 1 (San Francisco: HarperSanFrancisco, 1973), p. 342.

29. Quoted in Francis McCullagh, *The Bolshevik Persecution of Christianity* (New York: Dutton, 1924), p. 358.

30. Nikolai Bukharin and E. Preobrazhensky, *The ABC of Communism—A Popular Explanation of the Program of the Communist Party of Russia* (Ann Arbor: University of Michigan Press, 1966), p. 256.

31. Quoted in Curtiss, *Russian Church*, pp. 82–83.

32. Alexander Solzhenitsyn, *The Gulag Archipelago, 1918–1956*, vol. 2 (San Francisco: HarperSanFrancisco, 1974), pp. 18–19, 74.

33. Curtiss, *Russian Church*, p. 83.

34. Serge Bolshakov, *The Christian Church and the Soviet State* (London: Society for Promoting Christian Knowledge, 1942), page number lost; William Henry Chamberlin, "The Struggle for the Russian Soul: A Phase of Soviet Russia," *Atlantic Monthly*, September 1929, p. 395; Curtiss, *Russian Church*, p. 84; Hecker, *Religion and Communism*, p. 204n1; Julius Hecker, *Religion under the Soviets* (New York: Vanguard, 1927), p. 70; and "Bolsheviks Begin Attacking Church: Start New Paper Caricaturing Orthodoxy and Religion in Russia," *New York Herald*, June 9, 1921, quoted in Szczesniak, *Russian Revolution*, document 18.

35. Quoted in "Religious Conditions in Russia," *Hibbert Journal* 24, no. 3 (April 1926): 459.

36. Curtiss, *Russian Church*, p. 84.

37. *Komsomolskaya Pravda*, April 10, 1928, quoted in *Religion in Soviet Russia*, ed. William Chauncey Emhardt (London: Morehouse, 1929), p. 279.

38. Jim Forest, *Religion in the New Russia: The Impact of Perestroika on the Varieties of Religious Life in the Soviet Union* (New York: Crossroad, 1990), p. 9.

39. Curtiss, *Russian Church*, pp. 84–85; and Timasheff, *Religion*, p. 25.

40. Curtiss, *Russian Church*, p. 194; Gregory L. Freeze, "Counter-Reformation in Russian Orthodoxy: Popular Response to Religious Innovation, 1922–1925," *Slavic Review* 54, no. 2 (Summer 1995): 332n106; Jane Swan, *A Biography of Patriarch Tikhon* (Jordanville, NY: Holy Trinity Russian Orthodox Monastery, 1964), p. 30; Szczesniak, *Russian Revolution*, document 10; and Ariadna Williams, "Atheism and Religion in Russia," *Nineteenth Century and After* 106, no. 631 (September 1929): 339.

41. Altrichter, "Insoluble Conflicts," p. 201.

42. Freeze, "Counter-Reformation," p. 333n111.

43. McCullagh, *Bolshevik Persecution*, pp. 115–16; and Pospielovsky, *Russian Church*, p. 32.

44. Curtiss, *Russian Church*, p. 79; Freeze, "Counter-Reformation," p. 331n100; Rothenberg, "Legal Status," p. 66; and Zatko, *Descent into Darkness*, p. 123.

45. H. M. Kallen, "Religion in Russia," *New Republic* 52, no. 674 (November 2, 1927): 280.

46. Rothenberg, "Legal Status," pp. 79–80; and Swan, *Biography*, p. 31.

47. Hecker, *Religion and Communism*, p. 194.

48. Curtiss, *Russian Church*, p. 193; and Pospielovsky, *History*, pp. 58–59.

49. McCullagh, *Bolshevik Persecution*, p. 72.

50. "The End of a Church," *Pravda*, September 21, 1923 (summary), in Szczesniak, *Russian Revolution*, document 150.

51. Quoted in Pospielovsky, *History*, p. 38.

52. Chamberlin, "Russian Soul," p. 395.

53. Ibid.; and *Komsomolskaya Pravda*, June 19, 1928, quoted in Emhardt, *Religion*, p. 272.

54. Philip S. Bernstein, "Religion in Russia," *Harpers*, May 1930, p. 735.

55. Bernstein, "Religion in Russia," p. 735; Forest, *Impact of Perestroika*, p. 14n6;

and Edgar S. Furniss, "Religion in the Soviet Union: I—The History of the Conflict," *Current History* 32, no. 1 (April 1930): 28.

56. Quoted in David E. Powell, *Antireligious Propaganda in the Soviet Union: A Study of Mass Persuasion* (Cambridge, MA: MIT Press, 1975), p. 31.

57. Ibid.

58. Rothenberg, "Legal Status," p. 81.

59. H. N. Brailsford, "Religion and the Soviets," *New Republic* 62, no. 805 (May 7, 1930): 322; Chamberlin, "Russian Soul," p. 395; William C. White, "The Triple-Barred Cross," *Scribner's*, July 1930, p. 67; and Glennys Young, *Power and the Sacred in Revolutionary Russia: Religious Activists in the Village* (University Park: University of Pennsylvania Press, 1997), pp. 229–30.

60. Hecker, *Religion and Communism*, p. 203n2.

61. *Krasnaya Gazeta*, June 11, 1928.

62. Pospielovsky, *Russian Church*, p. 101n10; and Timasheff, *Religion*, p. 62.

63. Maurice Hindus, *Humanity Uprooted* (New York: J. Cape and H. Smith, 1929), pp. 31–32.

64. White, "Triple-Barred Cross," p. 77; and Emelyan Yaroslavsky, *Religion in the USSR* (New York: International Publishers, 1934), p. 10.

65. Williams, "Atheism and Religion," p. 337.

66. Quoted in Paul Miliukov, *Outlines of Russian Culture*, Part I: Religion and the Church (Philadelphia: University of Pennsylvania Press, 1943), p. 163.

67. "Instructions to the Orthodox Church against Government Acts," quoted in Paul B. Anderson, *People, Church and State in Modern Russia* (London: Student Christian Movement, 1944), pp. 55–57; and Szczesniak, *Russian Revolution*, document 9.

68. William C. Fletcher, *The Russian Orthodox Church Underground, 1917–1970* (London: Oxford University Press, 1971), pp. 84, 93.

69. Curtiss, *Russian Church*, p. 60; and Husband, *Godless Communists*, pp. 51–53.

70. William B. Husband, "Soviet Atheism and Russian Orthodox Strategies of Resistance, 1917–1932," *Journal of Modern History* 70 (March 1998): 88, 91.

71. Miliukov, *Outlines*, p. 164.

72. Quoted in Fletcher, *Church Underground*, pp. 22–23; Donald A. Lowrie, *The Light of Russia: An Introduction to the Russian Church* (Prague: YMCA Press, 1923), p. 223; and Edward Alsworth Ross, *The Russian Soviet Republic* (New York: Century, 1923), pp. 385, 386. There are many versions of this letter, probably because it was copied so many times.

73. Solzhenitsyn, *Gulag Archipelago*, vol. 1, p. 323.

74. Curtiss, *Russian Church*, p. 82; Matthew Spinka, *Church in Soviet Russia* (New York: Oxford University Press, 1956), p. 20; and Swan, *Biography*, p. 47.

75. Quoted in McCullagh, *Bolshevik Persecution of Christianity*, p. 59.

76. Quoted in Powell, *Antireligious Propaganda*, p. 22.

77. Miliukov, *Outlines*, p. 165; "Report of the U.S. Ambassador in Rome," December 9, 1921, quoted in Szczesniak, *Russian Revolution*, document 23; and Timasheff, *Religion*, p. 93.

CHAPTER 8

1. James W. Cunningham, "The Russian Patriarchate and the Attempt to Recover Symphonia," *Canadian-American Slavic Studies* 26, nos. 1–3 (1992): 278–79.

2. From Edwin Vail in *The American Friend*, summarized in "Religion and Anti-Religion in Russia: Observations by Recent Visitors," *Missionary Review of the World* 48, no. 5 (May 1925): 377.

3. Nikolai Bukharin and E. Preobrazhensky, *The ABC of Communism—A Popular Explanation of the Program of the Communist Party of Russia* (Ann Arbor: University of Michigan Press, 1966), p. 251.

4. Louis Fischer, "Soviet Russia's Grim Battle against Religion," *Current History* 18, no. 4 (July 1923): 594; and Julius F. Hecker, *Religion and Communism: A Study of Religion and Atheism in Soviet Russia* (Westport, CT: Hyperion, 1934), p. 52.

5. Quoted in Francis McCullagh, *The Bolshevik Persecution of Christianity* (New York: Dutton, 1924), p. 116.

6. Richard J. Cooke, *Religion in Russia under the Soviets* (New York: Abingdon, 1924), p. 76; Hecker, *Religion and Communism*, p. 200; and William B. Husband, *Godless Communists: Atheism and Society in Soviet Russia, 1917–1932* (DeKalb: Northern Illinois University Press, 2000), pp. 46, 81. Hecker sets the number at 37,000, and Husband sets it at 42,000.

7. Larry E. Holmes, *The Kremlin and the Schoolhouse: Reforming Education in Soviet Russia, 1917–1931* (Bloomington: Indiana University Press, 1991), p. 15.

8. Bukharin and Preobrazhensky, *The ABC of Communism*, p. 253.

9. Joan Delaney, "The Origins of Soviet Antireligious Organizations," in *Aspects of Religion in the Soviet Union: 1917–1967*, ed. Richard H. Marshall Jr. (Chicago: University of Chicago Press, 1971), p. 106; and Dimitry Pospielovsky, *A History of Marxist-Leninist Atheism and Soviet Antireligious Policies* (London: Macmillan, 1987), pp. 29, 45.

10. Delaney, "The Origins," p. 120; and William C. White, "The Triple-Barred Cross," *Scribner's*, July 1930, p. 77.

11. Husband, *Godless Communists*, p. 84.

12. Yaroslavsky writing in *Revolution and Culture*, no. 5 (1928), quoted in *Religion in Soviet Russia*, ed. William Chauncey Emhardt (London: Morehouse, 1929), p. 287.

13. William Henry Chamberlin, "The Struggle for the Russian Soul: A Phase of Soviet Russia," *Atlantic Monthly*, September 1929, p. 394.

14. Quoted ibid.

15. Husband, *Godless Communists*, p. 82; and McCullagh, *Bolshevik Persecution*, p. 53.

16. *Pravda*, April 17, 1923.

17. *Pravda*, May 4, 1923.

18. Yaroslavsky writing in *Revolution and Culture*, no. 5 (1928), quoted in Emhardt, *Religion*, p. 287.

19. Paul Miliukov, *Outlines of Russian Culture, Part I: Religion and the Church* (Philadelphia: University of Pennsylvania Press, 1943), p. 200.

20. Quoted in Joshua Rothenberg, "The Legal Status of Religion in the Soviet Union," in Marshall, *Aspects of Religion*, pp. 63–65.

21. Bukharin and Preobrazhensky, *ABC of Communism*, p. 252.

22. Husband, *Godless Communists*, p. 80.

23. Ibid., p. 81.

24. Quoted in N. S. Timasheff, *Religion in Soviet Russia, 1917–1942* (London: Religious Book Club, 1943), p. 27.

25. *The Communist Party of the Soviet Union in Resolutions and Decisions*, 7th ed. (Moscow, 1954), p. 551, quoted in Delaney, "The Origins," pp. 113–14.

26. Husband, *Godless Communists*, p. 85; and Pospielovsky, *History*, p. 46.

27. McCullagh, *Bolshevik Persecution*, p. 357.

28. Quoted in John Shelton Curtiss, *The Russian Church and the Soviet State, 1917–1950* (Boston: Little, Brown, 1953), p. 76.

29. Robert Conquest, *Religion in the USSR* (London: Bodley Head, 1968), p. 19; "Religion and Anti-Religion," p. 373; Rothenberg, "Legal Status," p. 69; and Jane Swan, *A Biography of Patriarch Tikhon* (Jordanville, NY: Holy Trinity Russian Orthodox Monastery, 1964), pp. 31–32.

30. McCullagh, *Bolshevik Persecution*, p. 375.

31. Pospielovsky, *History*, pp. 37–38.

32. Conquest, *Religion in the USSR*, p. 18; and Pospielovsky, *History*, p. 45.

33. Pospielovsky, *History*, p. 46.

34. Curtiss, *Russian Church*, pp. 76–77.

CHAPTER 9

1. Dimitry Pospielovsky, *The Russian Church under the Soviet Regime: 1917–1982*, vol. 1 (Crestwood, NY: St. Vladimir's Seminary Press, 1984), p. 147n55.

2. Quoted in Andrew Q. Blane, "Protestant Sectarians in the First Year of Soviet Rule," in *Aspects of Religion in the Soviet Union: 1917–1967*, ed. Richard H. Marshall Jr. (Chicago: University of Chicago Press, 1971), p. 308; and Peter Kenez, *The Birth of the Propaganda State: Soviet Methods of Mass Mobilization, 1917–1929* (New York: Cambridge University Press, 1985), p. 67.

3. Blane, "Protestant Sectarians," p. 310.

4. Robert Conquest, *Religion in the USSR* (London: Bodley Head, 1968), p. 14; Edward E. Roslof, "The Heresy of 'Bolshevik' Christianity: Orthodox Rejection of Religious Reform during NEP," *Slavic Review* 55, no. 3 (Autumn 1996): 628–29; and Joshua Rothenberg, "The Legal Status of Religion in the Soviet Union," in Marshall, *Aspects of Religion*, p. 80.

5. Edgar S. Furniss, "Religion in the Soviet Union: I—The History of the Conflict," *Current History* 32, no. 1 (April 1930): 30; and Edward Alsworth Ross, *The Russian Soviet Republic* (New York: Century, 1923), p. 388.

6. Dimitry Pospielovsky, *A History of Marxist-Leninist Atheism and Soviet Antireligious Policies* (London: Macmillan, 1987), p. 44; and Rothenberg, "Legal Status," p. 80.

7. Pospielovsky, *History*, p. 56.

8. Rothenberg, "Legal Status," pp. 80–81.

9. G. P. Fedotov, *The Russian Church since the Revolution* (New York: Macmillan, 1928), p. 47.

10. William B. Husband, *Godless Communists: Atheism and Society in Soviet Russia, 1917–1932* (DeKalb: Northern Illinois University Press, 2000), p. 58.

11. Joan Delaney, "The Origins of Soviet Antireligious Organizations," in Marshall, *Aspects of Religion*, pp. 111–12; and an article in *Izvestia*, January 10, 1923, quoted in *Religion in Soviet Russia*, ed. William Chauncey Emhardt (London: Morehouse, 1929), pp. 32–33.

12. Quoted in Kenez, *Propaganda State*, p. 183.

13. Louis Fischer, "Soviet Russia's Grim Battle against Religion," *Current History* 18, no. 4 (July 1923): 590; J. Zatko, *Descent into Darkness: The Destruction of the Roman Catholic Church in Russia, 1917–1923* (Notre Dame, IN: University of Notre Dame Press, 1965), p. 118; Husband, *Godless Communists*, p. 59; Richard Stites, *Revolutionary Dreams: Utopian Vision and Experimental Life in the Russian Revolution* (New York: Oxford University Press, 1989), p. 109; and Isabel A. Tirado, "The Revolution, Young Peasants, and the Komsomol's Antireligious Campaigns: 1920–1928," *Canadian-American Slavic Studies* 26, nos. 1–3 (1992): 105.

14. Husband, *Godless Communists*, pp. 59, 65.

15. Nikolai Bukharin and E. Preobrazhensky, *The ABC of Communism—A Popular Explanation of the Program of the Communist Party of Russia* (Ann Arbor: University of Michigan Press, 1966), p. 255.

16. Jennifer Wynot, *Russian Orthodox Monasteries' Response to the Relics Exposing Campaign, 1917–1922*, p. 20.

17. Alexander Solzhenitsyn, *The Gulag Archipelago, 1918–1956*, vol. 1 (New York: Harper and Rowe, 1973), p. 325.

18. Ross, *Russian Soviet Republic*, p. 389; and Timothy Ware, *The Orthodox Church* (Baltimore: Penguin, 1963), pp. 239–40.

19. Ivan Prokhanoff, *In the Cauldron of Russia, 1869–1933* (New York: All-Russian Evangelical Christian Union, 1933), p. 246.

20. Prokhanoff, *Cauldron of Russia*, pp. 243–44.

21. John Shelton Curtiss, *The Russian Church and the Soviet State, 1917–1950* (Boston: Little, Brown, 1953), p. 85.

22. Quoted in Peter J. Popoff, "The Religious Revolution in Russia," *Current History* 12, no. 1 (April 1920): 95–96. The priest was M. T. Fomin, and the letter was addressed to the bishop of Olonetsk and Petrozavodsk, originally published by the *Friend of Russia*, December 1919.

23. Ibid., p. 94.

24. Ibid.

25. Solzhenitsyn, *Gulag Archipelago*, vol. 1, p. 326.

26. Popoff, "Religious Revolution," p. 95.

27. Fischer, "Grim Battle," pp. 592–93.

28. Telegram of Chicherin to Cardinal Gasparri, April 2, 1919, quoted in *The Russian Revolution and Religion: A Collection of Documents concerning the Suppression of Religion by the Communists, 1917–1925*, ed. Boleslav Szczesniak (Notre Dame, IN: University of Notre Dame Press, 1959), document 17.

29. Zatko, *Descent Into Darkness*, p. 89.

30. Bohdan Bociurkiw, "Lenin and Religion," in *Lenin: The Man, the Theorist, the Leader—A Reappraisal*, ed. Leonard Schapiro and Peter Reddaway (New York: Praeger, 1967), p. 125; and Husband, *Godless Communists*, pp. 185–86 (endnotes).

31. Quoted in Curtiss, *Russian Church*, p. 86.

32. Ibid., pp. 86–87; Kenez, *Propaganda State*, p. 69; and Prokhanoff, *Cauldron of Russia*, p. 244.

33. Stites, *Revolutionary Dreams*, p. 108.

34. Quoted in Gregory L. Freeze, "Counter-Reformation in Russian Orthodoxy: Popular Response to Religious Innovation, 1922–1925," *Slavic Review* 54, no. 2 (Summer 1995): 314n35.

35. Quoted in Pospielovsky, *Russian Church*, p. 39.

36. David E. Powell, *Antireligious Propaganda in the Soviet Union: A Study of Mass Persuasion* (Cambridge, MA: MIT Press, 1975), p. 34. For a (somewhat feeble) defense of Russian relic veneration, see Leonid Turkevich, "Remains of Saints and the Russian Church," *Current History* 12, no. 1 (April 1920): 97–99.

37. Helmut Altrichter, "Insoluble Conflicts: Village Life between Revolution and Collectivization," in *Russia in the Era of NEP: Explorations in Soviet Society and Culture*, ed. Sheila Fitzpatrick (Bloomington: Indiana University Press, 1991), p. 202; and Stites, *Revolutionary Dreams*, p. 108.

38. Quoted in Waldemar Gurian, *Bolshevism: Theory and Practice* (London: Sheed and Ward, 1933), p. 351.

39. Nicolas Berdyaev, *The Origin of Russian Communism* (Ann Arbor: University of Michigan Press, 1960), p. 170.

40. Quoted in Tirado, "Revolution," p. 113.

41. Alexander Bogdanov, discussed in Jay Bergman, "The Image of Jesus in the Russian Revolutionary Movement: The Case of Russian Marxism," *International Review of Social History* 35 (1990): 230.

42. Quoted in Bergman, "Image of Jesus," p. 231.

43. Quoted in Stites, *Revolutionary Dreams*, p. 102; and Nina Tumarkin, "Religion, Bolshevism and the Origins of the Lenin Cult," *Russian Review* 40, no. 1 (January 1981): 42.

44. Richard Stites, "Bolshevik Ritual Building in the 1920s," in Fitzpatrick, *Russia in the Era of NEP*, p. 297.

45. D. Balashov, "The Traditional and the Modern," *Nauka I Religiya*, no. 12,

(1965): 30, quoted in Nikita Struve, "Pseudo-Religious Rites Introduced by the Party Authorities," in *Religion and the Search for New Ideals in the USSR*, ed. William C. Fletcher and Anthony J. Strover (New York: Praeger, 1967), p. 46.

46. Quoted in James Thrower, *Marxism-Leninism as the Civil Religion of Soviet Society: God's Commissar* (Lewiston, NY: E. Mellen, 1992), p. 39.

47. Ibid.

48. Bergman, "Image of Jesus," p. 245; and Tumarkin, "Lenin Cult," p. 44.

49. Quoted in Stites, *Revolutionary Dreams*, p. 120.

50. Bergman, "Image of Jesus," p. 244.

51. Ibid., pp. 239–45; and George Humphrey, *UA Professor Emeritus Publishes First English Translation of Rare Book by Intriguing Russian Figure, Alexander Bogdanov.*

52. Stanley High, "The Triumph of Atheism in Russia," *Atlantic Monthly*, January 1925, p. 123.

53. Stites, *Revolutionary Dreams*, p. 110.

54. Ibid., pp. 110–11.

55. Ibid., p. 108.

56. Ibid.

57. H. N. Brailsford, "Religion and the Soviets," *New Republic*, May 7, 1930, p. 322.

58. Quoted in Tirado, "Revolution," pp. 113–14.

CHAPTER 10

1. Richard Stites, *Revolutionary Dreams: Utopian Vision and Experimental Life in the Russian Revolution* (New York: Oxford University Press, 1989), p. 108.

2. Quoted in William B. Husband, *Godless Communists: Atheism and Society in Soviet Russia, 1917–1932* (DeKalb: Northern Illinois University Press, 2000), p. 95.

3. From a letter by Robert Crozier Long to the *New York Evening Post*, April 10, 1919, quoted in "Failure of Religion in Russia," *Literary Digest*, June 14, 1919, p. 32.

4. Edward Alsworth Ross, *The Russian Soviet Republic* (New York: Century, 1923), p. 391.

5. Richard Stites, "Bolshevik Ritual Building in the 1920s," in *Russia in the Era of NEP: Explorations in Soviet Society and Culture*, ed. Sheila Fitzpatrick (Bloomington: Indiana University Press, 1991), p. 301.

6. Quoted in David E. Powell, *Antireligious Propaganda in the Soviet Union: A Study of Mass Persuasion* (Cambridge, MA: MIT Press, 1975), p. 71.

7. Stites, "Ritual Building," p. 300.

8. Roger Pethybridge, *One Step Backwards, Two Steps Forward: Soviet Society and Politics in the New Economic Policy* (Oxford: Clarendon Press, 1990), p. 40; and Stites, "Ritual Building," pp. 300–301. Also see Stites, *Revolutionary Dreams*, pp. 111–12, where he offers a more complete list of creative names.

9. From an obscure 1920s publication, which can no longer be obtained for citation.

10. Lynne Viola, "The Peasant Nightmare: Visions of Apocalypse in the Soviet Countryside," *Journal of Modern History* 62, no. 4 (December 1990): 754.

11. Joshua Rothenberg, "The Legal Status of Religion in the Soviet Union," in *Aspects of Religion in the Soviet Union: 1917–1967*, ed. Richard H. Marshall Jr. (Chicago: University of Chicago Press, 1971), p. 63.

12. Stites, "Ritual Building," p. 302.

13. Story related by Louis Fischer.

14. John Shelton Curtiss, *The Russian Church and the Soviet State, 1917–1950* (Boston: Little, Brown, 1953), p. 104.

15. Quoted in Pethybridge, *One Step Backwards*, p. 42.

16. Stites, "Ritual Building," p. 302.

17. Helmut Altrichter, "Insoluble Conflicts: Village Life between Revolution and Collectivization," in Fitzpatrick, *Russia in the Era of NEP*, p. 203; Roger Pethybridge, *The Social Prelude to Stalinism* (London: Macmillan, 1974), p. 55; and Maurice Hindus, *Humanity Uprooted* (New York: J. Cape and H. Smith, 1929), p. 13.

18. Husband, *Godless Communists*, p. 46; and N. S. Timasheff, *Religion in Soviet Russia, 1917–1942* (London: Religious Book Club, 1943), p. 28.

19. Curtiss, *Russian Church*, p. 75.

20. Emelyan Yaroslavsky, *Religion in the USSR* (New York: International Publishers, 1934), p. 28.

21. Curtiss, *Russian Church*, p. 81.

22. Hindus, *Humanity Uprooted*, p. 44.

23. Stites, *Revolutionary Dreams*, p. 113.

24. Stites, "Ritual Building," p. 304.

25. Archbishop John Shahovskoy, "The Church and the Cremation Problem," Holy Trinity Cathedral *Church Life Bulletin*, November 1962, p. 1.

26. Curtiss, *Russian Church*, p. 79; Shahovskoy, "Cremation Problem," p. 1; and Stites, "Ritual Building," pp. 303–304.

27. Stites, "Ritual Building, pp. 305–306.

28. Curtiss, *Russian Church*, pp. 74–75; and Rothenberg, "Legal Status," p. 67.

29. *The Holy Easter*, quoted in A. Valentinov, *The Assault of Heaven: A Collection of Facts and Documents Relating to the Persecution of Religion and Church in Russia, Based Mainly upon Official Sources* (Berlin: Max Mattisson, 1924), pp. 97–98.

30. Sir Bernard Pares, *Russia between Reform and Revolution—Fundamentals of Russian History and Character* (New York: Schocken, 1962), pp. 134–35.

31. "Bolshevism out to Abolish God," *Literary Digest*, January 17, 1920, p. 36.

32. Timasheff, *Religion*, pp. 60–61.

33. From an obscure 1920s publication, which can no longer be obtained for citation.

34. Quoted in Richard J. Cooke, *Religion in Russia under the Soviets* (New York: Abingdon, 1924), p. 84.

35. Quoted in Stanley High, "The Triumph of Atheism in Russia," *Atlantic Monthly*, January 1925, pp. 124–25.

36. Stites, "Ritual Building," pp. 297–98.

37. Altrichter, "Insoluble Conflicts," p. 201.

38. Ibid., pp. 201–202.

39. Ibid., p. 203.

40. Quoted in *Religion in Soviet Russia*, ed. William Chauncey Emhardt (London: Morehouse, 1929), p. 275.

41. *Krasnaya Gazeta*, November 20, 1927, quoted in Emhardt, *Religion*, p. 274.

42. Larry E. Holmes, *The Kremlin and the Schoolhouse: Reforming Education in Soviet Russia, 1917–1931* (Bloomington: Indiana University Press, 1991), p. 102.

43. "Bolshevism out to Abolish God," p. 36.

44. Quoted in Annie Gérin, *Godless at the Workbench: Soviet Illustrated Humoristic Antireligious Propaganda* (Regina, Canada: Dunlop Art Gallery, 2003), p. 27.

45. Altrichter, "Insoluble Conflicts," pp. 195–96; and Husband, *Godless Communists*, p. 88.

46. Stites, "Ritual Building," p. 298.

47. Gregory L. Freeze, "Counter-Reformation in Russian Orthodoxy: Popular Response to Religious Innovation, 1922–1925," *Slavic Review* 54, no. 2 (Summer 1995): 320n60; Anne O'Hare McCormick, *The Hammer and the Scythe: Communist Russia Enters the Second Decade* (New York: Knopf, 1928), p. 213; Dimitry Pospielovsky, *A History of Marxist-Leninist Atheism and Soviet Antireligious Policies* (London: Macmillan, 1987), p. 56; and Timasheff, *Religion*, p. 37.

48. Altrichter, "Insoluble Conflicts," pp. 199–200; and Stites, "Ritual Building," p. 306.

49. D. Balashov, "The Traditional and the Modern," *Nauka I Religiya*, no. 12, (1965): 29, quoted in Nikita Struve, "Pseudo-Religious Rites Introduced by the Party Authorities," in *Religion and the Search for New Ideals in the USSR*, ed. William C. Fletcher and Anthony J. Strover (New York: Praeger, 1967), p. 46; Kolarz, *Religion*, p. 31; and a conversation by e-mail with Galina Nomokonova in St. Petersburg.

50. Julius F. Hecker, *Religion and Communism: A Study of Religion and Atheism in Soviet Russia* (Westport, CT: Hyperion, 1934), p. 217; Walter Kolarz, *Religion in the Soviet Union* (New York: St. Martin's, 1961), p. 31; Alexander Solzhenitsyn, *The Gulag Archipelago, 1918–1956*, vol. 1 (New York: Harper and Rowe, 1973), p. 50; and William C. White, "The Triple-Barred Cross," *Scribner's*, July 1930, p. 74.

51. Kolarz, *Religion*, pp. 30–31.

52. Curtiss, *Russian Church*, p. 80.

53. Quoted ibid., p. 80.

54. Ibid., pp. 80–81; and Rothenberg, "Legal Status," pp. 67–68.

CHAPTER 11

1. Harold H. Fisher, *The Famine in Soviet Russia, 1919–1923: The Operations of the American Relief Administration* (Freeport, NY: Books for Libraries, 1971), p. 98;

Francis Haller, *Famine in Russia: The Hidden Horrors of 1921*, p. 1; Jennifer Kao and John McCrory, *The Political Economy of Disaster: Famine in Russia, 1921–1922*, pp. 7–9; and Alexander Solzhenitsyn, *The Gulag Archipelago, 1918–1956*, vol. 1 (New York: Harper and Rowe, 1973), p. 342. See also the quotation from the Pomgol periodical *Pomoshch [Relief]* in Nathaniel Davis, *A Long Walk to Church: A Contemporary History of Russian Orthodoxy* (San Francisco: Westview, 1995), p. 3.

2. Quoted in Albert Galter, *The Red Book of the Persecuted Church* (Dublin, Ireland: M. H. Gill and Son, 1957), p. 34n4.

3. Kao and McCrory, *Disaster*, pp. 1–3, 6.

4. Emma Goldman, *My Disillusionment in Russia* (Mineola, NY: Dover, 2003), pp. 233–36.

5. Fisher, *Famine*, p. 51; Kao and McCrory, *Disaster*, p. 6; R. O. G. Urch, "Bolshevism and Religion in Russia," *Atlantic Monthly*, March 1923, p. 398; and J. Zatko, *Descent into Darkness: The Destruction of the Roman Catholic Church in Russia, 1917–1923* (Notre Dame, IN: University of Notre Dame Press, 1965), pp. 102–103.

6. Goldman, *Disillusionment*, pp. 233–36; Richard Pipes, *Russia under the Bolshevik Regime* (New York: Vintage, 1994), pp. 411–19; *Revelations from the Russian Archives—Early Cooperation: American Famine Relief*; and Zatko, *Descent into Darkness*, p. 102.

7. Fisher, *Famine*, pp. 51–52; and Zatko, *Descent into Darkness*, p. 103.

8. Quoted in Fisher, *Famine*, pp. 51–52. For the entire text of Gorky's appeal, see *Soviet Russia and the West: 1920–1927, A Documentary Survey*, ed. Xenia Joukoff Eudin and Harold H. Fisher (Stanford, CA: Stanford University Press, 1957), document 18.

9. Solzhenitsyn, *Gulag Archipelago*, vol. 1, p. 343.

10. Goldman, *Disillusionment*, pp. 233–36.

11. Fisher, *Famine*, p. 553.

12. Roger Pethybridge, *One Step Backwards, Two Steps Forward: Soviet Society and Politics in the New Economic Policy* (Oxford: Clarendon Press, 1990), p. 98.

13. Quoted in Fisher, *Famine*, p. 93.

14. Quoted in John Shelton Curtiss, *The Russian Church and the Soviet State, 1917–1950* (Boston: Little, Brown, 1953), p. 116.

15. Francis McCullagh, *The Bolshevik Persecution of Christianity* (New York: Dutton, 1924), p. 16; Dimitry Pospielovsky, "The Renovationist Movement in the Orthodox Church in the Light of Archival Documents," *Journal of Church and State* 39, no. 1 (January 1, 1997): 1–3; Matthew Spinka, *Church and the Russian Revolution* (New York: Macmillan, 1927), p. 165; Jane Swan, *A Biography of Patriarch Tikhon* (Jordanville, NY: Holy Trinity Russian Orthodox Monastery, 1964), p. 53; Urch, "Bolshevism and Religion," p. 399; and Zatko, *Descent into Darkness*, pp. 102, 104.

16. Pethybridge, *One Step Backwards*, p. 98; Dimitry Pospielovsky, *A History of Marxist-Leninist Atheism and Soviet Antireligious Policies* (London: Macmillan, 1987), p. 158n21; and Zatko, *Descent into Darkness*, p. 105.

17. Spinka, *Church and the Russian Revolution*, p. 163; and Zatko, *Descent into Darkness*, pp. 113–14.

18. Robert Pierce Casey, *Religion in Russia* (New York: Harper, 1946), p. 99.

19. Dimitry Pospielovsky, *The Russian Church under the Soviet Regime: 1917–1982*, vol. 1 (Crestwood, NY: St. Vladimir's Seminary Press, 1984), p. 118.

20. Paul D. Steeves, *The Canonization of Patriarch Tikhon as a Reflection of New Thinking in the Glasnost Era*, p. 9. Kalinin was nominally in charge, but Trotsky ran the show.

21. Quoted in Curtiss, *Russian Church*, p. 63.

22. Pospielovsky, *History*, pp. 36, 38.

23. I. Demidov, "Fight for Survival," *Living Age*, September 30, 1922, p. 829; and Urch, "Bolshevism and Religion," p. 399.

24. McCullagh, *Bolshevik Persecution*, p. 76.

25. Quoted in McCullagh, *Bolshevik Persecution*, p. 98.

26. Spinka, *Church and the Russian Revolution*, pp. 172, 177.

27. Ibid., p. 15.

28. William B. Husband, *Godless Communists: Atheism and Society in Soviet Russia, 1917–1932* (DeKalb: Northern Illinois University Press, 2000), p. 55; and Michael A. Meerson, "The Renovationist Schism in the Russian Orthodox Church," *Canadian-American Slavic Studies* 26, nos. 1–4 (1992): 299.

29. Fisher, *Famine*, p. 422; Husband, *Godless Communists*, pp. 55–56, 184; Pospielovsky, "Renovationist Movement," pp. 1–3; Spinka, *Church and the Russian Revolution*, pp. 173–74; and *Izvestia*, no. 46, February 26, 1922 (full text), quoted in Swan, *Biography*, pp. 55–56.

30. McCullagh, *Bolshevik Persecution*, p. 16.

31. Demidov, "Fight for Survival," p. 829; Vladimir Moss, *The Orthodox Church at the Crossroads: From 1900 to the Present Day*, p. 20 (my pagination); Matthew Spinka, *Church in Soviet Russia* (New York: Oxford University Press, 1956), p. 28; Swan, *Biography*, pp. 56–58; and *The Russian Revolution and Religion: A Collection of Documents concerning the Suppression of Religion by the Communists, 1917–1925*, ed. Boleslav Szczesniak (Notre Dame, IN: University of Notre Dame Press, 1959), document 25.

32. Quoted in Swan, *Biography*, p. 58.

33. Information from the Trotsky Archives held at Harvard University Press, discussed in Joan Delaney, "The Origins of Soviet Antireligious Organizations," in *Aspects of Religion in the Soviet Union: 1917–1967*, ed. Richard H. Marshall Jr. (Chicago: University of Chicago Press, 1971), p. 108.

34. Gregory L. Freeze, "Counter-Reformation in Russian Orthodoxy: Popular Response to Religious Innovation, 1922–1925," *Slavic Review* 54, no. 2 (Summer 1995): 315n37; McCullagh, *Bolshevik Persecution*, p. 8; and Moss, *Orthodox Church*, pp. 21–22 (my pagination).

35. Quoted in Paul B. Anderson, *People, Church and State in Modern Russia* (London: Student Christian Movement, 1944), p. 76.

36. *V Let Vlasti Sovetov* (Moscow, 1922), pp. 291–92, quoted in Zatko, *Descent into Darkness*, p. 157n36.

37. Quoted in Marcus Bach, *God and the Soviets* (New York: Thomas Y. Crowell, 1958), p. 93.

38. Spinka, *Church and the Russian Revolution*, p. 170.

39. Ibid., p. 180.

40. Richard J. Cooke, *Religion in Russia under the Soviets* (New York: Abingdon, 1924), p. 140; *Izvestia*, March 26, 1922, quoted in Curtiss, *Russian Church*, p. 113; Edward Alsworth Ross, *The Russian Soviet Republic* (New York: Century, 1923), p. 390; and Urch, "Bolshevism and Religion," p. 398.

41. Quoted in Pospielovsky, *Russian Church*, p. 81n92.

42. *Hieromartyr Benjamin, Metropolitan of Petrograd, and Those with Him*, p. 2 (my pagination).

43. Quoted in Spinka, *Church and the Russian Revolution*, pp. 178–79.

44. Stanley High, "The Triumph of Atheism in Russia," *Atlantic Monthly*, January 1925, p. 128; and Swan, *Biography*, p. 54.

45. Cooke, *Religion*, p. 148; McCullagh, *Bolshevik Persecution*, p. 4; Pethybridge, *One Step Backwards*, pp. 39–40; Spinka, *Church in Soviet Russia*, p. 28; Urch, "Bolshevism and Religion," pp. 398–99; and Zatko, *Descent into Darkness*, p. 105.

46. Quoted in Freeze, "Counter-Reformation," p. 314n35.

47. A March 17, 1922, coded telegram from chairman of the Smolensk regional executive committee Bulatov to the Moscow GPU, quoted in Felix Corley, *Religion in the Soviet Union: An Archival Reader* (New York: New York University Press, 1996), document 8.

48. All three quotations are from the notes of the March 20, 1922, Politburo meeting, attended by Stalin, Molotov, Kamenev, and Trotsky, quoted in Corley, *Religion*, document 9.

49. Ibid., p. 28.

50. *Izvestia*, March 28, 1922, quoted in N. S. Timasheff, *Religion in Soviet Russia, 1917–1942* (London: Religious Book Club, 1943), p. 29.

51. Curtiss, *Russian Church*, p. 119; and Husband, *Godless Communists*, p. 56.

52. Moss, *Orthodox Church*, p. 21 (my pagination); Pethybridge, *One Step Backwards*, pp. 39–40; and Urch, "Bolshevism and Religion," p. 399.

53. McCullagh, *Bolshevik Persecution*, p. 20.

54. Moss, *Orthodox Church*, p. 21 (my pagination); and Pospielovsky, *History*, pp. 34–36. This is a merging of the two translations.

55. Pospielovsky, *History*, p. 36.

56. *Letter from Lenin*; Moss, *Orthodox Church*, p. 21 (my pagination); and McCullagh, *Bolshevik Persecution*, p. 17.

57. William Chauncey Emhardt, ed., *Religion in Soviet Russia* (London: Morehouse, 1929), pp. 49–50.

58. McCullagh, *Bolshevik Persecution*, p. 27.

59. Daniel Peris, *Storming the Heavens: The Soviet League of the Militant Godless* (Ithaca, NY: Cornell University Press, 1998), p. 27; "Church Valuables Delivered to the

State Fund," Moscow *Bednota*, September 2, 1922, in Szczesniak, *Russian Revolution*, document 46; and Zatko, *Descent into Darkness*, p. 122.

60. Quoted in Dr. Roman Serbyn, "The First Man-Made Famine in Soviet Ukraine, 1921–1923," *Ukrainian Weekly*, November 6, 1988, p. 13 (my pagination).

61. McCullagh, *Bolshevik Persecution*, p. 8; Serbyn, "Man-Made Famine," p. 12; and Edmund A. Walsh, *The Catholic Church in Present Day Russia* (report delivered before the American Catholic Historical Association in Minneapolis, MN, on December 29, 1931), pp. 11–13.

62. Goldman, *Disillusionment*, pp. 233–36.

63. "Collection of Church Valuables," *Izvestia*, September 3, 1922 (document 47), and "Report of the U.S. Commissioner in Riga Concerning Divisions in the Russian Orthodox Church," July 17, 1922 (document 41), in Szczesniak, *Russian Revolution*.

64. Curtiss, *Russian Church*, p. 125; McCullagh, *Bolshevik Persecution*, p. 8; and Pospielovsky, *History*, p. 36. In terms of early 1920s US dollars, Louis Fischer, "Soviet Russia's Grim Battle against Religion," *Current History* 18, no. 4 (July 1923): 594, came up with a figure of $1.5 million, but the Russian Official Bureau of Statistics claimed the value of the confiscations equaled $5 million. Julius F. Hecker, *Religion and Communism: A Study of Religion and Atheism in Soviet Russia* (Westport, CT: Hyperion, 1934), p. 209, calculated much higher numbers for confiscated precious metals and gems, but he was sympathetic to the Communist cause and may have wanted to make the churches look bad for their prior hoarding of wealth. The government, paradoxically, may have wanted to underestimate these figures in order to avoid foreign criticism right after the Genoa Conference.

65. Curtiss, *Russian Church*, pp. 166–67.

66. Ibid., p. 126; Ross, *Russian Soviet Republic*, p. 388; Urch, "Bolshevism and Religion," p. 399; and Meerson, "The Renovationist Schism," p. 305n47.

67. Emhardt, *Religion*, pp. 49–50.

68. Casey, *Religion in Russia*, p. 98; and Moss, *Orthodox Church*, p. 22 (my pagination). Spinka, *Church and the Russian Revolution*, p. 171, says that when he saw the crown jewels in 1926 they were worth 500 million rubles.

69. Fisher, *Famine*, p. 320.

70. Cooke, *Religion*, p. 149.

CHAPTER 12

1. Cheka member Latzis, quoted in *Religion in Soviet Russia*, ed. William Chauncey Emhardt (London: Morehouse, 1929), p. 31.

2. Details and summaries of all Criminal Code laws having any relationship whatsoever to religious issues can be found in Francis McCullagh, *The Bolshevik Persecution of Christianity* (New York: Dutton, 1924), appendix II.

3. Quoted in Albert Galter, *The Red Book of the Persecuted Church* (Dublin, Ireland: M. H. Gill and Son, 1957), p. 42n13.

4. Krylenko, *Za Pyat Let (1918–1922)*, various pages, quoted in Alexander Solzhenitsyn, *The Gulag Archipelago, 1918–1956*, vol. 1 (New York: Harper and Rowe, 1973), pp. 307–309.

5. Wladyslav Kania, *Bolshevism and Religion* (New York: Polish Library, 1946), pp. 8–9.

6. Vladimir Moss, *The Orthodox Church at the Crossroads: From 1900 to the Present Day*, p. 57 (my pagination).

7. Michael Bourdeaux, *Religious Minorities in the Soviet Union* (London: Minority Rights Group, 1984), p. 5.

8. Stenographic notes of the questioning of Patriarch Tikhon, quoted in Solzhenitsyn, *Gulag Archipelago*, vol. 1, p. 348.

9. Jerome Davis, "Religion in Soviet Russia," *Missionary Review of the World* 45, no. 3 (March 1922): 191; McCullagh, *Bolshevik Persecution*, pp. 36–37; Jane Swan, *A Biography of Patriarch Tikhon* (Jordanville, NY: Holy Trinity Russian Orthodox Monastery, 1964), pp. 50, 60; and "The Confiscation of Church Property in Russia" (A report of the US Commissioner in Riga), April 21, 1922, in *The Russian Revolution and Religion: A Collection of Documents concerning the Suppression of Religion by the Communists, 1917–1925*, ed. Boleslav Szczesniak (Notre Dame, IN: University of Notre Dame Press, 1959), document 28.

10. Robert Conquest, *Religion in the USSR* (London: Bodley Head, 1968), p. 15.

11. McCullagh, *Bolshevik Persecution*, p. 22; and Solzhenitsyn, *Gulag Archipelago*, vol. 1, pp. 346–50.

12. Quoted in McCullagh, *Bolshevik Persecution*, p. 23.

13. McCullagh, *Bolshevik Persecution*, pp. 23–24; and R. O. G. Urch, "Bolshevism and Religion in Russia," *Atlantic Monthly*, March 1923, p. 400.

14. From an obscure 1920s publication, which can no longer be obtained for citation.

15. Ivan M. Andreyev, *Is the Grace of God Present in the Soviet Church?* (Wildwood, Alberta, Canada: Monastery, 2000), p. 95.

16. Quoted ibid.

17. Quoted ibid., p. 96; and Urch, "Bolshevism and Religion," p. 400.

18. *Izvestia*, May 6, 1922, quoted in McCullagh, *Bolshevik Persecution*, p. 29.

19. Swan, *Biography*, p. 60.

20. Stalin's May 8, 1922, letters to politburo members, quoted in Felix Corley, *Religion in the Soviet Union: An Archival Reader* (New York: New York University Press, 1996), document 13.

21. McCullagh, *Bolshevik Persecution*, pp. 7, 24, 26; and Solzhenitsyn, *Gulag Archipelago*, vol. 1, p. 347.

22. McCullagh, *Bolshevik Persecution*, p. 26.

23. *Pravda*, no. 99, May 6, 1922, quoted in John Shelton Curtiss, *The Russian Church and the Soviet State, 1917–1950* (Boston: Little, Brown, 1953), p. 120.

24. Quoted in *Hieromartyr Benjamin, Metropolitan of Petrograd, and Those with Him*, p. 6.

25. According to Curtiss, *Russian Church*, p. 122, there were ninety accused.

26. Solzhenitsyn, *Gulag Archipelago*, vol. 1, p. 345.

27. Quoted ibid., p. 346.

28. Ibid.

29. Dimitry Pospielovsky, "The Renovationist Movement in the Orthodox Church in the Light of Archival Documents," *Journal of Church and State* 39, no. 1 (January 1, 1997).

30. Solzhenitsyn, *Gulag Archipelago*, vol. 1, p. 346.

31. Quoted ibid., p. 351; and Matthew Spinka, *Church and the Russian Revolution* (New York: Macmillan, 1927), pp. 185–86.

32. Solzhenitsyn, *Gulag Archipelago*, vol. 1, p. 351.

33. *Hieromartyr Benjamin*, p. 5; and Moss, *Orthodox Church*, p. 27 (my pagination).

34. Quoted in *Hieromartyr Benjamin*, p. 5.

35. Ibid., p. 6.

36. Quoted in Solzhenitsyn, *Gulag Archipelago*, vol. 1, p. 351.

37. Constantin de Grunwald, *The Churches and the Soviet Union* (New York: Macmillan, 1962), p. 47.

38. Quoted in Conquest, *Religion in the USSR*, p. 15.

39. Quoted in Sergius Troitsky, *The Living Church*, bound inside of Emhardt, *Religion*, p. 363n36.

40. *Hieromartyr Benjamin*, p. 7. There are versions of the execution date ranging from August 25 to August 27.

41. John Haynes Holmes, "Religion in Revolutionary Russia," *Nation* 116, no. 3018 (May 9, 1923): 541–42.

42. H. N. Brailsford, "Religion and the Soviets," *New Republic* 62, no. 805 (May 7, 1930): 321, 323.

43. Harold Kellock, "Religion in the Soviet Union: IV—The Soviet Point of View," *Current History* 32, no. 1 (April 1930): 40.

44. From an obscure 1920s publication, which can no longer be obtained for citation.

45. Szczesniak, *Russian Revolution*, document 32.

CHAPTER 13

1. Quoted in Stanley High, "The Triumph of Atheism in Russia," *Atlantic Monthly*, January 1925, p. 129.

2. Francis McCullagh, *The Bolshevik Persecution of Christianity* (New York: Dutton, 1924), p. 35; Paul Miliukov, *Outlines of Russian Culture, Part I: Religion and the Church* (Philadelphia: University of Pennsylvania Press, 1943), p. 152; and Philip Walters, "The Renovationist Coup: Personalities and Programs," in *Church, Nation and State in Russia and Ukraine*, ed. Geoffrey A. Hosking (London: Macmillan, 1991), p. 250.

3. Quoted in Matthew Spinka, *Church in Soviet Russia* (New York: Oxford University Press, 1956), p. 33.

4. Robert Pierce Casey, *Religion in Russia* (New York: Harper, 1946), p. 108; and High, "Triumph of Atheism," p. 130.

5. Dimitry Pospielovsky, *The Russian Church under the Soviet Regime: 1917–1982*, vol. 1 (Crestwood, NY: St. Vladimir's Seminary Press, 1984), p. 145; and Edward E. Roslof, "The Heresy of 'Bolshevik' Christianity: Orthodox Rejection of Religious Reform During NEP," *Slavic Review* 55, no. 3 (Autumn 1996): 622.

6. Jane Swan, *A Biography of Patriarch Tikhon* (Jordanville, NY: Holy Trinity Russian Orthodox Monastery, 1964), p. 62.

7. Casey, *Religion in Russia*, p. 107.

8. Swan, *Biography*, p. 62.

9. Quoted ibid., pp. 63–65.

10. Felix Corley, *Religion in the Soviet Union: An Archival Reader* (New York: New York University Press, 1996), p. 23.

11. Corley, *Religion*, document 6; and Pospielovsky, *Russian Church*, p. 52.

12. Samsonov letter to Dzerzhinsky, December 1920, quoted in Corley, *Religion*, document 6.

13. Vladimir Moss, *The Orthodox Church at the Crossroads: From 1900 to the Present Day*, p. 22 (my pagination).

14. Quoted in Roslof, "Heresy," p. 616.

15. Walters, "Renovationist Coup," p. 251.

16. A record of the March 20, 1922, Politburo meeting, quoted in Corley, *Religion*, document 9.

17. Quoted in Moss, *Orthodox Church*, p. 20 (my pagination).

18. Quoted in Pospielovsky, "Renovationist Movement," p. 3 (my pagination).

19. Quoted in Elesha Coffman, "Soviets, Schism and Sabotage: How the Government Manipulated Division in the Russian Orthodox Church," *Christianity Today*, August 14, 2000.

20. Bohdan Bociurkiw, "Lenin and Religion," in *Lenin: The Man, the Theorist, the Leader—A Reappraisal*, ed. Leonard Schapiro and Peter Reddaway (New York: Praeger, 1967), p. 126.

21. Roslof, "Heresy," p. 616.

22. Quoted in Moss, *Orthodox Church*, p. 19 (my pagination).

23. Quoted in Corley, *Religion*, document 12.

24. Ibid.

25. Swan, *Biography*, p. 95.

26. John Haynes Holmes, "Religion in Revolutionary Russia," *Nation* 116, no. 3018 (May 9, 1923): 543.

27. Quoted in Richard J. Cooke, *Religion in Russia under the Soviets* (New York: Abingdon, 1924), p. 202.

28. McCullagh, *Bolshevik Persecution*, pp. 30–31; and Moss, *Orthodox Church*, p. 23 (my pagination).

29. McCullagh, *Bolshevik Persecution*, pp. 30–31; and Moss, *Orthodox Church*, p. 23 (my pagination).

30. Dmitry Safonov, "Eighty Years Ago Holy Martyr Ilarion Reconsecrated the Church of the Presentation Monastery after Expelling Renovationists," July 7, 2003, p. 4 (my pagination); McCullagh, *Bolshevik Persecution*, pp. 30–31; Moss, *Orthodox Church*, p. 23 (my pagination); and Swan, *Biography*, p. 65.

31. Ivan Tregubov, "Church Revolution in Soviet Russia," *Living Age*, September 2, 1922, p. 586; Sergius Troitsky, *The Living Church*, bound inside of *Religion in Soviet Russia*, ed. William Chauncey Emhardt (London: Morehouse, 1929), p. 346; Safonov, "Eighty Years Ago," p. 5 (my pagination); and Walters, "Renovationist Coup," pp. 260, 263.

32. Pospielovsky, *Russian Church*, p. 53.

33. Troitsky, *Living Church*, p. 364.

34. Maurice Hindus, *Humanity Uprooted* (New York: J. Cape and H. Smith, 1929), p. 23.

35. Walters, "Renovationist Coup," p. 262.

36. Quoted ibid., p. 263.

37. Ibid.

38. Nathaniel Davis, *A Long Walk to Church: A Contemporary History of Russian Orthodoxy* (San Francisco: Westview, 1995), p. 4; Pospielovsky, *Russian Church*, p. 83n95; Troitsky, *Living Church*, p. 329; and R. O. G. Urch, "Bolshevism and Religion in Russia," *Atlantic Monthly*, March 1923, p. 403.

39. Pospielovsky, *Russian Church*, p. 54.

40. John Shelton Curtiss, *The Russian Church and the Soviet State, 1917–1950* (Boston: Little, Brown, 1953), p. 172; and McCullagh, *Bolshevik Persecution*, pp. 33–34.

41. Quoted in Walters, "Renovationist Coup," p. 257.

42. Miliukov, *Outlines*, p. 181; and Walters, "Renovationist Coup," p. 257.

43. Quoted in Walters, "Renovationist Coup," p. 257.

44. Interview with a *New York World* reporter, quoted in Cooke, *Religion*, pp. 203–204.

45. Urch, "Bolshevism and Religion," p. 401; and Walters, "Renovationist Coup," p. 260.

46. McCullagh, *Bolshevik Persecution*, p. 34; and Daniel Peris, "Commissars in Red Cassocks: Former Priests in the League of the Militant Godless," *Slavic Review* 54, no. 2 (Summer 1995): 350.

47. Moss, *Orthodox Church*, p. 22 (my pagination); and Pospielovsky, *Russian Church*, p. 50.

48. Quoted in Troitsky, *Living Church*, p. 307.

49. N. S. Timasheff, *Religion in Soviet Russia, 1917–1942* (London: Religious Book Club, 1943), p. 31.

50. Quoted in Swan, *Biography*, pp. 65–67.

51. Ibid., p. 82.

52. McCullagh, *Bolshevik Persecution*, pp. 37–38. For the entire list of Tikhon's "crimes," see Swan, *Biography*, p. 67. The room description is based on Matthew Spinka, *Church and the Russian Revolution* (New York: Macmillan, 1927), pp. 201–202. It is not clear whether there were two meetings held on May 12 or just the one that began at 11:00 PM.

53. McCullagh, *Bolshevik Persecution*, p. 39.

54. The Paris newspaper *Les Dernieres Nouvelles*, April 21, 1923, carried this story.

55. *The Messenger of the Synod*, no. 3 (1925), quoted in Spinka, *Church and the Russian Revolution*, p. 200.

56. Robert Conquest, *Religion in the USSR* (London: Bodley Head, 1968), p. 15; and Spinka, *Church and the Russian Revolution*, pp. 201–202.

57. Quoted in McCullagh, *Bolshevik Persecution*, p. 40.

58. "Patriarch Tikhon Has of His Own Accord Temporarily Resigned," May 17, 1922, in *The Russian Revolution and Religion: A Collection of Documents concerning the Suppression of Religion by the Communists, 1917–1925*, ed. Boleslav Szczesniak (Notre Dame, IN: University of Notre Dame Press, 1959), document 31.

59. Urch, "Bolshevism and Religion," p. 402.

60. Quoted in Spinka, *Church and the Russian Revolution*, p. 256.

61. Urch, "Bolshevism and Religion," p. 402.

62. "Report of the U.S. Commissioner in Riga concerning the Situation of the Church in Russia," July 17, 1922, in Szczesniak, *Russian Revolution*, document 40; and Swan, *Biography*, p. 89.

63. Quoted in Troitsky, *Living Church*, p. 306.

64. Ibid., p. 314n38.

65. Quoted in Cooke, *Religion*, p. 211.

66. Curtiss, *Russian Church*, p. 119.

67. Quoted in *Hieromartyr Benjamin, Metropolitan of Petrograd, and Those with Him*, p. 3 (my pagination).

68. *Hieromartyr Benjamin*, pp. 3–4 (my pagination).

69. Ibid., p. 4 (my pagination).

70. Michael A. Meerson, "The Renovationist Schism in the Russian Orthodox Church," *Canadian-American Slavic Studies* 26, nos. 1–4 (1992): 307n55; Moss, *Orthodox Church*, p. 27 (my pagination); Spinka, *Church and the Russian Revolution*, p. 187; and Troitsky, *Living Church*, p. 312n25.

CHAPTER 14

1. Quoted in Francis McCullagh, *The Bolshevik Persecution of Christianity* (New York: Dutton, 1924), p. 33.

2. Paul Miliukov, *Outlines of Russian Culture, Part I: Religion and the Church* (Philadelphia: University of Pennsylvania Press, 1943), p. 175; and Jane Swan, *A Biography of Patriarch Tikhon* (Jordanville, NY: Holy Trinity Russian Orthodox Monastery, 1964), p. 71.

3. Quoted in Swan, *Biography*, p. 86.

4. McCullagh, *Bolshevik Persecution*, p. 55.

5. *Hieroconfessor Agathangelus, Metropolitan of Yaroslavl*; and Vladimir Moss,

The Orthodox Church at the Crossroads: From 1900 to the Present Day, p. 26 (my pagination).

6. McCullagh, *Bolshevik Persecution*, p. 43; and Moss, *Orthodox Church*, p. 27 (my pagination).

7. Quoted in William C. Fletcher, *The Russian Orthodox Church Underground, 1917–1970* (London: Oxford University Press, 1971), p. 27; and Moss, *Orthodox Church*, p. 27 (my pagination).

8. "Epistle of the Locum Tenens of the Holy Patriarch of Moscow and of All Russia, Metropolitan of Yaroslavl, Agathangel, to the Priests and All the Children of the Russian Orthodox Church," June 18, 1922, in *The Russian Revolution and Religion: A Collection of Documents concerning the Suppression of Religion by the Communists, 1917–1925*, ed. Boleslav Szczesniak (Notre Dame, IN: University of Notre Dame Press, 1959), document 36.

9. Sergius Troitsky, *The Living Church*, bound inside of *Religion in Soviet Russia*, ed. William Chauncey Emhardt (London: Morehouse, 1929), pp. 328–29.

10. Gregory L. Freeze, "Counter-Reformation in Russian Orthodoxy: Popular Response to Religious Innovation, 1922–1925," *Slavic Review* 54, no. 2 (Summer 1995): 319n55; and Philip Walters, "The Renovationist Coup: Personalities and Programs," in *Church, Nation and State in Russia and Ukraine*, ed. Geoffrey A. Hosking (London: Macmillan, 1991), p. 261.

11. Quoted in Walters, "Renovationist Coup," p. 258.

12. R. O. G. Urch, "Bolshevism and Religion in Russia," *Atlantic Monthly*, March 1923, pp. 402–403.

13. Quoted in Swan, *Biography*, p. 72.

14. Ibid., pp. 72–73.

15. Edward E. Roslof, "The Heresy of 'Bolshevik' Christianity: Orthodox Rejection of Religious Reform during NEP," *Slavic Review* 55, no. 3 (Autumn 1996): 617; and Walters, "Renovationist Coup," p. 262.

16. Louis Fischer, "Soviet Russia's Grim Battle against Religion," *Current History* 18, no. 4 (July 1923): 595–96; Dimitry Pospielovsky, *The Russian Church under the Soviet Regime: 1917–1982*, vol. 1 (Crestwood, NY: St. Vladimir's Seminary Press, 1984), p. 80; Arthur Ruhl, "The Bolshevik Drive on the Church," *Nation* 116, no. 3014 (April 11, 1923): 418; Urch, "Bolshevism," p. 403; and Walters, "Renovationist Coup," p. 262.

17. Ruhl, "Bolshevik Drive," p. 418.

18. Jacob Okunev, *The Change of Landmarks in the Church* (Kharkov, 1923), pp. 20–21 (in Russian), quoted in Troitsky, *Living Church*, p. 353.

19. *Izvestia*, August 28, 1922, in Miliukov, *Outlines*, p. 178; and Urch, "Bolshevism and Religion," p. 404.

20. Freeze, "Counter-Reformation," p. 318n50.

21. Ibid., p. 331.

22. Quoted in Richard J. Cooke, *Religion in Russia under the Soviets* (New York: Abingdon, 1924), p. 189.

23. Quoted in Walters, "Renovationist Coup," p. 264.

24. Matthew Spinka, *Church in Soviet Russia* (New York: Oxford University Press, 1956), pp. 17, 33.

25. Cooke, *Religion*, p. 165; February 27, 1923, meeting of the Antireligious Commission, in Felix Corley, *Religion in the Soviet Union: An Archival Reader* (New York: New York University Press, 1996), document 26; and William B. Stroyen, *Communist Russia and the Russian Orthodox Church, 1943–1962* (Washington, DC: Catholic University of America Press, 1967), p. 21. For a more naive view that "this council [sobor] actually represented the will of Greek Catholicism in Russia," see L. O. Hartman, "The Religious Situation in Russia," *Missionary Review of the World* 46, no. 8 (August 1923): 614–16. Hartman attended the sobor.

26. Cooke, *Religion*, p. 166; and Matthew Spinka, *Church and the Russian Revolution* (New York: Macmillan, 1927), p. 234.

27. Cooke, *Religion*, pp. 166–67; Freeze, "Counter-Reformation," p. 318; and Stroyen, *Communist Russia*, p. 21.

28. Cooke, *Religion*, pp. 167–68; and John Shelton Curtiss, *The Russian Church and the Soviet State, 1917–1950* (Boston: Little, Brown, 1953), p. 155.

29. Cooke, *Religion*, p. 167; and Alexander Solzhenitsyn, *The Gulag Archipelago, 1918–1956*, vol. 1 (New York: Harper and Rowe, 1973), p. 37.

30. Robert Conquest, *Religion in the USSR* (London: Bodley Head, 1968), p. 16; and Cooke, *Religion*, p. 165. Sources give varying figures for total dismissals by this time, ranging from the high sixties to the low eighties. Tikhon claimed eighty bishops had been deposed.

31. Curtiss, *Russian Church*, p. 155; Miliukov, *Outlines*, p. 179; and Spinka, *Church and the Russian Revolution*, p. 234. For a more detailed discussion of how the delegates to the Second Sobor were chosen and who attended, see Spinka, *Church and the Russian Revolution*, pp. 232–36. According to Troitsky, *Living Church*, p. 316n45, *Izvestia* listed only 200 delegates for the Living Church, 116 for Vedensky's Union, and 10 for Antonin's group. Pospielovsky, *Russian Church*, p. 58, says that the Soviet press labeled 66 delegates as "moderate Tikhonites."

32. Tikhon's June 28, 1923, proclamation from the Donskoy Monastery, quoted in Cooke, *Religion*, p. 233.

33. Curtiss, *Russian Church*, p. 156.

34. Freeze, "Counter-Reformation," p. 318n52; and Spinka, *Church and the Russian Revolution*, p. 236.

35. *Acts of the Second All Russian Local Sobor of the Orthodox Church*, May 2, 1923, quoted in Spinka, *Church and the Russian Revolution*, p. 237.

36. Quoted in McCullagh, *Bolshevik Persecution*, pp. 68–69. See Moss, *Orthodox Church*, p. 30 (my pagination), for a slightly different translation and Cooke, *Religion*, p. 185, for a little more of Vedensky's speech.

37. Moss, *Orthodox Church*, p. 30 (my pagination).

38. Quoted in Cooke, *Religion*, p. 189.

39. From an obscure 1920s publication, which can no longer be obtained for citation.

40. *Living Church*, no. 2, quoted in McCullagh, *Bolshevik Persecution*, p. 58.

41. Quoted in Curtiss, *Russian Church*, p. 157; and Spinka, *Church in Soviet Russia*, pp. 36–37.

42. Moss, *Orthodox Church*, p. 31 (my pagination); and Spinka, *Church and the Russian Revolution*, p. 240.

43. McCullagh, *Bolshevik Persecution*, p. 68; and Moss, *Orthodox Church*, p. 31 (my pagination).

44. Cooke, *Religion*, p. 183; Freeze, "Counter-Reformation," p. 313n29; and Troitsky, *Living Church*, p. 318.

45. M. M. Sheinman, *Religion and Church in the USSR* (Moscow: Cooperative Publishing Society of Foreign Workers in the USSR, 1933), p. 28.

46. Spinka, *Church and the Russian Revolution*, p. 247; and Troitsky, *Living Church*, p. 318.

47. McCullagh, *Bolshevik Persecution*, p. 66.

48. Freeze, "Counter-Reformation," p. 311; and McCullagh, *Bolshevik Persecution*, p. 67.

49. McCullagh, *Bolshevik Persecution*, p. 64.

50. Ibid., p. 35; Spinka, *Church and the Russian Revolution*, pp. 246–47; and quoted in Walters, "Renovationist Coup," pp. 258–59.

51. Cooke, *Religion*, p. 193; Curtiss, *Russian Church*, pp. 156, 158; and Spinka, *Church in Soviet Russia*, pp. 36–37.

52. Quoted in Moss, *Orthodox Church*, p. 30 (my pagination). It is possible that this event occurred on May 8, the second-to-last day of the sobor.

53. Fletcher, *Church Underground*, p. 33; and Spinka, *Church and the Russian Revolution*, p. 282.

54. Rene Fueloep-Miller, *The Mind and Face of Bolshevism: An Examination of Cultural Life in Soviet Russia* (New York: Harper and Row, 1965), pp. 250–51.

55. From an obscure 1920s publication, which can no longer be obtained for citation.

56. Quoted in Marcus Bach, *God and the Soviets* (New York: Crowell, 1958), pp. 97–98; and Nicolas de Basily, *Russia under Soviet Rule: Twenty Years of Bolshevik Experiment* (London: Allen and Unwin, 1938), p. 421.

57. Curtiss, *Russian Church*, p. 156; Moss, *Orthodox Church*, p. 30 (my pagination); and Pospielovsky, *Russian Church*, p. 51 n.

58. Ruhl, "Bolshevik Drive," pp. 418–19.

59. Adam B. Ulam, *The Bolsheviks: The Intellectual, Personal and Political History of the Origins of Russian Communism* (New York: Macmillan, 1965), pp. 553, 559.

60. Quoted in Ruhl, "Bolshevik Drive" (correction), p. 495.

61. Curtiss, *Russian Church*, p. 153.

62. Emhardt, *Religion*, pp. 70–72.

63. Quoted in Troitsky, *Living Church*, pp. 364–65.

64. Ibid., p. 309.

65. Pospielovsky, *Russian Church*, pp. 60, 65n56.

66. From an obscure 1920s publication, which can no longer be obtained for citation.

67. Fueloep-Miller, *Face of Bolshevism*, pp. 249–50.

68. Emhardt, *Religion*, pt. 3, chap. 5; and Moss, *Orthodox Church*, p. 31 (my pagination).

69. Miliukov, *Outlines*, pp. 171–72n1.

70. Ibid., p. 171.

CHAPTER 15

1. Matthew Spinka, *Church in Soviet Russia* (New York: Oxford University Press, 1956), p. 31.

2. John Shelton Curtiss, *The Russian Church and the Soviet State, 1917–1950* (Boston: Little, Brown, 1953), p. 159; and Spinka, *Church in Soviet Russia*, p. 38.

3. Curtiss, *Russian Church*, p. 91.

4. William C. Fletcher, *The Russian Orthodox Church Underground, 1917–1970* (London: Oxford University Press, 1971), pp. 33–34.

5. Letter from Chicherin to Stalin (as Central Committee secretary) on April 10, 1923, quoted in Felix Corley, *Religion in the Soviet Union: An Archival Reader* (New York: New York University Press, 1996), document 15.

6. Quoted in Constantin de Grunwald, *The Churches and the Soviet Union* (New York: Macmillan, 1962), p. 53.

7. Summary of the January 30 and February 27, 1923, meetings of the Antireligious Commission, quoted in Corley, *Religion*, document 26.

8. Curtiss, *Russian Church*, p. 159; N. S. Timasheff, *Religion in Soviet Russia, 1917–1942* (London: Religious Book Club, 1943), p. 33; and Philip Walters, "The Renovationist Coup: Personalities and Programs," in *Church, Nation and State in Russia and Ukraine*, ed. Geoffrey A. Hosking (London: Macmillan, 1991), p. 264.

9. Stanley High, "The Triumph of Atheism in Russia," *Atlantic Monthly*, January 1925, p. 127; and Spinka, *Church in Soviet Russia*, p. 31.

10. Vladimir Moss, *The Orthodox Church at the Crossroads: From 1900 to the Present Day*, p. 31 (my pagination).

11. Summary of the June 12, 1923, meeting of the Antireligious Commission, quoted in Corley, *Religion*, document 26; and Gregory L. Freeze, "Counter-Reformation in Russian Orthodoxy: Popular Response to Religious Innovation, 1922–1925," *Slavic Review* 54, no. 2 (Summer 1995): 322n69.

12. Curtiss, *Russian Church*, p. 155.

13. Quoted ibid., pp. 159–60; and Spinka, *Church in Soviet Russia*, p. 38. Each offers a slightly different translation of the same document.

14. Freeze, "Counter-Reformation," p. 323; and "Report of the U.S. Commissioner in Riga Concerning the Situation of the Church in Russia," July 17, 1922, in *The Russian Revolution and Religion: A Collection of Documents concerning the Suppression of Reli-*

gion by the Communists, 1917–1925, ed. Boleslav Szczesniak (Notre Dame, IN: University of Notre Dame Press, 1959), document 40.

15. *Izvestia, no.* 143, summarized in Jane Swan, *A Biography of Patriarch Tikhon* (Jordanville, NY: Holy Trinity Russian Orthodox Monastery, 1964), p. 84n13; and Francis McCullagh, *The Bolshevik Persecution of Christianity* (New York: Dutton, 1924), p. 73.

16. Matthew Spinka, *Church and the Russian Revolution* (New York: Macmillan, 1927), pp. 251–52.

17. Curtiss, *Russian Church*, p. 162.

18. *Manchester Guardian* interview with Tikhon, quoted in Spinka, *Church in Soviet Russia*, p. 38.

19. Quoted in Moss, *Orthodox Church*, p. 32 (my pagination).

20. Swan, *Biography*, pp. 80–81.

21. Quoted in Spinka, *Church and the Russian Revolution*, pp. 253–54. The interview was held on July 15, 1923.

22. Quoted in Richard J. Cooke, *Religion in Russia under the Soviets* (New York: Abingdon, 1924), p. 223.

23. Curtiss, *Russian Church*, p. 162; and Spinka, *Church in Soviet Russia*, p. 39.

24. Quoted in Curtiss, *Russian Church*, p. 163.

25. Quoted in Szczesniak, *Russian Revolution*, document 127.

26. Curtiss, *Russian Church*, p. 163.

27. Quoted in Spinka, *Church and the Russian Revolution*, p. 253.

28. Swan, *Biography*, pp. 89–90 (including n18).

29. Summary of the July 17, 1923, meeting of the Antireligious Commission, quoted in Corley, *Religion*, document 26.

30. Quoted in Spinka, *Church in Soviet Russia*, p. 39.

31. Quoted in Cooke, *Religion*, p. 227.

32. Curtiss, *Russian Church*, p. 165.

33. Quoted in *Hieromartyr Tikhon, Patriarch of Moscow and All Russia*.

34. Summary of the August 14, 1923, meeting of the Antireligious Commission, quoted in Corley, *Religion*, document 26; and Szczesniak, *Russian Revolution*, document 116.

35. Moss, *Orthodox Church*, p. 35 (my pagination).

36. Quoted ibid.

37. Swan, *Biography*, p. 91n20.

38. Freeze, "Counter-Reformation," p. 320.

39. Quoted ibid.

40. Ibid., p. 322; Moss, *Orthodox Church*, p. 36 (my pagination); Edward E. Roslof, "The Heresy of 'Bolshevik' Christianity: Orthodox Rejection of Religious Reform during NEP," *Slavic Review* 55, no. 3 (Autumn 1996): 622; and Swan, *Biography*, p. 91.

41. Quoted in Freeze, "Counter-Reformation," p. 325.

42. Ibid., pp. 324–25.

43. Quoted ibid., p. 321.

44. Ibid., p. 327nn81–82.

45. Curtiss, *Russian Church*, pp. 168–69.

46. Dimitry Pospielovsky, *The Russian Church under the Soviet Regime: 1917–1982*, vol. 1 (Crestwood, NY: St. Vladimir's Seminary Press, 1984), p. 63.

47. Curtiss, *Russian Church*, p. 173; and *Hieromartyr Tikhon*.

48. Quoted in Moss, *Orthodox Church*, p. 37 (my pagination).

49. Ibid.

50. Paul Miliukov, *Outlines of Russian Culture, Part I: Religion and the Church* (Philadelphia: University of Pennsylvania Press, 1943), p. 184; Pospielovsky, *Russian Church*, pp. 81, 83; and Spinka, *Church and the Russian Revolution*, p. 271.

51. Quoted in Curtiss, *Russian Church*, p. 173.

52. Fletcher, *Church Underground*, p. 38; and Moss, *Orthodox Church*, p. 33 (my pagination).

53. Curtiss, *Russian Church*, pp. 165–66.

54. Krasnitsky's "repentance" is discussed ibid., pp. 169–71.

55. Quoted in Sergius Troitsky, *The Living Church*, bound inside of *Religion in Soviet Russia*, ed. William Chauncey Emhardt (London: Morehouse, 1929), p. 320.

56. Quoted in Spinka, *Church and the Russian Revolution*, p. 281.

57. Curtiss, *Russian Church*, pp. 169–70; and Walters, "Renovationist Coup," p. 266.

58. Summary of the December 12, 1923, meeting of the Antireligious Commission, quoted in Corley, *Religion*, document 26; and Swan, *Biography*, pp. 91–92, 96.

59. Summary of the July 2, 1924, meeting of the Antireligious Commission, quoted in Corley, *Religion*, document 26.

60. Quoted in *Hieromartyr Tikhon*.

61. Spinka, *Church and the Russian Revolution*, p. 284.

62. Emhardt, *Religion*, p. 15.

63. Swan, *Biography*, pp. 93–94; and *Tikhon, Saint, Enlightener of America and Patriarch of Moscow*, p. 7 (my pagination).

64. Swan, *Biography*, pp. 95–96.

65. Quoted in *Hieromartyr Tikhon*; and Moss, *Orthodox Church*, p. 40 (my pagination).

66. Swan, *Biography*, pp. 25, 98.

67. Peter Kenez, *The Birth of the Propaganda State: Soviet Methods of Mass Mobilization, 1917–1929* (New York: Cambridge University Press, 1985), p. 68; Spinka, *Church in Soviet Russia*, p. 42; and Swan, *Biography*, p. 99.

68. *Tikhon, Saint, Enlightener*, p. 8 (my pagination).

69. Pospielovsky, *Russian Church*, pp. 123–24.

70. All quotations from Tikhon's will are taken from either Pospielovsky, *Russian Church*, pp. 123–24; or Spinka, *Church in Soviet Russia*, pp. 43–45. The complete text was published in *Izvestia* on April 15, 1925, and can be found in Swan, *Biography*, pp. 101–105.

71. Pospielovsky, *Russian Church*, pp. 63n52, 122, 124; and Spinka, *Church in Soviet Russia*, p. 43.

72. *Hieromartyr Tikhon*.

73. Most of these points concerning the fraudulent nature of the will were unearthed by Ivan Andreyev in *A Short History of the Russian Church from the Revolution to Our Time*, discussed in Swan, *Biography*, pp. 105–108.

74. Quoted in Miliukov, *Outlines*, p. 188.

75. Fletcher, *Church Underground*, p. 45.

76. Quoted in Roslof, "Heresy," p. 617.

77. *Hieromartyr Peter, Metropolitan of Krutitsa*; and Troitsky, *Living Church*, p. 324.

78. Miliukov, *Outlines*, p. 189 (Miliukov mistakenly gives the year as 1926); and Troitsky, *Living Church*, p. 327.

79. Quoted in Miliukov, *Outlines*, p. 190.

80. Troitsky, *Living Church*, p. 323.

81. Pospielovsky, *Russian Church*, pp. 124–25.

CHAPTER 16

1. Quoted in Ivan Tregubov, "Church Revolution in Soviet Russia," *Living Age*, September 2, 1922, p. 586.

2. John Shelton Curtiss, *The Russian Church and the Soviet State, 1917–1950* (Boston: Little, Brown, 1953), p. 144; Paul Miliukov, *Outlines of Russian Culture, Part I: Religion and the Church* (Philadelphia: University of Pennsylvania Press, 1943), p. 181; B. Titlinov, *Novaya Tserkov* (Petrograd-Moscow, 1923), p. 51, quoted in Edward E. Roslof, "The Heresy of 'Bolshevik' Christianity: Orthodox Rejection of Religious Reform During NEP," *Slavic Review* 55, no. 3 (Autumn 1996): 618; and Sergius Troitsky, *The Living Church*, bound inside of *Religion in Soviet Russia*, ed. William Chauncey Emhardt (London: Morehouse, 1929), pp. 318–19.

3. K. Rychkov, "Pod Svezhim Vpechatleniem," *Tserkovnaya Zaria*, Vologda, no. 1, September 15, 1922, pp. 10–11, quoted in Gregory L. Freeze, "Counter-Reformation in Russian Orthodoxy: Popular Response to Religious Innovation, 1922–1925," *Slavic Review* 54, no. 2 (Summer 1995): 315.

4. Quoted in Freeze, "Counter-Reformation," p. 306n5.

5. Constantin de Grunwald, *The Churches and the Soviet Union* (New York: Macmillan, 1962), pp. 50–51; and Freeze, "Counter-Reformation," p. 306n5.

6. Quoted in Freeze, "Counter-Reformation," p. 326.

7. Ibid., p. 306.

8. Ibid., pp. 313–14.

9. Ibid., p. 322.

10. Ibid., pp. 322–23.

11. Troitsky, *Living Church*, p. 302.

12. Quoted in Dimitry Pospielovsky, *The Russian Church under the Soviet Regime: 1917–1982*, vol. 1 (Crestwood, NY: St. Vladimir's Seminary Press, 1984), p. 62.

13. Daniel Peris, *Storming the Heavens: The Soviet League of the Militant Godless* (Ithaca, NY: Cornell University Press, 1998), p. 27.

14. William C. Fletcher, *The Russian Orthodox Church Underground, 1917–1970* (London: Oxford University Press, 1971), p. 35; and Freeze, "Counter-Reformation," p. 337.

15. Curtiss, *Russian Church*, p. 168; Fletcher, *Church Underground*, p. 36; and Roslof, "Heresy," p. 618.

16. William Henry Chamberlin, "The Struggle for the Russian Soul: A Phase of Soviet Russia," *Atlantic Monthly*, September 1929, p. 397; and Roslof, "Heresy," p. 632.

17. Quoted in Freeze, "Counter-Reformation," p. 317.

18. Quoted in Fletcher, *Church Underground*, p. 36.

19. Pospielovsky, *Russian Church*, pp. 37–38.

20. Freeze, "Counter-Reformation," p. 319.

21. Quoted in Roslof, "Heresy," p. 624.

22. Pospielovsky, *Russian Church*, p. 79; and Roslof, "Heresy," p. 631n57.

23. Quoted in Robert Pierce Casey, *Religion in Russia* (New York: Harper, 1946), p. 109.

24. Quoted in Pospielovsky, *Russian Church*, p. 84.

25. William B. Husband, *Godless Communists: Atheism and Society in Soviet Russia, 1917–1932* (DeKalb: Northern Illinois University Press, 2000), p. 58; and Roslof, "Heresy," p. 626.

26. Curtiss, *Russian Church*, p. 167; Freeze, "Counter-Reformation," pp. 314–15n36; and N. S. Timasheff, *Religion in Soviet Russia, 1917–1942* (London: Religious Book Club, 1943), pp. 32–33.

27. Freeze, "Counter-Reformation," p. 318.

28. Anne Applebaum, *Gulag: A History* (New York: Doubleday, 2003), pp. 18–22.

29. Ibid., pp. 27–28.

30. *To the Government of the USSR—Appeal of Orthodox Bishops from the Solovetsky Islands (1926)*, p. 1. Complete text.

31. Quoted in Miliukov, *Outlines*, p. 194.

32. Pospielovsky, *Russian Church*, p. 143.

33. Ibid., p. 146.

34. *To the Government of the USSR*, p. 1. See also Vladimir Moss, *The Orthodox Church at the Crossroads: From 1900 to the Present Day*, pp. 49–51 (my pagination); and Pospielovsky, *Russian Church*, pp. 144–45.

35. *To the Government of the USSR*, p. 3 (my pagination).

36. Quoted in Moss, *Orthodox Church*, pp. 50–51 (my pagination).

37. Matthew Spinka, *Church in Soviet Russia* (New York: Oxford University Press, 1956), p. 41; and Jane Swan, *A Biography of Patriarch Tikhon* (Jordanville, NY: Holy Trinity Russian Orthodox Monastery, 1964), p. 71.

38. Julius F. Hecker, *Religion and Communism: A Study of Religion and Atheism in Soviet Russia* (Westport, CT: Hyperion, 1934), p. 202n1.

39. Quoted in *Hieromartyr Peter, Metropolitan of Krutitsa*.

40. Ibid.; and Moss, *Orthodox Church*, p. 40 (my pagination). For more detail on Peter's early life and rise to prominence, see Spinka, *Church in Soviet Russia*, pp. 58–59.

41. Stanley High, "The Triumph of Atheism in Russia," *Atlantic Monthly*, January 1925, p. 129; and Moss, *Orthodox Church*, p. 41 (my pagination).

42. Quoted in Pospielovsky, *Russian Church*, p. 70.

43. *Hieromartyr Peter*, p. 3; and Spinka, *Church in Soviet Russia*, p. 58. For more details on the fabrication of this "plot," see Pospielovsky, *Russian Church*, pp. 65–66.

44. Quoted in *Hieromartyr Peter*, p. 4; and Moss, *Orthodox Church*, pp. 42–43 (my pagination).

45. Quoted in *Hieromartyr Peter*.

46. Spinka, *Church in Soviet Russia*, p. 59.

47. *Hieromartyr Peter*.

48. Quoted in Moss, *Orthodox Church*, pp. 44–45, 52 (my pagination).

49. Bohdan Bociurkiw, "Lenin and Religion," in *Lenin: The Man, the Theorist, the Leader—A Reappraisal*, ed. Leonard Schapiro and Peter Reddaway (New York: Praeger, 1967), p. 116n2; and Nicolas Zernov, *The Russians and Their Church* (Crestwood, NY: St. Vladimir's Seminary Press, 1994), p. 148.

50. Curtiss, *Russian Church*, p. 168; Moss, *Orthodox Church*, p. 7 (my pagination); Spinka, *Church in Soviet Russia*, pp. 55, 57; and Timothy Ware, *The Orthodox Church* (Baltimore, MD: Penguin, 1963), p. 161.

51. Moss, *Orthodox Church*, p. 51 (my pagination); Paul D. Steeves, *Keeping the Faiths: Religion and Ideology in the Soviet Union* (New York: Holmes and Meier, 1989), pp. 74–75; and Ware, *Orthodox Church*, p. 162.

52. Quoted in Moss, *Orthodox Church*, pp. 43–44 (my pagination).

53. Fletcher, *Church Underground*, p. 46; *Hieromartyr Peter*; and Pospielovsky, *Russian Church*, p. 66.

54. *Hieromartyr Peter*.

55. Quoted in Pospielovsky, *Russian Church*, p. 71n73.

56. Ibid., pp. 67, 71.

57. Fletcher, *Church Underground*, pp. 47–49; Moss, *Orthodox Church*, p. 46 (my pagination); and Pospielovsky, *Russian Church*, p. 72.

58. Pospielovsky, *Russian Church*, p. 150.

59. *Hieroconfessor Agathangel, Metropolitan of Yaroslavl*; Moss, *Orthodox Church*, p. 48 (my pagination); and Spinka, *Church in Soviet Russia*, pp. 60–61.

60. Quoted in Spinka, *Church in Soviet Russia*, p. 62.

61. Ibid., pp. 157–60.

62. Ibid., pp. 64–65.

63. Steeves, *Keeping the Faiths*, p. 37.

64. Quoted in *A Letter of Bishop Victor, and Others*.

65. Quoted in Freeze, "Counter-Reformation," p. 334n119.

66. Moss, *Orthodox Church*, p. 54 (my pagination); and Pospielovsky, *Russian Church*, p. 139.

67. For quotations from Sergei's Declaration, see Moss, *Orthodox Church*, pp. 55–56 (my pagination); Spinka, *Church in Soviet Russia*, pp. 66–67; and Ware, *Orthodox Church*, p. 162.

68. Mikhail V. Shkarovsky, "The Russian Orthodox Church vs. the State: The Josephite Movement, 1927–1940," *Slavic Review* 54, no. 2 (Summer 1995): 365, 368.

69. Roslof, "Heresy," p. 625; and Ware, *Orthodox Church*, p. 162.

70. Quoted in Miliukov, *Outlines*, p. 197.

71. Spinka, *Church in Soviet Russia*, pp. 68–69.

72. Ibid., pp. 51, 65; Ware, *Orthodox Church*, p. 162; and Zernov, *Russians*, pp. 160–61.

73. Ivan M. Andreyev, *Is the Grace of God Present in the Soviet Church?* (Wildwood, Alberta, Canada: Monastery, 2000), p. 34; Shkarovsky, "Orthodox Church," p. 368; and Spinka, *Church in Soviet Russia*, p. 68.

74. Miliukov, *Outlines*, p. 195: Spinka, *Church in Soviet Russia*, p. 70; and William B. Stroyen, *Communist Russia and the Russian Orthodox Church, 1943–1962* (Washington, DC: Catholic University of America Press, 1967), p. 24.

75. Andreyev, *Grace of God*, p. 45; Ethel Dunn,and Stephen P. Dunn, "Religion as an Instrument of Cultural Change: The Problem of the Sects in the Soviet Union," *Slavic Review* 23, no. 3 (September 1964): 466–67; and Pospielovsky, *Russian Church*, p. 159.

76. Fletcher, *Church Underground*, p. 59n66; Moss, *Orthodox Church*, p. 57 (my pagination); Pospielovsky, *Russian Church*, p. 155; and Spinka, *Church in Soviet Russia*, p. 70.

77. Protodeacon Christopher Birchall, in his introduction to Andreyev, *Grace of God*, p. 14; Fletcher, *Church Underground*, p. 60; Pospielovsky, *Russian Church*, p. 156; and Roslof, "Heresy," p. 632.

78. Quoted in Spinka, *Church in Soviet Russia*, pp. 70–71; and Ware, *Orthodox Church*, p. 163.

79. *Compassionate Love—Metropolitan Anthony Khrapovitsky; A Historical Survey of the Parish of St. John the Baptist*; and Ware, *Orthodox Church*, p. 163.

80. Paul B. Anderson, *People, Church and State in Modern Russia* (London: Student Christian Movement, 1944), pp. 70–72; and *Written Address of the Bishops in Solovky to Metropolitan Sergei*.

81. Quoted in Andreyev, *Grace of God*, p. 26; and Moss, *Orthodox Church*, p. 59 (my pagination).

82. Philaret (Metropolitan), *A Letter from Metropolitan Philaret to Father Victor Potapov of the Church Abroad Concerning Father Dimitry Dudko and the Moscow Patriarchate*, p. 3 (my pagination).

83. *A Letter of Bishop Victor.*

84. Ibid.; and Moss, *Orthodox Church*, p. 59 (my pagination).

85. Fletcher, *Church Underground*, pp. 58–59, 61.

86. Confirmed by Agathangel's niece, A. V. Preobrazhenskaya. Much of this material on Agathangel is based on *Hieroconfessor Agathangel*.

87. Quoted in Fletcher, *Church Underground*, p. 62.

88. Quoted in *Hieromartyr Peter*.

89. Ibid.

90. Quoted in Ware, *Orthodox Church*, p. 165.

91. Quoted in Nathaniel Davis, *A Long Walk to Church: A Contemporary History of Russian Orthodoxy* (San Francisco: Westview, 1995), p. xvi.

92. Ware, *Orthodox Church*, pp. 164–65 (footnote).

CHAPTER 17

1. Zvi Gitelman, "The Communist Party and Soviet Jewry: The Early Years," in *Aspects of Religion in the Soviet Union: 1917–1967*, ed. Richard H. Marshall Jr. (Chicago: University of Chicago Press, 1971), p. 337; and Joshua Rothenberg, "The Legal Status of Religion in the Soviet Union," in Marshall, *Aspects of Religion*, p. 71.

2. From an obscure 1920s publication, which can no longer be obtained for citation.

3. Monsignor M. D'Herbigny, *Militant Atheism: The Worldwide Propaganda of Communism* (London: Society for Promoting Christian Knowledge, 1933), p. 12.

4. *Komsomolskaya Pravda*, May 15, 1928, quoted in *Religion in Soviet Russia*, ed. William Chauncey Emhardt (London: Morehouse, 1929), p. 35; and Isabel A. Tirado, "The Revolution, Young Peasants, and the Komsomol's Antireligious Campaigns: 1920–1928," *Canadian-American Slavic Studies* 26, nos. 1–3 (1992): 101, 108.

5. Maurice Hindus, *Humanity Uprooted* (New York: J. Cape and H. Smith, 1929), pp. 40, 45.

6. Tirado, "Revolution," p. 98.

7. Quoted in William Henry Chamberlin, "Russian Crusade against Belief in God," *Current History* 25, no. 1 (October 1926): 29.

8. Daniel Peris, *Storming the Heavens: The Soviet League of the Militant Godless* (Ithaca, NY: Cornell University Press, 1998), pp. 39–40; and Tirado, "Revolution," pp. 97–98.

9. Quoted in Peris, *Storming the Heavens*, p. 39.

10. Hindus, *Humanity Uprooted*, p. 13; and Tirado, "Revolution," pp. 100–101.

11. Communist Party Central Committee, "On Antireligious Agitation and Propaganda among Women Workers and Peasants," in William G. Rosenberg, *Bolshevik Visions: First Phase of the Cultural Revolution in Soviet Russia, Part I: The Culture of a New Society—Ethics, Gender, the Family, Law and Problems of Tradition* (Ann Arbor: University of Michigan Press, 1990), p. 244.

12. Peter Kenez, *The Birth of the Propaganda State: Soviet Methods of Mass Mobilization, 1917–1929* (New York: Cambridge University Press, 1985), pp. 183–84.

13. *Krasnaya Gazeta*, no. 124, May 1928, quoted in Emhardt, *Religion*, p. 36; and Tirado, "Revolution," p. 115.

14. Quoted in Emhardt, *Religion*, p. 269.

15. Dimitry Pospielovsky, *A History of Marxist-Leninist Atheism and Soviet Antireligious Policies* (London: Macmillan, 1987), p. 46.

16. Walter Kolarz, *Religion in the Soviet Union* (New York: St. Martin's, 1961), pp. 8–10; David E. Powell, *Antireligious Propaganda in the Soviet Union: A Study of Mass*

Persuasion (Cambridge, MA: MIT Press, 1975), p. 35; Tirado, "Revolution," p. 110; and J. Zatko, *Descent into Darkness: The Destruction of the Roman Catholic Church in Russia, 1917–1923* (Notre Dame, IN: University of Notre Dame Press, 1965), p. 119.

17. Chamberlin, "Russian Crusade," p. 29; Julius F. Hecker, *Religion and Communism: A Study of Religion and Atheism in Soviet Russia* (Westport, CT: Hyperion, 1934), p. 222; Peris, *Storming the Heavens*, p. 45; Powell, *Antireligious Propaganda*, p. 35; and Richard Stites, *Revolutionary Dreams: Utopian Vision and Experimental Life in the Russian Revolution* (New York: Oxford University Press, 1989), p. 106.

18. Kolarz, *Religion*, pp. 7–8.

19. Chamberlin, "Russian Crusade," p. 29.

20. William Henry Chamberlin, "The Struggle for the Russian Soul: A Phase of Soviet Russia," *Atlantic Monthly*, September 1929, p. 395; Hecker, *Religion and Communism*, p. 219; Kolarz, *Religion*, pp. 6–7; and Stites, *Revolutionary Dreams*, p. 106. The figure of 123,000 for 1928 is from "There Are Many Godless But There Are No Workers on the Antireligious Front," *Pravda*, April 13, 1928.

21. Fyodor Oleshchuk, *Revolution and Culture*, nos. 3 and 4, 1928, quoted in Emhardt, *Religion*, pp. 37–38; Paul Miliukov, *Outlines of Russian Culture, Part I: Religion and the Church* (Philadelphia: University of Pennsylvania Press, 1943), p. 202; Daniel Peris, "The 1929 Congress of the Godless," *Soviet Studies* 43, no. 4 (1991): 713; and Powell, *Antireligious Propaganda*, pp. 37–38.

22. Quoted in Leon Trotsky, *My Life* (New York: Pathfinder, 1970), p. 476.

23. Peris, *Storming the Heavens*, p. 51; and Lewis H. Siegelbaum, *Soviet State and Society between Revolutions: 1918–1929* (New York: Cambridge University Press, 1992), p. 161.

24. Joan Delaney, "The Origins of Soviet Antireligious Organizations," in Marshall, *Aspects of Religion*, p. 121; and Stites, *Revolutionary Dreams*, p. 106.

25. Delaney, "The Origins," pp. 109, 122–23, 126–27.

26. Zeth Höglund, "Communism and Religion," pp. 236–38, and Emelyan Yaroslavsky, "Is the Communist Movement Antireligious? (An Answer to Höglund)," pp. 239–43, both in Rosenberg, *Bolshevik Visions*.

27. Delaney, "The Origins," pp. 117–19; and Daniel Peris, "Commissars in Red Cassocks: Former Priests in the League of the Militant Godless," *Slavic Review* 54, no. 2 (Summer 1995): 353–54.

28. Pospielovsky, *History*, p. 51; and Stites, *Revolutionary Dreams*, p. 106.

29. Robert Pierce Casey, *Religion in Russia* (New York: Harper, 1946), p. 81; and Delaney, "The Origins," pp. 115, 117–20.

30. Peris, *Storming the Heavens*, p. 53.

31. Chamberlin, "Russian Crusade," p. 32; and "Religious Conditions in Russia," p. 451.

32. Delaney, "The Origins," p. 104; and Peris, "Commissars," p. 358.

33. Pospielovsky, *History*, p. 52.

34. Philip Walters, "The Renovationist Coup: Personalities and Programs," in *Church, Nation and State in Russia and Ukraine*, ed. Geoffrey A. Hosking (London: Macmillan, 1991), p. 266.

35. Tirado, "Revolution," p. 116.

36. Emhardt, *Religion*, p. 269.

37. Tirado, "Revolution," p. 116.

38. William B. Husband, *Godless Communists: Atheism and Society in Soviet Russia, 1917–1932* (DeKalb: Northern Illinois University Press, 2000), p. 66.

39. Rothenberg, "Legal Status," pp. 72–73.

40. Alexander A. Bogolepov, "The Legal Position of the Russian Orthodox Church in the Soviet Union," in Marshall, *Aspects of Religion*, p. 196; Edgar S. Furniss, "Religion in the Soviet Union: I—The History of the Conflict," *Current History* 32, no. 1 (April 1930): 29; and Dimitry Pospielovsky, *The Russian Church under the Soviet Regime: 1917–1982*, vol. 1 (Crestwood, NY: St. Vladimir's Seminary Press, 1984), p. 148.

41. Pospielovsky, *Russian Church*, p. 149; Rothenberg, "Legal Status," pp. 76, 79; Richard Stites, "Bolshevik Ritual Building in the 1920s," in *Russia in the Era of NEP: Explorations in Soviet Society and Culture*, ed. Sheila Fitzpatrick (Bloomington: Indiana University Press, 1991), p. 306; and Nicolas Zernov, *The Russians and Their Church* (Crestwood, NY: St. Vladimir's Seminary Press, 1994), p. 161.

42. Powell, *Antireligious Propaganda*, p. 30; Rothenberg, "Legal Status," p. 82; and Zernov, *Russians*, p. 161.

43. Wladyslav Kania, *Bolshevism and Religion* (New York: Polish Library, 1946), p. 13.

44. Quoted in Bogolepov, "Legal Position," pp. 199–200; and Zernov, *Russians*, p. 160.

45. Bogolepov, "Legal Position," p. 200; and Matthew Spinka, *Church in Soviet Russia* (New York: Oxford University Press, 1956), p. 74.

46. Quoted in Bogolepov, "Legal Position," p. 200.

47. *Pravda*, June 11, 1929, retold by Kolarz, *Religion*, p. 9.

48. Delaney, "The Origins," pp. 116–17; and N. S. Timasheff, *Religion in Soviet Russia, 1917–1942* (London: Religious Book Club, 1943), pp. 42–43.

49. Helmut Altrichter, "Insoluble Conflicts: Village Life between Revolution and Collectivization," in Fitzpatrick, *Russia in the Era of NEP*, p. 205.

50. Husband, *Godless Communists*, p. 67; and Peris, "1929 Congress," p. 721.

51. Quoted in Mikhail V. Shkarovsky, "The Russian Orthodox Church vs. the State: The Josephite Movement, 1927–1940," *Slavic Review* 54, no. 2 (Summer 1995): 377.

52. Pospielovsky, *Russian Church*, p. 150.

53. Ibid., p. 153.

54. Ibid., pp. 152–53.

55. Quoted in Shkarovsky, "Orthodox Church," p. 376.

56. William C. Fletcher, *The Russian Orthodox Church Underground, 1917–1970* (London: Oxford University Press, 1971), p. 68; L. N. Mitrokhin, "Education in Atheism and Methodology of Studying the Survival of Religious Beliefs," *Soviet Sociology* 1, no. 1 (Summer 1962): 28; and Pospielovsky, *Russian Church*, p. 158.

57. Fletcher, *Church Underground*, p. 68; and Shkarovsky, "Orthodox Church," p. 368.

58. Quoted in *Metropolitan Joseph of Petrograd and the Beginning of the Catacomb Church*, p. 6.

59. Vladimir Moss, *The Orthodox Church at the Crossroads: From 1900 to the Present Day*, 58, pp. 60–61 (my pagination).

60. Ivan M. Andreyev, *Is the Grace of God Present in the Soviet Church?* (Wildwood, Alberta, Canada: Monastery, 2000), pp. 64, 66, 68; Shkarovsky, "Orthodox Church," pp. 365–67, 378; and Spinka, *Church in Soviet Russia*, pp. 74–75.

61. Pospielovsky, *Russian Church*, p. 156.

62. Moss, *Orthodox Church*, p. 39 (my pagination).

63. Shkarovsky, "Orthodox Church," p. 377.

64. *Orthodox Life*, no. 4 (1959) : 30–31, quoted in Timothy Ware, *The Orthodox Church* (Baltimore: Penguin, 1963), p. 19.

65. Andreyev, *Grace of God*, pp. 24–26.

66. Lynne Viola, "The Peasant Nightmare: Visions of Apocalypse in the Soviet Countryside," *Journal of Modern History* 62, no. 4 (December 1990): 759–63.

67. Andreyev, *Grace of God*, p. 46; and Moss, *Orthodox Church*, p. 66 (my pagination).

CHAPTER 18

1. "Bolshevism out to Abolish God," *Literary Digest*, January 17, 1920, p. 36.

2. Nikolai Bukharin and E. Preobrazhensky, *The ABC of Communism—A Popular Explanation of the Program of the Communist Party of Russia* (Ann Arbor: University of Michigan Press, 1966), p. 253.

3. R. O. G. Urch, "Bolshevism and Religion in Russia," *Atlantic Monthly*, March 1923, p. 398.

4. Gregory L. Freeze, "Counter-Reformation in Russian Orthodoxy: Popular Response to Religious Innovation, 1922–1925," *Slavic Review* 54, no. 2 (Summer 1995): 335n121; and George L. Kline, *Religious and Antireligious Thought in Russia* (Chicago: University of Chicago Press, 1968), p. 150.

5. Quoted in Donald A. Lowrie, *The Light of Russia: An Introduction to the Russian Church* (Prague: YMCA Press, 1923), pp. 220–21.

6. From an article by Richard Washburn Child in the *Saturday Evening Post*, summarized in "Religion and Anti-Religion in Russia: Observations by Recent Visitors," *Missionary Review of the World*, May 1925, p. 372.

7. Philip S. Bernstein, "Religion in Russia," *Harpers' Magazine*, May 1930, p. 735; William Henry Chamberlin, "The Struggle for the Russian Soul: A Phase of Soviet Russia," *Atlantic Monthly*, September 1929, p. 396; Dimitry Pospielovsky, *The Russian Church under the Soviet Regime: 1917–1982*, vol. 1 (Crestwood, NY: St. Vladimir's Seminary Press, 1984), p. 32; and Timothy Ware, *The Orthodox Church* (Baltimore: Penguin, 1963), p. 154.

8. Quoted in Felix Corley, *Religion in the Soviet Union: An Archival Reader* (New York: New York University Press, 1996), p. 14; N. S. Timasheff, *Religion in Soviet Russia, 1917–1942* (London: Religious Book Club, 1943), 37; and J. Zatko, *Descent into*

Darkness: The Destruction of the Roman Catholic Church in Russia, 1917–1923 (Notre Dame, IN: University of Notre Dame Press, 1965), p. 116.

9. Daniel Peris, *Storming the Heavens: The Soviet League of the Militant Godless* (Ithaca, NY: Cornell University Press, 1998), pp. 38–39.

10. Jerome Davis, "*Religion in Soviet Russia,*" *Missionary Review of the World*, March 1922, p. 191.

11. Francis McCullagh, *The Bolshevik Persecution of Christianity* (New York: Dutton, 1924), pp. 85–86; Prince Eugene Trubetzkoy, "The Bolshevist Utopia and the Religious Movement in Russia," *Hibbert Journal*, January 1920, p. 216; and Urch, "Bolshevism and Religion," p. 405.

12. Lynne Viola, "The Peasant Nightmare: Visions of Apocalypse in the Soviet Countryside," *Journal of Modern History* 62, no. 4 (December 1990): 756.

13. Quoted in Wladyslav Kania, *Bolshevism and Religion* (New York: Polish Library, 1946), pp. 41–42.

14. Quoted in Constantin de Grunwald, *The Churches and the Soviet Union* (New York: Macmillan, 1962), pp. 41–42.

15. Quoted in Kania, *Bolshevism and Religion*, p. 20.

16. Peter Kenez, *The Birth of the Propaganda State: Soviet Methods of Mass Mobilization, 1917–1929* (New York: Cambridge University Press, 1985), p. 68.

17. See Krylenko's closing statement in the Cieplak (Catholic) Trial in McCullagh, *Bolshevik Persecution of Christianity*, pp. 222–32.

18. Ivan Skvortsov-Stepanov, "Summary of the Argument in the Living Church," quoted in William Chauncey Emhardt, ed., *Religion in Soviet Russia* (London: Morehouse, 1929), p. 70.

19. Joshua Rothenberg, "The Legal Status of Religion in the Soviet Union," in *Aspects of Religion in the Soviet Union: 1917–1967*, ed. Richard H. Marshall Jr. (Chicago: University of Chicago Press, 1971), p. 70.

20. Ibid.

21. Quoted in Joan Delaney, "The Origins of Soviet Antireligious Organizations," in Marshall, *Aspects of Religion*, p. 110; and William B. Husband, *Godless Communists: Atheism and Society in Soviet Russia, 1917–1932* (DeKalb: Northern Illinois University Press, 2000), p. 59.

22. From an obscure 1920s publication, which can no longer be obtained for citation.

23. Quoted in "Failure of Religion in Russia," *Literary Digest*, June 14, 1919, p. 32.

24. Isabel A. Tirado, "The Revolution, Young Peasants, and the Komsomol's Antireligious Campaigns: 1920–1928," *Canadian-American Slavic Studies* 26, nos. 1–3 (1992): 109.

25. Quoted in Husband, *Godless Communists*, p. 60.

26. Husband, *Godless Communists*, pp. 87–88.

27. Quoted in "Religion and Anti-Religion in Russia," p. 373.

28. Robert Conquest, *Religion in the USSR* (London: Bodley Head, 1968), p. 9.

29. Roger Pethybridge, *The Social Prelude to Stalinism* (London: Macmillan, 1974), p. 156.

30. Peris, *Storming the Heavens*, p. 37.

31. Richard Stites, *Revolutionary Dreams: Utopian Vision and Experimental Life in the Russian Revolution* (New York: Oxford University Press, 1989), p. 107.

32. Glennys Young, *Power and the Sacred in Revolutionary Russia: Religious Activists in the Village* (University Park: University of Pennsylvania Press, 1997), p. 96.

33. Delaney, "The Origins," p. 105; and Dimitry Pospielovsky, *A History of Marxist-Leninist Atheism and Soviet Antireligious Policies* (London: Macmillan, 1987), p. 39.

34. Quoted in Lewis H. Siegelbaum, *Soviet State and Society between Revolutions: 1918–1929* (New York: Cambridge University Press, 1992), p. 163.

35. Young, *Power*, pp. 95–97.

36. Ivan Skvortsov-Stepanov, *The Problems and Methods of Antireligious Propaganda*.

37. Lowrie, *Light of Russia*, p. 226.

38. Husband, *Godless Communists*, p. 50; Hindus's story is summarized in Stites, *Revolutionary Dreams*, p. 107; and Young, *Power*, p. 99.

39. Lowrie, *Light of Russia*, p. 230.

40. Quoted in Pospielovsky, *History*, p. 40.

41. Quoted in Peris, *Storming the Heavens*, p. 32.

42. Young, *Power*, p. 99.

CHAPTER 19

1. Stalin, *Problems of Leninism*, p. 192, quoted in Wladyslav Kania, *Bolshevism and Religion* (New York: Polish Library, 1946), p. 16.

2. Quoted in William Henry Chamberlin, "The Struggle for the Russian Soul: A Phase of Soviet Russia," *Atlantic Monthly*, September 1929, p. 394.

3. Peter Reddaway, "Literature, the Arts and the Personality of Lenin," in *Lenin: The Man, the Theorist, the Leader—A Reappraisal*, ed. Leonard Schapiro and Peter Reddaway (New York: Praeger, 1967), p. 55; and James Thrower, *Marxist-Leninist "Scientific Atheism" and the Study of Religion and Atheism in the USSR* (New York: Mouton, 1983), p. 102.

4. William Henry Chamberlin, "Russian Crusade against Belief in God," *Current History* 25, no. 1 (October 1926): 31; Albert Galter, *The Red Book of the Persecuted Church* (Dublin, Ireland: M. H. Gill and Son, 1957), p. 33; Maurice Hindus, *Humanity Uprooted* (New York: J. Cape and H. Smith, 1929), pp. 44–45; William B. Husband, *Godless Communists: Atheism and Society in Soviet Russia, 1917–1932* (DeKalb: Northern Illinois University Press, 2000), p. 134; and Richard Stites, *Revolutionary Dreams: Utopian Vision and Experimental Life in the Russian Revolution* (New York: Oxford University Press, 1989), p. 107.

5. Robert Pierce Casey, *Religion in Russia* (New York: Harper, 1946), pp. 101–103.

6. Julius F. Hecker, *Religion and Communism: A Study of Religion and Atheism in Soviet Russia* (Westport, CT: Hyperion, 1934), p. 264.

7. Leon Trotsky, "Vodka, the Church and the Cinema," *Pravda*, July 12, 1923, in William G. Rosenberg, *Bolshevik Visions: First Phase of the Cultural Revolution in Soviet Russia*, part 2 (Ann Arbor: University of Michigan Press, 1990), p. 109.

8. Chamberlin, "Russian Soul," p. 31; Joan Delaney, "The Origins of Soviet Antireligious Organizations," in *Aspects of Religion in the Soviet Union: 1917–1967*, ed. Richard H. Marshall Jr. (Chicago: University of Chicago Press, 1971), p. 127; Hecker, *Religion and Communism*, p. 265; and David E. Powell, *Antireligious Propaganda in the Soviet Union: A Study of Mass Persuasion* (Cambridge, MA: MIT Press, 1975), p. 36.

9. Chamberlin, "Russian Soul," p. 389; Hecker, *Religion and Communism*, p. 247; Hindus, *Humanity Uprooted*, p. 43; Lewis H. Siegelbaum, *Soviet State and Society between Revolutions: 1918–1929* (New York: Cambridge University Press, 1992), p. 162; and Lynne Viola, "The Peasant Nightmare: Visions of Apocalypse in the Soviet Countryside," *Journal of Modern History* 62, no. 4 (December 1990): 753.

10. A. J. Mackenzie, *Propaganda Boom* (London: Right Book Club, 1938), p. 98, cited in Powell, *Antireligious Propaganda*, p. 37.

11. "The Attack of the Church Members (The Condition of Contemporary Church Literature in the USSR)," *Bezbozhnik*, May 6, 1928, quoted in *Religion in Soviet Russia*, ed. William Chauncey Emhardt (London: Morehouse, 1929), p. 284.

12. Hecker, *Religion and Communism*, p. 268.

13. Hindus, *Humanity Uprooted*, p. 41.

14. Quotation compiled from both Anne O'Hare McCormick, *The Hammer and the Scythe: Communist Russia Enters the Second Decade* (New York: Knopf, 1928), p. 209; and Paul D. Steeves, *Keeping the Faiths: Religion and Ideology in the Soviet Union* (New York: Holmes and Meier, 1989), p. 65.

15. Quoted in Daniel Peris, *Storming the Heavens: The Soviet League of the Militant Godless* (Ithaca, NY: Cornell University Press, 1998), p. 23.

16. Quoted in Francis McCullagh, *The Bolshevik Persecution of Christianity* (New York: Dutton, 1924), p. 376.

17. Husband, *Godless Communists*, p. 74.

18. Emelyan Yaroslavsky, *Religion in the USSR* (New York: International Publishers, 1934), p. 31.

19. "Religion and Anti-Religion in Russia: Observations by Recent Visitors," p. 377.

20. Quoted in Glennys Young, *Power and the Sacred in Revolutionary Russia: Religious Activists in the Village* (University Park: University of Pennsylvania Press, 1997), p. 100.

21. Isabel A. Tirado, "The Revolution, Young Peasants, and the Komsomol's Antireligious Campaigns: 1920–1928," *Canadian-American Slavic Studies* 26, nos. 1–3 (1992): 113.

22. Emhardt, *Religion*, p. 40.

23. Walter Kolarz, *Religion in the Soviet Union* (New York: St. Martin's, 1961), pp. 19–20.

24. A story told in Chlebzevich's book, *The Proletarian Reader and the Antireli-*

gious Campaign: Suggestions for the Literature, Forms and Methods of Antireligious Propaganda and Lecturing, quoted in Waldemar Gurian, *Bolshevism: Theory and Practice* (London: Sheed and Ward, 1933), pp. 350–51.

25. Fyodor Oleshchuk, *Revolution and Culture*, nos. 3 and 4, 1928, quoted in Emhardt, *Religion*, p. 38.

26. Kolarz, *Religion*, pp. 19–20.

27. Ibid., p. 20.

28. Quoted in Kolarz, *Religion*, p. 21.

29. Quoted in Viola, "Peasant Nightmare," p. 754n29.

30. Quoted in Siegelbaum, *Soviet State*, p. 255 (endnote 58).

31. Husband, *Godless Communists*, p. 75.

32. Quoted in Gurian, *Bolshevism*, p. 382.

33. Husband, *Godless Communists*, p. 88.

34. John Shelton Curtiss, *The Russian Church and the Soviet State, 1917–1950* (Boston: Little, Brown, 1953), p. 88; and M. Sherwood, *The Soviet War on Religion* (New York: Workers' Library Publishers, ca. 1930), pp. 16, 24.

35. Husband, *Godless Communists*, pp. 76–77.

36. Siegelbaum, *Soviet State*, p. 161.

37. Louis Fischer, "Soviet Russia's Grim Battle against Religion," *Current History* 18, no. 4 (July 1923): 590.

38. J. C. Hallman, *The Chess Artist: Genius, Obsession, and the World's Oldest Game* (New York: Dunne, 2003), pp. 44–45.

39. Hecker, *Religion and Communism*, pp. 260, 262; and Fedor Oleshchuk, "The Association of the Godless," *Revolution and Culture*, nos. 3 and 4 (1928), quoted in Emhardt, *Religion*, p. 40.

40. Chamberlin, "Russian Soul," p. 396; Hecker, *Religion and Communism*, p. 260; and William C. White, "The Triple-Barred Cross," *Scribner's*, July 1930, pp. 73–74.

41. Powell, *Antireligious Propaganda*, p. 36.

42. "Report on Informational and Agent Work of the Cheka among the Clergy," 1921, quoted in Felix Corley, *Religion in the Soviet Union: An Archival Reader* (New York: New York University Press, 1996), document 7.

43. October 1924 internal GPU circular, quoted in Corley, *Religion*, document 24.

44. Emelyan Yaroslavsky, "Is the Communist Movement Antireligious? (An Answer to Höglund)," in *Bolshevik Visions: First Phase of the Cultural Revolution in Soviet Russia, Part I: The Culture of a New Society—Ethics, Gender, the Family, Law and Problems of Tradition*, ed. William G. Rosenberg (Ann Arbor: University of Michigan Press, 1990), pp. 239–43, esp. p. 240.

45. Stanley High, "The Triumph of Atheism in Russia," *Atlantic Monthly*, January 1925, p. 122.

46. Bohdan Bociurkiw, "Lenin and Religion," in Schapiro and Reddaway, *Lenin*, p. 126; and Daniel Peris, "Commissars in Red Cassocks: Former Priests in the League of the Militant Godless," *Slavic Review* 54, no. 2 (Summer 1995): 345–46.

47. Peris, "Commissars," pp. 346–47.

48. Ibid., p. 347.

49. Quoted ibid., p. 350.

50. Ibid., p. 358.

51. Ibid., p. 356.

52. Stites, *Revolutionary Dreams*, p. 104.

53. Roger Pethybridge, *The Social Prelude to Stalinism* (London: Macmillan, 1974), p. 31.

54. Quoted in Jerome Davis, "Religion in Soviet Russia," *Missionary Review of the World*, March 1922, p. 192.

55. J. Zatko, *Descent into Darkness: The Destruction of the Roman Catholic Church in Russia, 1917–1923* (Notre Dame, IN: University of Notre Dame Press, 1965), p. 117.

56. Bociurkiw, "Lenin and Religion," p. 128.

57. Hecker, *Religion and Communism*, pp. 258–59.

58. Quoted in Chamberlin, "Russian Crusade," p. 31.

59. Ibid., p. 28; Richard J. Cooke, *Religion in Russia under the Soviets* (New York: Abingdon, 1924), pp. 77–78; Husband, *Godless Communists*, p. 62; Dimitry Pospielovsky, *A History of Marxist-Leninist Atheism and Soviet Antireligious Policies* (London: Macmillan, 1987), p. 29; and "Soviet Russia and Religion," *Missionary Review of the World*, November 1923, p. 887.

60. Chamberlin, "Russian Soul," p. 396.

61. Ibid., p. 30; Stites, *Revolutionary Dreams*, pp. 106–107; and N. S. Timasheff, *Religion in Soviet Russia, 1917–1942* (London: Religious Book Club, 1943), p. 35.

62. Corley, *Religion*, p. x.

63. Quoted in Cooke, *Religion*, pp. 77–78.

64. Hecker, *Religion and Communism*, p. 255.

65. Fischer, "Grim Battle," p. 597; and Hecker, *Religion and Communism*, p. 255.

66. Emhardt, *Religion*, p. 37; and R. O. G. Urch, "Bolshevism and Religion in Russia," *Atlantic Monthly*, March 1923, p. 405.

67. Pospielovsky, *History*, p. 57.

68. Hecker, *Religion and Communism*, p. 224; Kolarz, *Religion*, p. 8; and Pospielovsky, *History*, p. 57.

69. Hecker, *Religion and Communism*, pp. 223–24.

70. Trotsky, "Vodka," p. 109.

71. "There Are Many Godless, But There Are No Workers on the Antireligious Front," *Pravda*, April 13, 1928, quoted in Emhardt, *Religion*, p. 288.

72. "The Attack of the Church Members," *Bezbozhnik*, May 6, 1928, quoted in Emhardt, *Religion*, p. 282.

73. William B. Husband, "Soviet Atheism and Russian Orthodox Strategies of Resistance, 1917–1932," *Journal of Modern History* 70 (March 1998): 87.

74. Kolarz, *Religion*, p. 6; Timasheff, *Religion*, pp. 58–59, 61, 93; and Young, *Power*, pp. 161–62.

75. Husband, "Soviet Atheism," pp. 92–93; Peter Kenez, *The Birth of the Propaganda State: Soviet Methods of Mass Mobilization, 1917–1929* (New York: Cambridge University Press, 1985), p. 67; and Stites, *Revolutionary Dreams*, p. 108.

76. Husband, "Soviet Atheism," pp. 84–85.

77. Quoted in Nicolas Zernov, *The Russians and Their Church* (Crestwood, NY: St. Vladimir's Seminary Press, 1994), p. 145n3.

78. "There Are Many Godless," quoted in Emhardt, *Religion*, p. 289.

79. Timasheff, *Religion*, p. 62.

80. Emhardt, *Religion*, p. 290.

81. Ariadna Williams, "Atheism and Religion in Russia," *Nineteenth Century and After*, September 1929, p. 337.

82. Peris, "Commissars," p. 355; and Edward E. Roslof, "The Heresy of 'Bolshevik' Christianity: Orthodox Rejection of Religious Reform During NEP," *Slavic Review* 55, no. 3 (Autumn 1996): 628.

83. Peris, "Commissars," pp. 342, 354.

84. Quoted in Emhardt, *Religion*, p. 284.

85. Ibid.

CHAPTER 20

1. James Zatko, *Descent into Darkness: The Destruction of the Roman Catholic Church in Russia, 1917–1923* (Notre Dame, IN: University of Notre Dame Press, 1965), p. 86.

2. Joseph McCabe, *Atheist Russia Shakes the World: How the Wicked Bolsheviks Save Our Christian World*; Francis McCullagh, *The Bolshevik Persecution of Christianity* (New York: Dutton, 1924), p. 108; and Zatko, *Descent into Darkness*, p. 64.

3. From an obscure 1920s publication, which can no longer be obtained for citation.

4. Albert Galter, *The Red Book of the Persecuted Church* (Dublin, Ireland: M. H. Gill and Son, 1957), pp. 36–38; and Paul Mailleux, "Catholics in the Soviet Union," in *Aspects of Religion in the Soviet Union: 1917–1967*, ed. Richard H. Marshall Jr. (Chicago: University of Chicago Press, 1971), pp. 360–61.

5. Deacon Herman Ivanov-Treenadzaty, *The Vatican and Russia: The Eastern Rite and the Bolshevik Revolution*.

6. McCabe, *Atheist Russia*; and Robert Royal, *Soviet Terror*, p. 1.

7. Mailleux, "Catholics," p. 360.

8. Joseph Lins, *Siberia*.

9. Roger Pethybridge, *One Step Backwards, Two Steps Forward: Soviet Society and Politics in the New Economic Policy* (Oxford: Clarendon Press, 1990), pp. 42–43.

10. Galter, *Red Book*, p. 38.

11. Emelyan Yaroslavsky, *Religion in the USSR* (New York: International Publishers, 1934), p. 36.

12. Edmund A. Walsh, "Religion in the Soviet Union: III—A Roman Catholic Indictment," *Current History* 32, no. 1 (April 1930): 36.

13. Louis Fischer, "The Vatican and the Kremlin," *Nation* 130, no. 3367 (January 15, 1930): 83.

14. Martha Edith Almedingen, *The Catholic Church in Russia Today* (New York: P. J. Kenedy, 1923), pp. 33–34.

15. Maurice Hindus, *Humanity Uprooted* (New York: J. Cape and H. Smith, 1929), p. 20.

16. Royal, *Soviet Terror*, p. 1.

17. Zatko, *Descent into Darkness*, appendix.

18. McCullagh, *Bolshevik Persecution*, p. 367. The whole of Article VII is included.

19. Quoted in Zatko, *Descent into Darkness*, p. 100n24.

20. McCullagh, *Bolshevik Persecution*, pp. 110–11.

21. Zatko, *Descent into Darkness*, pp. 99–100, 125.

22. Almedingen, *Catholic Church*, pp. 54–63.

23. Ibid., pp. 58–59.

24. "Memorandum from the Polish Executive Committee in Byelorussia and the Ukraine concerning Defense of the Catholic Religion in Soviet Russia," May 12, 1925, in *The Russian Revolution and Religion: A Collection of Documents concerning the Suppression of Religion by the Communists, 1917–1925*, ed. Boleslav Szczesniak (Notre Dame, IN: University of Notre Dame Press, 1959), document 156.

25. *Bezbozhnik*, April 3, 1923, quoted in McCullagh, *Bolshevik Persecution*, p. 118.

26. Testimony of Exarch Fyodorov at his trial, quoted in Zatko, *Descent into Darkness*, p. 65.

27. Fischer, "Vatican," p. 82.

28. Zatko, *Descent Into Darkness*, pp. 68, 70, 83.

29. McCullagh, *Bolshevik Persecution*, p. 161; and Zatko, *Descent into Darkness*, p. 73.

30. Zatko, *Descent into Darkness*, pp. 74–75.

31. Budkiewicz's letter, "The Question of Signing the Agreement under Existing Conditions," excerpts of which were included in the Statement of Accusation at the Catholic Trial of May 1923, quoted in McCullagh, *Bolshevik Persecution*, pp. 156–59; and Zatko, *Descent into Darkness*, pp. 75–76, 80, 82.

32. Mailleux, "Catholics," p. 361; Royal, *Soviet Terror*, p. 1; and Zatko, *Descent into Darkness*, pp. 77–79.

33. Zatko, *Descent into Darkness*, pp. 79–80.

34. Quoted in McCullagh, *Bolshevik Persecution*, pp. 161–62. See also Joseph Ledit, *Archbishop John Baptist Cieplak* (Montreal: Palm, 1963), p. 60.

35. Zatko, *Descent into Darkness*, p. 79 (including n19). Here Zatko says this letter was written on July 1, 1921, but in 130n38 he says it was written in July 1922.

36. Ibid., pp. 81–82.

37. William Chauncey Emhardt, ed., *Religion in Soviet Russia* (London: Morehouse, 1929), p. 182.

38. *Pravda*, March 22, 1923, quoted in Emhardt, *Religion*, p. 185.

39. Zatko, *Descent into Darkness*, pp. 126–27.

40. Ibid., p. 133.

41. Moise Beilinson, "Two Internationals: Red and Black, Rapprochement between the Church of Rome and the Soviet Government," *New Republic*, September 27, 1922, p. 124.

42. Recorded by Deacon Herman Ivanov-Treenadzaty, quoted in Vladimir Moss, *The Orthodox Church at the Crossroads: From 1900 to the Present Day*, p. 67 (my pagination).

43. "How Bolshevism Is Overwhelming the Russian Church," *Current Opinion* 74, no. 6 (June 1923): 726; "Report of the U.S. Commissioner in Riga Concerning the Situation of the Church in Russia," July 17, 1922, in Szczesniak, *Russian Revolution*, document 40; and Zatko, *Descent into Darkness*, pp. 109–11.

44. *Osservatore Romano*, September 16, 1922, as cited in Zatko, *Descent into Darkness*, p. 114.

45. Fischer, "Vatican," p. 82.

46. Ibid.

47. McCullagh, *Bolshevik Persecution*, pp. 74–75.

48. Zatko, *Descent into Darkness*, p. 113.

49. McCabe, *Atheist Russia*.

50. Zatko, *Descent into Darkness*, pp. 111–12.

51. Almedingen, *Catholic Church*, quoted in McCabe, *Atheist Russia*.

52. "Report of the U.S. Commissioner in Riga to the Secretary of State concerning the Vatican and the Orthodox," May 29, 1922, quoted in Szczesniak, *The Russian Revolution*, document 34. The only problem with this theory is that Young's source was a Latvian bishop with close ties to Metropolitan Anthony in Yugoslavia who had a fierce anti-Bolshevik agenda.

53. Quoted in Fischer, "Vatican," p. 82. Fischer gives several examples of Walsh's misrepresentations.

54. McCabe, *Atheist Russia*.

55. Fischer, "Vatican," p. 82; and Galter, *Red Book*, p. 35.

56. Mailleux, "Catholics," p. 362; and Zatko, *Descent into Darkness*, p. 110 (and n34).

57. Zatko, *Descent into Darkness*, pp. 111–12.

58. Quoted ibid., p. 115n50.

59. Fischer, "Vatican," pp. 82–83.

60. Felix Corley, *Religion in the Soviet Union: An Archival Reader* (New York: New York University Press, 1996), p. 12; and Jane Swan, *A Biography of Patriarch Tikhon* (Jordanville, NY: Holy Trinity Russian Orthodox Monastery, 1964), p. 8n13.

61. Serge Bolshakov, *Russian Nonconformity: The Story of "Unofficial" Religion in Russia* (Philadelphia: Westminster, 1950), p. 149.

62. Quoted in Galter, *Red Book*, p. 41.

63. Mailleux, "Catholics," p. 362; and Zatko, *Descent into Darkness*, pp. 84, 107.

64. Recorded by Deacon Herman Ivanov-Treenadzaty, quoted in Moss, *Orthodox Church*, p. 68 (my pagination).

65. Almedingen, *Catholic Church*, p. 89.

66. McCullagh, *Bolshevik Persecution*, p. 111; and Pethybridge, *One Step Backwards*, p. 42.

67. Quoted in Zatko, *Descent into Darkness*, p. 121.

68. Ibid., p. 124.

69. Almedingen, *Catholic Church*, pp. 89–90; and Zatko, *Descent into Darkness*, p. 124.

70. Zatko, *Descent into Darkness*, p. 130.

71. Quoted in Mailleux, "Catholics," pp. 362–63; and Zatko, *Descent into Darkness*, pp. 124–25.

72. Edmund A. Walsh, *The Catholic Church in Present Day Russia* (Minneapolis, MN, December 29, 1931), pp. 11–13.

CHAPTER 21

1. This account is based upon "Letter of Rev. Xavier Klimaszewski to Archbishop John Baptist Cieplak concerning His Experiences in Saratov Diocese," May 2, 1924, in *The Russian Revolution and Religion: A Collection of Documents concerning the Suppression of Religion by the Communists, 1917–1925*, ed. Boleslav Szczesniak (Notre Dame, IN: University of Notre Dame Press, 1959), document 155.

2. This story was inspired by material in "Report of the U.S. Legation in Riga Concerning Mistreatment of the Catholic Nuns in Moscow," December 7, 1923, in Szczesniak, *Russian Revolution*, document 153.

3. Quoted in Emelyan Yaroslavsky, *Religion in the USSR* (New York: International Publishers, 1934), p. 60.

4. J. Zatko, *Descent into Darkness: The Destruction of the Roman Catholic Church in Russia, 1917–1923* (Notre Dame, IN: University of Notre Dame Press, 1965), p. 124.

5. Francis McCullagh, *The Bolshevik Persecution of Christianity* (New York: Dutton, 1924), p. 117.

6. *Pravda*, March 11, 1923, quoted in *Religion in Soviet Russia*, ed. William Chauncey Emhardt (London: Morehouse, 1929), p. 182; and Zatko, *Descent into Darkness*, pp. 74, 88.

7. Zatko, *Descent into Darkness*, p. 132.

8. McCullagh, *Bolshevik Persecution*, pp. 113, 136, 169, 172; and Paul Mailleux, "Catholics," in *Aspects of Religion in the Soviet Union: 1917–1967*, ed. Richard H. Marshall Jr. (Chicago: University of Chicago Press, 1971), p. 363.

9. Zatko, *Descent into Darkness*, p. 137.

10. Ibid., p. 158.

11. For descriptions of the personalities and details of courtroom testimony I have relied on Captain Francis McCullagh, who was a witness to these events. The Soviets never made a transcript of the trial available to the public.

12. McCullagh, *Bolshevik Persecution*, p. 112

13. Emhardt, *Religion*, p. 182; and Albert Galter, *The Red Book of the Persecuted Church* (Dublin, Ireland: M. H. Gill and Son, 1957), pp. 43–44.

14. McCullagh, *Bolshevik Persecution*, pp. 383–85.

15. Ibid., p. 129, appendix IX.

16. Ibid., pp. 130–32.

17. Ibid., p. 135.

18. See McCullagh, *Bolshevik Persecution*, pp. 229–32, for a thorough discussion of all charges against Budkiewicz.

19. Zatko, *Descent Into Darkness*, pp. 149–51.

20. Quoted ibid., p. 120.

21. Ibid., p. 144.

22. Quoted in McCullagh, *Bolshevik Persecution*, pp. 177–78.

23. Ibid., pp. 215–17.

24. Galter, *Red Book*, p. 44n16.

25. Quoted in McCullagh, *Bolshevik Persecution*, p. 201.

26. Zatko, *Descent into Darkness*, pp. 147–48, 151.

27. Quoted in Szczesniak, *Russian Revolution*, document 62.

28. For more on Cieplak's defense arguments, see the letter he wrote to the British representative in Petrograd in January 1923, quoted in full in McCullagh, *Bolshevik Persecution*, pp. 113–14.

29. Zatko, *Descent into Darkness*, pp. 153–54.

30. Quoted in Edmund A. Walsh, *The Catholic Church in Present Day Russia* (Minneapolis, MN, December 29, 1931), p. 15.

31. *London Times*, March 23, 24 and 27, 1923, quoted in Emhardt, *Religion*, p. 184.

32. Quoted in Zatko, *Descent into Darkness*, p. 154.

33. "Methodist Split on Russia's New Church," *Literary Digest*, July 28, 1923, p. 31.

34. *The Servant of God Exarch Leonid Fyodorov.*

35. McCullagh, *Bolshevik Persecution*, pp. 364–65; and *Servant of God*. For a fuller version of the verdict, see *Izvestia*, March 27, 1923, quoted in Emhardt, *Religion*, p. 185.

36. *Gazetta Poranna*, April 4, 1923, quoted in Emhardt, *Religion*, p. 188.

37. See Zatko, *Descent into Darkness*, pp. 158–67, for a full discussion of diplomatic protests in the days prior to the execution.

38. *Izvestia*, March 30, 1923, quoted in Emhardt, *Religion*, pp. 190–91.

39. Emhardt, *Religion*, p. 190.

40. Ibid., pp. 187–88.

41. Quoted in "How Bolshevism Is Overwhelming the Russian Church," *Current Opinion*, June 1923, p. 727; and Szczesniak, *Russian Revolution*, document 78.

42. *Izvestia*, March 30, 1923, quoted in Emhardt, *Religion*, p. 191.

43. Ibid.

44. Felix Corley, *Religion in the Soviet Union: An Archival Reader* (New York: New York University Press, 1996), p. 15; "How Bolshevism Is Overwhelming the Russian Church," p. 726; and *Servant of God*.

45. Mailleux, "Catholics," p. 368; *Servant of God*; and Zatko, *Descent into Darkness*, pp. 175–76.

46. Quoted in Galter, *Red Book*, p. 45n17.

47. Ibid.

48. Ibid.

49. Ibid., pp. 49–50; and Robert Royal, *Soviet Terror*, p. 1.

50. Galter, *Red Book*, p. 46; and Royal, *Soviet Terror*, p. 2.

51. Source lost.

52. Deacon Herman Ivanov-Treenadzaty, quoted in Vladimir Moss, *The Orthodox Church at the Crossroads: From 1900 to the Present Day*, p. 69 (my pagination).

53. Deacon Herman Ivanov-Treenadzaty, *The Vatican and Russia: The Eastern Rite and the Bolshevik Revolution*.

54. Paul Lesourd, *They Doubly Tear Down: How the Church Functions in Time of Crisis—Historical Precedents and Modern Practice*, p. 1; Mailleux, "Catholics," p. 363; and Sergius Troitsky, *The Living Church*, bound inside of Emhardt, *Religion*, pp. 346–47.

55. *The Generals of the Society of Jesus*; and Mailleux, "Catholics," p. 363.

56. Joseph McCabe, *Atheist Russia Shakes the World: How the Wicked Bolsheviks Save Our Christian World*.

57. Dimitry Pospielovsky, *A History of Marxist-Leninist Atheism and Soviet Antireligious Policies* (London: Macmillan, 1987), p. 48.

58. Quoted in J. De Bivort de la Saudée, *Communism and Antireligion* (London: Burns Oates and Washbourne, 1938), p. 35.

59. Edgar S. Furniss, "Religion in the Soviet Union: I—The History of the Conflict," *Current History* 32, no. 1 (April 1930): 25; and Ivanov-Treenadzaty, *Vatican and Russia*.

60. Quoted in McCabe, *Atheist Russia*.

61. Dimitry Pospielovsky, *The Russian Church under the Soviet Regime: 1917–1982*, vol. 1 (Crestwood, NY: St. Vladimir's Seminary Press, 1984), pp. 40–41.

CHAPTER 22

1. Quoted in David Chidester, *Christianity: A Global History* (San Francisco: HarperSanFrancisco, 2000), p. 374.

2. Glennys Young, *Power and the Sacred in Revolutionary Russia: Religious Activists in the Village* (University Park: University of Pennsylvania Press, 1997), p. 90n54.

3. Ethel Dunn and Stephen P. Dunn, "Religion as an Instrument of Cultural Change: The Problem of the Sects in the Soviet Union," *Slavic Review* 23, no. 3 (September 1964): 469.

4. Felix Corley, *Religion in the Soviet Union: An Archival Reader* (New York: New York University Press, 1996), pp. 5–6; Alan G. Hefner, *Khlysty*; George Vernadsky, *A History of Russia* (New Haven, CT: Yale University Press, 1929), p. 117; and Nicolas Zernov, *The Russians and Their Church* (Crestwood, NY: St. Vladimir's Seminary Press, 1994), p. 150.

5. Ethel Dunn, "Russian Sectarianism in New Soviet Marxist Scholarship," *Slavic Review* 26, no. 1 (March 1967): 137.

6. Engels, "Ludwig Feuerbach and the End of Classical German Philosophy," in Karl Marx and Friedrich Engels, *On Religion* (New York: Schocken, 1964), p. 264.

7. Zernov, *Russians*, p. 142.

8. Serge Bolshakov, *The Christian Church and the Soviet State* (London: Society for Promoting Christian Knowledge, 1942), pp. 119–20; L. N. Mitrokhin, "Education in Atheism and Methodology of Studying the Survival of Religious Beliefs," *Soviet Sociology* 1, no. 1 (Summer 1962): 30; and Ivan Prokhanov, *In the Cauldron of Russia, 1869–1933* (New York: All-Russian Evangelical Christian Union, 1933), p. 150.

9. Michael Bourdeaux, *Religious Minorities in the Soviet Union* (London: Minority Rights Group, 1984), p. 19; Dunn, "Russian Sectarianism," pp. 131, 139; Andrei Gogolev, "Tragedy of Kazan Adventists," *Kommersant-Daily*, November 21, 1997, pp. 1–2; and *Seventh-Day Adventist Church/Fundamental Beliefs*.

10. Sir Donald MacKenzie Wallace, *Russia on the Eve of War and Revolution* (New York: Vintage, 1961).

11. Dunn, "Russian Sectarianism," p. 129; and Mitrokhin, "Education in Atheism," pp. 27–28.

12. Dunn, "Russian Sectarianism," p. 131; H. M. Kallen, "Religion in Russia," *New Republic*, November 2, 1927, p. 281; and Zernov, *Russians*, p. 142.

13. Pavel Pavlov in *The Word of Truth*, 1917.

14. Quoted in Vladimir Lenin, *Draft Resolution on the Publication of a Periodical for Members of Religious Sects.*

15. William Henry Chamberlin, "The Struggle for the Russian Soul: A Phase of Soviet Russia," *Atlantic Monthly*, September 1929, p. 392; and Mitrokhin, "Education in Atheism," p. 27.

16. Chamberlin, "Russian Soul," pp. 392–93; Lynne Viola, "The Peasant Nightmare: Visions of Apocalypse in the Soviet Countryside," *Journal of Modern History* 62, no. 4 (December 1990): 754; and William C. White, "The Triple-Barred Cross," *Scribner's*, July 1930, p. 71.

17. Dunn, "Russian Sectarianism," p. 135.

18. Walter Kolarz, *Religion in the Soviet Union* (New York: St. Martin's, 1961), p. 288.

19. Quoted in Serge Bolshakov, *Russian Nonconformity: The Story of "Unofficial" Religion in Russia* (Philadelphia: Westminster, 1950), p. 119.

20. Kolarz, *Religion*, pp. 288–89.

21. Quoted in Anne O'Hare McCormick, *The Hammer and the Scythe: Communist Russia Enters the Second Decade* (New York: Knopf, 1928), p. 214.

22. Quoted in Dimitry Pospielovsky, *A History of Marxist-Leninist Atheism and Soviet Antireligious Policies* (London: Macmillan, 1987), p. 47.

23. Quoted in Dunn and Dunn, "Cultural Change," p. 470.

24. Pospielovsky, *History*, p. 58.

25. Chamberlin, "Russian Soul," pp. 393–94; and Maurice Hindus, *Humanity Uprooted* (New York: J. Cape and H. Smith, 1929), p. 21.

26. Quoted in Andrew Q. Blane, "Protestant Sectarians in the First Year of Soviet Rule," in *Aspects of Religion in the Soviet Union: 1917–1967*, ed. Richard H. Marshall Jr. (Chicago: University of Chicago Press, 1971), p. 304n7.

27. Viola, "Peasant Nightmare," p. 755.

28. June 12, 1923, meeting of the Antireligious Commission, quoted in Corley, *Religion*, document 26; and Kolarz, *Religion*, p. 131.

29. Dunn, "Russian Sectarianism," p. 130; and Matthew Spinka, *Church and the Russian Revolution* (New York: Macmillan, 1927), p. 320.

30. Dunn and Dunn, "Cultural Change," p. 469; and Lewis H. Siegelbaum, *Soviet State and Society between Revolutions: 1918–1929* (New York: Cambridge University Press, 1992), p. 163.

31. From an obscure 1920s publication, which can no longer be obtained for citation.

32. Christel Lane, "The Case of the Molokan Sect in Soviet Society," *Comparative Studies in Society and History* 17, no. 2 (April 1975): 221–37.

33. Mitrokhin, "Education in Atheism," p. 29.

34. M. Sherwood, *The Soviet War on Religion* (New York: Workers' Library Publishers, ca. 1930), pp. 33–34; and Didier Diers and Xavier Valla, *The Russian Sect of the Castrated from the 18th to the 20th Century*.

35. McCormick, *Hammer and the Scythe*, pp. 214–15.

36. Charles Karner, "Protestant World Report," *Hungarian Protestant Almanac*, 1933, p. 1.

37. Blane, "Protestant Sectarians," p. 303.

38. Quoted in "Religious Conditions in Russia," *Hibbert Journal* (April 1926): 453.

39. Edward E. Roslof, "The Heresy of 'Bolshevik' Christianity: Orthodox Rejection of Religious Reform during NEP," *Slavic Review* 55, no. 3 (Autumn 1996): 627; and Spinka, *Church and the Russian Revolution*, p. 319.

40. Bolshakov, *Russian Nonconformity*, p. 119; Dunn, "Russian Sectarianism," p. 140; Dimitry Pospielovsky, *The Russian Church under the Soviet Regime: 1917–1982*, vol. 1 (Crestwood, NY: St. Vladimir's Seminary Press, 1984), p. 41; Prokhanov, *In the Cauldron of Russia*, p. 175; and Paul D. Steeves, *Keeping the Faiths: Religion and Ideology in the Soviet Union* (New York: Holmes and Meier, 1989), p. 86.

41. Spinka, *Church and the Russian Revolution*, p. 318.

42. Blane, "Protestant Sectarians," pp. 309–12.

43. Ibid., pp. 312–17.

44. Paul D. Steeves, *Russian Baptists and the Military Question, 1920–1929*; and Viola, "Peasant Nightmare," p. 755.

45. October 9, 1918, meeting of the Revolutionary Military Soviet, quoted in Corley, *Religion*, document 5.

46. Quoted in Chamberlin, "Russian Soul," p. 397.

47. From a memo by Tuchkov dated February 27, 1924, quoted in Corley, *Religion*, document 25.

48. Steeves, *Russian Baptists*, p. 6 (my pagination). See also Chamberlin, "Russian Soul," p. 397.

49. From a memo by Tuchkov dated February 27, 1924, quoted in Corley, *Religion*, document 25.

50. Steeves, *Russian Baptists*, pp. 8–9 (my pagination).

51. Sherwood, *Soviet War*, p. 12.

52. Steeves, *Russian Baptists*, p. 9 (my pagination).

53. Bolshakov, *Russian Nonconformity*, p. 120.

54. Chamberlin, "Russian Soul," p. 395.

55. Frank H. Epp, "Mennonites in the Soviet Union," in Marshall, *Aspects of Religion*, pp. 285, 289–90.

56. Ibid., p. 290; and M. M. Sheinman, *Religion and Church in the USSR* (Moscow: Cooperative Publishing Society of Foreign Workers in the USSR, 1933), p. 21.

57. Epp, "Mennonites," pp. 291–92.

58. Emelyan Yaroslavsky, *Religion in the USSR* (New York: International Publishers, 1934), p. 26.

59. Epp, "Mennonites," p. 292; Edgar S. Furniss, "Class War Linked with Anti-–Religion in Soviet Policy," *Current History* 31, no. 3 (December 1929): 607; and White, "Triple-Barred Cross," p. 75.

60. Bourdeaux, *Religious Minorities*, p. 20.

61. Kolarz, *Religion*, p. 328.

62. Quoted in Bourdeaux, *Religious Minorities*, p. 19.

63. Ibid., p. 20.

64. Quoted in Klibanov, "The Dissident Denominations in the Past and Today," *Soviet Sociology* 3, no. 4 (Spring 1965): 55.

65. February 27, 1923, and December 14, 1928, meetings of the Antireligious Commission, quoted in Corley, *Religion*, document 26; Louis Fischer, "Soviet Russia's Grim Battle against Religion," *Current History* 18, no. 4 (July 1923): 593; and Edgar S. Furniss, "Religion in the Soviet Union: I—The History of the Conflict," *Current History* 32, no. 1 (April 1930): 29.

CHAPTER 23

1. Quoted in Nicolas de Basily, *Russia under Soviet Rule: Twenty Years of Bolshevik Experiment* (London: George Allen and Unwin, 1938), p. 423.

2. Quoted in William C. White, "The Triple-Barred Cross," *Scribner's*, July 1930, p. 76.

3. Quoted in Dimitry Pospielovsky, *A History of Marxist-Leninist Atheism and Soviet Antireligious Policies* (London: Macmillan, 1987), p. 52.

4. Paul B. Anderson, "The Council for Religious Affairs and the Shaping of Soviet Religious Policy," *Soviet Studies* 43, no. 4 (1991): 690; and Paul D. Steeves, *Keeping the Faiths: Religion and Ideology in the Soviet Union* (New York: Holmes and Meier, 1989), p. 89.

5. Serge Bolshakov, *Russian Nonconformity: The Story of "Unofficial" Religion in Russia* (Philadelphia: Westminster, 1950), p. 120; Albert Galter, *The Red Book of the Persecuted Church* (Dublin, Ireland: M. H. Gill and Son, 1957), p. 50; Lino Gussoni and Aristede Brunello, *The Silent Church: Facts and Documents concerning Religious Persecution behind the Iron Curtain* (New York: Veritas, 195), p. 19; and Steeves, *Keeping the Faiths*, p. 89.

6. Quoted in Paul B. Anderson, "Reflections on Religion in Russia: 1917–1967," in *Aspects of Religion in the Soviet Union: 1917–1967*, ed. Richard H. Marshall Jr. (Chicago: University of Chicago Press, 1971), p. 22; and N. S. Timasheff, *Religion in Soviet Russia, 1917–1942* (London: Religious Book Club, 1943), p. 65.

7. Walter Kolarz, *Religion in the Soviet Union* (New York: St. Martin's, 1961), p. 12.

8. Robert Pierce Casey, *Religion in Russia* (New York: Harper, 1946), p. 94; Timasheff, *Religion*, p. 65; and Kolarz, *Religion*, pp. 12–13.

9. *Orthodox Church of Russia*, p. 2; and Pospielovsky, *History*, p. 65.

10. Anderson, "Reflections," p. 20; Nathaniel Davis, *A Long Walk to Church: A Contemporary History of Russian Orthodoxy* (San Francisco: Westview, 1995), p. 1; and William B. Stroyen, *Communist Russia and the Russian Orthodox Church, 1943–1962* (Washington, DC: Catholic University of America Press, 1967), pp. 29, 34.

11. Marcus Bach, *God and the Soviets* (New York: Crowell, 1958), p. 99; and Alexander A. Bogolepov, "The Legal Position of the Russian Orthodox Church in the Soviet Union," in Marshall, *Aspects of Religion*, p. 201.

12. Patricia Blake, "Alliance with the Unholy," *Life*, September 14, 1959, p. 122.

13. *The Truth about Religion in Russia* (Moscow: Moscow Patriarchate, 1942), pp. 15–17, quoted in Steeves, *Keeping the Faiths*, pp. 92–93. See also Constantin de Grunwald, *The Churches and the Soviet Union* (New York: Macmillan, 1962), pp. 54–56; and Stroyen, *Communist Russia*, p. 32.

14. Blake, "Alliance," p. 122; and Steeves, *Keeping the Faiths*, p. 14.

15. Boris Talantov, *The Moscow Patriarchate and Sergianism*.

16. Kolarz, *Religion*, pp. 13, 15.

17. Stroyen, *Communist Russia*, pp. 33–34.

18. Ibid.

19. Gerald Buss, *The Bear's Hug: Christian Belief and the Soviet State, 1917–1986* (Grand Rapids, MI: Eerdman, 1987), pp. 33–34; Steeves, *Keeping the Faiths*, pp. 94–95; and Stroyen, *Communist Russia*, pp. 35, 37.

20. Anderson, "Religious Affairs," pp. 690–91, 702; Michael Bourdeaux, *Risen Indeed: Lessons in Faith from the USSR* (London: Darton, Longman and Todd, 1983), p. 18; Buss, *Bear's Hug*, p. 34; and Stroyen, *Communist Russia*, p. 35.

21. Vladimir Moss, *The Orthodox Church at the Crossroads: From 1900 to the Present Day*, p. 28 (my pagination); and Stroyen, *Communist Russia*, p. 38.

22. Anderson, "Reflections," pp. 25, 28; Dimitry Pospielovsky, *The Russian Church under the Soviet Regime: 1917–1982*, vol. 1 (Crestwood, NY: St. Vladimir's Seminary Press, 1984), p. 161; and Stroyen, *Communist Russia*, pp. 38–39.

23. Quoted in Anderson, "Religious Affairs," p. 690; and G. Karpov, *Rapprochement between the Orthodox Church and Soviet Government*, p. 1.

24. Bogolepov, "Legal Position," pp. 201–202, 204.

25. Ibid., pp. 203–204.

26. Alexander Solzhenitsyn, *The Gulag Archipelago, 1918–1956*, vol. 1 (New York: Harper and Rowe, 1973), p. 86.

27. Bogolepov, "Legal Position," p. 206; and Steeves, *Keeping the Faiths*, pp. 99–100.

28. Michael Bourdeaux, *Religious Minorities in the Soviet Union* (London: Minority Rights Group, 1984), p. 6.

29. Kolarz, *Religion*, pp. 16–17.

30. Steeves, *Keeping the Faiths*, pp. 99–100.

31. Kolarz, *Religion*, pp. 34–35.

32. Quoted in Blake, "Alliance," pp. 122, 124.

33. Quoted in James Thrower, *Marxist-Leninist "Scientific Atheism" and the Study of Religion and Atheism in the USSR* (New York: Mouton, 1983), pp. 397–99.

34. Kolarz, *Religion*, p. 30.

35. Blake, "Alliance," p. 124; and Bogolepov, "Legal Position," pp. 206–207.

36. Serhii Plokhy, "A Review of John Anderson's *Religion, State and Politics in the Soviet Union and Successor States*," *Journal of Ukrainian Studies* 21, nos. 1–2 (Summer–Winter 1996): 1.

37. Bohdan Bociurkiw, "Religion and Atheism in Soviet Society," in Marshall, *Aspects of Religion*, p. 48; and Donald A. Lowrie and William C. Fletcher, "Khrushchev's Religious Policy: 1959–1964," in Marshall, *Aspects of Religion*, p. 132.

38. Quoted in Lowrie and Fletcher, "Khrushchev's Religious Policy," pp. 133–34.

39. Anderson, "Religious Affairs," p. 691; and Lowrie and Fletcher, "Khrushchev's Religious Policy," p. 133.

40. Jim Forest, *Religion in the New Russia: The Impact of Perestroika on the Varieties of Religious Life in the Soviet Union* (New York: Crossroad, 1990), pp. 2, 18.

41. Anderson, "Religious Affairs," p. 699; Bociurkiw, "Religion and Atheism," p. 50; George L. Kline, *Religious and Antireligious Thought in Russia* (Chicago: University Press of Chicago, 1968), p. 168; Lowrie and Fletcher, "Khrushchev's Religious Policy," pp. 152–53; and Father Victor Potapov, *Legacies of Communism for Russian Churches*.

42. N. Riabinsky, quoted in Lowrie and Fletcher, "Khrushchev's Religious Policy," pp. 139–40.

43. Bourdeaux, *Religious Minorities*, p. 5; and Lowrie and Fletcher, "Khrushchev's Religious Policy," pp. 143–44, 147.

44. Lowrie and Fletcher, "Khrushchev's Religious Policy," pp. 144–45.

45. Bourdeaux, *Religious Minorities*, p. 5.

46. Lowrie and Fletcher, "Khrushchev's Religious Policy," pp. 146–47.

47. Peter Kenez, professor of Russian History at the University Press of California at Santa Cruz, personal communication.

48. *Pravda*, September 26, 1962, quoted in Lowrie and Fletcher, "Khrushchev's Religious Policy," p. 141.

49. Lowrie and Fletcher, "Khrushchev's Religious Policy," pp. 141–43.

50. Ibid., pp. 135–38.

51. James H. Billington, *Religious Revival in Russia: Discovery and Change*; and Bourdeaux, *Religious Minorities*, p. 3.

52. Quoted in Bourdeaux, *Religious Minorities*, pp. 3–4.

53. For a full discussion of churches open both before and after Khrushchev's anti-religious campaign, see Nathaniel Davis, "The Number of Orthodox Churches before and after the Khrushchev Antireligious Drive," *Slavic Review* 50, no. 3 (Fall 1991): 612–20; Lowrie and Fletcher, "Khrushchev's Religious Policy," pp. 153–54; and Steeves, *Keeping the Faiths*, pp. 104–105.

54. Anderson, "Religious Affairs," pp. 691, 695–97, 706.

55. Felix Corley, *Religion in the Soviet Union: An Archival Reader* (New York: New York University Press, 1996), p. 8.

56. Bourdeaux, *Religious Minorities*, pp. 13–14.

57. Steeves, *Keeping the Faiths*, pp. 101–102.

58. Compiled from quotations in Bociurkiw, "Religion and Atheism," pp. 50–51; and Steeves, *Keeping the Faiths*, p. 109.

59. Bociurkiw, "Religion and Atheism," pp. 50–51.

60. Quoted in Bociurkiw, "Religion and Atheism," p. 50.

61. *Man and the World*, 1966, no. 11 (Kiev), quoted in Bogolepov, "Legal Position," p. 208n30.

62. *Informations Catholiques Internationales* (Paris), quoted in Bogolepov, "Legal Position," p. 206.

63. Bogolepov, "Legal Position," pp. 219–20.

64. Bociurkiw, "Religion and Atheism," p. 55; Zvi Gitelman, "The Communist Party and Soviet Jewry: The Early Years," in Marshall, *Aspects of Religion*, p. 165; and Steeves, *Keeping the Faiths*, pp. 107–108.

65. Quoted in Bourdeaux, *Risen Indeed*, p. 26.

66. Bociurkiw, "Religion and Atheism," pp. 55–56; and L. N. Mitrokhin, "Education in Atheism and Methodology of Studying the Survival of Religious Beliefs," *Soviet Sociology* 1, no. 1 (Summer 1962): 27.

67. Father Hilarion Alfeyev, *Atheism and Orthodoxy in Modern Russia*; and Bociurkiw, "Religion and Atheism," pp. 59–60.

68. Quoted in Bourdeaux, *Religious Minorities*, p. 9.

69. Quoted in Bourdeaux, *Risen Indeed*, p. 25.

70. Bourdeaux, *Religious Minorities*, p. 9.

71. Ibid., pp. 4, 21.

72. Billington, *Religious Revival*.

73. Bourdeaux, *Religious Minorities*, p. 8; Forest, *Impact of Perestroika*, p. 4; and "Orthodox Church of Russia," p. 3.

74. Bourdeaux, *Religious Minorities*, p. 10.

75. Ibid., p. 4; and Steeves, *Keeping the Faiths*, pp. 66–67.

76. Quoted in Steeves, *Keeping the Faiths*, pp. 66–67.

77. Father James Thornton, "Communists Go Up and Down: Yo-Yo Tactics Regarding Religion," pp. 4–5.

78. The story and the quotation are from Forest, *Impact of Perestroika*, pp. 14–15.

79. Quoted ibid., pp. 6, 7, 190.

80. Ibid., pp. 8–10.

81. Quoted ibid., pp. 188–89.

82. Ibid., pp. 20, 189–90.

83. Ibid., p. 199n17; and Thornton, "Yo-Yo Tactics," p. 5.

84. Corley, *Religion*, p. 12; Forest, *Impact of Perestroika*, p. 19n8; and Paul D. Steeves, *The Canonization of Patriarch Tikhon as a Reflection of New Thinking in the Glasnost Era*, pp. 3, 10. The hagiographies conveniently neglected to mention Tikhon's early anti-Bolshevik activities. Konstantin Kharchev, the former chairman of the Council on Religious Affairs, gave interviews in 1989 and 1991 supporting the view that Gorbachev and the Party Central Committee were behind the canonization of Tikhon.

85. J. Patrick Gray, "The Long Alliance of Patriarch Aleksy II and the Communist Party of Russia," *Washington Times*, n.d.

86. Quoted in Harold J. Berman, *Freedom of Religion in Russia: An Amicus Brief for the Defendant*, pp. 6–7 (my pagination).

CHAPTER 24

1. Herbert Aptheker, "Marxism and Religion," in *Marxism and Christianity: A Symposium*, ed. Herbert Aptheker (New York: Humanities, 1968), p. 39.

2. Louis Fischer, "Soviet Russia's Grim Battle against Religion," *Current History* 18, no. 4 (July 1923): 588.

3. Quoted in Yaroslav Onyschuk, "What's behind the Russian Antireligious Campaign?" *Texas Quarterly* 10, no. 2 (Summer 1967): 211–14, 213.

4. Ibid.

5. Quoted in Father Hilarion Alfeyev, *Atheism and Orthodoxy in Modern Russia*, p. 2 (my pagination).

6. Leon Trotsky, "Vodka, the Church and the Cinema," *Pravda*, July 12, 1923, in William G. Rosenberg, *Bolshevik Visions: First Phase of the Cultural Revolution in Soviet Russia*, part 2 (Ann Arbor: University of Michigan Press, 1990), p. 108.

7. Maurice Hindus, *Humanity Uprooted* (New York: J. Cape and H. Smith, 1929), p. 18.

8. Quoted in Richard J. Cooke, *Religion in Russia under the Soviets* (New York: Abingdon, 1924), p. 13.

9. Quoted in Timothy Ware, *The Orthodox Church* (Baltimore: Penguin, 1963), p. 159.

10. Anne O'Hare McCormick, *The Hammer and the Scythe: Communist Russia Enters the Second Decade* (New York: Knopf, 1928), p. 217.

11. Hindus, *Humanity Uprooted*, p. 28.

12. Quoted in Vladimir Moss, *The Orthodox Church at the Crossroads: From 1900 to the Present Day*, p. 59 (my pagination).

13. Quoted in Harold J. Berman, *Freedom of Religion in Russia: An Amicus Brief for the Defendant*, pp. 5–6 (my pagination).

14. Michael Bakunin, *God and the State* (New York: Dover, 1970), pp. 55–56.

15. All quotes in this paragraph from Steven Pinker, *The Blank Slate: The Modern Denial of Human Nature* (New York: Viking, 2002), pp. 155–56.

16. Pethybridge, *The Social Prelude to Stalinism* (London: Macmillan, 1974), p. 39.

17. Quoted in Pinker, *Blank Slate*, p. 286.

18. *Orlovskaya Pravda*, May 30, 1937, quoted in Paul B. Anderson, *People, Church and State in Modern Russia* (London: Student Christian Movement, 1944), p. 114.

19. Joseph McCabe, *Atheist Russia Shakes the World: How the Wicked Bolsheviks Save Our Christian World*.

20. Emma Goldman, *My Disillusionment in Russia* (Mineola, NY: Dover, 2003), p. 247.

21. Ibid., p. 248.

22. Ibid., pp. 249–50, 258.

23. December 4, 1920, Samsonov memo, quoted in Felix Corley, *Religion in the Soviet Union: An Archival Reader* (New York: New York University Press, 1996), document 6.

24. "The Moscow Committee of the Communist Party on the Antireligious Front," *Pravda*, June 15, 1928, quoted in *Religion in Soviet Russia*, ed. William Chauncey Emhardt (London: Morehouse, 1929), p. 291.

25. William B. Husband, *Godless Communists: Atheism and Society in Soviet Russia, 1917–1932* (DeKalb: Northern Illinois University Press, 2000), pp. 64–65.

26. Dimitry Pospielovsky, *A History of Marxist-Leninist Atheism and Soviet Antireligious Policies* (London: Macmillan, 1987), p. 54.

27. Quoted in William B. Husband, "Soviet Atheism and Russian Orthodox Strategies of Resistance, 1917–1932," *Journal of Modern History* 70 (March 1998): 91.

28. "Those Who Think and Those Who Miss Their Chance," *Komsomolskaya Pravda*, June 22, 1928, quoted in Emhardt, *Religion*, p. 293.

29. William C. White, "The Triple-Barred Cross," *Scribner's*, July 1930, pp. 67–78, 72.

30. Ibid., pp. 37–38, 54–55.

31. Robert Pierce Casey, *Religion in Russia* (New York: Harper, 1946), p. 105.

32. H. N. Brailsford, "Religion and the Soviets," *New Republic*, May 7, 1930, p. 322.

33. Richard Dawkins, *A Devil's Chaplain: Reflections on Hope, Lies, Science and Love* (Boston: Houghton Mifflin, 2003), pp. 128, 241, 247.

34. Richard Dawkins, "Now Here's a Bright Idea," *Free Inquiry* (October/ November 2003): 12.

CHAPTER 25

1. Rita Carter, *Mapping the Mind* (Berkeley and Los Angeles: University of California Press, 1998), p. 129; David Chidester, *Christianity: A Global History* (San Francisco: HarperSanFrancisco, 2000), p. 345; and Julius F. Hecker, *Religion and Communism: A Study of Religion and Atheism in Soviet Russia* (Westport, CT: Hyperion, 1934), pp. 1n1, 5, 163–64.

2. Clifford Geertz, quoted in Stewart Elliott Guthrie, *Faces in the Clouds: A New Theory of Religion* (New York: Oxford University Press, 1993), p. 32.

3. Quoted in Steven Pinker, *The Blank Slate: The Modern Denial of Human Nature* (New York: Viking, 2002), p. 131.

4. Guthrie, *Clouds*, p. 45.

5. Quoted in Michael Bourdeaux, *Risen Indeed: Lessons in Faith from the USSR* (London: Darton, Longman and Todd, 1983), p. 24.

6. Michael Bakunin, *God and the State* (New York: Dover, 1970), pp. 19–22.

7. Quoted in William Henry Chamberlin, "The Struggle for the Russian Soul: A Phase of Soviet Russia," *Atlantic Monthly*, September 1929, p. 399.

8. Quoted in Nathaniel Davis, *A Long Walk to Church: A Contemporary History of Russian Orthodoxy* (San Francisco: Westview, 1995), p. xviii.

9. Nathaniel Davis, *Long Walk*, p. xviii.

10. Quoted in David E. Powell, *Antireligious Propaganda in the Soviet Union: A Study of Mass Persuasion* (Cambridge, MA: MIT Press, 1975), p. 2.

11. Emelyan Yaroslavsky, *Religion in the USSR* (New York: International Publishers, 1934), p. 32.

12. Pinker, *Blank Slate*, pp. 169–70.

13. Bakunin, *God and the State*, p. 30.

14. Ibid., p. 56; and quoted in Pinker, *Blank Slate*, p. 157.

15. Maurice Hindus, *Humanity Uprooted* (New York: J. Cape and H. Smith, 1929), pp. 40–41.

16. Yaroslavsky, *Religion in the USSR*, p. 31.

17. Quoted in Martha Edith Almedingen, *The Catholic Church in Russia Today* (New York: P. J. Kenedy, 1923), p. 84.

18. William B. Husband, *Godless Communists: Atheism and Society in Soviet Russia, 1917–1932* (DeKalb: Northern Illinois University Press, 2000), p. 82.

19. Gregg Easterbrook, *The Vatican's Turn to Recant: Scientists Censured in the Past Are Being Posthumously Redeemed.*

20. Quoted in Paul Miliukov, *Outlines of Russian Culture, Part I: Religion and the Church* (Philadelphia: University of Pennsylvania Press, 1943), p. 201.

21. Marx, *Critique of the Gotha Program*, quoted in Powell, *Antireligious Propaganda*, p. 14.

22. Emelyan Yaroslavsky, "Is the Communist Movement Antireligious? (An Answer to Höglund)," in *Bolshevik Visions: First Phase of the Cultural Revolution in Soviet Russia, Part I: The Culture of a New Society—Ethics, Gender, the Family, Law and Problems of Tradition*, ed. William G. Rosenberg (Ann Arbor: University of Michigan Press, 1990), p. 242.

23. Bohdan Bociurkiw, "Lenin and Religion," in *Lenin: The Man, the Theorist, the Leader—A Reappraisal*, ed. Leonard Schapiro and Peter Reddaway (New York: Praeger, 1967), p. 129.

24. E. F. Muravyev and Y. V. Dmitryev, "Atheism and Religion in the USSR," *Soviet Review* 2, no. 7 (July 1961): 52.

25. George L. Kline, *Religious and Antireligious Thought in Russia* (Chicago: University of Chicago Press, 1968), p. 162.

26. Christel Lane, "Some Explanations for the Persistence of Christian Religion in Soviet Society," *Sociology* 8 (1974): 237–38.

27. Ibid., pp. 238–39.

28. Quoted in Paul Edwards, "Pierre Bayle (1647–1706)," *Free Inquiry* (Summer 2003): 57.

29. Fyodor Dostoevsky, *The Brothers Karamazov* (New York: Modern Library, 1996), p. 676.

30. Prince Eugene Trubetzkoy, "The Bolshevist Utopia and the Religious Movement in Russia," *Hibbert Journal* (January 1920): 217.

31. Yaroslavsky, *Religion in the USSR*, p. 19.

32. Lynne Viola, "The Peasant Nightmare: Visions of Apocalypse in the Soviet Countryside," *Journal of Modern History* 62, no. 4 (December 1990): 753.

33. Quoted in Bociurkiw, "Lenin and Religion," p. 128.

34. Richard Stites, *Revolutionary Dreams: Utopian Vision and Experimental Life in the Russian Revolution* (New York: Oxford University Press, 1989), p. 115.

35. *Pravda*, November 3, 1961, quoted in Paul D. Steeves, *Keeping the Faiths: Religion and Ideology in the Soviet Union* (New York: Holmes and Meier, 1989), p. 136.

36. Kline, *Thought in Russia*, p. 160.

37. Quoted in N. S. Timasheff, *Religion in Soviet Russia, 1917–1942* (London: Religious Book Club, 1943), p. 12.

38. Bakunin, *God or Labor: The Two Camps*.

39. James Rachels, *Elements of Moral Philosophy* (New York: Random House, 1986), page number lost.

40. *Catholic Encyclopedia* (New York: Robert Appleton, 1907–1909), vol. 5, pp. 557, 562, quoted in Joseph Wheless, *Forgery in Christianity: A Documented Record of the Foundations of the Christian Religion* (New York: Knopf, 1930), p. 341.

41. A. Tokarev, *Religion in the History of the Peoples of the World* (Moscow, 1964), quoted in James Thrower, *Marxist-Leninist "Scientific Atheism" and the Study of Religion and Atheism in the USSR* (New York: Mouton, 1983), pp. 412–13.

42. Guthrie, *Clouds*, p. 18.

43. Quoted in Jim Zwick, ed., *Mark Twain's Religion*.

44. Walter Kolarz, *Religion in the Soviet Union* (New York: St. Martin's, 1961), pp. 18–19.

BIBLIOGRAPHY

Listed Web sites were in existence at the listed access date. If a site can no longer be located at the Web address given, perhaps the additional information will assist in locating it. Because Web sites do not normally have pages in the traditional book sense, I have numbered my pages as I have printed them in order to make it a little more convenient for any reader referring to them.

Achelis, Elisabeth. "Russia's Difficulties." *Journal of Calendar Reform* (1954). http://www.personal.ecu.edu/mccartyr/Russia.html (accessed May 18, 2005).

Alfeyev, Father Hilarion. *Atheism and Orthodoxy in Modern Russia.* A speech delivered (by the Russian Orthodox Church of Three Saints, Garfield, NJ) at the Orthodox Peace Fellowship retreat in Vezelay, France, May 5–7, 2001. http://www.geocities.com/frgeorgek/atheism_orthodoxy.html (accessed May 18, 2005).

Almedingen, Martha Edith. *The Catholic Church in Russia Today.* New York: P. J. Kenedy and Sons, 1923.

Altrichter, Helmut. "Insoluble Conflicts: Village Life between Revolution and Collectivization." In Fitzpatrick, *Russia in the Era of NEP.*

Anderson, Paul B. "The Council for Religious Affairs and the Shaping of Soviet Religious Policy." *Soviet Studies* 43, no. 4 (1991): 689–710.

———. *People, Church and State in Modern Russia.* London: Student Christian Movement Press, 1944.

———. "Reflections on Religion in Russia: 1917–1967." In Marshall, *Aspects of Religion in the Soviet Union.*

Andreyev [Andreyevsky, pseud.], Ivan M. *Is the Grace of God Present in the Soviet Church?* Introduction by Protodeacon Christopher Birchall. Written and originally published in Jordanville, NY, 1948. This edition (Wildwood, Alberta, Canada: Monastery Press, 2000) contains two essays: "Is the Grace of God Present in the Soviet Church?" and "Notes about the Catacomb Church in the USSR."

Anthony, Metropolitan of Kiev and Galich. *How Does Orthodoxy Differ from the Western Denominations?* Pamphlet extracted from Anthony, *The Moral Teaching of the Orthodox Church.* New York: 1967.

Applebaum, Anne. *Gulag: A History.* New York: Doubleday, 2003.

Aptheker, Herbert. "Marxism and Religion." In Aptheker, *Marxism and Christianity.*

———, ed. *Marxism and Christianity: A Symposium.* New York: Humanities, 1968.

Bach, Marcus. *God and the Soviets.* New York: Crowell, 1958.

Bakunin, Michael. *God or Labor: The Two Camps.* http://home.thirdage.com/education /ralphdavid/godlabor.html (accessed May 18, 2005). Excerpted from Guy A. Aldred, *Bakunin's Writings.* New York: Modern Publishers, 1947.

———. *God and the State.* New York: Dover, 1970.

Batalden, Stephen. *Modern Russian Bible Translation: Four Questions That Prevent Consensus.* http://www.samford.edu/groups/global/ewcmreport/articles/ew07205.htm (accessed May 18, 2005). Excerpted from *East-West Church and Ministry Report* 7, no. 2 (Spring 1999): 9–10.

Beilinson, Moise. "Two Internationals: Red and Black, Rapprochement between the Church of Rome and the Soviet Government." *New Republic* 32, no. 408 (September 27, 1922): 123–24.

Belinsky, Vissarion. *Selected Philosophical Works.* Moscow: Foreign Language Publishing House, 1948.

Belliustin, Ioann. *Description of the Clergy in Rural Russia: The Memoir of a Nineteenth-Century Parish Priest.* Ithaca, NY: Cornell University Press, 1985. Originally published in 1850 as *Opisanie sel'skogo dukhovenstva.*

Benet, Sula, ed. *The Village of Viriatino: An Ethnographic Study of a Russian Village from before the Revolution to the Present.* Garden City, NY: Doubleday, 1970. First published in Moscow in 1958.

Berdyaev, Nicolas. *The Origin of Russian Communism.* Ann Arbor: University of Michigan Press, 1960.

———. *The Russian Revolution.* Ann Arbor: University of Michigan Press, 1961.

Bergman, Jay. "The Image of Jesus in the Russian Revolutionary Movement: The Case of Russian Marxism." *International Review of Social History* 35 (1990): 220–48.

Berman, Harold J. *Freedom of Religion in Russia: An Amicus Brief for the Defendant.* http://www.law.emory.edu/EILR/volumes/win98/berman.html (accessed June 10, 2004, but no longer available). This essay can now be found on pages 265–84 in John Witte Jr. and Michael Bourdeaux, *Proselytism and Orthodoxy in Russia: The New War for Souls.* New York: Orbis, 1999.

Bernstein, Philip S. "Religion in Russia." *Harpers*, May 1930, pp. 733–39.

Billington, James H. *Religious Revival in Russia: Discovery and Change.* http://www .georgetown.edu/centers/woodstock/report/r-fea31.htm (accessed May 18, 2005). *Woodstock Report* no. 31 (October 1992): 3–8. One of a number of presentations encompassed under the title "Religion in the Former Soviet Republics," sponsored by the Woodstock Theological Center.

Bird, Thomas E. *Conservative Trends within the Russian Church.* http://www.george-town.edu/centers/woodstock/report/r-fea31.htm (accessed May 18, 2005). *Woodstock Report* no. 31 (October 1992): 3–8. One of a number of presentations encompassed under the title "Religion in the Former Soviet Republics," sponsored by the Woodstock Theological Center.

———. "The Party, the Patriarch and the World Council." *Commonweal,* April 13, 1962.

Blake, Patricia. "Alliance with the Unholy." *Life,* September 14, 1959, pp. 114–26.

Blane, Andrew Q. "Protestant Sectarians in the First Year of Soviet Rule." In Marshall, *Aspects of Religion in the Soviet Union.*

Bociurkiw, Bohdan. "Lenin and Religion." In Schapiro and Reddaway, *Lenin: The Man, the Theorist, the Leader,* pp. 107–34.

———. "Religion and Atheism in Soviet Society." In Marshall, *Aspects of Religion in the Soviet Union,* pp. 45–60.

Bogolepov, Alexander A. "The Legal Position of the Russian Orthodox Church in the Soviet Union." In Marshall, *Aspects of Religion in the Soviet Union.*

Bolshakov, Serge. *The Christian Church and the Soviet State.* London: Society for Promoting Christian Knowledge, 1942.

———. *Russian Nonconformity: The Story of "Unofficial" Religion in Russia.* Philadelphia: Westminster, 1950.

"Bolshevism out to Abolish God." *Literary Digest,* January 17, 1920, pp. 36–37.

Bourdeaux, Michael. *Religious Minorities in the Soviet Union.* Rev. 4th ed. London: Minority Rights Group, 1984.

———. *Risen Indeed: Lessons in Faith from the USSR.* London: Darton, Longman, and Todd, 1983.

Bowman, Herbert E. *Vissarian Belinski, 1811–1848: A Study in the Origins of Social Criticism in Russia.* Cambridge, MA: Harvard University Press, 1954.

Brailsford, H. N. "Religion and the Soviets." *New Republic,* May 7, 1930, pp. 321–23.

Bukharin, Nikolai, and E. Preobrazhensky. *ABC of Communism—A Popular Explanation of the Program of the Communist Party of Russia.* Ann Arbor: University of Michigan Press, 1966.

Bulgakov, Sergius. *The Orthodox Church.* Crestwood, NY: St. Vladimir's Seminary Press, 1988.

Bunyan, James, and H. H. Fisher. *The Bolshevik Revolution, 1917–1918: Documents and Materials.* Palo Alto, CA: Stanford University Press, 1934. Reprinted by Stanford University Press in 1961.

Buss, Gerald. *The Bear's Hug: Christian Belief and the Soviet State, 1917–1986.* Grand Rapids, MI: W. B. Eerdmans, 1987.

Carr, E. H. *Michael Bakunin.* London: Macmillan, 1937.

Carter, Rita. *Mapping the Mind.* Berkeley and Los Angeles: University of California Press, 1998.

Casey, Robert Pierce. *Religion in Russia.* New York: Harper, 1946.

Chamberlin, William Henry. "Russian Crusade against Belief in God." *Current History* 25, no. 1 (October 1926): 28–33.

———. "The Struggle for the Russian Soul: A Phase of Soviet Russia." *Atlantic Monthly*, September 1929, pp. 388–99.

———. "Who's Who in Soviet Russia." *Atlantic Monthly*, October 1924, pp. 545–55.

Cherkasov, Andrei. *In the Town Surovkino, Even Cossacks Sympathize with Old Believers.* http://english.pravda.ru/region/2001/10/06/17248.html (accessed May 18, 2005).

Chernyshevsky, Nikolai. *Selected Philosophical Essays.* Moscow: Foreign Language Publishing House, 1953.

Chidester, David. *Christianity: A Global History.* San Francisco: HarperSanFrancisco, 2000.

Cianfarra, Camille M. *The Vatican and the Kremlin.* New York: Dutton, 1950.

Cloutier, H. Handley. "Belinsky—Advocate of Liberty." *Russian Review* 8, no. 1 (January 1949): 20–33.

Coffman, Elesha. "Soviets, Schism and Sabotage: How the Government Manipulated Division in the Russian Orthodox Church." *Christianity Today*, August 14, 2000. http://www.christianitytoday.com/ct/2000/133/54.0.html (accessed May 18, 2005).

Communist Party Central Committee. "On Antireligious Agitation and Propaganda among Women Workers and Peasants." In Rosenberg, *Bolshevik Visions*, pp. 244–47.

Compassionate Love—Metropolitan Anthony Khrapovitsky. Nikodemos Orthodox Publication Society, 2000. http://www.roca.org/OA/61/61f.htm (accessed May 18, 2005).

Conquest, Robert. *Religion in the USSR.* London: Bodley Head, 1968.

Cooke, Richard J. *Religion in Russia under the Soviets.* New York: Abingdon, 1924.

Corley, Felix. *Religion in the Soviet Union: An Archival Reader.* New York: New York University Press, 1996.

Crystal, David, ed. *The Cambridge Biographical Encyclopedia.* 2nd ed. Cambridge: Cambridge University Press, 1998.

Cunningham, James W. "The Russian Patriarchate and the Attempt to Recover Symphonia." *Canadian-American Slavic Studies* 26, nos. 1–3 (1992): 267–92.

Curtiss, John Shelton. *Church and State in Russia, 1900–1917.* New York: Columbia University Press, 1940.

———. *The Russian Church and the Soviet State, 1917–1950.* Boston: Little, Brown, 1953.

Davis, Jerome. "Religion in Soviet Russia." *Missionary Review of the World* 45, no. 3 (March 1922): 189–92.

Davis, Nathaniel. *A Long Walk to Church: A Contemporary History of Russian Orthodoxy.* San Francisco: Westview, 1995.

———. "The Number of Orthodox Churches before and after the Khrushchev Antireligious Drive." *Slavic Review* 50, no. 3 (Autumn 1991): 612–20.

Dawkins, Richard. *A Devil's Chaplain: Reflections on Hope, Lies, Science, and Love.* Boston: Houghton Mifflin, 2003.

———. "Now Here's a Bright Idea." *Free Inquiry* (October/November 2003): 12–13.

De Basily, Nicolas. *Russia under Soviet Rule: Twenty Years of Bolshevik Experiment.* London: Allen and Unwin, 1938.

De Bivort de la Saudée, J. *Communism and Antireligion.* London: Burns, Oates, and Washbourne, 1938.

De Grunwald, Constantin. *The Churches and the Soviet Union.* New York: Macmillan, 1962.

Delaney, Joan. "The Origins of Soviet Antireligious Organizations." In Marshall, *Aspects of Religion in the Soviet Union.*

Demidov, I. "Fight for Survival." *Living Age,* September 30, 1922, pp. 826–29. Originally published in *Sovremennya Zapiski* (a Parisian Russian language liberal periodical), July 14, 1922.

Dewey, John. "Religion in the Soviet Union: II—An Interpretation of the Conflict." *Current History* 32, no. 1 (April 1930): 31–36.

D'Herbigny, Monsignor M. *Militant Atheism: The Worldwide Propaganda of Communism.* London: Society for Promoting Christian Knowledge, 1933.

Diers, Didier, and Xavier Valla. *The Russian Sect of the Castrated from the 18th to the 20th Century.* http://www.nocirc.org/symposia/fourth/diers.html (accessed May 18, 2005). Presented at the Fourth International Symposium on Sexual Mutilations, University of Lausanne, Lausanne, Switzerland, August 9–11, 1996.

Dostoevsky, Fyodor. *The Brothers Karamazov.* New York: Modern Library, 1996. Originally written in 1879–1880.

Dukhobors. http://www.encyclopedia.com/html/D/Dukhobor.asp (accessed May 18, 2005).

Dunn, Ethel. "Russian Sectarianism in New Soviet Marxist Scholarship." *Slavic Review* 26, no. 1 (March 1967): 128–40.

Dunn, Ethel, and Stephen P. Dunn. "Religion as an Instrument of Cultural Change: The Problem of the Sects in the Soviet Union." *Slavic Review* 23, no. 3 (September 1964): 459–78.

Easterbrook, Gregg. *The Vatican's Turn to Recant: Scientists Censured in the Past Are Being Posthumously Redeemed.* http://www.beliefnet.com/story/13/story_1349 _1.html (accessed May 18, 2005).

Edwards, Paul. "Pierre Bayle (1647–1706)." *Free Inquiry* (Summer 2003): 55–58.

Emhardt, William Chauncey, ed. *Religion in Soviet Russia.* London: Morehouse, 1929.

Epp, Frank H. "Mennonites in the Soviet Union." In Marshall, *Aspects of Religion in the Soviet Union.*

Eudin, Xenia Joukoff, and Harold H. Fisher, eds. *Soviet Russia and the West: 1920–1927: A Documentary Survey.* Stanford, CA: Stanford University Press, 1957.

Eudin, Xenia Joukoff, and Robert C. North, eds. *Soviet Russia and the East: 1920–1927: A Documentary Survey.* Stanford, CA: Stanford University Press, 1957.

Evtuhov, Catherine. "The Church in the Russian Revolution: Arguments for and against Restoring the Patriarchate at the Church Council of 1917–1918." *Slavic Review* 50, no. 3 (Autumn 1991): 497–511.

"Failure of Religion in Russia." *Literary Digest,* June 14, 1919, p. 32.

Fedotov, G. P. *The Russian Church since the Revolution.* New York: Macmillan, 1928.

Feuerbach, Ludwig. *The Essence of Christianity*. Amherst, NY: Prometheus Books, 1989. Originally published in Germany in 1841.

Fischer, Louis. "Soviet Russia's Grim Battle against Religion." *Current History* 18, no. 4 (July 1923): 588–97.

———. "The Vatican and the Kremlin." *Nation*, January 15, 1930, pp. 82–83.

Fisher, Harold H. *The Famine in Soviet Russia, 1919–1923: The Operations of the American Relief Administration*. Freeport, NY: Books for Libraries, 1971.

Fitzgerald, Rev. Thomas. *The Great Schism*. Holy Cross School of Theology, Department of Religious Education, Greek Orthodox Archdiocese of America, 1996. http://www.goarch.org/en/ourfaith/articles/article7102.asp (accessed May 18, 2005).

Fitzpatrick, Sheila, et al., eds. *Russia in the Era of NEP: Explorations in Soviet Society and Culture*. Bloomington: Indiana University Press, 1991.

Fletcher, William C. *The Russian Orthodox Church Underground, 1917–1970*. London: Oxford University Press, 1971.

Fletcher, William C. and Anthony J. Strover, eds. *Religion and the Search for New Ideals in the USSR*. New York: Praeger, 1967.

Forest, Jim. *Religion in the New Russia: The Impact of Perestroika on the Varieties of Religious Life in the Soviet Union*. New York: Crossroad, 1990.

Freeze, Gregory L. "Counter-Reformation in Russian Orthodoxy: Popular Response to Religious Innovation, 1922–1925." *Slavic Review* 54, no. 2 (Summer 1995): 305–39.

Fried, Albert, and Ronald Sanders. *Socialist Thought: A Documentary History*. Garden City, NY: Anchor Books, 1964.

Fueloep-Miller, René. *The Mind and Face of Bolshevism: An Examination of Cultural Life in Soviet Russia*. New York: Harper and Row, 1965.

Furniss, Edgar S. "Class War Linked with Anti-Religion in Soviet Policy." *Current History* 31, no. 3 (December 1929): 606–608.

———. "Religion in the Soviet Union: I—The History of the Conflict." *Current History* 32, no. 1 (April 1930): 25–30.

Galter, Albert. *The Red Book of the Persecuted Church*. Dublin, Ireland: M. H. Gill, 1957. *The Generals of the Society of Jesus*. http://www.sogang.ac.kr/~gesukr /sj /sjgen15.html (accessed June 10, 2004, but no longer available).

Georgi Valentinovich Plekhanov. http://www.marxists.org/glossary/people/p/l.htm (accessed May 18, 2005). *Encyclopedia of Marxism*: glossary of people.

Gérin, Annie. *Godless at the Workbench: Soviet Illustrated Humoristic Antireligious Propaganda*. Regina, Canada: Dunlop Art Gallery, 2003.

Gitelman, Zvi. "The Communist Party and Soviet Jewry: The Early Years." In Marshall, *Aspects of Religion in the Soviet Union*.

"Going to Church in Russia." *Literary Digest*, December 13, 1919, p. 36.

Gogolev, Andrei. "Tragedy of Kazan Adventists." *Kommersant-Daily*, November 21, 1997.

Goldman, Emma. *My Disillusionment in Russia*. Mineola, New York: Dover, 2003. Originally published in 1923. Chapter 21 ("Exploiting the Famine") is excerpted online at http://www.marxists.org.

Graham, James. *The Russian Civil War.* http://www.historyorb.com/russia/civil_war .shtml (accessed May 18, 2005).

Graham, Stephen. *Undiscovered Russia.* http://www.vologda-oblast.ru/main.asp?V=403 &LNG=ENG (accessed May 18, 2005).

Gray, J. Patrick. "The Long Alliance of Patriarch Aleksy II and the Communist Party of Russia." *Washington Times.* http://www.episcopalian.org/rmn/ANEDITOR.htm (accessed May 18, 2005).

Greater Love Hath No Man: New Martyr Metropolitan Benjamin of Petrograd. Nikodemos Orthodox Publication Society, Orthodox America, 1998–2000. http://www.roca.org/OA/66-68/66h.htm (accessed May 18, 2005).

Gurian, Waldemar. *Bolshevism: Theory and Practice.* London: Sheed and Ward, 1933.

Gussoni, Lino, and Aristede Brunello. *The Silent Church: Facts and Documents concerning Religious Persecution behind the Iron Curtain.* New York: Veritas, 1954.

Guthrie, Stewart Elliott. *Faces in the Clouds: A New Theory of Religion.* New York: Oxford University Press, 1993.

Haller, Francis. *Famine in Russia: The Hidden Horrors of 1921.* http://www.icrc .org/Web/eng/siteeng0.nsf/html/5RFHJY (accessed May 18, 2005).

Halliday, E. M. *Russia in Revolution.* New York: American Heritage, 1967.

Hallman, J. C. *The Chess Artist: Genius, Obsession, and the World's Oldest Game.* New York: Dunne, 2003.

Hare, Richard. *Pioneers of Russian Social Thought: Studies of Non-Marxian Formation in Nineteenth-Century Russia and of Its Partial Revival in the Soviet Union.* New York: Oxford University Press, 1951.

Harrigan, Steve. "Russian, Italian Leaders Agree to Boost Relations." *Cable News Network, Inc.* (contributions by Associated Press and Reuters), February 10, 1998.

Hartman, L. O. "The Religious Situation in Russia." *Missionary Review of the World* 46, no. 8 (August 1923): 611–19.

Hazard, John N. *The Soviet System of Government.* Rev. ed. Chicago: University of Chicago Press, 1957.

Hecker, Julius F. *Religion and Communism: A Study of Religion and Atheism in Soviet Russia.* Westport, CT: Hyperion, 1973. This is a reprint of the 1934 John Wiley and Sons edition.

———. *Religion under the Soviets.* New York: Vanguard, 1927.

Hefner, Alan G. *Khlysty.* http://www.themystica.com/mystica/articles/k/khlysty.html (accessed May 18, 2005).

Hieroconfessor Agathangelus, Metropolitan of Yaroslavl. Nikodemos Orthodox Publication Society, Orthodox America, 1998–2000. http://www.orthodox.net/russiannm /agath-angelus-metropolitan-and-hieroconfessor-of-yaroslavl.html (accessed May 18, 2005).

Hieromartyr Benjamin, Metropolitan of Petrograd, and Those with Him. St. Nicholas Russian Orthodox Church. Priest Seraphim Holland. http://www.orthodox.net/russiannm/benjamin-metropolitan-and-hieromartyr-of-petrograd-and-those-with-him.html (accessed May 18, 2005).

Hieromartyr Peter, Metropolitan of Krutitsa. St. Nicholas Russian Orthodox Church. Priest Seraphim Holland. http://www.orthodox.net/russiannm/peter-metropolitan-and-hieromartyr-of-krutitsa.html (accessed May 18, 2005).

Hieromartyr Tikhon, Patriarch of Moscow and All Russia. St. Nicholas Russian Orthodox Church. Priest Seraphim Holland. http://www.orthodox.net/russiannm/hieromartyr-tikhon-patriarch-of-moscow-and-all-russia.html (accessed May 18, 2005).

High, Stanley. "The Triumph of Atheism in Russia." *Atlantic Monthly,* January 1925, pp. 122–30.

Hindus, Maurice. *Humanity Uprooted.* New York: J. Cape and H. Smith, 1929. *A Historical Survey of the Parish of St. John the Baptist.* Russian Orthodox Cathedral of St. John the Baptist, Washington, DC, September 1999. http://www.stjohndc.org/Jubilee/History.htm (accessed May 18, 2005).

Höglund, Zeth. "Communism and Religion." In Rosenberg, *Bolshevik Visions.*

Holmes, John Haynes. "Religion in Revolutionary Russia." *Nation,* May 9, 1923, pp. 541–44.

Holmes, Larry E. *The Kremlin and the Schoolhouse: Reforming Education in Soviet Russia, 1917–1931.* Bloomington: Indiana University Press, 1991.

"How Bolshevism Is Overwhelming the Russian Church." *Current Opinion* 74, no. 6 (June 1923): 726–27.

Hulmes, Edward. "Marx and the Bible." In Metzger and Coogan, *The Oxford Companion to the Bible.*

Humphrey, George. "UA Professor Emeritus Publishes First English Translation of Rare Book by Intriguing Russian Figure, Alexander Bogdanov." http://www.ahsc.arizona.edu/opa/news/sep02/russia.htm (accessed May 18, 2005).

Husband, William B. *Godless Communists: Atheism and Society in Soviet Russia, 1917–1932.* DeKalb, IL: Northern Illinois University Press, 2000.

———. "Soviet Atheism and Russian Orthodox Strategies of Resistance, 1917–1932." *Journal of Modern History* 70 (March 1998): 74–107.

Ivanov-Treenadzaty, Deacon Herman. *The Vatican and Russia: The Eastern Rite and the Bolshevik Revolution.* Orthodox Christian Information Center. http://www.orthodox-info.com/ecumenism/vatican_russia.aspx (accessed May 18, 2005).

Jaeger, John. *The Religious Interrelationship between Hegel, Feuerbach and Marx.* http://www.wordtheque.com/pls/wordtc/new_wordtheque.w6_start.doc?code=56909&lang=EN (accessed May 18, 2005). Theological Gathering 3, Spring 1997, Urbana-Champaign, IL, April 10, 1997.

Kallen, H. M. "Religion in Russia." *New Republic* 52, no. 674 (November 2, 1927): 279–82.

Kania, Wladyslav. *Bolshevism and Religion.* New York: Polish Library, 1946.

Kao, Jennifer, and John McCrory. *The Political Economy of a Disaster: Famine in Russia, 1921–1922.* http://www.johnmccrory.com/articles/article.asp?this=243 (accessed May 18, 2005).

Karner, Charles. "Protestant World Report." *Hungarian Protestant Almanac,* 1933. Also published online as "Persecution of Christians in Bolshevik Russia." http://www.cry-ingvoice.com/Christian_martyrs/Bols1.html (accessed May 18, 2005).

Karpov, G. *Rapprochement between the Orthodox Church and Soviet Government*. The Internet Modern History Sourcebook, part of the Internet History Sourcebooks Project (created in 1997). http://darkwing.uoregon.edu/~sshoemak/325/texts/karpov.htm (accessed May 18, 2005). Speech delivered at the Orthodox Church Sobor in Moscow in 1945.

Kartashev, A. A. "Church Reform." In Raeff, *Peter the Great*.

Kellock, Harold. "Religion in the Soviet Union: IV—The Soviet Point of View." *Current History* 32, no. 1 (April 1930): 38–40.

Kenez, Peter. *The Birth of the Propaganda State: Soviet Methods of Mass Mobilization, 1917–1929*. New York: Cambridge University Press, 1985.

———. *The Defeat of the Whites: Civil War in South Russia, 1919–1920*. Berkeley and Los Angeles: University of California Press, 1977.

———. "Pogroms and White Ideology in the Russian Civil War." In Klier and Lambroza, *Pogroms*.

Klibanov, A. I. "The Dissident Denominations in the Past and Today." *Soviet Sociology* 3, no. 4 (Spring 1965): 44–60.

Klier, John D., and Shlomo Lambroza, eds. *Pogroms: Anti-Jewish Violence in Modern Russian History*. New York: Cambridge University Press, 1992.

Kline, George L. *Religious and Antireligious Thought in Russia*. Chicago: University of Chicago Press, 1968.

Kohn, Hans, ed. *The Mind of Modern Russia: Historical and Political Thought of Russia's Great Age*. New York: Harper and Row, 1955.

Kolarz, Walter. *Religion in the Soviet Union*. New York: St. Martin's, 1961.

Kutash, Archpriest Ihor. *A Brief History of the Ukrainian Orthodox Church*. http://www.unicorne.org/orthodoxy/articles/contributors/articles/historyuocc.htm (accessed May 18, 2005).

Lampert, E. *Studies in Rebellion*. London: Routledge, 1957.

Lane, Christel. "The Case of the Molokan Sect in Soviet Society." *Comparative Studies in Society and History* 17, no. 2, (April 1975): 221–37. http://www.molokane.org/molokan/History/Lane.htm (accessed May 18, 2005).

———. "Some Explanations for the Persistence of Christian Religion in Soviet Society." *Sociology* 8 (1974): 233–44.

Lauer, Quentin. "The Atheism of Karl Marx." In Aptheker, *Marxism and Christianity*.

Ledit, Joseph. *Archbishop John Baptist Cieplak*. Montreal: Palm, 1963.

Lenin, V. I. *The Attitude of the Workers' Party to Religion*. http://www.marxists.org/archive/lenin/works/1909/may/13.htm (accessed May 18, 2005). This essay can also be found in Lenin, *Collected Works*, vol. 15. Moscow: Progress Publishers, n.d., 402–13.

———. *Draft Resolution on the Publication of a Periodical for Members of Religious Sects*. August 1903. http://www.marxists.org/archive/lenin/works/1903/2ndcong/6.htm

(accessed May 18, 2005). Section 6 of the minutes of the Second Regular Congress of the Russian Social Democratic Labor Party. These minutes can also be found in Lenin, *Collected Works*, 4th English ed. Moscow: Progress Publishers, 1965, pp. 359–424.

———. "Socialism and Religion." *Novaya Zhizn*, no. 28 (December 3, 1905). http://www.marxists.org/archive/lenin/works/1905/dec/03.htm (accessed May 18, 2005). See also Lenin, *Collected Works*, 4th English ed. Moscow: Progress Publishers, 1972.

———. *Speech at the First All-Russia Congress of Working Women*. http://www.marxists.org/archive/lenin/works/1918/nov/19.htm (accessed May 18, 2005). See also Lenin, *Collected Works*, vol. 28. Moscow: Progress Publishers, 1974, pp. 180–82.

Lesourd, Paul (Society of Jesus). *They Doubly Tear Down: How the Church Functions in Time of Crisis—Historical Precedents and Modern Practice*. http://www.olfatima.com/they_doubly_tear_down.htm (accessed May 18, 2005). An excerpt from *Le Jesuite Clandestin*, translated by Reverend Terence Fulham. Lethielleux: 1976, pp. 65–66.

Letkemann, Peter. *Mennonite Victims of Revolution Anarchy, Civil War, Disease and Famine: 1917–1923*. http://old.mbconf.ca/old/historian/98-06/feature-2.html?view=l (accessed May 18, 2005).

Letter from Lenin. Library of Congress archives. May 19, 1922. http://www.ibiblio.org/expo/soviet.exhibit/ae2bkhun.html (accessed May 18, 2005).

A Letter of Bishop Victor, and Others. http://www.monasterypress.com/martyropinions.html (accessed May 18, 2005). Various statements from the New Martyrs and Confessors of Russia on the question as to whether the Moscow Patriarchate is a valid church organization containing life-saving mysteries. Found in the Archives of the Orthodox St. Tikhon Theological Institute.

Lewin, Moshe. *The Making of the Soviet System: Essays in the Social History of Interwar Russia*. New York: Pantheon, 1985.

Lichtman, Richard. "The Marxian Critique of Christianity." In Aptheker, *Marxism and Christianity*.

Lins, Joseph. *Siberia*. http://www.newadvent.org/cathen/13767b.htm (accessed May 18, 2005). Transcribed by Joseph E. O'Connor from *The Catholic Encyclopedia*, vol. 13, 1912.

Lobkowicz, Nicholas. "Karl Marx's Attitude toward Religion." *Review of Politics* 26, no. 3 (July 1964): 319–52.

Lowrie, Donald A. *The Light of Russia: An Introduction to the Russian Church*. Prague: YMCA Press, 1923.

Lowrie, Donald A., and William C. Fletcher. "Khrushchev's Religious Policy: 1959–1964." In Marshall, *Aspects of Religion in the Soviet Union*.

Mackenzie, A. J. *Propaganda Boom*. London: Right Book Club, 1938.

Mailleux, Paul. "Catholics in the Soviet Union." In Marshall, *Aspects of Religion in the Soviet Union*.

Malia, Martin. *Alexander Herzen and the Birth of Russian Socialism: 1812–1855*. Cambridge, MA: Harvard University Press, 1961.

Marshall, Richard H., Jr. *Aspects of Religion in the Soviet Union: 1917–1967*. Chicago: University of Chicago Press, 1971.

Marx, Karl. Introduction to *A Contribution to the Critique of Hegel's "Philosophy of Right."* *Deutsch-Franzosische Jahrbucher*, February 1844. http://www.marxists .org/archive/marx/works/1843/critique-hpr/ (accessed May 18, 2005).

Marx, Karl, and Friedrich Engels. *On Religion*. New York: Schocken, 1964.

Maximoff, G. P., ed. *The Political Philosophy of Bakunin: Scientific Anarchism*. Glencoe, IL: Free Press, 1953.

McCabe, Joseph. *Atheist Russia Shakes the World: How the Wicked Bolsheviks Save Our Christian World*, edited by E. Haldeman-Julius. http://www.infidels.org/library/histor-ical/joseph_mccabe/big_blue_books/book_09.html (accessed May 18, 2005). Chapters used: "The Vatican Courts Russia for Years" and "Supposed Persecution of Religion."

McClung, Britt. *Molokans, Stundists, and Pashkovites: A Historical and Sociological Exami-nation of the Baptist Schism in the Soviet Union—History of Russian Baptists*. Baylor Uni-versity, Waco, TX. December 8, 1999. http://www.geocities.com/Athens/Olympus/5357 /mcclung.html (accessed May 18, 2005).

McCormick, Anne O'Hare. *The Hammer and the Scythe: Communist Russia Enters the Second Decade*. New York: Knopf, 1928.

McCullagh, Captain Francis. *The Bolshevik Persecution of Christianity*. New York: Dutton, 1924.

Meerson, Michael A. "The Renovationist Schism in the Russian Orthodox Church." *Canadian-American Slavic Studies* 26, nos. 1–4 (1992): 293–314.

Meisel, James H., and Edward S. Kozera, eds. *Materials for the Study of the Soviet System: State and Party Constitutions, Laws, Decrees, Decisions and Official State-ments of the Leaders in Translation*. 2nd ed. Ann Arbor, MI: G. Wahr, 1953.

"Methodist Split on Russia's New Church." *Literary Digest*, July 28, 1923, pp. 30–31.

Metropolitan Joseph of Petrograd and the Beginning of the Catacomb Church. http://www.sisqtel.net/~williams/rcs/metropolitanjoseph.html (accessed May 18, 2005).

Metzger, Bruce M., and Michael D. Coogan, eds. *The Oxford Companion to the Bible*. New York: Oxford University Press, 1993.

Miliukov, Paul. *Outlines of Russian Culture, Part I: Religion and the Church*. Philadel-phia: University of Pennsylvania Press, 1943.

Mitrokhin, L. N. "Education in Atheism and Methodology of Studying the Survival of Religious Beliefs." *Soviet Sociology* 1, no. 1 (Summer 1962): 23–31.

Moss, Vladimir. *The Orthodox Church at the Crossroads: From 1900 to the Present Day*. http://www.romanitas.ru/eng/THE%20ORTHODOX%20CHURCH%20-%20I.htm (accessed May 18, 2005).

Muravyev, E. F., and Y. V. Dmitryev. "Atheism and Religion in the USSR." *Soviet Review* 2, no. 7 (July 1961): 41–56. Originally published in the Soviet Union as "Concrete-ness in the Study and Overcoming of Religion," *Voprosy Filosofi*, no. 3, 1961.

Occult Roots of the Russian Revolution. New Dawn International News Service. http://www.geocities.com/countermedia/1.html (accessed May 18, 2005).

O'Meara, William. *Marx's Atheism and the Ideal of Self-Realization.* http://eserver.org /clogic/3-1&2/omeara.html (accessed May 18, 2005).

Onyschuk, Yaroslav. "What's behind the Russian Antireligious Campaign?" *Texas Quarterly* 10, no. 2 (Summer 1967): 211–14.

Onyshkevych. *Folklore behind the Ivana Kupala Stamp.* http://myweb.wvnet.edu/~roman /potpourri/ivano_kupalo.html (accessed May 18, 2005).

Orthodox Church of Russia. http://www.cnewa.org/ecc-orthodox-russia.htm (accessed May 18, 2005).

Pares, Sir Bernard. *Russia between Reform and Revolution:Fundamentals of Russian History and Character.* New York: Schocken, 1962. Originally published in 1905.

Peris, Daniel. "Commissars in Red Cassocks: Former Priests in the League of the Militant Godless." *Slavic Review* 54, no. 2 (Summer 1995): 340–64.

———. "The 1929 Congress of the Godless." *Soviet Studies* 43, no. 4 (1991): 711–32.

———. *Storming the Heavens: The Soviet League of the Militant Godless.* Ithaca, NY: Cornell University Press, 1998.

Pethybridge, Roger. *One Step Backwards, Two Steps Forward: Soviet Society and Politics in the New Economic Policy.* Oxford: Clarendon, 1990.

———. *The Social Prelude to Stalinism.* London: Macmillan, 1974.

Philaret (Metropolitan). *A Letter from Metropolitan Philaret to Father Victor Potapov of the Church Abroad Concerning Father Dimitry Dudko and the Moscow Patriarchate.* St. Vladimir's Russo-Greek Orthodox Church, 2002. http://www.stvladimirs .ca/library/metropolitan-philaret-potapov-letter.html (accessed May 18, 2005).

Pinker, Steven. *The Blank Slate: The Modern Denial of Human Nature.* New York: Viking, 2002.

Pipes, Richard. *Russia Under the Bolshevik Regime.* New York: Vintage, 1994.

Plokhy, Serhii. "A Review of John Anderson's *Religion, State and Politics in the Soviet Union and Successor States.*" *Journal of Ukrainian Studies* 21, nos. 1–2 (Summer–Winter 1996): 339 and following.

Popoff, Peter J. "The Religious Revolution in Russia." *Current History* 12, no. 1 (April 1920): 94–97.

Pospielovsky, Dimitry. *A History of Marxist-Leninist Atheism and Soviet Antireligious Policies.* London: Macmillan, 1987.

———. "The Renovationist Movement in the Orthodox Church in the Light of Archival Documents." *Journal of Church and State* 39, no. 1 (January 1, 1997): 85–105.

———. *The Russian Church under the Soviet Regime: 1917–1982.* Vol. 1. Crestwood, NY: St. Vladimir's Seminary Press, 1984.

Potapov, Father Victor. *Legacies of Communism for Russian Churches.* http://www .georgetown.edu/centers/woodstock/report/r-fea31.htm (accessed May 18, 2005). *Woodstock Report*, October 1992, no. 31, pp. 3–8. One of a number of presentations encompassed under the title "Religion in the Former Soviet Republics," sponsored by the Woodstock Theological Center.

Powell, David E. *Antireligious Propaganda in the Soviet Union: A Study of Mass Persua-*

sion. Cambridge, MA: MIT Press, 1975.

Prokhanov, Ivan. *In the Cauldron of Russia, 1869–1933*. New York: All-Russian Evangelical Christian Union, 1933.

Rachels, James. *The Elements of Moral Philosophy*. New York: Random House, 1986.

Raeff, Marc, ed. *Peter the Great: Reformer or Revolutionary?* Boston: Heath, 1963.

Randall, Francis B. "Introduction to Karl Marx and Friedrich Engels." In *The Communist Manifesto*. New York: Washington Square, 1964.

Rasputin, Maria. *My Father*. New Hyde Park, NY: University Books, 1970.

Reddaway, Peter. "Literature, the Arts and the Personality of Lenin." In Schapiro and Reddaway, *Lenin: The Man, the Theorist, the Leader*.

"Religion and Anti-Religion in Russia: Observations by Recent Visitors." *Missionary Review of the World* 48, no. 5 (May 1925): 371–80.

"Religious Conditions in Russia." *Hibbert Journal* 24, no. 3 (April 1926): 449–62.

Revelations from the Russian Archives. Early Cooperation: American Famine Relief.http://www.loc.gov/exhibits/archives/eara.html (accessed May 18, 2005).

Rosenberg, William G., ed. *Bolshevik Visions: First Phase of the Cultural Revolution in Soviet Russia—Part I: The Culture of a New Society: Ethics, Gender, the Family, Law and Problems of Tradition*. Ann Arbor: University of Michigan Press, 1990.

Roslof, Edward E. "The Heresy of 'Bolshevik' Christianity: Orthodox Rejection of Religious Reform during NEP." *Slavic Review* 55, no. 3 (Autumn 1996): 614–35.

Ross, Edward Alsworth. *The Russian Soviet Republic*. New York: Century, 1923.

Rothenberg, Joshua. "The Legal Status of Religion in the Soviet Union." In Marshall, *Aspects of Religion in the Soviet Union*.

Royal, Robert. *The Soviet Terror*. Arlington Catholic Herald, Inc. Crossroads, 2000. http://www.catholicherald.com/royal/royal10.htm (accessed May 18, 2005). The tenth in a series of online articles based on his book: *The Catholic Martyrs of the Twentieth Century—A Comprehensive Global History*.

Ruhl, Arthur. "The Bolshevik Drive on the Church." *Nation*, April 11, 1923, pp. 417–19. Including "A Correction" [to the April 11 article], *Nation*, April 25, 1923, 495, that printed a quotation by J. Okunov in *Pravda* that had been inadvertently omitted in the original article.

"Russians Standardize Religion." *Literary Digest*, March 13, 1920, p. 37.

Safonov, Dmitry. "Eighty Years Ago Holy Martyr Ilarion Reconsecrated the Church of the Presentation Monastery after Expelling Renovationists." http://www.stetson.edu/~psteeves/relnews/0307d.html (accessed May 18, 2005).

Saint John of Shanghai and San Francisco. "Holy Righteous John of Kronstadt: On the Occasion of his Glorification." *Parish Life*, October 1997. http://www.stjohndc.org/stjohndc/English/Saints/9711c1.htm (accessed May 18, 2005).

Schapiro, Leonard, and Peter Reddaway, eds. *Lenin: The Man, the Theorist, the Leader— A Reappraisal*. New York: Praeger, 1967.

Selezneva, Ludmilla. Lectures delivered by this professor of history at Rostov State University aboard the ship *Viking Kirov*, June 2003.

Serbyn, Dr. Roman. "The First Man-Made Famine in Soviet Ukraine, 1921–1923." *Ukrainian Weekly*, November 6, 1988. http://www.ukrweekly.com/Archive/1988 /458814.shtml (accessed May 18, 2005).

The Servant of God Exarch Leonid Feodorov. Transalpine Redemptorists. http://www .redemptorists .org.uk/red/mag/russian1.htm (accessed May 18, 2005).

Seventh-Day Adventist Church/Fundamental Beliefs. http://www.adventist.org/beliefs /index.html (accessed May 18, 2005).

Shahovskoy, Archbishop John. "The Church and the Cremation Problem." Holy Trinity Cathedral *Church Life Bulletin*, November 1962 (modified November 21, 1998). http://www.holy-trinity.org/morality/shahovskoy-cremation.html (accessed May 18, 2005).

Sheinman, M. M. *Religion and Church in the USSR*. Moscow: Cooperative Publishing Society of Foreign Workers in the USSR, 1933.

Sherwood, M. *The Soviet War on Religion*. New York: Workers' Library Publishers, c. 1930.

Shkarovsky, Mikhail V. "The Russian Orthodox Church vs. the State: The Josephite Movement, 1927–1940." *Slavic Review* 54, no. 2 (Summer 1995): 365–84.

Siegelbaum, Lewis H. *Soviet State and Society between Revolutions: 1918–1929*. New York: Cambridge University Press, 1992.

Smith, Norman J. "The Evangelical Christians in Russia." *Missionary Review of the World* 48, no. 7 (July 1925): 525–32.

Solzhenitsyn, Alexander. *The Gulag Archipelago, 1918–1956*. Vols. 1 and 2. San Francisco: HarperSanFrancisco, 1973 and 1974.

"Soviet Russia and Religion." *Missionary Review of the World* 46, no. 11 (November 1923): 886–88.

"Soviet Russia's Grim Battle against Religion." *Current History* 18, no. 4 (July 1923): 588–97.

Spinka, Matthew. *The Church and the Russian Revolution*. New York: Macmillan, 1927.

———. *The Church in Soviet Russia*. New York: Oxford University Press, 1956.

Stalin, Joseph. *The Foundations of Leninism*. http://ptb.lashout.net/marx2mao/Stalin /FL24.html (accessed June 10, 2004, but no longer available)

———. *Mastering Bolshevism*. New York: Workers Library Publishers, 1937. http://www.marx2mao.com/Stalin/MB37.html (accessed May 18, 2005).

Steeves, Paul D. *The Canonization of Patriarch Tikhon as a Reflection of New Thinking in the Glasnost Era*. http://www.stetson.edu/~psteeves/canonizationoftikhon.html (accessed May 18, 2005). Paper presented at the Berlin-Brandenburgisches Staat-Kirche-Kolloquium, May 22–24, 1996.

———. *Keeping the Faiths: Religion and Ideology in the Soviet Union*. New York: Holmes and Meier, 1989.

———. *Russian Baptists and the Military Question, 1920–1929*. Stetson University, January 1996. http://www.stetson.edu/~psteeves/rusbaptistpacifism.html (accessed May 18, 2005).

Stepniak. *Underground Russia: Revolutionary Profiles and Sketches From Life.* New York: Charles Scribner's Sons, 1885. "Stepniak" is a pseudonym for a former editor of the Populist newspaper *Land and Liberty.*

Stites, Richard. "Bolshevik Ritual Building in the 1920s." In Fitzpatrick, *Russia in the Era of NEP.*

————. *Revolutionary Dreams: Utopian Vision and Experimental Life in the Russian Revolution.* New York: Oxford University Press, 1989.

Stroyen, William B. *Communist Russia and the Russian Orthodox Church, 1943–1962.* Washington, DC: Catholic University of America Press, 1967.

Struve, Nikita. "Pseudo-Religious Rites Introduced by the Party Authorities." In Fletcher and Strover, *Religion and the Search for New Ideals,* pp. 44–48.

Swan, Jane. *A Biography of Patriarch Tikhon.* Jordanville, NY: Holy Trinity Russian Orthodox Monastery, 1964.

Szczesniak, Boleslav, ed. *The Russian Revolution and Religion: A Collection of Documents concerning the Suppression of Religion by the Communists, 1917–1925.* Notre Dame, IN: University of Notre Dame Press, 1959.

Talantov, Boris. *The Moscow Patriarchate and Sergianism.* http://www.orthodoxinfo .com/resistance/cat_tal.aspx (accessed June 10, 2004). Also found in Ivan Andreyev, *Russia's Catacomb Saints.* Platina, CA: St. Herman of Alaska Press, 1982, pp. 463–86.

Thornton, Father James. "Communists Go Up and Down: Yo-Yo Tactics Regarding Religion." Our Lady's Library/The Fatima Crusader. http://www.fatimacrusader.com /cr35/cr35pg28.asp (accessed May 18, 2005). Condensation of an article originally published in *New American,* July 16, 1990, under the title "Pragmatic Atheists."

Thrower, James. *Marxism-Leninism as the Civil Religion of Soviet Society: God's Commissar.* Lewiston, NY: E. Mellen, 1992.

————. *Marxist-Leninist "Scientific Atheism" and the Study of Religion and Atheism in the USSR.* New York: Mouton, 1983.

Tikhon: Saint, Enlightener of America, and Patriarch of Moscow. http://www.antiochian .org/Bishops/tikhon.htm (accessed May 18, 2005).

Timasheff, N. S. *Religion in Soviet Russia, 1917–1942.* London: Religious Book Club, 1943.

Tirado, Isabel A. "The Revolution, Young Peasants, and the Komsomol's Antireligious Campaigns: 1920–1928." *Canadian-American Slavic Studies* 26, nos. 1–3 (1992): 97–117.

Tolstoy, Leo. *Letter to a Non-Commissioned Officer.* Anarchy Archives: An Online Research Center on the History and Theory of Anarchism. http://dwardmac .pitzer.edu/Anarchist_Archives/bright/tolstoy/officer.html (accessed May 18, 2005).

To the Government of the USSR—Appeal of Orthodox Bishops from the Solovetsky Islands (1926). Apparently this document is no longer available online (where I found it). Contact the Keston Institute at www.keston.org and they might be able to produce it.

Treadgold, Donald W. *Twentieth Century Russia.* 2nd ed. Chicago: Rand McNally, 1964.

Tregubov, Ivan. "Church Revolution in Soviet Russia." *Living Age*, September 2, 1922, pp. 585–86. Originally published in *Izvestia*, June 4, 1922.

Troitsky, Sergius. *The Living Church*. This edition is bound inside of William Chauncey Emhardt, *Religion in Soviet Russia*. London: Morehouse, 1929.

Trotsky, Leon. *My Life*. New York: Pathfinder, 1970. Originally written in 1929.

———. "Vodka, the Church and the Cinema." *Pravda*, July 12, 1923. Also in *Bolshevik Visions: First Phase of the Cultural Revolution in Soviet Russia*, pt. 2, edited by William G. Rosenberg. Ann Arbor: University of Michigan Press, 1990, pp. 106–109.

Trubetzkoy, Prince Eugene. "The Bolshevist Utopia and the Religious Movement in Russia." *Hibbert Journal* 18, no. 2 (January 1920): 209–24.

Tumarkin, Nina. "Religion, Bolshevism and the Origins of the Lenin Cult." *Russian Review* 40, no. 1, (January 1981): 35–46.

Turkevich, Leonid. "Remains of Saints and the Russian Church." *Current History* 12, no. 1 (April 1920): 97–99.

Ukraine before World War II. http://insight.busadm.wayne.edu/irene/wwii.htm (accessed June 12, 2004, but no longer available).

Ulam, Adam B. *The Bolsheviks: The Intellectual, Personal and Political History of the Origins of Russian Communism*. New York: Macmillan, 1965.

Urch, R. O. G. "Bolshevism and Religion in Russia." *Atlantic Monthly*, March 1923, pp. 394–406.

Utechin, S. V. *A Concise Encyclopedia of Russia*. New York: Dutton, 1964.

Valentinov, A. A. *The Assault of Heaven: A Collection of Facts and Documents Relating to the Persecution of Religion and Church in Russia, Based Mainly upon Official Sources*. Berlin: M. Mattisson, 1924.

"The Vatican and the Kremlin." *Nation*, January 15, 1930, pp. 82–83.

Vernadsky, George. *A History of Russia*. New Haven, CT: Yale University Press, 1929.

Viola, Lynne. "The Peasant Nightmare: Visions of Apocalypse in the Soviet Countryside." *Journal of Modern History* 62, no. 4 (December 1990): 747–70.

Vladimir, Metropolitan and Hieromartyr of Kiev. St. Nicholas Russian Orthodox Church, Dallas, TX. http://www.orthodox.net/russiannm/vladimir-metropolitan-and-hiero-martyr-of-kiev.html (accessed May 18, 2005).

Wallace, Sir Donald Mackenzie. Originally written in 1877, then revised and published in 1905 as *Russia*. Revised again in 1912 and published as *Russia on the Eve of War and Revolution*. New York: Vintage, 1961. http://emotionalliteracyeducation.com /classic_books_online/rsdmw10.htm (accessed May 18, 2005).

Walsh, Edmund A. *The Catholic Church in Present Day Russia*. Minneapolis, MN, December 29, 1931. A report to the American Catholic Historical Association.

———. "Religion in the Soviet Union: III—A Roman Catholic Indictment." *Current History* 32, no. 1 (April 1930): 36–38.

Walters, Philip. "The Renovationist Coup: Personalities and Programs." In *Church, Nation, and State in Russia and Ukraine*, edited by Geoffrey A. Hosking. London: Macmillan, 1991.

Ware, Timothy. *The Orthodox Church*. Baltimore, MD: Penguin, 1963.

Weiant, Edmund T. *Sources of Modern Mass Atheism in Russia*. Mt. Vernon, OH: Printing Arts, 1953.

Wheless, Joseph. *Forgery in Christianity: A Documented Record of the Foundations of the Christian Religion*. New York: Knopf, 1930.

White, William C. "The Triple-Barred Cross." *Scribner's*, July 1930, pp. 67–78.

Whiteford, Father John. *The Orthodox Approach to Truth/Sola Scriptura: In the Vanity of Their Minds/An Orthodox Examination of the Protestant Teaching*. http://www.philthompson.net/pages/library/solascriptura.html (accessed May 18, 2005).

Whittemore, Thomas. "The Rebirth of Religion in Russia." *National Geographic*, November 1918, pp. 378–401.

Williams, Albert Rhys. *The Russian Land*. New York: New Republic, 1928.

Williams, Ariadna. "Atheism and Religion in Russia." *Nineteenth Century and After* 106, no. 631 (September 1929): 335–45.

Written Address of the Bishops in Solovky to Metropolitan Sergei. Apparently this document is no longer available online (where I found it). Contact the Keston Institute at www.keston.org; they might be able to produce it.

Wynot, Jennifer. *Russian Orthodox Monasteries' Response to the Relics Exposing Campaign, 1917–1922*. http://www.georgefox.edu/academics/undergrad/departments/soc-swk/ree/2003/wynot03.doc (accessed May 18, 2005). Excerpt from Wynot, *Keeping the Faith: Russian Orthodox Monasticism in the Soviet Union, 1917–1939*. College Station: Texas A&M University Press, 2004.

Yaroslavsky, Emelyan. "Is the Communist Movement Antireligious? (An Answer to Höglund)." In Rosenberg, *Bolshevik Visions*.

———. *Religion in the USSR*. New York: International Publishers, 1934. This book was written for foreign consumption.

Young, Glennys. *Power and the Sacred in Revolutionary Russia: Religious Activists in the Village*. University Park: University of Pennsylvania Press, 1997.

Zatko, James J. "A Contemporary Report on the Condition of the Catholic Church in Russia, 1922." *Harvard Theological Review* 53, no. 4 (October 1960): 277–95.

———. *Descent into Darkness: The Destruction of the Roman Catholic Church in Russia, 1917–1923*. Notre Dame, IN: University of Notre Dame Press, 1965.

Zenkovsky, V. V. *A History of Russian Philosophy*. Vol. 1. New York: Columbia University Press, 1953.

Zernov, Nicolas. *The Russians and Their Church*. 3rd ed. Crestwood, NY: St. Vladimir's Seminary Press, 1994.

Zwick, Jim, ed. *Mark Twain's Religion*. http://www.boondocksnet.com/twaintexts/biography/paine_bio295.html (accessed May 18, 2005).

INDEX

Abbreviations:

GPU	State Political Administration (secret police)
HCA	Higher Church Administration
Met.	Metropolitan
ROC	Russian Orthodox Church
RSFSR	Russian Soviet Federated Socialist Republic

See "biblical quotations" for New Testament books.
See "stories" for any one of the six fictional vignettes.